# MEASUREMENT

AND

# EVALUATION

THIRD EDITION

# MEASUREMENT AND EVALUATION

In Physical Education and Exercise Science

DOUGLAS N. HASTAD
UNIVERSITY OF WISCONSIN–LA CROSSE

ALAN C. LACY
INDIANA STATE UNIVERSITY

Allyn and Bacon
Boston   London   Toronto   Sydney   Tokyo   Singapore

| | |
|---|---|
| *Publisher:* | Joseph E. Burns |
| *Composition and Prepress Buyer:* | Linda Cox |
| *Manufacturing Buyer:* | Megan Cochran |
| *Cover Administrator:* | Jenny Hart |
| *Electronic Composition:* | Publishers' Design and Production Services, Inc. |

**Library of Congress Cataloging-in-Publication Data**

Hastad, Douglas N.
    Measurement and evaluation in physical education and exercise
science / Douglas N. Hastad, Alan C. Lacy. — 3rd ed.
        p.   cm.
    Includes bibliographical references and index.
    ISBN 0-205-27977-5 (casebound)
    1. Physical fitness—Testing.   2. Physical education and training—
Testing.   I. Lacy, Alan C.   II. Title.
    GV436.H35   1998
    613.7—dc21                                                        97-43905
                                                                          CIP

Printed in the United States of America.

10 9 8 7 6 5 4 3 2        02 01 00 99 98

To my wife, Nancy, and our wonderful children, Jacob and Rebekah.

D.N.H.


To Patti, Sarah, Thomas, Clyde, and Lena Mary—many thanks for your unconditional love and support in my life.

A.C.L.

# Contents

Preface    xvii

▶ 1    **INTRODUCTION TO MEASUREMENT AND EVALUATION    1**

Key Terms    1
Objectives    1
Historical Perspective of Measurement and Evaluation    3
Current Trends    7
    Increased Accountability    7
    Importance of Health-Related Physical Fitness    8
    Altering Physical Fitness Patterns    9
    Increased Sophistication of Measurement Instruments    10
    Advent of Private Physical Activity-Based Programs    11
    More Rigorous Program Standards    12
    New Assessment Tools for All Ages and Abilities    12
    Subjective Techniques    13
    Use of Systematic Observation Instruments    13
    Competency-Based Testing    14
    Authentic Assessment and Portfolios    14
    Research    15
    Computers    15
    Future Directions    15
Definitions of Test, Measurement, and Evaluation    16
    Test    16
    Measurement    17
    Evaluation    17
    Relationships among Test, Measurement, and Evaluation    18
Use of Measurement and Evaluation in Physical Education    19
    Student Performance    19
    Teacher Performance    21
Use of Measurement and Evaluation in the Nonschool,
    Exercise Setting    23
Summary    24
Discussion Questions    25
References    25
Representative Readings    26

► 2 **LINKING PROGRAM DEVELOPMENT WITH MEASUREMENT AND EVALUATION** 27

*Key Terms* 27
*Objectives* 27
The Four Learning Domains of Physical Education 29
    Health-Related Physical Fitness Domain 29
    Psychomotor Domain 30
    Cognitive Domain 31
    Affective Domain 31
Needs Assessment 32
Program Development 34
    Phase 1 Establishing a Realistic Philosophical Approach 35
    Phase 2 Developing Attainable Program Goals 36
    Phase 3 Determining Unit Outcomes 37
    Phase 4 Establishing Performance-Based Objectives 38
    Phase 5 Evaluation and Improving the Program 39
*Summary* 41
*Discussion Questions* 41
*References* 42
*Representative Readings* 42

► 3 **BASIC STATISTICS** 43

*Key Terms* 43
*Objectives* 43
Levels of Measurement 44
    Nominal Level 45
    Ordinal Level 45
    Interval Level 47
    Ratio Level 47
Frequency Distributions 47
    Simple Frequency Distribution 48
    Grouped Frequency Distribution 48
Graphical Representation of Data 50
    Symmetry and Skewness 53
Measures of Central Tendency 56
    Mode 56
    Median 57
    Mean 58
Measures of Variability 60
    Range 61
    Interpercentile Range 61

Variance    62
Standard Deviation    63
Properties of the Normal Curve    68
Standard Scores    69
Percentile Rank    69
Z-Scores    73
T-Score    76
Correlation    77
Spearman Rho Rank-Order Correlation    79
Pearson Product-Moment Correlation    81
Regression    83
Tests for Differences between Groups    85
t-test for Independent Samples    86
t-test for Dependent Samples    88
Simple Analysis of Variance (ANOVA)    90
*Summary    91*
*Discussion Questions    91*
*References    92*
*Representative Readings    92*

▶ 4    **CRITERIA FOR TEST SELECTION    93**

*Key Terms    93*
*Objectives    93*
Validity    94
Face Validity    95
Content Validity    95
Construct Validity    96
Concurrent Validity    96
Predictive Validity    97
Reliability    97
Test-Retest Reliability    98
Alternate Form Reliability    98
Split-Half or Odd-Even Reliability    99
Objectivity    100
Relationship between Validity, Reliability, and Objectivity    101
Administrative Concerns in Test Selection    102
Relevance    102
Educational Value    103
Economy    104
Time    104
Enjoyment    104

      Norms    105

      Discrimination    107

      Independence    107

      Sex Appropriateness    108

      Reliance on Another's Performance    108

      Safety    109

      Testing Large Groups    110

      Ease of Scoring, Interpreting, and Reporting    110

Planning Test Administration    111

      Securing Materials and Preparing the Testing Area    111

      Knowledge of the Test    112

      Recording the Scores    113

      Training Testers    114

      Practicing Test Items    114

      Warming Up    115

      Standardizing Instructions    115

      Converting, Interpreting, and Evaluating the Results    116

*Summary*    *117*

*Discussion Questions*    *118*

*References*    *118*

*Representative Readings*    *118*

**▶ 5   MEASURING THE HEALTH-RELATED PHYSICAL FITNESS DOMAIN    121**

*Key Terms*    *121*

*Objectives*    *121*

Health-Related Physical Fitness    123

Test Batteries to Measure Health-Related Physical Fitness    125

      Measuring Cardiorespiratory Fitness    137

      Measuring Muscular Strength and Endurance    150

      Strength Tests Using Weight Machines    159

      Measuring Flexibility    164

      Measuring Body Composition    172

Basic Anthropometric Measurements    179

Valuing and Assessing the Process of Physical Activity    183

      Physical Education Environment    184

      Exercise Science Environment    184

*Summary*    *185*

*Discussion Questions*    *185*

*References*    *185*

*Representative Readings*    *188*

► 6 **MEASURING THE PSYCHOMOTOR DOMAIN** **191**

*Key Terms* *191*
*Objectives* *191*
Skill-Related Physical Fitness 194
    Uses of Skill-Related Physical Fitness Tests 194
    Measuring Agility
    Measuring Balance 203
    Measuring Speed and Reaction Time 212
    Test Batteries to Measure Skill-Related Physical Fitness 215
Sports Skills Tests 229
    Team Sports 230
    Individual and Dual Sports 252
*Summary* *265*
*Discussion Questions* *265*
*References* *265*
*Representative Readings* *267*


► 7 **MEASURING THE COGNITIVE DOMAIN** **273**

*Key Terms* *273*
*Objectives* *273*
Measuring Cognitive Achievement 275
    School Settings 275
    Nonschool Settings 277
Planning the Written Test 277
    Matching Test Items to Objectives 277
    Taxonomy of Educational Objectives 278
    Knowledge 279
    Comprehension 279
    Application 280
    Analysis 280
    Synthesis 280
    Evaluation 280
    Table of Specifications 281
Selection of Test Items 284
    True-False 285
    Matching 285
    Multiple-Choice 286
    Completion Items 287
    Short-Answer Questions 288
    Essay 288
Administering the Written Test 291

Assembling the Test     291
Giving the Test     292
Grading the Test     292
Analyzing the Test     293
Quantitative Item Analysis     293
Qualitative Item Analysis     297
Sources for Test Questions     298
Other Sources     299
*Summary     299*
*Discussion Questions     300*
*References     301*
*Representative Readings     301*


► 8   **MEASURING THE AFFECTIVE DOMAIN     303**

*Key Terms     303*
*Objectives     303*
Measuring Attitude Toward Physical Activity     306
Review of Literature     306
Data Gathering and Analysis     307
Uses of Attitudinal Scales     311
Problems Associated with Attitudinal Testing     311
Tests     312
Measuring Self-Concept     329
Review of the Literature     330
Data Gathering and Analysis     331
Tests     331
Measuring Social Competence     335
Data Gathering and Analysis     335
Problems Associated with Measuring Social Variables     340
*Summary     342*
*Discussion Questions     342*
*References     342*
*Representative Readings     344*


► 9   **GRADING     345**

*Key Terms     345*
*Objectives     345*
Controversies of Grading     346
To Grade or Not to Grade     347
Issues in Grade Determination     349

Methods of Grading 357
    Norm-Referenced Approach 358
    Criterion-Referenced Approach 364
    Other Methods to Determine Grades 367
Reporting Student Performance Data 372
    Report Card 373
    Student Portfolios 373
    Personal Letter 374
    Conference 375
    Graphic Profile 376
*Summary* 377
*Discussion Questions* 378
*References* 378
*Representative Readings* 379

**10 USING SELF-EVALUATION TO IMPROVE INSTRUCTION 381**

*Key Terms* 381
*Objectives* 381
Traditional Methods of Observation 384
    Eyeballing 384
    Note Taking 384
    Checklists 385
    Rating Scales 385
Systematic Observation Methodology 388
Data Recording Procedures 389
    Event Recording 391
    Interval Recording 394
    Duration Recording 397
    Group Time Sampling 400
Validity and Reliability of Systematic Observation 404
    Validity 404
    Reliability 404
Using Systematic Observation for Self-Evaluation 407
    Practice Time 408
    Instructional Time 409
    Management Time 409
    Response Latency 410
    Instructor Movement 410
    Specific Instructional Behaviors 412
Selected Instruments for Systematic Observation 416
    All-Purpose Event-Recording Form (Instructor Behaviors) 417

All-Purpose Duration-Recording Form (Student Time Analysis)   417
Group Time Sampling Form (Class Analysis)   420
General Supervision Instrument   421
System for Observing Fitness Instructions (SOFIT)
Arizona State University Observation Instrument (ASUOI)   425
Academic Learning Time-Physical Education (ALT-PE)   426
*Summary*   *430*
*Discussion Questions*   *431*
*References*   *431*

◣ **11   ASSESSING INDIVIDUALS WITH DISABILITIES   433**

*Key Terms*   *433*
*Objectives*   *433*
Linking Curriculum Development and Measurement of Students
   with Disabilities   436
Phase 1: Establishing a Realistic Philosophical Approach   436
Phase 2: Developing Attainable Program Goals   436
Phase 3: Determining Unit Outcomes   437
Phase 4: Establishing Performance-Based Objectives   438
Phase 5: Evaluating and Improving the Program   438
The Importance of an Individualized Program   438
Preliminary Considerations for Testing   439
Tests for Students with Disabilities   444
Physical/Motor Fitness Tests   444
Fundamental Motor Patterns   455
Putting it All Together: The Individualized Education
   Program (IEP)   462
The Written IEP Document   463
*Summary*   *473*
*Discussion Questions*   *473*
*References*   *474*
*Representative Readings*   *475*

◣ **12   MEASUREMENT AND EVALUATION IN SCHOOL
SETTINGS   479**

*Key Terms*   *479*
*Objectives*   *479*
NASPE Projects—New Visions for Assessment   480
Guidelines for Effective Measurement and Evaluation   485

Variables Affecting Measurement and Evaluation Models     486
        Characteristics and Interests of Students     487
        Class Size     489
        Class Time     489
        Personnel Support     489
        Technological Support     490
        State and Local Mandates     490
        Curricular Content     490
Examples of Measurement and Evaluation Models     493
        Case Study #1     494
        Case Study #2     495
        Case Study #3     497
        Case Study #4     497
        Case Study #5     499
        Case Study #6     501
        Case Study #7     501
        Case Study #8     503
*Summary     505*
*Discussion Questions     505*
*References     506*
*Representative Readings     506*

## ▶ 13   MEASUREMENT AND EVALUATION IN NONSCHOOL SETTINGS     507

*Key Terms     507*
*Objectives     507*
The Role of Measurement and Evaluation in the Nonschool
    Setting     509
Characteristics of Nonschool Fitness and Exercise Programs     510
        Athletic Training     511
        Corporate and Community Exercise and Fitness Programs     513
        Hospital- and University-Based Health and Fitness Programs     513
        Therapeutic Recreation     515
Considerations for Measurements and Evaluation in Adult Fitness
        Environments     516
Tests Used in the Nonschool Exercise Setting     518
        Testing Maximal Oxygen Uptake     518
        Other Tests     521
*Summary     537*
*Discussion Questions     537*
*References     538*
*Representative Readings     538*

► **14   USING COMPUTER TECHNOLOGY      541**

*Key Terms      541*
*Objectives      541*
Uses of the Personal Computer in Physical Education
   and Exercise Science      542
Basic Personal Computing      543
Functions of the Personal Computer      544
   Input and Storage      545
   Processing      546
   Output Devices      547
   Other Peripherals      548
Networking      549
How to Select a Microcomputer System      550
Personal Computer Software      552
   Communications      552
   Computer-Assisted Instruction      553
   Database management      554
   Electronic Spreadsheet      554
   Grading      555
   Graphics      556
   Statistics      557
   Utilities      558
   Word Processing      559
*How to Select Software      559*
*Software for Measurement and Evaluation      560*
*Summary      561*
*Representative Readings      561*


**INDEX      563**

# Preface

*Measurement and Evaluation in Physical Education and Exercise Science,* Third Edition, links theory and practice and provides a practical approach to measurement and evaluation in physical education (grades K–12) and in nonschool exercise environments.

As with the second edition, one of the commitments of this text is to emphasize how the processes of measurement and evaluation can and should be used as vital tools to enhance physical education and exercise programs in nonschool settings. Future teachers will learn to set and meet teaching goals; accurately measure and evaluate students, including those with special needs; and create and administer effective programs. This text articulates clearly the role of measurement and evaluation in developing curriculum and in assessing it. The third edition has been expanded to include a more indepth discussion about process versus product outcomes in physical education. And, provides the reader up-to-day information and suggestions regarding outcomes in physical education.

This third edition broadens the discussion about the role of measurement and evaluation in nonschool exercise settings. Chapter 13 addresses the needs of practitioners who will work in adult and youth exercise environments such as hospitals, health clubs, sports medicine programs, YMCA and YWCA's, recreation programs, and the corporate world. This text includes discussions of tests, equipment, goals, training, and venues relevant to contemporary measurement and evaluation techniques used outside the school setting.

The text as a whole has been updated and revised to include new tests, norms, and techniques. As before, Chapter 1 provides an introduction to and a historical perspective for the use of measurement and evaluation in physical education programs. Current trends are identified and discussed. Chapter 2 stresses the rationale for including measurement and evaluation procedures as part of the curriculum decision-making process. This chapter reviews the four learning domains of physical education, discusses the roles of needs assessment and of measurement and evaluation in curriculum development, provides useful application statements, and differentiates between qualitative and quantitative assessment.

Chapter 3 takes a "cookbook" approach to statistics, focusing less on theory and more on approaching data collection and analysis in a sequential manner appropriate to the needs of the students. More information on tests of differences has been added. Chapter 4 addresses criteria for test selection and discusses the concepts of validity, reliability, and objectivity for both quantitative and qualitative measurement and evaluation. Practical concerns in selecting, planning, and administering tests are also included.

To maintain knowledge consistent with current thought and technology, several other key topics have been selected. Chapters 5–8 introduce the most widely used, valid, and reliable field-based tests and test batteries that have been proven successful in measuring performance in the health-related physical fitness domain, psychomotor domain, cognitive domain, and affective domain. Techniques presented in these chapters can be used as part of the day-to-day operation of a physical education program or the nonschool fitness environment.

Chapter 9 discusses the many aspects to be considered when incorporating measurement and evaluation procedures into the grading scheme. The advantages and disadvantages of a variety of grading systems are thoroughly covered. Chapter 10 focuses on the use of systematic observation to improve instruction—a topic not usually included in standard measurement and evaluation textbooks. This important topic receives thorough attention, and various approaches used to evaluate behaviors in activity settings are identified and explained. This chapter has been expanded to include discussion of self-evaluation of instruction in school and non-school settings.

Chapter 11, written by Garth Tymeson, a well-known authority in the field of adapted physical education, is devoted to assessment and evaluation techniques for youths with disabilities and details the most popular field-based tests. This chapter is aimed specifically at the implementation of P.L. 94-142, which requires practitioners who work with individuals with disabilities to be more accountable in the assessment and evaluation of students.

Chapter 12 presents *models* of measurement and evaluation as they apply to school settings. Information on authentic assessment has been added. This information will assist teachers (1) in incorporating measurement strategies from each of the four learning domains and (2) in developing a sound model on which to base evaluation of the program and justification of subsequent instructional modifications. Case studies apply the information, illustrating different teaching situations. This edition includes the addition of case studies which utilize qualitative measurement techniques.

As mentioned above, Chapter 13 is expanded and addresses the use of measurement and evaluation in nonschool settings. Students should be aware that increasing numbers of jobs involve such settings and that the success of fitness programming and exercise prescription in nonschool settings is very dependent upon techniques described in this chapter. The chapter characterizes four categories of adult fitness and exercise programs and describes various movement and fitness tests utilized in nonschool settings.

Because technological advances have made personal computers a useful tool to physical educators, Chapter 14 updates the reader about current computing technology, software considerations, and applications that can be used by professionals in the measurement and evaluation process.

As with the second edition, chapters begin with concise objectives and a list of key words. They conclude with a summary and a series of discussion questions designed to assist students in synthesizing information presented in the chapter. The third edition continues to provide a practical and useful Instructor's Research Manual. This manual contains discussion points, lecture outlines, a test bank of true/false, multiple choice, and essay questions, overhead transparency masters, and other helpful teaching aids.

## Acknowledgments

There are many individuals who have made contributions to this textbook. Without their help, all of the changes and improvements in the third edition would not have been possible.

We appreciate the efforts and suggestions made by each of the reviewers: Richard Clower, Western Maryland College; Emma Gibbons, Texas A & M University; Julee Illner, Southern Illinois University at Carbondale; and Charles Jackson, The College of William and Mary. Our thanks also to reviewers of past editions.

The initiation of this project was made possible by the support of Colette Kelly, Gay Pauley, and their coworkers at GSP. Over the years, we had a great working relationship with them. Their contributions during the revision process and the support they provided in past editions is greatly appreciated. We thank them and wish them well in future endeavors.

Since GSP was acquired by Allyn and Bacon, we have had the opportunity to get to know and work with many new people. Our appreciation goes to Joe Burns, Mary Beth Finch, Sara Sherlock, and Suzy Spivey for their hard work and good counsel during the transitional phase and final production stages of this textbook. We look forward to working with them in the future.

We also acknowledge Dr. Garth Tymeson of University of Wisconsin—La Cross. He is the author of Chapter 11, which deals with measuring students with special needs. Thank you for contributing your time and expertise in the original writing and subsequent revisions of this chapter. Last but not least, special thanks is given to Dr. Robert P. Pangrazi of Arizona State University. He has provided continual guidance and support not only to this textbook but also in many other professional endeavors.

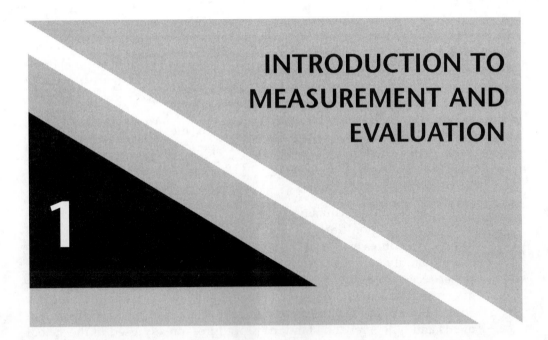

# INTRODUCTION TO MEASUREMENT AND EVALUATION

**1**

## ► KEY TERMS

achievement
authentic assessment
classification
competency-based testing
diagnosis
evaluation
improvement
measurement
portfolio
qualitative
quantitative
test
test reliability
test validity

## ► OBJECTIVES

*After reading this chapter, the student should be able to:*

1. Discuss measurement and evaluation from a historical perspective.
2. Identify current trends and future directions of measurement and evaluation.
3. Define and understand the relationship among test, measurement, and evaluation.
4. List and describe various ways that measurement and evaluation can be used in conjunction with student performance.
5. List and describe various ways that measurement and evaluation can be used in conjunction with teacher performance.
6. Identify nonschool exercise programs that employ measurement and evaluation techniques as part of activity or exercise programs.

Measurement and evaluation are interrelated processes. Generally speaking, measurement is the task of administering a test for the purpose of obtaining a quantifiable score. The number of abdominal curls successfully completed in one minute, the distance run in 12 minutes, the number of questions answered correctly on a written examination, and the score attained on a personality inventory are some examples of **quantitative** information derived from measurement techniques. Assigning "very good" to an individual's performance or rating a team's performance on the basketball floor as "average" are examples of **qualitative** measurement information.

Physical educators have at their disposal a variety of measurement tools to assist in the acquisition of useful data about student performance in the psychomotor, fitness, cognitive, and affective domains. Improved testing procedures also assist administrators and supervisors in systematically quantifying information pertaining to teaching effectiveness. The rather recent advent of physical activity programs in nonschool settings has created new possibilities for measurement and evaluation techniques. Some of these applications require the use of sophisticated testing instruments and others rely on standard procedures already used in the school setting.

Evaluation refers to the translation of test results into meaningful information that will aid the practitioner and other professionals in making judgments and unbiased decisions about the data obtained through measurement. Results of physical fitness testing that show below average performance by students may cause the physical education teacher to alter program offerings. Because of poor hitting, a baseball coach may decide to rotate his or her line-up. In both of these cases, the results of measurement were used for evaluative purposes and the results of the evaluation caused a decision to be rendered and a change to occur. Similarly, an exercise physiologist may develop, after a particular testing protocol on the treadmill, a personalized exercise regimen for a client.

Thus, evaluation translates test results into meaningful information. Measurement, evaluation, and decision making are intertwined. It is important that reliable, solid, objective measurement take place to be used in making sound evaluation upon which a decision can be based. Measurement precedes evaluation, and evaluation precedes decision making. With respect to physical education and exercise science, decisions need to be based on measurement techniques that can be carefully evaluated.

It is important to remember that physical education has gained a place of prominence and partnership with other facets of the educational curriculum in direct proportion to the development and refinement of its measurement and evaluation techniques. Likewise, activity programs in nonschool settings are rapidly attaining credibility in the area of health promotion and disease prevention. If physical education and nonschool exercise programs are to survive and flourish, it is imperative that physical educators and exercise specialists rely on measurement and evaluative techniques in the decision-making process.

## HISTORICAL PERSPECTIVE OF MEASUREMENT AND EVALUATION

The origin of testing and measurement coincides with that period of history often cited as the beginning of formal physical education, the mid-1800s. The appointment of Dr. Edward Hitchcock, in 1861, to the position of director of the department of hygiene and physical education at Amherst College gave academic status to the discipline of physical education. Of more important historical significance, Dr. Hitchcock's work in the science of anthropometrics (body symmetry and proportion) introduced a quantifiable and objective approach to physical education. The pioneer efforts of Hitchcock and other medical doctors turned physical educators marked the beginning of an era in which measurement was developed, implemented, and promoted.

During the period from 1860 to 1880, measurement techniques were most commonly used in the continued study of anthropometrics and the resulting longitudinal studies to develop normative data about the physical dimensions and growth patterns of youth. Dr. Dudley Sargent of Harvard University devised more than 40 different anthropometric measurements. While his research was used to describe the "typical" college male and female, Sargent went one step further in the process of using data: from obtained measurements, he prescribed a program of exercises for individuals. Although Sargent's efforts were reported in journals and in a manual on measurement and testing, his impact was greatest on American youth. His testing system was adopted by public schools, colleges, and the YMCA. There is no doubt that the use of measurement in physical education contributed to its rise to a more respected position in the overall educational scheme during the latter part of the nineteenth century.

Around 1880, the use of measurement in the field of physical education broadened to include more than the study of anthropometrics. The high interest in competitive athletics and strength development to improve performance caused leaders in physical education to focus attention on capacities of performance rather than on body symmetry. Sargent devised a battery of tests measuring the strength of the arms, legs, back, grip, and vital capacity. This test battery, known as the *Intercollegiate Strength Test*, became an integral component of intercollegiate competition.

As the medical profession made advances in the areas of cardiac and respiratory function, physical educators began to tap newly acquired knowledge and sought methods of testing the cardiovascular efficiency of the body. Results of these studies suggested a relationship between the functional capacity of the body during movement and the efficiency of the heart and circulatory system. From its birth in the late 1800s, assessment of the cardiorespiratory system has matured into one of the most vital areas associated with physical education.

In the beginning of the twentieth century, public schools and colleges began to introduce achievement tests into their curricula. Using tests for the purposes of assigning a grade and classifying students by skill level marked the beginning of an application practice widely used today. In the area of physical education, this period was marked by further refinement of strength testing and the onset of achievement tests. No longer was strength considered to be the prime factor in performance. Measures of muscular endurance and speed were found to be independent of strength and identified as variables that enhanced athletic performance. Test batteries that measured the endurance of various muscle groups were developed.

The 1920s were particularly significant for the area of measurement and evaluation. New statistical techniques were developed and more precise methods to construct tests became available. Reliability, validity, and objectivity of tests were enhanced. The development of tests to measure

▰ **FIGURE 1.0**    Physical Education Class.

motor ability, and capacity flourished. The public's increased interest in sport spawned a wide assortment of skills tests designed to measure selected components of athletic performance. Standards of performance once arbitrarily assigned were now clearly and accurately defined. Modern test construction continues to be modeled on what was learned in the 1920s.

The concept of measuring social skills was also introduced in the 1920s. Since physical education and sport programs claimed to positively affect the social competence of participants, efforts to measure such effects were necessary. Rating scales and inventories to assess social and moral attributes were developed. The assessment of social qualities is often overlooked, but is nevertheless a viable measurement area, important in the overall evaluation of physical education and sport programs.

World War II prompted a renewed national concern for physical fitness. College and public school physical education curricula responded to the need for physically fit citizens by shifting program emphasis from a sports orientation to physical training. Not surprisingly, a change in the focus of measurement in physical education accompanied this trend toward physical fitness. New physical fitness tests, developed at a rapid rate and designed to meet the needs of a nation at war, could be easily administered to large groups, and scores could be quickly tabulated and interpreted. While initially devised for the various branches of the armed forces, many items included in these test batteries evolved into appropriate tools for today's practitioner.

Though the major thrust in physical education and measurement techniques following World War II was away from fitness testing and back to a more eclectic course and study emphasis, the United States' involvement in the Korean conflict brought with it a resurgence of physical training of U.S. youth. Of greater programmatic significance, however, were the results of the Kraus-Weber tests of minimal muscular strength. These tests were used in a project that compared the minimum muscular strength of European and U.S. youth. The findings reported that U.S. youth were dramatically less fit than their European counterparts. The outgrowth of this study was the establishment of the President's Council on Youth Fitness and the development of the AAHPER (American Association for Health, Physical Education, and Recreation) Youth Fitness Test.

It is arguable that the successful launching of Sputnik I by the Soviets in 1957 had greater impact on U.S. education than any other single event in history. Almost overnight, schools shifted educational philosophy. Science courses quickly became the core of most academic programs. This trend, of course, prompted a rethinking about the place of nonscientific disciplines in the total curriculum. Physical education's place in the overall educational scheme was in jeopardy. In response to criticism about its apparent lack of a scientific knowledge base, and in an attempt to establish quantifiable evidence to retain programs, university physical education departments began undertaking various empirically based research projects. This research was aided by a dramatic increase in funding for facilities and equipment for scientific investigations during the 1960s. Further, graduate programs in physical education experienced rapidly increasing enrollments. These factors, coupled with advancing technology, contributed to the need for enhanced measurement and evaluation techniques in physical education.

In many respects, physical education prospered during the 1970s. Enrollment in school and college programs reached all-time highs. External and internal funds were available to support programs, and the demand for teachers remained high during the early part of the decade. Equipment used for measurement and evaluation became more sophisticated and reasonably priced. Physical education programs seemed secure, but this was not the case for long. The dawn of the 1980s brought with it declining enrollments, budget cuts, drastic decreases in federal and state grant funds, the elimination of school and college teaching positions, and a rethinking about how educational programs should be held accountable. State and local governments were under pressure to improve the quality of education for students. Physical education was not exempted from these eroding factors.

Physical education in the 1980s was characterized by relaxed requirements in the schools. Many school districts began to reduce the time devoted to physical education that once was a vital part of the curriculum. Fewer students in the United States were taking high school physical education than during the mid-1970s. The U. S. Center for Disease Control reported that of a sample of students in grades 9–12 only 48 percent were enrolled in physical education classes during 1985. This compared to 65 percent in 1984 (*Chicago Tribune*, 1991). Not surprisingly, this trend was accompanied by a "dramatic decline in the fitness of the nation's youth" (AAHPERD, 1990, p. 1). The total enrollment of school-age youth reached its long-predicted low in the latter part of the decade. During this period the general public was demanding greater accountability of school boards and schools. Physical education programs needed to provide quantifiable evidence of demonstrated improvement and progress toward goals.

In the 1980s and early 1990s physical educators and exercise scientists began to establish clearer definitions for what it means to be physically fit and physically educated. Physical education and exercise programs began to encourage students and clients to develop higher levels of basic fitness and physical competence as needed for many work situations and active leisure participation. Improving student/client health-related fitness components of cardiorespiratory endurance, muscular strength and endurance, flexibility, and body composition became prominent goals. Beyond broadening the general public's understanding of what it means to be physically fit, exercise professionals and physical educators began to develop programs that would take into account variations in an individual's level of fitness. This meant more personal attention for clients and more focused exercise programs to attain specific goals. In addition to improving health-related fitness as measured by selected fitness tests, programs began to recognize the value having clients and students better understand the importance of being physically fit (NASPE, 1995). Programs developed written materials that better described the why and how of fitness. The ultimate goal was no longer to simply develop fitness. Rather, it was becoming increasingly important to assist the student and client in developing the ability and willingness to accept responsibility for personal fitness. Measurement and evaluation were critical procedures in this process.

Today, physical education and exercise programs must justify their existence with quantifiable outcomes—no longer is physical education able to develop or continue programs that are supported only on philosophical beliefs and professional opinion. To this end, physical educators and exercise scientists must seek and properly use methods and techniques to gather data to support programs. During the past 125 years physical education and exercise professions have taken great steps forward, and many of these steps coincided with advances in research, measurement, and evaluation. To continue to progress, physical educators and exercise practitioners must recognize the importance of measurement and evaluation techniques in developing effective physical education programs, promoting adult health and fitness programs, and generally moving the American public toward a more active lifestyle. Intervention in the early years will facilitate the commitment to an active and healthy lifestyle.

## CURRENT TRENDS

While the history of measurement and evaluation in physical education has been somewhat fragmented and without focus, a clearer perspective of the purpose of measurement and evaluation in the educational scheme is emerging. Current events suggest that physical education and other physical activity-based programs are at a crossroads. Reacting properly and with expediency to current trends could greatly solidify the position of physical education within the educational experience and further broaden the exercise science's extension into the private sector. Understandably, measurement and evaluation play important roles in the response to each trend.

## Increased Accountability

The verification of educational attainment is an essential application of measurement and evaluation. The 1990s are witnessing a renewal of educational reform. At the heart of this revival is the public's growing interest in greater educational effectiveness. For example, never before in the history of education have legislators, boards of education, and the general public placed such a premium on the quality of student that schools and colleges produce. Many states are requiring undergraduate students to pass preprofessional exams before entering the sequence of teacher preparation courses; states are implementing competency tests for certified teachers; and local boards are demanding that teachers be held accountable for their performance and the achievement of their students. Declining physical fitness scores, increasing numbers of obese individuals, and poor health habits do little to exempt physical education from critical review.

To respond to these trends and restore credibility to physical education, practitioners must reevaluate their present programs in terms of the product (wellness) and the culture. Curriculum can no longer be viewed simply in terms of attaining objectives associated with the learning domains. The increased emphasis on accountability has created an all-important niche for measurement and evaluation. Undergraduate and graduate offerings must link the relationship between measurement and evaluation with other dimensions of curriculum building. Incorporating techniques of measurement and evaluation into the yearly plan becomes vital. Given the readily quantifiable nature of our discipline and the high interest in physical activity, this task is definitely achievable.

## Importance of Health-Related Physical Fitness

The American public is more aware than ever of the importance of being physically fit. Obesity, poor cardiovascular functioning, low back pain, and inadequate muscular strength and endurance are factors attributable to a sedentary lifestyle. It is encouraging that these health problems can be positively altered through planned programs of exercise and physical activity.

The burgeoning interest in health-related physical fitness is responsible for the rapid increase in private enterprises dedicated to physical activity programming. Health clubs and studios are enjoying financial success by offering a wide assortment of supervised fitness activities. Corporate centers, colleges and universities, and even small businesses are offering exercise programs to enhance the health and well-being of their employees. A central ingredient in the success of many of these programs is the measurement and evaluation component: minimal fitness testing to provide the participant with baseline information about his or her level of physical fitness and a follow-up evaluation to prescribe activities are necessary to ensure proper fitness development and maintenance. An encouraging trend is that there has been a recent and dramatic shift from evaluating individual fitness levels by means of motor performance tests to the use of health-related fitness tests (Symons and Grascoigne, 1990).

Physical educators are opting to measure health fitness components such as cardiovascular endurance, body composition, muscular strength and endurance, and flexibility of the low back areas. These measurements seem to be replacing traditional testing practices which are designed to determine skill performance in such areas as balance, coordination, speed, and power.

The ironic aspect of this fitness boom is that it primarily involves middle- and upper-middle-class adults 30–50 years old. A recent study by the U. S. Department of Health and Human Services concluded that about half of American children and adolescents are not developing the exercise and fitness skills to maintain an adequate level of health. Results from the California Physical and Health-Related Fitness Test published in the late 1980s indicated that only 16 percent of fifth graders, 20 percent of seventh graders, and 26 percent of ninth graders met the minimum standards for abdominal strength, arm and shoulder strength, flexibility of lower back, and cardiorespiratory fitness as measured by the AAHPERD *Physical Best* test (AAHPERD, 1990). Another national fitness study conducted in the mid-1980s showed that youth in grades 5–12 were becoming fatter and not achieving the minimum appropriate physical activity to maintain effectively functioning cardiorespiratory systems (Ross and Gilbert, 1985).

These findings confirm a trend of deterioration in the overall physical fitness status of youth (Hunsicker and Reiff, 1977; Kirshenbaum and Sullivan, 1983). Unfortunately, physical education has been in the schools for years and the fitness levels of youngsters have not substantially improved (Corbin and Pangrazi, 1992). This claim has done little to support the importance of professionally taught school programs. This is disappointing, especially since more and more people recognize the value of fitness and means to achieve a healthy lifestyle. It has been shown that school attendance decreases the activity patterns of children, which should lend support to implementation and continuation of physical education programs *that positively alter the fitness of the participants.* Verification of such positive fitness outcomes is possible only through a well-planned, objective, valid, and reliable measurement and evaluation scheme.

## Altering Physical Activity Patterns

A national objective for the year 2000 is to increase at least 75 percent the number of youth aged 6–17 years who engage in vigorous activity that promotes cardiorespiratory fitness (Public Health Service, 1991). Data suggest that current levels of vigorous physical activity among high school youth will have to more than double to attain this objective. More disturbing, however, is the finding that indicates participation in vigorous physical activity among high school students may be decreasing. This is not surprising, given the fact that participation in school physical education also may be decreasing (Center for Disease Control, 1991).

Increasing the amount of time adults devote to vigorous physical activity is becoming an important challenge. Only 22 percent of adult Americans are active at the level recommended for health benefits. Conversely, 24 percent of the nation's adults are totally sedentary, and the remaining 54 percent are inadequately active. Promotion of and participation in increased physical activity as a means of disease prevention must become an integral part of health care reform. In fact, federal regulations have been issued that not only permit but also encourage government agencies to include structured physical fitness programs in their overall occupational health programs. Nationwide we need to employ strategies that alter the physical activity patterns of our citizenry, young and old. Without a strong health promotion/disease prevention component, health reform could quickly become unaffordable (American College of Sports Medicine, 1993).

In sum, physical inactivity is a major chronic disease risk factor that crosses all demographic boundaries. At the school level, physical educators need to make youth more aware of the relationships between inactivity and chronic health problems. The trend is to emphasize the process of physical activity rather than fitness scores and award systems. Physical education programs are placing a renewed emphasis on developing activity habits that carry over to out-of-school activities. Measurement and evaluation techniques can assist in this challenge. Children and adults can learn to quantitatively monitor and chart their activity patterns. Teachers and employers can provide computer technology to assist individuals in evaluating their activity habits and better understanding their overall lifestyle.

## Increased Sophistication of Measurement Instruments

The rapid technological advances of the past 15 years have resulted in the design and development of equipment to aid in measuring human performance parameters. Physiological responses can be readily monitored by electronic apparatus. Using sophisticated scientific equipment to obtain computer-generated readouts of heart rate, oxygen consumption, blood pressure, and other variables associated with cardiovascular efficiency is becoming a common learning experience for undergraduate students. Improvements in the area of high-speed cinematography, e.g., allowing simultaneous computer analysis of movement in several planes, are responsible for the rapid advancement of knowledge of motor behavior. Human performance laboratories at colleges and universities are strengthening teaching and research components of physical education programs through the acquisition of laboratory equipment.

Technology has also benefitted the practitioner. Items such as computerized pulse-o-meters and skinfold calipers, which give a digitized accounting of heart rate and electronically convert thickness of skinfold to percentage of body fat, respectively, are now available as over-the-counter items. Retailers and wholesalers are responding to the consumer's need to know. Home exercise equipment usually includes information concerning the intensity and duration of the workout. It is becoming fashionable to measure one's own level of physical fitness. The accuracy and ease with which physical performance factors can be measured has positively contributed to the field of measurement and evaluation.

## Advent of Private Physical Activity–Based Programs

In recent years there has been a marked trend toward the establishment of private enterprises offering directed programs of exercise. Health clubs, fitness centers, and exercise studios have targeted the sedentary adult population as a viable market. Undergraduate and graduate programs in fitness leadership have sprung up in response to this trend. Students in

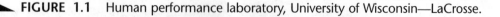

▶ **FIGURE 1.1**   Human performance laboratory, University of Wisconsin—LaCrosse.

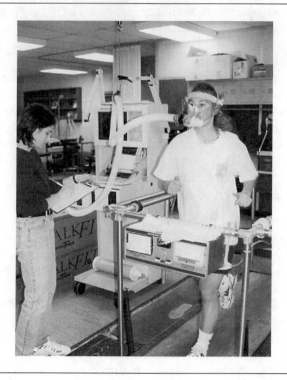

these programs are usually required to successfully complete a program of study in exercise science. Central to the program is a course in measurement and evaluation. It is important to respond to the expanding perspectives on physical education and the variety of nonteaching careers that are available to students in movement-based programs.

Providing personalized testing and evaluation on selected human performance parameters is a vital aspect of many of these programs. The types of assessment procedures vary from simple fitness and psychomotor tests to sophisticated protocols such as underwater weighing, submaximal stress tests, and, in some cases, blood analysis. Whatever the type, personal health evaluation is an essential and attractive feature of most nonschool physical activity–based programs. Chapter 13 provides a broader discussion of measurement and evaluation in the nonschool setting.

## More Rigorous Program Standards

There seems to be no escaping the trend to reform educational practices to establish higher standards in both public and private education. It appears that the time has also come for physical education to reestablish programmatic standards and goals. School districts throughout the country are embarking on extensive curricular reviews. There are broad efforts to establish national content standards for each area in the school curriculum. Nationwide, children and youth are repeating grades and classes as school districts make promotion and graduation standards more rigorous. Curricular reform and the redefining of standards require insightful planning and evaluation. Program administrators, supervisors, and teachers have relied on various paper-and-pencil instruments to make decisions regarding the status of current program offerings, facilities, equipment, and, of course, student performance. By raising program standards and student expectations and relying on measurement and evaluation processes to make decisions, physical educators could join this quest to make educational programs more challenging and fruitful.

## New Assessment Tools for All Ages and Abilities

Historically, measurement and evaluation have been restricted to school-age, college, and young adult populations. However, renewed interest in the physical performance capabilities of all individuals has prompted the development of new testing techniques appropriate for preschool children and older adults. These assessment tools are being used to find out more about the capabilities of individuals at the two ends of the life cycle. In addition, empirical research is being conducted to learn more about the physical activity patterns of our nation's very young and old.

Public Law 94-142 (The Education for All Handicapped Children Act of 1975), assuring all individuals the right to a free public education in the least restrictive environment, regardless of disabilities, brought with it a need to develop, refine, and modify testing procedures for special populations. Since in most cases results from such tests are used to place the person with a disability in the appropriate educational setting and develop an individual educational program, assessment and evaluation are central to the education of students with disabilities.

## Subjective Techniques

While physical education has as its primary goals motor skill and physical fitness development, there are other program objectives that pertain to elements associated with the affective domain. Such objectives might be concerned with student attitudes, self-concept, and personal values in relationship to physical activity. While laudable, efforts of physical educators to verify attainment of such goals have been hampered by the heretofore subjective nature of evaluation of the affective domain.

Recently, subjective techniques such as rating scales, inventories, checklists, and other instruments used to assess areas of the affective domain have been modified. The focus of this modification has been on adding objectivity to the instruments. Perceived behavior can now be readily translated into quantifiable terms and subjected to proper statistical analysis. Resulting information can be used to better evaluate the impact of the program or activities on the whole person, not just the program's physical aspects.

## Use of Systematic Observation Instruments

The advent of systematic observation instrumentation, which will be discussed in detail in Chapter 10, has contributed more quantifiable information about teacher and student behavior than any other measurement technique. The development of descriptive analytic techniques has enabled physical educators to collect and isolate specific objective data about such teacher and student behaviors as appropriateness, productivity, activity, management, negative reactions, and rates of information feedback. Systematic observation relies on procedures that measure the number of events, duration of the events, and/or occurrence of events over time. Specifically, systematic observation allows a trained person following stated guidelines and procedures to observe, record, and analyze interactions with the assurance that others viewing the same sequence of events would agree with the recorded data. There are a number of systems currently being used throughout the country to analyze teacher and student behaviors during organized physical activity.

## Competency-Based Testing

The movement toward **competency-based** testing is a trend affecting all levels of American education. Students in elementary and secondary schools are being required to pass a selected sequence of courses in basic subjects before they can be promoted or graduated. At many colleges and universities undergraduates seeking careers in teaching must demonstrate proficiency in math, reading comprehension, and grammar before being admitted to the professional sequence of teacher preparation courses. Minimally, a preprofessional skills test must be passed before a teaching certificate is issued. In some states, certified teachers are being required to pass competency tests in order to retain their professional credentials.

In addition to ensuring quality, competency-based testing may be used to classify students according to ability. Ability grouping has been and will continue to be an efficient and effective method to enhance the instructional setting. On the whole, grouping students with similar interests and skills positively contributes to the attainment of program objectives.

## Authentic Assessment and Portfolios

**Authentic assessment** is an ongoing feedback system that monitors and records student learning and outcomes. Originating in the regular classroom, authentic assessment is aligned with student outcomes. Outcomes are assertions about learning that guide instruction and are closely linked to unit plans and assessment. Sequential outcome statements can profile student learning through the school years and, oftentimes, form the basis for grade-level benchmarks (competencies) that amplify the definition of the physically educated person (Melograno, 1994). Spawned by the accountability movement, student outcomes assist the teacher in organizing classroom data and student performance in a manner that is more easily understood by all constituencies. Student outcomes are somewhat of a departure from the more rigid standardized achievement test and reflect society's interest in performance-based approaches to assessment. For example, in physical education students' performance in a "real" game of basketball (i.e., chest pass is evaluated relative to performing the skill during a scrimmage) is assessed rather than the number of chest passes successfully completed during a standardized test. Portfolios are featured as the most promising method to exhibit and record student performance. Portfolio assessment is designed to present a broader, more genuine picture of student learning (Zessoules & Garner, 1991).

**Portfolio** assessment offers a visual presentation of students' performance, including their strengths and areas for improvement. Just recently, we are seeing portfolios used in the physical education assessment process. Physical educators can maintain records of fitness progress, demonstrated skill competencies, physical activity behavior, and social interactive behaviors. Teachers can utilize video technology to document performance and assist in evaluation and computer technology to record, store, and report this valuable information. The practitioner needs to become accustomed to think in terms of student outcomes and be prepared to effectively handle the accompanying portfolio assessment. Portfolios are discussed in Chapter 12 as an alternative assessment strategy.

## Research

Basic or applied research requires a fundamental knowledge of measurement and evaluation techniques. In this era of increased accountability it is becoming essential for practitioners to possess at least the minimum skills needed to conduct field-based research. Providing students with fundamental skills in statistics and data analysis and hands-on experience with standardized tests is necessary if we expect them to produce the quantifiable evidence needed to strengthen the role of physical education in the total educational experience. A working knowledge of the measurement and evaluation processes will greatly assist the practitioner in determining programmatic needs, selecting testing instruments, administering tests, compiling and analyzing data, and reporting results.

## Computers

Like most new education technologies, the popularization of the computer brought with it apprehension and confusion. However, recognizing both the rapidly expanding role and the potential of this educational tool, once-cautious practitioners now seek to develop and apply their computer skills. Personnel affiliated with physical activity–based programs use the personal computer for improved recordkeeping, word processing, statistical analyses, and graphics, which are but a few of the functions performed by the personal computer that improve efficiency and accuracy of measurement and evaluation tasks. Computer software and hardware that aid in the testing, tutoring, and teaching of students are also available. Chapter 14 provides a more thorough explanation of the role of the computer in physical education.

## Future Directions

Measurement and evaluation will become increasingly integrated with a physical educator's responsibilities. Nationwide efforts are being initiated to promote assessment and evaluation of youth in areas of physical fitness and skill, and these large-scale campaigns are designed to alter the activity habits of youth to produce positive changes in lifestyle. Further, school districts are initiating mechanisms that focus on the product—the student. Learning will need to be evidenced by a change of behavior in the direction of the stated objectives. Physical education is moving away from teaching traditional sports skills in favor of specific movement skills and patterns used in sports. The ever-changing, diverse nature of our population will accelerate this shift. Technology will continue to provide efficient and effective means to measure learner outcomes, and measurement and evaluation will be an integral part of the physical education curriculum. Measurement and evaluation should be approached as a means of helping physical educators perform their jobs more effectively rather than being viewed as an additional burden ("just one more thing to do"). Physical educators who can provide quantifiable evidence of progress toward goals will be in a position to gain resources for their programs. Educators who ignore the importance of measurement and evaluation will place programs in serious jeopardy.

## DEFINITIONS OF TEST, MEASUREMENT, AND EVALUATION

Many terms in the area of measurement and evaluation are closely related, and terms may at times be used interchangeably and improperly in informal discussion. Though many terms will be introduced throughout this textbook, it is important to establish some operational definitions of basic terminology before embarking on further topics. It is critical for the reader to understand the interrelationships and differences between test, measurement, and evaluation.

## Test

Three terms that are used interchangeably are *test*, *examination*, and *quiz*. Each of these words refers to a type of instrument or procedure that measures attributes or properties of an individual. In most subject areas, these terms refer to some type of paper-and-pencil instruments used to measure content knowledge. A "quiz" is most often thought of as a brief version of a test, while "examination" carries the connotation of a lengthy, comprehensive testing process.

In physical education, there is a need to test content knowledge, fitness levels, motor skills, and attitudes and feelings related to physical activity. Paper-and-pencil quizzes and examinations can certainly be administered in many circumstances, but because of the wide variety of areas to be measured, the term "test" is most appropriate for the majority of physical education situations. Thus, in this textbook, **test** is an all-encompassing term that refers to instruments, protocols, or techniques used to measure a quantity or quality of properties or attributes of interest. In physical education, properties or attributes included in areas such as cognitive knowledge, components of fitness, values, general motor skills, and motor skills specific to certain sports are subject to testing. Many types of tests may be effectively utilized in physical education settings. For example, students' knowledge of fitness concepts or understanding of a particular sport's rules and strategies may be measured with written tests. Certain questionnaires or inventories may be used to measure attitudes or feelings about physical activity. A shuttle run can measure agility; a 40-yard sprint can test running speed; the 12-minute run is commonly used to test cardiovascular endurance. Numerous tests have been designed to measure particular sports skills such as serving in tennis or dribbling in basketball.

Whatever test is chosen, it is crucial that it meet the criteria of being a valid and reliable test for the group being measured. The **reliability** of the test refers to the precision, consistency, or repeatability of the measurement, while the **validity** of a test is the degree to which it measures what it purports to measure. The concepts of validity and reliability will be discussed in detail in Chapter 4.

## Measurement

After choosing or constructing an appropriate test, the next step is to administer the chosen measuring instrument. During the administration of this test, measurement takes place when a score is obtained. **Measurement** is the process of collecting data on the property or attribute of interest. Measurement should be as precise, reliable, and objective as possible, and the results expressed in a numerical form that indicates the quantity of the property or attribute being measured. If a multiple-choice test is administered on the rules and strategies of tennis, then the student's knowledge should be reflected by the score on the test. This score serves as a measurement of the individual student's knowledge of the topic. When a sprint is used as a test of running speed, the performance is measured by timing the trials. The final measurement in seconds will indicate how much running speed each particular sprinter possesses.

It is important to remember that an appropriate test must be chosen and properly administered before any confidence can be placed in the final measurement. Even a highly valid and reliable test will yield inaccurate measurements if the administration of the test is carried out under varied conditions. The environment of the test must be as controlled as possible, with educators following a standardized plan of administration to ensure accuracy of measurement.

## Evaluation

**Evaluation** is the process of interpreting the collected measurement and determining some worth or value. Often this interpretation of worth will be done by comparing results to predetermined criteria or objectives. Without the availability of tests and the resulting measurements and norms to be used for comparison, the evaluative process would lack crucial information necessary for informed and impartial decisions.

Without the evaluative processes, the scores collected would have little value. With some tests, the criterion by which to judge the score is common knowledge. If a college sprinter runs 100 meters in 9.4 seconds, a value judgment, or evaluation, of this time can be made based on our knowledge of performances in this event. Evaluations resulting from measurements in other tests may not be as simple. On a treadmill stress test, a 45-year-old female is measured to have a maximal oxygen uptake of 60 millimeters of oxygen per kilogram of body weight. How would you evaluate that measurement? Is her cardiovascular condition good, fair, or bad?

By comparing the results of this test with similar scores, you would be able to evaluate the cardiovascular condition of this subject. However, without administering the test and completing the measurement, you would have no basis for evaluation. Thus, it becomes obvious that the selection of the test and the measurement process are integral to evaluation.

There is no substitute for good judgment and common sense in choosing the testing instrument and in attaining and evaluating the measurement. Though we strive for objectivity, evaluation is a judgment. If there were no place for judgment in the measurement and evaluation process, people could be replaced by computers. Nevertheless, there is no place for judgments that are made without supporting quantitative data in today's educational process.

## Relationships Among Test, Measurement, and Evaluation

From the preceding definitions and accompanying discussion, it should be obvious that the terms *test*, *measurement*, and *evaluation* are interrelated but not synonymous. Tests are specific instruments of measurement. Administering the test is a process of measurement; without tests, measurement would be impossible. The quantitative data resulting from the test represent the measurement.

Measurement is a technique necessary for evaluation. Measurement represents status of a certain attribute or property and is a terminal process. Evaluation is a broader term representing a more complex process than the other two, and many times will be expressed in qualitative terms. Evaluation determines the extent to which objectives are met and is an ongoing and continuous process. By comparing measurements and comparing them to objectives, it is possible to form conclusions based on sound judgment and rationale to improve the quality of the physical education program.

In summary, tests are tools or instruments of measurement; measurement is a major step in evaluation; and evaluation is an all-encompassing process that makes qualitative decisions based on quantitative data derived from tests and measurement.

# USES OF MEASUREMENT AND EVALUATION IN PHYSICAL EDUCATION

It would be impossible to have quality physical education without utilization of measurement and evaluation strategies. Good teachers should test continuously to measure and evaluate in order to gain insights about student progress and the effectiveness of instruction. The process of measurement and evaluation is not an end unto itself. Everything in a program should have a purpose, with the measurement providing data with which to evaluate predetermined objectives. Student outcomes can be measured and evaluated in relation to objectives concerning skills, fitness, knowledge, and values included in the curriculum. Program effectiveness, including teaching behaviors and curricular offerings, can also be evaluated based on this information. With this perspective established, more specific uses of measurement and evaluation regarding student and teacher performance in physical education can be detailed.

## Student Performance

Measurement undertaken in conjunction with student performance can take many forms, with tests running the gamut from simple to complex. Whatever the scope of the measurement, a certain amount of data is critical to giving both the teacher and the student needed information about whether objectives are being met. The effective teacher can use measurement in a variety of ways to impact upon the student.

### Diagnosis

In certain physical education settings, it is appropriate to use measurement tools for **diagnosis** of specific student competencies. By diagnosing weaknesses, the teacher is able to concentrate on these areas to help the student learn. Diagnosis is obviously important in improving motor skills and in pinpointing cognitive areas that need to be emphasized and can be effective in areas concerning health-related physical fitness. Perhaps more important, it can enable the teacher to plan and instruct more effectively. It furnishes the teacher information with which to formulate objectives and determine curricular content. If particular weaknesses surface, remedial programs can be prescribed after the students are assessed.

## Classification

Related to the issue of diagnosis is the measurement strategy of **classification**. From an educational standpoint, it is sometimes advantageous to divide students into either homogeneous or heterogeneous groups based on some attribute. An obvious example of this is in sport when coaches use performance to group players into teams (e.g., varsity, junior varsity). Certain units of instruction might be taught most effectively to groups of students with similar abilities, while other units of instruction may be taught more effectively if student groups comprise a wide range of abilities. Decisions regarding classification by group are based on the teacher's philosophy, unit objectives, the nature of the unit, and the type of students involved.

## Achievement

Perhaps the most important role of measurement is that of determining student **achievement**. Achievement is not to be confused with improvement. Achievement refers to the final ability level at a designated point in time, often coinciding with the end of a unit. The measurement of achievement is normally made relative to some standard or criterion.

The achievement of an individual student gives information to the teacher and student about the level of performance. The collective achievement of a group or class of students supplies data needed to evaluate teacher effectiveness and determine whether the objectives of the program are being met.

## Improvement

**Improvement** is the difference in performance between an initial point and a later point of time. Improvement may be measured over the length of an individual unit, semester, or year. Information concerning improvement in a given area can be valuable to both the teacher and the student. It is particularly encouraging for a student with low initial levels of a certain attribute to be able to measure his or her progress.

Assessing improvement is a viable role of measurement and, in some instances, can be implemented into a grading scheme. However, the teacher must be aware of the inequities of grading on improvement in the case of students who exhibit outstanding initial performance levels and so may not be able to show dramatic gains. It would seem that the best reason to measure improvement is to provide encouragement and information on performance to lower-skilled members of the group.

## Motivation

Measurement of different facets of physical education can provide an important motivation factor. For example, if skill tests are given at the beginning and end of a unit, many students will be motivated to try to improve their performance scores. Likewise, if an examination on rules and strategies of a sport is announced, this may motivate students to learn material that they might not otherwise study.

There are occasions when physical educators encourage students to monitor their performance levels through self-testing activities. For example, youngsters could be encouraged to complete some or all of the items included on the AAHPERD *Physical Best* test battery. Self-assessment of levels of performance on the distance run, skinfold, sit-and-reach, sit-up, or pull-up tests is a useful approach to keep students up-to-date on their progress toward goals. A word of caution should be mentioned. Educators must always be aware of the situation in which a student might become frustrated by the lack of improvement and/or poor performance. If a student is not meeting personal expectations or is obviously deficient compared to classmates, the process of measuring this weakness might serve to discourage rather than to motivate the student.

# Teacher Performance

Measurement and evaluation can perform a variety of roles in relation to the performance of the teacher. Determining grades, assessing improvement, and motivating students are a few examples of ways in which measurement and evaluation can aid teacher effectiveness. Teachers can utilize measurement procedures to evaluate their students, themselves, and their programs. A competent teacher views this process as a way to evaluate students in a fair and consistent manner and as a vehicle for program development and an opportunity for professional growth.

## Assignment of Grades

When measurement and evaluation are mentioned, most physical educators immediately think of the grading process, since measurement is used for grading more than any other purpose. Grades should convey a sense of achievement and status as compared to the stated objectives of the curriculum. The construction/selection of proper measuring instruments to gather information on students becomes integral to the grading process.

The teacher should have a strong rationale and supporting evidence to justify why certain grades are assigned to particular students. There are several methods of grading, and setting up an equitable system to assign grades is not a task to be taken lightly. Chapter 9 examines the many facets of grading to be considered by the physical education teacher. The point to be made at this time is that assignment of grades in an accountable manner is a major component of teacher performance. Without measurement and evaluation procedures, this would be impossible.

## Evaluation of Units of Instruction

Student achievement in individual units of instruction may be measured and compared with the predetermined objectives of the unit. The teacher is then able to make an evaluation of the unit based on this information. This evaluation may affect several areas. Teaching performance comes under scrutiny; if students did not achieve as well as was expected, then course content and teaching methods may need to be altered; or perhaps the objectives of the unit need to be modified to reflect more realistic expectations. All instruments used for measurement during the unit should be examined to determine if they accurately assess student achievement.

## Evaluation of the Curriculum

The cumulative evaluation of the individual units in comparison with general or global curricular objectives provides information for teachers and administrators to use in assessing the effectiveness of the overall program. This broad-based evaluation may result in modifying the length of a unit, adding or dropping a unit from the curriculum, forming the rationale for procuring equipment and/or facilities, or justifying the request for additional faculty members.

The evaluation of curriculum should be ongoing, and the results of the process should be incorporated into the program. A curriculum must be continually modified to meet the changing needs of students. If a program is allowed to continue the status quo, then it runs the chance of becoming stagnant and outdated. Constant fine-tuning can help ensure a dynamic physical education curriculum based on sound education philosophy. Without a solid measurement and evaluation foundation, this process cannot be effective.

## Teacher Effectiveness

Measurement instruments may be utilized to determine teacher effectiveness by assessing student performance or by direct observation of the teaching–learning setting. If a majority of students fails to meet desired objectives in a unit, then certainly teacher effectiveness could be questioned. However, valid reasons other than the effectiveness of the teacher may contribute to this situation. A particularly unskilled group of students and/or unrealistic objectives could be the root of the problem. No doubt, the teaching style and resultant learning environment that is created should be evaluated on a regular basis as well, regardless of levels of student achievement. This assessment may be in the form of a self-evaluation, peer evaluation, or formal evaluation by an administrator.

With the advent of systematic observation instrumentation, behaviors of teachers in the teaching–learning environment can be observed, coded, and quantified. This type of measurement offers objective insights to teachers by which they can evaluate and improve their teaching style. Teaching behaviors such as the praise-to-scold ratio, use of first names and instructional feedback, and management of time can be crucial to creating an environment in which students have the best chance for success.

Student behaviors as they relate to teaching effectiveness may also be measured. For example, time on task has been identified as a crucial element of learning, so it is possible now to measure the amount of time that students are actively engaged in appropriate versus inappropriate activities. Student interactions may also be observed and quantified.

Until recent years, teacher effectiveness was measured by subjective means such as rating scales and anecdotal records. With the development of objective observation systems, these subjective methods are of limited value. Chapter 10 is devoted to a thorough discussion of systematic observation of teacher and student behaviors.

### Public Relations and Physical Education

Physical educators should use every opportunity to publicize the contributions that a quality physical education program can make. If by using measurement it can be demonstrated that the program is meeting worthwhile objectives, continued support for physical education is more likely. It is well worth the effort to publicize outstanding fitness scores of physical education students to other students, administrators, parents, and the general community. Physical educators should take advantage of every chance to justify their place in the curriculum of contemporary schools.

## USES OF MEASUREMENT AND EVALUATION IN THE NONSCHOOL, EXERCISE SETTING

Although the majority of this text focuses on measurement and evaluation in the school setting, a chapter is specifically dedicated to measurement and evaluation techniques for the nonschool exercise setting. There is an ever-increasing number of movement-based academic programs that prepare students for careers in nonschool settings, including fitness management, cardiac rehabilitation, fitness leadership, athletic training, therapeutic recreation, and sports administration. Graduates from such programs are prepared for employment in hospital settings, YMCAs or YWCAs, health clubs, university wellness programs, corporate fitness programs, and many other exercise- and fitness-related organizations and programs.

Even though these nonschool exercise settings differ from the traditional school environment for physical education, certain skills, strategies, and techniques are needed to develop and design successful programs in both types of settings. Measurement and evaluation are integral factors in the operation of exercise and fitness programs in the nonschool environment. For example, techniques to assess initial fitness level are essential for determining fitness programming and exercise prescription for clients. Simple statistical techniques are useful for analyzing data from facility-use surveys. Employee performance can be measured and evaluated. Athletic trainers use a variety of measurement techniques to diagnose the extent of sports injuries. The rehabilitation of a sports injury may require utilization of sophisticated electronic equipment. The use of microcomputers is essential in monitoring budget, inventory, and other components of a successful business. Clearly, a working knowledge of measurement and evaluation techniques is needed to develop and manage successful nonschool exercise and fitness programs.

Common testing protocols found in the nonschool setting include use of the treadmill and bicycle ergometer to measure cardiorespiratory fitness, hydrostatic (underwater) weighing to determine body fat percentage, and specialized field tests for adults. Although a detailed description of the complete protocols is beyond the scope of this text and would likely be covered in a fitness assessment/exercise prescription course, Chapter 13 provides a synopsis of some of these tests. It also discusses similarities and differences among measurement and evaluation techniques in various nonschool settings and describes measurement and evaluation models for the nonschool setting.

## SUMMARY

This chapter provides a basic introduction and orientation to the importance of measurement and evaluation in physical education. A historical perspective, current trends, and contemporary issues in measurement and evaluation are included.

A discussion of the definitions of *test*, *measurement*, and *evaluation* clarifies this terminology for the reader. An understanding of these terms and their relationship is basic to understanding their roles in physical education.

Different facets of a quality physical education program are examined in conjunction with their utilization of measurement and evaluation techniques. It should be clear that the use of these techniques is critical both to students as they participate in physical education activities and to teachers as they strive to deliver a quality program. It is hoped that the crucial nature of the role of measurement and evaluation in physical education will become increasingly clear as the reader progresses through this textbook.

## ► DISCUSSION QUESTIONS

1. How did the work of Edward Hitchcock and Dudley Sargent contribute to the development of measurement and evaluation in physical education from 1860 until the turn of the century?
2. What significant events in history had an impact on the evolution of measurement and evaluation procedures from 1900 to 1970?
3. What were the significant events in the 1970s and 1980s in which the measurement and evaluation process helped portray the fitness status of our nation's school-age youth?
4. What current trends in physical education have a direct relationship to the importance of measurement and evaluation?
5. What is the interrelationship between test, measurement, and evaluation?
6. What is the role of measurement and evaluation in assessing student performance in physical education?
7. How can measurement and evaluation procedures be used in relation to the performance of the teacher?
8. How can measurement and evaluation procedures be used in exercise and sport settings outside the school?

## ► REFERENCES

AAHPERD. (1990). Poor student test scores give boost to fitness education awareness in California. *Update,* p. 1, March.

American College of Sports Medicine (1991). *Prevention and President Clinton's Health Care Reform Proposal.* Paper presented before the Subcommittee on Health Committee on Ways and Means, U.S. House of Representatives, October 26, 1993.

Centers for Disease Control (1991). Participation of high school students in school physical education-United States, 1990. *Morbidity and Mortality Weekly Report* 40: 607-615.

*Chicago Tribune.* (1991). Physical education classes shrinking. *Chicago Tribune,* p. 22, September 8.

Corbin, C. B. & Pangrazi, R. P. (1992). Are American children and youth fit? *Research Quarterly for Exercise and Sports,* 63(2): 96–106.

Hunsicker, P., and Reiff, G. (1977). Youth fitness report: 1958–1965–1975. *Journal of Health and Physical Education* 48:31–33.

Kirshenbaum, J., and Sullivan, R. (1983). Hold on there, America. Sports Illustrated 58:60–64, February 7.

Melagrano, V. J. (1994). Portfolio assessment: Documenting authentic student learning. *Journal of Physical Education, Recreation, and Dance* 65: 50–61.

National Association for Sport and Physical Education (1995). Moving into the future: National Standards for Physical Education. St. Louis: Mosby.

National Commission on Excellence in Education. (1983). *A nation at risk: The imperatives of educations reform.* Washington, DC: U. S. Department of Education.

Public Health Service (1991). *Healthy people 2000: National health promotion and disease prevention objectives.* Washington, D.C.: U. S. Department of Health and Human Services.

Ross, J., and Gilbert, G. (1985). The National Council on Youth Fitness study: A summary of findings. *Journal of Physical Education, Recreation, and Dance* 56:45–50.

Symons, C. W., & Gascoigne, J. L. (1990). The nation's health objectives—a means to school-wide fitness advocacy. *Journal of Physical Education, Recreation, and Dance* 61: 59–63.

U.S. Department of Health and Human Services (1990). *Standards and criteria for the development and evaluation of comprehensive federal physical fitness programs.* Washington, D.C.: U.S. Department of Health and Human Services.

Zessoules, R., & Gardner, H. (1991). Authentic assessment: Beyond the buzzword and to the classroom. In V. Perrone (Ed.), *Expanding student assessment* (pp. 47–71). Alexandria, VA: Association for Supervision and Curriculum Development.

## ▶ REPRESENTATIVE READINGS

Barrow, H. M., and McGee, R. (1979). *A practical approach to measurement in physical education.* 3d ed. Philadelphia, PA: Lea and Febiger.

Johnson, B. L., and Nelson, J. K. (1986). *Practical measurements for evaluation in physical education.* 4th ed. Minneapolis, MN: Burgess.

Kirkendall, D. R.; Gruber, J. J.; and Johnson, R. E. (1980). *Measurement and evaluation for physical educators.* Dubuque, IA: Wm. C. Brown.

Kraus, H., and Hirschland, R. P. (1954). Minimum muscular fitness tests in school children. *The Research Quarterly* 25:178–188.

Miller D. K. (1994). *Measurement by the physical educator: Why and how.* 2nd ed. Dubuque, IA: Brown and Benchmark.

Mood, D. P. (1980). *Numbers in motion: A balanced approach to measurement and evaluation in physical education.* Palo Alto, CA: Mayfield.

Nelson, M. A. (1991). The role of physical education and children's activity in the public health. *Research Quarterly for Exercise and Sport* 62:148–150.

Pangrazi, R. P. and Dancer, V. P. (1995). *Dynamic Physical Education for Elementary School Children.* Boston: Allyn and Bacon.

Raithel, K. S. (1988). Are American children really unfit? *The Physician and Sportsmedicine* 16(10):146–154.

Ross, J. G., and Pate, R. R. (1987). The national children and youth fitness study II: A summary of findings. *JOPERD* 58(9): 51–56.

Symons, C. W., and Gascoigne, J. L. (1990). The nation's health objectives— A means to schoolwide fitness advocacy. *JOPERD* 61(6):59–63.

U. S. Department of Health and Human Services. (1990). *Promoting health/ preventing disease: Year 2000 objectives for the nation.* Washington, DC: Author.

Verducci, F. M. (1980). *Measurement concepts in physical education.* St. Louis, MO: C. V. Mosby.

# LINKING PROGRAM DEVELOPMENT WITH MEASUREMENT AND EVALUATION

**2**

## ► KEY TERMS

affective domain
cognitive domain
curriculum development
health-related physical fitness domain
learning domain
needs assessment
performance-based objectives
physical fitness
program continuity
program goals
psychomotor domain
sports-related fitness
student interest surveys
unit outcomes

## ► OBJECTIVES

*After reading this chapter, the student should be able to:*

1. Characterize the four learning domains associated with physical education and analyze them from the perspective of different school settings and teaching situations.

2. Understand how to plan a needs assessment and cite occasions for use.

3. Identify and describe the five phases of program development and understand the role of measurement and evaluation in this process.

4. Distinguish relationships among program goals, unit objectives, and performance-based objectives.

5. Discuss the ongoing nature of the program development process.

6. Articulate the relationship of measurement and evaluation procedures to program development.

When measurement and evaluation are mentioned, most physical educators automatically think only of the issue of grading. While grading is obviously a critical part of these processes, it is only one area in which measurement and evaluation can make important contributions to a quality physical education program. In nonschool settings, exercise science practitioners often do not recognize the importance of measurement and evaluation activities to program development.

The planning of the curriculum, the subsequent delivery of the activities, and the effectiveness of the overall program are seldom discussed in relationship to measurement and evaluation practices. One of the shortcomings of many measurement and evaluation courses is that they do not sufficiently address practical issues relevant to the contemporary physical educator and exercise science practitioner. Many practitioners never consider their measurement and evaluation practices as tools to use in improving their programs.

In nonschool settings, measurement and evaluation activities are also critical to program development and continuity. In athletic training, physical therapy, adult fitness settings, and other exercise science environments, the use of measurement and evaluation is the foundation of the program. For instance, in fitness settings, a client typically undergoes an initial screening to assess current levels of body composition, cardiovascular endurance, and flexibility. An exercise program is then designed based on this initial assessment, and the individual's progress is monitored as she or he progresses through the program.

Without measurement and evaluation of the components of health-related physical fitness, there would be no way to ascertain initial fitness levels, monitor the program, or know when the person had met prescribed goals. The same sort of model would typically be used in athletic training for assessing injury, monitoring the effectiveness of rehabilitation, and knowing when an athlete should be released to return to activity. Beyond these individual programs, program administrators can use measurement and evaluation to assess total program goals by looking at collective outcomes of all clients currently engaged in the program.

The physical education curriculum also should provide experiences that promote students' growth and development. These activities need to be planned and categorized based on their contributions to the various learning domains. The traditional learning domains—cognitive, affective, and psychomotor—represent logical classifications for directed learning. This conceptualization of the learning domains, as related to physical education, needs to be upgraded to include a fourth domain: health-related physical fitness.

The ultimate success of a school-based or nonschool-based program depends on the instructor's effectiveness in helping students or clients achieve goals related to each of the four learning domains. Planning and implementing various learning experiences is a multiphase, ongoing process that relies on quantifiable data to assist in determining the effectiveness of learning experiences. In this era of concern regarding accountability, measurement and evaluation are inextricably linked to decisions made concerning program development. Practitioners need to become more familiar with assessment tools that can be used to measure performance in each of the four domains.

Thus, the main purpose of this chapter is to discuss and emphasize the natural connections between the program development and the measurement and evaluation processes. To do this, it is first necessary to identify and briefly describe each of the four learning domains integral to physical education. (Each of these domains, and its appropriate measurement and evaluation procedures, is presented in depth in subsequent chapters.) A five-phase approach to program development is then presented, emphasizing the role of measurement and evaluation in each phase.

# THE FOUR LEARNING DOMAINS OF PHYSICAL EDUCATION

Program structure should provide educational experiences that foster growth and development in the four learning domains of physical education and exercise science: health-related physical fitness, psychomotor, cognitive, and affective. Each **learning domain** should be viewed as a sphere in which certain outcomes are targeted for attainment through specific educational experiences. An individual's progress toward objectives in each domain can and should be monitored. Chapters 5–8 describe specific measurement tools and strategies that can be used appropriately to measure performance or qualities associated with each of the four domains. The establishment of goals in these domains is equally important in school and nonschool settings.

## Health-Related Physical Fitness Domain

A review of curriculum and measurement texts shows that most authors include health-related physical fitness within the psychomotor domain. However, it is proposed in this textbook that curricular development and accompanying measurement techniques could be more effective and easily understood if the health-related physical fitness domain and the psychomotor domain were viewed as separate realms. Proposed initially by Annarino, Cowell, and Hazelton (1980), this view is becoming an accepted way to classify learning domains in physical education. The current emphasis on health-related fitness as determined by the increased interest in fitness activities for a lifetime and the number of texts devoted specifically to health fitness also support the emergence of a separate learning domain.

The **health-related physical fitness domain** is characterized by those aspects of physical fitness that affect an individual's functional health and physical well-being. The importance of good eating and activity habits to increase the chances for good health has received much publicity in recent years. Regular aerobic exercise, combined with good nutrition, helps prevent hypokinetic conditions such as cardiovascular disease, low back pain, obesity, and hypertension. The importance of emphasizing these areas in the physical education curriculum warrants its being included as a separate domain. In many nonschool settings, health-related physical fitness is a primary goal.

In the physical education field, confusion exists about the term **physical fitness.** Some physical education textbooks include health-related physical fitness tests, such as the Prudential FITNESSGRAM (1992) in the psychomotor domain. Various physical fitness test batteries include tests of speed, agility, quickness, upper body strength, and jumping ability. While these are important skills for playing competitive or recreational sports, they have little bearing on maintaining good health for a lifetime. In order to distinguish these tests of athletic skills from those of physical fitness, we can classify them as measuring **sports-related fitness**. Sports-related fitness tests also should be included in measurement and evaluation schemes, but it should be remembered that they are more appropriately grouped in the psychomotor domain.

It is becoming accepted practice for **physical fitness** testing to emphasize health-related components, including body composition (ratio of leanness to fatness), cardiovascular efficiency, muscular strength and endurance, and flexibility of lower back and posterior thigh area. While sports-related skill test scores are dependent on genetic predisposition and, thus, difficult to improve, virtually any student can improve scores on health-related components with a systematic conditioning program and proper motivation. To avoid confusion with the sports-related fitness components and to ensure proper emphasis of the health-related components, a separate learning domain is not only helpful, but necessary. Chapter 5 describes the components of health-related physical fitness and discusses tests designed to measure cardiovascular fitness, muscular strength and endurance, flexibility, and body composition.

## Psychomotor Domain

The **psychomotor domain** includes fundamental movement patterns that are skill-related and emphasizes specialized skills needed in particular sports. Skill-related fitness components include balance, speed, agility, coordination, and power associated with quality performance in sport. Of the four demains, this one is more specific to school settings than to nonschool settings. Typically, adult fitness settings would not include sport skill development as a goal.

While the psychomotor domain includes traits specific to general motor ability tests, test batteries are also available to measure skills that are specific to a particular sport. Therefore, sports skills are also included in the psychomotor domain. The ability to shoot free throws in basketball, putt a golf ball, or serve a tennis ball can be measured in a very accurate way. Chapter 6 identifies and discusses specific facets of skill fitness and describes various assessment techniques to evaluate general motor ability and specific sports skills.

## Cognitive Domain

Though not often associated with physical education by the general public and many physical educators, the cognitive domain is a critical area that should be addressed in the measurement and evaluation scheme. The **cognitive domain** includes processes of acquiring and using knowledge such as thinking, recognizing, memorizing and recalling, creating, and understanding. The classification of educational objectives for this domain is typically linked to Bloom's *Taxonomy of Educational Objectives* (1956). The various levels of Bloom's taxonomy represent an ascending order of cognitive processes. These hierarchical levels can be matched to students' cognitive abilities at the various stages of development in order to provide proper cognitive activities and realistic objectives.

Inasmuch as there is a renewed emphasis on the importance of teaching the how and why of physical activity, it is necessary to develop proper techniques designed to measure and evaluate performance in the cognitive domain. A knowledge of the rules, strategies, skill techniques, safety procedures, equipment, and the underlying concepts of movement and fitness should be addressed in the program. The use of valid and reliable procedures allows us to know if students are achieving in the cognitive area. Chapter 7 describes how to construct, administer, and evaluate a written test. It is an area that should be addressed in nonschool settings as well as school settings. It is critical that individuals in fitness and rehabilitation settings have a clear understanding of their personal programs.

## Affective Domain

The **affective domain** includes development of socioemotional skills, good sportsmanship, cooperation, self-concept, and positive attitudes toward physical activity. Within the whole scope of education, there are lofty goals about improving areas associated with the affective domain. Nevertheless, little has been done to substantiate these claims or hold teachers accountable in this area. Virtually every set of goals or objectives in physical education contains statements concerning the affective domain; however, these objectives are seldom measured and evaluated in an objective and quantifiable manner. If objectives about such things as improving attitudes toward physical activity are included, then these areas should be included in the measurement and evaluation scheme. While goals in this area are often not emphasized, they are a very important area in both school and nonschool settings.

The assessment of the affective domain can be accomplished with measurement tools such as attitudinal surveys, sociometric inventories, self-concept scales, and value appraisals. Chapter 8 provides a thorough explanation of the affective domain and identifies various measurement tools that can provide objective and quantifiable information about the areas included in the affective domain.

## NEEDS ASSESSMENT

Prior to any stage of program development, an assessment should be conducted to determine the needs of the program. These needs may be classified according to philosophical beliefs, content requirements, fitness levels, or students' performance. The procedure used to identify strengths and weaknesses associated with the various aspects of the program, a critical tool for obtaining information important to program decision making, is called a **needs assessment**.

In physical education, a needs assessment is a process for determining the appropriateness of the goals for the program, teacher, or student and for determining what specific activities to include in a physical education curriculum. In nonschool settings, needs assessments can take the form of initial screening of injuries, fitness levels, etc. This initial assessment forms the basis for subsequent treatments or fitness prescriptions Even though general program goals are broad and easily understood, the specific unit outcomes and performance-based student objectives should be geared toward the needs of the particular program or students involved. The needs assessment may also serve as an initial pretest to obtain baseline data, which enables the progress of the students to be regularly monitored and evaluated through periodic testing during the unit, semester, or year. Whatever the format, the needs assessment is clearly based on sound measurement and evaluation practices.

Through comparative procedures, results of the assessment are translated into more meaningful descriptive data. This information can then be utilized to determine the relative status of the program, teacher effectiveness, and student performance in relation to expected standards.

For example, a needs assessment could be conducted to determine the health-related physical fitness status of the students in a particular school. The Prudential FITNESSGRAM test battery (1992) could be administered to students during the fall. Raw scores could be collected and means calculated for each age and gender. Group means could be compared to national standards. The relationship of the group means to the national criteria would provide information about the relative health-related physical fitness status of youth in the school. Based on this comparison, the physical education teacher would have the information necessary to draw conclusions regarding health-related physical fitness needs of the students.

The prevalence and sophistication of assessment tools make the type and extent of information that can be obtained about the program, teachers, and students almost limitless. Remember, the needs assessment can be utilized to evaluate any of the four learning domains associated with physical education. See Figure 2.0 for an outline for conducting a needs assessment. Once the needs have been determined, physical educators and

**► FIGURE 2.0** Map for conducting needs assessment.

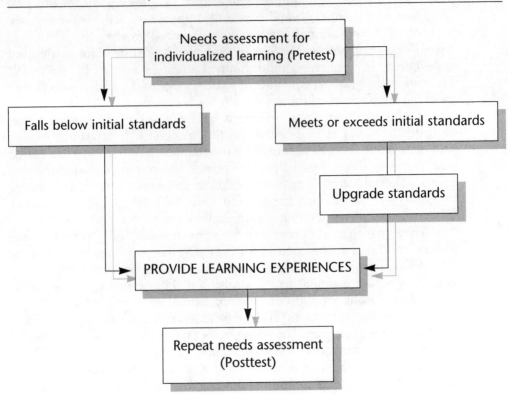

exercise science practitioners can rely on the results of recent scientific findings to assist in the selection of appropriate activities to best meet those needs.

The importance and utility of the needs assessment should not be underestimated. Both physical educators and exercise science practitioners are encouraged to implement a needs assessment during any phase of program development, always keeping in mind that the quantifiable information derived from a needs assessment can be useful in making the transition from one phase of curriculum development to the next.

## PROGRAM DEVELOPMENT

Program development takes place in both school and nonschool settings. The steps of program development are very similar in these different activity-based environments. The role of measurement and evaluation in the development and maintenance of any type of program is crucial.

Many physical education textbooks are dedicated to **curriculum development,** with each offering a different approach to the teaching of physical education. Despite this variety, most long-term goals for physical education are the same. What differs is the approach to achieve those goals. Lack of agreement among nationally recognized experts in curriculum design does not necessarily imply that physical education curriculum development is fragmented and unrefined. Rather, it typifies the pattern of curriculum development in virtually all subject areas and suggests that more than one approach can achieve the same outcome.

Programmatic decision making is neither an exact science nor a simple operation, yet it is essential to the successful functioning of any program. While consensus cannot be reached on all of the steps associated with program development, several phases are common to quality programs: (1) establishing a realistic philosophical approach; (2) developing program goals; (3) determining unit outcomes; (4) establishing performance objectives; and, (5) evaluating and improving the program.

These five phases of program development should flow in a sequential pattern. Although the procedures for the respective phases vary, each of the five phases depends upon measurement and evaluation techniques to provide information essential to the decision-making process. For example, establishing a realistic philosophical approach requires a database that accurately depicts the parameters (budget, facilities, equipment, supplies, and so on) that limit the program. The successes of phases two through four, which deal with program goals, unit outcomes, and performance objectives, depend on quantitative information that accurately indicates the status of individuals in the various learning domains. The final phase, evaluating and improving the curriculum, needs to work from a baseline of quantifiable information if subsequent alterations in program are to be recommended and successfully implemented. Each of these phases is discussed below.

## Phase 1: Establishing a Realistic Philosophical Approach

Perhaps the most important task confronting physical educators and exercise science practitioners during the various stages of program building is establishing a realistic philosophical approach. The philosophical aims of a program are the foundation on which the other phases of program development are built. Certainly, not everyone endorses the same philosophical beliefs. However, there are several philosophical aims that, in all likelihood, would be a part of any quality program, including commitment to maximum participation by all students, a focus on fitness-related activities, accommodating students with special needs, and assurances to provide quality instruction. At first thought, measurement and evaluation do not seem necessary in the development of philosophical aims. Nevertheless, some measurement techniques provide invaluable assistance in the process of finalizing the philosophical aims of a physical education program.

**Student interest surveys** provide important information related to diversity and balance of curricular offerings at various grade levels. These surveys should take into account facilities, equipment, administrative policies, and so on. Results of such a survey are often surprising and may offer suggestions on new activities that can be included to update the curriculum. A survey of physical education programs may also yield helpful information about innovations in curriculum design. By studying program offerings in an objective way, a determination can be made as to whether a curriculum is sufficiently diverse to meet the philosophical aims of a physical education program. Similar surveys can be used to gather valuable information for nonschool programs.

The philosophy of a program should reflect the characteristics and needs of the students. A clear understanding of the various attributes and stages of development of the different ages of boys and girls and the relationship of these attributes to the four domains of physical education provide a basis for philosophical decisions. Research provides excellent descriptive information on the general characteristics and developmental stages of school-age youth. The best way to collect specific information about students is to utilize selected performance tests to measure the current status of students. Knowing the status of the students makes it possible to construct the curricular framework to meet the characteristics and needs of the students.

A dilemma in forming philosophical aims for a program is what emphasis to put on the various learning domains. Should more concern be displayed toward the health-related fitness levels, cognitive understanding, motor skill development, or the attitudes and socioemotional skills of the students? Which domain is most important and, as a result, receives more emphasis? While all domains are certainly important, formal needs assessment may indicate that a particular area needs more emphasis. This type of decision influences many later decisions made in regard to curriculum planning and the measurement and evaluation model.

Part of the philosophical underpinnings of a quality physical education program should be the expectations of teacher performance. Too often, all of the attention centers on student expectations, and teacher performance is taken for granted. Certain teacher behaviors promote an effective teaching–learning environment and facilitate the management of students in physical education. High rates of specific, positive feedback to students; high rates of using students' first names; an active teaching style; low percentages of management activities; and high rates of appropriate on-task student behaviors are examples of behaviors that indicate effective teaching. Systematic observation procedures enable us to measure and analyze behaviors in physical education in a quantifiable and objective way. Chapter 10 describes systematic observation procedures that can be readily implemented in the physical education setting.

**Program continuity** is another important philosophical area to be considered. Successful continuity planning requires a great deal of time and effort. A quality program should include a sequenced physical education curricular offering from K–12. Unfortunately, this area is not commonly addressed because physical educators in elementary and secondary levels tend to work independently of each other. The needs assessment in each learning domain for each grade level provides a starting point to plan program continuity.

Philosophically, an ongoing evaluation of any activity-based program is essential. Properly chosen measurement tools based on philosophical tenets should be utilized to provide a quantifiable basis for this evaluation to take place. The primary purpose for the evaluation is to determine if program objectives are being achieved. Because various constituencies demand educational accountability, the concept of ongoing evaluation based on sound measurement procedures assumes even more importance. This evaluation should focus on both student performance and teacher performance. The evaluation model should enable teachers and administrators to make decisions on successful and unsuccessful facets of the physical education program. Areas of deficiency then can be corrected, and what is judged as satisfactory can be retained and enhanced.

## Phase 2: Developing Attainable Program Goals

Once a realistic philosophical approach to the program has been developed, it becomes appropriate to develop global program goals that are challenging, yet attainable and realistic. This is the second phase of curriculum development. **Program goals** evolve from the fundamental philo-sophical aims and serve as the primary link between the philosophy and activities of the program. Failure to develop and attain predetermined pro-gram goals makes any type of accountability difficult and, based on current trends in education, places the program in jeopardy of being cut back or eliminated.

Similar to the process that leads to establishing a program philosophy, Phase 2 depends on proper techniques of measurement and evaluation to develop attainable program goals. To evaluate whether program goals have been attained obviously is a function of sound measurement procedures. Determining the degree to which program goals are being met is vital to the process and is best achieved through objective inquiry.

Many of the same areas in which needs assessments are used to deter-mine philosophical aims are also used to formulate program goals. Written goals cannot be finalized without investigating student needs, characteris-tics, and interests. A predetermined set of program goals provides students, teachers, parents, and administrators with an overview of expectancies of the physical education program. Program goals should be measurable and realistic and lend themselves to objective assessment.

The goals of a program are broader and more global than the unit out-comes (Phase 3) and the performance objectives (Phase 4). The measurement and evaluation of performance objectives and unit outcomes serve as infor-mation for the evaluation of program goals. Program goals should reflect each of the four learning domains. One or more goals should be included concerning the development of health-related physical fitness, psychomo-tor skills, cognitive processes, and the affective areas. The following list is a good example of program goals for a physical education program. Consider these goals and decide if others should be included.

1. Establish and maintain health-related physical fitness.
2. Develop competence in movement.
3. Understand the importance of health-related physical fitness and the benefits of an active lifestyle.
4. Comprehend the rules, strategies, techniques, and safety procedures associated with games and sports.
5. Develop socioemotional skills.
6. Display a positive attitude toward physical activity.

## Phase 3: Determining Unit Outcomes

As noted earlier, the goals of a physical education program are broad and global in nature. After Phase 2 is completed, the tasks of choosing units, sequencing units in a logical order, and determining outcomes for each unit make up Phase 3. Just as measurement and evaluation play an integral part in the first two phases, they also are crucial to this phase.

Information on student needs, characteristics, and interests is critical in the selection of units. Availability of facilities and equipment, number and length of units, teacher expertise, balance of activities, and climate also must be considered when selecting and sequencing units. The units should be organized in a horizontal progression during any given school year and in a vertical progression from grades K–12.

**Unit outcomes** are developed to serve as targets for students and teachers during the individual activity and can be linked to any of the program goals. For example, assume we are defining unit outcomes for a seventh grade basketball unit. A unit outcome could be

The student will learn the fundamentals of shooting a free throw.

This unit outcome is directly linked to the program goal of developing competence of movement, which in basketball includes the ability to shoot free throws.

From this example, one can readily see that there could be a number of unit outcomes. Remember that the length of the unit, the age of the students, their initial competence, the size of class, and many other factors will affect what can be accomplished. Since unit outcomes are related to attainable program goals, make certain that the unit outcomes are attainable as well.

## Phase 4: Establishing Performance-Based Objectives

After units have been selected for the curriculum, the scope and sequence of those units must be determined. Integral to this process is writing **performance-based objectives** specific to each unit. In writing performance-based objectives, the same factors are considered as when defining unit outcomes. Performance-based objectives break down unit outcomes into measurable and observable terms. Just as unit outcomes are linked to program goals, performance-based objectives are linked to unit outcomes.

Care must be taken in writing these objectives so that expectancies of the students are clear. Also called behavioral objectives, performance-based objectives are statements about what the student should be able to perform. An example of a performance-based objective is

The student will be able to make 5 of 10 free throws.

The achievement of this performance-based objective has obvious evaluative implications on the unit outcome stated previously. Because of this relationship, the achievement of the performance-based objective also has influence on the related program goal. The achievement-based objective is crucial to the measurement and evaluation scheme of the overall program.

A series of performance-based objectives written for different levels of competence can furnish a more complete evaluation picture for a given task. For instance, the example above could be stated with different criteria: "3 free throws of 10" or "7 free throws of 10."

Performance-based objectives can and should be written for each of the four learning domains. The clarity of performance-based objectives and the accurate measurement of student outcomes based on these objectives provide the basis for evaluating achievement. The effectiveness of any program should be evaluated in light of the achievement of the participants.

## Phase 5: Evaluating and Improving the Program

The final phase of the program development process is concerned with evaluating and improving the program. The process of teaching can be represented by three basic questions:

What do I want to teach?

How do I want to teach it?

How well did I teach it?

The fifth phase deals with the last question. In an age of increased accountability, the effectiveness of the program is often measured by achievement of the participants. In a very real sense, how well one teaches is also measured by how well students meet the objectives set forth in the program. Thus, the answer to the question of "How well did I teach it?" can relate to the effectiveness of the program.

A program must be continually monitored and revised as needed. When areas of the program are recognized as needing improvement, it may be that units need to be added, modified, or deleted. This relates directly back to the question of "What do I want to teach?" Or it may be determined that the activity units are appropriate, but change is needed in the teaching methodologies, sequence, or structure of the unit. This type of decision relates to the second question, "How do I want to teach it?" Thus, the process of teaching should not be linear as shown previously but, rather, ongoing or cyclical as shown below.

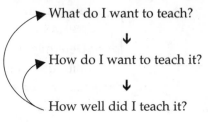

Phase 5 follows this model. If areas of the program need improvement, it may be necessary to return to any or all of the previous four phases. Addressing the first two questions could affect any of the first four phases of program development. In addition, decisions made in Phase 5 can directly impact other phases as the program is revised. Figure 2.1 illustrates this concept.

Evaluating the effectiveness of the program is an ongoing process, since a program never should be in its final form. It continually needs to be fine-tuned for improvement and to remain current. Measuring the performance of participants, surveying their interests, and assessing their needs are all sources of information for program evaluation. A periodic evaluation, usually yearly, is done based on the information gathered from measurement procedures in each of the first four phases. The evaluation includes each of the four learning domains.

After quantifiable and objective information is gathered, qualitative judgments based on sound logic and the data collected are made to evaluate and improve the program. Some activities will be added, others will be

▶ **FIGURE 2.1**    The ongoing program development process.

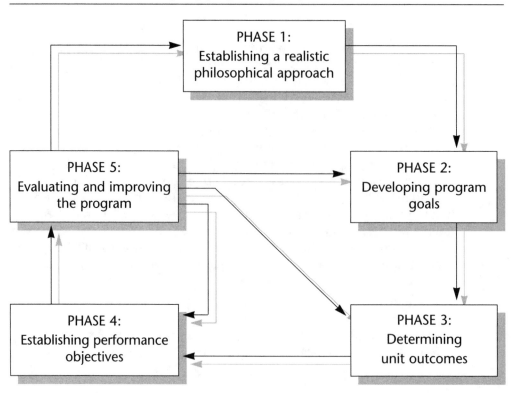

PHASE 1:
Establishing a realistic
philosophical approach

PHASE 5:
Evaluating and improving
the program

PHASE 2:
Developing program
goals

PHASE 4:
Establishing performance
objectives

PHASE 3:
Determining
unit outcomes

dropped, and others will undergo various types of modification. The utilization of information collected from the variety of measurement procedures is critical to programmatic decision making. With the wide range of available measurement tools, it would be foolish to make any decisions concerning the program without making full use of these assessment procedures. It is impossible to construct and maintain a quality program without having a solid measurement and evaluation model.

## SUMMARY

The primary goal of this chapter is to establish the critical linkages between measurement and evaluation strategies and program development processes in physical education and exercise science. The five phases of program development and the role of measurement and evaluation in each phase are presented. The importance of the program development process as dynamic rather than static is discussed.

Measurement and evaluation are critical components of this ongoing program development process. Informed decisions in any phase depend on sound measurement and evaluation strategies. Accuracy of measurement followed up with sound evaluation are essential to ensuring initial and continued quality in school and nonschool programs.

## ▶ DISCUSSION QUESTIONS

1. Describe each of the four learning domains in physical education. Explain what measurement and evaluation procedures could be used to assess achievement in each domain.

2. Provide a rationale for the treatment of health-related physical fitness as a separate learning domain in physical education. Include a discussion about the differences between health-related fitness and sports-related fitness in your answer.

3. Which learning domain merits the most instructional time during the year? The least? Give reasons for your opinions.

4. Provide examples of situations in which a needs assessment should be used. How often should a needs assessment be conducted?

5. Select any phase of program development. What are the various ways measurement and evaluation strategies can be used to make informed decisions about the status of this phase?

6. Explain how Phase 5 of program development is related to the previous four phases. In your answer discuss how the relationship among the five phases affects program development as an ongoing process.

◤ **REFERENCES**

Annarino, A. A.; Cowell, C. C.; and Hazelton, H. W. (1980). *Curriculum theory and design in physical education.* St. Louis, MO: C. V. Mosby.

Bloom, B.; Englehart, M.; Furst, E.; and Kratwohl, D. (1956). *Taxonomy of educational objectives: The classification of educational goals, handbook 1: Cognitive domain.* New York: Longmans, Green.

Cooper Institute for Aerobics Research (1992). *The Prudential FITNESSGRAM: Test Administration Manual.* Dallas, TX: Cooper Institute for Aerobics Research.

◤ **REPRESENTATIVE READINGS**

Corbin, C. B., ed. (1980). *A textbook of motor development.* 2d ed. Dubuque, IA: Wm. C. Brown.

Harrison, J. M. (1996). *Instructional strategies for secondary school physical education.* 4th ed. Dubuque, IA: Wm. C. Brown.

Siedentop, D.; Herkowitz, H.; and Rink, J. (1984). *Elementary physical education methods.* Englewood Cliffs, NJ: Prentice-Hall.

Wessel, J. A., and Kelly, L. (1986). *Achievement-based curriculum development in physical education.* Philadelphia, PA: Lea & Febiger.

Willgoose, C. E. (1984). *The curriculum in physical education.* 4th ed. Englewood Cliffs, NJ: Prentice-Hall.

Zaichkowsky, L. D.; Zaichkowsky, L. B.; and Martinek, T. J. (1980). *Growth and development: The child and physical activity.* St. Louis, MO: C. V. Mosby.

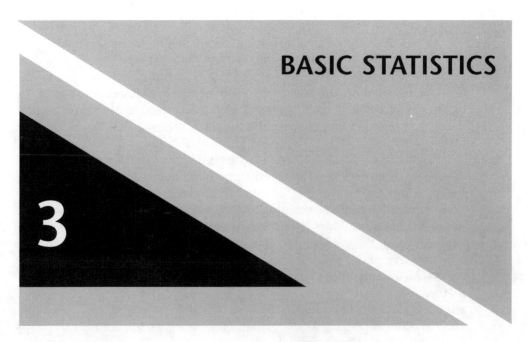

# BASIC STATISTICS

## 3

### ▶ KEY TERMS

abscissa
apparent limits
bar graph
ceiling effect
continuous data
correlation
correlation coefficient
cumulative frequency
   graph
discrete data
frequency polygon
grouped frequency
   distribution
histogram
interpercentile range
interquartile range
interval
leptokurtic
mean
median
mode
nominal
normal curve
ordinal
ordinate
Pearson product-
   moment correlation

percentile
platykurtic
range
ratio
real limits
scattergram
simple analysis of
   variance (ANOVA)
simple frequency
   distribution
simple regression
skewed
Spearman rho rank-
   order correlation
standard deviation
standard scores
statistics
T-score
t-test for dependent
   samples
t-test for
   independent
   samples
variance
z-score

### ▶ OBJECTIVES

*After reading this chapter, the student should be able to:*

1. Classify data according to the four measurement levels.

2. Recognize and use data display techniques.

3. Identify, understand the role of, and calculate the measures of central tendency and the measures of variability.

4. Describe the properties of the normal curve.

5. Give the general properties of standard scores and transform raw scores into percentile ranks, z-scores, and T-scores.

6. Utilize appropriate correlational procedures to ascertain relationships between sets of data.

7. Develop simple regression formulas from sets of data with high correlation coefficients.

8. Provide a rudimentary explanation of appropriate applications for t-tests and simple ANOVA.

A t the mention of the word "statistics," people exhibit a variety of reactions—cynicism, suspicion, awe, anxiety. A popular notion sees statistics as numerical information that may be manipulated to defend any position while appearing analytical and objective. True, statistics can be used in this way, but keep in mind that nonsense may be expressed verbally as well as statistically. A knowledge of logic is a good defense against verbal nonsense. By the same token, a basic knowledge of statistics is a good safeguard against numerical nonsense.

This chapter is designed as a basic guide to the most common statistical procedures used in physical education and exercise science. Very little theory is presented, and the "cookbook" approach to the statistical operations included is geared to helping the practitioner feel comfortable with the various techniques. Many statistical textbooks present in-depth theoretical explanations if the student desires more information. For students who are apprehensive about studying statistics, they should discard any preconceived ideas and approach this chapter with an open mind. The only mathematical skills needed to master the statistical procedures presented are the basic computational skills of addition, subtraction, multiplication, and division. A pocket calculator will make it easier to complete the steps involved in the various procedures.

Simply defined, **statistics** is the science of collecting, classifying, presenting, and interpreting numerical data. A basic knowledge of statistics helps to organize and analyze data collected, or measured, from tests. For instance, it is common for a curl-up test to be administered as a part of fitness testing. The teacher administers the test to all the students in her classes. This could easily be 150 students or more. All scores are recorded, but raw data in this form means very little to the teacher or the students. What kind of information does the teacher need to make these data meaningful?

An average score for all students would certainly be helpful, as would average scores per class or by age and gender. By looking at the highest score and the lowest score, the teacher gets an idea of the spread of the scores or the range of ability of students in the group. If students are to be tested later in the year, improvement can also be calculated. All of this information is statistical in nature and helps the teacher and student understand the results of the sit-up test. Without statistical procedures, this information would be meaningless.

## LEVELS OF MEASUREMENT

Prospective physical education teachers and exercise science practitioners should become familiar with the four levels of measurement: nominal, ordinal, interval, and ratio. These four kinds of measurement represent different levels of precision in gathering data and measuring variables. An understanding of the differences in these levels of measurement is basic to using various statistical procedures properly. Certain statistical procedures assume a specific level of measurement, and if this criterion is not met, then the data will be analyzed in an improper manner, resulting in misinterpretation.

## Nominal Level

The **nominal** level is the simplest and least precise of the four measurement scales. Numbers are often assigned for the sole purpose of differentiating an attribute or property of one object from another. The following are examples of a nominal level of measurement with numbers assigned for identification:

> Basketball jersey #34
>
> Interstate Highway 20
>
> Locker #80

Nominal measurements do not always assign numbers for differentiation. Rather than numbers, letters of the alphabet or names can easily be assigned. Gender is differentiated by male and female; male could be assigned M and female assigned F. Eye color can be identified by the terms *blue*, *brown*, *gray*, or *hazel*. Nationality can be American, Canadian, or Mexican. By totalling the number of each nationality, a frequency count for each category can be reported.

Other than a frequency count, no other calculation can be made with nominal measures. Locker #80 and locker #40 are merely two different lockers that are assigned numbers for identification. No arithmetic procedures would be appropriate for these locker numbers. No comparisons between 40 and 80 can be made. Locker #40 is not viewed as being smaller than locker #80. A Social Security number is a nominal measurement that identifies a person as distinct from other people. As simple as the nominal scale is, it is a form of measurement that is very useful in making differentiation between objects or people and in reporting the frequency of something that occurs or exists.

## Ordinal Level

The **ordinal** level of measurement is more precise than the nominal level because it has the property of order. The numbers assigned represent relative amounts of the quality or attribute being measured. A differentiation between one object and another can be made as with nominal measurement, but ordinal measurement also specifies the direction of the difference. Thus, one can say "more than" or "less than."

If a student did more sit-ups than anyone in the class, that student's name would be first on a list showing order of scores. The statement can be made that this student did "more sit-ups than the second-place student." Similarly, the second-place student did "more than the third-place student." Without knowing the actual scores, it cannot be known how many is "more than." The top-ranked student may have done 60 sit-ups, the second-ranked student 59, while the third-ranked student may have done 55. Though first place is one place higher than second place, and second place is one place higher than third place, the differences between the raw scores of the three students are not equal.

This is an important level of measurement, but it does not allow for meaningful arithmetic calculations to be made. As illustrated by the sit-up example above, ordinal differences do not imply equal differences in the amount of the attribute being measured. Ranking teams or players is common in physical education and athletics. Any type of ranking is an example of ordinal measurement.

## *Assigning Ranks to Raw Data*

If two scores are identical, then those scores logically should share the same rank. The scores below represent the score of a 10-point pop quiz. In the example, the score "6" occurs twice and shares the rank of 3.5.

| Score | Rank |
|-------|------|
| 9 | 1 |
| 7 | 2 |
| 6 | 3.5 |
| 6 | 3.5 |
| 5 | 5 |
| 3 | 6 |
| 2 | 7 |

If three scores are the same, then their shared rank would be the middle-rank of the three.

| Score | Rank |
|-------|------|
| 9 | 1 |
| 8 | 2 |
| 7 | 3 |
| 6 | 5 |
| 6 | 5 |
| 6 | 5 |
| 5 | 7 |
| 4 | 8 |

## Interval Level

Scores at the **interval** level are more precise than nominal and ordinal data. With data at the interval level, the equal differences in measurements reflect equal differences in the amount of the characteristic being assessed. In an interval scale, the zero point of the interval scale is arbitrary, but it does not represent absence of the attribute. A temperature scale is an example of an interval level measurement. If it is 0 degrees outside, the measurement does not reflect absence of temperature. The temperature can go below zero as well. However, a change in the temperature from 0° to 4° F is the same amount of difference if the temperature changes from 72° to 76° F. Calendar time is also an example of an interval measurement scale.

With interval data, calculations are meaningful. Arithmetic operations can be done, but ratio statements cannot be made. For instance, is 80° F twice as hot as 40° F? Because there is no value in an interval scale that represents absence of an attribute, in this case temperature, ratio statements of this sort are incorrect; 80° F is 40° F warmer than the temperature of 40° F, but it does not represent a temperature that is twice as hot.

## Ratio Level

The most precise and most useful of all levels is that of **ratio** measurement. It has all the same characteristics of the interval scale with the added advantage of having an absolute zero that reflects absence of the attribute or quality being measured. Because of the absolute zero quality, ratio statements such as "twice as high" or "half as fast" have meaning.

Assume that a student took an exam that had 100 possible points. If she scored 90 on the exam and a classmate scored 45, one score is twice as high as the other. If someone scored zero on the exam, the score reflects the fact that the person did not get any answers correct. A child who is three feet tall is only half as tall as an adult who is six feet tall. With ratio level data, this type of statement is meaningful. Fortunately, most measurements in physical education and exercise science settings are ratio in nature so that arithmetic operations can be calculated and comparative statements can be made.

## FREQUENCY DISTRIBUTIONS

Frequency distributions are a simple way to present a set of collected scores in an organized way. Frequency refers to how often a score occurs. Distribution refers to how the scores are dispersed. When data such as test scores are collected, the result is usually a list of unorganized numbers. Listed below is a short list of raw scores from a one-minute curl-up test.

41, 22, 40, 38, 58, 44, 49, 15, 28, 46, 35, 55, 33

For any interpretation of the scores to be made, it is helpful to organize it into some type of logical format. The most common method of organization is to list the scores in rank order fashion as shown below:

58, 55, 49, 46, 44, 41, 40, 38, 35, 33, 28, 22, 15

## Simple Frequency Distribution

With a larger amount of curl-up scores, a similar list can be made to show each score separately:

58, 55, 54, 50, 49, 48, 46, 45, 44, 43, 42, 41, 40, 40, 40, 40, 39, 39, 39,
39, 38, 38, 38, 38, 38, 38, 37, 37, 37, 37, 37, 36, 36, 36, 36, 35, 35, 34,
34, 34, 34, 34, 34, 33, 33, 33, 33, 33, 33, 32, 32, 32, 32, 31, 31, 31,
31, 31, 30, 30, 30, 29, 29, 29, 29, 28, 28, 28, 28, 27, 27, 27, 26, 26, 26,
26, 25, 25, 24, 24, 24, 23, 22, 22, 22, 21, 21, 20, 19, 18, 17, 16, 15, 15,
13, 12, 10, 9

However, to avoid a long, cumbersome list of numbers such as this, it is helpful to form the numbers into a **simple frequency distribution**. The first step is to rank the scores from best to worst in order to gain additional information about the relative position of each score in the list. In most cases, the highest score is the best. In some situations, however, lower scores represent better results. For instance, faster (lower) times in the 100-meter dash and lower golf scores represent better performance. Typically, a lower resting heart rate represents better cardiovascular fitness. Then add a frequency column (f) to indicate how many times each score (X) occurred. Table 3.0 illustrates the long list of individual scores shown above transformed into a simple frequency distribution. The "N = 100" indicates that 100 scores are in this group of data. By briefly examining the simple frequency distribution, one can see which score occurred most often and least often and how the scores are dispersed throughout the range of scores. Even though the simple frequency distribution is more compact than a long listing of individual scores, it is sometimes advantageous to use another method to summarize data.

## Grouped Frequency Distribution

Sometimes it is more convenient to create a **grouped frequency distribution.** Grouped frequency distributions further compact the data and are particularly appropriate for large groups of data. The first step is to decide how many groups should be formed and what size the interval should be for a group to adequately display the data. A rule that should almost always be followed is that there should be somewhere between 10 and 20 groups.

▶ **TABLE 3.0**   Simple frequency distribution for curl-up scores on one-minute test.

| X | f | X | f | X | f |
|---|---|---|---|---|---|
| 58 | 1 | 38 | 6 | 24 | 3 |
| 55 | 1 | 37 | 5 | 23 | 1 |
| 54 | 1 | 36 | 4 | 22 | 3 |
| 50 | 1 | 35 | 2 | 21 | 2 |
| 49 | 1 | 34 | 7 | 20 | 1 |
| 48 | 1 | 33 | 5 | 19 | 1 |
| 46 | 1 | 32 | 4 | 18 | 1 |
| 45 | 2 | 31 | 5 | 17 | 1 |
| 44 | 1 | 30 | 3 | 16 | 1 |
| 43 | 1 | 29 | 4 | 15 | 2 |
| 42 | 1 | 28 | 4 | 13 | 1 |
| 41 | 2 | 27 | 3 | 12 | 1 |
| 40 | 4 | 26 | 4 | 10 | 1 |
| 39 | 4 | 25 | 2 | 9 | 1 |
| | | | | N = 100 | |

Fewer than 10 groups will result in too many scores in each group and obscure important data patterns, while more than 20 groups can cause too few or even zero scores to be in each group and make it difficult to see trends in data. Generally, try to keep the number of groups around 15.

By locating the highest and lowest curl-up scores in the data, the spread of the scores, called the **range**, can be determined. In the example used in Table 3.0, the lowest score is 9 and the highest score is 58. Thus, the range is 49, which can be rounded to 50. Knowing that it is desirable to have between 10 and 20 groups, divide those two numbers into 50. This will help determine the interval for each group and the number of groups to be formed.

$$50 \div 10 = 5$$
$$50 \div 20 = 2.5$$

The interval size should be a whole number, and it is advantageous for the whole number to be odd. The previous calculation tells us that the interval should be between 2.5 and 5. Since the interval should be both whole and odd, our choice is either 3 or 5. An interval of 5 will be used, although either of the two interval values would suffice.

Next, the limits of the interval must be determined for the set of data. The lowest number in the group should be a multiple of the interval. Since

▶ **TABLE 3.1**    Grouped frequency distribution for curl-up scores on one-minute test.

| GROUP X | f |
|:---:|:---:|
| 55–59 | 2 |
| 50–54 | 2 |
| 45–49 | 5 |
| 40–44 | 9 |
| 35–39 | 21 |
| 30–34 | 24 |
| 25–29 | 17 |
| 20–24 | 10 |
| 15–19 | 6 |
| 10–14 | 3 |
| 5–9 | 1 |
|  | N = 100 |

9 is the lowest score, the limit for the lowest group would be 5, and the interval for the lowest group would be 5–9. The next group would be 10–14, followed by 15–19, and so on. When the group intervals are established, tally the number of scores that fall into each interval. Table 3.1 lists a group frequency distribution for the curl-up scores.

The group limits discussed above, called **apparent limits**, are adequate as long as all the data are in whole numbers, called **discrete data**. Since partial curl-ups are not counted, results of a curl-up test would be an example of discrete data. However, a large amount of data in physical education can be in decimal form, known as **continuous data**. The **real limits** of the 5–9 interval would be 4.5 and 9.49 if the data were in continuous form. The apparent limits are used for convenience, but we must remember that the real limit is .5 below the lower apparent limit and .49 above the upper apparent limit. For example, a score of 14.5 would fall into the 15–19 group while a score of 14.49 would be placed in the 10–14 group.

## GRAPHICAL REPRESENTATION OF DATA

Graphs provide a visual representation of data and often present data in a more meaningful form than tables of numbers. In many situations, the old adage "a picture is worth a thousand words" can be adapted to "a graph is worth a thousand numbers." Graphs are particularly useful in comparing two sets of data or in illustrating a trend.

Usually, the frequency is placed on the Y-axis, or the **ordinate**, and the scores are placed on the X-axis, or the **abscissa**. The most common type of graph is the **histogram**, which is usually based on data from a group frequency distribution. Note that the frequency is placed on the Y-axis, or the ordinate, and the raw scores are placed on the X-axis, or the abscissa. By looking at relative heights of the various bars, one can quickly note the distribution of scores. The histogram in Figure 3.0 is based on the data in Table 3.1 and depicts grouped frequency distribution of curl-up scores on a one-minute test.

A **frequency polygon** is another type of graph that is used frequently to display data. Either the frequency polygon or histogram can be used to depict the same data. Figure 3.1 illustrates the same curl-up scores used in Figure 3.0 in a frequency polygon.

Another graph similar to the histogram is the **bar graph**. The difference in the two is that the bars are separated on a bar graph. Figure 3.2 shows scoring results of a conference basketball season on a bar graph.

If a physical education teacher wanted to determine cumulative frequencies and percentiles, these could be calculated and graphed for a visual representation. Table 3.2 shows cumulative frequencies and percentiles for the set of curl-up scores found in the grouped frequency distribution shown in Table 3.1. The cumulative frequencies are derived by starting at the lowest interval and adding each successive higher group interval to the total frequency below. By looking at the lowest interval, 5–9, a frequency of 1 is noted, and when added to the frequency of the next inter-

▲ **FIGURE 3.0** Histogram.

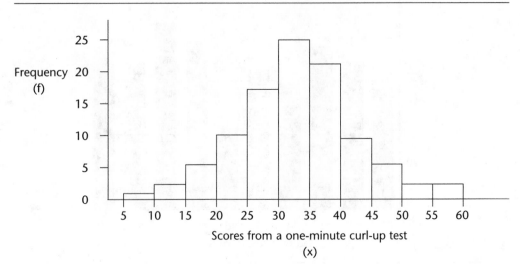

**► FIGURE 3.1**   Frequency polygon.

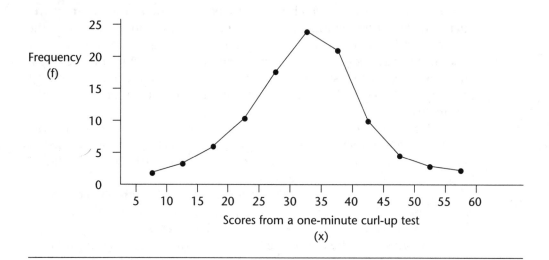

Scores from a one-minute curl-up test
(x)

**► FIGURE 3.2**   Bar graph.

# Desert Valley Basketball

## Scoring Results

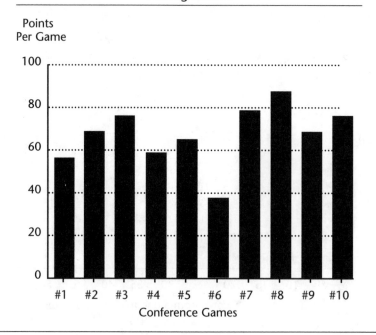

Conference Games

▶ **TABLE 3.2** Cumulative frequencies (Cum f) and percentiles (Cum %) for a grouped frequency distribution.

| GROUP X | f | CUM f | CUM % |
|---------|-----|-------|-------|
| 55–59 | 2 | 100 | 100 |
| 50–54 | 2 | 98 | 98 |
| 45–49 | 5 | 96 | 96 |
| 40–44 | 9 | 91 | 91 |
| 35–39 | 21 | 82 | 82 |
| 30–34 | 24 | 61 | 61 |
| 25–29 | 17 | 37 | 37 |
| 20–24 | 10 | 20 | 20 |
| 15–19 | 6 | 10 | 10 |
| 10–14 | 3 | 4 | 4 |
| 5–9 | 1 | 1 | 1 |
|  | N = 100 |  |  |

val, 10–14, which is 3, the cumulative frequency is 4. This process continues through each group interval.

The cumulative percentiles are calculated by dividing each cumulative frequency by the total number of scores in the distribution. For example, group interval 25–29 has a cumulative frequency of 37. This number divided by 100 yields the cumulative percentile of this interval, 37 percent. More information about calculating percentiles from raw scores is provided later in the chapter.

A **cumulative frequency graph** can be constructed from this type of information. This type of graph shows the number of students who scored at or below a certain score. This curve can be plotted using scores on the abscissa and cumulative frequency on the ordinate. The upper limits for each group interval should be used to plot the graph. A cumulative frequency graph depicting the data in Table 3.2 is shown in Figure 3.3.

## Symmetry and Skewness

When scores are plotted on the various graphs, as has been discussed in previous sections, many different types of curves can result. The most common curve is the **normal curve**. This symmetrical, bilateral, bell-shaped curve theoretically occurs when a large number of scores are normally distributed on each end of the curve. The typical normal curve is shown in Figure 3.4.

Both ends, or tails, of the curve are symmetrical, and they represent extremely low or high scores in the distribution. Most scores are at the mid-

▶ **FIGURE 3.3**    Cumulative frequency graph.

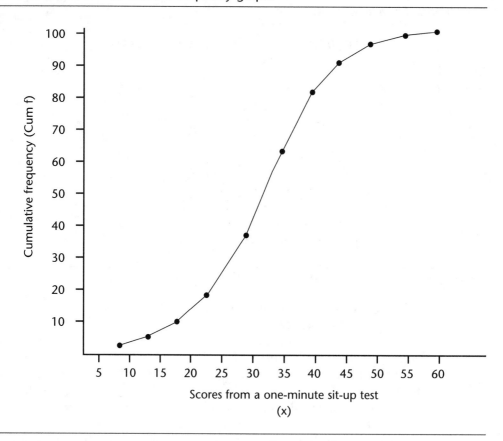

dle of the scale with very few scores falling at the ends. However, many sets of data are not normally distributed, which results in several variations of the normal curve.

If the range of scores in the distribution is limited, which results in the extreme scores being closer to the middle, the curve is steeper and called **leptokurtic**. If the scores of the group are spread out with fewer scores in the middle, the resulting flat curve is called **platykurtic**. Illustrations of these two curves are shown in Figure 3.5. Notice that either of these conditions can be created artificially by compressing or spreading the scale of scores on the abscissa.

While leptokurtic or platykurtic variations of the normal curve are still symmetrical, distributions of scores have a disproportionate number of scores that do not fall in the middle of the distribution. This causes the tails

► **FIGURE 3.4**   Normal curve.

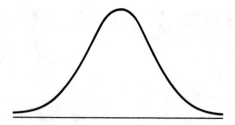

of the curve to be asymmetrical. For data of this sort, the frequency is described as being **skewed**. With skewed data, the high point, or the hump, of the curve will be shifted to the left or right with a longer than normal tail going the opposite direction. If most scores in a group are high on a test and a small number do poorly, the high point of the curve shifts to the right with a longer tail to the left. This type of distribution is skewed negatively, or skewed to the left. A curve that has the hump to the left and the longer tail to the right is skewed positively, or to the right. Examples of skewed curves are also shown in Figure 3.5.

► **FIGURE 3.5**   Leptokurtic, platykurtic, skewed positive, and skewed negative curves.

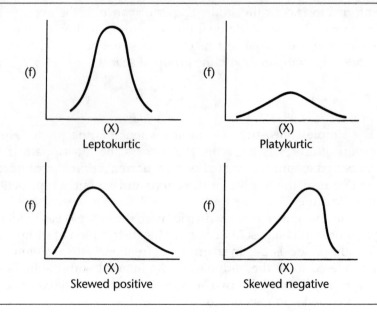

► **FIGURE 3.6**    Graphing data.

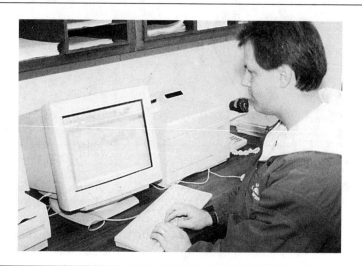

## MEASURES OF CENTRAL TENDENCY

Measures of central tendency are numerical values that describe the middle or central characteristics of a set of scores. If measures of central tendency are known, any given score can be compared to the middle scores. If a student takes an exam and attains a score of 85, that score provides some information about the student's performance. If the average score on the exam was 70, then additional important information is available to use in evaluating individual test results. Measures of central tendency allow a score to be compared with the group of scores.

## Mode

The simplest measure of central tendency is the **mode**. The mode of a group of scores is the score that occurs the most often. If the variable measured assumes a normal or near normal curve distribution, the mode will be near the middle of the curve and be fairly representative of the middle scores.

In a simple frequency distribution, the mode is easily identifiable; it is the score with highest frequency. In the distribution of sit-up scores in Table 3.0, the mode is 34. In a grouped frequency distribution, the mode is considered to be the midpoint of the interval with the highest frequency. Some groups may have two or more modes if several scores tie for the highest occurrence in a set of scores.

There are several advantages in using the mode over other measures of central tendency: It is easy to identify, no calculations are necessary, and it gives a quick estimate of the center of the group that is fairly accurate when the distribution is normal. Disadvantages in using the mode are as follows: it is a terminal statistic—that is, it does not give information that can be used for further calculation; it is unstable compared to other measures of central tendency, since it can change depending on the methods of grouping the intervals; and it disregards extreme scores and does not reflect their number, their size, or the distance from the center of the group. Notice in the two groups of scores below that the mode is 80 in both.

95, 90, 90, 90, 85, 85, 80, 80, 80, 80, 75, 75, 75, 70, 70

99, 99, 90, 85, 85, 80, 80, 80, 80, 70, 70, 50, 45, 45, 20

Because the mode is not a precise measure of central tendency, it is the same in two groups of numbers that are quite different.

## Median

The **median** of a group of scores is the point at which half of the scores are below and half are above. It represents the 50th percentile in the group of scores. If the number of scores in the group is odd, the median is the middle score. If the number of scores is even, the median falls between the middle two scores. Thus, the median of the scores 4, 5, 6, 7, 8 would be 6, while the median of the scores 4, 5, 6, 7, 8, 9 would be 6.5. The median can be used with ordinal, interval, or ratio data.

Like the mode, the median is unaffected by extreme scores. The calculation of the median does not take into consideration the value of the scores. It is based on the number of scores and their rank order. Consider the example of nine employees making $10,000 a year and the owner making $100,000 a year. In this case, the mode and the median are both $10,000. They are unaffected by the size of the extreme score.

In the example above, the median would be more representative than the average salary of the central tendency of the group. The average salary of the company would not be as accurate, because of the extreme score. When the distribution is skewed with extreme scores, it is more appropriate to use the median. The lack of effect by extreme scores on the median can also be a disadvantage in certain instances. Because the median does not consider the size of the scores, important information given by the data is lost. Another disadvantage is that the median is also a terminal statistic so that no further calculations can be made to divulge more information about the data.

# Mean

The numerical average of a group of numbers is the **mean**, which is calculated by adding all the scores and dividing by the total number of scores. The mean is not always a whole number—it is continuous rather than discrete. The mean is the most commonly used measure of central tendency.

Unlike the mode and median, the calculation of the mean considers both the number of scores and their size. It gives weight to each of the scores according to its relative distance from other scores in the group. Because of this feature, it is the most sensitive of all central measures. Slight changes in some of the scores in the group will probably not affect the mode or median, but even minor changes in any score will be reflected in the mean. Thus, the chief advantage of the mean is that it considers all information about the data. Further, it is not a terminal statistic because it provides a basis for many additional calculations that yield even more information.

The critical disadvantage of the mean is that it is very sensitive to extreme scores. When one or more of the scores is extreme, the mean is pulled toward that extreme and may not represent the true central measure of the group. The example cited concerning the nine employees making $10,000 per year with the employer making $100,000 illustrates this characteristic of the mean. The mean of $19,000 would not accurately represent the central tendency of this group of salaries.

The mean assumes at least a level of measurement that is either interval or ratio. Whereas the mode requires only nominal measures and the median assumes an ordinal level, the mean cannot be calculated with these levels of measurement. The mode and median can be applied to interval/ratio data, but since the mean uses the greatest amount of information about the data, it is the most stable.

The formula for finding the mean ($\bar{X}$) with ungrouped data is shown in Formula 3.0.

◤ **FORMULA 3.0**

| Calculation of mean for ungrouped data |
|---|

$$\bar{X} = \frac{\Sigma X}{N}$$

where
$\Sigma X$ is the sum of all scores
$N$ is the total number of scores

Table 3.3 shows scores for 13 students from a one-minute curl-up test and illustrates the calculation of the mean with Formula 3.0.

When calculating the mean for a simple frequency distribution, as illustrated in Table 3.4, a slight modification is made in the formula. Instead of taking the sum of the 13 individual scores, multiply the frequency (f) by

▶ **TABLE 3.3** Calculation of the mean for ungrouped data.

| X |
|---|
| 58 |
| 55 |
| 49 |
| 46 |
| 44 |
| 41 |
| 40 |
| 38 |
| 35 |
| 33 |
| 28 |
| 22 |
| 15 |
| ΣX = 504     N = 13 |

$$\bar{X} = \frac{\Sigma X}{N}$$

$$\bar{X} = \frac{504}{13}$$

$$\bar{X} = 38.77$$

the score and add the products to find the sum of all scores. Note also that N is calculated by adding the f column since this represents the total number of scores. The formula for finding the mean of data listed in a frequency distribution is listed below:

▶ **FORMULA 3.1**

| Calculation of mean for frequency distribution |
|---|

$$\bar{X} = \frac{\Sigma fX}{N}$$

Table 3.4 lists data from a one-minute curl-up test in a simple frequency distribution to illustrate the use of this formula.

The formula for calculating the mean of a simple frequency distribution is also used when figuring the mean for a grouped frequency distribution. Since all scores are not known in this situation, let the midpoint of each interval represent X. The midpoint is the median of the interval in question. For example, the midpoint of the 5–9 interval is 7. The computation for the mean of a grouped frequency distribution is illustrated in Table 3.5.

By assuming that the midpoint represents all the scores in the particular group interval, a small amount of accuracy is sacrificed. Actually, the sum of the original 100 scores used in this example (see Table 3.0) is 3210. When this sum is divided by 100 (N), the true mean is 32.1. This type of small error can be tolerated for the sake of convenience.

▶ **TABLE 3.4**    Calculation of the mean for a simple frequency distribution.

| X | f | fX | |
|---|---|---|---|
| 58 | 1 | 58 | |
| 55 | 1 | 55 | $\bar{X} = \dfrac{\Sigma fX}{N}$ |
| 49 | 2 | 98 | |
| 44 | 4 | 176 | |
| 41 | 5 | 205 | |
| 40 | 7 | 280 | $\bar{X} = \dfrac{1777}{49}$ |
| 38 | 6 | 228 | |
| 35 | 6 | 210 | |
| 33 | 7 | 231 | $\bar{X} = 36.27$ |
| 28 | 5 | 140 | |
| 22 | 3 | 66 | |
| 15 | 2 | 30 | |
| | N = 49 | ΣfX = 1777 | |

## MEASURES OF VARIABILITY

Knowing the mean, median, and mode gives little information about the variability of the scores. After determining the central tendencies of a set of data, information about the variability, or the spread, of the scores is desirable. The scores of the group can be clustered or spread out around the mean. Normal, leptokurtic, and platykurtic curves (see Figure 3.5) illustrate these situations.

When the variability of data is known, it allows for further analysis of the scores to be made, as well as a comparison of two groups of scores.

▶ **TABLE 3.5**    Calculation of the mean for a grouped frequency distribution.

| GROUP X | MID-X | f | fX | |
|---------|-------|---|----|--|
| 55–59 | 57 | 2 | 114 | |
| 50–54 | 52 | 2 | 104 | $\bar{X} = \dfrac{\Sigma fX}{N}$ |
| 45–49 | 47 | 5 | 235 | |
| 40–44 | 42 | 9 | 378 | |
| 35–39 | 37 | 21 | 777 | $\bar{X} = \dfrac{3200}{100}$ |
| 30–34 | 32 | 24 | 768 | |
| 25–29 | 27 | 17 | 459 | |
| 20–24 | 22 | 10 | 220 | $\bar{X} = 32$ |
| 15–19 | 17 | 6 | 102 | |
| 10–14 | 12 | 3 | 36 | |
| 5–9 | 7 | 1 | 7 | |
| | | N = 100 | ΣfX = 3200 | |

Typically, the means of two sets of data are compared when, in fact, it may be more appropriate to compare the variability of the groups, especially when the means are similar but the scores are decidedly different. Like measures of central tendency, several statistical methods give information about the variability of scores in a group.

## Range

The range gives a quick estimate about the spread of scores in a list of data. At best, it is a rough estimate of the variability of the group but offers an advantage because it is easily calculated. The range is the difference between the highest and lowest score in the group. Because it is determined by only two scores in the group and is, thus, directly affected by an extreme score, it is not a sensitive indicator of the variability.

The range has been previously mentioned in reference to determining appropriate intervals for group frequency distributions. When grouped frequency distributions are illustrated with graphs, the range is typically placed on the abscissa with the frequency on the ordinate. When large groups of scores are collected from normal populations, these graphs are usually in the form of a normal curve.

## Interpercentile Range

If it is desirable to look only at the spread of the middle scores, **interpercentile range** may be utilized. The most common type of interpercentile range is the **interquartile range**. Interquartile range gives information about the variability of the scores around the median, or 50th percentile. The interquartile range is calculated by subtracting the score representing the 25th percentile from the score representing the 75th percentile. The formula for interquartile range is given in Formula 3.2.

▶ **FORMULA 3.2**

| Calculation of interquartile range |
|---|

$$Q3 - Q1 = IQR$$
where $IQR$ = interquartile range
$Q3$ = 75th percentile score
$Q1$ = 25th percentile range

If the score equivalent to the 75th percentile is 125 and the 25th percentile is 80, the interquartile range would be 125 minus 80, or 45.

Other interpercentile ranges are not utilized as often as interquartile range, but they can easily be calculated in the same manner as long as equal amounts of scores are eliminated from each end of the distribution. For instance, the range between the 90th and 10th percentile or the 80th and 20th percentile might be of interest.

## Variance

Another method of examining the spread of the scores is by examining the distance of each score from the mean, called the deviation from the mean. If the mean of the group of scores is 5, and one of the scores (X) is 7, then the deviation from the mean is +2. If another score is 3, then the deviation is –2. The deviation score is derived by subtracting the mean from the raw score $(X–\bar{X})$. Notice in the example below that the mean is 5, and the sum of all deviation scores equals zero. When the mean is correct, the sum of the deviations will equal zero. This is a good way to check the accuracy of the mean.

| Group 1 | | Group 2 | |
|---|---|---|---|
| X | X–X̄ | X | X–X̄ |
| 7 | +2 | 9 | +4 |
| 6 | +1 | 7 | +2 |
| 5 | 0 | 5 | 0 |
| 4 | –1 | 3 | –2 |
| 3 | –2 | 1 | –4 |
| X = 25 | | X = 25 | |
| N = 5 | | N = 5 | |
| X̄ = 5 | | X̄ = 5 | |

The scores in group 2 have a greater spread around the mean as reflected in the higher deviation scores. If the signs are ignored and only the absolute number of units from the mean is considered, the total deviation $\Sigma(X–\bar{X})$ is indicative of the variability of the group. Total deviation around the mean for Group 1 is 6 and for Group 2 is 12. If the $\Sigma(X–\bar{X})$ is divided by the number of scores (N) in the group, the resultant value for Group 1 is 1.2 and for Group 2, 2.4. This value is called the average deviation. It should be noted that the range for Group 1 is 4 while the range for Group 2 is 8. This range corresponds perfectly to the average deviation for each group.

Though this statistic gives information about the variability of the scores, it is a terminal statistic because it is mathematically incorrect to ignore the positive and negative values. Because of this, the average deviation is not often utilized other than to help conceptualize variance and standard deviation. A mathematical way of eliminating the negative numbers is to square the deviation scores of each score. By performing this simple operation, all the squared deviation scores, i.e. $(X–\bar{X})$, would be expressed in positive numbers.

By adding all the $(X–\bar{X})^2$ values, we find the sum of squared deviation scores $\Sigma(X–\bar{X})^2$ from the mean. When the $\Sigma(X–\bar{X})^2$ is divided by N, the statistic called the **variance** has been calculated. Thus, the formula for variance is given in Formula 3.3.

▶ **FORMULA 3.3**

| Calculation of the variance |
|---|

$$s^2 = \frac{\Sigma(X-\bar{X})^2}{N}$$

where

$s^2$ = variance

X = score

$\bar{X}$ = mean

N = total number of scores

Below, a third column for $(X-\bar{X})^2$ is added to our example to illustrate how the variance ($s^2$) is derived.

| | Group 1 | | | Group 2 | |
|---|---|---|---|---|---|
| X | X–$\bar{X}$ | $(X-\bar{X})^2$ | X | X–$\bar{X}$ | $(X-\bar{X})^2$ |
| 7 | +2 | 4 | 9 | +4 | 16 |
| 6 | +1 | 1 | 7 | +2 | 4 |
| 5 | 0 | 0 | 5 | 0 | 0 |
| 4 | –1 | 1 | 3 | –2 | 4 |
| 3 | –2 | 4 | 1 | –4 | 16 |

Group 1: X = 25, N = 5, $\bar{X}$ = 5, $\Sigma(X-\bar{X})^2 = 10$

Group 2: X = 25, N = 5, $\bar{X}$ = 5, $\Sigma(X-\bar{X})^2 = 40$

$$s^2 = \frac{\Sigma(X-\bar{X})^2}{N} \qquad s^2 = \frac{\Sigma(X-\bar{X})^2}{N}$$

$$s^2 = \frac{10}{5} \qquad s^2 = \frac{40}{5}$$

$$s^2 = 2 \qquad s^2 = 8$$

The $s^2$ is an accurate indicator of variability of a group of scores. Unfortunately, $s^2$ is expressed in squared units.

## Standard Deviation

The problem of squared units can easily be remedied by taking the square root of the variance, which is called the **standard deviation** (s). Just as the mean is the most commonly used measure of central tendency, the standard deviation is the most common statistic of measures of variability. Thus, the previous sections on average deviation and variance have been leading to the concept of standard deviation. Remember that in calculating the variance, the deviation scores were squared to eliminate the negative signs. To eliminate the squared units that represent the value of the variance, it is logical to take the square root. Therefore, the deviation formula for calculating the standard deviation for a group of scores is given in Formula 3.4.

### ▶ FORMULA 3.4

| Calculation of standard deviation (deviation method) | $$s = \sqrt{\dfrac{\Sigma(X-\bar{X})^2}{N}}$$ |
| --- | --- |

The standard deviation for Group 1 and Group 2 is calculated with the deviation formula as follows:

| *Group 1* | *Group 2* |
| --- | --- |
| $s = \sqrt{\dfrac{\Sigma(X-\bar{X})^2}{N}}$ | $s = \sqrt{\dfrac{\Sigma(X-\bar{X})^2}{N}}$ |
| $s = \sqrt{\dfrac{10}{5}}$ | $s = \sqrt{\dfrac{40}{5}}$ |
| $s = \sqrt{2}$ | $s = \sqrt{8}$ |
| $s = 1.41$ | $s = 2.82$ |

The standard deviation values for both groups remain consistent with the range. If the standard deviation for a group of scores is small, then this indicates that the deviations of the scores from the mean are small. There could still be extreme scores in the set of data, but a majority of scores are clustered near the mean. As the standard deviation becomes larger, the scores of the group are spread farther from the mean. A leptokurtic curve would have a small standard deviation, while a platykurtic curve would have a larger standard deviation.

This statistic gives an accurate and mathematically correct description of the variability of the group. It is the most commonly used measure of variability since many advanced statistical applications are based on the mean and standard deviation of a set of data. It is also quite useful in its applications to the normal curve and standard scores. These applications will be discussed later in this chapter.

In statistics, the symbol "$\sigma$" is often used to represent the standard deviation of a population, while "s" is used to represent the standard deviation of a sample selected from that population. For convenience and because it is appropriate for the statistical scope of this textbook, the symbol "s" will be used in this chapter.

Similarly, in formulas for standard deviation for a sample selected from a population, N–1 may be used in the denominator. If the standard deviation is calculated for specific groups, or populations, it is appropriate to use N in the denominator. Since most applications for the practitioner in physical education and the exercise sciences are with specific groups rather than samples, all standard deviation formulas in this textbook use N in the denominator.

The method for calculating the standard deviation used in the examples above is called the "deviation method." The steps entailed in using this method offer a conceptual framework underlying the standard deviation statistic. When the mean is a whole number and there are a small number of scores in the group, the deviation method is an effective way to calculate the standard deviation. Although the deviation method is of value to help understand the derivation of the standard deviation, it is rarely used for computational purposes. When the mean is a fractional number and a large number of cases are in the group, the "raw score method" is much easier than the deviation method.

Use of a hand calculator will expedite the calculations necessary for the raw score method. The raw score formula for calculating the standard deviation for ungrouped data is given in Formula 3.5.

▶ **FORMULA 3.5**

| Calculation of standard deviation for ungrouped data (raw score method) | $s = \sqrt{\dfrac{N \Sigma X^2 - (\Sigma X)^2}{N(N)}}$ |
|---|---|

Table 3.6 illustrates the use of this formula.

**TABLE 3.6**  Calculation of standard deviation with ungrouped data.

| X | X² |
|---|---|
| 16 | 256 |
| 14 | 196 |
| 13 | 169 |
| 11 | 121 |
| 10 | 100 |
| 8 | 64 |
| 7 | 49 |
| 5 | 25 |
| 4 | 16 |
| 2 | 4 |
| $\Sigma X = 90$ | $\Sigma X^2 = 1000$ |
| $N = 10$ | |

*continued on page 66*

**TABLE 3.6**    *Continued*

The steps in computing the standard deviation for these data are as follows:

1. Determine N by counting the total number of scores.
2. Determine the sum of ($\Sigma$X).
3. Create an $X^2$ column by squaring each score.
4. Sum the $X^2$ column to calculate $\Sigma X^2$.
5. Substitute the values into the formula and solve for s.

$$s = \sqrt{\frac{N\Sigma X^2 - (\Sigma X)^2}{N(N)}}$$

$$s = \sqrt{\frac{10(1000) - (90)^2}{10(10)}}$$

$$s = \sqrt{\frac{10,000 - 8100}{100}}$$

$$s = \sqrt{\frac{1900}{100}}$$

$$s = \sqrt{19}$$

$$s = 4.36$$

The same steps can be followed to calculate the s for a simple or group frequency distribution, except the frequency column must be included in the computation. The raw score formula for a frequency distribution would be as given in Formula 3.6.

► **FORMULA 3.6**

| Calculation of standard deviation for a frequency distribution (raw score method) | $s = \sqrt{\dfrac{N\Sigma fX^2 - (\Sigma fX)^2}{N(N)}}$ |
| --- | --- |

Table 3.7 illustrates the computations involved in finding the standard deviation for a frequency distribution.

When a grouped frequency distribution is involved, the midpoint of each interval serves as the value in the X column. Otherwise, the computations are the same for both types of frequency distributions.

There are other methods of calculating the standard deviation for different groups of scores. Unless there is a relatively small group of data,

▶ **TABLE 3.7**    Calculation of standard deviation from frequency distribution.

| X | f | fX | X² | fX² |
|---|---|---|---|---|
| 16 | 1 | 16 | 256 | 256 |
| 14 | 2 | 28 | 196 | 392 |
| 13 | 4 | 52 | 169 | 676 |
| 11 | 5 | 55 | 121 | 605 |
| 10 | 5 | 50 | 100 | 500 |
| 8 | 7 | 56 | 64 | 448 |
| 7 | 6 | 42 | 49 | 294 |
| 5 | 4 | 20 | 25 | 100 |
| 4 | 3 | 12 | 16 | 48 |
| 2 | 2 | 4 | 4 | 8 |
| | N = 39 | ΣfX = 335 | | ΣfX² = 3327 |

The steps in computing the standard deviation for these data are as follows:
1. Determine N by adding the frequency (f) column.
2. Multiply f by X to create the fX column.
3. Add the fX column to determine ΣfX.
4. Square scores in the X column to create X² column.
5. Multiply f by X² to create the fX² column.
6. Add the fX² column.
7. Substitute the values into the formula and solve for s.

$$s = \sqrt{\frac{N\Sigma fX^2 - (\Sigma fX)^2}{N(N)}}$$

$$s = \sqrt{\frac{39(3327) - (335)^2}{39(39)}}$$

$$s = \sqrt{\frac{129{,}753 - 112{,}225}{1521}}$$

$$s = \sqrt{\frac{17528}{1521}}$$

$$s = \sqrt{11.52}$$

$$s = 3.39$$

it is desirable to utilize a programmable desk calculator or statistical software designed for microcomputers to derive the standard deviation. In situations where the standard deviation is calculated by hand, the raw score method is an effective choice.

When the standard deviation and the mean are known for a set of data, it is easier to analyze the group of scores. The average score as well as the spread of the scores helps describe the data. A better understanding of what these statistics mean should evolve as the relationship of these statistics and the properties of the normal curve are discussed.

## PROPERTIES OF THE NORMAL CURVE

The normal frequency distribution curve, known as the normal curve, was mentioned briefly earlier in this chapter. After presenting the measures of central tendency and variability, it is now appropriate to further discuss the properties of the normal curve. The normal curve represents a theoretical distribution of data based on a mathematical formula. Shown in Figure 3.6, the normal curve suggests that, for normally distributed interval/ratio data, the scores will be symmetrically distributed around the mean. The scores cluster in the vicinity of the mean and gradually taper off in the tails of the curve. The tails of the curve never reach the baseline so that it allows infinite variation in either direction.

The center of a perfectly normal curve is the highest point of the curve representing the greatest frequency of scores. As such, it also represents the mode, median, and mean of the group of scores. This center point divides the curve in half so that 50 percent of the scores fall above and 50% fall below the mean. The standard deviation of the curve is measured along the baseline. (See Figure 3.7.)

The properties of the normal curve are such that practically all scores (99.74 percent) will fall ±3 standard deviations from the mean. Further,

▶ **FIGURE 3.7**   Mean, median, and mode in normal curve.

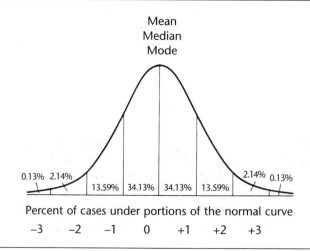

Mean
Median
Mode

0.13%  2.14%          2.14%  0.13%

13.59% | 34.13% | 34.13% | 13.59%

Percent of cases under portions of the normal curve

−3    −2    −1    0    +1    +2    +3

95.44 percent of all scores will occur within ±2 standard deviation units from the mean, while 68.26 percent are found ±1 standard deviation from the mean.

## STANDARD SCORES

The direct result of measurement is the raw score. These raw scores may reflect time, distance, weight, number of successful attempts, and so on. In most instances, raw scores from one set of data are not directly comparable to scores from another set of data. If a student runs 1.5 miles in 11:45 and does 48 sit-ups in one minute, which is better? A track athlete ran 400 meters in 55 seconds and threw the discus a distance of 129 feet. In which event was the performance superior?

Without more information about these raw scores, it is impossible to make any meaningful comparisons. Seconds in the 400-meter run and feet in the discus throw cannot be logically compared. By knowing more about the set of scores, **standard scores** can be calculated that provide a commonality, which allows meaningful comparisons of different sets to be made. Several types of standard scores may be used. The most widely used types are the percentile rank, the z-score, and the T-score.

## Percentile Rank

One of the most common statistics and, certainly the most popular standard score, is the **percentile**. Most people in the general public have some understanding of percentiles. As a result, practitioners in physical education and the exercise sciences find this statistical method to be particularly useful in interpreting scores. Percentile rank provides a quick comparison with all other scores in the group.

A score at the 66.7th percentile is equal to or surpasses at least two-thirds of the scores in the group. A 90th percentile score indicates that a score is equal or better than 9 of 10 scores earned on the particular test. If a student scores in the 25th percentile on a test of aerobic endurance, then three-quarters of the persons who took the test had a better performance than that student.

Using percentile rank, it becomes possible to compare raw scores from different sets of data. If 400 meters is run in 55 seconds and is in the 71st percentile, and the discus is thrown 129 feet and is in the 64th percentile, then it is obvious which is the best performance.

Since the 50th percentile is, by definition, the median for the group of scores, information about the relative value of any percentile rank is known. The mathematical conversion of raw scores to standard scores, such as a percentile, allows logical comparisons to be made and is a common technique in statistics.

As discussed previously in the chapter, percentiles can be calculated from frequency distributions. When scores are arranged in a simple frequency distribution, it is necessary to determine how many scores are equal to or below the raw score in question. Consider the following data:

| Group X | f | Cum f | Cum % |
|---------|-----|-------|-------|
| 23–25   | 3   | 66    | 100   |
| 20–22   | 7   | 63    | 95    |
| 17–19   | 15  | 56    | 85    |
| 14–16   | 19  | 41    | 62    |
| 11–13   | 11  | 22    | 33    |
| 8–10    | 9   | 11    | 14    |
| 5–7     | 2   | 2     | 1     |

$$N = 66$$

By creating the cumulative frequency (Cum f) and cumulative percentile (Cum %) columns, the percentile for each group of scores can be ascertained. For instance, 22 scores are equal to or lower than the group of scores from 11 to 13. By dividing that number found in the cumulative frequency column for the 11–13 group by the total number of scores ($N = 66$), it can be calculated that this group of scores is at the 33rd percentile.

Suppose the exact percentile rank of a score in the 11–13 interval is needed. For instance, what is the percentile rank for the score of 12? For a more exact calculation of percentile rank, Formula 3.7 can be used:

► **FORMULA 3.7**

| Calculation of percentile rank |
|---|

$$\text{Percentile of rank score} = 100 \left[ \frac{(\text{score} - \text{LRL of group})}{i} \times (\text{f of group}) + (\text{cum f of the group below}) \right] \div N$$

The values to be substituted into the formula to calculate the percentile rank of the raw score of 12 are as follows:

score = 12
LRL (lower real limits) of group = 10.5
i (size of interval of group) = 3
f (frequency) of group = 11
cum f (cumulative frequency) of group below = 11
N (total number of scores) = 66

The formula used for this calculation may look complex. However, by making the necessary substitutions from the grouped frequency distribution as shown, it is a simple task to calculate the percentile rank of 12.

$$\text{Percentile of score} = 100 \left[ \frac{(\text{score} - \text{LRL of group})}{i} \times (\text{f of group}) + (\text{cum f of the group below}) \right] \div N$$

$$\text{Percentile of 12} = 100 \left[ \frac{12-10.5}{3} \times 11 + 11 \right] \div 66$$

$$\text{Percentile of 12} = 100 \left[ \frac{1.5}{3} \times 11 + 11 \right] \div 66$$

$$\text{Percentile of 12} = 100 \left[ .5 \times 11 + 11 \right] \div 66$$

$$\text{Percentile of 12} = 100 \left[ 5.5 + 11 \right] \div 66$$

$$\text{Percentile of 12} = 100 \left[ 16.5 \right] \div 66$$

$$\text{Percentile of 12} = 1650 \div 66$$

$$\text{Percentile of 12} = 25$$

It is also possible to calculate the score that corresponds to a specific percentile rank. Using the same grouped frequency distribution data, suppose it were desirable to know the score that falls at the 75th percentile. Formula 3.8 can be used to make this calculation:

▶ **FORMULA 3.8**

| Calculation of score corresponding to percentile rank |
|---|

$$\text{Score} = (\text{LRL of group}) + i \left[ \frac{(\text{nth case}) - \left( \begin{array}{c} \text{cum f of} \\ \text{group below} \end{array} \right)}{\text{f of group}} \right]$$

The values to be substituted into this formula are as follows:

nth case = 75% of N = .75 × 66 = 49.5
cum f of group below = 41 (In the Cum f column, this is the cum f of the group that does not exceed the nth case.)
f of group = 15 (In the Cum % column, it can be noted that the 75th percentile falls in the 35–39 group.)
i (interval of group) = 3
LRL (lower real limit) of group = 16.5

The calculation of this sample problem is as follows:

$$\text{Score} = (\text{LRL of group}) + i \left[ \frac{(\text{nth case}) - (\text{cum f of group below})}{\text{f of group}} \right]$$

$$\text{Score} = 16.5 + 3 \left[ \frac{(49.5) - (41)}{15} \right]$$

$$\text{Score} = 16.5 + 3\left[\frac{8.5}{15}\right]$$

$$\text{Score} = 16.5 + 3\,[.57]$$

$$\text{Score} = 16.5 + 1.71$$

$$\text{Score} = 18.21$$

Thus, the score from the data that corresponds to the 75th percentile would be 18.21.

Though percentile ranks are a very useful statistical tool, some limitations exist. Percentile ranks are ordinal in nature and, as such, represent a terminal statistic. They cannot be added or subtracted logically. Equal differences in percentile ranks do not represent equal differences in the corresponding raw scores. Percentiles are based on the number of scores on a particular test. In a normal frequency distribution, it is much more difficult to improve from the 90th to the 95th percentile than to improve from the 45th to the 50th percentile. Because there are so many scores, a small improvement in the raw score in the middle of the group could be a relatively large jump in percentile rank. The opposite holds true on the extreme ends of the scale. This phenomenon is called a **ceiling effect**.

In Figure 3.8, note that a student who improved from 30 sit-ups to 35 sit-ups shows an improvement from the 50th percentile to the 74th

▶ **FIGURE 3.8**   Illustration of ceiling effect.

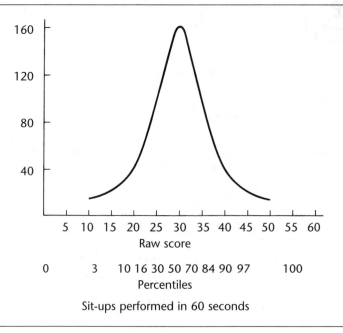

percentile. A student who had a better initial performance of 45 sit-ups, 96th percentile, and improved to 50 sit-ups shows an increase to the 98th percentile. Though both students improved by five sit-ups, the resultant percentile ranks can be deceiving. This example shows that percentile ranks should be used with caution when considering improvement in performance.

## Z-Scores

A standard score that is expressed in terms of standard deviation units on a normal curve is called a z-**score**. A z-score indicates how far from the mean the raw score is located. The farther above the mean the raw score is, the higher the z-score will be. If the score is lower than the mean of the group, the z-score will be negative. The mean of a group of scores is represented by a z-score of 0. If the mean and standard deviation of the group of scores are known, the z-score for any raw score in the group can be calculated using Formula 3.9.

▶ **FORMULA 3.9**

| Calculation of z-score |
|---|

$$z = \frac{X - \bar{X}}{s}$$

In a group of scores with a mean of 50 and a standard deviation of 6, what would be the z-score value of the raw score of 59? By applying Formula 3.9, the z-score for 59 can be calculated as follows:

$$z = \frac{X - \bar{X}}{s}$$

$$z = \frac{59 - 50}{6}$$

$$z = \frac{9}{6}$$

$$z = 1.5$$

The z-score of 1.5 represents a raw score that is 1.5 standard deviation units above the mean. A raw score smaller than the mean will always result in a negative z-score unless the lower score represents the better performance.

In physical education, exercise science, and athletics, there are certain tests in which a lower score is better. Golf scores, time in any type of race, and percentage of body fat are examples. In these situations, subtract the raw score from the mean in the numerator of the equation. Thus, the equation is as shown in Formula 3.10.

▶ **FORMULA 3.10**

| Calculation of z-score when lower score represents better performance | $z = \dfrac{\overline{X} - X}{s}$ |
|---|---|

If the mean for a group of golf scores is 86.8 with a standard deviation of 9.4, what is the z-score for a raw score of 79?

$$z = \frac{\overline{X} - X}{s}$$

$$z = \frac{86.8 - 79}{9.4}$$

$$z = \frac{7.8}{9.4}$$

$$z = .83$$

A z-score is useful in comparing scores in two separate distributions. The raw scores may represent time in the 50-yard dash and distance in the standing long jump. By converting both raw scores to z-scores, there is a basis for comparison to determine which is the best score. The size of the z-score also gives important information about how far above or below the mean the score is located.

With the properties of the normal curve in mind (see Figure 3.6), the z-score gives information about what percent of scores of the population falls between the z-score and the mean. A z-score of 1.0 represents one standard deviation unit above the mean. It is characteristic of the normal curve that exactly 34.13 percent of the population of scores lies between the mean and one standard deviation unit.

Since 50 percent of the scores lie on each side of the mean, it can be deduced that a z-score of 1.0 is equal to or better than 84.13 percent of the scores in the distribution. This assumes that the group of scores is normally distributed. Table 3.8 shows the percentage of area that falls between the mean and any z-score in a group. The far left-hand column represents z-values to the nearest tenth. The figures across the top represent the hundredths value. If the z-score was 1.57, then move down the left-hand column to 1.5 and then across the table to the .07 column. The number located by this procedure should be 0.4418. This means that 44.18 percent of the area of the normal curve lies between the mean and the z-score of 1.57.

Because the normal curve is symmetrical, 44.18 percent of the area of the normal curve lies between the mean and a z-score of –1.57. Further, 88.36 percent of the area lies between the z-scores of 1.57 and –1.57.

**TABLE 3.8** The normal distribution.

Percentage area under the standard normal curve from 0 to z (shown shaded) is the value found in the body of the table.

| z | 0.00 | 0.01 | 0.02 | 0.03 | 0.04 | 0.05 | 0.06 | 0.07 | 0.08 | 0.09 |
|---|------|------|------|------|------|------|------|------|------|------|
| 0.0 | 0.0000 | 0.0040 | 0.0080 | 0.0120 | 0.0160 | 0.0199 | 0.0239 | 0.0279 | 0.0319 | 0.0359 |
| 0.1 | 0.0398 | 0.0438 | 0.0478 | 0.0517 | 0.0557 | 0.0596 | 0.0636 | 0.0675 | 0.0714 | 0.0753 |
| 0.2 | 0.0793 | 0.0832 | 0.0871 | 0.0910 | 0.0948 | 0.0987 | 0.1026 | 0.1064 | 0.1103 | 0.1141 |
| 0.3 | 0.1179 | 0.1217 | 0.1255 | 0.1293 | 0.1331 | 0.1368 | 0.1406 | 0.1443 | 0.1480 | 0.1517 |
| 0.4 | 0.1554 | 0.1591 | 0.1628 | 0.1664 | 0.1700 | 0.1736 | 0.1772 | 0.1808 | 0.1844 | 0.1879 |
| 0.5 | 0.1915 | 0.1950 | 0.1985 | 0.2019 | 0.2054 | 0.2088 | 0.2123 | 0.2157 | 0.2190 | 0.2224 |
| 0.6 | 0.2257 | 0.2291 | 0.2324 | 0.2357 | 0.2389 | 0.2422 | 0.2454 | 0.2486 | 0.2517 | 0.2549 |
| 0.7 | 0.2580 | 0.2611 | 0.2642 | 0.2673 | 0.2704 | 0.2734 | 0.2764 | 0.2794 | 0.2823 | 0.2852 |
| 0.8 | 0.2881 | 0.2910 | 0.2939 | 0.2967 | 0.2995 | 0.3023 | 0.3051 | 0.3078 | 0.3106 | 0.3133 |
| 0.9 | 0.3159 | 0.3186 | 0.3212 | 0.3238 | 0.3264 | 0.3289 | 0.3315 | 0.3340 | 0.3365 | 0.3389 |
| 1.0 | 0.3413 | 0.3438 | 0.3461 | 0.3485 | 0.3508 | 0.3531 | 0.3554 | 0.3577 | 0.3599 | 0.3621 |
| 1.1 | 0.3643 | 0.3665 | 0.3686 | 0.3708 | 0.3729 | 0.3749 | 0.3770 | 0.3790 | 0.3810 | 0.3830 |
| 1.2 | 0.3849 | 0.3869 | 0.3888 | 0.3907 | 0.3925 | 0.3944 | 0.3962 | 0.3980 | 0.3997 | 0.4015 |
| 1.3 | 0.4032 | 0.4049 | 0.4066 | 0.4082 | 0.4099 | 0.4115 | 0.4131 | 0.4147 | 0.4162 | 0.4177 |
| 1.4 | 0.4192 | 0.4207 | 0.4222 | 0.4236 | 0.4251 | 0.4265 | 0.4279 | 0.4292 | 0.4306 | 0.4319 |
| 1.5 | 0.4332 | 0.4345 | 0.4357 | 0.4370 | 0.4382 | 0.4394 | 0.4406 | 0.4418 | 0.4429 | 0.4441 |
| 1.6 | 0.4452 | 0.4463 | 0.4474 | 0.4484 | 0.4495 | 0.4505 | 0.4515 | 0.4525 | 0.4535 | 0.4545 |
| 1.7 | 0.4554 | 0.4564 | 0.4573 | 0.4582 | 0.4591 | 0.4599 | 0.4608 | 0.4616 | 0.4625 | 0.4633 |
| 1.8 | 0.4641 | 0.4649 | 0.4656 | 0.4664 | 0.4671 | 0.4678 | 0.4686 | 0.4693 | 0.4699 | 0.4706 |
| 1.9 | 0.4713 | 0.4719 | 0.4726 | 0.4732 | 0.4738 | 0.4744 | 0.4750 | 0.4756 | 0.4761 | 0.4767 |
| 2.0 | 0.4772 | 0.4778 | 0.4783 | 0.4788 | 0.4793 | 0.4798 | 0.4803 | 0.4808 | 0.4812 | 0.4817 |
| 2.1 | 0.4821 | 0.4826 | 0.4830 | 0.4834 | 0.4838 | 0.4842 | 0.4846 | 0.4850 | 0.4854 | 0.4857 |
| 2.2 | 0.4861 | 0.4864 | 0.4868 | 0.4871 | 0.4875 | 0.4878 | 0.4881 | 0.4884 | 0.4887 | 0.4890 |
| 2.3 | 0.4893 | 0.4896 | 0.4898 | 0.4901 | 0.4904 | 0.4906 | 0.4909 | 0.4911 | 0.4913 | 0.4916 |
| 2.4 | 0.4918 | 0.4920 | 0.4922 | 0.4925 | 0.4927 | 0.4929 | 0.4931 | 0.4932 | 0.4934 | 0.4936 |
| 2.5 | 0.4938 | 0.4940 | 0.4941 | 0.4943 | 0.4945 | 0.4946 | 0.4948 | 0.4949 | 0.4951 | 0.4952 |
| 2.6 | 0.4953 | 0.4955 | 0.4956 | 0.4957 | 0.4959 | 0.4960 | 0.4961 | 0.4962 | 0.4963 | 0.4964 |
| 2.7 | 0.4965 | 0.4966 | 0.4967 | 0.4968 | 0.4969 | 0.4970 | 0.4971 | 0.4972 | 0.4973 | 0.4974 |
| 2.8 | 0.4974 | 0.4975 | 0.4976 | 0.4977 | 0.4977 | 0.4978 | 0.4979 | 0.4979 | 0.4980 | 0.4981 |
| 2.9 | 0.4981 | 0.4982 | 0.4982 | 0.4983 | 0.4984 | 0.4984 | 0.4985 | 0.4985 | 0.4986 | 0.4986 |
| 3.0 | 0.4987 | 0.4987 | 0.4987 | 0.4988 | 0.4988 | 0.4989 | 0.4989 | 0.4989 | 0.4990 | 0.4990 |

# T-Score

Another type of standard score derived from the z-score is the **T-score**. Because the z-score is usually a fractional number and half of the z-scores are negative numbers, it is sometimes desirable to transform the z-score into a T-score. The value for a T-score is represented by a positive, whole number, which may help students or parents comprehend the meaning of the standard score. To calculate the T-score, the Formula 3.11 is used:

▶ **FORMULA 3.11**

| Calculation of T-score |

$$T = 10\left(\frac{X - \overline{X}}{s}\right) + 50$$

or

$$T = 10z + 50$$

Using this formula, convert a z-score of –1.2 to the corresponding T-score. Simply multiply the z-score by 10 and add 50. The substitutions into the formula above should read

$$T = 10z + 50$$
$$T = 10\,(-1.2) + 50$$
$$T = -12 + 50$$
$$T = 38$$

While a distribution of z-scores has a mean of zero and a standard deviation of 1, the T-score distribution has a mean of 50 and a standard deviation of 10. This means that a z-score of –1.0 is equivalent to a T-score of 40, a z-score of 0 is the same as a T-score of 50, and a z-score of 1.0 corresponds to a T-score of 60. T-scores are used because it is sometimes easier to conceptualize standard scores from 0 to 100 with a mean of 50. It is rare to have a T-score less than 20 or higher than 80 since these represent a –3 and a +3 standard deviation from the mean. Figure 3.9 should clarify the relation-

▶ **FIGURE 3.9**   Normal curve with standard score scales.

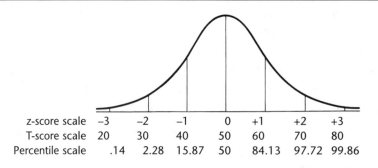

| | | | | | | | |
|---|---|---|---|---|---|---|---|
| z-score scale | –3 | –2 | –1 | 0 | +1 | +2 | +3 |
| T-score scale | 20 | 30 | 40 | 50 | 60 | 70 | 80 |
| Percentile scale | .14 | 2.28 | 15.87 | 50 | 84.13 | 97.72 | 99.86 |

ships between the various standard scores that have been discussed in the previous sections. As noted in the figure, a z-score of 1.0, a T-score of 60, and a percentile score of 84.13 percent are equivalent. These various scales represent different ways to compare raw scores in standard score formats.

# CORRELATION

The statistical technique of correlation can be quite valuable in physical education. The concept of **correlation** refers to the relationship between two variables. The **correlation coefficient** is the statistic that represents the relationship, or association, between the variables. When information is desired about the relationship between one set of values and another set of values, a correlation procedure is employed. To use correlation, two or more variables from the same population are required. When more than two variables are examined, multiple correlation procedures are appropriate. The discussion in this chapter will be limited to correlation between two variables.

Consider a group of 30 physical education students. What type of relationship is there between the height and weight of these 30 students? In most circumstances, the taller a student is, the more he or she weighs. This illustrates a positive correlation. Similarly, when variable X is smaller and variable Y also decreases, this also represents a positive correlation. A perfect positive correlation coefficient would be +1.00. The correlation coefficient can never be larger than this value.

Suppose the same group of 30 students were timed in the 50-yard dash and measured in the long jump. Usually the faster a person can sprint, the better long jumper he or she will be. Thus, the lower the time (variable X) in the 50-yard dash, the greater the distance (variable Y) in the long jump. As variable X gets smaller, variable Y gets larger. This is an example of a negative correlation. A perfect negative correlation coefficient would be −1.00. A correlation coefficient can never be lower than this value.

Thus, the correlation coefficient that represents the relationship between two sets of variables is always between −1.00 and +1.00. If two sets of values have absolutely no relationship, then the correlation coefficient would be 0. Correlation coefficients of −1.00, +1.00, or 0 are rarely obtained. A correlation of −.75 indicates just as strong of a relationship between the two variables as +.75. As the correlation coefficient approaches 0 from either the positive or negative side, it is an indication of less relationship between the variables. Therefore, a −.50 correlation coefficient indicates a stronger relationship between two sets of variables than a +.49.

As the correlation coefficient nears +1 or −1, there is a stronger linear relationship between the variables in question. A visual description of the correlation coefficient may be shown on a graph called a **scattergram** (see

Figure 3.10). The X variable is placed on the abscissa, and the Y variable on the ordinate. By plotting the points for each subject on variables X and Y, a pattern of points will emerge. If the pattern formed is linear, the relationship between variables is great, and the correlation coefficient will be high. A perfectly straight line would represent a +1.00 or −1.00 correlation coefficient. Figure 3.10 includes several scattergrams to illustrate the various relationships between variables.

Safrit and Wood (1995) present general guidelines on how the size of the correlation coefficient should be interpreted. They are

± .80 – 1.00 High
± .60 – 0.79 Moderately high
± .40 – 0.59 Moderate
± .20 – 0.39 Low
± .00 – 0.19 No relationship

**FIGURE 3.10**    Scattergrams representing various correlation coefficients.

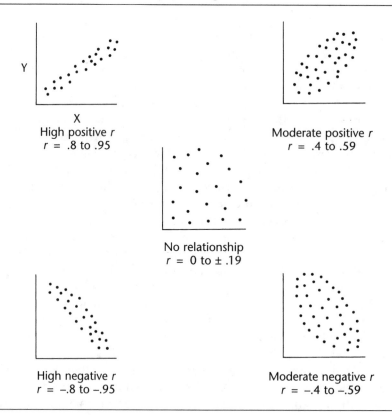

Y

X
High positive *r*
*r* = .8 to .95

Moderate positive *r*
*r* = .4 to .59

No relationship
*r* = 0 to ± .19

High negative *r*
*r* = −.8 to −.95

Moderate negative *r*
*r* = −.4 to −.59

The correlation coefficient for the relationship between two sets of variables can be squared to interpret the amount of shared variance between the two sets of data. Thus, if the correlation between pull-ups and chin-ups is .9, the shared variance is .81. This can be interpreted to mean that the two sets of data have 81 percent shared variance, or overlap. These two sets of data are highly related by one or more common characteristics, which can be logically assumed to be strength of the arms and shoulders.

It should be emphasized that highly correlated variables show a strong relationship, or association between the two sets of variables. However, high correlation never proves causation. Being tall does not cause someone to be heavy nor does being short guarantee weighing less. A very fast sprinter may be a poor long jumper. If a correlation coefficient is high enough, it can have some predictive potential. Unless there is a perfect correlation, however, the prediction cannot be foolproof.

## Spearman Rho Rank-Order Correlation

When one or both groups of data involved in a correlation procedure are at the ordinal level of measurement, then the **Spearman rho rank-order correlation** should be used. Team rankings and order of finish in tournaments are examples of ordinal data often used in physical education. If one group of scores happens to be interval or ratio data, change them to the ordinal level by rank ordering them before using the Spearman rho formula.

Suppose a racquetball instructor gave a serving test that yielded a raw score at the ratio level and then had a single round-robin class tournament at the end of the unit. The teacher wants to know if the scores on the serving test correlate highly with the final ranking in the class tournament.

To calculate the Spearman rho rank-order correlation, Formula 3.12 is used.

► **FORMULA 3.12**

| Spearman rho rank-order correlation | $r' = 1 - \dfrac{6\Sigma d^2}{N(N^2 - 1)}$ |

Table 3.9 illustrates the calculation of a Spearman rho rank-order correlation coefficient.

The correlation coefficient in this calculation is .66. This represents a moderately high relationship between the results of the serving test and finish in the class standings.

▶ **TABLE 3.9**   Calculation of Spearman rho rank-order correlation coefficient.

| SERVING SCORE (X) | RANK X | RANK OF FINISH (Y) | d | $d^2$ |
|:---:|:---:|:---:|:---:|:---:|
| 95 | 1 | 2 | −1 | 1 |
| 92 | 2 | 4 | −2 | 4 |
| 88 | 3 | 1 | 2 | 4 |
| 87 | 4 | 5 | −1 | 1 |
| 85 | 5 | 8 | −3 | 9 |
| 82 | 6 | 3 | 3 | 9 |
| 80 | 7 | 9 | −2 | 4 |
| 77 | 8 | 10 | −2 | 4 |
| 75 | 9 | 7 | 2 | 4 |
| 72 | 10 | 6 | 4 | 16 |
| N = 10 | | | $\Sigma d = 0$ | $\Sigma d^2 = 56$ |

The steps in computing the Spearman rho rank-order correlation coefficient are as follows:

1. Determine N by counting the number of paired scores, N = 10.
2. Convert the raw scores on the serving test to ordinal data.
3. Subtract the rank of variable Y from the rank of variable X to create the d column, d = Rank X − Rank Y. If subtraction is done correctly, the $\Sigma d$ will always be zero.
4. Square each value of d to create the $d^2$ column and add the $d^2$ values, $\Sigma d^2 = 56$.
5. Substitute the values into the formula to solve for r'.

$$r' = 1 - \frac{6\Sigma d^2}{N(N^2 - 1)}$$

$$r' = 1 - \frac{6(56)}{10(10^2 - 1)}$$

$$r' = 1 - \frac{336}{10(100 - 1)}$$

$$r' = 1 - \frac{336}{10(99)}$$

$$r' = 1 - \frac{336}{990}$$

$$r' = 1 - .34$$

$$r' = .66$$

## Pearson Product-Moment Correlation

If the two sets of variables in question are represented by interval or ratio data, then the **Pearson product-moment correlation** method should be used. The correlation coefficient value derived from this procedure is represented by the symbol $r$. When using correlation procedures, 30 or more subjects are desirable so that extreme scores of one subject do not affect the coefficient. For convenience, the examples included here will have fewer subjects.

The raw score formula for the Pearson product-moment correlation is shown in Formula 3.13.

▶ **FORMULA 3.13**

| Pearson product-moment correlation | $r = \dfrac{N\Sigma XY - \Sigma X\Sigma Y}{\sqrt{[N\Sigma X^2 - (\Sigma X)^2]\,[N\Sigma Y^2 - (\Sigma Y)^2]}}$ |
|---|---|

Though the formula may appear complex, it is simply a matter of substituting the proper values and completing the calculation. The use of a hand calculator makes this task easier. Table 3.10 shows the scores attained by 10 students on pull-up and chin-up tests. By surveying the scores and from intuition, it is easy to note a positive relationship between the scores. By implementing the raw score formula, the exact nature of the relationship between the scores on these two tests can be calculated.

A correlation coefficient of .985 represents a high positive relationship between pull-ups and chin-ups.

The data in the Pearson product-moment correlation example (Table 3.10) can be changed to ordinal data by ranking each set of data. If this were done, the Spearman rho formula could be utilized. The coefficients for the two correlation techniques would not be identical, but they would be very similar, because when ratio scores are converted to ordinal scores, less information is known about the original ratio-level scores.

In summary, when two sets of scores are collected from the same set of subjects, the relationship between the two variables can be estimated using a correlation procedure. The Pearson product-moment method is used with interval or ratio data and is usually preferred since it utilizes a higher level of measurement. However, if ordinal data are involved, the Spearman rho formula should be used. Correlation procedures provide the basis for more important applications in physical education and the exercise sciences. When there is a high correlation coefficient, regression equations can be developed to make meaningful predictions from known data. In Chapter 4, validity and reliability of tests are discussed. Correlation procedures play an integral role in establishing validity and reliability of tests used in both school and nonschool settings.

▶ **TABLE 3.10** Calculation of Pearson product-moment correlation.

| PULL-UPS (X) | CHIN-UPS (Y) | X² | Y² | XY |
|:---:|:---:|:---:|:---:|:---:|
| 10 | 13 | 100 | 169 | 130 |
| 16 | 20 | 256 | 400 | 320 |
| 4 | 6 | 16 | 36 | 24 |
| 8 | 11 | 64 | 121 | 88 |
| 9 | 11 | 81 | 121 | 99 |
| 6 | 10 | 36 | 100 | 60 |
| 1 | 2 | 1 | 4 | 2 |
| 12 | 15 | 144 | 225 | 180 |
| 7 | 8 | 49 | 64 | 56 |
| 5 | 6 | 25 | 36 | 30 |
| $\Sigma X = 78$ | $\Sigma Y = 102$ | $\Sigma X^2 = 772$ | $\Sigma Y^2 = 1276$ | $\Sigma XY = 989$ |

The steps in computing the Pearson product-moment correlation coefficient are as follows:

1. Determine N by counting the number of pairs of scores. In this example, N = 10.
2. Add column X, $\Sigma X = 78$.
3. Add column Y, $\Sigma Y = 102$.
4. Create an $X^2$ column by squaring each score in the X column and add the $X^2$ column, $\Sigma X^2 = 772$.
5. Create a $Y^2$ column by squaring each score in the Y column and add the $Y^2$ column, $\Sigma Y^2 = 1276$.
6. Multiply each X score by the corresponding Y score to create an XY column and add the XY column, $\Sigma XY = 989$.
7. Substitute the values into the formula and solve for $r$.

$$r = \frac{N\Sigma XY - \Sigma X \Sigma Y}{\sqrt{[N\Sigma X^2 - (\Sigma X)^2][N\Sigma Y^2 - (\Sigma Y)^2]}}$$

$$r = \frac{10(989) - 78(102)}{\sqrt{[10(772) - (78)^2][10(1276) - (102)^2]}}$$

$$r = \frac{9890 - 7956}{\sqrt{(7720 - 6084)(12,760 - 10,404)}}$$

$$r = \frac{1934}{\sqrt{(1636)(2356)}}$$

$$r = \frac{1934}{\sqrt{3,854,416}}$$

$$r = \frac{1934}{1963.27}$$

$$r = .985$$

Thus correlation procedures are quite valuable in many areas of measurement and evaluation.

## Regression

Using the mean and standard deviation from the sets of data for two variables having a high correlation coefficient, it is possible to predict the value of variable Y from variable X and vice versa. When working with two sets of data, this process is known as **simple regression**. The higher the correlation coefficient, the more accurate will be the prediction of the regression equation. While regression equations can be calculated for two sets of data with a moderate or low correlation coefficient, it makes little sense to do so since they would reflect a wide range of possible error in the prediction. Only when the correlation coefficient is ±1.00 is the resulting prediction from the regression equation completely accurate. However, when the correlation is high (±.8 or higher) the range of error for the predicted values is relatively small.

A simple regression is also called a linear regression since the analysis tries to find a straight line that best fits the data from variable X and variable Y. Formula 3.14 for a simple regression analysis is the formula for a straight line.

► **FORMULA 3.14**

| Calculation of simple regression | $$Y' = a + bX$$ |

The values to be substituted into this formula are as follows:

$Y'$ = predicted value of variable Y
$a$ = Y intercept (where line crosses the Y axis)
$b$ = slope of the regression line
$X$ = known value of variable X

Before applying the formula, calculate the slope (b) and the Y intercept. Formula 3.15 is used for calculating the slope (b).

► **FORMULA 3.15**

| Calculation of the slope | $$b = r\left(\frac{s_y}{s_x}\right)$$ |

$r$ = correlation coefficient

$s_y$ = standard deviation of variable Y

$s_x$ = standard deviation of variable X

The formula for calculating the Y intercept (a) is as follows:

### ▶ FORMULA 3.16

| Calculation |
| of the Y |
| intercept |

$a = \bar{Y} - b\bar{X}$

$\bar{Y} = $ mean of variable Y

$\bar{X} = $ mean of variable X

$b = $ slope

Using the data from the previous Pearson product-moment correlation example (Table 3.10), $r$ is calculated as .985. For variable X (pull-ups), the mean is 7.8 and the standard deviation is 4.04. For variable Y (chin-ups), the mean is 10.2 and the standard deviation is 4.85. With this information, the calculation of a regression equation allows an accurate prediction of how many chin-ups a student can do when the number of pull-ups that student is capable of doing is known. For instance, if a student can do 15 pull-ups, how many chin-ups could a teacher expect the student to do? To answer this question using regression analysis, calculate as follows:

1. Calculate the mean and standard deviation for each set of data. Since these procedures were performed previously in this chapter, the values are provided.

2. Calculate the Pearson product-moment correlation coefficient. This was done in Table 3.10.

3. Calculate the slope (b).

$$b = r\left(\frac{s_y}{s_x}\right)$$

$$b = .985\left(\frac{4.85}{4.04}\right)$$

$$b = .985(1.2)$$

$$b = 1.18$$

4. Calculate the Y intercept (a).

$a = \bar{Y} - b\bar{X}$

$a = 10.2 - 1.18(7.8)$

$a = 10.2 - 9.22$

$a = .98$

5. Using the regression formula, compute Y′ (called "Y prime"), which is the predicted number of chin-ups the student will be able to complete.

$Y' = a + bX$

$Y' = .98 + 1.18 (15)$

$Y' = .98 + 17.7$

$Y' = 18.68$

The Y' value of 18.68 is a prediction of the number of chin-ups the student can do. Since fractional chin-ups would not be counted, the predicted Y value can be rounded to 19. Remember that while there is some margin of error in the prediction, the closer the correlation coefficient is to ±1.00, the more accurate the prediction is. The exact standard error of the estimate can be calculated for any regression equation, but this information is beyond the intended scope of this chapter. The reader should refer to a textbook with more advanced statistical procedures for a discussion of determining confidence intervals for regression analysis.

This introduction to simple or linear regression is based on working with only two sets of variables. This is quite common in physical education and the exercise sciences. For instance, predicting a person's maximal oxygen uptake based on results of a 12-minute run test would be based on simple regression. Completing a 12-minute run test is much simpler, cheaper, and time efficient than a maximal oxygen uptake test protocol. While giving up a small amount of accuracy is a disadvantage, the advantages far outweigh this disadvantage in many situations.

It should be pointed out that multiple regression equations can also be calculated from more than two sets of data. For example, a variable Y might be predicted from variables A, B, and C. This type of statistical work is typically done on a computer because of the complexity of the calculations. An example of this is skinfold formulas using multiple sites for measurement. If a skinfold formula were to use the chest, abdominal, and thigh sites to measure millimeters of fat, then three variables would be used to predict the percentage of body fat. This prediction of body fat would be based on multiple correlation of skinfold sites to underwater weighing procedures for determining body fat. Both simple and multiple regression procedures are quite useful in the physical education and exercise science areas.

## TESTS FOR DIFFERENCES BETWEEN GROUPS

The previous section of this chapter has dealt with the relationship, or correlation, between two sets of data. In some situations, it is desirable to know if significant differences exist between groups of scores. A number of different statistical tests are appropriate to use based on a number of different factors. Among these factors are the number of groups involved, number of subjects in the groups, and sampling procedures used for selection of subjects within the groups. Many other research design and methodological factors are also involved in determining differences between groups. In addition, the student needs a thorough conceptual knowledge of probability theory, assumptions underlying the tests, and other more advanced statistical concepts to interpret the results of these tests used to determine differences between groups.

These areas of information are typically included in introductory statistics and research methods courses. Entire textbooks are devoted to these areas. While it is important that a student recognize the existence of such tests, a cursory examination of the tests and their accompanying formulas can often lead to misuse and faulty interpretations of results. Clearly, an introductory measurement and evaluation textbook such as this one cannot present the depth of information necessary for the reader to have sufficient knowledge to use and interpret these tests properly. Thus, the following brief descriptions of two types of t-tests and simple analysis of variance (ANOVA) are intended simply to provide the reader with a brief introduction to the role and function of these commonly used statistical procedures. They are referred to as inferential statistics because results can be inferred to apply to the population from which the sample was selected.

## t-test for Independent Samples

A **t-test for independent samples** can be used to determine if there are differences between the sets of scores from two groups of subjects taking the same test. Suppose a physical education teacher wants to examine whether being in physical education class improves the cardiorespiratory fitness levels of students. In this hypothetical situation, two groups of 31 students are randomly selected from the entire 10th-grade population at a school. One group of 31 students enrolls in daily physical education class during the year while the other group does not take physical education. At the end of the year, the 12-minute run/walk test is administered to all students to measure cardiorespiratory fitness. In the 12-minute run/walk, the score on the test is the number of yards covered in 12 minutes.

The PE group has a mean score of 2,400 yards, with a standard deviation of 300, while the non-PE group has a mean score of 2,150, with a standard deviation of 375. The t-test for independent samples can be used to determine if there is a statistically significant difference in the results of the two groups in the 12-minute run/walk test. In some cases, small differences in the mean can be statistically significant, while in other sets of data, larger differences are not significantly, different. The calculation of statistical significance takes into account sample size and variability of group scores. Thus, the t-test takes into account not only the difference in the means of the two groups but also the difference in the variability of the scores.

The steps for calculating this type of t-test using the data above are as follows:

1. Calculate the standard error of the difference between the means ($S_{d\bar{x}}$) using the standard deviations of the two groups. The formula is

$$S_{d\bar{x}} = \sqrt{\frac{N_1 s_1^2 + N_2 s_2^2}{N_1 + N_2 - 2}\left(\frac{1}{N_1} + \frac{1}{N_2}\right)}$$

where $s_1$ is the standard deviation of the PE group
$s_2$ is the standard deviation of the non-PE group
$N_1$ is the size of the PE group
$N_2$ is the size of the non-PE group
By substituting the values, the $S_{d\bar{x}}$ is calculated as follows:

$$S_{d\bar{x}} = \sqrt{\frac{31(300^2) + 31(375^2)}{31 + 31 - 2}\left(\frac{1}{31} + \frac{1}{31}\right)}$$

$$S_{d\bar{x}} = \sqrt{\frac{31(90,000) + 31(140,625)}{60}}\,(.032 + .032)$$

$$S_{d\bar{x}} = \sqrt{\frac{2,790,000 + 4,359,375}{60}}\,(.064)$$

$$S_{d\bar{x}} = \sqrt{\frac{7,149,375}{60}}\,(.064)$$

$$S_{d\bar{x}} = \sqrt{119,156.25}\,(.064)$$

$$S_{d\bar{x}} = \sqrt{7626}$$

$$= 87.32$$

2. Calculate the t-value by using the following formula:

$$t = \frac{\bar{X}_1 - \bar{X}_2}{S_{d\bar{x}}}$$

where $X_1$ is the mean of the PE group
$X_2$ is the mean of the non-PE group
$S_{dx}$ is the standard error of difference between means
By substituting the appropriate values, the t-value is calculated as follows:

$$t = \frac{2400 - 2150}{87.32}$$

$$t = \frac{250}{87.32}$$

$$t = 2.86$$

3. Determine the degrees of freedom (df) by adding the two number of scores in each group and subtracting 2 (df = $N_1 + N_2 - 2$). In this example the df are calculated as follows:

df = 31 + 31 – 2 = 62 – 2 = 60

4. Refer to Table 3.11, which is an abbreviated table of the critical values of t. The t-value in this sample problem is 2.86. If this obtained value is greater than the table value, it is concluded that the means are significantly different from one another. To use this table, the degrees of freedom must be known and a level of significance must be selected. The .05 level of significance should be used. This level indicates a 95 percent probability that the conclusions being reached by the t-test are actually true (5 chances out of 100 not true). In physical education and exercise science, .05 is typically used. By checking Table 3.11 for 60 degrees of freedom at the .05 level, you can see that the critical value is 2.00. Since the t-value of 2.86 exceeds the critical value of 2.00, it an be concluded that there is a significant difference in cardiorespiratory fitness in the two groups.

## t-test for Dependent Samples

A second type of t-test is the **t-test for dependent samples.** When a group of subjects is measured on two different occasions (usually a pretest and posttest situation), this test can be used to see if significant differences exist between the two sets of scores. This t-test is done in a manner similar to the independent t-test, the difference being that the two sets of scores are related. The two most common designs for this type of t-test are repeated measures and matched pairs. Repeated measures typically uses a pretest and a posttest to generate two groups of scores from one set of subjects. Matched pairs deliberately matches subjects according to one or more variables and then assigns them to two different groups. In either case, the two groups are not independent of each other.

If a fitness instructor assesses a group of 20 clients prior to prescribing an exercise program, the assessment (pretest) typically includes body composition testing. After the clients are involved in a supervised exercise program for eight weeks, a second body composition assessment (posttest) might be done. A repeated measures t-test would determine if any significant changes in body composition occurred for the group. The t-value would be calculated the same way as the example given for independent samples, except that the values for the means and standard deviations would come from the pretest and posttest data. Another slight difference is that the degrees of freedom is calculated by using the formula df = n-1. Thus, for this example the degrees of freedom would be 19.

▶ **TABLE 3.11** Critical value of t.

| Degrees of freedom | Level of significance (two-tailed) | |
|:---:|:---:|:---:|
| | **.05** | **.01** |
| 1 | 12.71 | 63.66 |
| 2 | 4.30 | 9.93 |
| 3 | 3.18 | 5.84 |
| 4 | 2.78 | 4.60 |
| 5 | 2.57 | 4.03 |
| 6 | 2.45 | 3.71 |
| 7 | 2.37 | 3.50 |
| 8 | 2.31 | 3.36 |
| 9 | 2.26 | 3.25 |
| 10 | 2.23 | 3.17 |
| 11 | 2.20 | 3.11 |
| 12 | 2.18 | 3.06 |
| 13 | 2.16 | 3.01 |
| 14 | 2.15 | 2.98 |
| 15 | 2.13 | 2.95 |
| 16 | 2.12 | 2.92 |
| 17 | 2.11 | 2.90 |
| 18 | 2.10 | 2.89 |
| 19 | 2.09 | 2.86 |
| 20 | 2.08 | 2.85 |
| 25 | 2.06 | 2.79 |
| 30 | 2.04 | 2.75 |
| 40 | 2.02 | 2.70 |
| 60 | 2.00 | 2.66 |

If a football coach wants to experiment with two different off-season strength training regimens, the matched pairs t-test can be used. The coach can match pairs of players by their one-repetition bench press maximum and their weight at the start of off-season. For instance, the coach might match two players weighing 270 pounds each and both able to bench press 300 pounds. By repeating this type of matching with 25 pairs of players and splitting them into two matched groups of 25 players, the coach creates two groups equally matched on bench press strength and weight. Each group would go through a different weight training regimen in the off-season workouts. At the end of the off-season, the players would be tested for their bench press maximum again. This data collected at the end of the off-season would form two groups of scores for the t-test computation. Degrees of freedom for this type of dependent t-test is calculated with number of pairs - 1 (N-1) being the formula. Thus, if the coach were to match 25 pairs of players and assign them to separate groups, the degrees of freedom would be 24.

## Simple Analysis of Variance (ANOVA)

The **simple analysis of variance (ANOVA)** is an extension of the t-test for independent samples. Recall that the t-test is used when two groups of scores are involved. The simple ANOVA test is used when there are three or more groups. Suppose a secondary physical education instructor wants to know if the type of curricular offerings makes a difference in student attitudes toward physical activity. In this sample, three different 10th grade classes might be taught physical education with the same instructional methods but different curricular design. Group A might participate only in team sports for the semester. Group B might participate only in lifetime sports during the same semester, while Group C is involved in a curriculum that alternates a team sports unit with a lifetime sports unit. It would be time-consuming and statistically incorrect to do three different t-tests (A–B, A–C, B–C).

The simple ANOVA, sometimes called a one-way ANOVA, enables the teacher to compare the differences among the three groups in one statistical procedure. In the example above, a fourth group (group D) could be formed that took no physical education at all. Again, multiple t-tests (A–B, A–C, A–D, B–C, B–D, C–D) should not be computed. Rather, a 1 (attitude scores) × 4 (groups) ANOVA would be the proper test for significant differences. If the ANOVA procedure indicates significant differences, it is then necessary to use a post hoc test (i.e., Scheffe test for multiple comparisons) to ascertain exactly which groups are significantly different from the others.

This brief overview of tests for significant differences between groups indicates the breadth of this area of statistics. The three tests mentioned are but a few of the statistical procedures used to determine significant differences. Other procedures include Chi-square, two-way ANOVA, and multiple analysis of variance (MANOVA). With the broad array of concepts and procedures included in this area of statistics, the information provided here only scratches the surface. The examples discussed provide illustrations to help the reader understand possible applications of these statistical procedures. While more detailed information is beyond the intended scope of this textbook, in-depth study of this area would be beneficial to any person in the physical education or exercise science professions.

# SUMMARY

This chapter examines basic statistical terminology and techniques that are important to practitioners in physical education and exercise science. A number of statistical concepts are presented, including levels of measurement, frequency distribution, graphical presentation of the data, measures of central tendency, measures of variability, properties of the normal curve, standard scores, correlational procedures, simple regression, and tests for differences between groups. An understanding of this information should prepare the reader for more in-depth understanding of the issues in the chapters that follow.

## ▶ DISCUSSION QUESTIONS

1. Describe the characteristics of the four levels of measurement. Give an example of each. Why is it important to understand the differences in these levels of measurement?

2. What are the advantages of using data display techniques to illustrate results of a test? What are some different methods of illustrating data?

3. List five characteristics of the normal curve.

4. Explain what is meant by the term "correlation." How can the use of correlational procedures help in teaching physical education?

5. Give the definition of a standard score. How are standard scores used in analyzing performance on tests given in physical education?

6. Below is a set of data representing measurement to the nearest millimeter of tricep skinfold of 7th grade boys:

4, 7, 13, 12, 10, 6, 7, 17, 9, 8, 13, 21, 6, 9, 10, 9, 8, 7, 5, 9, 15, 17, 19, 8, 9, 10, 7, 4, 20, 10, 9, 15, 12, 18, 12, 8, 9, 9, 11, 10, 7, 8, 15, 6, 19, 10, 9, 9, 7, 13, 12, 8, 22, 10, 5, 8, 9, 11, 13, 15, 19, 17, 11, 9, 8, 9, 10, 11, 7, 9, 14, 7, 16, 10, 9, 8, 9, 6, 14, 11, 12, 9, 8, 15, 6, 10, 17

Complete the following using the above data:
   a. Organize the data into a group frequency distribution.
   b. Draw a histogram of the data.
   c. Draw a frequency polygon of the data.
   d. Calculate cumulative frequency and cumulative percentiles for the data.
   e. From the grouped frequency distribution, find the mode, median, and range.
   f. From the grouped frequency distribution, calculate mean and standard deviation.
   g. Transform the raw scores of 7, 10, 13, and 16 into corresponding z-scores, T-scores, and percentiles.

7. Calculate the correlation coefficient for the following sets of scores.

| X (Pull-ups) | Y (Push-ups) |
|---|---|
| 3 | 12 |
| 12 | 30 |
| 7 | 27 |
| 10 | 37 |
| 5 | 21 |
| 9 | 35 |
| 6 | 21 |
| 1 | 9 |
| 4 | 17 |
| 0 | 4 |

8. From the data above, using simple regression procedures, predict how many push-ups can be done by a student who is able to complete 8 pull-ups.

## ▶ REFERENCE

Safrit, M. J., and Wood, Terry M. (1995) *Introduction to measurement in physical education and exercise science,* 3rd ed. St. Louis, MO: Times Mirror/Mosby.

## ▶ REPRESENTATIVE READINGS

Garrett, H. E. (1966). *Statistics in psychology and education,* 6th ed. New York: Longmans, Green.

Mood, D. P. (1980). *Numbers in motion: A balanced approach to measurement and evaluation in physical education.* Palo Alto, CA: Mayfield.

Turney, B. L., and Robb, G. P. (1973). *Statistical methods for behavioral science.* New York: Harper and Row.

Vincent, W. J. (1995). *Statistics in kinesiology.* Champaign, IL: Human Kinetics.

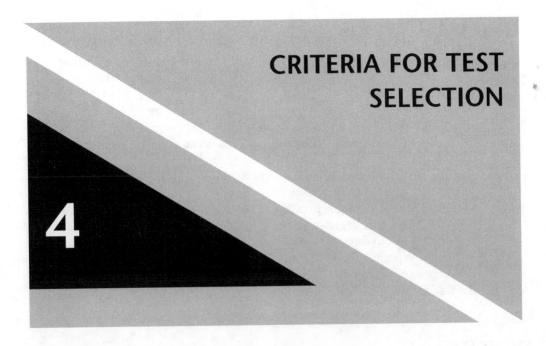

# CRITERIA FOR TEST SELECTION

**4**

## ▶ KEY TERMS

*- due w. Nov.3*

- alternate form reliability
- concurrent validity
- construct validity
- content validity
- criterion measure
- discrimination
- face validity
- independence
- norms
- objectivity
- odd-even reliability
- predictive validity
- relevant
- reliability
- Spearman-Brown prophecy formula
- split-half reliability
- test-retest reliability
- validity

## ▶ OBJECTIVES

*After reading this chapter, the student should be able to:*

1. Understand methods of establishing validity of various types of testing instruments.
2. Understand methods of establishing reliability of various types of testing instruments.
3. Explain the relationship between the validity, reliability, and objectivity of a testing instrument.
4. Discuss administrative concerns involved with selection of appropriate testing instruments.
5. Realize the importance of thorough planning for the administration of the test to ensure the collection of valid scores.

When the term "test" is mentioned, the thought of paper and pencil examinations taken in most classes usually comes to mind. While this is an important type of testing in the cognitive area, other types of tests exist to assess components of health and skill-related fitness, measure specific sports skills, and determine attitudes and feelings related to physical activity that are important in physical education and exercise science. One of the responsibilities of a physical educator or other exercise professional is to select appropriate test instruments based on certain criteria. This chapter presents criteria critical to the effectiveness of any type of test.

A "test" has been defined as an instrument, protocol, or technique used to measure a quantity or quality of properties or attributes of interest. A wide variety of tests is available to evaluate content in the various domains of physical education and exercise science. In some cases, it may be necessary to construct a test to measure some trait or attribute if an appropriate test is not available. Whether the instructor is constructing a test or using an existing one, certain characteristics, or criteria, are necessary if the measurements from the test are to be useful. These criteria are validity, reliability, and objectivity.

## VALIDITY

A test is said to possess **validity** if it accurately measures the attribute that it is designed to measure. This may seem to be a simple idea, but surprisingly, many tests being used lack this crucial quality. If a student won the class ladder tournament in racquetball but did not score well on the battery of racquetball skills test, then it is likely that the tests administered were not indicative of racquetball skill. Assuming that the tests were administered correctly, the battery of tests was not a valid measure of racquetball skill. Conversely, a student who is a mediocre player scoring high on a skills test would cast doubts on the validity of the particular test.

Suppose an instructor scheduled an examination on the statistical concepts presented in the previous chapter. When the students receive a copy of the test, they notice that all the questions pertain to the measures of central tendency. Would this be a valid test regarding their knowledge of Chapter 3? It might be a valid test of knowledge specific to the mode, median, and the mean, but it would not measure the knowledge of the information included in the whole chapter. Thus, it would lack validity. It would not measure what it was supposed to measure.

Validity of tests can be established using either a qualitative or quantitative approach. Although numerical techniques can be included, the qualitative approach depends upon the use of common sense and logic in making subjective judgments about the test in question. The quantitative approach is a data-based approach that involves calculating correlation coefficients to determine the validity. Choosing a procedure for establishing validity of a test often depends on the type of test that is being administered. With this in mind, five procedures for establishing validity will be discussed, starting with qualitative, or data-free, techniques and followed by the more powerful quantitative, or data-based, methods.

## Face Validity

The weakest procedure for establishing validity is called **face validity**. This argument is based on cursory examination of the testing instrument to see if it measures what it purports to measure. Because face validity is based on subjectivity, it does not present a strong argument for validity. The nature of some tests, however, allows them to be validated by this means.

If an instructor wanted to test the ability of a group of students to shoot free throws in basketball, the obvious test would be to let the students shoot a predetermined number of free throws and count the number of successful attempts. Certainly, this test would measure what it intended to measure. Logic tells the instructor that this is a valid way to test the ability to shoot free throws. No other more powerful procedure for determining validity needs to be considered.

Suppose an instructor wanted to give a written examination of fitness concepts and prepared a 50-item test. After reading the exam, it is noticed that all the items refer in some way to the concepts of fitness. If face validity is accepted, then this test would be considered valid. However, this type of logic contains pitfalls that demand more than a superficial examination to ensure validity. The test may contain an overabundance of questions in one area of fitness or contain questions that are poorly written. These weaknesses would cause the scores to reflect inaccurately the student's comprehension, or lack thereof, of the fitness concepts covered in class. Consider the next type of validity procedure to understand why face validity is not acceptable in this situation.

## Content Validity

For many assessment techniques used in physical education or fitness settings, (e.g., certain questionnaires, attitude surveys), **content validity** is the strongest method available. To establish content validity of an instrument, a more in-depth study is made of the test to ensure the representativeness of the items. Content validity argues that there is a rationale for each item based on what the instrument is designed to measure. The test items should represent the educational objectives of the unit.

When some type of physical performance is being measured, content validity can be established by logically determining the actions and demands made by the particular performance. The "content" of swimming

25 yards is a valid test for swimming speed. On closer inspection, however, some physical performance tests may not measure what they are intended to measure.

Suppose a test were constructed to measure the ability to throw a softball. The students being tested throw at the target from a distance of 25 feet. One might consider this a valid test until realizing that from that distance a person could hit the target and have a high score on the test without exhibiting good throwing form or velocity. Consequently, the "content" of this test does not test all facets of softball throwing ability, so it is not valid for measuring overall softball throwing ability.

## Construct Validity

A statistical extension of content validity is called **construct validity**. To use this procedure, one must first locate two groups that are known to differ significantly on the variable, or construct, being tested. A test is then administered to both groups to determine if there is a significant statistical difference between the scores in the groups. If there is no significant difference, then the test is not valid. Because extreme groups are normally used in determining construct validity, it is, at best, evidence of a general level of validity.

## Concurrent Validity

A stronger quantitative procedure for establishing validity is called **concurrent validity**. To use this method, one must have a known valid instrument to measure the variable of interest. Both the established test and the new test are administered to the same students. The results of the two tests are then correlated. A high correlation coefficient shows concurrent validity. The higher the correlation coefficient, the stronger the rationale is for the validity of the new test.

Concurrent validity procedures provide an estimate of the validity of the test. Few tests are perfectly valid. A weakness of the previous procedures discussed is that they assume an "either-or" stance on the validity of a test and provide no estimate—either they are valid or they are not. Because quantitative procedures can give an estimated degree of validity, they provide a stronger, more powerful argument for validity.

If a new test is easier to administer, less expensive, requires less equipment, or is in some way more adaptable to local needs, then there is good reason to develop and validate it. For instance, a maximal oxygen uptake treadmill test has proved to be a valid way to measure cardiorespiratory endurance. This type of test requires thousands of dollars of equipment, several people to administer it properly, and is time-consuming. Therefore, it is not be practical for mass testing in schools and colleges. However, other tests of cardiorespiratory endurance, such as the 12-minute run, have shown high concurrent validity to treadmill testing. Additionally, the 12-minute run can be administered inexpensively to a large number of people in field situations. Though it may not be as accurate as the more sophisticated treadmill test, it is an excellent test for most needs.

## Predictive Validity

The final method for establishing validity is **predictive validity.** This procedure can provide more powerful evidence of validity than any of the techniques that have been previously discussed. If an instrument has strong predictive validity, its scores will correlate highly with some type of measure in the future. Predictive validity is considered the ultimate evidence of an instrument's validity when the instrument predicts the behavior it seeks to measure.

For example, based on the score of a valid test, one should be able to predict how well a person will perform in the future in a competitive situation. Thus, to establish predictive validity, we correlate the scores on the test with performance in a game or meet. If the correlation coefficient is .80 or above, that is a strong argument for the predictive validity of the test. Unfortunately, this procedure is time-consuming and requires longitudinal study of the variable in question; that is, the subjects must be followed to the actual performance in the future.

## RELIABILITY

A test that gives consistent results is said to possess **reliability.** If a class of students takes the same test on two different days, the scores obtained should be about the same. A reliable test will yield data that are stable, repeatable, and precise. Some qualities or attributes can be measured more reliably than others. A person's height or weight can be measured precisely, and several trials are not likely to show much variation. Conversely, time on a mile run will fluctuate over several trials.

To ensure reliability, measurement techniques and conditions should be standardized to reduce measurement error. For example, consider what would happen to scores on a sit-up test if it were administered the first time on a gym floor and the next time on cushioned gym mats. Less than precise directions, inconsistent scoring procedures, different equipment, and different environmental conditions are examples of factors that can affect test reliability and the value of the scores collected. The subject's motivational state and general health, the presence of an audience, and length of the test are other elements that can affect reliability.

Because vastly different types of tests are given in physical education and exercise science, a number of different methods have been developed to estimate the reliability testing instruments. To determine the reliability of a test, at least two sets of scores must be obtained. Three procedures for establishing reliability are presented below.

## Test-Retest Reliability

The **test-retest reliability** procedure is exactly what the name implies. By administering the test, the first set of data is produced. After an appropriate period of time, the test is administered again in conditions as much the same as possible. The two sets of data are correlated to determine the reliability coefficient. Thus, this technique requires administering the same test to the same subjects on two separate occasions.

The tricky part of this procedure is to determine what is an "appropriate period of time" between the test and retest. The time interval between tests must consider the relationship between the variable being measured and factors such as maturation, learning, or changes in physical condition. The test-retest procedure is a good way to determine reliability for tests measuring stable information or measuring a variable or characteristic that is slow to change or develop.

If the test in question is a physical performance test, it can be given on the same day (e.g., free throw test) or on separate days (e.g., 12-minute run) if fatigue is a factor. In some physical performance tests, learning may take place during the first trial that would cause improvement in the second trial. Could this "learning effect" be a cause of concern in a free throw test? If "learning effect" is probable, then the test-retest may not be effective for estimating reliability.

In many types of written tests, students can remember the questions and their answers. If enough time elapses so that they forget the items on the test, there is a chance that the level of knowledge may have changed. The same is true for instruments that measure changeable traits such as attitudes and values. In these instances, other procedures to estimate reliability may be more appropriate.

## Alternate Form Reliability

The **alternate form reliability** procedure requires two equivalent forms of the test in question. The two tests should be of the same length with the same type of questions included on both instruments. The same group of respondents is given both tests. Depending on whether fatigue is a factor, the tests may be administered consecutively or with a suitable interval of rest. Intervals should be short, however, to avoid any change in condition or learning that would compromise reliability.

It is important to alternate the order in which the forms are administered. Part of the group should take form 1 first, followed by form 2, while the other half should take form 2 followed by form 1. This alternation protects against fatigue and boredom distorting the scores of the second test.

After both forms have been scored, the correlation of the scores on forms 1 and 2 can be calculated to determine the reliability of the instrument. The biggest problem with this method is that it is difficult enough to develop one testing instrument, and alternate form reliability requires the formulation of two tests. In most instances, it is not practical for teachers to devote this much time to test construction.

## Split-Half or Odd-Even Reliability

A third procedure, called **split-half** or **odd-even reliability**, can alleviate some of the problems encountered in the alternate form reliability and the test-retest methods. This technique is often used with written tests but can also be used with physical performance tests when an even number of trials are given. The advantage of this procedure is that it requires only one administration of one instrument to the group of respondents. The instrument is either split in half or the odd and even items are separated to form two sets of scores from the test. The two sets of scores are then correlated to estimate the reliability of the instrument.

The odd-even version is generally preferred because it ensures that fatigue or boredom will not bias scores, and more importantly, both sets of questions will be representative of the test. If split-halves are used, it opens the possibility that each half of the test covers different material or one is easier than the other. The odd-even split eliminates this concern.

A major problem with this procedure is that, generally, greater length provides more reliability in an instrument. If reliability is related to the number of items on the instrument, then splitting the instrument in half can reduce its reliability. Because of this situation, a procedure called the **Spearman-Brown prophecy formula** was developed. This formula uses the actual reliability coefficient obtained from the correlation of the two halves of the instrument to predict the reliability of the entire instrument. It is given in Formula 4.0.

▶ **FORMULA 4.0**

| Spearman-Brown Prophecy Formula |
|---|

$$\text{Reliability of whole test} = \frac{2 \text{ (reliability of } \frac{1}{2} \text{ test)}}{1 + \text{(reliability of } \frac{1}{2} \text{ test)}}$$

As an example, assume that after administering an exam, it was scored by separating the odd and even questions. The correlation computed between the odd and even scores was .70. Using the formula shown above, the estimated reliability of the whole test would be calculated as follows:

$$\text{Reliability of whole test} = \frac{2(.70)}{1 + .70} = \frac{1.40}{1.70} = .82$$

As illustrated, the reliability of the whole test is estimated to be higher (.82) than the correlation between the odd and even scores (.70). The odd-even method followed by the Spearman-Brown prophecy formula is one of the most frequently used procedures to estimate reliability.

## OBJECTIVITY

A third criterion for a good test is **objectivity.** Objectivity is a type of reliability that concerns the administration of tests. Giving directions, scoring, and behavior of the administrator can affect the reliability of a test. If a test is administered and scored independently by two people, the resulting scores should be similar. The only differing condition of the two testing procedures is *who* administered the test.

Suppose a group of students was given a pull-up test on successive days by two different teachers. On the first day, the administrator of the test allowed students to kick and swing on the bar to help perform their pull-ups. The teacher on the second day did not allow this technique. If the scores from the first trial and second trial were correlated, the coefficient would probably not be very high. This would be due to the lack of objectivity during the two test administrations.

Tests that measure height, weight, length, or that use counting are usually highly objective. Two timers with accurate stopwatches should be able to measure the same runner in an accurate and objective way. Similarly, two testers independently measuring the high jump or long jump on the same attempt should be able to obtain the same reading.

When tests have a high degree of subjectivity, such as the judging of diving or the form of a golf swing, objectivity coefficients are typically lower. Rating scales are frequently used in physical education and athletic settings. Unless properly constructed with specific criteria in mind, these rating scales can be very subjective. This is caused by a difference in interpretation or bias, usually unintentional, on the part of the judges. To increase the objectivity of the judging, a **criterion measure** is used, which is based on detailed specifics of the skill to be performed and how it should be judged. When a teacher is evaluating form of a sport skill in a class, the evaluation should be based on a criterion list to improve the objectivity of the analysis.

In many physical education settings, classes are large and time is limited. Rather than a formalized skills test, teachers often use formative assessment techniques, described in Chapter 1, of observing students in real game situations to evaluate student performance. This observation made in the actual context of the game may actually provide a more realistic appraisal of student outcomes, with the bonus of being time-efficient. However, the teacher must be aware of systematically applying the same performance criteria to all students to maintain objectivity. Also mentioned in Chapter 1, the term "authentic assessment" has gained popularity in recent years to describe the direct evaluation of student performance in a real-life setting. In authentic assessment, examples of student performance, not highly inferential estimates provided by group testing, are used to measure learning. For instance, student performance in real game settings is assessed rather than assessing skill with a more artificial skills test. Authentic assessment is ongoing and can include many types of documentation. Performance samples, anecdotal reports, student journals or logs, and fitness profiles are some of the things included in authentic assessment that may be compiled in a portfolio. More detailed information concerning authentic assessment is in Chapter 12.

Written tests involving true-false, matching, or multiple choice questions can be graded in a highly objective manner since the answer given is clearly right or wrong. Objectivity can become more of a problem on essay questions. If two different graders evaluate an essay answer, it is likely that they will give differing amounts of credit. This problem can be alleviated somewhat by composing a criterion answer and scoring the question based on specific points mentioned in the criterion.

Objectivity also depends on the clarity of directions. The test administrator must understand how to properly administer the test, and the students must understand how the test is performed and how it will be scored. A trial test is often appropriate to ensure that testing and scoring procedures are clear. By carefully planning the test and conscientiously following the protocol for test administration and scoring, objectivity of the test can be improved. Results of a test that are biased by a lack of objectivity waste the time and efforts of both the students and the teacher and are of little value in evaluating students.

# RELATIONSHIP BETWEEN VALIDITY, RELIABILITY, AND OBJECTIVITY

For a test to yield results that are an accurate reflection of the ability or attribute being measured, it must possess the characteristics of validity, reliability, and objectivity. A definite relationship exists among these three criteria.

There is a one-way relationship between validity and reliability. A test may be reliable but not valid. An instrument might give consistent results but not measure what it claims to measure. However, a test cannot be valid if it is not reliable. If a test cannot provide stable and repeatable results, it is not possible for it to be valid. The reliability of a test should be established before examining the validity of the instrument. In a sense, a test's degree of reliability places a ceiling on how valid the instrument can be.

As stated earlier, objectivity is related to reliability. Without objectivity, an instrument will lack reliability. Thus, the relationship between objectivity and validity is the same as between reliability and validity. An instrument may be objective without being valid but cannot be valid without being objective. Therefore, both objectivity and reliability are prerequisites to validity. To summarize, if a test is to be of any value, it must yield the same results regardless of who administers it; it must measure the quality or attribute in a stable and repeatable manner; and it must measure the quality or attribute that it claims to measure.

## ADMINISTRATIVE CONCERNS IN TEST SELECTION

Because physical education performance tests are generally more complex than written tests and the time period available to physical education is usually shorter than that of other academic classes, other criteria must also be met if a test is to be useful. Even a valid, reliable, and objective test may be eliminated from consideration if it fails to meet some of these additional administrative concerns.

For a testing program to be effective, it is necessary to avoid the pitfall of selecting tests that, due to a particular teaching situation, may cause logistical nightmares. A careless approach to test administration can result in invalid scores. Since testing in physical education should consume no more than 10 percent of the total instructional time, it becomes only prudent to select tests that are compatible with various aspects of the overall program. Therefore, during the curricular planning stages, several practical criteria for selecting a test and planning for test administration need to be considered.

After acceptable validity, reliability, and objectivity of a test have been determined, it is the responsibility of the program planners to identify factors that affect the efficiency and management of the testing program. Only after thorough deliberations about these factors should a test or testing program be considered for inclusion in the yearly physical education program.

## Relevance

Yearly, unit, and weekly lesson plans should include learning activities that are designed to achieve stated goals and objectives. To be meaningful, the selection of tests should be **relevant,** or linked, to measurement of program, unit, student, or teacher goals and the specific learning experiences planned to achieve those goals. Further, tests should require that the students use proper technique, adhere to the rules of the activity, and perform skills associated with the activity. For example, a tennis serve test that does not demand that the performer execute a proper toss and legal foot placement is not requiring proper technique.

Outcome statements, learning activities, and testing programs associated with physical education should be closely linked. Simply testing for the sake of testing has no place in a physical education program, particularly when the viability of a physical education program may rest on test scores to show success in meeting predetermined objectives.

*The National Association of Sport and Physical Education (NASPE)* sponsored a project resulting in Outcomes of Quality Physical Education (1992) that includes 20 outcome statements that were expanded into sample benchmarks for selected grade levels. To complement this work, *Moving Into the Future: National Physical Education Standards —A Guide to Content and Assessment* (1995) was completed to clarify content standards and provide assessment guidelines. These two related projects illustrate how curricular goals and assessment should be aligned so that the measurement and evaluation activities are relevant and meaningful to the students. More detailed discussion of the application of these publications is in Chapter 12.

## Educational Value

As an integral part of the education process, testing should not just be an evaluation process, but a learning experience for the students as well. As a result of test taking, they should learn something about themselves and the qualities being assessed. A key feature of contemporary health fitness test batteries is their educational component. The *AAHPERD Physical Best* and *Prudential FITNESSGRAM* have been combined to provide a comprehensive health-related physical fitness test battery accompanied by educational materials. Student knowledge and attitudes about physical fitness are considered more important than actual results of the test administration. Test results can be used to profile the level of physical performance capacities, thereby broadening the student's awareness of, and interest in, personal health and functional well-being. On a written test, it is feasible that students can learn facts or concepts by comparing their responses with the answer key.

Many microcomputer software packages are available that offer tutorials about physical fitness, nutrition, sports, and health. Often these learning packages contain review questions that give students an opportunity to test their knowledge about a particular topic. Utilizing the microcomputer in testing can be an effective method to assist students in learning. It also can be a way to greatly reduce the amount of class time dedicated to testing. Chapter 14 discusses various ways the microcomputer can be used to facilitate instruction in physical education. Keep in mind that testing can be educational and that allowing it to become separate from instruction can be deleterious to the overall program.

## Economy

Tests should be economically feasible in terms of equipment and personnel. Since school districts do not have the financial resources to purchase elaborate instruments, machines, and high-tech equipment that measure human performance with great precision, it is imperative that tests selected are affordable. This is one reason that the AAHPERD *Physical Best* and the *Revised Program for the Presidential Physical Fitness Award* are such popular test batteries. Each test requires minimal monetary expenditure for equipment and supplies.

Equipment and materials are not the only cost factor associated with test administration. To ensure valid results, tests need to be monitored by trained individuals. Since most test batteries contain several items, it is economical to have more than one person available to function as a test administrator. When students, parents, college students, or other teachers assist in testing, time must be devoted to training them. A test that takes a great deal of time to complete, demands a high degree of skill and experience to administer, and requires extensive training and practice time may not be a judicious use of personnel.

## Time

Tests should be administered in a relatively short period of time. With the demands placed on teacher accountability, it is appropriate that the majority of time in physical education be devoted to learning experiences designed to meet predetermined objectives. Recognizing this, most experts in program design and measurement recommend that formal testing programs consume no more than 10 percent of total instructional time (Baumgartner and Jackson, 1995; Barrow and McGee, 1979; and Johnson and Nelson, 1986). The task of test selection based on the availability of time becomes increasingly more difficult in situations in which instructional units are short, and time for instruction and practice are at a premium. As we know, the validity and reliability of a test often depend on the administration of a certain number of trials. Deviating from the standard instructions may cause invalid results. Compromising the testing program by offering an abbreviated version of a particular test can result in gathering useless data and wasting valuable class time.

While tests that require precise equipment may be costly in terms of dollars, they also may take a significant amount of time to administer. Other tests may need extensive preliminary arrangements, such as lines drawn on the floor, stations set up at various locations throughout the test area, specific dimensions marked on the playing field, or other tasks that take time. The bottom line is that all tests demand some set-up time. Always be aware of the time allocated for testing and select tests accordingly.

## Enjoyment

Tests should be a nonthreatening and relatively enjoyable experience. Most people have experienced anxiety and apprehension associated with taking a test. These feelings are often due to a threatening environment. Particularly with physical performance tests, test administrators need to take measures to ensure that the testing session is as enjoyable as possible and in no way discourages participation in physical activity. When participants enjoy taking a test and understand why they are being tested, they may become motivated to do well. A youngster who wants to improve her time on the mile run may be motivated by the fact that a faster time reflects a higher level of cardiovascular functioning.

Enjoyability is related to comfort. Providing mats for tests that require students to be on the floor, ensuring pleasant climatic conditions, and planning on privacy for certain tests are examples of how teachers can make the testing environment more comfortable. Even though certain cardiorespiratory endurance tests and other maximum-effort tests can be uncomfortable, students can learn to view them as challenging and important. Also, if a test is too repetitive, extremely easy or difficult, or viewed by the students as unimportant, the chances of it being an enjoyable experience are diminished.

## Norms

Selection of tests should be made only after considering the availability of current normative tables. **Norms** are values representative of a particular population. These values are usually reported as the mean and percentile equivalents of performance scores on a standardized test. In physical education, normative tables are available for many tests that measure performance in the physical and psychomotor learning domains. While results of tests of cognition and affective behavior lack a normative database, the scores may be either compared to an existing standard or used to determine change over a period of time.

Normative tables provide the means to compare individual performance with a larger population. These comparisons can provide valuable information to assist the test administrator and participant in determining the relationship of individual performance scores to scores of others of the same age and gender. If comparisons show students scoring below the national average, it is probably necessary to seriously review the existing curriculum. While the categorization of norms according to age and gender is common, some normative tables further classify scores by height and weight. Since these maturational factors affect physical performance, it is only prudent to consider them when making comparisons of performance scores. The important point to remember is that norms are a reflection of a specific group from which the norms were compiled and should be interpreted accordingly. For example, completing 60 sit-ups in one minute would not be as impressive if done by a high school senior as if performed by a second grade youngster. Similarly, norms based on the performance of secondary girls are not appropriate for kindergarten boys.

Several other important factors should be considered before using norms. Specifically, the adequacy of the norms must be evaluated.

1. The normative database should include a sufficiently large number of subjects. Generally, the larger the sample, the more closely it represents the total population. While there is no clear-cut rule indicating how large the sample should be, any normative table with fewer than several hundred scores for each age, sex, and test should be interpreted with caution.

2. The normative database should be representative of the performance of the population for which it was devised. Sampling a population that is in some way unique could result in erroneous interpretation of obtained scores. For example, using performance scores of college football players to develop norms for a particular test of minimal muscular strength and endurance would result in disproportionately high norms and would not be representative of the general population. To allow for a fair interpretation of student scores, comparisons should be made with a similar population.

3. The directions and manner of scoring need to be clear enough to ensure that the procedures used to administer the test are identical to those used in compiling the norms. If the procedures are different, any attempt to compare scores legitimately is impossible.

4. The geographic location of the population should be considered in devising the norms. Climate, socioeconomic level, cultural influence, and other environmental conditions could bias the sample. Variation in the norms can be controlled somewhat by devising local norms. Using computers, tables generated from raw performance scores can be quickly compiled and formatted into normative tables that display the percentile equivalents for the range of scores.

5. Norms should be current and updated on a regular basis. Computers allow for frequent revision. Maintaining a current bank of raw scores

and revising the norms on a yearly basis will take into account the ever-changing characteristics and abilities of youth.

## Discrimination

A test must take into account the wide range of performance capacities and abilities of students and should place a score on a continuum and be sensitive enough to make discriminations among all the students taking the test. **Discrimination** refers to the ability of a test to differentiate between good, average, and poor students. In selecting a test, a instructor may wish to choose one that is difficult enough so that no student receives a perfect score, but easy enough so that no student receives a zero. For example, assessment of percentage of body fat allows each student an opportunity to receive a score. That score falls along a continuum that discriminates among individuals who are extremely lean and those who are extremely fat. Similarly, a student completing a softball throw for distance will receive a perfomance score that falls somewhere between an extremely short distance and an extremely long distance. Tests that allow for a score of zero are problematic and may not truly discriminate among the performances of students, as Baumgartner and Jackson (1982) demonstrate:

> Consider the problem of students' receiving the minimum or maximum score. How would you determine who is the better student: Although two students who receive a zero on a pull-up test are both weak, they are probably not equal in strength per pound of body weight. Remember, however, that the fact that no student receives a perfect score or a zero is no guarantee that a test discriminates satisfactorily; conversely, the fact that someone does receive a perfect score or a zero is no guarantee that the test is a poor one.

Finding a test that totally discriminates among students' performance scores is a difficult task. The AAHPERD *Physical Best* fitness battery is one such test. Each test item is designed to measure the qualities of a function, along a continuum from severely deficient to high levels of functional capacity.

## Independence

Usually a single test is insufficient to measure the overall physical abilities or performance capacities of an individual. To obtain an overall profile of a student's physical skills or physical fitness requires administration of a test battery, composed of several tests that are each designed to measure a specific component. Each test should be **independent** of, or unrelated to, other items in the battery. Having students run the 50-yard dash, 100-yard dash, and the 100-meter dash to measure running speed would be a waste of time.

Each of these tests is a true measure of running speed, and hence highly related. Giving just one of the tests would provide all the information necessary to determine running speed performance.

If the measures in a test battery are unrelated, the correlation (see Chapter 3) between them is low. When scores from two tests are highly correlated, they are probably measuring the same trait. The practice of using related tests to measure performance is not only time-consuming, but also unfair to students who consistently score poorly on tests that measure that particular trait. When two (or more) tests in a battery are not mutually exclusive (i.e., they are highly correlated), retain only the one that is most appropriate for the situation.

## Sex Appropriateness

Tests should take into account the differences between males and females in such a way that the process does not bias in favor of one sex or another. In selecting and administering tests, instructors should be continually aware of the inherent differences that exist between boys and girls. From a physiological perspective, boys generally have more muscular strength and endurance, are taller and heavier, possess a lower percentage of body fat, and display greater cardiovascular endurance. On the other hand, girls tend to have greater flexibility, rhythmic coordination, and buoyancy.

Physical educators need to develop procedures for assessment and evaluation that take into account these differences in a nondiscriminating way. Administering tests with available norms allows the instructor to compare students' raw performance scores with those of others of the same age and sex. This type of evaluative procedure is more acceptable than having a criterion-referenced scale that applies to all students, regardless of sex. Differences attributed to sex are pertinent only on measures of physical ability or functional capacity and need not be a concern when selecting a test to measure abilities or behavior traits associated with the cognitive or affective learning domains.

## Reliance on Another's Performance

One student's test score should not depend on the performance of another student. The practice of administering tests that require interaction among students during the test trials with the results of that interaction being recorded as a test score should be avoided. Suppose a teacher was interested in testing students' ability to catch the forward pass in football. Using another student as the thrower could result in inconsistent throws. In this case, the performance score, number of caught balls, would depend on the ability of another person.

Students' performances should be based entirely on their abilities and not those of classmates or other individuals. Skills tests for such sportsas racquetball, tennis, and basketball should be constructed so that an individual's ability is measured and the score is not biased by interaction with a classmate.

## Safety

Teachers should always select tests that can be conducted in a safe environment and that are not inherently dangerous. Criteria to be considered in determining whether a test is safe include station site, the potential for students to overexert, and the capabilities of students. Selecting a safe site to conduct tests of motor ability or physical fitness is important. Most of the time this means exercising good judgment and common sense. Finding a smooth, unlittered outdoor area for the distance run, providing mats for the sit-up test, and securing spotters for tests of balance are examples of prudent measures to make the testing site as safe as possible. The use of marking devices that are soft, unbreakable, and highly visible is recommended. Fluorescent boundary cones are much preferred to chairs, bottles, or portable metal standards.

On tests of physical performance, students should be encouraged to do as well as possible. However, safeguards need to be provided that will protect against the likelihood of students overexerting themselves to the extent of causing injury. All tests of flexibility require that a muscle, or group of muscles, be stretched as far as possible. To prevent the injury of muscle tissue during the test, a warm-up session stretching the particular muscle group to be tested should be conducted immediately before test administration.

Protecting students from overexertion is a result of proper planning and a thorough knowledge about the purposes of the test. As a general rule, physical education teachers should consult with the school nurse prior to administering any strenuous test. This not only assists the teacher in identifying students who may have health problems that would prohibit participation, but it also displays prudent behavior on the part of the teacher. Proper conditioning should precede the administration of tests that require great efforts of muscular strength and endurance or cardiovascular expenditure.

Maturation is a factor that affects test performance. Expecting young children to perform at the same level as high school students on measures of strength and endurance is ludicrous. Asking students to perform skills on a test that is on a higher level than that which they are capable of could jeopardize their safety. Be sure to check the age appropriateness of the test prior to final test selection and be familiar with the abilities of students before placing them in a testing situation.

The instructor also needs to be knowledgeable about the test and the characteristics to be measured if the environment is to be safe. If the test administrator does not understand potential dangers associated with the test, problems could arise. In order to secure a safe testing environment, the instructor must know what to do and how to do it.

## Testing Large Groups

Physical education teachers are usually responsible for more students than other faculty members are. Planning, organizing, and actual testing to accommodate such large numbers seems overwhelming. Selecting tests under these circumstances can be made easier if attention is given to tests that lend themselves to mass testability. With large classes it is imperative that students be measured as quickly, yet accurately, as possible. This can be accomplished by testing students successively or simultaneously. For example, a large number of students can be tested in a single class period in physical performance tests such as the flexed arm hang, pull-ups, sit-and-reach, and shuttle run. Using the partner system, half of the class can be tested at the same time. Having a partner count the number of sit-ups correctly completed in a given time period or keeping track of elapsed time on a distance run are examples of how administration time can be reduced by simultaneously testing large numbers of students. Using the school nurse, other teachers, aides, parents, or local college students to assist in test administration is another way to reduce the time associated with testing large numbers of students. Another feature of simultaneous testing is that it keeps most students occupied and discourages class disruptions resulting from inactivity.

## Ease of Scoring, Interpreting, and Reporting

A test should allow for easy and accurate scoring and should be used as a self-assessment technique by students. Selecting tests that can be easily scored on specially designed forms or that provide microcomputer software for quick and accurate interpretation and reporting are time-saving procedures and should be considered. While important to test administration, ease of scoring should not be the primary factor in test selection. It should, however, be considered if the test is to be utilized for educational purposes. For instance, a sit-and-reach apparatus could be located in a particular area of the school and made available for students to self-test their flexibility. Similarly, a tumbling mat with permanently marked distance increments could be used by students to regularly monitor their performance on standing long jump.

As previously discussed, if a test is to provide valid and reliable results, the test administrator must follow the standardized instructions.

Deviating from the proper procedures will result in worthless scores. Learning correct test procedures and developing an understanding of assessment instruments used to measure the learning domains in physical education is crucial. Attending training sessions or working with someone who is familiar with the test are good ways to acquire the knowledge and skills to conduct a testing session. Students can learn how to administer many of the physical performance tests simply through the process of taking the test. Special tutoring sessions before or after school and brief training episodes during class time are opportunities for teachers to provide students with the skills needed to benefit from self-testing. If one of the major goals of physical education is to develop students' knowledge and understanding about the value of physical activity, then they must be taught self-appraisal techniques.

## PLANNING TEST ADMINISTRATION

Once the assessment instruments to be used in the physical education program have been determined, planning for the testing session can begin. Proper planning increases the likelihood of smooth and efficient testing sessions and of obtaining valid and reliable scores. Several suggestions related to test selection, administration, scoring, and objectivity have already been discussed in this chapter. Specific organizational hints are also provided in Chapters 5–8 along with the directions for each of the tests presented in those chapters. However, some general recommendations for planning are given here.

## Securing Materials and Preparing the Testing Area

Proper use of space, equipment, and supplies reduces the amount of time required for administering the test. Competent test administration begins with compiling a detailed list of needed test equipment, supplies, and other necessary materials. Planning for appropriate utilization of space can reduce set-up time, ensure a safer environment, eliminate confusion, and minimize crowding.

### *Equipment and Supplies*

The test directions should indicate the type and amount of equipment and supplies necessary for administration of the test. While materials vary among tests, items usually needed include stopwatches, tape measures, signs, pencils, score cards, tumbling mats, and boundary cones. Examples of specialized items include hand dynamometers, skinfold calipers, and a sit-and-reach apparatus. Remember, all necessary equipment and supplies should be in their proper location before the testing session. Scurrying around during the test session looking for necessary items is a waste of precious time. Be prepared!

### Testing Area

Because the condition of a test area can affect performance, the area to be used should be a safe environment in which to conduct a test. A properly prepared test area eliminates hazards to students' safety. Advance preparation to ensure safety includes mowing the field, sweeping the asphalt area, trimming border shrubs, replacing burned-out light fixtures, cleaning the floor, and repairing the walls.

### Arrangement of the Testing Area

Proper sequential ordering of test items is essential and requires careful advance preparation. If the standardized instructions detail a specific arrangement for the testing area, then that blueprint must be precisely followed. If not, establish an order and arrangement that meets the needs of the testing program. Several factors should be kept in mind as plans are made. First, the sequence of test items should be arranged to offset fatigue and provide functional rest periods for students. For example, strenuous tests should not be administered in succession. Alternating a fatigue test with a test requiring minimal locomotor movement is an appropriate practice. As a standard rule, distance runs should not be scheduled first. In fact, distance runs can serve as an exciting culminating experience to a testing program. Second, the number of possible test stations may be limited by availability of equipment and supplies. If more than one piece of necessary equipment is available, however, test time can be decreased by increasing the number of test stations used for the particular activity. Third, test situations should be clearly marked and students made aware of the rotational sequence before beginning the tests. Finally, the tester needs to know how long it takes to administer each of the tests. A test that requires a particularly long time to administer may be handled best by using multiple test sites.

## Knowledge of the Test

As a test administrator, the instructor should have a thorough knowledge of the test and a precise understanding of its administrative procedures. It also helps if the students are familiar with the test and know its purpose. If the instructor is inexperienced with a particular test, it may be helpful to write out a list of all the instructional and organizational procedures. Knowing the number of trials, exact measurement techniques, and recommended organizational procedures associated with each test ensures accuracy of scores and allows judicious use of valuable class time. If a test will not take the entire class period, the instructor should plan some instructional activity for the remaining time.

## Recording the Scores

The manner in which raw scores are recorded on score cards is integral to the efficiency of the testing program. Scoring forms should be designed and printed in advance of the test session. Many test batteries have preprinted score cards available. Adopting these forms may save time and serve the purpose. Keep in mind, however, that a cost is usually associated with requesting these forms.

In most cases, the instructor will be responsible for devising the score sheet used in recording the individual performance scores. Two common types of score cards are the class roll sheet and the individual score card.

### Class Roll Sheet

The class roll sheet contains the names of all members of a particular class. Usually alphabetized by last name, this sheet provides spaces to record the scores that students achieve on all tests as well as to report other pertinent data (e.g., age, height, weight, sex). This type of form is appropriate when one test administrator is responsible for the recording of all raw scores. Because all the names are listed in a sequential manner, use of a class roll sheet facilitates the time taken to record scores. In addition, posting scores on sheets gives students the opportunity to readily view their performance on the different tests in relation to others in their class. Having all the raw scores on sheets also expedites the conversion from raw scores to percentile equivalents. The likelihood of misplacing any student's performance scores is also decreased by using roll sheets.

### Individual Score Card

The most popular, and perhaps the best, way to record students' test scores is to use an individual score card. Even in the elementary schools, the individual score card offers numerous advantages. If the students are tested in the order in which the score cards are arranged, the tester does not have to look through a long list of names. Trained assistants in the form of parents, college students, or members of the class can accurately record raw scores. With individual score cards, students have an opportunity to become more aware of their performance and to share in the testing procedure. They can examine and reflect on their performance scores and have a better idea of their achievement status. Posting normative tables on a convenient bulletin board will allow students to receive immediate feedback regarding their relative performance.

The design and contents of the card depend, of course, on the test or test battery selected. Space should be provided for information such as the student's name, age, height, weight, class, homeroom, and teacher. Generally, the 5" × 8" index card provides enough space for all the necessary categories.

If a school or district has the capability to store raw scores on a computer, the design of either the roll sheet or score card becomes important. Organizing the information in such a way that it can be easily input on to a microcomputer diskette or mainframe computer can be a tremendous timesaver. Chapter 14 discusses the use of computers in physical education and exercise science and describes ways in which raw data can be transcribed onto an electronic recording device.

## Training Testers

An important step in the testing process is the training of testers. Simply because a person reads the instruction manual does not guarantee that the directions are understood. Some tests, such as body composition, also require proficiency on the part of the tester. In this case, the tester must be skilled with the skinfold calipers in order to obtain accurate and reliable readings of subcutaneous fat. To better prepare testers and assistants, practice sessions should be conducted with a sample of subjects. These sessions can be used to clarify instructions, standardize procedures, and develop technical skills necessary to administer the test. The advent of several new batteries of physical fitness and performance tests has prompted many schools and districts to devote inservice workshop time to training physical education personnel in methods and procedures associated with test administration. While the use of paraprofessionals, college students, parents, and class members as assistants for testing is encouraged, it is advisable to conduct formal practice sessions so they become familiar with their responsibilities.

## Practicing Test Items

In physical education, a primary source of measurement error is not allowing students the opportunity to become familiar with and practice test items. Reliability, the ability of a test to consistently measure what it is supposed to measure, depends on whether a student has practiced the skills related to the test. Students often perform better in a test on the second administration since they are familiar with techniques and protocols of the test from the first administration. This is the "learning effect." The second score is more indicative of their true abilities. Thus, it is important that students become thoroughly familiar with the test before their scores are actually collected to evaluate their proficiency.

Students should be informed well in advance of upcoming tests so that they can prepare accordingly. In the 1.5 mile run, for instance, it is important for students to understand the concept of pace, be aware of their optimal pace, and have experience in running for an extended duration. In another case, improved muscular strength and endurance as measured by free weight lifting may be related more to efficiency and familiarity with the technique than to actual strength gains.

Students should be given ample time to develop some degree of physical fitness prior to taking tests that require extreme physical exertion. Expecting the students to complete a distance run test the first week of classes is unacceptable practice from a medical point of view and may also promote resentment and poor attitudes toward physical education and activity.

## Warming Up

An initial period of 5–10 minutes should be devoted to physiologically and psychologically preparing for taking a test. Proper warm-up and stretching exercises may also help prevent muscle and joint injury, which could occur as a result of maximum effort on a test. The warm-up is not only a safety precaution but it also improves performance on tests. Some tests are specific in nature and require a special kind of warm-up. The sit-and-reach test to measure flexibility of the lower back and posterior thigh requires a thorough warm-up session to prepare those particular muscle groups for the actual test. Remember, it is the responsibility of the test administrator to properly warm up students for each of the test items. Make certain that students do not cool down as they wait their turn to perform the test.

## Standardizing Instructions

Once the test site has been designed and procedures determined, it is time to develop specific instructions. Most tests require two types of directions, one for the test administrators and the other for the students. Instructions for testers contain information related to explanation, demonstration, administration, and scoring of the test. Instructions for students include how to perform the test, hints on techniques to improve scores, and other information. These directions should be standardized and prepared in written form. Caution must be taken that some students are not given different or additional information about what is considered good performance or suggested goals. While viewed as motivating, this type of information may also have a deleterious effect on performance.

## Converting, Interpreting, and Evaluating the Results

The reason for testing students is to obtain meaningful information about their abilities. Once obtained, this information can be used in a variety of ways to enhance program and individual performance. Interestingly, many physical educators test for the sake of satisfying an imposed administrative mandate and fail to complete the final stage of test administration—converting, interpreting, and evaluating the results.

### Converting Scores

Recording scores is usually a simple process of placing raw scores onto roll sheets or individual score cards. However, scores in raw form are generally meaningless and difficult to interpret. Therefore, it sometimes becomes necessary to convert raw scores into standard scores. Chapter 3 describes different types of standard scores and their calculations. Chapter 14 identifies microcomputer software that quickly converts raw scores into more meaningful standard scores.

The most common procedure for obtaining a standard score is converting a raw score to a percentile equivalent. Percentile scores describe the individual's performance relative to the performance of others in the same age and gender categories. Some normative tables even classify scores according to height and weight.

### Interpreting Scores

Once the scores have been converted to a more meaningful standard score, the next phase of the posttest procedure is interpretation of the results. Students should always be apprised of their performance and made aware of the meaning of the results. A score of 32 centimeters on the sit-and-reach test is more easily interpreted by a 12-year-old girl if she knows that her performance is at the 60th percentile. She can translate this to mean that her performance on this test of flexibility is better than 60 percent of the population of same age and gender students who made up the normative sample. Many microcomputer programs can also quickly convert raw scores into percentile equivalents and provide students with immediate feedback in the form of a personalized fitness profile. The use of local norms is an asset, especially when students have a working knowledge of norms and have ready access to them. Chapter 14 discusses ways to use the microcomputer to facilitate the conversion, interpretation, and evaluation of test scores. Interpretation of standard scores enables the instructor and students to monitor the students' progress and identify their strengths and weaknesses.

### Evaluating Scores

A vital phase of the posttest procedure is the evaluation of scores in relation to the process and product. This follow-up procedure usually results in the refocus of aims or goals of the program and a concomitant change in the process used to attain stated goals. For example, if students in a school district display poor performance relative to national percentile equivalents on a test of cardiorespiratory fitness, physical educators could rightfully redirect the program to attain higher levels of cardiorespiratory performance. To do so would require the inclusion of more vigorous learning activities into the curriculum. Always be mindful that evaluation is an ongoing process designed to improve the standards of the program.

## SUMMARY

This chapter deals with many criteria that a teacher or administrator must consider in selecting testing instruments. Because of the many types of tests available, the instructor must be aware of the various pitfalls in test selection and administration that can contaminate the results.

A portion of the chapter presents the concepts of validity, reliability, and objectivity. Regardless of the type of test, any instrument must possess these critical characteristics. It is important that the reader understand these criteria for test selection and their interrelationships.

Even if a test possesses these three characteristics, many other concerns need to be considered in test selection. A test may be valid, reliable, and objective yet not meet the needs of a particular situation. A detailed listing of additional administrative concerns is presented and discussed.

Once it is determined that a test is valid, reliable, and objective and that it satisfies other criteria specific to the testing situation, careful planning of the test administration is necessary to ensure the accuracy of the results. No matter how good a test is, it will yield scores of little value if it is not administered properly.

A number of steps important to test administration are presented as suggestions for good planning. It should be emphasized that there is no substitute for common sense in selecting and properly administering a test. Hopefully, the information in this chapter, coupled with a healthy dose of common sense, will simplify the task of test selection and administration and ensure scores that reflect the true abilities and/or attributes of the students.

## ► DISCUSSION QUESTIONS

1. What are two qualitative methods for determining validity of a testing instrument? Describe testing instruments for which it would be appropriate to use these procedures.

2. What are three quantitative methods of determining validity of a testing instrument? Describe testing instruments for which it would be necessary to use these methods.

3. What are four methods used to determine the reliability of a test? Compare and contrast the advantages and disadvantages of each of these procedures. Give an example of when it would be appropriate to use each of these methods.

4. What is the one-way relationship between validity and reliability of a testing instrument?

5. What are some administrative concerns that a teacher should have when selecting a test? Which are most important and why?

6. Thorough planning is essential when preparing to administer a test. What things should an instructor consider to ensure valid scores when planning the test?

## ► REFERENCES

American Alliance for Health, Physical Education, Recreation, and Dance. (1992). *Outcomes of quality physical education programs.* Reston, VA.

Barrow, H. M., and McGee, R. (1989) *A practical approach to measurement in physical education.* 4th ed. Philadelphia, PA: Lea and Febiger.

Baumgartner, T. A., and Jackson, A. S. (1995). *Measurement for evaluation in physical education.* 5th ed. Dubuque, IA: Wm. C. Brown.

Johnson, B. L., and Nelson, J. K. (1986). *Practical measurements for evaluation in physical education.* 4th ed. Edina, MN: Burgess Publishing.

National Association of Sport and Physical Education. (1995). *Moving into the Future: National physical education standards—A guide to content and assessment.* St. Louis: Mosby.

## ► REPRESENTATIVE READINGS

American Alliance for Health, Physical Education, Recreation and Dance. (1976). *AAHPERD youth fitness test manual.* Reston, VA.

_____. (1980). *AAHPERD Health Related Fitness Manual.* Reston, VA.

_____. (1988). *Physical best: The American Alliance physical fitness education and assessment program.* Reston, VA.

Crowl, T. K. (1986). *Fundamentals of research: A practical guide for educators and special educators.* Columbus, OH: Publishing Horizons.

Fox, D. J. (1969). *The research process in education.* New York: Holt, Rinehart and Winston.

Institute for Aerobic Research. (1992). *The Prudential FITNESSGRAM.* Dallas, TX: Institute.

Mood, D. P. (1980). *Numbers in motion: A balanced approach to measurement and evaluation in physical education.* Palo Alto, CA: Mayfield.

Pangrazi, R. P., and Hastad, D. N. (1986). *Fitness in the elementary schools.* Reston, VA: American Alliance for Health, Physical Education, and Recreation.

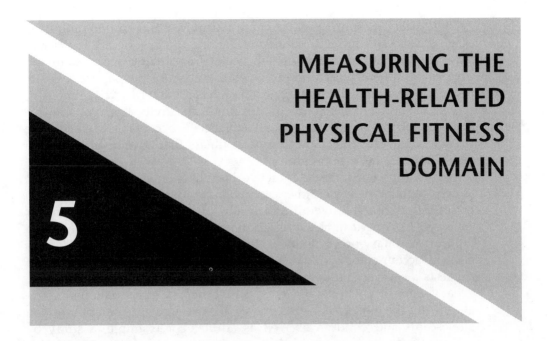

# MEASURING THE HEALTH-RELATED PHYSICAL FITNESS DOMAIN

**5**

## ► KEY TERMS

anthropometric measurement
body composition
cardiorespiratory fitness
distance run
extension
fat weight
field-based tests
flexibility
flexion
health-related physical fitness
lean weight
muscular endurance
muscular strength

## ► OBJECTIVES

*After reading this chapter, the student should be able to:*

1. Describe the components of health-related physical fitness and discuss the relationship of each to an individual's physical health and well-being.
2. Understand the importance of incorporating learning experiences that are designed to develop health-related physical fitness.
3. Recognize and describe the importance of valuing and assessing the process of physical activity.
4. Identify valid and reliable tests used to measure components of health-related physical fitness.
5. Follow standardized procedures in administering tests that measure various components of health-related physical fitness.

Physical fitness and regular physical activity are central to producing physically educated individuals. During the past decade, participation in physical activity for the sake of improving one's health and physical well-being has increased. More and more people are jogging, cycling, swimming, and joining health clubs and other exercise centers to receive the health benefits of vigorous physical activity. It is now fashionable to be attired in exercise apparel and socially acceptable to discuss the positive changes in one's own physical fitness that have resulted from a newly initiated exercise program.

This apparent increase in active lifestyles, however, is misleading. Slowly, but effectively, the American public is being lulled into a false sense of security about the overall fitness and physical activity levels in our country. The American Heart Association estimates that the annual death toll from coronary heart disease in the United States is over 600,000. This not only accounts for over one-half of all deaths in this country, but it also suggests a severely limited lifestyle for an enormous number of people. What is more frightening, however, is that the risk factor patterns associated with the onset of degenerative heart diseases are apparent in adolescents and children as well as adults. For example, a study by Gilliam, Katch, Thorland, and Weltman (1977) in which 47 boys and girls ages 7 to 12 were tested found that 65 percent of the children had at least one coronary heart disease risk factor; 11 percent were obese; 18 percent and 11 percent had elevated triglycerides and cholesterol, respectively; and another 11 percent had low physical work capacity as measured by maximal oxygen uptake. Moreover, findings of a 1991 report suggest that participation in vigorous physical activity among high school students may be decreasing (Public Health Service, 1991).

The evidence to support a negative relationship between habitual physical activity and coronary heart disease morbidity and mortality is substantial (Breslow and Enstrom, 1980; Fox and Skinner, 1964; Paffenbarger et al., 1977, 1978). In fact, it has been estimated that as many as 250,000 deaths per year in the United States, approximately 12 percent of the total, are attributable to lack of regular physical activity (Hohn, Teutsch, Rothenberg, and Marks, 1986; McGinnis and Foege, 1993). It has been proven that cardiorespiratory fitness in persons of both sexes, all ages, and with or without cardiovascular health problems can be improved through regular programs of aerobic exercise (American College of Sports Medicine, 1978, 1993.)

In perhaps the most comprehensive study ever conducted to investigate the relationship between physical fitness and the risk of dying, Blair et al. (1989) found the following:

1. Death rates for the least fit men were 3.4 times higher than for the most fit men and for the least fit women, 4.6 times higher than for the most fit women.

2. Higher levels of physical fitness were beneficial even in those with other risk factors such as high blood pressure, elevated cholesterol levels, history of cigarette smoking, and family history of heart disease.

3. Cancer death rates were much lower in physically fit men and women.

4. Even moderate levels of exercise will result in a fitness level associated with a greatly reduced risk of death.

Obesity and lower back pain are also serious problems in this country. Medical experts agree that obesity has reached epidemic proportions in the United States. Conservative estimates suggest that 30–60 percent of the 10 million or more school-age children in this country are obese, and as many as 75 million Americans have problems associated with the lower back, with 7 million new victims each year (Toufexis, 1980).

The key to reducing back pain and preventing its onset lies in strengthening and stretching the muscles in the back and abdomen. Several decades ago, this recommended regimen of exercise was unheard of. Now, many medical specialists believe back patients should start doing gentle exercise as soon as their pain allows and should continue exercising for the rest of their lives. In many programs sponsored by YMCAs, fitness centers, and hospitals, individuals learn how to work, play, and exercise in ways that reduce strain and strengthen the muscles of the lower back. Physical education teachers are becoming increasingly aware of the role exercise plays in reducing lower back problems and are responding by including static stretching and abdominal strengthening activities into daily lessons.

Physical health and well-being is undeniably associated with an active lifestyle. Promotion of increased physical activity as a means of disease prevention as well as prevention of obesity, lower back pain, and degenerative diseases and processes is critical (American College of Sports Medicine, 1993). As such, physical education and exercise science become valuable means to enhance the functional health of individuals. Given that two of the primary goals of physical education are to develop and maintain a level of health-related physical fitness commensurate with an individual's needs and to promote the value of a physically active lifestyle, it is only appropriate that tests to measure the health and physical well-being of students be included as a vital part of the physical education curriculum. The following sections define health-related physical fitness and discuss tests that can be used to measure and evaluate students and adults in the areas of cardiovascular fitness, muscular endurance, flexibility, and body composition.

## HEALTH-RELATED PHYSICAL FITNESS

Although it is generally agreed that physical fitness is an important part of normal growth and development, a generic definition of the precise nature of physical fitness has not been universally accepted. Through research and scholarly inquiry, it is clear that the multidimensional characteristics of physical fitness can be divided into two areas: health-related physical fitness and skill-related physical fitness (AAHPERD, 1980; Corbin and Lindsey, 1988). This departure from the traditional notion of fitness has resulted in a clear differentiation between physical fitness related to functional health and well-being and physical performance related primarily to athletic ability. A practitioner must be aware that this distinction has program implications. Understanding the distinctive features of health-related and skill-related fitness and the components of each will help physical educators and exercise scientists develop program goals and performance-based objectives and measure progress toward those goals. It is suggested that dichotomizing the definition of fitness should not lessen the importance of each aspect in the program construction.

**Health-related physical fitness** includes those aspects of physiological function that offer protection from diseases resulting from a sedentary lifestyle. It can be improved and/or maintained through a regular program of physical activity that adheres to the principles of exercise. Specific components of health-related physical fitness include cardiovascular fitness, muscular strength and endurance, flexibility of the lower back, and body composition.

**Cardiorespiratory fitness** is the ability to exercise the entire body for extended periods of time without undue fatigue. A strong heart is necessary to supply oxygenated blood effectively to the muscles of the body. Poor cardiorespiratory fitness has been identified as an antecedent to heart disease.

**Muscular strength** is the ability of muscles to exert force. **Muscular endurance** is the ability of muscles to exert force over an extended period of time. Maintenance of minimal levels of trunk and hip strength/endurance are important to prevent and alleviate low back pain and tension.

**Flexibility** of the lower back refers to the range of motion available in the musculature of the lower back. Muscles, tendons, and ligaments tend to retain or increase their elasticity through stretching activities. People who are flexible are less subject to injury during physical activity, usually possess sound posture, and experience less back pain.

**Body composition** refers to the amount of body fat a person carries. A fit person has a relatively low percentage of body fat. As discussed earlier, obesity has been linked with the onset of various health problems.

Laboratory-based testing is the most accurate means to measure components of health-related physical fitness. These tests are conducted on an individual basis in a laboratory setting using trained personnel operating sophisticated equipment. For example, maximal oxygen uptake is most accurately determined by measuring expired gases during maximal exercise. Underwater weighing to determine body composition is another lab technique that permits an accurate calculation of body fat percentage. Like measuring oxygen uptake, hydrostatic weighing requires the use of expensive electronic equipment and trained technicians. Lab testing apparatus may also be available to athletic and personal trainers. Although a detailed description of these tests is beyond the scope of this text, the reader is encouraged to study Chapter 13 for a brief summary of some tests to measure health-related physical fitness. The remainder of this chapter is devoted to identifying and describing field tests that have been found to correlate highly with lab tests and are suitable for use with individuals of all ages. Each of the test batteries or individual test items will include, where available, examples of norms and criteria. Even though the trend is toward criterion-referenced evaluation, we have assured the reader a choice.

## TEST BATTERIES TO MEASURE HEALTH-RELATED PHYSICAL FITNESS

Fitness testing has undergone significant changes in recent years. Once dedicated to measuring skills, test items now focus on components of health-related physical fitness. Most test batteries currently in use evaluate performance on the basis of its relationship to a criterion or standard rather than to the group being tested. Normative information, while useful to profile group performance, is assuming a less prominent role in judging the fitness of individuals. With the movement toward the use of standards has come a movement to encourage and recognize improvement and alteration of exercise behavior, rather than merely performance. The reader is reminded that this movement toward criterion-referenced scores reflects the fact that there is little correlation between activity and fitness test results. It is important, therefore, to reinforce behavior rather than simply a score. With this rapidly changing focus in fitness testing comes the responsibility for educators and program administrators to remain up-to-date on testing goals, procedures, and award systems.

Tests described in the following sections were selected based on health-related criteria discussed earlier in this chapter. Choosing a battery of test items rather than individually selected tests can be advantageous. First, often a test battery has been checked for reliability and validity and efforts have been made to avoid testing the same component twice. Second, batteries may provide a way to calculate an overall score for each participant. And finally, test batteries can serve as common denominators among schools within the same locale. Only test batteries that are easily administered, include software support systems, measure components of health-related physical fitness, are economically feasible for the schools, and are supported by practical and appropriate award systems were selected for inclusion.

## *Prudential FITNESSGRAM*

(Cooper Institute for Aerobics Research, 1994)

*Purpose:* The Prudential FITNESSGRAM is a comprehensive fitness program designed to measure the components of health-related physical fitness that have been identified as important to total health and optimal function. The goals of the program are to promote enjoyable regular physical activity and to provide a thorough fitness assessment and reporting program for children and youth. Several test options are provided for most items, with one option recommended. The recommended test for each item is described first in each section.

*Description:* The items of the test battery are (1) one-mile walk/run or a multistage 20-meter shuttle run called the PACER to measure cardiorespiratory capacity; (2) skinfold thickness or body mass index to measure body composition; (3) timed curl-up test to measure abdominal strength and muscular endurance; (4) the trunk lift to measure trunk extensor strength and flexibility; (5) push-ups, modified pull-ups, pull-ups, or flexed arm hang to measure muscular strength and endurance of the upper body; and (6) back-saver sit-and-reach or shoulder stretch to measure flexibility.

The Prudential FITNESSGRAM test battery is a reporting system able to provide meaningful feedback to students, teachers, and parents, with an awards program that acknowledges achievement and exercise behavior. The test battery also includes modifications for special populations (see Chapter 11). For additional information regarding the Prudential FITNESSGRAM write directly to Prudential FITNESSGRAM, Cooper Institute for Aerobics Research, 12330 Preston Road, Dallas, TX 75230.

*Validity:* Content validity is assumed for the test battery. Validity coefficients for some of the test items have been reported by the Cooper Institute for Aerobics Research (1986, 1992).

*Age Level:* Ages 5–16+

*Norms:* Results of the Prudential FITNESSGRAM are communicated in the form of desirable health standards.

*Test Area:* Any spacious gymnasium or multipurpose room and outdoor area are suitable for administering the test battery.

### *Test 1: One-Mile Walk/Run (Recommended)*

*Instructions:* Students are instructed to run/walk the one-mile distance as fast as possible. Students begin on the command "Ready, start."

*Equipment Needed:* Stopwatch, pencil and scoresheet, and boundary markers for the running area.

*Scoring Procedure:* The time taken to cover the one-mile distance is recorded in minutes and seconds. Students in grades K–3 should not be timed but should simply complete the distance.

*Organizational Hints:* Instruction emphasizing pacing and practice should precede test administration. Administering the test under conditions of high temperature and/or humidity or windy conditions should be avoided. A proper warm-up should precede test administration. It is important that a system be devised to accurately count laps and record times (e.g., partnering with older children).

### The Progressive Aerobic Cardiovascular Endurance Run-PACER (Recommended for K–3)

*Instructions:* A 20-meter course is marked with boundary cones and a taped line at each end. Each student should have a space for running that is 40–60 inches wide. A PACER audiotape (includes music and prerecorded beeping sound) is used and students are to run the distance of the marked area and touch the line before the beep on the audiotape sounds. At the sound of the beep students reverse direction and run back to the other taped line. Students who get to the line before the beep must wait for the beep before running in the other direction. Students continue this pattern until they have twice failed to reach the line before the beep sounds. Two missed arrivals constitutes completion of the test.

*Equipment Needed:* Tape playback machine with good volume, PACER tape, boundary cones, masking tape, pencils, and score sheets.

*Scoring Procedure:* A partner should record the lap number on a pre-designed score sheet. The reported score is the total number of laps completed.

*Organizational Hints:* Students should be encouraged to pace themselves. When testing groups of students, older students or adults can be used to assist in the scorekeeping. Students who have twice missed the pace should depart the testing area being careful not to interfere with others still running.

### Test 2: Skinfold (Recommended)

*Instructions:* The triceps and calf are the two sites for the skinfold test. Specific instructions for locating and measuring these sites can be found later in this chapter.

*Equipment Needed:* Skinfold caliper.

*Scoring Procedure:* The median of three measurements for each site is recorded as the student's score.

*Organizational Hints:* All measurements are taken on the right side of the body. Skinfolds should be measured in a setting that assures privacy for the child. When possible, it is suggested that the same tester administer all skinfold measurements.

### Body Mass Index (Optional)

*Instructions:* The body mass index (BMI) is defined as the ratio of body weight (measured in kilograms) and the square of the height (measured in meters). Body weight is measured with the individual clad in lightweight shorts and shirt. Reading is recorded to nearest 0.5 kilogram. Standing height is measured with the individual in stocking feet, fully erect, and stretched to full height while keeping the heels flat on the floor. The body mass index is determined as follows:

$$BMI = \text{Body weight (Kg)} / \text{Height (m)}^2$$

### Test 3: Curl-Up (Required)

*Instructions:* Students lie on their back on a mat or piece of carpet, with legs bent at the knee (approximately 140° angle). Legs should be slightly apart, arms straight and parallel to the trunk with palms of hands resting on the mat or carpet, and fingers stretched out. The head is in contact with the hands of a partner sitting or kneeling at the student's head. When the student has assumed the correct start position, another partner places the appropriate measuring strip on the mat under the student's knees so that the fingertips are resting on the edge of the measuring strip. Figure 5.0

▶ **FIGURE 5.0**   Curl-up.

shows the start and up positions for this test and the responsibilities of each partner. On the command "Go" the student curls up slowly, sliding the fingers across the measuring strip until they reach the other side of the strip, then returns to start position (head returns to contact the partner's hands on the floor). This movement should be slow and deliberate (approximately 20 curl-ups per minute or one every three seconds). The teacher should call the cadence for the class. The student maintains this pattern without pausing until completing 75 curl-ups or becoming unable to continue.

***Equipment Needed:*** Stopwatch or prerecorded audiotape to monitor cadence, mat or piece of carpet, Prudential FITNESSGRAM measuring strip, and pencils and scoresheets.

***Scoring Procedure:*** The number of correctly performed curl-ups is recorded as the score.

***Organizational Hints:*** Students should be placed in groups of three with one student designated to secure the measuring strip, another to place his/her hands under the head of the test taker, and the third to do the curl-up. The upward movement should consist of a flattening of the lower back followed by a slow curl of the upper spine. A curl-up is considered completed when the back of the head returns to the partner's hands.

### Test 4: Trunk Lift (Required)

***Instructions:*** The student lies face down on a mat or piece of carpet. Hands are placed under thighs and toes are pointed. The student is instructed to lift the upper body off the floor to a height of 12 inches. See Figure 5.1.

**FIGURE 5.1** Trunk lift.

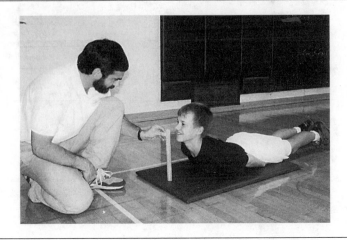

***Equipment Needed:*** Mat or piece of carpet and a yardstick or 12-inch ruler.

***Scoring Procedure:*** The greatest height maintained by the student's chin from the mat/carpet, recorded to the nearest inch, is the score, with the better of two trials recorded. Maximum score is 12 inches.

***Organizational Hints:*** Students should be encouraged to use slow, static movements to attain the highest score. Marking the yardstick/ruler at 6 inches and 12 inches will be helpful in accurately measuring the chin height.

### Test 5: Push-Up (Recommended)

***Instructions:*** The student is instructed to complete as many push-ups as possible, keeping time with the cadence provided by the audiotape. Figure 5.2 shows the correct up and down positions for the push-up.

***Equipment Needed:*** Mat or piece of carpet and PACER test audiotape to indicate cadence.

**FIGURE 5.2**    Push-up.

*Scoring Procedure:* The total number of push-ups completed successfully is recorded as the score.

*Organizational Hints:* A partner should be used to count. Incorrectly completed push-ups, usually the result of knees touching floor, swaying of back, inability to fully extend arms, or failing to bend arms to 90°, should not be counted.

### Modified Pull-Up (Optional)

*Instructions:* Student lies on back with shoulders directly under the bar, which is set 1–2 inches above the student's reach. An elastic band is positioned approximately 7–8 inches below and parallel to the bar. Using an overhand grip and from the down position, the student pulls up on the bar until chin is above the elastic band. Legs should remain straight and heels on the floor throughout this upward movement. Upon completing the pull-up, the student returns to the start position. Figure 5.3 shows the start and up positions for this test.

*Equipment Needed:* Modified pull-up apparatus, elastic band, mat or piece of carpet, and pencils and scoresheets.

*Scoring Procedure:* The number of correctly completed modified pull-ups is recorded as the score.

▶ **FIGURE 5.3**   Modified pull-up.

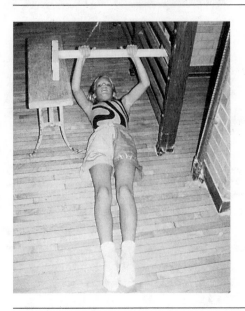 

*Organizational Hints:* Movement should be rhythmical and continuous. Resting or stopping is not allowed.

### Pull-Up (Optional)

*Instructions:* The student hangs from a horizontal bar with arms and legs fully extended and feet off the floor. The hands grasp the bar with palms away from the body. Once the body is still the student pulls up with the arms until the chin is over the bar, then lowers the body to the starting position. This movement is repeated as many times as possible.

*Equipment Needed:* A horizontal bar approximately 1.5 inches in diameter. This bar should be of adequate height or adjustable to accommodate the tallest person in class. Figure 5.4 shows the down and up positions for the pull-up.

*Scoring Procedure:* The number of successfully completed pull-ups (chin over bar) is recorded as the student's score.

*Organizational Hints:* This option should not be selected for students unable to complete one pull-up. Pull-ups should be completed smoothly and with minimal horizontal motion. Test administrators may lift the student to reach the bar and assist in minimizing unnecessary movement by placing their arms across the front of the student's thighs. Legs must remain fully extended throughout the test.

► **FIGURE 5.4**    Pull-up.

### Flexed-Arm Hang (Optional)

*Instructions:* Instructions for the flexed-arm hang are given later in this chapter. The stopwatch is stopped if the head tilts backward to keep the chin above the bar or when the chin touches or falls below the bar.

*Equipment Needed:* A horizontal bar approximately 1.5 inches in diameter. This bar should be of adequate height or adjustable to accommodate the tallest person in class. A stopwatch is required.

*Scoring Procedure:* The score is the number of seconds (to the nearest second) the student holds the hanging position, with one trial only.

*Organizational Hints:* The height of the bar should be adjusted for each student, as necessary, to be approximately equal to the standing height of the student. Spotters should be positioned in front of and behind the student. The timer should start the stopwatch as soon as the student is free from both spotters' assistance and assumes the flexed-arm hang position. Knees must not be raised and kicking is not permitted.

### Test 6: Back-Saver Sit-and-Reach (Recommended)

*Instructions:* The student sits on the floor, shoes off, with one leg extended so the bottom of the foot is flat against the box. The other leg is bent at the knee with the foot flat on the floor 2–3 inches to the side of the extended leg. Arms are extended over the measuring scale with one hand on top of the other, palms down, finger pads on fingernails. Keeping palms down, the student reaches forward along the scale four times and holds the fourth reach for one second. Repeat with other side. Figure 5.5 shows the hold positions for one side of the body.

▶ **FIGURE 5.5** Back-saver sit-and-reach.

*Equipment Needed:*  Solid box, 12 inches tall and 9 inches long (any width). Measuring scale is marked on top of box with 9-inch mark at far end and zero-inch mark at end near student.

*Scoring Procedure:*  The number of inches (rounded to nearest inch) reached for each side is recorded. Maximum score per side is 12 inches.

*Organizational Hints:*  To keep the student's extended leg from bending, the tester may place one hand on the student's knee. The student's hips should remain square with the box.

### Shoulder Stretch (Optional)

*Instructions:*  Student reaches with right hand over right shoulder and down the back. At the same time, the student places the left hand behind the back and reaches up, trying to touch the fingers of the right hand. Figure 5.6 shows shoulder stretch for right side.

*Equipment Needed:*  None necessary.

*Scoring Procedure:*  The test is scored pass/fail. If the student is able to touch the fingers of opposite hands, the score is recorded as pass.

*Organizational Hints:*  A partner should be used to determine touch. A proper warm-up should precede the test.

**FIGURE 5.6**  Shoulder stretch.

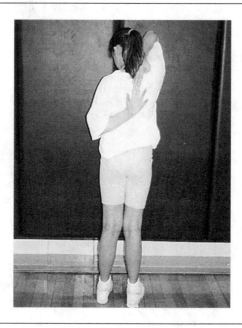

## FYT — Fit Youth Today

(American Health and Fitness Foundation, Inc., 1986)

*Purpose:* The aims of this program are to (1) educate and condition students for a lifetime of healthy living; (2) assess the level of health-related physical fitness of youth; and (3) evaluate each student's personal level of fitness by comparing scores to a desirable level of health fitness.

*Description:* The FYT program is more than an assessment tool. FYT offers a complete approach to health-related physical fitness and includes (1) a planned curriculum; (2) an extensive health fitness question and answer section; (3) an exercise program; (4) a three-level integrated awards program; and (5) a four-item health-related physical fitness test battery. The items of this battery are the steady-state jog, two-minute bent-knee curl-up, sit-and-reach test, and two-site skinfold caliper measurement.

*Validity:* Validity coefficients reported ranged from .60 to .90 for the steady-state run and body composition tests, respectively. The curl-up and sit-and-reach test are supported by content validity.

*Reliability:* Reliability coefficients for the distance run typically exceed .70. Pearson $r$'s for the flexed knee curl-up were greater than .77. The sit-and-reach and body composition tests had reported reliabilities higher than .84 and .90, respectively.

*Age Level:* Ages 9–18.

*Norms:* Criteria standards for skinfolds are given in Table 5.0.

▶ **TABLE 5.0**  Sum of calf and triceps skinfolds.

| | MALE | | | FEMALE | |
|---|---|---|---|---|---|
| Grade | Sum of Calf & Triceps | Approximate % Body Fat | Grade | Sum of Calf & Triceps | Approximate % Body Fat |
| 4 | 23 | 19 | 4 | 32 | 26 |
| 5 | 26 | 21 | 5 | 32 | 26 |
| 6 | 29 | 23 | 6 | 33 | 27 |
| 7 | 29 | 23 | 7 | 34 | 28 |
| 8 | 29 | 23 | 8 | 34 | 28 |
| 9 | 27 | 22 | 9 | 34 | 28 |
| 10 | 25 | 20 | 10 | 34 | 28 |
| 11 | 23 | 19 | 11 | 34 | 28 |
| 12 | 23 | 19 | 12 | 34 | 28 |

Reprinted by permission of The American Health and Fitness Foundation, Austin, Texas.

*Test Area:* Spacious outdoor area for the steady state jog (preferably a track) and a gymnasium or multipurpose room.

### Test 1: Steady State Jog

*Instructions:* On the command "Ready, go," students are instructed to jog continuously for 20 minutes.

*Equipment Needed:* Accurately measured outdoor running area.

*Scoring Procedure:* The distance covered at the conclusion of 20 minutes is recorded to the nearest tenth of a mile.

*Organizational Hints:* Students should be actively involved in a program of aerobic conditioning for at least eight weeks before test administration. The concept of pace should be understood by all test participants. At the conclusion of the test all students should engage in a three- to five-minute cool-down activity. Administering the test during inclement weather, including extremely hot or cold days, should be avoided.

### Test 2: Bent-Knee Curl-Up

*Instructions:* Students assume the starting position by lying on their backs with knees flexed, feet and back flat on the floor, with the heels approximately 12–18 inches from the buttocks. Arms are folded across the chest with hands on opposite shoulders. On the command "Ready, Go," the participant curls to a sitting position until the elbows contact the thighs. The curl-up is completed when the student returns to the "ready" position.

*Equipment Needed:* Individual mats or pieces of carpet and a stopwatch.

*Scoring Procedure:* The number of successfully completed curl-ups in two minutes is recorded as the student's score.

*Organizational Hints:* Students should be instructed to pace themselves throughout the test. Peer assistance may be used to facilitate test administration.

### Test 3: Sit-and-Reach

*Instructions:* The participant sits comfortably on the floor with shoes off, legs extended, and feet flat against the sit-and-reach apparatus. The student places one hand on top of the other with finger pads on fingernails. On the signal, the student gradually reaches as far forward as possible and holds this position until the test administrator places a marker at the end of the student's finger tips. Students are permitted three additional consecutive attempts to push the marker further.

*Equipment Needed:* Sit-and-reach apparatus consisting of a box with a yardstick on top. The end of the box against which the students place their feet should measure 12 inches high. The yardstick should be securely fastened on top of the box with the 9-inch mark just above the end of the box where the student's feet rest.

*Scoring Procedure:* The farthest point reached in the four attempts is recorded to the nearest half-inch.

*Organizational Hints:* Proper stretching activities should be conducted prior to administration of the test. Multiple boxes allow more than one student to be tested at a time.

### Test 4: Body Composition

*Instructions:* This is a two-site skinfold measurement. The triceps skinfold is measured with the right arm relaxed at the side of the body. The calf skinfold is taken on the inside of the right calf, at the level of the maximal calf girth (see Figure 5.24).

*Equipment Needed:* Skinfold calipers.

*Scoring Procedure:* The median of three measurements at each site is recorded. The sum of the two sites is recorded as the student's score.

*Organizational Hints:* If there is disparity on any of the three measurements, redo the three trials for that particular site. See Chapter 13 for additional hints about administering the skinfold test.

## Measuring Cardiorespiratory Fitness

The relationship between cardiorespiratory fitness and health is well documented. Increases in cardiorespiratory fitness permit a higher quality of life by increasing the rate at which energy can be provided to support work and play activities. Individuals with higher levels of cardiorespiratory fitness can accomplish more physical work in a given period of time and can complete work tasks with less physiological stress than persons with low levels of cardiorespiratory fitness.

Cardiorespiratory fitness involves numerous physiological variables. No single measurement protocol can be expected to accurately evaluate every variable associated with the cardiorespiratory system. The laboratory test that has earned the widest acceptance as a composite measure of cardiorespiratory fitness is direct measurement of maximal aerobic power. This measurement is reported in terms of maximal oxygen uptake relative to body weight.

Maximal oxygen uptake (usually identified as $VO_2$ max) is the greatest rate at which oxygen can be consumed during exercise at sea level. This precise measurement is typically expressed as milliliters of oxygen consumed per kilogram of body weight per minute (ml. $kg^{-1}min^{-1}$) and represents an overall indicator of the functional capacity of the cardiorespiratory system. Exercise physiology classes provide more detailed discussions regarding cardiorespiratory fitness and introduce laboratory methods used to directly measure $VO_2$ max. Fox and Mathews (1981) and McArdle, Katch, and Katch (1981) serve as good references and provide background on the procedures associated with measuring cardiorespiratory fitness in a laboratory setting. In this chapter assessment of cardiorespiratory fitness will be confined to field-based tests. See Chapter 13 for a more detailed description of laboratory tests to measure cardiorespiratory fitness.

**Field-based tests** refer to assessment protocols that can be conducted away from the confines of the laboratory. Because the setting is less restricting than the laboratory, procedures are less sophisticated, accommodate larger numbers of subjects, and are significantly less expensive and time-consuming. Losses in precision and accuracy are offset by gains in practicality.

Whether the test should be laboratory or field based depends on how the test results are to be used. For example, if the intent is to measure the aerobic capacity of a world-class athlete in order to develop an Olympic training program, the inclination may be to opt for the laboratory test. On the other hand, if the purpose is to provide a class of third grade children with information about their level of cardiorespiratory fitness, it is more practical and every bit as useful to administer a field-based test that provides an estimate of their aerobic capacity.

Field-based tests to measure cardiorespiratory fitness have been developed by identifying either measures of endurance performance or physiological markers that correlate highly with $VO_2$ max (AAHPERD, 1984). A common physiological marker in assessing cardiorespiratory fitness is heart rate response to submaximal exercise. This method necessitates controlling the work rate and accurately measuring the heart rate either during or after the exercise bout. Several field-based tests such as bicycle ergometry and step tests have been used to control work rate. Estimations of heart rate response to exercise can be obtained through electrocardiography or pulse rate. While considered field based, both the bicycle ergometer tests and step tests are somewhat limiting because of the need for specific equipment.

The most widely used approach to field measurement of cardiorespiratory fitness is the **distance run**. Distance runs are similar to $VO_2$ max in that subjects are encouraged to expend maximum effort. Even though distance runs are dependent on other factors, such as body composition and running efficiency, these tests of long duration can be used to accurately estimate cardiorespiratory fitness. Field-based tests that can be used by the practitioner to measure cardiorespiratory fitness are described below.

## 1-Mile or 1.5-Mile Run

*Purpose:* The purpose of these distance runs is to measure maximal function and endurance of the cardiorespiratory system.

*Instructions:* Students are instructed to run the required distance in the fastest possible time. A signal, "Ready, go," or a whistle is used to begin the test. Test participants, or their partners, are informed of the total elapsed time as the participants cross the finish line. Students should be encouraged to keep moving (running, jogging, or walking) throughout the test.

*Validity:* Endurance running is widely accepted as a valid method to measure cardiorespiratory fitness. Performance on running of one mile farther has been shown to correlate significantly with laboratory-tested maximum aerobic capacity (AAHPERD, 1984). (See Table 5.1.) The longer distance runs provide more precise information about the functional state of the cardiorespiratory system.

*Reliability:* The high validity correlations depicted in Table 5.1 support the reliability of distance run tests. Further, distance run tests indicate a high consistency of repeated performance (Doolittle et al., 1969).

*Age Level:* The mile run is recommended for children 5–12 years of age. For individuals 13 years of age and older the 1.5-mile run is suggested.

*Test Area:* Any smooth, flat area safe for running on which distance can be accurately measured. Figure 5.7 offers some suitable layouts for administering the distance run.

**FIGURE 5.7** Schematic drawings of suggested layouts to use in administering the one-mile run/walk test. Increase laps 50 percent for the 1.5-mile run.

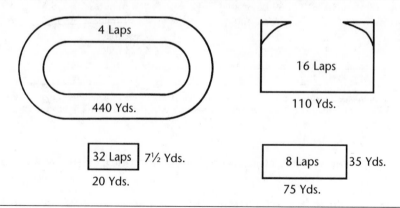

▶ **TABLE 5.1**  Means and standard deviations of maximal oxygen uptake and concurrent validity of distance run tests.

| SOURCE | SAMPLE | RUN | Max VO$_2$ (ml/kg•min) $\overline{X}$ | S | $^r$xy* |
|--------|--------|-----|-----|---|------|
| Burke (1976) | 44 college men | 12 minutes | 52.8 | 6.1 | .90 |
| Burris (1970) | 30 college women | 12 minutes | | | .74 |
| Cooper (1968) | 115 men, ages 17–52 | 12 minutes | | | .90 |
| Cureton et al. (1977) | 140 boys, age 10 | 1 mile | 48.0 | 6.7 | −.66 |
| | 56 girls, age 10 | 1 mile | 45.4 | 5.9 | −.66 |
| Doolittle and Bigbee (1968) | 9 boys, grade 9 | 12 minutes | | | .90 |
| Getchell et al. (1977) | 21 college women | 12 minutes | 46.2 | 5.9 | .91 |
| Gutin et al. (1976) | 15 boys and girls, age 11 | 1800 yards | 47.5 | 5.8 | −.76 |
| Jackson and Coleman (1976) | 22 boys, grades 1–6 | 9 minutes | 44.5 | 4.6 | .82 |
| | | 12 minutes | | | .82 |
| | 25 girls, grades 1–6 | 9 minutes | 40.6 | 4.1 | .71 |
| | | 12 minutes | | | .71 |
| Katch et al. (1973) | 36 college women | 12 minutes | 38.9 | 4.6 | .67 |
| Kitagawa et al. (1977) | 39 college men | 2400 meters | 51.8 | 6.6 | −.63 |
| | 33 college women | 2400 meters | 50.0 | 3.9 | −.42 |
| Krahenbuhl et al. (1977) | 20 boys, age 8 | ¾ mile | 47.6 | 7.1 | −.64 |
| | | 1 mile | | | −.71 |
| | 18 girls, age 8 | ¾ mile | 42.9 | 5.7 | −.22 |
| | | 1 mile | | | −.26 |
| Maksud and Coutts (1971) | 17 boys, ages 11–14 | 12 minutes | 47.4 | 4.0 | .65 |
| Maksud et al. (1976) | 26 college women | 12 minutes | 41.0 | 3.8 | .70 |
| Mayhew and Andrew (1975) | 24 college women | 1½ miles | 55.5 | 7.9 | −.74 |
| Ribisi and Kachadarian (1969) | 24 middle-aged men | 2 miles | 48.6 | 5.4 | −.86 |
| | 11 college men | 1 mile | 57.4 | 3.6 | −.79 |
| | | 2 miles | | | −.85 |
| Shaver (1975) | 30 college men | 1 mile | 53.5 | 5.6 | −.43 |
| | | 2 miles | | | −.76 |
| | | 3 miles | | | −.82 |
| Vodak and Wilmore (1975) | 69 boys, ages 9–12 | 6 minutes | 53.6 | 5.6 | .50 |
| Wiley and Shaver (1972) | 35 college men | 1 mile | 52.6 | 6.3 | −.29 |
| | | 2 miles | | | −.47 |
| | | 3 miles | | | −.43 |

*Correlation between Max VO$_2$ and distance run.

***Equipment Needed:*** Fluorescent boundary cones, stopwatch, clipboard, and pencil.

***Scoring Procedure:*** The 1-mile and 1.5-mile runs are scored to the nearest second.

▶ **TABLE 5.2** Percentile norms for the 12-minute (yards) and 1.5-mile (minutes and seconds) run for boys ages 13–18 (1980).

| PERCENTILE | 12-MIN. RUN | 1.5-MILE RUN |
|:---:|:---:|:---:|
| 90 | 3140 | 9:15 |
| 80 | 2952 | 10:01 |
| 70 | 2819 | 10:34 |
| 60 | 2699 | 11:02 |
| 50 | 2592 | 11:29 |
| 40 | 2485 | 11:55 |
| 30 | 2365 | 12:24 |
| 20 | 2232 | 12:56 |
| 10 | 2044 | 13:42 |

Reprinted by permission of American Alliance for Health, Physical Education, Recreation and Dance, Reston, Virginia.

*Norms:* Norms for the 1.5-mile run can be found in Tables 5.2 and 5.3. Norms for the 1-mile run can be found in Tables 5.4 and 5.5.

*Organizational Hints:* When testing elementary-age children, it is advisable to use youngsters from the upper grades (i.e., fifth and sixth) to serve as lap counters and recorders during the testing of the younger grades (i.e., K–4). Figure 5.8 is an example of a lap card used to keep track of a child's performance. Peer age assistants, in the form of partners, can be used to collect raw distance run scores for youth older than 12 years of age. Partners who are counting laps and

▶ **TABLE 5.3** Percentile norms for the 12-minute (yards) and 1.5-mile (minutes and seconds) run for girls ages 13–18.

| PERCENTILE | 12-MIN. RUN | 1.5-MILE RUN |
|:---:|:---:|:---:|
| 90 | 2318 | 13:19 |
| 80 | 2161 | 14:34 |
| 70 | 2050 | 15:26 |
| 60 | 1950 | 16:14 |
| 50 | 1861 | 16:57 |
| 40 | 1772 | 17:39 |
| 30 | 1672 | 18:27 |
| 20 | 1561 | 19:19 |
| 10 | 1404 | 20:34 |

Norms from the Texas Physical Fitness Test (1973).

Reprinted by permission of American Alliance for Health, Physical Education, Recreation and Dance, Reston, Virginia.

▲ **TABLE 5.4** Percentile norms for the one-mile run (minutes and seconds) for boys ages 5–18 (1980).

| AGE | 5 | 6 | 7 | 8 | 9 | 10 | 11 | 12 | 13 | 14 | 15 | 16 | 17–18 |
|---|---|---|---|---|---|---|---|---|---|---|---|---|---|
| Percentile | | | | | | | | | | | | | |
| 99 | 7:45 | 8:15 | 7:17 | 6:14 | 6:43 | 6:25 | 6:04 | 5:40 | 5:44 | 5:36 | 5:44 | 5:40 | 5:41 |
| 90 | 9:41 | 9:30 | 8:35 | 8:12 | 7:29 | 7:26 | 7:19 | 6:44 | 6:22 | 6:05 | 6:08 | 6:02 | 6:13 |
| 80 | 11:13 | 10:23 | 9:18 | 8:45 | 8:22 | 7:57 | 7:48 | 7:12 | 6:42 | 6:21 | 6:29 | 6:22 | 6:30 |
| 70 | 11:50 | 11:20 | 9:45 | 9:31 | 8:50 | 8:23 | 8:08 | 7:37 | 7:00 | 6:41 | 6:42 | 6:41 | 6:42 |
| 60 | 12:48 | 11:47 | 10:46 | 10:20 | 9:14 | 8:49 | 8:39 | 7:59 | 7:14 | 6:54 | 7:02 | 6:53 | 7:07 |
| 50 | 13:46 | 12:29 | 11:25 | 11:00 | 9:56 | 9:19 | 9:06 | 8:20 | 7:27 | 7:10 | 7:14 | 7:11 | 7:25 |
| 40 | 14:17 | 13:20 | 12:04 | 11:49 | 11:01 | 9:45 | 9:46 | 8:51 | 7:51 | 7:24 | 7:30 | 7:27 | 7:45 |
| 30 | 15:18 | 14:13 | 13:30 | 12:30 | 11:44 | 10:38 | 10:40 | 9:30 | 8:24 | 7:54 | 7:52 | 7:51 | 8:06 |
| 20 | 16:37 | 15:18 | 14:37 | 13:56 | 12:25 | 11:31 | 12:02 | 10:42 | 8:50 | 8:15 | 8:26 | 8:41 | 8:38 |
| 10 | 17:21 | 16:56 | 15:50 | 15:16 | 14:19 | 13:00 | 13:37 | 12:07 | 9:39 | 9:30 | 9:25 | 9:52 | 10:37 |

Reprinted by permission of American Alliance for Health, Physical Education, Recreation and Dance, Reston, Virginia.

▲ **TABLE 5.5** Percentile norms for the one-mile run (minutes and seconds) for girls ages 5–18 (1980).

| AGE | 5 | 6 | 7 | 8 | 9 | 10 | 11 | 12 | 13 | 14 | 15 | 16 | 17–18 |
|---|---|---|---|---|---|---|---|---|---|---|---|---|---|
| Percentile | | | | | | | | | | | | | |
| 99 | 9:03 | 8:06 | 7:58 | 7:45 | 7:21 | 7:09 | 7:07 | 6:57 | 6:20 | 6:44 | 6:36 | 6:33 | 6:54 |
| 90 | 11:23 | 9:52 | 9:35 | 9:30 | 8:44 | 8:30 | 8:10 | 7:44 | 7:45 | 7:39 | 8:01 | 7:47 | 8:05 |
| 80 | 12:48 | 11:06 | 10:27 | 10:17 | 9:31 | 9:10 | 8:57 | 8:18 | 8:12 | 8:03 | 8:24 | 8:33 | 8:44 |
| 70 | 13:26 | 11:46 | 10:55 | 10:50 | 10:07 | 9:47 | 9:29 | 8:55 | 8:27 | 8:23 | 8:59 | 9:26 | 9:10 |
| 60 | 14:14 | 12:46 | 11:43 | 11:30 | 10:32 | 10:23 | 10:00 | 9:21 | 8:56 | 8:55 | 9:38 | 10:06 | 9:28 |
| 50 | 15:08 | 13:48 | 12:30 | 12:00 | 11:12 | 11:06 | 10:27 | 9:47 | 9:27 | 9:35 | 10:05 | 10:45 | 9:47 |
| 40 | 16:20 | 14:19 | 13:42 | 12:45 | 12:00 | 11:41 | 11:12 | 10:22 | 9:57 | 10:20 | 10:51 | 11:35 | 10:04 |
| 30 | 17:32 | 15:06 | 14:08 | 13:47 | 12:42 | 12:09 | 11:51 | 11:00 | 10:31 | 11:11 | 12:05 | 12:32 | 10:50 |
| 20 | 18:19 | 15:55 | 15:10 | 14:56 | 13:52 | 13:31 | 12:36 | 11:57 | 11:23 | 12:21 | 13:04 | 14:05 | 12:12 |
| 10 | 18:38 | 18:11 | 16:03 | 16:30 | 15:25 | 15:12 | 14:41 | 13:34 | 13:09 | 15:20 | 15:25 | 15:02 | 13:05 |

Reprinted by permission of American Alliance for Health, Physical Education, Recreation and Dance, Reston, Virginia.

▶ **FIGURE 5.8**   Lap card for scoring distance runs.

Lap #1 _____   Lap #5_____

Lap #2 _____   Lap #6_____

Lap #3 _____   Lap #7_____

Lap #4 _____   Lap #8_____

Mile Run Time [          ]                 In Seconds [          ]

recording times should be positioned near the finish line in order to clearly hear the timer call out the time as the runners finish the test.

Before testing, the teacher should examine the records of each student and visit with the school nurse to ensure that participants with known medical problems that would contraindicate vigorous exercise are not allowed to take the test. Students should practice distance running, with emphasis placed on the concept of pace, before being tested. The purpose of the test should be explained to the students and steps taken to ensure a high level of motivation so that meaningful results are obtained.

### 9- or 12-Minute Run

*Purpose:* The purpose of the timed distance run is to measure maximal function and endurance of the cardiorespiratory system.

*Instructions:* Students are instructed to run as far as possible in 9 or 12 minutes. A signal, "Ready, go," or a whistle is used to begin the test. A loud signal such as a whistle or gun is used to stop the test. Participants continue to run or walk until they hear the signal to stop.

*Validity:* Timed distance running has been widely accepted as a valid method to measure cardiorespiratory fitness. Further, timed distance runs seem to provide as much information about a participant's cardiorespiratory fitness as the mile or 1.5-mile runs. Runs greater than one mile seem to provide more precise information about the functional state of the cardiorespiratory system than do shorter length runs.

*Reliability:* The high validity correlations depicted in Table 5.1 support the reliability of timed distance run tests. Further, timed distance run tests indicate a high consistency of repeated performance (Askew, 1966; Burris, 1970).

*Age Level:* The 9-minute run is for students 6–12 years of age. The 12-minute run is recommended for youth 13 years of age and older.

*Test Area:* Either of the timed distance runs can be administered properly on a flat, safe area suitable for running. Figure 5.7 provides examples of acceptable layouts.

*Equipment Needed:* Fluorescent boundary cones, stopwatch, clipboard, pencil, and whistle.

*Scoring Procedure:* The distance covered during the allotted time is recorded (to the nearest 10 yards) as the score. Performances should be immediately recorded on a scorecard.

*Norms:* Norms for the 12-minute run are found in Tables 5.2 and 5.3. Norms for the 9-minute run are found in Tables 5.6 and 5.7.

*Organizational Hints:* The distance of the course should be measured so that the number of laps completed can be counted and easily multiplied by the course distance. Marking the course at 10-yard intervals enables the test participants or partners to easily calculate distances less than a full lap. On the signal to finish all runners stop, and partners immediately run to the spot where their runner stopped and calculate the laps run multiplied by the distance per lap, adding yards covered on the last lap (laps run 2 distance per lap + additional yards). This distance is recorded on the scorecard.

## LSU Step Test

(Nelson, 1976)

*Purpose:* To measure heart rate response to submaximal exercise.

*Description:* This test is designed to provide participants with a graphic profile of heart rate change during exercise and recovery.

*Instructions:* Participants work as partners with half of the class or group serving as test participants and the other half as counters. Counters are positioned behind the test takers so that they are in position to readily take the stepper's pulse at the carotid artery. Practice in finding and counting the pulse at the carotid artery should be given prior to test administration because undue pressure placed on the artery can cause a decrease in blood flow to the brain.

First, the preexercise pulse rate is recorded. This is determined by counting the pulse rate while participants are seated on the floor. Test participants are not allowed to begin the test until three consecutive 10-second count pulse rates have indicated a stabilization of the heart rate.

**TABLE 5.6** Percentile norms for the 9-minute run (yards) for boys ages 5–18 (1980).

| AGE | 5 | 6 | 7 | 8 | 9 | 10 | 11 | 12 | 13 | 14 | 15 | 16 | 17–18 |
|---|---|---|---|---|---|---|---|---|---|---|---|---|---|
| **Percentile** | | | | | | | | | | | | | |
| 99 | 1975 | 2000 | 2400 | 2520 | 2450 | 2520 | 2520 | 2880 | 2615 | 2686 | 2757 | 2828 | 2899 |
| 90 | 1530 | 1650 | 1900 | 2100 | 2040 | 2120 | 2109 | 2175 | 2320 | 2391 | 2462 | 2533 | 2604 |
| 80 | 1370 | 1525 | 1733 | 1870 | 1875 | 1950 | 1970 | 2000 | 2150 | 2221 | 2292 | 2363 | 2434 |
| 70 | 1310 | 1440 | 1640 | 1770 | 1800 | 1859 | 1890 | 1900 | 2049 | 2120 | 2191 | 2262 | 2333 |
| 60 | 1220 | 1350 | 1540 | 1695 | 1740 | 1780 | 1808 | 1810 | 1964 | 2035 | 2106 | 2177 | 2248 |
| 50 | 1170 | 1280 | 1440 | 1595 | 1660 | 1690 | 1725 | 1760 | 1885 | 1956 | 2027 | 2098 | 2169 |
| 40 | 1100 | 1200 | 1370 | 1500 | 1600 | 1600 | 1640 | 1680 | 1806 | 1877 | 1948 | 2019 | 2090 |
| 30 | 1010 | 1130 | 1310 | 1420 | 1490 | 1536 | 1575 | 1590 | 1721 | 1792 | 1863 | 1934 | 2005 |
| 20 | 940 | 1050 | 1195 | 1340 | 1370 | 1420 | 1440 | 1450 | 1620 | 1691 | 1762 | 1833 | 1904 |
| 10 | 830 | 940 | 1070 | 1180 | 1243 | 1250 | 1275 | 1300 | 1450 | 1521 | 1592 | 1663 | 1734 |

Reprinted by permission of American Alliance for Health, Physical Education, Recreation and Dance, Reston, Virginia.

**TABLE 5.7** Percentile norms for the 9-minute run (yards) for girls ages 5–18 (1980).

| AGE | 5 | 6 | 7 | 8 | 9 | 10 | 11 | 12 | 13 | 14 | 15 | 16 | 17–18 |
|---|---|---|---|---|---|---|---|---|---|---|---|---|---|
| **Percentile** | | | | | | | | | | | | | |
| 99 | 1584 | 1980 | 2340 | 2260 | 2300 | 2240 | 2170 | 2370 | 2197 | 2235 | 2273 | 2311 | 2349 |
| 90 | 1410 | 1620 | 1710 | 1750 | 1870 | 1900 | 1930 | 2070 | 2005 | 2043 | 2081 | 2119 | 2157 |
| 80 | 1320 | 1520 | 1570 | 1600 | 1700 | 1750 | 1780 | 1840 | 1837 | 1875 | 1913 | 1951 | 1989 |
| 70 | 1243 | 1390 | 1490 | 1520 | 1590 | 1596 | 1650 | 1733 | 1738 | 1776 | 1814 | 1852 | 1890 |
| 60 | 1220 | 1253 | 1402 | 1440 | 1515 | 1525 | 1570 | 1690 | 1655 | 1693 | 1731 | 1769 | 1807 |
| 50 | 1140 | 1208 | 1344 | 1358 | 1425 | 1460 | 1480 | 1590 | 1577 | 1615 | 1653 | 1691 | 1729 |
| 40 | 1060 | 1140 | 1280 | 1315 | 1350 | 1375 | 1405 | 1500 | 1499 | 1537 | 1575 | 1613 | 1651 |
| 30 | 1000 | 1060 | 1190 | 1250 | 1290 | 1290 | 1356 | 1420 | 1416 | 1454 | 1492 | 1530 | 1568 |
| 20 | 866 | 990 | 1110 | 1180 | 1225 | 1230 | 1300 | 1220 | 1317 | 1355 | 1393 | 1431 | 1469 |
| 10 | 750 | 850 | 997 | 1056 | 1080 | 1100 | 1125 | 1130 | 1149 | 1187 | 1225 | 1263 | 1301 |

Reprinted by permission of American Alliance for Health, Physical Education, Recreation and Dance, Reston, Virginia.

Once preexercise heart rate has been determined, the steppers stand in front of the bench and, on command, begin stepping at the cadence of 24 steps/minute for females and 30 steps/minute for males. The cadence should be established with a metronome. This can be done by multiplying the required steps per minute by 4 (i.e., the metronome is set at 96 for 24 steps/minute and at 120 for 30 steps/minute). After participants have completed two minutes of continuous stepping, the command "stop, sit down, find your pulse" is given, and after five seconds a 10-second pulse count is taken. Three recovery pulse counts are taken (each for 10 seconds) at one minute, two minutes, and three minutes after exercise. After the four postexercise heart rate counts are completed, the steppers and pulse counters reverse roles and the other half of the class or group is ready to begin the test.

The following directions are read to students. The language may be modified to the comprehension level of the students.

> Today we are going to take a test that is designed to reflect your cardiorespiratory fitness. This refers to your body's ability to adjust to exercise and then recover. You know that when you exercise, such as when you run, play a sport, or dance vigorously, your heart beats faster and then it gradually slows down afterward. If you are in good shape—have good cardiorespiratory fitness—you can exercise longer and harder than someone who is not in as good shape, and also you can recover faster.
>
> We will count our pulse rate before exercise, then step up and down on a bench for two (or three) minutes and then count our pulse immediately afterward, then again at one, two, and three minutes after exercise to see how quickly the pulse rate returns to normal. Talking, laughing, and moving about will cause the heart rate to fluctuate. Therefore, it is very important that you sit down right away after exercise and remain quiet for the three minutes during which the pulse counts are taken.
>
> When counting pulse rate, if you feel a beat at the same instant that you are told to begin counting, count that beat as zero.
>
> Later you will plot your pulse rates on a graph so you can see how your heart adjusts to exercise and recovers. (Johnson and Nelson, 1986, p. 162)

**Validity:** Construct validity has been demonstrated through experimental research. Further, the sensitivity of the test in determining alterations in heart rate due to a conditioning program was evidenced in a study completed by Patterson and Nelson (1976).

**Reliability:** Test-retest reliability coefficients for the five pulse counts have been reported as follows (Johnson and Nelson, 1986):

Before exercise, .86

Five seconds after exercise, .88

One minute after exercise, .85
Two minutes after exercise, .87
Three minutes after exercise, .80

***Age Level:*** Grade 9 to adult.

***Test Area:*** Gymnasium or other spacious indoor area.

***Equipment Needed:*** Stopwatch, benches or bleachers (17–18 inches high), and a metronome.

***Scoring Procedure:*** Each of the five 10-second pulse counts is recorded on a scoresheet. Each of these counts is multiplied by 6 to convert the scores into heartbeats per minute. The beats-per-minute scores are plotted on a personalized chart for each student to show the heart's response before, during, and after exercise. (See Figure 5.9.) The same chart should be used to plot the performance on subsequent test sessions to show the heart's response to any intervening cardiovascular conditioning program.

***Organizational Hints:*** Recording the instructional sequence on video or audio tape greatly increases test objectivity and releases test administrators

**FIGURE 5.9** Graphic profile of heart rate after LSU step test.

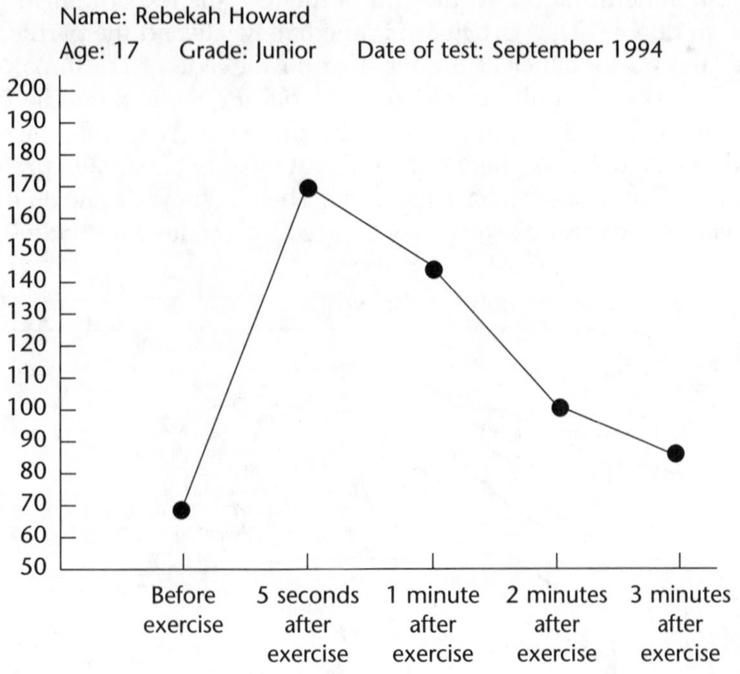

from tedious duties, allowing them to assist students in pulse counting, recording, and other tasks related to the test.

Students should be allowed at least one day to practice the protocol associated with the test and should be encouraged to practice self-testing their heart rate recovery. Information derived from this test may assist in explaining key concepts associated with cardiorespiratory fitness development and maintenance.

### Kasch Pulse Recovery Test (1968)

**Purpose:** To determine the heart's ability to adapt to and recover from exercise.

**Instructions:** The class or group is divided in half, with each individual assigned a partner. One partner takes the test while the other serves as a counter. The test administrator gives the following commands:

*"Ready" . . . "Up" . . . "Two" . . . "Three" . . . "Four."*

The command "Up" is repeated every four seconds and signals the test taker to step up on the bench with one foot. On the command "Two" the test taker steps the other foot onto the bench. On the command "Three" the test taker steps the lead foot (the first foot onto the bench) back to the floor. On the command "Four" the foot remaining on the bench is brought to the floor and the original starting position is assumed. This sequence is followed for a three-minute duration. At the end of the test, the test administrator says, "Stop, sit down." The participant immediately sits and the partner quickly locates the pulse (either at the wrist or on the side of the throat over the carotid artery). The pulse is measured by placing the two middle fingers of the right hand on the thumb side of the subject's wrist while the subject is seated (see Figure 5.10.) Taking the pulse at the wrist is usually preferable to using the carotid artery (along the neck). There is some debate on this point, however, so the carotid artery may be used by a trained individual.

▶ ·**FIGURE 5.10**   Taking the pulse at the wrist.

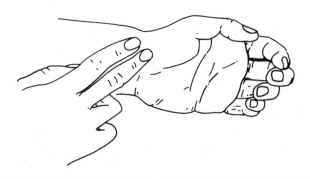

When counting the pulse, the beat felt at the moment of the signal to "start" should be designated as zero. The counter needs to understand that an error of one pulse count represents a six-beat error in a 10-second count and a four-beat error in a 15-second count.

Ten seconds after the "Stop" command, the test administrator gives the command "Start." This signals the partners to begin counting the pulse. After one minute, the test administrator calls "Stop." The number of heartbeats counted during this one-minute period is immediately recorded as the student's score. The partners reverse roles and repeat the procedure.

*Validity:* Test-retest procedures yielded a Pearson *r* of –.53 when compared to maximal oxygen uptake as measured on a bicycle ergometer.

*Age Level:* Ages 6–adult.

*Test Area:* Gymnasium or large indoor area.

*Equipment Needed:* Stopwatch or large sweep hand wall clock, 12-inch-high benches or bleachers, and a metronome.

*Scoring Procedure:* The recorded score is the total number of pulse counts in the 60-second time period.

*Norms:* Suggested standards can be found in Table 5.8.

► **TABLE 5.8**  Suggested standards (1976)—recovery heart rate, 0–1 minute post-exercise in sitting position.

| Classification | 6–12 YRS. | | 18–26 YRS. | | 27–60 YRS. | |
|---|---|---|---|---|---|---|
| | Boys | Girls | Men | Woman† | Men | Woman† |
| Superior | 74 | 82 | 68 | 73 | 69 | 74 |
| Excellent | 75–83 | 89–93 | 69–75 | 74–82 | 70–78 | 75–83 |
| Good | 84–92 | 94–103 | 76–83 | 83–90 | 79–87 | 84–92 |
| Average | 93–103 | 104–115 | 84–92 | 91–100 | 88–99 | 93–103 |
| Fair | 104–112 | 116–125 | 93–99 | 101–107 | 100–107 | 104–112 |
| Poor | 113–121 | 126–136 | 100–106 | 108–114 | 108–115 | 113–121 |
| Very poor | 122 | 137 | 107 | 115 | 116 | 122 |
| Mean | 98 | 111 | 88 | 95 | 93 | 98 |
| Range | 74–126 | 83–142 | 72–104 | – | 60–115 | – |
| SD | 9.9 | 11.2 | 9.8 | – | 9.5 | – |

†Arbitrary data.

From F. W. Kasch and J. L. Boyer, *Adult Fitness: Principles and Practices.* Palo Alto, California. Mayfield Publishing Co., 1968. Used by permission of the authors. Reprinted by permission of Mayfield Publishing Co., Palo Alto, California.

*Organizational Hints:* Benches should be secured to the floor or heavy enough not to move around when students are stepping up and down. Students should have a minimum of five minutes to rest before taking the test. The test administrator should be observant for fatigue displayed by students during the test.

## Measuring Muscular Strength and Endurance

Strength is the amount of force a muscle can exert. Strength is required to perform work, decrease chances of injury, prevent low back pain, improve posture, and curb the onset of diseases that result from a sedentary lifestyle.

Endurance is the ability of the muscles to work for long periods of time without undue fatigue. Endurance prevents unwanted fatigue from daily routines and enhances opportunities for success and enjoyment in sport and recreational activities. Muscular strength and endurance are important for good health.

Physical training programs to improve muscular strength and endurance differ. Strength training requires an overload in the amount of resistance, while muscular endurance training programs require an overload in the number of exercise repetitions. Weight training, specific exercises, isometrics, isokinetics, and various continuous activities such as jogging, cycling, swimming, hiking, and aerobic dance can all be designed to improve muscular strength and endurance.

Strength is measured by the amount of force produced with a single maximal effort, and endurance is assessed by the number of repeated muscular contractions over a long period of time against light-to-moderate resistance. Tests of muscular endurance may be either dynamic or static. Dynamic tests are concerned with the ability of muscle to repeat a movement against submaximal resistance or pressure. Static tests measure the ability of a muscle to maintain a certain degree of tension over time. Examples of cited in the subsequent sections.

### AAHPERD Modified Sit-Ups

(AAHPERD, 1980)

*Purpose:* The purpose of the sit-up test is to measure strength and endurance of the abdominal muscles.

*Instructions:* Students are positioned on their backs with legs flexed at the knees, feet flat on the floor, and the heels 12 to 18 inches from the buttocks. The arms should be crossed and in contact with the chest with the hands on opposite shoulders. The hands must remain in contact with the shoulders during the complete curl. The head should be tucked (curled) with the chin to chest. A partner holds the feet on the floor and counts the number of correctly executed sit-ups. On the signal to begin, the student curls to a sitting position until the forearms touch the thigh. One sit-up is complete when the midback makes contact with the testing surface on the down portion. The student is instructed to execute as many sit-ups as possible in 60 seconds. A signal to stop should be given at the end of 60 seconds.

*Validity:* On the basis of content validity, the one-minute timed modified sit-up is acceptable as a test to measure muscular strength and endurance of the abdominal muscles. Evidence from studies of muscle activity during the execution of a sit-up have shown that abdominal muscles are being utilized during the execution of the test (Godfrey et al., 1977; Kendall, 1965; Walters and Partridge, 1957).

*Reliability:* The reliability of sit-up tests has been considered acceptable. Test-retest correlation coefficients have ranged from .68 to .94. Further research is needed on the reliability of the test when administered to children in the early elementary and middle school years (AAHPERD, 1984).

*Age Level:* Ages 6–adult.

*Test Area:* Any large flat area (preferably indoors).

*Equipment Needed:* A stopwatch and exercise mat or piece of carpet.

*Scoring Procedure:* The number of successfully completed sit-ups in one minute is recorded as the score.

*Norms:* Norms for the AAHPERD modified sit-ups test are given in Tables 5.9 and 5.10. Criterion-referenced standards for the two-minute modified sit-ups test can be found in Table 5.11.

**TABLE 5.9** Percentile norms for sit-ups for boys ages 5–18 (1980).

| AGE | 5 | 6 | 7 | 8 | 9 | 10 | 11 | 12 | 13 | 14 | 15 | 16 | 17–18 |
|---|---|---|---|---|---|---|---|---|---|---|---|---|---|
| Percentile | | | | | | | | | | | | | |
| 99 | 47 | 47 | 53 | 55 | 52 | 59 | 61 | 68 | 70 | 70 | 69 | 70 | 65 |
| 90 | 27 | 33 | 39 | 42 | 43 | 47 | 48 | 52 | 54 | 54 | 55 | 59 | 59 |
| 80 | 24 | 28 | 34 | 38 | 39 | 42 | 44 | 48 | 50 | 51 | 50 | 53 | 54 |
| 70 | 22 | 25 | 31 | 35 | 36 | 39 | 41 | 45 | 46 | 48 | 48 | 50 | 51 |
| 60 | 20 | 22 | 29 | 32 | 34 | 36 | 39 | 42 | 44 | 45 | 46 | 47 | 49 |
| 50 | 18 | 20 | 26 | 30 | 32 | 34 | 37 | 39 | 41 | 42 | 44 | 45 | 46 |
| 40 | 15 | 18 | 24 | 29 | 30 | 31 | 34 | 36 | 39 | 40 | 41 | 42 | 44 |
| 30 | 13 | 16 | 21 | 26 | 27 | 29 | 31 | 33 | 36 | 38 | 39 | 39 | 40 |
| 20 | 9 | 13 | 17 | 23 | 24 | 25 | 28 | 30 | 33 | 35 | 36 | 35 | 37 |
| 10 | 5 | 9 | 14 | 19 | 20 | 19 | 23 | 25 | 29 | 31 | 31 | 30 | 31 |

▶ **TABLE 5.10**    Percentile norms for sit-ups for girls ages 5–18 (1980).

| AGE | 5 | 6 | 7 | 8 | 9 | 10 | 11 | 12 | 13 | 14 | 15 | 16 | 17–18 |
|---|---|---|---|---|---|---|---|---|---|---|---|---|---|
| **Percentile** | | | | | | | | | | | | | |
| 99 | 35 | 42 | 51 | 55 | 51 | 54 | 55 | 61 | 60 | 57 | 64 | 63 | 65 |
| 90 | 27 | 32 | 37 | 41 | 41 | 44 | 46 | 48 | 48 | 48 | 50 | 50 | 50 |
| 80 | 24 | 29 | 32 | 36 | 37 | 40 | 42 | 43 | 43 | 43 | 45 | 45 | 45 |
| 70 | 23 | 26 | 30 | 34 | 34 | 37 | 39 | 40 | 40 | 40 | 41 | 39 | 43 |
| 60 | 20 | 24 | 28 | 31 | 31 | 34 | 36 | 39 | 37 | 38 | 40 | 35 | 40 |
| 50 | 19 | 22 | 25 | 29 | 29 | 32 | 34 | 36 | 35 | 35 | 37 | 33 | 37 |
| 40 | 16 | 19 | 23 | 27 | 27 | 29 | 32 | 33 | 33 | 33 | 33 | 31 | 35 |
| 30 | 13 | 16 | 21 | 23 | 25 | 26 | 29 | 31 | 30 | 31 | 31 | 30 | 32 |
| 20 | 10 | 13 | 19 | 20 | 21 | 23 | 26 | 29 | 27 | 28 | 28 | 26 | 29 |
| 10 | 6 | 9 | 13 | 17 | 17 | 19 | 21 | 23 | 23 | 24 | 25 | 23 | 25 |

Reprinted by permission of American Alliance for Health, Physical Education, Recreation and Dance, Reston, Virginia.

*Organizational Hints:* Students should have prior experience executing the sit-up. One of the controversial points about this test is whether students are able to accurately count and identify a proper sit-up. Therefore, time should be devoted to explaining what constitutes a properly executed sit-up. Beginning several days before the test, students should be given time to practice administering the test to each other.

## Bent Knee Sit-Ups

*Purpose:* To measure strength and endurance of the abdominal muscles.

*Instructions:* Student lies on back with legs flexed at the knees and feet approximately 12 inches apart. The hands are placed behind the head with fingers interlaced. A partner holds the student's ankles and keeps the feet in contact with the floor while counting each sit-up. On the signal to begin,

▶ **TABLE 5.11**    Bent-knee sit-ups test: criterion-referenced standards, males and females (1980).

| | GRADE LEVEL | | | |
|---|---|---|---|---|
| | **4** | **5** | **6** | **7–12** |
| Number of sit-ups Completed in two minutes | 34 | 36 | 38 | 40 |

Reprinted by permission of The American Health and Fitness Foundation, Austin, Texas (1986).

the student sits up, turns the trunk touching one elbow to the opposite knee, and returns to the starting position. The next sit-up is performed touching the other elbow to the opposite knee. This alternating sequence is repeated as many times as possible. One complete sit-up is counted each time the pupil returns to the starting position. Students should be informed that credit will not be given for sit-ups completed when fingertips do not maintain contact behind the head, when the knee is not touched by the opposite elbow, or when the performer pushes off the floor with the elbow.

*Validity:* Face validity is accepted for this test.

*Reliability:* A Pearson *r* as high as .94 has been reported for this test (Johnson and Nelson, 1986). Berger (1966) reported a correlation of .71 between a timed sit-up and an unlimited sit-up test.

*Age Level:* Ages 10–adult.

*Test Area:* Any large, flat area (preferably indoors).

*Equipment Needed:* An exercise mat or piece of carpet.

*Scoring Procedure:* The total number of sit-ups successfully completed is recorded as the score. Variations of the test allow for a one- or two-minute time limit.

*Organizational Hints:* The counters should be constantly reminded to watch for release of the interlaced fingers. Further, counters should be alerted to stringently enforce the instruction that states that no sit-up will be counted unless it is properly executed.

## Pull-Ups

*Purpose:* To measure strength and endurance of the arm and shoulder girdle muscles.

*Description:* The test is designed to assess the relative muscular strength and endurance of the arm and shoulder girdle region in pulling the body upward.

*Instructions:* Student hangs from a horizontal bar with arms and legs fully extended. Feet should be off the floor with hands grasping the bar, and hands have palms away from the body. Once the body is still, the student pulls the body up with the arms until the chin is over the upper portion of the bar. The body is then lowered to the original starting position. The exercise should be repeated as many times as possible.

*Validity:* Face validity is accepted for this test.

*Reliability:* Test-retest protocol has resulted in an r as high as .87 (Johnson and Nelson, 1986).

▶ **TABLE 5.12**   Eighty-fifth percentile criterion-referenced norms for pull-ups for boys and girls ages 6–17 years.

| Age | Pull-Ups | Age | Pull-Ups |
|---|---|---|---|
| | BOYS | | GIRLS |
| 6 | 2 | 6 | 2 |
| 7 | 4 | 7 | 2 |
| 8 | 5 | 8 | 2 |
| 9 | 5 | 9 | 2 |
| 10 | 6 | 10 | 3 |
| 11 | 6 | 11 | 3 |
| 12 | 7 | 12 | 2 |
| 13 | 7 | 13 | 2 |
| 14 | 10 | 14 | 2 |
| 15 | 11 | 15 | 2 |
| 16 | 11 | 16 | 1 |
| 17 | 13 | 17 | 1 |

Reprinted by permission of The President's Council on Physical Fitness and Sports, Washington, D.C.

*Age Level:* Ages 6–adult.

*Test Area:* An uncluttered area free of potential sources of accidents (i.e., chairs, walls, etc.).

*Equipment Needed:* A horizontal bar approximately 1.5 inches in diameter. This bar should be of adequate height or adjustable to accommodate the tallest person to be tested.

*Scoring Procedure:* The number of successfully completed pull-ups is recorded as the student's score.

*Norms:* 85th percentile criterion-referenced norms for the Presidential Physical Fitness Award are found in Table 5.12.

*Organizational Hints:* The pull-up should be smooth and completed with minimal horizontal motion. Test administrators may assist in minimizing superfluous movement by placing their arms across the front of the performer's thighs. Legs must remain fully extended throughout the entire test.

## Flexed-Arm Hang

*Purpose:* To measure strength and endurance of the arm and shoulder girdle muscles.

*Description:* The test is designed to assess the relative muscular strength and endurance of the arm and shoulder girdle region by holding the body stationary using a flexed-arm position.

*Instructions:* The performer grasps the bar with palms facing forward (away from the body). Using spotters, the student raises the body off the floor until the chin is over the bar and the arms flexed at the elbow (Figure 5.11). Feet should be free from the floor with legs straight and body held still throughout the duration of the test. The student holds the position as long as possible.

*Validity:* Face validity is accepted for this test.

*Reliability:* Correlation coefficients ranging from .74 to .90 have been reported for this test (Cotton and Marwitz, 1971; Johnson and Nelson, 1986).

*Age Level:* Ages 9–adult.

*Test Area:* An uncluttered area free of potential sources of accidents (e.g., chairs, walls).

*Equipment Needed:* A horizontal bar approximately 1.5 inches in diameter. This bar should be of adequate height or adjustable to accommodate the tallest person to be tested.

► **FIGURE 5.11**   Flexed-arm hang.

► **TABLE 5.13**   Eighty-fifth percentile criterion-referenced norms for flexed-arm hang (AAHPERD, 1976).

| Age | Flexed Arm Hang |
|:---:|:---:|
| | **GIRLS** |
| 10 | 21 sec. |
| 11 | 20 sec. |
| 12 | 19 sec. |
| 13 | 18 sec. |
| 14 | 19 sec. |
| 15 | 18 sec. |
| 16 | 19 sec. |
| 17 | 19 sec. |

Reprinted by permission of The President's Council on Physical Fitness and Sports, Washington, D.C.

*Scoring Procedure:* The score is the number of seconds (to the nearest second) the student holds the hanging position, in one trial only.

*Norms:* 85th percentile criterion-referenced norms for the Presidential Physical Fitness Award for girls are found in Table 5.13.

*Organizational Hints:* The height of the bar should be approximately equal to the standing height of the performer. Spotters should be positioned in front of and behind the performer. The timer should start the stopwatch as soon as the student is free from both spotters' assistance and assumes the flexed-arm hang position. The stopwatch should be stopped if the chin touches the bar, tilts backward or upward, or moves below the horizontal bar. Legs and trunk should remain motionless throughout the entire test. Knees must not be raised and kicking is not permitted.

## Modified Pull-Ups

*Purpose:* To measure strength and endurance of the arm and shoulder girdle muscles.

*Description:* The test requires the student to perform pull-ups on an incline board and move the body weight with arms until muscles are completely fatigued.

*Instructions:* The student lies in a prone position on the apparatus with hands placed shoulder-width apart grasping a horizontal bar. The student assumes a straight-arm hanging position, pulls the body up the incline board until the chin is over the bar, and returns to the original straight-arm position. This action is repeated as many times as possible.

*Validity:* Face validity is accepted for this test.

*Reliability:* Intraclass reliability estimates of .90 and higher have been reported for this test.

*Age Level:* Elementary age children to adults.

*Test Area:* Indoor area.

*Equipment Needed:* The apparatus necessary to conduct this test can be either purchased from a commercial vendor or constructed for approximately $50. The commercial apparatus has been improved to make it safer (Baumgartner et al., 1984). The incline board is constructed from two 10-foot boards, each 2 inches by 12 inches. These boards are fastened together with three 12-inch hinges (this allows the board to be folded for ease of transportation and storage). The 18-inch bar is made of .75-inch plumbing pipe and connected to the top of the board with right-angle attachments so the bar is 6 inches off the board. An angle iron is fastened underneath near the top of the incline board (this is used to hook over a bar, such as a doorway bar 5 feet from the floor, which gives the desired 30-degree angle from the floor). An ordinary four-wheel scooter is needed for the student to lie on. The testing position and equipment are shown in Figure 5.12.

*Scoring Procedure:* The recorded score is the number of completed repetitions.

*Norms:* Table 5.14 shows available percentile norms.

*Organizational Hints:* Students should be informed to pull in a smooth, even manner. The scooter wheels should not swivel. Practice prior to actual test administration is recommended.

**FIGURE 5.12** The incline board with rail system and scooter board (underside).

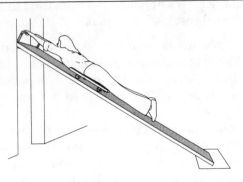

◥ **TABLE 5.14**   Descriptive statistics and percentile norms for modified pull-ups test (subjects from Denton, TX area public school).

|  | Boys | Girls |
|---|---|---|
|  | N = 345 | N = 318 |
| Percentile |  |  |
| 90 | 47 | 38 |
| 80 | 40 | 30 |
| 70 | 35 | 26 |
| 60 | 31 | 23 |
| 50 | 28 | 20 |
| 40 | 25 | 18 |
| 30 | 23 | 16 |
| 20 | 19 | 13 |
| 10 | 15 | 11 |
|  | X = 30.37 | X = 22.74 |
|  | S.D. = 12.85 | S.D. = 10.68 |
|  | S.E. = 0.69 | S.E. = 0.60 |

Reprinted by permission of American Alliance for Health, Physical Education, Recreation and Dance, Reston, Virginia.

## Dynamometer

*Purpose:* The dynamometer is a piece of equipment designed to measure static strength (force exerted against an immovable resistance) and endurance.

*Description:* While the dynamometer may be used to test several groups of muscles, it is most commonly used to measure grip strength. Explanation of its use is limited to this particular function. Figure 5.13 shows a variety of dynamometers and one being used for testing purposes.

The dynamometer traditionally has been used to collect research data. Its relatively nominal cost ($45–150) makes it affordable for school use.

*Instructions:* The dynamometer must first be adjusted to fit the student's handgrip size. In a standing position, the student holds the dynamometer out to the side and squeezes the grip as hard as possible without moving the arm. Three trials are recommended, with a one-minute rest between trials (Heyward, 1984).

To be measured on grip endurance, the student should squeeze the handgrip as hard as possible for 60 seconds. The force is recorded in kilograms every 10 seconds. As Safrit (1990) explains, relative endurance can be calculated by dividing the final force by the initial force and multiplying that quotient by 100.

**▶ FIGURE 5.13**   Hand dynamometers.

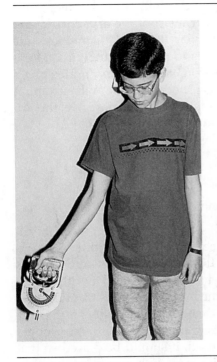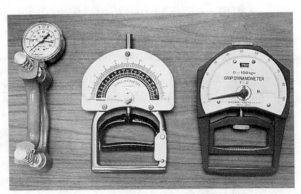

*Validity:* Unreported.

*Reliability:* Reliability coefficients of .90 and higher have been reported.

*Age Level:* Elementary school age to adults.

*Test Area:* Indoors or outdoors.

*Equipment Needed:* Grip dynamometer.

*Scoring Procedure:* Scores are measured in kilograms (0–100). If more than one trial is given, record the average of the number of trials.

## Strength Tests Using Weight Machines

Weight machines are multipurpose in nature and are becoming more popular as teaching aids and testing devices for middle and secondary school physical education. The Universal Gym apparatus is one of the more common weight-training stations. It has multiple lifting stations and is an appropriate device to measure dynamic muscular strength of various muscle groups for students in grades 8–12.

One criterion to determine muscular strength is maximum weight lifted in one repetition. This method can be used to measure various muscle groups. The more commonly practiced lifts consist of the arm curl, lateral pull-down, and bench press. These particular lifts and instructions are shown in Figures 5.14–5.16. Lifting activities to measure strength and endurance of leg muscles include knee extension, knee flexion, and leg press.

There is a positive correlation between body weight and maximum weight lifted. This means that heavier youngsters lift more weight. All scores should be interpreted considering the test-taker's weight.

## Arm Curl for Muscular Endurance

(Jackson and Smith, 1974)

*Purpose:* To measure muscular strength and endurance of the arm flexors.

*Instructions:* The performer assumes a standing position with head, shoulders, and buttocks against a wall. Feet are shoulder-width apart and positioned approximately 12 to 15 inches from the wall. To ensure that this position is maintained throughout the test, Jackson and Smith (1974) suggest placing a sheet of paper behind the buttocks. The performer must keep the paper pinned to the wall while executing consecutive arm curls. The test is terminated when the paper falls or the individual can no longer perform the curl. If a weight machine is used, it should be placed so that when the participant holds the weight with arms fully extended the exercise weight is suspended slightly above the remaining weights. A complete repetition occurs when the arms are flexed and the bar touches the performer's chin. A three-second cadence is used to assist in executing each repetition of the test. Each repetition must be completed in the three-second limit, and each new repetition cannot begin until a new three-second interval begins. Figure 5.14 shows an arm curl from a seated position.

*Validity:* Face validity is assumed for this test.

*Reliability:* Since a maximum endurance effort is being tested, consistency of performance should be quite high.

*Age Level:* Eighth grade to adult.

*Test Area:* A small indoor multipurpose room, large enough to accommodate a Universal Gym apparatus.

*Equipment Needed:* Universal Gym or similar station weight-training apparatus. A metronome is useful to assist in keeping exercise cadence constant.

*Scoring Procedure:* The number of repetitions successfully completed is recorded as the score.

**FIGURE 5.14** Arm curls.

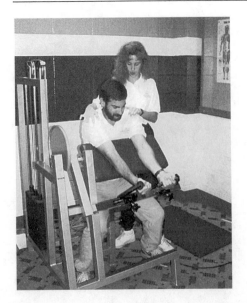 

*Norms:* Since normative data are not available for middle school or high school students, test scores can be used as criterion measures, standard scores can be calculated from raw scores, or local norms can be developed.

*Organizational Hints:* A weight that all members of the group can successfully lift one time should be selected. If free weights are used, two spotters should watch each performer.

### Lat Pull Down

(Jackson and Smith, 1974)

*Purpose:* To measure the muscular endurance of the latissimus dorsi muscle and the elbow flexors.

*Instructions:* From a kneeling position, the student grasps the handle grips of the bar with elbows extended. The bar is pulled down behind the head to touch the juncture of the neck and shoulders, just below the hairline. The weight is brought back smoothly to the original starting position (see Figure 5.15). The knees must remain in contact with the floor throughout the duration of the test. Each repetition must be completed in the three seconds and each new repetition cannot begin until a new three-second interval begins. The exercise is repeated as many times as possible.

► **FIGURE 5.15**    Lateral pull-down.

*Validity:* Face validity is assumed for this test.

*Reliability:* Since a maximum endurance effort is being tested, consistency of performance should be quite high.

*Age Level:* Eighth grade to adult.

*Test Area:* A small indoor multipurpose room, large enough to accommodate a Universal Gym apparatus.

*Equipment Needed:* Universal Gym or similar station weight-training apparatus. A metronome is useful to assist in keeping exercise cadence constant.

*Scoring Procedure:* The number of repetitions successfully completed is recorded as the score.

*Norms:* Since normative data are not available for middle school or high school students, test scores can be used as criterion measures, standard scores can be calculated from raw scores, or local norms can be developed.

*Organizational Hints:* A weight that all members of the group in class can successfully lift one time should be selected. In order to keep the knees from rising, it may be necessary to have a spotter hold the performer's lower legs on the floor. This can be accomplished by applying pressure to the performer's calves. Participants should be reminded not to drop the weights.

An alternative to using the same weight for everyone would be to individualize the test by selecting a weight that requires a percentage of maximum strength to be lifted. Pollock, Schmidt, and Jackson (1977) suggest using a weight that is 70 percent of the subject's maximum lift.

### Bench Press
(Jackson and Smith, 1974)

*Purpose:* To measure muscular endurance of the chest and posterior arm.

*Instructions:* The student assumes a back-lying position on the bench with knees bent and feet on the bench, slightly more than shoulder-width apart. The back rests comfortably, flat on the bench, and the hands grip the bar with palms facing upward. The weight is lifted upward until the arms are fully extended, then lowered until the weights lifted touch the weights beneath them. Each repetition must be completed in the three-second limit, and each new repetition cannot begin until a new three-second interval begins. Figure 5.16 shows use of the bench press.

*Validity:* Face validity is assumed for this test.

*Reliability:* Since a maximum endurance effort is being tested, consistency of performance should be quite high.

*Age Level:* Eighth grade to adult.

▶ **FIGURE 5.16**   Bench press.

*Test Area:* A small indoor multipurpose room, large enough to accommodate a Universal Gym apparatus.

*Equipment Needed:* Universal Gym or similar station weight-training apparatus. A metronome is useful to assist in keeping exercise cadence constant.

*Scoring Procedure:* The number of repetitions successfully completed is recorded as the score.

*Norms:* Since normative data are not available for middle school or high school students, test scores can be used as criterion measures, standard scores can be calculated from raw scores, or local norms can be developed.

*Organizational Hints:* A weight that can be lifted by all the students in class should be used. If free weights are used, spotters should stand at each end of the bar and the bar should be brought to the chest on the return phase of the exercise.

## Measuring Flexibility

Flexibility is a measure of the range of motion available at a joint or group of joints. Individuals who can freely move the joints of the ankles, knees, hips, wrists, elbows, and shoulders without stiffness are said to have good flexibility. They can move better and enjoy their activities more. Most important, people who display high degrees of flexibility seem to be healthier than those who do not.

In the past, flexibility has been the most ignored component of health-related physical fitness. Recently, however, there has been a resurgence of interest in exercise and physical activity designed to promote and develop flexibility. Research has shown that lower back–posterior thigh flexibility is important for the prevention and rehabilitation of lower back disorders. And as we already know, lower back pain and muscular tension are significant health problems for the American population (AAHPERD, 1984). In fact, it has been estimated that 25 to 30 million Americans, or approximately 16 percent of the population, have suffered from lower back pain syndrome and that nearly 8 out of 10 persons have at one time or another suffered from backache (Corbin and Lindsey, 1988; Vitale, 1973). According to the American Medical Association, in 1983 some 7 million Americans were undergoing treatment for chronic back problems. It has been estimated that 2 million people have been added to this list yearly (Shaw, 1983). In financial terms, lower back pain has cost the American workplace over $1 billion in lost productivity per year (AAHPERD, 1984).

Flexibility varies among individuals, and great differences can occur among the joints of one person. Structure as well as the amount of muscle and fatty tissue around the joint can affect the range of motion. Measuring and evaluating flexibility is usually discussed in terms of *flexion* or *extension*. **Flexion** occurs when the angle of the body with its articulations is decreased through movement. Getting the lower leg in position to punt a football by moving it backward and upward to the upper leg is an example of flexion. Angle increase of the body in relationship to its articulations is referred to as **extension.** Extending the lower leg to punt the football is an example of extension. Tests of flexibility may be used to determine potential in a particular athletic activity, assess change of flexibility performance as part of a physical education unit or rehabilitation process, and diagnose joint or muscular dysfunction. The following are examples of tests used to measure flexibility.

### Sit-and-Reach Test

*Purpose:* The purpose of the sit-and-reach test is to evaluate the flexibility of the low back and posterior thigh.

*Description:* The sit-and-reach test requires the performer to stretch forward and extend the hamstring and low back muscles.

*Instructions:* The student assumes a sitting position with legs extended, feet shoulder-width apart, and shoes off. The arms are extended forward with one hand on top of the other and finger pads on top of fingernails. The student reaches directly forward, palms down, along the measuring scale four times, holding the position of maximum reach the last time for one full second. Only one trial is given.

*Validity:* The validity of this test is supported by logic. This particular test has been used in clinical settings to determine the range of motion in the hamstring muscles and lower back (Manitoba Department of Education, 1977).

*Reliability:* Coefficients ranging from .70 to .96 have been reported for the sit-and-reach test when used with school-age youth (Buxton, 1957; Mathews, Shaw, and Bohnen, 1957; Mathews, Shaw, and Woods, 1959).

*Age Level:* Elementary school age to adult.

*Test Area:* Room with level floor.

*Equipment Needed:* A special apparatus consisting of a box with a measuring scale in which 23 centimeters is at the edge against which the bottom of the feet rest. (See Figure 5.17 for specifications.)

*Scoring Procedure:* The score is the most distant point reached, measured to the nearest centimeter.

*Norms:* Percentile norms for boys and girls are found in Tables 5.15 and 5.16.

▶ **FIGURE 5.17**    Schematic drawing of constructed sit-and-reach apparatus.

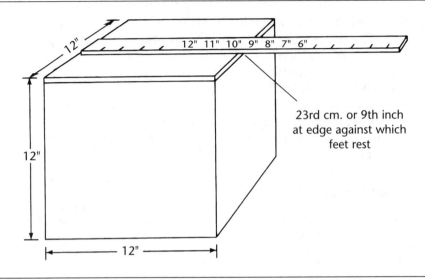

*Organizational Hints:* Legs must remain straight throughout the entire stretch. The test administrator may need to hold the legs down at the knees. Students take the test with their shoes off. Extreme scores as a result of disproportionate arm length/leg length may affect the results. Students can be taught to administer the test to one another. The score recorded as the most distant point must be reached with both hands. Students should warm up

▶ **TABLE 5.15**    Percentile norms for sit-and-reach (cm) for boys ages 5–18.

| AGE | 5 | 6 | 7 | 8 | 9 | 10 | 11 | 12 | 13 | 14 | 15 | 16 | 17–18 |
|---|---|---|---|---|---|---|---|---|---|---|---|---|---|
| Percentile | | | | | | | | | | | | | |
| 99 | 36 | 37 | 38 | 38 | 37 | 37 | 38 | 52 | 41 | 43 | 47 | 45 | 48 |
| 90 | 31 | 32 | 31 | 32 | 32 | 31 | 32 | 32 | 34 | 37 | 39 | 40 | 43 |
| 80 | 29 | 30 | 29 | 30 | 30 | 29 | 30 | 30 | 32 | 34 | 36 | 37 | 40 |
| 70 | 28 | 28 | 27 | 28 | 28 | 28 | 28 | 29 | 29 | 31 | 33 | 35 | 38 |
| 60 | 26 | 27 | 26 | 27 | 27 | 26 | 26 | 27 | 27 | 30 | 32 | 32 | 36 |
| 50 | 25 | 26 | 25 | 25 | 25 | 25 | 25 | 26 | 26 | 28 | 30 | 30 | 34 |
| 40 | 24 | 24 | 24 | 24 | 24 | 23 | 23 | 24 | 24 | 26 | 28 | 28 | 32 |
| 30 | 23 | 23 | 22 | 23 | 22 | 21 | 22 | 22 | 22 | 24 | 26 | 26 | 30 |
| 20 | 22 | 22 | 20 | 21 | 21 | 19 | 20 | 20 | 19 | 22 | 23 | 23 | 26 |
| 10 | 19 | 18 | 18 | 18 | 18 | 17 | 16 | 16 | 15 | 18 | 19 | 18 | 23 |

Reprinted by permission of American Alliance for Health, Physical Education, Recreation and Dance, Reston, Virginia.

▶ **TABLE 5.16**   Percentile norms for sit-and-reach (cm) for girls ages 5–18.

| AGE | 5 | 6 | 7 | 8 | 9 | 10 | 11 | 12 | 13 | 14 | 15 | 16 | 17–18 |
|---|---|---|---|---|---|---|---|---|---|---|---|---|---|
| Percentile | | | | | | | | | | | | | |
| 99 | 37 | 38 | 37 | 39 | 39 | 41 | 41 | 46 | 49 | 49 | 49 | 48 | 47 |
| 90 | 32 | 33 | 33 | 34 | 34 | 34 | 36 | 38 | 40 | 42 | 44 | 43 | 43 |
| 80 | 31 | 31 | 31 | 32 | 32 | 32 | 33 | 35 | 37 | 39 | 42 | 41 | 41 |
| 70 | 29 | 29 | 30 | 30 | 30 | 30 | 31 | 33 | 35 | 36 | 40 | 38 | 40 |
| 60 | 28 | 28 | 29 | 29 | 29 | 29 | 30 | 32 | 32 | 35 | 37 | 36 | 37 |
| 50 | 27 | 27 | 27 | 28 | 28 | 28 | 29 | 30 | 31 | 33 | 36 | 34 | 35 |
| 40 | 25 | 25 | 26 | 26 | 26 | 27 | 27 | 28 | 29 | 31 | 33 | 33 | 33 |
| 30 | 24 | 24 | 25 | 24 | 24 | 25 | 25 | 26 | 26 | 29 | 32 | 31 | 32 |
| 20 | 23 | 22 | 23 | 22 | 22 | 22 | 23 | 23 | 23 | 26 | 30 | 28 | 29 |
| 10 | 20 | 20 | 20 | 19 | 20 | 19 | 20 | 20 | 20 | 23 | 25 | 23 | 26 |

prior to taking the test. A bench with a metric ruler may be used as a substitute for the sit-and-reach apparatus. The sit-and-reach apparatus should be placed against the wall to prevent it from sliding on the floor.

### Kraus-Weber Floor Touch
(Kraus and Hirschland, 1954)

*Purpose:* To measure flexibility of the lower trunk and the posterior thigh.

*Description:* This test is part of the Kraus-Weber Tests of Minimum Muscular Fitness.

*Instructions:* The student assumes a standing position with feet together. Shoes are off. Arms hang comfortably by the sides. Using static movement and not flexing the leg at the knee, the student bends forward and down, attempting to touch the floor with the tips of the fingers and to hold this position for three counts. Figure 5.18 depicts the movement associated with this test. One trial is allowed.

*Validity:* Face validity is assumed.

*Reliability:* Not reported for this specific test.

*Age Level:* Elementary school age to adult.

*Test Area:* Any room with flat floor.

*Equipment Needed:* Stopwatch.

▶ **FIGURE 5.18**    Kraus-Weber floor touch.

**Scoring Procedure:** Traditionally, the test has been scored on a pass-fail basis. If the student is able to hold the floor-touch position for the full three seconds, a grade of pass is recorded. If not, the student receives a fail. Another method of scoring this test has been reported by Safrit (1990). This option uses numerical ratings from 0 to 10. If the floor-touch position is held for the full three seconds, the student receives a 10. If the floor is not touched, 1 point is subtracted for every inch between the floor and the student's fingertips.

**Norms:** Not relevant when using a pass-fail scale.

**Organizational Hints:** As with the sit-and-reach, the test administrator may have to hold the legs straight to prevent the student from flexing at the knee.

### Trunk Extension
(Cureton, 1941)

**Purpose:** To assess the hyperextension limits of the lower trunk.

**Instructions:** The student assumes a prone position on the floor or mat and places the hands on the lower back, one on top of the other. A partner, or an assigned assistant, straddles the performer's legs and places pressure on the posterior thigh region in order to keep the hips touching the floor. The student raises the trunk from the floor as far as possible and holds that position. Using a tape measure, the distance from the mat to the depression at the base of the neck and upper end of the sternum (suprasternal notch) is measured to the nearest quarter inch. Figure 5.19 provides an example of how to administer this test.

*Validity:*　Face validity is assumed for this test.

*Reliability:*　Not reported for this specific test.

*Age Level:*　Elementary school age to adult.

*Test Area:*　A room with a level floor.

*Equipment Needed:*　Mat or piece of carpet and tape measure.

*Scoring Procedure:*　The recorded score is derived from a simple procedure. First, a standard measure of the student's trunk is taken by measuring the distance between the suprasternal notch and the floor while the student is in a seated position. This trunk length is recorded to the nearest quarter inch. Second, the measured trunk extension is multiplied by 100 and the resultant number is divided by trunk length. This number is recorded as the student's score.

*Organizational Hints:*　For the sake of comfort, the student should perform the test on a carpeted floor or mat.

▶ **FIGURE 5.19**　Trunk extension.

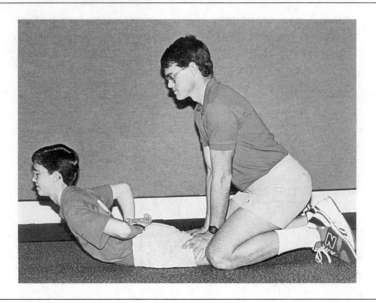

◣  **FIGURE 5.20**    Goniometer.

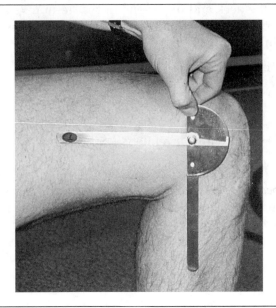

## Goniometer

*Purpose:* To measure the joint angle at the two extremes of the total range of movement.

*Description:* The goniometer is like a protractor. It consists of two levers, one with a circle at the end and the other attached to the pivotal center of the circle (see Figure 5.20). The goniometer is designed to measure angles in degrees.

*Instructions:* The pivotal center of the goniometer is placed on the joint so that it coincides with the fulcrum of the joint movement. For example, if the flexion and extension of the lower trunk is to be measured, one lever of the goniometer is placed along the vertical axis of the lower trunk, and the other lever along the vertical axis of the upper leg (see Figure 5.21). The degree of the angle for each extreme is recorded. The range of motion for the flexion and extension of the lower trunk is the difference between the scores obtained at full extension and full flexion.

*Validity:* Since it accurately measures angles around joints, logical validity is assumed.

*Reliability:* Calibration ensures accurate measurement. Consistent measurement may be obtained through constant practice with this particular instrument.

**FIGURE 5.21** Measuring angle of movement of lower trunk using the goniometer.

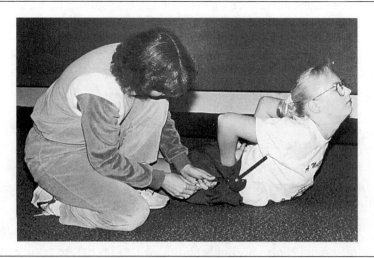

*Age Level:* Elementary school age to adult.

*Test Area:* A small room.

*Equipment Needed:* Goniometer.

*Scoring Procedure:* The difference between the extremes in flexion and extension is the recorded score.

*Norms:* Not available.

*Organizational Hints:* To facilitate test administration, testers should have prior training in using the goniometer and calculating the recorded score. Students should warm up prior to test administration.

### Leighton Flexometer (1942)

*Purpose:* To measure the angles (in degrees) of body segment movement.

*Description:* The Leighton flexometer has a weighted 360-degree dial and a weighted pointer that rotate on an axle. Gravity pulls the weighted end and pointer downward to obtain a measurement. The flexometer measures limb flexion and extension for various sports skills, such as throwing, kicking, etc. It has been used to measure flexibility at 30 anatomical sites (Verducci, 1980).

*Instructions:* The instrument is attached to the appropriate segment of the body. The starting position is the point at which one of the levers to be moved is at its extreme. The zero marks on the pointer and dial should be in the vertical position. The dial is locked in place. As the body segment (and the lever) is moved to its other extreme, the dial begins to swing freely. Once the segment reaches its extreme the dial should be locked in place.

*Validity:* Construct validity is established.

*Reliability:* Test-retest reliability coefficients of .98 were obtained in 30 different measures of flexibility (Forbes, 1950).

*Age Level:* Elementary school age to adult.

*Test Area:* A small room.

*Equipment Needed:* Leighton Flexometer and bench or table.

*Scoring Procedure:* The reading on the dial after taking the segment through its range of motion estimates the arc through which the movement occurred and is recorded as the score.

*Norms:* Not available.

*Organizational Hints:* Students should warm up before taking the test.

## Measuring Body Composition

Medical experts agree that obesity has reached epidemic proportions in the United States. Obesity is probably the most widespread handicap facing 10 million school-age children and adolescents today. One of the unfortunate myths associated with obesity is that children will grow out of the condition when they enter adolescence. Sadly, this does not occur. Instead, children grow more deeply into obesity until the problem becomes almost irreversible.

Basically, total body weight can be divided into two components, fat weight and lean weight. **Lean weight** comprises all organ tissue, muscle, and bone. **Fat weight** refers to the body tissue that can be defined as chemically fat. Percent body fat, or the percent of total weight represented by fat weight, is the index used to describe individual body composition. For example, a youngster who weighs 100 pounds and whose body composition is 20 percent fat, has a fat weight of 20 pounds and a lean weight of 80 pounds.

Measuring fatness and leanness of the body has been of interest to physical educators for years. Measuring body composition is important because being misinformed about healthful body fat levels or having a distorted body image may result in physiological and psychological problems (Thomas and Whitehead, 1993). Researchers in physical education and related disciplines have developed many methods to assess and evaluate body composition. Historically, educators and scientists have used height and weight ratios to determine overweight, making the assumption that overweight and overfat were synonymous. We now know that overweight and overfat are not interchangeable terms. Overweight is defined as a condition that exists when people's weight is in excess of recommended limits for their body type. Overfatness refers to a state of poor health that results from possessing an unacceptable ratio of fat to lean body mass. For example, many athletes participating in sports that require a great deal of strength to be successful (e.g., football, shot put, discus throw) would be classified as overweight according to age-height-weight scales, when in fact their body composition indicates that they are lean. Their apparent overweight is related to heavy bone structure and high amounts of muscle tissue. Because of the misinterpretations associated with the definitional differences between overweight and overfat, methods other than weight/height ratio should be used to quantify the fat component of total body weight (AAHPERD, 1984). The following skinfold tests have been used to estimate percentage of body fat.

### Skinfolds (Abdomen, Calf, Chest, Scapula, Thigh, and Triceps)

*Purpose:* To measure the level of body fatness.

*Description:* A skinfold consists of a double layer of skin and subcutaneous fat (see Figure 5.22). Measurements are usually taken on the right side of the body with the subject standing. Through extensive research, certain anatom-

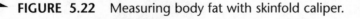

**FIGURE 5.22** Measuring body fat with skinfold caliper.

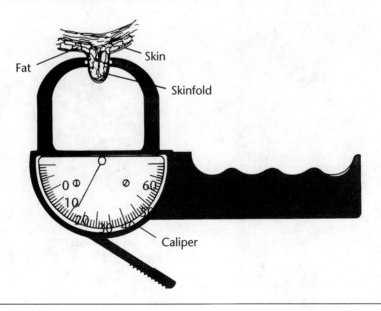

ical sites have been identified as landmarks for skinfold testing. Some of the more common sites are the abdomen, calf, scapula, suprailiac, thigh, and triceps.

*Instructions:* The proper sequence for administering the skinfold test consists of firmly grasping the skinfold between thumb and forefinger and lifting it away; placing the caliper one-half inch above or below the skinfold; slowly releasing the pressure on the caliper trigger so the pinchers can exert full tension on the skinfold; and then reading the scale.

### Abdomen

The abdominal skinfold is measured on a vertical fold approximately one inch to the right of the umbilicus (Figure 5.23).

### Calf

The calf skinfold is taken on the inside of the right calf, at the level of the maximal calf girth (Figure 5.24).

### Scapula

The subscapular skinfold is measured on the right side of the body approximately one-half inch below the inferior angle of the scapula following the natural lines of the fold (Figure 5.25).

**FIGURE 5.23**
Abdominal skinfold.

**FIGURE 5.24**
Calf skinfold.

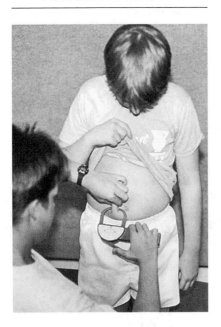

**FIGURE 5.25**
Subscapular skinfold.

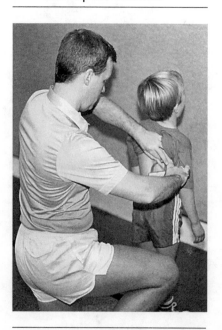

**FIGURE 5.26**
Suprailiac skinfold.

### Suprailiac

The suprailiac skinfold is a diagonal fold measured at the front of the hips immediately above the crest of the ilium (Figure 5.26).

### Thigh

The thigh skinfold is measured halfway between the inguinal ligament (where the hip joint bends in front) and the top of the patella (knee-cap). The skinfold is vertical in the anterior midline of the thigh (Figure 5.27).

### Triceps

The triceps skinfold is measured over the triceps muscle of the right arm midway between the olecranon process of the elbow and the acromial process of the scapula, i.e., the tip of the shoulder and parallel to the longitudinal axis of the upper arm (Figure 5.28).

*Validity:* Skinfolds have been found to be more valid than height–weight ratio in estimating body fatness as determined by laboratory procedure (hydrostatic weighing) and have a higher correlation with percent fat than most other indices. See Table 5.17 for studies showing correlations between skinfolds and percent fat. The most accurate measure available to schools is the skinfold assessment (Thomas and Whitehead, 1993).

▶ **FIGURE 5.27**
Thigh skinfold.

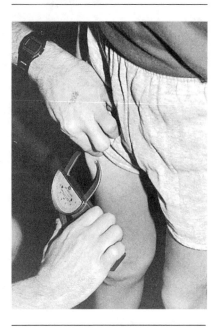

▶ **FIGURE 5.28**
Triceps skinfold.

Many different combinations of skinfold measurements can be used to predict percentage of body fat. Jackson and Pollock (1976) have demonstrated that skinfold fat measurements taken at various anatomical landmarks measure body fatness and are highly correlated. This finding means that if an individual tends to have a relatively high skinfold value at one site, a correspondingly high value will be found at another site. From the test administrator's point of view, this means that measuring skinfolds at multiple sites may provide no more accurate information than could be obtained by measuring at one or two sites. While measuring multiple sites increases consistency of measurement, the gain in validity is minimal (Pollock, 1975, 1976).

*Age Level:* Elementary school age to adult.

*Test Area:* Small room with private area.

*Equipment Needed:* A skinfold caliper (e.g., Lange, Harpenden, Slim Guide, Fat-O-Meter, Ross Laboratories) is necessary for taking these measurements (Figure 5.29). The caliper should be capable of accurate calibration and exert a constant pressure of 10 gm/sq mm throughout the measurement range.

*Scoring Procedure:* To ensure accuracy, several readings should be taken at a particular site with the median score in millimeters (to the nearest .5mm) recorded as the score.

▶ **TABLE 5.17** Correlations between skinfolds and percent fat.*

| | SKINFOLDS | | |
| | Triceps | Subscapular | Triceps and Subscapular |
| Investigator and Sample | r | r | R** |
|---|---|---|---|
| Parizkova (1961) | | | |
| 9–12-year-old girls | .74 | .80 | .81 |
| 9–12-year-old boys | .85 | .88 | .89 |
| 13–16-year-old girls | .74 | .80 | .82 |
| 13–16-year-old boys | .93 | .89 | .95 |
| Young et al. (1968) | | | |
| Non-menarche girls | .76 | .72 | — |
| Menarche girls | .58 | .52 | — |
| Katch and Michael (1968) | | | |
| 16–17-year-old boys | .84 | .81 | — |
| Lohman et al. (1975) | | | |
| 8–12-year-old boys | .79 | .73 | — |
| Parizkova and Rath (1972) | | | |
| 8–12-year-old boys | — | — | .86 |
| Harsha et al. (1978) | | | |
| 6–16-year-old boys (white) | .76 | .75 | — |
| 6–16-year-old girls (white) | .75 | .80 | — |
| 6–16-year-old girls (black) | .82 | .75 | — |
| 6–16-year-old boys (black) | .82 | .87 | — |
| Boileau et al. (1981) | | | |
| 8–11-year-old boys — Illinois | .77 | .64 | .78 |
| 8–11-year-old boys — California | .83 | .80 | .85 |

*% fat estimated from body density or 40K.
**Multiple correlation based on use of both triceps and subscapular as predictors.

*Norms:* Tables 5.18 and 5.19 show normative data for skinfold measurements. Equations to convert raw skinfold data to percentage of body fat have been developed by Lohman, Boileau, and Massey (1975) and are as follows:

Males:   % of fat = (1.35(sum of 2sk)) − (.012(sum of 2 sk))² − 4.4

Females: % of fat = (1.35(sum of 2sk)) − (.012(sum of 2 sk))² − 2.4

*Organizational Hints:* The test administrator needs to be sensitive to the manner in which this test is conducted. This is particularly true in the school setting, where the teacher encounters many subjects who might feel

▶ **FIGURE 5.29**    Skinfold calipers.

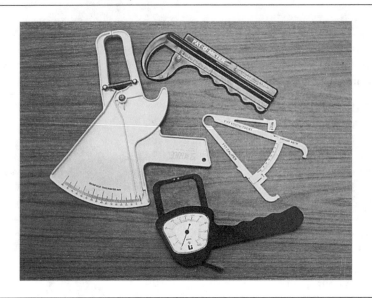

▶ **TABLE 5.18**    Percentile norms for sum of triceps plus subscapular skinfolds (mm) for boys ages 6–18b.

| AGE | 6 | 7 | 8 | 9 | 10 | 11 | 12 | 13 | 14 | 15 | 16 | 17 |
|---|---|---|---|---|---|---|---|---|---|---|---|---|
| Percentile | | | | | | | | | | | | |
| 99 | 7 | 7 | 7 | 7 | 7 | 8 | 8 | 7 | 7 | 8 | 8 | 8 |
| 90 | 9 | 9 | 9 | 10 | 10 | 10 | 10 | 10 | 9 | 10 | 10 | 10 |
| 80 | 10 | 10 | 10 | 11 | 11 | 12 | 11 | 11 | 11 | 11 | 11 | 12 |
| 70 | 11 | 11 | 11 | 12 | 12 | 12 | 12 | 12 | 12 | 12 | 12 | 13 |
| 60 | 12 | 12 | 12 | 13 | 13 | 14 | 13 | 13 | 13 | 13 | 13 | 14 |
| 50 | 12 | 12 | 13 | 14 | 14 | 16 | 15 | 15 | 14 | 14 | 14 | 15 |
| 40 | 13 | 13 | 14 | 15 | 16 | 17 | 16 | 17 | 15 | 16 | 16 | 16 |
| 30 | 14 | 14 | 16 | 17 | 18 | 20 | 19 | 19 | 18 | 18 | 18 | 19 |
| 20 | 15 | 16 | 18 | 20 | 21 | 24 | 24 | 25 | 23 | 22 | 22 | 24 |
| 10 | 18 | 18 | 21 | 26 | 28 | 33 | 33 | 36 | 31 | 30 | 29 | 30 |

*aBased on data from F. E. Johnston, D. V. Hamill, and S. Lemeshow. (1) Skinfold Thickness of Children 6–11 Years (Series II, No. 120, 1972), and (2) Skinfold Thickness of Youths 12–17 Years (Series II, No. 132, 1974). U.S. National Center for Health Statistics, U.S. Department of HEW, Washington, D.C.*

*bThe norms for age 17 may be used for age 18.*

Reprinted by permission of American Alliance for Health, Physical Education, Recreation and Dance, Reston, Virginia.

▶ **TABLE 5.19** Percentile norms for sum of triceps plus subscapular skinfolds (mm) for girlsa ages 6–18b.

| AGE | 6 | 7 | 8 | 9 | 10 | 11 | 12 | 13 | 14 | 15 | 16 | 17 |
|---|---|---|---|---|---|---|---|---|---|---|---|---|
| Percentile | | | | | | | | | | | | |
| 99 | 8 | 8 | 8 | 9 | 9 | 8 | 9 | 10 | 10 | 11 | 11 | 12 |
| 90 | 10 | 11 | 11 | 12 | 12 | 12 | 12 | 13 | 15 | 16 | 16 | 16 |
| 80 | 12 | 12 | 12 | 13 | 13 | 14 | 14 | 15 | 17 | 18 | 19 | 19 |
| 70 | 12 | 13 | 14 | 15 | 15 | 16 | 16 | 17 | 19 | 21 | 21 | 22 |
| 60 | 13 | 14 | 15 | 16 | 17 | 17 | 17 | 19 | 21 | 23 | 23 | 24 |
| 50 | 14 | 15 | 16 | 17 | 18 | 19 | 19 | 20 | 24 | 25 | 25 | 27 |
| 40 | 15 | 16 | 18 | 19 | 20 | 21 | 22 | 23 | 26 | 28 | 29 | 30 |
| 30 | 16 | 18 | 20 | 22 | 24 | 23 | 25 | 27 | 30 | 32 | 32 | 34 |
| 20 | 18 | 20 | 23 | 26 | 28 | 28 | 31 | 33 | 35 | 37 | 37 | 40 |
| 10 | 22 | 25 | 30 | 34 | 35 | 36 | 40 | 43 | 42 | 48 | 46 | 46 |

*aBased on data from Johnston, F. E., D. V. Hamill, and S. Lemeshow. (1) Skinfold Thickness of Children 6–11 Years (Series II, No. 120, 1972), and (2) Skinfold Thickness of Youths 12–17 Years (Series II, No. 132, 1974). U.S. National Center for Health Statistics, U.S. Department of HEW, Washington, D.C.*

*bThe norms for age 17 may be used for age 18.*

uncomfortable with this test. Always use good judgement. To avoid placing the students in a potentially embarrassing situation, the skinfold test should be administered in a private setting out of view of other students. Results of this test should be completely confidential. Students should be given an opportunity to learn how to use the caliper. Self-testing using partners is a good way for the students to become comfortable with the skinfold test. To ensure accuracy in testing, the test administrator should have prior training and practice working with the caliper. It is important to maintain records of these measures over time so as to assist the subject in better understanding the interplay of growth, maturation, diet, and physical activity. Doing so will also reinforce the important concept that fitness is a process that has to be maintained, and not just a product to be stored indefinetely (Corbin and Lindsey, 1990).

## BASIC ANTHROPOMETRIC MEASUREMENTS

**Anthropometric measurement** measures the growth changes that occur in the body. Height and weight are the two most common anthropometric measurements. In many situations, the physical education teacher is assigned the responsibility of charting the height and weight of students. Obtaining this information requires very little time and usually can become part of procedures associated with other tests. As with other assessments, this information should not simply be obtained and allowed to collect dust on some shelf. It can be valuable information and should be used in conjunction with other pertinent data. Keep in mind that height and weight measures do not provide information on body fatness (Thomas and Whitehead, 1993). Given the wide variations in growth and development among youngsters, we urge educators to exercise caution in reaching broadranging conclusions only from data derived from these charts.

Students should be encouraged to monitor their height and weight in relationship to others of the same age and sex. In so doing, they need to become familiar with growth charts and with plotting their positions on the chart. Understanding their relationship to others may provide insights about why their performance or health status differs from that of their peers. A number of procedures may be used to monitor the physical growth and development of youth. The following is one of the more popular methods used to chart height and weight.

## The NCHS Physical Growth Chart

(Ross Laboratories, 1982)

*Purpose:* To plot the growth of youth 2 to 18 years of age.

*Description:* Two charts are available, one for boys and one for girls. The most recent version was adapted from Hamill, Drizd, Johnson, Reed, Roche, and Moore (1979) and produced by Ross Laboratories (1982). Figures 5.30 and 5.31 depict the growth charts for boys and girls, respectively.

*Instructions:* Locate the student's age line on the bottom of the chart and plot the weight and height on the respective portions of the chart. Determine the percentile equivalent for height and weight by simple interpolation procedure.

*Validity:* The charts were developed after many years of studying the growth patterns of youth.

*Reliability:* None reported.

*Age Level:* Ages 2–18.

*Test Area:* Small room.

*Equipment Needed:* Accurate scale and tape measure.

*Scoring Procedure:* Record weight to nearest pound and height to nearest 1/2 inch.

*Norms:* Figures 5.30 and 5.31 show percentile equivalents.

**FIGURE 5.30**   Boys ages 2 to 18 years, physical growth NCHS percentiles.

Name _____ Record #_____

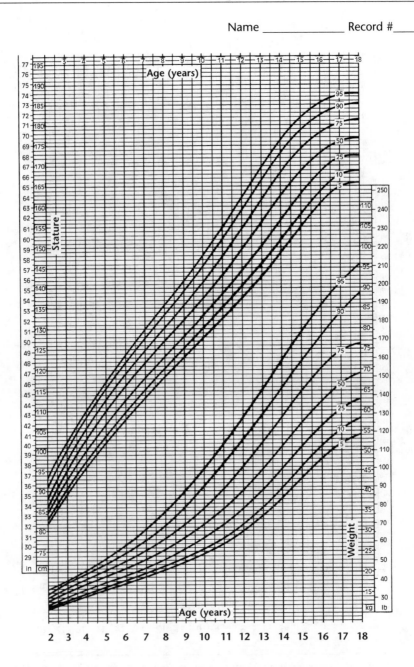

### ◢ FIGURE 5.31   Girls ages 2 to 18 years, physical growth NCHS percentiles.

Name _____ Record #_____

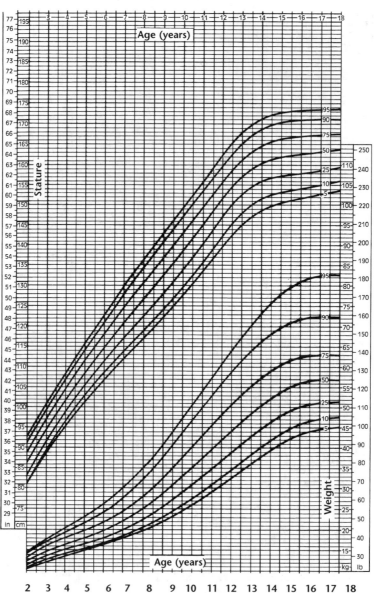

***Organizational Hints:*** This assessment should be conducted at the same time other testing procedures are being administered. Often, a school nurse is responsible for taking these measurements. Arrangements can sometimes be made for the nurse to maintain records of the students and identify those who appear to exhibit disproportionate growth patterns.

## VALUING AND ASSESSING THE PROCESS OF PHYSICAL ACTIVITY

Physical inactivity contributes to more than 250,000 deaths each year. Based on a wealth of information, the American Heart Association now lists a sedentary lifestyle as an official major risk factor for coronary heart disease. As might be expected, increased levels of habitual physical activity are associated with lower all-cause death rates. Even so, only one in four adult Americans is active at the level recommended for health benefits (ACSM, 1993). Recent evidence suggests that teenagers are not as active as children. In fact, one study reported that teenagers are less active than they were 10 years ago (Centers for Disease Control, 1992). And, even at the elementary school there are concerns about the activity level of children (Ross, Pate, Caspersen, Damberg, and Svilar, 1987).

Regardless of age, physical activity influences the degree of health-related physical fitness. The extent to which it directly affects health fitness depends on a number of factors. Some variables, such as heredity, growth, development, and diet, to name a few, are nearly impossible for the practitioner to consider in the typical health fitness evaluation. It is unwise to merely deduce that because a youngster demonstrates health fitness she must be active. Physical activity generally increases health-related fitness, but the idea that activity builds fitness may lead teachers or exercise practitioners to believe that individuals who score well on fitness tests are active and those who do not score well are inactive (Pangrazi and Corbin, 1993).

Because of this relationship, it is increasingly more important to devote attention to valuing and assessing the process of physical activity. If physical educators are attempting to promote an active lifestyle among students, then there must be a means to measure the results of their efforts. Similarly, if an adult exercise leader wants to increase the exercise habits of participants, there need to be mechanisms in place to assess and evaluate the behaviors of these individuals. These tactics can be stand-alone efforts or woven into the fabric of a health related physical fitness test.

Following are some suggestions and recommendations that incorporate the assessment of physical activity into the evaluation of health related physical fitness.

## Physical Education Environment

1. Fitness experiences and testing should help students clearly understand the relationship between good health fitness and physical activity. Employ strategies that encourage activity and participation.

2. Criterion-referenced standards should be emphasized rather than normative standards that compare students to each other. Criterion referenced standards that convey a level of health allow students to decide whether they need to alter their physical activity in order to improve their health fitness.

3. Avoid concluding that low fitness scores mean that the student is inactive. The result of this may negatively influence youngsters' self-esteem and deter them from activity.

4. Work with students to help them assess their level of activity outside the school. Activities such as keeping an activity diary of type and extent of exercise, using computer programs to calculate caloric consumption and expenditure, and following a specially designed fitness regime are examples of measurable homework activities that students can complete for physical education. By doing so, individuals will be able to ascertain a pattern of behavior over time. This is useful for individuals to better understand their actual activities, thus enhancing their decision-making process.

5. Consider employing a self-testing procedure. This allows students an opportunity to work together to develop fitness profiles. The goal is to teach students the process of fitness testing so they will be able to evaluate their health status during adulthood (Pangrazi and Corbin, 1993).

## Exercise Science Environment

1. Utilize computer technology to assist adults in recording, monitoring, and analyzing their physical activity patterns and other healthy lifestyle behaviors.

2. Encourage exercise participants to assess and evaluate the frequency, intensity, and duration of their physical activity to ensure that fitness benefits are derived.

3. Provide older youth and adults with quantitative information that portrays the value of physical activity in positively altering health related fitness factors.

4. Teach self-testing and monitoring techniques that assist the client in participating in physical activity that is of at least moderate intensity.

5. Help participants understand the influence that extraneous factors (i.e., heredity, social and physical environment, and lifestyle) have on health-related fitness performance.

# SUMMARY

This chapter reviews the components of health-related physical fitness and summarizes selected field-based tests designed to measure cardiorespiratory fitness, muscular strength, flexibility, and body composition. Summaries for respective tests include purpose, instructions for test administration, validity and reliability, age level, test area, equipment needed, scoring procedure, norms, and organizational hints. The tests cited in this chapter are appropriate for youth of all ages, require little expense, and can be administered in most school settings. In addition, this chapter discusses the practice of valuing and assessing the process of physical activity. It presents suggestions and recommendations that incorporate the assessment of physical activity into the evaluation of health related physical fitness.

## ▶ DISCUSSION QUESTIONS

1. What test items would you select for assessing components of health-related physical fitness? What factors would influence your decision?

2. Identify the factors that should be considered before administering tests of cardiorespiratory fitness, muscular strength, flexibility, and body composition.

3. How frequently would you test students to measure components of health-related physical fitness? Could students administer any of these tests (i.e., self testing)? How would self-tests or peer assessment affect the validity and reliability of a test?

4. What sites would you select for determining body composition? Why? What caliper would you select? Why?

5. Would you report skinfold scores in millimeters or convert to percentage of body fat? Explain.

6. Describe the importance of valuing a healthy lifestyle. What strategies can be used in the assessment process to promote the importance of being physically active.

## ▶ REFERENCES

American Alliance for Health, Physical Education, Recreation and Dance. (1980). *Health related physical fitness test manual.* Reston, VA.

_____. (1984). *Technical manual: Health related physical fitness.* Reston, VA.

_____. (1988). *Physical best: The American Alliance physical fitness education and assessment program.* Reston, VA.

American College of Sports Medicine. (1978). The recommended quantity and quality for developing and maintaining fitness in healthy adults. *Medicine and Science in Sports* 10:vii–x.

American College of Sports Medicine (1993). *The Role of Physical Activity and Prevention in Health Care Reform in the United States.* Presented to House Ways and Means

Subcommittee in Health, October 26, 1993.

American Health and Fitness Foundation, Inc. (1986). *FYT-FIT youth today.* Austin, TX.

Askew, N. (1966). Reliability of the 600-yard run/walk test at the secondary school level. *Research Quarterly* 37:451–54.

Baumgartner, T. A.; East, W. B.; Frye, P. A.; Hensley, L. D.; Knox, D. F.; and Norton, C. J. (1984). Equipment improvements and additional norms for the modified pull-up test. *Research Quarterly for Exercise and Sport* 55:64–68.

Berger, R. A. (1966). Evaluation of the 2-minute sit-up test as a measure of muscular endurance and strength. *Journal of the Association for Physical and Mental Rehabilitation* 20:140.

Blair, S.; Kuhl, H.; Pattenbarger, R.; Clark, D.; Cooper, K.; and Gibbons, L. (1989). Physical fitness and all-cause mortality: A prospective study of healthy men and women. *Journal of the American Medical Association* 262:2395–2401.

Breslow, L., and Enstrom, J. E. (1980). Persistence of health habits and their relationships to mortality. *Preventive Medicine* 9:469–83.

Burris, B. (1970). *Reliability and validity of the twelve-minute run test for college women.* Paper presented at AAHPERD Convention, Seattle, WA.

Buxton, D. (1957). Extension of the Kraus-Weber test. *Research Quarterly* 28(3):210–17.

Cooper Institute for Aerobics Research (1994). The *Prudential FITNESSGRAM: Test Administration Manual.* Dallas, TX: Cooper Institute for Aerobics Research.

Corbin, C. B., and Lindsey, R. (1990). *Concepts of physical fitness with laboratories.* 6th ed. Dubuque, IA: William C. Brown.

Cotton, D. J., and Marwitz, B. (1971). Relationship between two flexed-arm hangs and pull-ups for college women. *Research Quarterly* 40:415–16.

Cureton, T. K. (1941). Flexibility as an aspect of physical fitness. *Research Quarterly Supplement* 12:388–89.

Doolittle, T. L.; Dominic, J. C.; and Doolittle, J. (1969). The reliability of selected cardiorespiratory endurance field tests with adolescent female populations. *American Corrective Therapy Journal* 23:135–38.

Forbes, J. M. (1950). *Characteristics of flexibility of boys.* Unpublished doctoral dissertation, University of Oregon, Eugene.

Fox, A., and Skinner, J. (1964). Physical activity and cardiovascular health. *American Journal of Cardiology* 14:31–46.

Fox, E. L., and Mathews, D. K. (1981). *The physiological basis of physical education and athletics.* 3d ed. Philadelphia, PA: Saunders College Publishing.

Gilliam, T. B.; Katch, V. L.; Thorland, W. G.; and Weltman, A. W. (1977). Prevalence of coronary heart disease risk factors in active children 7 to 12 years of age. *Medicine and Science in Sports* 9(1):21–25.

Godfrey, K. E.; Kindig, L. E.; and Windell, E. J. (1977). Electromyographic study of duration of muscle activity in sit-up variations. *Archives of Physical Medicine and Rehabilitation* 58:132–35.

Hahn, R. A., Teutsch, S. M., Rothenberg, R. B. and Marks, J. S. (1986). Excess deaths from nine chronic diseases in the United States. *Journal of the American Medical Association.* 264:2654–2659.

Hamill, P. V. V., et al. (1979). Physical growth: National Center for Health Statistics Percen-tiles. *American Journal of Clinical Nutrition* 32:607–29.

Heyward, V. H. (1984). *Designs for fitness.* Minneapolis, MN: Burgess.

Institute for Aerobics Research and Campbell's Soup. (1986). *FITNESSGRAM.* Dallas, TX: Institute for Aerobics Research.

Jackson, A. S., and Pollock, M. L. (1976). Factor analysis and multivariate scaling of anthropometric variables for the assessment of body composition. *Medicine and Science in Sports* 8:196–203.

Jackson, A. S., and Smith, L. (1974). *The validation of an evaluation system for weight training.* Presented at AAHPERD Conference, March 1977, Anaheim, CA.

Johnson, B. L., and Nelson, J. K. (1986). *Practical measurements for evaluation in physical education.* 4th ed. Minneapolis, MN: Burgess.

Kasch, F. W., and Boyer, J. L. (1968). *Adult fitness: Principles and practices.* Palo Alto, CA: Mayfield Publishing.

Kendall, F. P. (1965). A criticism of current tests and exercises for physical fitness. *Physical Therapy* 45:187–97.

Kraus, H., and Hirschland, R. (1954). Minimum muscular fitness tests in school children. *Research Quarterly* 25:177–88.

Leger, L.; Mercier, D.; Gaderuz, C.; and Lambert, J. (1988). The multistage 20 metre shuttle run test for aerobic fitness. *Journal of Sport Sciences.* 6:93–101.

Leighton, J. (1942). A simple, objective and reliable measure of flexibility. *Research Quarterly* 13:205–16.

Lohman, T. G.; Boileau, R. A.; and Massey, B. H. (1975). Prediction of lean body mass in young boys from skinfold thickness and body weight. *Human Biology* 47: 245–62.

Manitoba Department of Education. (1977). *Manitoba physical fitness performance test manual and fitness objectives for Manitoba youth 5–18 years of age.* Winnipeg, Manitoba: Manitoba Department of Education.

Mathews, D. K.; Shaw, V.; and Bohnen, M. (1957). Hip flexibility of college women as related to length of body segments. *Research Quarterly* 28:352–56.

Mathews, D. K.; Shaw, V.; and Woods, J. B. (1959). Hip flexibility of elementary school boys as related to body segments. *Research Quarterly,* 30(3):297–302.

McArdle, W. D.; Katch, F. I.; and Katch, V. L. (1981). *Exercise physiology: Energy, nutrition, and human performance.* Philadelphia, PA: Lea and Febiger.

McGinnis, J. M. and Foege, W. (1993). Actual causes of death in the United States. *Journal of the American Medical Association* 270:2207–2212.

Nelson, J. K. (1976). Fitness testing as an educational process. In Jan Broekhoff, ed. *Physical education, sports and the sciences.* Eugene, OR: Microform Publications, pp. 65–74.

Paffenbarger, R. S., et al. (1977). Work energy level, personal characteristics and fatal heart attack: A birth-cohort effect. *American Journal of Epidemiology* 106:200–13.

_____. (1978). Physical activity as an index of heart attack risk in college alumni. *American Journal of Epidemiology* 108:161–75.

Patterson, M. L., and Nelson, J. K. (1976). Influence of an aquatic conditioning program on selected heart rate responses. *Proceedings of the international conference on underwater education.* Montclair, CA: National Association of Underwater Instructors.

Pollock, M. L. (1975). Prediction of body density in young and middle-aged women. *Journal of Applied Physiology* 38:745–49.

_____. (1976). Prediction of body density in young and middle-aged men. *Journal of Applied Physiology* 40:300–04.

Pollock, M. L.; Schmidt, D. H.; and Jackson, A. S. (1977). Body composition: Measurement and changes resulting from physical training. *Proceedings of the NCPEAM and NCPEAW,* Orlando, Florida.

Public Health Service. *Healthy People 2000: National health promotion and disease precaution objectives—full report with commentary.* Washinton, DC: U. S. Department of Health and Human Service, 1991, 101–103 [DHHS Publication #(PHS) 91–50212.]

Safrit, M. J. (1990). *Introduction to measurement in physical education and exercise science.* 2d ed. St. Louis, MO: Times Mirror/ Mosby.

Shaw, D. A. (1983). Back to back fitness. *Corporate Fitness and Recreation* 2:31–37.

Thomas, D. Q. and Whitehead, J. R. (1993). Body composition assessment—some practical answers to teachers' questions. *Journal of Physical Education, Recreation, and Dance.* May–June, pp. 16–19.

Toufexis, A. (1980). That aching back! *Time,* July 14, pp. 30–38.

Verducci, F. M. (1980). *Measurement concepts in physical education.* St. Louis, MO: C. V. Mosby.

Vitale, F. (1973). *Individualized fitness programs.* Englewood Cliffs, NJ: Prentice-Hall.

Walters, C. E., and Partridge, M. J. (1957). Electro-myographic study of the differential action of the abdominal muscles during exercise. *American Journal of Physical Medicine* 36:259–68.

## ▶ REPRESENTATIVE READINGS

American Alliance for Health, Physical Education, Recreation and Dance. (1976). *AAHPERD youth fitness test manual.* Reston, VA.

Baumgartner, T. A. (1978). Modified pull-up test. *Research Quarterly* 49:80–84.

Boileau, R. A.; Wilmore, J. H.; Lohman, T. G.; Slaughter, M. H.; and Riner, W. F. (1981). Estimation of body density from skinfold thicknesses, body circumference and skeletal widths in boys aged 8 to 11 years: Comparison of two samples. *Human Biology* 53:575–92.

Cooper, K. H.; Pollock, M. L.; Martin, R. P.; White, S. R.; Linnerud, A. C.; and Jackson, A. S. (1976). Physical fitness levels vs. selected coronary risk factors. *Journal of the American Medical Association* 236:166–69.

Cotton, D. J., and Marwitz, B. (1971). Relationship between two flexed-arm hangs and pull-ups for college women. *Research Quarterly* 40:415–16.

Falls, H. B.; Baylor, A. M.; and Dishman, R. K. (1980). *Essentials of fitness.* Philadelphia, PA: Saunders College.

Gibbons, L. W.; Blair, S. N.; Cooper, K. H.; and Smith, M. (1983). Association between coronary heart disease risk factors and physical fitness in healthy adult women. *Circulation* 67:977–83.

Going, S. B. and Lohman, T. G. (1990). The skinfold test—a response. *Journal of Physical Education, Recreation, and Dance,* October, pp. 74–78.

Harsha, D. W.; Fredrichs, R. R.; and Berenson, G. S. (1978). Densitometry and anthropometry of black and white children. *Human Biology* 50:261–80.

Hastad, D. N. (1986). Physical fitness for elementary school children. *Thresholds in Education* 12:12–14.

Hastad, D. N.; Marett, J. R.; and Plowman, S. A. (1983). *Evaluation of the health related physical fitness status of youth in the state of Illinois.* Dekalb, IL: Northern Illinois University.

Hockey, R. V. (1985). *Physical fitness: The pathway to healthful living.* 5th ed. St. Louis, MO: Times Mirror/Mosby.

Jenson, C. R., and Hirst, C. C. (1980). *Measurement in physical education and athletics.* New York: Macmillan.

_____. (1974) *Skinfold thickness of children 12–17 years.* Series II, No. 132. Washington, DC: U.S. Center for Health Statistics.

Johnson, F. E.; Hamill, D. U.; and Lemeshow, S. (1972). *Skinfold thickness of children 6–11 years.* Series II, No. 120. Washington, D.C.: U.S. Center for Health Statistics.

Katch, F. I., and Michael, E. D. (1986). Prediction of body density from skinfold and girth measurements of college females. *Journal of Applied Physiology* 26:92–94.

Krahenbuhl, G. R.; Pangrazi, R. P.; Burkett, L.; Schneider, M. J.; and Petersen, G. (1977). Field estimation of $VO_2$ max in children eight years of age. *Medicine and Science in Sports* 9:37–40.

Lohman, T. G.; Pollock, M. L.; Slaughter, M. J.; Brandon, L. J.; and Boileau, R. A. (1984). Methodological factors and the prediction of body fat in female athletes. *Medicine and Science in Sports and Exercise* 16:1, 92–96.

Miller, D. K. (1994). *Measurement by the physical educator: why and how.* 2nd ed. Dubuque, IA: Brown and Benchmark.

Pangrazi, R. P., and Dauer, V. P. (1995). *Dynamic physical education for elementary school children.* Boston: Allyn and Bacon.

Pangrazi, R. P., and Hastad, D. N. (1986). *Fitness in the elementary schools.* Reston, VA: American Alliance for Health, Physical Education, Recreation and Dance.

Parizkova, J. (1961). Total body fat and skinfold thickness in children. *Metabolism* 10:794–807.

Riley, J. H. (1990). A critique of skinfold tests from the public school level. *Journal of Physical Education, Recreation and Dance.* October, pp. 71–73.

Woods, P. D.; Haskell, W.; Klein, H.; Lewis, S.; Stern, M. P.; and Farquhar, J. (1976). The distribution of plasma lipoprotein in middle-aged male runners. *Metabolism* 25:1249–57.

# MEASURING THE PSYCHOMOTOR DOMAIN

**6**

agility
balance
body management competence
coordination
dynamic balance
fundamental skills
higher skill attainment
power
reaction time
skill-related physical fitness
    components
specialized skills
speed
static balance

▶ OBJECTIVES

*After reading this chapter, the student should be able to:*

1. Define psychomotor performance and cite fundamental skills associated with general motor ability and sports.
2. Describe the sequence in which children acquire physical skills.
3. Explain components of skill-related physical fitness and state examples of how each can be measured and evaluated.
4. Follow directions for administering selected tests to measure general motor ability, selected team sports skills, and individual sports skills.
5. Understand the characteristics associated with conducting assessment and evaluation in the psychomotor domain.

primary goal of physical education is to develop movement competence. As physical educators, we must recognize that the essence of physical activity is movement and our task is to teach students how to become skillful movers. Whether it is by providing learning experiences that teach kindergarten children fundamental locomotor movements, teaching middle school youngsters how to play racquet sports, or refining complex techniques associated with selected sports, one of the primary roles of the physical educator is to develop and improve performance in the psychomotor domain.

In the elementary school, children should learn how to competently manage their bodies and develop useful physical skills (Pangrazi and Dauer, 1992). The hierarchy of skill development depends on the early acquisition of fundamental movement competencies. There are four stages in this hierarchy, the first of which is body management competence. **Body management competence** is achieved when a child learns how to control the body in personal space, in general space in relation to others, and while working with an object or an apparatus. To accomplish this requires repeated opportunity for practice and for experimentation with a wide variety of basic movement challenges. After youngsters are able to effectively demonstrate appropriate body management using good standards of posture and body mechanics, they are ready to move into stage two of skill acquisition: fundamental skill development.

**Fundamental skills** are the basic skills that children require to function in their environment. Classified into three groups—locomotor, nonlocomotor, and manipulative—these skills are stressed in the primary grades and are periodically reviewed in the intermediate grades. Locomotor skills get the body from one place to another or propel the body upward in a vertical manner. The eight basic locomotor movements are walking, running, hopping, jumping, galloping, sliding, leaping, and skipping. Nonlocomotor movements are those executed in place, without appreciable movement or utilization of space. Examples of nonlocomotor movement include bending, twisting, swaying, shaking, and bouncing. Hand-eye or foot-eye skills in which an individual handles some kind of object with one or more body parts are referred to as manipulative skills. Manipulation of objects leads to better coordination and tracking skills, which are important to the development of specialized skills, the third stage of skill development.

**Specialized skills** are those used in sports and other units of activity taught in physical education. Rhythmic activities, gymnastics, swimming, individual sports, team sports, fitness routines, rope jumping, and so on are examples of areas that require a foundation of fundamental skills. Many of these skills have critical points of technique and strongly emphasize correct performance. Only after students have acquired specialized skills can they be successful in the fourth stage of skill development: higher skill attainment.

**Higher skill attainment** usually is accomplished after an individual possesses a firm foundation of body management, fundamental skills, and specialized skills and expresses a willingness to participate in activities that will further refine selected skills. Intramural sports, organized youth sports, and interschool competition are a few examples of areas in which children may seek higher skill attainment.

From a psychomotor perspective, most students in junior and senior high school require movement opportunities associated with stages three and four of the hierarchy of skill attainment. By the time a youngster makes the transition from the elementary school to the middle school, learning experiences in physical education to enhance psychomotor development should focus on specialized skills and higher skill attainment. Junior and senior high school physical educators should begin to counsel students on procedures and opportunities for developing physical skills outside the school program. As students' skill levels improve, so does their interest in voluntary participation in physical activity.

Students need to be aware that physical skill development is not easy and demands long, continuous effort before visible dividends are returned. The notion that skill attainment is easy must be discouraged. A more realistic premise that physical activity can be enjoyed throughout life and that skill practice will result in enhanced performance must be emphasized. The use of practical assessment techniques at all grade levels will assist the practitioner in evaluating students and will provide a basison which students can better view their progress toward higher skill attainment.

The relationship between physical skill development and physical fitness development may be confusing, especially to a beginning teacher. As we discussed earlier, physical fitness has taken on a multidimensional definition. To be more effective in meeting the needs of students, curricular decision making in physical education should offer students planned experiences throughout the K–12 period in both the health-related physical fitness domain and psychomotor domain. Chapter 5 focused on the health-related physical fitness domain by providing a definition of health-related physical fitness and a look at tests to measure and evaluate a student's health and physical well-being. This chapter is designed to do the same for the psychomotor domain. The remainder of this chapter provides a clear definition of skill-related physical fitness and its components and suggests practical tests of motor ability and sports skills. It is important to note that testing should not take priority over teaching. First and foremost, teachers and directors of activity programs need to focus energy and time on instruction. Measurement and evaluation are to be used to assist the instructional process, not detract from it.

# SKILL-RELATED PHYSICAL FITNESS

To be successful in sports requires more than an optimal level of health-related physical fitness. An individual must possess qualities of function that enable him to perform sports skills. Due to heredity, many individuals are predisposed to a certain level of skill-related fitness. This is particularly important to remember when determining grades based on skill assessment. The particular attributes that assist an individual in displaying athletic prowess, but are not related to the degree of functional health, are referred to as **skill-related physical fitness components**. Basketball, football, and baseball are some of the more obvious sports that require harmonious interaction among various body parts. To be successful at receiving a pass while driving for a lay-up, taking a pitch-out from the quarterback, or fielding a ground ball hit to deep shortstop requires coordination. While coordination is essential for performance of certain athletic skills, it is not related to the overall health and well-being of an individual. In addition to coordination, six components of skill-related physical fitness are also clearly related to sport performance but are not directly linked to the health of an individual. The assessment of these components is important as the physical educator makes ongoing evaluations of progress toward program and student goals:

**Agility** is the ability to rapidly and accurately change the position of the body in space. Springboard diving, wrestling, and dynamic gymnastic moves are examples of activities that require agility.

**Balance** is the maintenance of equilibrium while stationary or moving. Performing a handstand, walking a balance beam, and maintaining a stable position throughout the golf swing are examples of skills that require balance.

**Coordination** is the ability to simultaneously perform multiple motor tasks smoothly and accurately. Hitting a return in tennis, juggling several objects, batting a pitched baseball, or punting a football are examples of athletic skills that require coordination.

**Power** is the ability to exert maximum force in a minimum length of time. Weight lifting and football blocking are examples.

**Reaction time** is the duration between the stimulation and the response to the stimulation. A swimmer's response to the starting gun or a tennis player's reaction to a booming serve are examples of situations that require short reaction times.

**Speed** is the ability to perform a movement in a short period of time. It is advantageous for a sprinter on a track team or a wide receiver on a football team to possess speed.

## Uses of Skill-Related Physical Fitness Tests

Because a primary goal of the physical education program is to improve the physical skill of students, it makes sense that a majority of class time be dedicated to skill practice. Further, if most of the class time is devoted to skill practice, then testing should include measures of the skill components that have been practiced. The actual selection of a skills test may be decided on the basis of one or more selected criteria. Considerations in using and selecting skills tests are as follows:

1. Validity and reliability. As discussed in previous chapters, two of the primary criteria in selecting a test are validity and reliability. If a particular test is the most valid and reliable instrument representing the skill that the teacher wants to measure, then it should be used.

2. Classifying students into learning groups. Placing students of similar abilities together for practice sessions is considered an appropriate teaching strategy. Homogenous grouping permits more desirable teaching situations from the standpoint of practice through drilling. Lessons then can be planned with the strengths and weaknesses of all students in class considered. Having students work with classmates of similar abilities allows for individualized instruction and facilitates skill improvement and a positive learning situation. The teacher is able to structure situations that challenge students of varying abilities, and students are placed in a setting in which they are working with someone of similar ability. And as we know, playing against someone who is far better, or worse, does little to enhance skill or foster a positive attitude toward that particular activity. Youngsters appreciate fairness, enjoy competing with other students of similar athletic ability, and favor homogenous grouping (Lockhart and Mott, 1951).

3. Inclusion in a comprehensive test of skill-related physical fitness. Oftentimes physical educators want to obtain a composite profile of motor skill performance. Although several test batteries measure general motor ability, in most instances some items of a test battery are not related to skills taught in a particular unit of instruction. When this is the case, instructors may wish to utilize individual tests that measure skills emphasized in class. Each test selected becomes part of a more useful whole.

4. Assessing performance to predict potential in different sport activities. There may be youths who do not realize their potential for success in sport and/or athletics. The results of assessment may help them recognize their innate potential. Armed with this information, a youngster may feel more confident about seeking participation in interschool or intraschool sport competition.

5. Motivating students to higher levels of skill performance. Youth can be motivated to achieve through knowledge of results and goal setting. The results of skill assessment can serve to provide the quantitative base upon which students monitor their progress. Trying to set a personal best on a test is a typical response of youth. The motivation to excel is greatly diminished unless a previous score or a criterion is available.

6. Determining student achievement and grades. As in other subject areas, testing may be used in physical education to monitor progress and assist in grading.

7. Developing class profiles. The content of yearly programs in physical education does not change much from one year to the next. Modifications in learning experiences are usually in response to recent research findings, state mandates, and new ideas. Since much of what a physical educator does is repeated on an annual basis, it is sometimes helpful to use tests for the purpose of profiling student performance. Establishing a rudimentary form of a normative database can assist the instructor in evaluating the skill performance of students. Comparing classes from different years or sections on similar test items can provide information useful in evaluating, developing, maintaining, or modifying the program.

8. Measuring the effectiveness of a specific unit of instruction. A test designed to measure specific student outcomes will provide a quantifiable appraisal of the effectiveness of instruction. Student learning, the primary goal of all teachers, can only be measured and monitored through assessment.

9. Diagnosing injury or deficiency. Some tests of skill can be used to determine the level of function associated with a particular aspect of skill-related physical fitness. Motor skill deficiencies apparent in the instructional setting may be more objectively viewed after an assessment session. Diagnosing a youngster's weaknesses in motor skill performance can assist in developing a series of meaningful and appropriate learning experiences.

10. As a teaching aid to supplement class instruction. Testing should be an educational experience. Once students become familiar with the test procedures they can periodically conduct their own self-tests, which allows them to monitor performance at their convenience. Teachers can even require students to complete tests during nonclass time. Many skill tests can be completed without the aid of an instructor and can be used as educational tools.

11. Explaining the physical education program to various publics. In this era of accountability, the use of test results to explain a program to various constituencies is crucial. Parents, administrators, and other groups can better understand the strengths and weaknesses of a program if it can be explained in quantifiable terms. Tests that have a normative database may help describe the effectiveness of the program. Comparing the performance of students on a specific skills test with other students of the same age and sex may be more easily understood by noneducators and nonphysical educators than simply reporting scores.

From the preceding list, we have seen that tests of skill-related physical fitness may be used for many purposes. It is important that any testing be used in a humane manner. Students should not feel undue pressure to perform at a high level. Rather, they should be encouraged to participate and demonstrate improvement. Regardless of the reason that tests are being used, physical education teachers have the opportunity to select and administer many different types of motor skills tests. The following sections provide a wide variety of skills tests designed to assess the various components of skill-related physical fitness.

## Measuring Agility

Agility enables an individual to rapidly and precisely alter the position and direction of the body and is an important ingredient for success in a wide variety of sports. Racquetball, for instance, requires participants to make sudden changes in court positioning in response to the ball coming off the wall. A basketball player must possess agility to guard an opponent. In soccer, a player must constantly be prepared to change direction in order to move with the ball.

Traditionally, agility has been viewed as inexorably linked to heredity. To a certain extent, this is a valid assumption. However, research has confirmed that agility may be improved through practice, training, and instruction (Bennett, 1956). Findings from other research studies indicate a positive correlation between physical growth and agility in boys and girls at the primary grade level (Seils, 1951). As children get older this linear relationship between agility and growth continues in boys, but reverses in girls. At about 14 years of age, girls' agility begins to decline, while boys begin to make significant gains (Espenschade, 1947). Thus, a person's level of agility is probably a combined result of heredity, training, and experience.

An agile person can quickly and efficiently mobilize the large muscle groups of the body in order to make rapid changes in direction of movement. These rapid changes in movement have been measured by such tests as zig-zag runs, side-steps, and obstacle runs. Agility assumes a vital role in predicting the success of an individual in sport and physical activity. Through appropriate testing, the physical educator can determine which students are most agile and which ones require additional practice to better perform an activity.

The following are examples of field-based tests that may be used by the practitioner to measure agility.

### Illinois Agility Run

(Cureton, 1951)

*Purpose:* The purpose of this test is to measure the agility.

*Description:* The Illinois Agility Run is a valid and reliable means of assessing agility. It is relatively easy to administer and requires little equipment and set-up. Figure 6.0 depicts the layout of the test area and appropriate floor markings.

*Instructions:* The student assumes a prone position with hands at the sides of the chest and on the starting line. On the command "Go," the student stands up and sprints 30 feet to the first turning point. At the turning point, with at least one foot crossing the turning point, the student reverses direction and sprints diagonally back toward the starting line. After reaching the starting line, the student begins to zig-zag through the chairs in such a way so as to return to the starting line. Upon completing the zig-zag through the chairs, the student sprints toward the final turning point. At this point, a stop and reverse is repeated and the student runs full speed across the finish line.

*Validity:* Correlation coefficients ranging from .33 to .46 were obtained with other measures of agility (Cureton, 1947; O'Connor and Cureton, 1945).

*Reliability:* The reliability coefficients ranged from .77 to .92, which suggest a high degree of consistency (Cureton, 1947; O'Connor and Cureton, 1945).

*Age Level:* Ages 6–adult.

*Test Area:* Any smooth flat area spacious enough to accommodate the movement.

◤ **FIGURE 6.0**    Diagram for Illinois agility run.

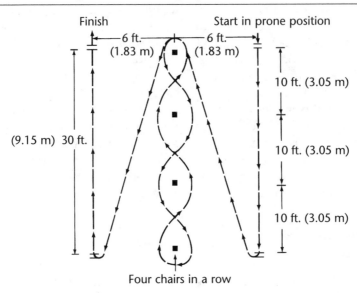

Four chairs in a row

From Thomas K. Cureton, *Physical Fitness of Champion Athletes.* Urbana, IL: University of Illinois Press, 1951, p. 68. Reprinted by permission.

*Equipment Needed:* Four chairs and a stopwatch.

*Scoring Procedure:* The time to the nearest half second is recorded as the student's score. If time permits, the best of three trials should be considered the score.

*Norms:* Standard score tables are available for young boys ages 7–13 and high school girls in Cureton (1964) and O'Connor and Cureton (1945), respectively.

*Organizational Hints:* Students should be given time to become acquainted with the path of the test. The test should be taken in court shoes or bare feet.

## Side-Stepping

(State of North Carolina, 1977)

*Purpose:* The purpose of this test is to measure agility.

*Instructions:* Two parallel lines are marked on the floor 12 feet apart. The student assumes a starting position with one foot touching one of the lines. On the command "Go," the student moves sideward with a side-step (sliding) toward the other line. Once the lead foot has crossed the other line, the student repeats the action back to the starting line and continues back and forth until time is called. The student must face the same direction throughout the test and the feet must not cross.

*Validity:* Face validity is assumed.

*Reliability:* Not reported.

*Age Level:* Ages 6–adult.

*Test Area:* Any smooth flat area is suitable.

*Equipment Needed:* Tape to mark the lines and a stopwatch.

*Scoring Procedure:* One point is scored each time the student touches a line. The total number of lines touched in 30 seconds is recorded as the score.

*Norms:* Normative tables for this test can be found in Table 6.0.

*Organizational Hints:* Utilizing an assistant to count lines touched and record the score is helpful.

## Squat Thrust

*Purpose:* The purpose of this test is to measure how fast the position of the body can be changed.

*Instructions:* The student assumes a standing position. On the signal to start, the student moves to a squat position (Count 1), a front leaning rest

**TABLE 6.0**  Percentile norms for side-step.*

**BOYS**

| Percentile | 9 | 10 | 11 | 12 | 13 | 14 | 15 | 16 | 17 |
|---|---|---|---|---|---|---|---|---|---|
| 95 | 19 | 19 | 20 | 21 | 23 | 23 | 25 | 23 | 26 |
| 90 | 17 | 18 | 19 | 19 | 21 | 21 | 23 | 22 | 25 |
| 85 | 16 | 17 | 18 |  | 20 |  | 22 | 21 | 23 |
| 80 | 15 |  | 17 | 18 | 19 | 20 | 21 | 20 | 22 |
| 75 |  | 16 |  |  |  |  | 20 |  | 21 |
| 70 |  | 16 | 16 | 17 | 18 | 19 |  |  |  |
| 65 | 14 | 15 |  | 16 |  |  | 19 | 19 | 20 |
| 60 |  | 15 | 15 | 16 | 17 | 18 |  |  |  |
| 55 | 13 | 14 | 14 |  | 17 | 18 | 18 | 18 | 19 |
| 50 |  |  |  | 15 |  |  | 18 |  | 18 |
| 45 |  |  | 14 |  | 16 | 17 |  | 17 | 18 |
| 40 | 12 | 13 |  | 14 |  |  | 17 |  | 17 |
| 35 | 11 | 13 | 13 | 14 | 15 | 16 | 16 | 16 | 17 |
| 30 | 11 | 12 |  | 13 | 14 | 15 | 16 | 16 | 16 |
| 25 | 10 | 12 | 12 | 13 | 14 | 15 | 15 | 15 | 16 |
| 20 | 10 | 11 | 11 | 12 | 13 | 14 | 15 | 15 | 15 |
| 15 | 9 | 10 | 11 | 12 | 13 | 14 | 14 | 14 | 14 |
| 10 | 8 | 9 | 10 | 11 | 11 | 13 | 13 | 13 | 12 |
| 5 | 7 | 8 | 8 | 9 | 10 | 11 | 11 | 10 | 10 |

**GIRLS**

| Percentile | 9 | 10 | 11 | 12 | 13 | 14 | 15 | 16 | 17 |
|---|---|---|---|---|---|---|---|---|---|
| 95 | 18 | 19 | 21 | 20 | 20 | 21 | 21 | 21 | 21 |
| 90 | 16 | 17 | 18 | 18 | 19 | 19 | 20 | 19 | 20 |
| 85 | 15 | 16 | 17 | 18 | 18 | 18 | 19 | 18 | 18 |
| 80 |  |  | 16 | 17 | 17 | 18 | 18 | 17 | 19 |
| 75 |  | 15 |  |  | 17 | 17 | 17 | 17 | 18 |
| 70 | 14 |  | 15 | 16 |  |  | 17 |  |  |
| 65 |  |  |  |  | 16 | 16 |  | 16 | 16 |
| 60 |  | 14 |  |  |  | 16 |  |  | 16 |
| 55 | 13 |  | 14 | 15 |  |  | 16 |  |  |
| 50 |  | 13 |  |  |  |  |  | 15 |  |
| 45 |  |  | 13 | 14 | 15 | 15 | 15 | 15 | 15 |
| 40 | 12 |  |  |  |  |  | 15 |  |  |
| 35 |  | 12 |  | 13 |  |  |  | 14 |  |
| 30 | 11 |  | 12 |  | 14 |  |  | 13 | 14 |
| 25 |  | 11 |  | 12 | 13 | 14 | 14 | 12 | 13 |
| 20 | 10 |  | 11 |  | 12 | 13 | 13 | 11 | 11 |
| 15 | 9 | 10 | 10 | 11 | 11 | 12 | 11 | 10 | 11 |
| 10 | 8 | 9 | 9 | 8 | 10 | 11 | 10 | 9 | 10 |
| 5 | 7 | 7 | 7 |  |  |  |  |  |  |

*Gaps (spaces with no numbers) indicate same number as above gap applies.

Reprinted by permission of the North Carolina State Department of Public Instruction (1977), Raleigh, North Carolina.

position (Count 2), a squat position (Count 3), and returns to the starting position (Count 4). Figure 6.1 shows the sequence of the movement. This movement is repeated as rapidly as possible until the signal to stop is given.

***Validity:*** An *r* of .553 was reported for boys and .341 for girls.

***Reliability:*** A correlation coefficient of .92 has been reported.

***Age Level:*** Ages 10–adult.

▶ **FIGURE 6.1** Sequence for squat thrust.

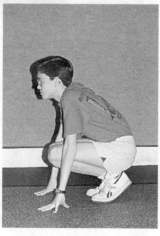

*Test Area:* Any smooth flat area free from debris is suitable for mass testing.

*Equipment Needed:* A stopwatch.

*Scoring Procedure:* Each movement is considered a part. For example, the squat position is counted as one, moving to the front-leaning rest position is two, and so on. The number of successfully executed movements completed in 10 seconds is recorded as the student's score.

*Organizational Hints:* Points may be deducted for improper execution of the movement, which includes the following: (1) moving the feet to the rear (or standing upright) before the hands are placed flat on the floor, (2) failing to assume a front leaning rest position (i.e., swayed back or piked position), and (3) assuming a nonerect standing position with the head down.

## Shuttle Run
(AAHPER, 1976)

*Purpose:* The purpose of this test is to measure speed and agility.

*Description:* This test assesses those components of skill fitness requiring quick and accurate movement of muscles.

*Instructions:* Two blocks of wood 2 inches by 2 inches by 4 inches are placed side by side on a line 30 feet from the starting line. On command to start, the student runs from behind the starting line to retrieve one of the blocks. After placing it behind the starting line, the student runs to pick up the second block and carries it back across the starting line. Two trials are given, with rest allowed between them.

*Validity:* Face validity is assumed.

*Reliability:* Not reported in the AAHPER booklet.

*Age Level:* Ages 9–adult.

*Test Area:* Any smooth flat area free of debris is suitable for administering this test.

*Equipment Needed:* Marking tape, a stopwatch, and two blocks of wood2 inches by 2 inches by 4 inches.

*Scoring Procedure:* The time taken to correctly retrieve both blocks is recorded in seconds to the nearest tenth. The better time of the two trials is reported as the student's score.

*Norms:* Criterion-referenced norms for this test can be found in Table 6.1.

*Organizational Hints:* Dropping or throwing a block disqualifies the subject for that particular trial. Youngsters should be given adequate time to warm up prior to taking this test.

▶ **TABLE 6.1** Criterion-referenced standards (85th percentile) for shuttle run: boys and girls ages 10–17.

| BOYS | | GIRLS | |
|---|---|---|---|
| Age | Shuttle Run | Age | Shuttle Run |
| 10 | 10.4 sec. | 10 | 10.8 sec. |
| 11 | 10.3 sec. | 11 | 10.6 sec. |
| 12 | 10.0 sec. | 12 | 10.5 sec. |
| 13 | 9.9 sec. | 13 | 10.5 sec. |
| 14 | 9.6 sec. | 14 | 10.4 sec. |
| 15 | 9.4 sec. | 15 | 10.5 sec. |
| 16 | 9.2 sec. | 16 | 10.4 sec. |
| 17 | 9.1 sec. | 17 | 10.4 sec. |

Reprinted by permission of the President's Council on Physical Fitness and Sports (1976), Washington, D.C.

## Measuring Balance

Balance is a vital component of efficient motor response and can be classified into two types, static and dynamic. **Static balance** is the ability to maintain equilibrium while in a stationary position. Remaining virtually motionless in a posed position while on the balance beam or standing on one's hands are examples of tasks requiring static balance. **Dynamic balance** is the ability to move through space in a steady and stable manner. Examples of movement requiring dynamic balance include activities such as tumbling, stunts, skating, and swimming. Both types of balance are important in everyday movement patterns and standing, as well as selected sports skills.

The ability to maintain balance is related to several factors. First of all, balance is a function of the mechanisms of the inner ear. These organs, called semicircular canals, affect the ability of an individual to maintain proper balance. Proper balance is also affected by an individual's ability to sense or "feel" the skill or movement. Many times we hear people say such things as, "She certainly has a feel for performing the floor exercise" or "He can't be knocked off his feet because of his exceptional balance." In these cases, it is likely that the persons in question do indeed have a kinesthetic sense for stability. Finally, balance is affected by visual perception. Those individuals who are able to visualize the body's position during a movement are more likely to maintain proper balance than those who cannot. Controlling and coordinating all these factors are essential to skills requiring balance.

Balance appears to be task-specific and differs from most other motor skills in that performance does not demonstrate marked improvement with age. Most studies of balance use static (one foot standing) and dynamic (beam walking) tests of balance. In the case of static balance ability usually increases with age. Research on the static balance abilities of children shows a linear trend toward improved performance from ages 2 through 12 (De Oreo, 1971; Van Slooten, 1973). Prior to age 2, children generally are not able to perform a one-foot static balance task, probably because of their still-developing abilities to maintain a controlled upright posture. De Oreo (1980) suggests that distinct boy-girl differences are not evident in static balance performance as with other motor performance tasks. In fact, girls tend to be more proficient in balance-related activities until about age 7 or 8, whereupon the boys catch up. Both sexes level off in performance around age 8, prior to a surge in abilities from ages 9 to 12. This increase, however, is small when compared to increases in other skills. Cratty and Martin (1969) found boys to be superior to girls in balance performance between the ages of 6 and 7, but no significant differences occurred beyond this age. Studies of dynamic balance also show only a slight improvement with age. Govatos (1966) and Keogh (1965) found that girls performed better than boys on tests of dynamic balance between the ages of 7 and 11.

A person who is able to maintain a stationary position or control the body while moving displays the characteristic of good balance, which is an important skill for participation in physical activity or sport. As such, ascertaining level of performance for balance may be useful for the physical educator. Examples of field-based tests that can be used by the physical educator to measure balance are provided in the following section.

## Stork Stand

**Purpose:** The purpose of this test is to measure the ability to balance in a stationary, upright position supported on the ball of the foot of the dominant leg.

**Description:** This is a test of static balance.

**Instructions:** The student stands erect on the dominant foot, placing the opposite foot flat on the medial (inside) part of the supporting knee, with the hands on hips. On the signal to begin, the subject raises the heel of the support foot off the floor and maintains this position as long as possible, as pictured in Figure 6.2.

Safrit (1990) describes a variation of this test in which the performers do not raise themselves on the ball of the foot.

**Validity:** Face validity is accepted.

**Reliability:** Test-retest reliability coefficients range from .85 to .87.

**Age Level:** Ages 6–adult.

▶ **FIGURE 6.2** Stork stand.

*Test Area:* Any smooth, flat area away from a wall is suitable for administration of this test.

*Equipment Needed:* Stopwatch.

*Scoring Procedure:* The highest of three trials is recorded to the nearest second.

*Norms:* Not available for K–12. Norms for college-age students are reported in Johnson and Nelson (1986).

*Organizational Hints:* This test also serves as a challenge activity to practice the skill of balancing. Subjects may be tested in pairs by having one person perform and the other monitor the seconds as they are called aloud by the test administrator.

### Johnson Modification of the Bass Test of Dynamic Balance
(Johnson and Leach, 1968)

*Purpose:* The purpose of this test is to measure the ability to maintain balance prior to, during, and after movement.

*Description:* This is a test to measure dynamic balance and is a modification of the Bass Test of Dynamic Balance (1939).

*Instructions:* Following the floor pattern shown in Figure 6.3 the subject assumes an upright position balancing on the right leg, leaps from starting line to mark #1, landing on the left foot, and balances on that foot as long as possible up to 5 seconds. The subject then leaps to mark #2, following the same process. This sequence is followed to the completion of the floor pattern.

*Validity:* An *r* of .46 was reported when this test was correlated with the Bass Test of Dynamic Balance (Johnson and Nelson, 1986).

*Reliability:* A test-retest reliability of .75 was reported for this test.

*Age Level:* High school to adult.

*Test Area:* Any smooth, flat area large enough to accommodate the floor pattern and free from wall space is appropriate.

*Equipment Needed:* Stopwatch, marking tape, and measuring tape.

◤ **FIGURE 6.3**   Layout for modified Bass dynamic balance test.

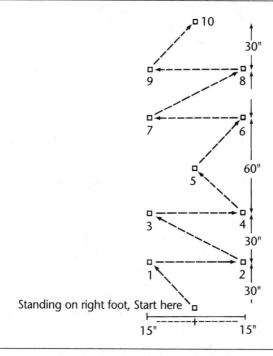

Reprinted with permission of Macmillan Publishing Company from *Practical Measurements for Evaluation in Physical Education* by Johnson and Nelson. Copyright © 1986 by Macmillan Publishing Company.

*Scoring Procedure:* Each mark successfully landed on earns five points. One point is scored for each second that the subject maintains balance on the mark, to a maximum of five seconds. Since there are 10 marks, it is possible to score 10 points per mark for a total of 100 points. The total number of points earned is recorded as the score. Penalty points are deducted for any of the following reasons:

1. Not stopping after landing on the mark
2. Touching the floor with a body part other than the supporting foot
3. Not covering the 1- by .75-inch tape mark with the supporting foot on landing
4. Moving the supporting foot while in a balanced position. If the subject loses balance, she should reposition herself on the proper marker before making the next leap.

*Norms:* Not reported for elementary and secondary school students.

*Organizational Hints:* The seconds elapsed during the balance phase of this test should be counted aloud. Scorecards that provide space for separate recording of the performance on each marker should be provided. Partners may be used to assist in recording the score as counted by the test administrator.

## Balance Beam Walk

(Jensen and Hirst, 1980)

*Purpose:* The purpose of this test is to measure the student's ability to balance while walking on a balance beam.

*Description:* This is a test of dynamic balance.

*Instructions:* The student is instructed to stand at one end of a four-inch-wide balance beam. When ready, the student begins to slowly walk (one foot in front of the other) the full length of the beam, pausing at the end for five seconds, turning 180 degrees, and returning to the starting point. Three trials are given.

*Validity:* Face validity is accepted.

*Reliability:* Not reported.

*Age Level:* Ages 6–adult.

*Test Area:* Any smooth, flat area with ample space to place the beam is suitable.

*Equipment Needed:* A standard balance beam.

*Scoring Procedure:* Pass-fail.

*Norms:* Not reported.

*Organizational Hints:* The participant should be encouraged to move at a steady pace. Using a low beam (4–6 inches off the ground) provides a safer setting than the typical Olympic-height beam.

## Measuring Coordination

Coordination is the ability to integrate separate motor systems with varying sensory modalities to produce efficient movement patterns (Gallahue, 1982). The more complex the movement pattern or sequence of patterns, the greater the degree of coordination necessary for successful performance. Although all movements use visual information in one way or another, some commonly accepted examples of gross visual-motor skills are throwing, catching, kicking, striking, and ball bouncing. Coordination is interrelated with other skill-related fitness components, such as balance, speed, reaction time, and agility, but not closely affiliated with muscular strength, endurance, or power. In sum, coordinated movement is that which is rhythmical, properly sequenced, and devoid of any superfluous actions.

Common movement patterns that require coordination are any skills that use foot-eye or hand-eye interaction. Each of these actions is characterized by incorporating visual information with some form of limb action. The success of the movement depends on the accuracy of the visual system. These skills usually involve an object such as a ball, bat, or racquet.

The development of coordinative skills is gradual, linearly related to age, and dependent on visual and motor maturation. Performance on tests of coordination tends to be superior for boys when compared to girls (Frederick, 1977; Van Slooten, 1973). Gross body coordination in children is associated with moving the body rapidly while performing various fundamental skills. Peterson et al. (1974) have reported a strong relationship among measures of the shuttle run, 30-yard dash, basic locomotor movement, and the standing long jump and gross body coordination. Charts depicting the various developmental stages associated with skills requiring coordination can be found in Corbin (1980), Gallahue (1982), Zaichkowsky, Zaichkowsky, and Martinek (1980) and other texts on motor development.

A person who displays coordination can hit a pitched ball, return a shot in badminton, catch a thrown ball on the run, harmoniously integrate multiple gross motor actions into a smooth movement pattern, and so on. Since it depends on maturation, the degree of coordination changes regularly and at times, rapidly. Carefully observing students performing fundamental skills during an instructional unit can assist the physical educator in evaluating the relative levels of coordination. Because of the interrelatedness of coordination with the skill components of balance, agility, reaction time, and speed, a physical education teacher can utilize results of tests in these areas to make evaluative statements regarding the level of coordination exhibited by students. A more effective means to assess coordination, however, is through selected test batteries that have been specifically designed to measure coordination. An example of a field-based test battery that can be used by the practitioner to measure coordination is discussed in the following section.

## Body Coordination Test

(Schilling and Kiphard, 1976)

*Purpose:* The purpose of this test battery is to measure total body control and coordination in children.

*Description:* This battery consists of four homogeneous subtests and was originally designed to identify motor retardation in children 5–14 years old.

### Test 1: Balance (Backward)

*Task:* Backward balancing, three times per beam.

*Equipment:* Three balance beams.

*Practice Trial:* Administrator demonstrates the task by walking forward and backward on the wide beam. The child has one practice trial walking forward and backward on each beam. When balance is lost on the practice trial the child steps back on the beam at that point and resumes the practice trial, covering the entire length of the beam.

*Test Trials:* After the practice trial on the appropriate beam, the tester asks the child to do as well as he or she can by going backward only (starting with the widest beam). There will be three trials per beam for a total of nine trials.

*Instructions:* "If you touch the floor with your foot you must start again from the beginning. Now begin going backward. I will count each step." The tester should call each step in a loud voice.

*Scoring Procedure:* One point is awarded for each backward step taken on the balance beam starting with the second step. The first step does not count. A maximum of 8 points can be awarded per trial. If the child travels the beam in less than 8 steps, 8 points are still awarded. Maximum score (3 beams × 3 trials × 8 points) = 72.

### Test 2: Hopping

*Task:* Hopping on one leg to and over foam blocks, maintaining balance.

*Equipment:* 12 foam rubber blocks, masking tape, tape measure.

*Practice Trials:* Administrator demonstrates task by hopping on one leg to a foam rubber block, hopping over it on the same leg and proceeding for at least two more hops (about 10 feet total). The children are shown that the blocks are soft. Two practice trials are allowed for each leg (five hops). A five-year-old child is given the practice trials without a block. If the child succeeds, one block is added for the first test trial. This rule applies separately for each leg. Children 6 years of age and older do two practice trials per leg, using one block. However, if the child fails the first practice trial, the block is removed. If the child succeeds, the appropriate number of blocks are added for the test trial.

*Test Trials:* A child starts the test trial at a block height determined by age and success on practice trials.

Starting levels:

5 years — 0 blocks
6 years — 1 block
7 and 8 years — 3 blocks
9 and 10 years — 5 blocks
11–14 years — 7 blocks

If a child seven years or older does not succeed at the starting height, the first trial is started using one block. A child is given three chances to perform the task.

*Instructions:* "Start hopping on one leg, hop over the blocks and hop at least two more times on the same leg. Do not touch the floor with your other leg."

*Scoring Procedure:* Three points are awarded each for levels 0–12 (13 levels) if the child succeeds on the first trial. Two points are awarded for success on the second trial and 1 point for success on the third trial. Failure occurs when (a) the opposite leg touches the floor, (b) the blocks are kicked over, or (c) after hopping over the pile, fewer than two hops are taken. The test is terminated when the child fails to accumulate 5 points on two successive trials. A maximum of 39 points may be awarded per leg for a total score of 78.

### Test 3: Lateral Jumping

*Task:* Lateral jumping as rapidly as possible for 15 seconds.

*Equipment:* Stopwatch and small wooden beam.

*Practice Trial:* Administrator demonstrates task by jumping laterally over the beam with two feet together. The student has five practice jumps.

*Instructions:* "Stand near the beam, feet together. On 'go,' jump across and back as quickly as possible until I say 'stop'." If the child touches the beam, the attempt is counted as successful; however, the child should be encouraged to try clearing the beam, feet together.

*Scoring Procedure:* Each jump across the beam (side A to side B) is worth one point. There are two trials, each across and back, with each lasting 15 seconds.

### Test 4: Lateral Movement

*Task:* Moving laterally as rapidly as possible.

*Equipment:* Two platforms (25 cm × 25 cm), stopwatch, masking tape.

*Practice Trials:* Administrator explains the position of the platforms (12.5 cm apart). The student steps on right platform, picks up the platform to the left using both hands, and places it on the right side. The student then steps on this platform and picks up the left platform, and so on. Allow one practice trial of three to five shifts emphasizing speed as well as the importance of proper positioning of the platform (for maximum scores). Note: If a child wishes to work toward the left it is permissible. Movement in a straight line should be encouraged.

*Test Trials:* Two trials, each of 20 seconds duration, are allowed with 70 seconds allowed between trials. The test administrator counts points aloud and assumes a position 7 to 10 feet from the child, moving laterally with the child.

*Instructions:* "Step on this platform. Take the other with both hands and place it on your other side. Now step on this platform. Do this as quickly as possible. I will count your score. Go when I say 'go' and stop when I say 'stop'."

*Scoring Procedure:* Score consists of shifts of the platform and shifts of the body within a 20-second time interval. The first point is awarded when the platform touches the floor at the right side of the body. The second point is awarded when the child has stepped on the "next" platform with both feet. A third point is given when the platform is placed on the right, and so on.

**Note:** If the child is distracted by noise, the trial is discontinued. If the child stumbles, falls, touches the floor with a hand or foot or takes the free platform with only one hand, the trial continues but no point is awarded for the error. The child should be encouraged to keep going on the task. The total score is the sum of the two trials.

*Validity:* Reported coefficients range from .50 to .60.

*Reliability:* The reliability of the individual test items ranges from .65 to .87. For the entire test, the reliability is .90, which suggests that the composite score should be used.

*Age Level:* Ages 6–14 years old.

*Test Area:* Classroom space or larger with ample area for four testing stations.

*Norms:* Not available.

# Measuring Speed and Reaction Time

Speed and quick reaction time are essential elements for successful performance in most sports skills. Speed is the ability to perform a movement in a short period of time. Reaction time is the time it takes to respond to a stimulus. Specifically, it is the elapsed time between the presentation of a stimulus and the movement of the body, body parts, or an object.

At first glance, speed and reaction time may seem to be two separate elements. While a sprinter may be slow getting out of the blocks in response to the starter's gun, he or she may be able to compensate with his or her sprinting ability. Similarly, a hitter in baseball may be slow on the base paths, but possess the reaction time to move the bat into position to hit a pitched ball. The instances that show the separateness of speed and reaction time are many; however, it is apparent that a relationship exists between speed and reaction time. Reaction time affects total speed of movement. A sprinter who reduces the time to get out of the blocks improves the total running time. A running back with quick reaction time improves his effectiveness by increasing his overall speed.

Speed of forward movement is generally measured through various tests of running speed. Running speed tends to increase as the child gets older, and generally sex differences favor boys. Frederick (1977) found that speed, as measured by the 20-yard dash, was linearly related to age in a group of 3- to 5-year-old children. Milne, Seefeldt, and Reuschlein (1976) reported that running speed varied among children in kindergarten through second grade, and boys' performance scores were significantly better than girls. Di Nucci (1976) found that age and sex differences favored boys on a number of running tasks with 6- to 8-year-olds. Keogh (1965) indicated that boys and girls were similar in running speed at ages 6 and 7, but boys were superior from age 8 to 12. Both boys and girls improve on measures of running speed until age 12, whereupon girls tend to level off in their performance and boys tend to continue improving throughout the adolescent years (AAHPER, 1976).

Reaction time has been found to decrease (get faster) in children as they get older. Cratty's (1979) review suggested that simple reaction time is approximately twice as long in 5-year-old children as it is in adults for an identical task and that there is rapid improvement in reaction time from age 3 to age 5. These differences in performance are likely due to maturation of the neurological mechanisms and differences in the information processing capabilities of children and adults. Fulton and Hubbard (1975) reported that reaction times of boys and girls ages 9 to 17 improved significantly with age, with girls demonstrating consistently faster times. Speed of movement also improved significantly with age, with boys being faster.

Speed, like reaction time, can be measured in the laboratory setting using sophisticated cinematography techniques or in field-based settings using reliable and valid tests. In most cases, the physical educator is not able to fund the expensive, technologically advanced equipment designed to measure speed and/or reaction time. Nevertheless, using some simple measuring devices (usually a stopwatch and meter stick), the physical educator can conduct meaningful and accurate assessment of the skill-related physical fitness components of speed and reaction time. Examples of field-based tests that can be used by the practitioner to measure speed and reaction time are provided in the following section.

### 50-Yard Dash

(AAHPER, 1976)

*Purpose:* The purpose of this test is to measure forward running speed.

*Description:* This is perhaps the most valid field test for predicting speed. Results can be used to establish ability groups on the basis of speed.

*Instructions:* The student assumes a ready position behind the marked starting line. The sequence for the command to start is (1) "Take your mark," (2) "Get set," (3) "Go." On the command "Go," the student runs 50 yards as fast as possible.

*Validity:* Construct validity has been established for this test.

*Reliability:* Test-retest reliability coefficients for this particular test ranged from .86 (Fleishman, 1964) to .94 (Jackson and Baumgartner, 1969).

*Age Level:* Ages 6–adult.

*Test Area:* A smooth, flat running area at least 75 yards in length, marked off with starting and finishing lines 50 yards apart, is suitable for this test.

*Equipment Needed:* Stopwatch and marking tape.

*Scoring Procedure:* The amount of time elapsed between the start and the moment the student crosses the finish line is the recorded score. Time is reported to the nearest tenth of a second.

*Norms:* This test is part of the AAHPER Youth Fitness Test Battery. Criterion-referenced norms for this battery are in Table 6.2.

*Organizational Hints:* The teacher should be positioned at the finish line and should simultaneously lower the arm from a raised position and shout "Go" to signal the start. Using an assistant to record the time (to the nearest tenth of a second) will allow more efficient test administration.

### Hand Reaction Time Test

*Purpose:* The purpose of this test is to measure the reaction time of the thumb and forefinger.

► **TABLE 6.2**   Criterion-referenced standards (85th percentile) for 50-yard dash: boys and girls ages 10–17.

| | BOYS | | GIRLS |
|---|---|---|---|
| Age | 50-Yard Dash | Age | 50-Yard Dash |
| 10 | 7.4 sec. | 10 | 7.5 sec. |
| 11 | 7.4 sec. | 11 | 7.6 sec. |
| 12 | 7.0 sec. | 12 | 7.5 sec. |
| 13 | 6.9 sec. | 13 | 7.5 sec. |
| 14 | 6.6 sec. | 14 | 7.4 sec. |
| 15 | 6.4 sec. | 15 | 7.5 sec. |
| 16 | 6.2 sec. | 16 | 7.5 sec. |
| 17 | 6.1 sec. | 17 | 7.5 sec. |

Reprinted by permission of the President's Council on Physical Fitness and Sports (1976), Washington, D.C.

*Description:* The test requires the student to react to a randomly dropped falling ruler by catching it with the thumb and forefinger.

*Instructions:* The student sits in a chair next to a table, with the elbow and lower arm resting on the table. The heel of the hand rests on the table so that only the fingers and thumb extend beyond the edge of the table. The test administrator holds the ruler from the very top, allowing the lower end of the ruler at the 1″ mark to dangle between the thumb and forefinger of the subject. The student is instructed to concentrate on the ruler. The test administrator signals "Ready." After this command the administrator has up to 10 seconds to release the ruler. Once the ruler is dropped, the student pinches the thumb and forefinger together as quickly as possible (see Figure 6.4). Twenty trials are administered.

*Validity:* Construct validity was established for this test.

*Reliability:* Johnson and Nelson (1986) reported a test-retest reliability coefficient of .89 for a similar test.

*Age Level:* Ages 6–adult.

*Test Area:* Any area large enough to comfortably accommodate the table and two chairs.

*Equipment Needed:* Ruler, chairs, and table.

*Scoring Procedure:* The point at which the top of the forefinger and thumb crosses the ruler is the initial value. One inch is subtracted from this reading on the ruler, since the starting position was at the one-inch line. The student's

▶ **FIGURE 6.4** Hand reaction.

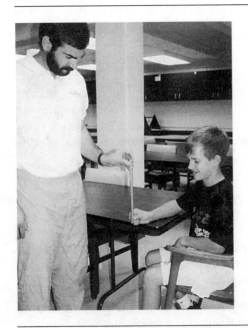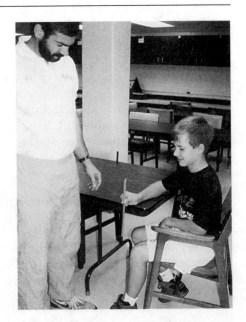

score is the sum of the middle 10 scores. The lower the total score, the faster the reaction time.

*Norms:* Not available.

*Organizational Hints:* When the ruler is positioned, it should not touch the thumb or index finger of the subject. The time between the ready command and ruler release should be varied.

## Test Batteries to Measure Skill-Related Physical Fitness

This section describes various batteries of tests designed to provide a composite picture of a student's performance on test items associated with the psychomotor domain. Theoretically, a comprehensive test to measure skill-related fitness would represent all factors that influence athletic performance. This, of course, is not the case. The sophistication and magnitude of such a test is unrealistic and, to date, not available. Nevertheless, test batteries are available that provide information about the performance of students on selected items of skill-related physical fitness. In general, the batteries cited comprise tests that measure performance in the areas of agility, balance, coordination, reaction time, and speed.

Tests described in this section were selected based on the criteria discussed in Chapter 4. The selected test batteries can be easily administered;

require little training; are economically feasible for the public school setting; measure traits that provide useful information to the student, teacher, and parents; have displayed longevity; and contain normative information. These are viable tools for any organization wishing to initiate an assessment protocol to profile the composite motor ability of students. The tests are functional and objective in measuring components of skill-related physical fitness. Teachers should consider program objectives and other variables (see Chapter 2) in selecting a battery that is appropriate for a particular situation. Examples of field-based test batteries that can be used by the physical educator to measure skill-related physical fitness are provided in the following section.

## North Carolina Motor Fitness Battery

(State of North Carolina, 1977)

*Purpose:* The purpose of this test battery is to measure achievement in the psychomotor domain. Specifically, individual tests measure components of strength, speed, endurance, agility, and power.

*Description:* This battery comprises five tests: sit-ups, side-stepping, standing broad jump, modified pull-ups, and squat thrust (Figure 6.5). Students should be divided into five groups and rotated from station to station so that no student will be utilizing the same muscle groups in succession.

*Validity:* Not reported. Face validity is assumed. Several test items are similar to other tests that have reported validity coefficients.

*Reliability:* Not reported for the test battery.

*Age Level:* Boys and girls ages 9–18.

*Norms:* Percentile norms are found in Tables 6.0 and 6.3–6.6 regarding test items.

*Test Area:* The entire test battery should utilize a mass testing format that has students rotating from station to station in a predetermined order. A large multipurpose room or gymnasium would provide appropriate space to administer this battery.

### Test 1: Sit-Ups

*Instructions:* The student lies on the back with fingers clasped behind the neck and elbows touching the floor. Knees should be flexed, feet flat on the floor, with a partner stabilizing the feet. The student sits up, turns the trunk, touches one elbow to the opposite knee, and returns to the starting position. This movement is repeated with the student alternately touching knees with opposite elbows. Students must be reminded to return to the original

▶ **FIGURE 6.5**   North Carolina motor fitness battery.

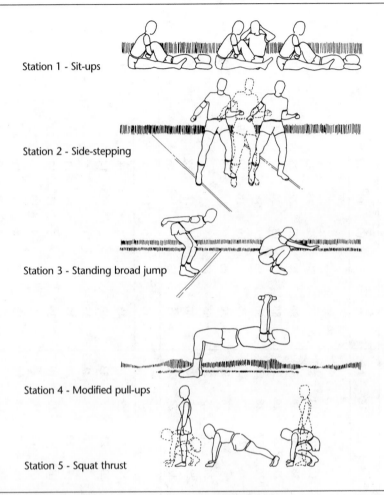

Station 1 - Sit-ups

Station 2 - Side-stepping

Station 3 - Standing broad jump

Station 4 - Modified pull-ups

Station 5 - Squat thrust

Reprinted by permission of the North Carolina State Department of Public Instruction, Raleigh, North Carolina.

starting position with the elbows touching the floor. Arching the back on the return should be discouraged (see Figure 6.5).

***Equipment Needed:*** Mat and stopwatch.

***Scoring Procedure:*** The score is the number of sit-ups correctly completed (returning to original down position) in 30 seconds.

***Organizational Hints:*** The test administrator can administer this test from a central position. To ensure uniformity in performance, students should have a chance to practice the test.

**TABLE 6.3** Percentile norms for sit-ups.

**BOYS**

| Percentile | Age 9 | 10 | 11 | 12 | 13 | 14 | 15 | 16 | 17 |
|---|---|---|---|---|---|---|---|---|---|
| 95 | 24 | 25 | 26 | 27 | 30 | 30 | 31 | 33 | 33 |
| 90 | 21 | 23 | 24 | 25 | 27 | 28 | 30 | 30 | 32 |
| 85 | 20 | 21 | 23 | 24 | 26 | 27 | 28 | 29 | 31 |
| 80 | 19 | 20 | 22 | 23 | 25 | 26 | 27 | 28 | 30 |
| 75 | 18 | 19 | 21 | 22 | 24 | 25 | 26 | 27 | 29 |
| 70 | 17 | 18 | 20 | 21 | 23 | 25 |    | 26 | 28 |
| 65 |    |    | 19 |    | 22 | 24 | 25 | 25 | 27 |
| 60 | 16 | 17 |    | 20 | 21 | 23 | 24 |    | 26 |
| 55 | 15 | 16 | 18 | 19 |    | 22 |    | 24 | 25 |
| 50 | 14 | 15 | 17 | 18 | 20 |    | 23 | 22 |    |
| 45 | 14 | 15 | 16 | 17 |    | 21 | 22 | 23 | 24 |
| 40 | 13 | 14 |    |    | 19 | 20 | 21 |    | 23 |
| 35 | 13 | 14 | 15 | 16 | 18 |    |    | 21 | 21 |
| 30 | 12 | 13 | 14 | 15 | 17 | 19 | 20 |    | 20 |
| 25 | 11 | 12 | 13 | 14 | 16 | 18 |    | 20 | 19 |
| 20 | 11 | 11 | 12 | 13 | 15 | 17 | 19 | 19 |    |
| 15 | 10 | 10 | 11 | 12 | 14 | 16 | 17 | 17 | 18 |
| 10 | 8 | 8 | 10 | 11 | 13 | 14 | 16 | 16 |    |
| 5 | 5 | 6 | 7 | 9 | 10 | 12 | 13 | 14 | 15 |

**GIRLS**

| Percentile | Age 9 | 10 | 11 | 12 | 13 | 14 | 15 | 16 | 17 |
|---|---|---|---|---|---|---|---|---|---|
| 95 | 20 | 22 | 23 | 25 | 25 | 25 | 25 | 24 | 23 |
| 90 | 19 | 20 | 22 | 23 | 23 | 23 | 23 | 22 | 22 |
| 85 | 17 | 18 | 20 | 21 | 21 | 22 | 22 | 21 | 20 |
| 80 | 16 | 17 | 19 | 20 | 20 | 21 | 21 | 20 | 20 |
| 75 | 15 | 16 | 18 | 19 | 19 | 20 | 19 | 19 |    |
| 70 | 15 |    | 17 | 18 | 18 | 19 |    | 18 | 19 |
| 65 | 14 | 15 | 16 |    | 17 | 18 | 18 | 17 |    |
| 60 | 13 | 14 | 15 | 17 | 17 | 18 |    |    | 18 |
| 55 | 13 |    | 15 | 16 |    |    |    | 16 |    |
| 50 | 13 | 14 | 15 | 16 | 16 | 17 | 17 | 16 | 17 |
| 45 | 12 | 12 | 13 | 15 | 15 | 16 | 16 | 15 |    |
| 40 | 11 | 11 | 13 | 14 | 15 | 16 | 15 | 14 | 16 |
| 35 |    | 11 |    | 13 | 15 | 15 | 15 | 14 |    |
| 30 | 10 | 10 | 12 | 13 | 14 | 14 |    | 13 | 15 |
| 25 |    |    | 11 | 12 | 13 | 14 | 14 | 12 | 13 |
| 20 | 9 | 9 | 10 | 11 | 12 | 13 | 13 | 11 |    |
| 15 | 7 | 8 | 9 | 11 | 11 | 12 | 11 |    | 12 |
| 10 | 6 | 6 | 8 | 9 | 10 | 11 | 10 | 9 | 9 |
| 5 | 3 | 3 | 5 | 7 | 8 | 9 | 7 | 6 | 7 |

Reprinted by permission of the North Carolina State Department of Public Instruction (1977), Raleigh, North Carolina.

**TABLE 6.4** Percentile norms for standing broad jump.

**BOYS**

| Age / Percentile | 9 | 10 | 11 | 12 | 13 | 14 | 15 | 16 | 17 |
|---|---|---|---|---|---|---|---|---|---|
| 95 | 70 | 72 | 75 | 80 | 85 | 92 | 96 | 97 | 98 |
| 90 | 66 | 68 | 71 | 75 | 80 | 87 | 91 | 94 | 96 |
| 85 | 63 | 66 | 69 | 72 | 78 | 84 | 89 | 92 | 94 |
| 80 | 61 | 64 | 67 | 71 | 76 | 82 | 87 | 90 | 93 |
| 75 | 60 | 62 | 65 | 69 | 74 | 80 | 85 | 88 | 92 |
| 70 | 59 | 61 | 64 | 67 | 73 | 78 | 83 | 86 | 91 |
| 65 | 58 | 60 | 63 | 66 | 72 | 77 | 82 | 85 | 87 |
| 60 | 57 | 59 | 62 | 65 | 71 | 75 | 81 | 83 | 86 |
| 55 | 55 | 58 | 61 | 64 | 69 | 74 | 79 | 82 | 85 |
| 50 | 54 | 57 | 59 | 63 | 68 | 72 | 78 | 80 | 83 |
| 45 | 53 | 55 | 58 | 61 | 66 | 71 | 76 | 78 | 82 |
| 40 | 52 | 54 | 57 | 60 | 65 | 70 | 75 | 76 | 81 |
| 35 | 50 | 53 | 56 | 59 | 64 | 69 | 74 | 74 | 79 |
| 30 | 49 | 52 | 54 | 58 | 62 | 67 | 72 | 73 | 78 |
| 25 | 48 | 50 | 53 | 56 | 61 | 65 | 71 | 72 | 75 |
| 20 | 46 | 49 | 51 | 54 | 59 | 63 | 69 | 70 | 74 |
| 15 | 44 | 47 | 50 | 52 | 56 | 61 | 66 | 68 | 72 |
| 10 | 41 | 45 | 47 | 49 | 53 | 59 | 63 | 63 | 70 |
| 5 | 38 | 41 | 41 | 41 | 46 | 54 | 56 | 60 | 63 |

**GIRLS**

| Age / Percentile | 9 | 10 | 11 | 12 | 13 | 14 | 15 | 16 | 17 |
|---|---|---|---|---|---|---|---|---|---|
| 95 | 63 | 66 | 71 | 73 | 74 | 75 | 79 | 77 | 76 |
| 90 | 60 | 62 | 67 | 70 | 72 | 72 | 75 | 76 | 73 |
| 85 | 58 | 60 | 65 | 68 | 69 | 70 | 73 | 73 | 72 |
| 80 | 56 | 58 | 63 | 66 | 67 | 68 | 71 | 71 | 71 |
| 75 | 54 | 57 | 61 | 64 | 66 | 66 | 68 | 68 | 70 |
| 70 | 53 | 55 | 60 | 63 | 64 | 65 | 67 | 66 | 68 |
| 65 | 51 | 54 | 59 | 61 | 63 | 64 | 66 | 63 |  |
| 60 | 51 | 53 | 58 | 60 | 62 | 62 | 64 | 61 | 67 |
| 55 | 50 | 52 | 56 | 59 | 61 | 61 | 63 |  | 66 |
| 50 | 49 | 50 | 55 | 58 | 60 | 60 | 62 | 60 | 64 |
| 45 | 48 | 49 | 54 | 57 | 59 | 59 | 60 | 59 | 63 |
| 40 | 47 | 48 | 53 | 56 | 58 | 58 | 59 | 57 | 62 |
| 35 | 46 | 47 | 51 | 54 | 56 | 57 | 58 | 55 | 59 |
| 30 | 45 | 46 | 49 | 53 | 55 | 55 | 57 | 54 | 56 |
| 25 | 43 | 44 | 48 | 50 | 53 | 54 | 56 | 53 | 51 |
| 20 | 41 | 43 | 46 | 49 | 52 | 52 | 54 | 51 | 50 |
| 15 | 39 | 40 | 44 | 47 | 50 | 50 | 52 | 49 | 48 |
| 10 | 37 | 37 | 42 | 44 | 47 | 48 | 48 | 47 | 46 |
| 5 | 35 | 34 | 38 | 38 | 42 | 44 | 44 | 44 | 41 |

Reprinted by permission of the North Carolina State Department of Public Instruction (1977), Raleigh, North Carolina.

**TABLE 6.5**   Percentile norms for modified pull-ups.

**BOYS**

| Percentile | Age 9 | 10 | 11 | 12 | 13 | 14 | 15 | 16 | 17 |
|---|---|---|---|---|---|---|---|---|---|
| 95 | 29 | 31 | 34 | 36 | 36 | 36 | 36 | 36 | 36 |
| 90 | 26 | 28 | 30 | 31 | 32 | 33 | 33 | 34 | 34 |
| 85 | 24 | 26 | 28 | 29 | 30 | 31 | 32 | 33 | 32 |
| 80 | 23 | 25 | 26 | 27 | 28 | 30 | 30 | 31 | 31 |
| 75 | 21 | 23 | 24 | 25 | 26 | 28 | 29 | 30 | 30 |
| 70 | 20 | 22 | 23 | 24 | 24 | 27 | 28 | 28 | 29 |
| 65 | 19 | 21 | 21 | 23 | 23 | 25 | 27 | 27 | 28 |
| 60 | 18 | 20 |  | 22 | 21 | 24 | 26 | 26 | 26 |
| 55 | 17 | 19 | 20 | 20 | 20 | 23 | 24 | 25 | 26 |
| 50 | 16 | 18 | 19 | 19 | 19 | 22 | 23 | 24 | 25 |
| 45 | 15 | 17 | 18 | 18 | 18 | 20 | 22 | 23 | 24 |
| 40 | 14 | 16 | 17 | 17 | 17 | 19 | 21 | 21 | 23 |
| 35 | 13 | 15 | 16 | 16 | 16 | 18 | 20 | 20 | 21 |
| 30 | 12 | 14 | 15 | 15 | 14 | 16 | 18 | 18 | 20 |
| 25 | 10 | 12 | 14 | 13 | 13 | 15 | 17 | 17 | 19 |
| 20 | 8 | 11 | 12 | 12 | 11 | 12 | 15 | 16 | 17 |
| 15 | 5 | 9 | 11 | 10 | 9 | 11 | 13 | 14 | 15 |
| 10 | 5 | 6 | 9 | 8 | 6 | 8 | 10 | 12 | 12 |
| 5 | 1 | 2 | 3 | 3 | 3 | 4 | 7 | 8 | 9 |

**GIRLS**

| Percentile | Age 9 | 10 | 11 | 12 | 13 | 14 | 15 | 16 | 17 |
|---|---|---|---|---|---|---|---|---|---|
| 95 | 26 | 29 | 31 | 30 | 29 | 30 | 33 | 25 | 30 |
| 90 | 24 | 26 | 27 | 27 | 25 | 25 | 28 | 24 | 25 |
| 85 | 22 | 23 | 23 | 24 | 24 | 23 | 25 | 20 | 23 |
| 80 | 20 | 21 | 21 | 22 | 21 | 22 | 23 | 19 |  |
| 75 | 19 | 19 | 20 | 21 | 19 | 21 | 22 | 18 | 21 |
| 70 | 18 | 18 | 19 | 20 | 18 | 20 | 21 | 17 | 20 |
| 65 | 17 | 17 | 18 | 19 | 17 | 19 | 20 | 16 |  |
| 60 | 16 | 16 | 17 | 18 | 16 | 18 | 19 |  | 14 |
| 55 | 15 | 15 | 16 | 17 | 15 | 17 | 18 | 15 | 13 |
| 50 | 14 | 14 | 15 | 16 |  | 16 | 16 | 14 | 12 |
| 45 | 13 | 13 | 14 | 15 | 14 | 15 |  | 13 | 11 |
| 40 | 12 | 12 | 13 | 14 | 13 | 14 | 15 | 12 | 10 |
| 35 | 11 | 11 | 12 | 13 | 12 | 13 | 14 | 11 |  |
| 30 | 10 | 10 | 11 | 11 | 11 | 12 | 13 | 10 | 9 |
| 25 | 9 | 9 | 10 | 10 | 10 | 11 | 11 | 8 | 8 |
| 20 | 8 | 7 | 9 | 9 | 9 | 10 | 10 | 5 | 7 |
| 15 | 6 | 5 | 7 | 7 | 7 | 9 | 8 | 4 | 6 |
| 10 | 3 | 3 | 4 | 5 | 5 | 7 | 6 | 3 | 5 |
| 5 | 1 | 1 | 1 | 1 | 2 | 4 | 3 | 1 | 4 |

Reprinted by permission of the North Carolina State Department of Public Instruction (1977), Raleigh, North Carolina.

**TABLE 6.6**  Percentile norms for squat thrust.

**BOYS**

| Age | 9 | 10 | 11 | 12 | 13 | 14 | 15 | 16 | 17 |
|---|---|---|---|---|---|---|---|---|---|
| Percentile | | | | | | | | | |
| 95 | 22 | 20 | 20 | 22 | 23 | 24 | 24 | 23 | 24 |
| 90 | 19 | 18 | 18 | 19 | 21 | 21 | 22 | 21 | 22 |
| 85 | 17 | 17 | 17 | 18 | 20 | 20 | 21 | 20 | 21 |
| 80 | 16 | 16 | 16 | 17 | 19 | 19 | 20 | 20 | 20 |
| 75 | 15 | 15 | 15 | | | 19 | | | |
| 70 | | | | | 18 | | 19 | 19 | |
| 65 | 14 | 14 | | 16 | 17 | 18 | | 18 | 19 |
| 60 | | | 14 | 15 | | | 18 | | |
| 55 | | | | | | 17 | | | 18 |
| 50 | 13 | 13 | 13 | 14 | 16 | 16 | 17 | 17 | 17 |
| 45 | | | | | | | 16 | | 16 |
| 40 | 12 | 12 | 13 | 14 | 15 | 15 | 16 | 16 | 16 |
| 35 | | | | 13 | 14 | | | 15 | |
| 30 | 11 | 11 | 11 | 12 | 14 | 14 | 15 | 15 | 15 |
| 25 | | | | | 12 | | | | |
| 20 | 10 | 10 | 10 | 11 | 13 | 13 | 14 | 14 | 14 |
| 15 | 9 | 9 | 9 | 10 | 12 | 12 | 13 | 13 | 13 |
| 10 | 8 | 8 | 8 | 9 | 10 | 11 | 12 | 12 | 12 |
| 5 | 6 | 6 | 6 | 7 | 8 | 10 | 11 | 10 | 9 |

**GIRLS**

| Age | 9 | 10 | 11 | 12 | 13 | 14 | 15 | 16 | 17 |
|---|---|---|---|---|---|---|---|---|---|
| Percentile | | | | | | | | | |
| 95 | 20 | 19 | 18 | 20 | 20 | 20 | 19 | 18 | 19 |
| 90 | 18 | 17 | 17 | 18 | 18 | 18 | 18 | 18 | 18 |
| 85 | 16 | 16 | 16 | 17 | 17 | 17 | 17 | 17 | 17 |
| 80 | 15 | 15 | 15 | 16 | 16 | 16 | 16 | 16 | |
| 75 | 15 | | | 15 | | | | | |
| 70 | 14 | 14 | 14 | | 15 | 15 | 15 | 15 | 16 |
| 65 | | | | | 15 | 15 | 15 | 14 | |
| 60 | 13 | 13 | 13 | 14 | 14 | 14 | 14 | 14 | 15 |
| 55 | | | | | 14 | 14 | 14 | | |
| 50 | 12 | 12 | 12 | 13 | 13 | 13 | 13 | 13 | 14 |
| 45 | 12 | | 12 | 12 | 13 | 13 | 13 | 12 | 13 |
| 40 | | 12 | | 12 | 12 | 13 | 12 | 12 | 13 |
| 35 | 11 | 11 | 11 | 11 | 12 | 12 | | | 13 |
| 30 | | 10 | | | | | 12 | 11 | 12 |
| 25 | 10 | | 11 | 11 | 11 | 11 | 12 | 11 | 11 |
| 20 | 10 | 9 | 10 | 10 | 10 | 11 | 11 | 11 | 10 |
| 15 | 9 | 9 | 9 | 9 | 9 | 10 | 10 | 10 | 9 |
| 10 | 8 | 8 | 8 | 8 | 8 | 9 | 9 | 9 | 8 |
| 5 | 6 | 6 | 7 | 6 | 6 | 7 | 7 | 5 | 3 |

Reprinted by permission of the North Carolina State Department of Public Instruction (1977), Raleigh, North Carolina.

### Test 2: Side-Stepping

*Instructions:* The student assumes a standing position with one foot touching one of two sidelines spaced 12 feet apart. On the command to "Go," the student moves sideward with a side-step (sliding), leading with the foot nearest the line that is being approached until that line is crossed with one foot. The movement is repeated to the other line in the same manner, and so on for 30 seconds. The student must face the same direction throughout the test.

*Equipment Needed:* Marking tape and a stopwatch.

*Scoring Procedure:* The score is the number of sidelines touched in the 30-second period.

*Organizational Hints:* Students should perform the test in proper court shoes or barefoot.

### Test 3: Standing Broad Jump

*Instructions:* The student assumes a starting (semicrouched) position behind the take-off line with feet approximately shoulder-width apart. When ready, the student takes off on two feet and jumps as far as possible. Students should be encouraged to swing their arms and flex their legs at the knees in preparation for the jump. The distance is measured from the point where the body touches nearest the take-off line to the take-off line. Three consecutive trials are permitted.

*Equipment Needed:* Measuring tape (12-foot), tumbling mats for use on hard surface or jumping pit for outdoor use, marking tape.

*Scoring Procedure:* The distance jumped on the best of the three trials is recorded to the nearest inch.

*Organizational Hints:* The test administrator should be kneeling in the landing area in order to be able to accurately mark the distance jumped. An assistant to help record scores is beneficial. If mats are used, students not being tested should be positioned on the corners to keep mats from sliding on the floor.

### Test 4: Modified Pull-Ups

*Instructions:* The student lies on his or her back with shoulders positioned directly under a horizontal bar that is 30 inches from the floor. Using a palms-away grip to grasp the bar and keeping feet flat on the floor to create a straight line from the knees to head, the student pulls up with the arms until they are completely bent and the chest and chin are touching the bar, then lowers to the original position. No rest is allowed between pull-ups, feet must be kept under knees, the body must remain rigid, and arms must be fully extended on return to the starting position.

**Equipment Needed:** Two chairs to support the bar, one horizontal bar approximately six feet in length, a stopwatch, and a tumbling mat or piece of carpet.

**Scoring Procedure:** The number of successfully completed pull-ups performed in 30 seconds is recorded as the score.

**Organizational Hints:** Students should be positioned in each chair to hold the chinning bar in place while the student is performing the test. An assistant should be used to spot and carefully monitor the subject.

### Test 5: Squat Thrust

**Instructions**
Students assume an upright standing position. On the signal to begin, they drop to a squat position with the hands flat on the floor about shoulder-width apart (count 1), fully extend the legs back, keeping them together, and assume a front leaning rest position (count 2), pull legs to the squat position (count 3), and return to the start position (count 4). The squat position must be maintained before thrusting legs back for count 2. The exercise must be continuous with no resting allowed (see Figure 6.1).

**Equipment Needed:** A stopwatch.

**Scoring Procedure:** The score is the number of fully completed repetitions in 30 seconds.

**Organizational Hints:** Using a partner system enables half the group to perform this test at a time.

## Texas Physical Motor Fitness/Developmental Tests
(American Heart Association in Texas and Governor's Commission on Physical Fitness, 1986)

**Purpose:** This is a battery of tests designed to assist teachers to determine the physical and motor abilities of students.

**Description:** The program comprises two test batteries that measure motor fitness and motor development, respectively. The motor fitness test consists of two items: the shuttle run and standing long jump. The motor development test comprises seven items and measures dynamic balance, static balance, kicking, throwing, catching, body awareness, and posture. The motor development battery is optional but is recommended as an aid to help teachers identify motor development deficiencies that could adversely affect a youngster's participation in physical activity in later years. The motor development test is described here to provide an example of an assessment instrument that can help provide a profile depicting the developmental stages of children and secure information essential to curriculum development.

*Validity:* Face validity is accepted for all items.

*Reliability:* Not reported.

*Age Level:* 5–9 years.

*Norms:* Tables 6.7 and 6.8 provide normative information regarding two motor fitness tests.

*Test Area:* Any smooth, safe indoor or outdoor area spacious enough to accommodate testing stations is appropriate.

▶ **TABLE 6.7**   Percentile norms for Texas Motor Fitness Test: boys ages 5–9.

| Percentile | STANDING LONG JUMP (in inches) | | | | | SHUTTLE RUN TIME (in seconds) | | | | |
|---|---|---|---|---|---|---|---|---|---|---|
| | 5 | 6 | 7 | 8 | 9 | 5 | 6 | 7 | 8 | 9 |
| 95 | 50 | 58 | 63 | 65 | 69 | 6.29 | 5.55 | 5.53 | 5.41 | 5.32 |
| 90 | 47 | 55 | 59 | 63 | 67 | 6.54 | 5.79 | 5.75 | 5.64 | 5.49 |
| 85 | 46 | 54 | 58 | 61 | 66 | 6.79 | 6.03 | 5.97 | 5.87 | 5.66 |
| 80 | 45 | 53 | 58 | 59 | 65 | 7.04 | 6.27 | 6.19 | 6.10 | 5.83 |
| 75 | 44 | 51 | 55 | 57 | 62 | 7.29 | 6.51 | 6.41 | 6.33 | 6.00 |
| 70 | 43 | 50 | 53 | 56 | 60 | 7.54 | 6.75 | 6.63 | 6.56 | 6.17 |
| 65 | 41 | 47 | 51 | 55 | 58 | 7.79 | 6.99 | 6.85 | 6.79 | 6.34 |
| 60 | 39 | 45 | 50 | 55 | 57 | 8.04 | 7.23 | 7.07 | 7.02 | 6.51 |
| 55 | 38 | 42 | 47 | 52 | 54 | 8.29 | 7.47 | 7.29 | 7.25 | 6.68 |
| 50 | 38 | 40 | 45 | 49 | 51 | 8.54 | 7.71 | 7.51 | 7.48 | 6.85 |
| 45 | 36 | 37 | 41 | 46 | 49 | 8.79 | 7.95 | 7.73 | 7.71 | 7.02 |
| 40 | 35 | 35 | 37 | 43 | 47 | 9.03 | 8.19 | 7.95 | 7.94 | 7.19 |
| 35 | 31 | 32 | 35 | 41 | 43 | 9.28 | 8.43 | 8.17 | 8.17 | 7.36 |
| 30 | 28 | 30 | 34 | 39 | 40 | 9.53 | 8.67 | 8.39 | 8.40 | 7.53 |
| 25 | 27 | 28 | 31 | 38 | 39 | 9.78 | 8.91 | 8.61 | 8.63 | 7.70 |
| 20 | 25 | 27 | 28 | 37 | 39 | 10.03 | 9.15 | 8.83 | 8.86 | 7.87 |
| 15 | 23 | 26 | 27 | 36 | 38 | 10.28 | 9.39 | 9.05 | 9.07 | 8.04 |
| 10 | 22 | 25 | 27 | 35 | 38 | 10.53 | 9.63 | 9.27 | 9.32 | 8.21 |
| 5 | 20 | 23 | 25 | 34 | 36 | 10.79 | 9.87 | 9.49 | 9.55 | 8.38 |

▶ **TABLE 6.8** Percentile norms for Texas Motor Fitness Test: girls ages 5–9.

| Percentile | STANDING LONG JUMP (in inches) | | | | | SHUTTLE RUN TIME (in seconds) | | | | |
|---|---|---|---|---|---|---|---|---|---|---|
| | 5 | 6 | 7 | 8 | 9 | 5 | 6 | 7 | 8 | 9 |
| 95 | 50 | 55 | 62 | 66 | 66 | 6.84 | 6.26 | 6.13 | 6.25 | 5.76 |
| 90 | 46 | 53 | 59 | 62 | 63 | 7.08 | 6.52 | 6.36 | 6.40 | 5.92 |
| 85 | 45 | 52 | 58 | 60 | 62 | 7.32 | 6.78 | 6.59 | 6.55 | 6.08 |
| 80 | 45 | 52 | 57 | 59 | 61 | 7.56 | 7.04 | 6.82 | 6.70 | 6.24 |
| 75 | 44 | 50 | 56 | 58 | 60 | 7.80 | 7.30 | 7.05 | 6.85 | 6.40 |
| 70 | 43 | 47 | 55 | 57 | 59 | 8.04 | 7.56 | 7.28 | 7.00 | 6.56 |
| 65 | 41 | 45 | 52 | 56 | 57 | 8.28 | 7.82 | 7.51 | 7.15 | 6.72 |
| 60 | 39 | 42 | 49 | 55 | 56 | 8.52 | 8.08 | 7.74 | 7.30 | 6.88 |
| 55 | 38 | 40 | 46 | 51 | 53 | 8.76 | 8.34 | 7.97 | 7.45 | 7.04 |
| 50 | 37 | 39 | 43 | 47 | 51 | 9.00 | 8.60 | 8.20 | 7.60 | 7.20 |
| 45 | 35 | 37 | 40 | 45 | 48 | 9.24 | 8.86 | 8.43 | 7.75 | 7.36 |
| 40 | 34 | 35 | 37 | 44 | 46 | 9.48 | 9.12 | 8.66 | 7.90 | 7.52 |
| 35 | 30 | 32 | 35 | 42 | 43 | 9.72 | 9.38 | 8.89 | 8.05 | 7.68 |
| 30 | 26 | 30 | 34 | 40 | 41 | 9.96 | 9.64 | 9.12 | 8.20 | 7.84 |
| 25 | 25 | 29 | 31 | 38 | 40 | 10.20 | 9.90 | 9.35 | 8.35 | 8.00 |
| 20 | 25 | 28 | 29 | 36 | 39 | 10.44 | 10.16 | 9.58 | 8.50 | 8.16 |
| 15 | 24 | 27 | 28 | 32 | 38 | 10.68 | 10.42 | 9.81 | 8.65 | 8.32 |
| 10 | 23 | 25 | 27 | 29 | 37 | 10.92 | 10.68 | 10.04 | 8.80 | 8.48 |
| 5 | 18 | 21 | 25 | 27 | 34 | 11.16 | 10.94 | 10.27 | 8.95 | 8.64 |

Reprinted by permission of The American Heart Association of Texas and Governor's Commission on Physical Education, Texas Affiliate (1986), Fort Worth, Texas.

### Motor Fitness Test: Shuttle Run

*Instructions:* The student is positioned behind a start/finish line. On the command to start, the student runs to retrieve an eraser located behind a line 17 yards from the start line. As the student passes the timing line, located 2 yards from the start/finish line, the teacher starts the stopwatch. The watch is stopped as the student crosses the start/finish line. One trial is permitted.

*Equipment Needed:* Stopwatch, marking tape, measuring tape, and standard chalkboard eraser.

*Scoring Procedure:* The elapsed time from the student first crossing the timing line until running through the start/finish line is recorded to the nearest hundredth of a second.

*Organizational Hints:* Proper footwear should be worn. A digital readout stopwatch is best suited to give accurate reading to the nearest hundredth of a second. Students should be given an opportunity to practice the test and should be encouraged to run through the finish line rather than stop at it.

### Motor Fitness Test: Standing Long Jump

*Instructions:* The student assumes a starting (semicrouched) position behind the take-off line with feet approximately shoulder-width apart. When ready, the student takes off on two feet and jumps as far as possible. Students should be encouraged to swing their arms and flex their legs at the knees in preparation for the jump. The distance is measured from the point where the body touches nearest the take-off line (usually the back of the heels) to the take-off line. Two consecutive trials are permitted.

*Equipment Needed:* Measuring tape (12 foot), tumbling mats for use on hard surface or jumping pit for outdoor use, marking tape.

*Scoring Procedure:* The distance jumped on the better of the two trials is recorded to the nearest inch.

*Organizational Hints:* The test administrator should be kneeling in the landing area in order to accurately mark the distance jumped. An assistant to help record scores is beneficial. If mats are used, students not being tested should be positioned on the corners to keep the mat from sliding on the floor.

### Motor Development Test: Walking a Line Forward/Backward

*Instructions:* The student stands at one end of a one-inch-wide line with one foot in front of the other, heel to toe. The student is requested to walk forward for six consecutive steps, always making sure that the heel of the front foot touches the toes of the back foot. Upon completing the forward walk, the student walks backward, heel to toe, for six consecutive steps. A second trial (for each test) is administered only if the student fails to achieve maximum points on the first trial.

*Equipment Needed:* Marking tape.

*Scoring Procedure:* The number of correctly executed steps (forward and backward) is recorded as the student's score (maximum score is 12).

*Organizational Hints:* If the student does not maintain a heel-to-toe step or steps off the line, the test should be repeated. Proper demonstration helps the students understand how they are to walk.

### Motor Development Test: Standing with Eyes Open/Closed

*Instructions:* This test consists of three sets of two static balance challenges. First, the student assumes a standing position with one foot in front of the other (heel touching toes) on a one-inch-wide line on the floor. The stopwatch is started when the student has established balance and can hold that position. The student repeats this test with eyes closed. In the second set of this test, the student is instructed to stand with only the right foot on the line and the left foot bent at the knee, with the left foot resting on the medial side of the right knee area (stork stand). The stopwatch is started when the student has assumed the starting position. The student repeats the test with the eyes closed. The third set of two tests is a repeat of the second set but balanced on the left foot. Two trials are permitted for each of these six tests. The maximum score possible for any of the six tests is 10 seconds.

*Equipment Needed:* Stopwatch and marking tape.

*Scoring Procedure:* The better of two trials for each test is recorded to the nearest second (maximum of 10).

*Organizational Hints:* On the one-foot balances, the student is allowed one warning for improper positioning of the bent leg. If the student drops the leg below a 45-degree angle a second time, the test is stopped. The supporting foot must be in contact with the line at all times.

### Motor Development Test: Kicking a Ball

*Instructions:* The student stands approximately 15–20 feet from the instructor, who rolls the ball to the child and observes the kicking pattern. Indicating which foot the student uses to kick the ball, the number of proper kicking techniques observed is recorded. Five consecutive trials are given.

*Equipment Needed:* 8.5-inch playground ball.

*Scoring Procedure:* One point is awarded for each of the following behaviors: steps toward the ball before kicking, foot contacts center of the ball, leg is fully extended at contact, and leg continues to follow through after contact. The number of observed behaviors (maximum of four) is recorded for each trial.

*Organizational Hints:* Student assistants can be used to retrieve balls.

### Motor Development Test: Throwing a Ball

*Instructions:* The student stands approximately 15 feet from the instructor and, using an overhand motion, throws a tennis ball to the instructor. The throwing hand and the number of proper throwing techniques observed are recorded. Five consecutive trials are administered.

*Equipment Needed:* Tennis balls.

*Scoring Procedure:* One point each is awarded for the following: holds the tennis ball with tips of fingers; stands with feet slightly spread, with foot opposite the throwing arm in a forward position; steps forward with the opposite foot when throwing; and follows through with arm fully extended. A score is recorded for each of the five trials.

*Organizational Hints:* Student assistants can be used to retrieve balls.

### Motor Development Test: Catching a Ball

*Instructions:* The student holds a standard playground ball (8.5-inch) with hands positioned on each side of ball at waist level in front of the body. The student drops and catches the ball with the instructor observing. Five trials are given.

*Equipment Needed:* 8.5-inch playground ball.

*Scoring Procedure:* The number of correct behaviors are recorded for each of the five trials. One point is scored for each of the following: elbows bent and in front of body, flight of ball watched throughout bounce and catch, ball caught entirely with hands, and the ball does not bounce higher than the shoulders. Record the correct number of observed behaviors for each trial (maximum of 4).

### Motor Development Test: Body Awareness

*Instructions:* The following sequence of instructions should be given to students: "Touch each of the body parts I ask you to touch. Touch your nose. Touch your mouth. Touch your foot. Touch your right shoulder. Touch your left ear. Touch your left knee with your right hand. Touch your right elbow with your left hand."

*Equipment Needed:* None.

*Scoring Procedure:* One point is awarded for each correct response (maximum of 7 points).

*Organizational Hints:* To prevent children from overhearing the sequence, the test should be administered privately to one child at a time.

### Motor Development Test: Posture

*Instructions:* The student assumes a standing position on a piece of tape located two feet from the modified posture grid (see Figure 6.6). The instructor is positioned approximately 15 feet directly behind the child in order to view the student's posture and the grid on the wall. The teacher should observe the position of the child's head, shoulders, and hips in relation to the grid. Specifically, the instructor is checking to see whether the head is tilted left or right, whether one shoulder is high or low, and whether either hip is high or low. The student is asked to stand sideways so the instructor can check if the head is tipped forward or backward in relation to the line.

▶ **FIGURE 6.6** Modified posture grid.

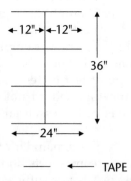

Any misalignments should be recorded on a scoresheet according to the following codes:

*Posterior View Codes*

| | | |
|---|---|---|
| Head: | HTL (head tilt left) | HTR (head tilt right) |
| Shoulder: | LSL (left shoulder low) | RSL (right shoulder low) |
| | LSH (left shoulder high) | RSH (right shoulder high) |
| Hips: | LHL (left hip low) | RHL (right hip low) |
| | LHH (left hip high) | RHH (right hip high) |

*Lateral View Codes*

| | | |
|---|---|---|
| Head: | HTF (head tilt forward) | HTB (head tilt backward) |

**Equipment Needed:** Modified posture grid (see Figure 6.6).

**Scoring Procedure:** No numeric rating is derived from this test. This test serves as an appraisal of posture and records appropriate misalignments.

**Organizational Hints:** The grid can be painted or constructed with tape on the gym wall. Youngsters should be encouraged to assume a comfortable position when taking this test.

## SPORTS SKILLS TESTS

Tests measuring psychomotor performance can be either fitness component-specific (i.e., agility, balance, coordination, power, speed, or reaction time) or sport-specific (e.g., badminton, baseball). It may be argued that many of the psychomotor tests discussed in the first portion of this chapter measure performance attributes associated with specific sport skills. However, evaluating units of instruction that teach techniques of certain sports is usually best accomplished by administering tests that require utilization of the objects and implements used in that particular sport. In other words, if a youngster is taught how to hit an overhead clear in badminton and is expected to perform it, then assessment should measure that sport skill. Similarly, if accuracy is emphasized in throwing a football, then tests measuring that goal should be utilized. Specific teaching situations will dictate the type of test or tests to use. When selecting tests of specific sport skills, educators should not use a skill test that does not meet the evaluation needs or the essential criteria of validity, reliability, and objectivity.

For the sake of clarity, the remainder of the chapter has been divided into two sections: tests for team sports and tests for individual and dual sports. The scope of this text is not sufficient to cover all the sports skills tests on the market. The tests selected represent only a small portion of the total number of sports skills tests in the literature, but are well suited for use in the schools. For additional tests see Barrow and McGee (1979), Baumgartner and Jackson (1987), Collins and Hodges (1978), Johnson and Nelson (1986), and Safrit (1990).

## Team Sports

The following section describes tests designed to assess specific skill performance in team sports.

### Measuring Baseball/Softball Skills

### AAHPER Softball Skills Tests for Boys and Girls (1966)

*Purpose:* The purpose of these test batteries is to measure fundamental skills associated with the sports of baseball and softball.

*Description:* The test batteries are similar for boys and girls. The primary difference between the two batteries is that the throwing for accuracy and underhand pitching distances are shorter for girls. Otherwise each battery consists of the following: base running, catching fly balls, fielding ground balls, fungo hitting, overhand throw for accuracy, softball throw for distance, speed throw, and underhand pitching.

*Validity:* Face validity accepted.

*Reliability:* Tests with reported coefficients of less than .70 were not included in the skills test.

*Age Level:* Boys and girls ages 10–18.

*Norms:* Reported in AAHPER Softball Skills Tests (1966).

*Test Area:* Large gymnasium with wall space and outdoor area.

### Test 1: Base Running

*Instructions:* The student assumes a standing position in the batting box. On the command "Hit," the student swings the bat, drops the bat, and runs the base paths in the proper sequence. Two trials are given.

*Equipment Needed:* Stopwatch, bat, and bases.

*Scoring Procedure:* The score is the elapsed time from the command "Hit" to the student touching home plate. The better of the two trials is recorded to the nearest tenth of a second.

*Organizational Hints:* In order for the trial to count, the student must touch all the bases.

### Test 2: Catching Fly Balls

*Instructions:* The student assumes a ready position at second base, which is the middle point of a 60 foot by 60 foot marked-off square (catching zone). A ball is thrown in the air, clearing a rope (8 feet high) fastened between two standards, which are located 5 feet in front of home plate toward the student. The ball is thrown at regular speed and targeted to land somewhere inside the catching zone. Each student is given two trials of 10 balls each.

*Equipment Needed:* Approximately 15 softballs, fluorescent boundary cones, tape measure, and bases.

*Scoring Procedure:* The number of balls successfully caught during the two trials is recorded as the student's score.

*Organizational Hints:* No practice trials are allowed. Approximately one-third of the balls should be thrown to the left of second base, one-third to the right, and one-third at second base.

### Test 3: Fielding Ground Balls

*Instructions:* The student assumes a ready position at least 50 feet from the thrower. On the signal to begin, the thrower begins throwing ground balls toward the student. The student attempts to successfully field each ball, holding it momentarily before tossing it aside (see Figure 6.7). Twenty ground balls constitute the number of trials for the test. One practice trial is permitted.

*Equipment Needed:* Approximately 15 softballs, fluorescent boundary cones to mark off fielding area, and 100-foot tape measure.

*Scoring Procedure:* The number of successfully fielded ground balls is recorded as the student's score.

◣ **FIGURE 6.7**   Fielding ground balls.

*Organizational Hints:*  Throws should be made at five-second intervals. Each throw must hit the ground inside the first 25-foot restraining line (see Figure 6.8). Some variation in speed and direction of the throw is encouraged.

### Test 4: Fungo Hitting

*Instructions:*  The student is instructed to stand at home plate, toss the ball into the air, and hit it alternately to right and left field. This process continues until 10 balls have been hit to each field. Practice trials are allowed to each side.

*Equipment Needed:*  Bat and approximately 15 softballs.

◣ **FIGURE 6.8**   Layout for fielding ground balls.

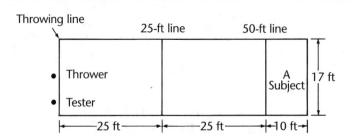

Reprinted by permission of American Alliance for Health, Physical Education, Recreation and Dance, Reston, Virginia.

*Scoring Procedure:* A fly ball to the designated field is worth two points, a ground ball one point. Two consecutive misses to the same field count as a trial. The score is the sum of the point values earned for each trial up to a maximum of 40 points.

*Organizational Hints:* If the bat touches the ball it is counted as a trial. Hits to right and left field must pass between first and second, or second and third base, respectively.

### Test 5: Overhand Throw for Accuracy

*Instructions:* The student throws the ball in an overhand manner at a circular target from a distance of 65 feet for boys or 40 feet for girls. Ten trials are allowed.

*Equipment Needed:* Softballs and target(s) with the following dimensions: Three concentric circles with 1-inch lines: the center circle is 24 inches in diameter, the second circle is 48 inches in diameter, and the outer circle is 72 inches in diameter. The bottom of the outer circle is 36 inches from the floor.

*Scoring Procedure:* A ball hitting in the center circle is worth three points, second circle two points, and the outer circle one point. The sum of the points accumulated in 10 throws is the score.

*Organizational Hints:* Balls hitting on the line are awarded the higher point value. One or two practice throws are allowed.

### Test 6: Softball Throw for Distance

*Instructions:* The student assumes a position in front of a restraining line six feet from the throwing line. Staying within these lines, the student is instructed to throw the softball as far as possible. Three trials are given.

*Equipment Needed:* Softballs, 250-foot tape measure, and boundary cones.

*Scoring Procedure:* The farthest of the three trials is recorded to the nearest foot.

*Organizational Hints:* The measurement of distance is made at right angles from the point of landing to the throwing line (the tape does not have to be moved in an arc to measure each throw). Each throw should be marked with a stake or some other visible but not easily moved object.

### Test 7: Speed Throw

*Instructions:* The student assumes a ready position behind a restraining line located nine feet from a smooth wall. On the signal to "Go," the student throws the ball (overhand) against the wall and catches it on the rebound. This sequence is repeated until 15 hits against the wall have been completed. Two trials are given.

*Equipment Needed:* Softballs, stopwatch, measuring tape, and marking tape.

*Scoring Procedure:* The score is the time elapsed between hitting the wall with the first ball and the 15th. The better of two trials is recorded to the nearest tenth of a second.

*Organizational Hints:* All throws must be made from behind the restraining line. If the ball eludes the student completely, a retrial may be given.

### Test 8: Underhand Pitching

*Instructions:* The student pitches the ball underhand at a rectangular target. Boys stand behind a 46 foot restraining line, girls behind a 38 foot restraining line. Fifteen trials are allowed.

*Equipment Needed:* Marking tape, measuring tape, softballs, and a rectangular target(s) constructed according to the following dimensions: The outer borders measure 42 by 29 inches wide and enclose an inner rectangle measuring 30 by 17 inches.

*Scoring Procedure:* Balls hitting the center area of the target count two points, balls hitting the outer area count one point. The sum of the points made on 15 pitches is recorded as the student's score.

*Organizational Hints:* One practice trial is allowed before the 15 pitches. The student must keep one foot on the restraining line while stepping forward to throw the ball toward the target.

For information on other tests measuring softball and baseball skills, see the *Representative Reading* list at the end of the chapter.

## Measuring Basketball Skills

### AAHPERD Basketball Skills Test (1984)

*Purpose:* The purpose of this test battery is to measure student performance of selected basketball skills.

*Description:* The test battery consists of four items: control dribble, defensive movement, passing, and speed spot shooting.

*Validity:* Juried validity ratings for test items ranged from .65 to .95.

*Reliability:* Intraclass reliability coefficients testing boys and girls separately ranged from .82 to .97 for all items.

*Age Level:* Males and females ages 10 through college.

*Norms:* Normative information is provided in the AAHPERD manual.

*Test Area:* Gymnasium with smooth court space and basketball goals.

### Test 1: Control Dribble

**Instructions:** On the signal to start, the student begins dribbling with the nondominant hand from the nondominant side of starting cone A to the nondominant side of the center cone B and proceeds through the course as depicted in Figure 6.9, using either hand for dribbling. A practice trial is followed by two timed trials.

**Equipment Needed:** A basketball, stopwatch, and six fluorescent boundary cones.

▶ **FIGURE 6.9** Layout for control dribble.

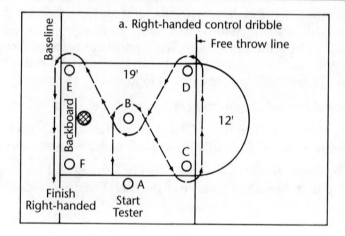

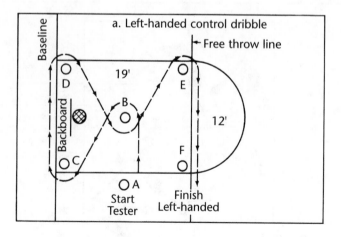

*Scoring Procedure:* The score for each trial will be the elapsed time required to correctly complete the course. Scores should be recorded to the nearest tenth of a second for each trial. The final score is the sum of the two trials.

*Organizational Hints:* The stopwatch is stopped as soon as the student passes both feet across the finishing line. Any ball handling violation (i.e., traveling or double dribbling) results in a retake of that particular trial. Movement in the wrong direction around the cone also results in a retake of the trial.

### Test 2: Defensive Movement

*Instructions:* The student assumes a defensive position (legs flexed at the knees with feet spread) on point A, facing away from the basket. On the signal "Ready, go," the student slides to the left to point B, touches the floor outside the freethrow lane with the left hand, performs a drop step (see Figure 6.10) and slides to point C and touches the floor outside the free throw lane with the right hand. The student continues through the course as mapped out in Figure 6.11 until both feet cross the finish line (diagonal return to point A). A practice trial is followed by two timed trials.

*Equipment Needed:* Stopwatch, measuring tape, and marking tape.

*Scoring Procedure:* The sum of the elapsed time for each trial is recorded as the student's score. Each trial is recorded to the nearest tenth of a second.

*Organizational Hints:* Crossing the feet or turning and running are considered faults and result in a retake of the trial. The drop step must occur after the hand touches outside the free throw lane.

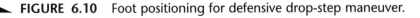

**FIGURE 6.10**    Foot positioning for defensive drop-step maneuver.

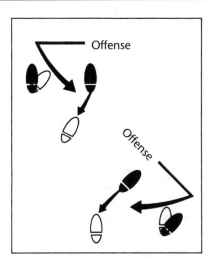

▶ **FIGURE 6.11**   Layout for defensive movement.

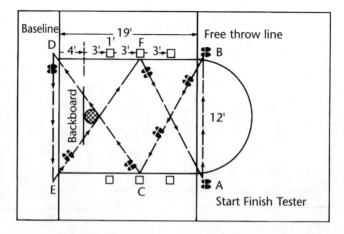

Reprinted by permission of American Alliance for Health, Physical Education, Recreation and Dance, Reston, Virginia.

### Test 3: Passing

*Instructions:* The student stands behind a restraining line, facing the wall, holding a basketball. On the signal "Ready, go," the student executes a chest pass toward the first target, retrieves the ball while moving into position facing the second target, and executes a chest pass toward target B. This sequence is continued until the student reaches target F. At target F, the student completes two passes toward the target and reverses the sequence back to target E, D, and so on. Figure 6.12 diagrams the arrangement for the wall pass test. One practice trial is followed by two timed 30-second trials.

*Equipment Needed:* A basketball, stopwatch, tape measure, and marking tape.

*Scoring Procedure:* Each pass hitting the target or the outline counts two points. A pass hitting wall space between the targets counts one point. The sum of points earned in each trial is recorded as the student's score.

*Organizational Hints:* Executing the pass in front of the restraining line results in no points for that pass. Passes other than chest passes are not allowed. Targets must be passed at in proper sequence.

### Test 4: Speed Spot Shooting

*Instructions:* The student assumes a ready position behind any one of five shooting spots appropriate for the age and grade. Shooting spots are 9 feet from the basket for grades 5 and 6, 12 feet for grades 7–9, and 15 feet for grades 10–12. Figure 6.13 shows the placement of the shooting spots. On the signal "Ready, go," the student shoots at the basketball goal, rebounds the

▶ **FIGURE 6.12**   Layout for basketball wall pass.

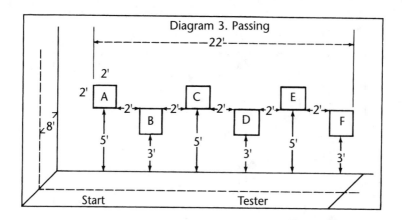

Reprinted by permission of American Alliance for Health, Physical Education, Recreation and Dance, Reston, Virginia.

ball, dribbles to another shooting spot, and shoots. The student must attempt at least one shot from each of the five spots. A maximum of four lay-ups are allowed during a trial, but no two may be in succession. A practice trial is followed by two timed 60-second trials.

***Equipment Needed:*** Stopwatch, basketball, tape measure, and marking tape.

***Scoring Procedure:*** Two points are awarded for each shot made. One point is awarded for each shot not made that hits the rim on its downward flight. The total points accumulated for both of the trials is recorded as the student's score.

***Organizational Hints:*** The student must have at least one foot behind the line when executing the shot. A scorecard that allows easy recording of shots taken facilitates scoring. Any ball-handling violation that precedes a shot negates the score of that attempt. Any lay-up in excess of four or immediately following a lay-up is scored as zero.

For information on other tests that measure basketball skills, see the *Representative Readings* list at the end of the chapter.

### *Measuring Football Skills*

### *AAHPER Football Skills Test (1966)*

***Purpose:*** The purpose of this test battery is to measure selected performance skills associated with the sport of football.

▶ **FIGURE 6.13** Layout and example for speed spot shooting.

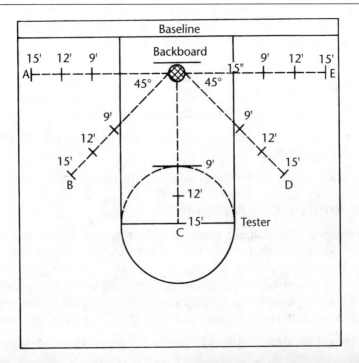

Diagrams reprinted by permission of American Alliance for Health, Physical Education, Recreation and Dance, Reston, Virginia.

*Description:* The items selected for presentation in this text consist of the following tests: ball-changing zigzag run, catching the forward pass, football pass for accuracy, football punt for distance, forward pass for distance, kickoff, pull-out, and 50-yard dash with football.

*Validity:* Face validity is accepted.

*Reliability:* Not reported.

*Age Level:* Ages 10–18. Originally designed for boys.

*Norms:* Normative information is available in the AAHPER testing manual for boys ages 10–18.

*Test Area:* A large indoor area and smooth outdoor area free of debris.

### Test 1: Ball-Changing Zigzag Run

*Instructions:* The student assumes a starting position behind a restraining line holding a football under the right arm. On the signal "Go," the student runs in a zigzag pattern through a series of five cones placed in a straight line 10 feet apart, changing the location of the ball to the outside arm as each cone is passed. The student circles the last (fifth) cone and repeats the in and out pattern back to the starting line. Two trials are given.

*Equipment Needed:* Stopwatch, football, tape measure, and five cones.

*Scoring Procedure:* The elapsed time from the signal "Go," until the student crosses the starting line on the return run is recorded to the nearest tenth of a second. The faster of the two trials is recorded as the student's score.

*Organizational Hints:* Touching a cone results in a retake of that particular trial. After switching the ball to the other arm, the free arm should be extended in a stiff-arm position.

### Test 2: Catching the Forward Pass

*Instructions:* The student assumes a ready position 9 feet to the left of the center on a line of scrimmage. On a signal, the student runs straight for 30 feet and turns at a 90-degree angle to the left and continues the pattern. A passer located 15 feet behind the center passes the football to the receiver. Ten passes are thrown. The same procedure is followed with the student lined up 9 feet to the right of center, running a pattern 30 feet straight downfield and cutting to the right. Figure 6.14 depicts the field specifications for this particular test.

*Equipment Needed:* Boundary cones to mark the starting point, cutting point, and passing point, and footballs.

*Scoring Procedure:* One point is awarded for each pass caught. The total number of passes caught is recorded as the student's score.

▶ **FIGURE 6.14** Layout for the AAHPERD football forward pass catching test.

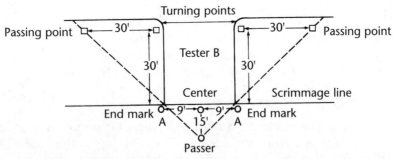

*"A" is the starting position of the subject.*

From AAHPERD Football Skills Test Manual, Washington, DC: American Alliance for Health, Physical Education, Recreation and Dance, 1966. Reprinted by permission.

*Organizational Hints:* The passer should be skilled in throwing a football. A passing point should be located 30 feet to the outside of each cutting point. Poorly thrown balls result in a retake of that trial. The ball should be thrown slightly above head height.

### Test 3: Football Pass for Accuracy

*Instructions:* The student assumes a standing position behind a restraining line located 15 yards from a target that is hung on the wall. Specifications for this target are the same as for the baseball throw for accuracy, previously discussed in this chapter. The student attempts 10 passes at the target. One sequence of 10 trials is given.

*Equipment Needed:* Target, measuring tape, marking tape, and footballs.

*Scoring Procedure:* Three points are awarded for a hit in the inner circle, two for the middle circle, and one for the outer circle. Throws hitting on the line are awarded the higher point value. The sum of 10 trials is recorded as the student's score.

*Organizational Hints:* To simulate a game situation, students should be encouraged to move either left or right before throwing. Students must remain behind the restraining line while throwing.

### Test 4: Football Punt for Distance

*Instructions:* The student assumes a position in front of a restraining line which is six feet from the punting line. Staying within these lines, the student is instructed to punt the football as far as possible. Three trials are given.

*Equipment Needed:* Footballs, 200-foot tape measure, and boundary cones.

*Scoring Procedure:* The farthest of the three trials is recorded to the nearest foot.

*Organizational Hints:* The measurement of distance is made at right angles from the point of landing to the punting line (the tape does not have to be moved in an arc to measure each throw). Each punt should be marked with a stake or some other visible but not easily moved object.

### Test 5: Forward Pass for Distance

*Instructions:* The student assumes a position in front of a restraining line which is six feet from the passing line. Staying within these lines, the student is instructed to pass the football as far as possible. Three trials are given.

*Equipment Needed:* Footballs, 200-foot tape measure, and boundary cones.

*Scoring Procedure:* The farthest of the three trials is recorded to the nearest foot.

*Organizational Hints:* The measurement of distance is made at right angles from the point of landing to the passing line (the tape does not have to be moved in an arc to measure each throw). Each pass should be marked with a stake or some other visible but not easily moved object.

### Test 6: Kickoff

*Instructions:* A football is placed on a kicking tee so that it tilts slightly back toward the kicker. The player kicks the ball as far as possible downfield. Three trials are given.

*Equipment Needed:* Footballs, 200-foot tape measure, kicking tee, and boundary cones.

*Scoring Procedure:* The farthest of the three trials is recorded to the nearest foot.

*Organizational Hints:* The measurement of distance is made at right angles from the point of landing to the kicking line (the tape does not have to be moved in an arc to measure each throw). Each kick should be marked with a stake or some other visible but not easily moved object. The student may take as long a run as desired.

### Test 7: Pull-out

*Instructions:* The student assumes a set position (football stance). On the signal "Go," the student pulls out to the right, runs around a goal post (or cone) located 9 foot 3 inches from the starting position, and straight downfield for 30 feet. Two trials are given.

*Equipment Needed:* Stopwatch, tape measure, and boundary cones.

*Scoring Procedure:* The score is the elapsed time from the signal "Go" until the student crosses the finish line. The better of the two trials is recorded.

*Organizational Hints:* The finish line should be clearly marked. A boundary cone may be substituted for a goal post.

### Test 8: 50-Yard Dash with Football

*Instructions:* The student assumes a ready position behind a starting line and, on the command "Go," runs 50 yards carrying the football under the arm. Two trials are given.

*Equipment Needed:* Stopwatch, football, measuring tape, and boundary cones.

*Scoring Procedure:* The amount of time elapsed between the start and the moment the student crosses the finish line is the score. The better of two trials is recorded.

*Organizational Hints:* The testing area should be a smooth, safe area free of debris.

For information on other tests that measure football skills, see the *Representative Readings* list at the end of the chapter.

## Measuring Soccer Skills

## The McDonald Soccer Test (1951)

*Purpose:* The purpose of this test is to measure general soccer ability.

*Description:* The test requires the student to display the fundamental skills of accurate kicking, ball control, and ability to receive a moving ball.

*Validity:* Validity coefficients derived by correlating coaches' ratings of playing abilities with test scores ranged from .63 to .94.

*Reliability:* Not reported for this test.

*Age Level:* Originally designed for college men and women, this test is also appropriate for high school boys and girls.

*Norms:* Not available for high school students.

*Test Area:* A smooth, flat area free of debris and long grass is suitable for this test.

*Instructions:* The student assumes a position behind a restraining line located nine feet from a wall, which is at least 30 feet wide by 11.5 feet high. On the signal to start, the student kicks the ball against the wall as many times as possible in 30 seconds. The student is allowed to retrieve the ball with any part of the body and return it to a position behind the restraining line. All kicks must occur from behind the restraining line. Four trials are given.

*Equipment Needed:* Wall space, three soccer balls, stopwatch, boundary cones or marking tape, and a tape measure.

*Scoring Procedure:* The highest number of successful kicks for one of the four trials is recorded as the student's score.

*Organizational Hints:* Two spare soccer balls should be placed along the nine-foot restraining line and may be used if the kicked ball gets out of control. The student may kick the ball on the fly or on the bounce.

## Soccer Battery

(Yeagley, 1972)

*Purpose:* The purpose of this test is to measure fundamental soccer skills of novice participants.

*Description:* The battery consists of the following four test items: dribbling, heading, juggling, and wall volleying.

*Validity:* A multiple correlation derived from comparing juried ratings with test scores was .78.

*Reliability:* Reliability coefficients ranged from .64 to .91.

*Age Level:* Originally administered to college physical education majors, this test battery is appropriate for use with youth 10–18 years old.

*Norms:* Not available.

*Test Area:* Gymnasium with ample wall space.

### Test 1: Dribble

*Instructions:* The student assumes a ready position behind a restraining line. On the signal "Go," the student dribbles the soccer ball through the obstacle course described in Figures 6.15 and 6.16. Two trials are given.

*Equipment Needed:* Soccer ball, stopwatch, and boundary cones.

*Scoring Procedure:* The time elapsed from the signal "Go," until the student crosses the finish line and brings the ball to a complete halt is recorded to the nearest tenth of a second. The best of two trials is recorded as the student's score.

*Organizational Hints:* While the course outline must be followed, a student is not penalized for touching or moving an obstacle with the feet or ball.

► **FIGURE 6.15**   Soccer ball dribble.

► **FIGURE 6.16**   Layout for soccer dribble.

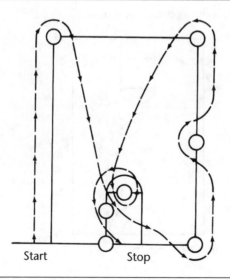

Start          Stop

Reprinted by permission of J. L. Yeagley, Indiana University, Bloomington, Indiana.

### Test 2: Heading

***Instructions:*** The student assumes a standing position on the inside of the backcourt portion of the center circle area of a basketball floor. Using the midcourt line as the restraining line, the student attempts to head a thrown soccer ball into the specified scoring area. Figure 6.17 shows the configuration for this test. Three tosses each are made from points A and C and four tosses from point B for a total of 10 attempts.

***Equipment Needed:*** Several soccer balls and marking tape.

***Scoring Procedure:*** The sum of points earned on all 10 trials is recorded as the student's score.

***Organizational Hints:*** We suggest that the distance be reduced from the heading area to the scoring area for youngsters. The toss should be made in a soft manner, reaching a height of no more than 15 feet. Any balls landing on the line are awarded the higher point value. The teacher should use caution and good judgment if employing this test at the elementary school level so as to reduce the potential for neck injury.

### Test 3: Juggling

***Instructions:*** The student assumes a standing position holding a soccer ball in the hands. On the signal "Go," the student bounces the ball on the floor

► **FIGURE 6.17**    Layout for heading test.

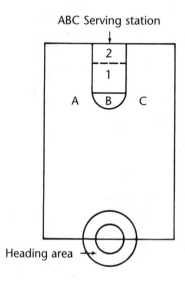

Reprinted by permission of J. L. Yeagley, Indiana University, Bloomington, Indiana.

and attempts to juggle the ball with the feet (or other parts of the body except the arms and hands) as many times as possible in 30 seconds. Two trials are given.

*Equipment Needed:* Stopwatch and soccer ball.

*Scoring Procedure:* The total number of legal juggles in 30 seconds is recorded. The better of two trials is reported as the student's score.

*Organizational Hints:* The half-court area of a basketball court serves as the testing area. One point is deducted each time the student touches the ball with arms or hands. The ball is allowed to bounce on the floor.

### Test 4: Wall Volley

*Instructions:* The student assumes a standing position behind a restraining line, which is located 15 feet from a smooth wall. Figure 6.18 describes the set-up specifications for this test. On the signal "Go," the student kicks the ball at the wall as many times as possible in 30 seconds. Two trials are given.

*Equipment Needed:* Stopwatch, marking tape, tape measure, and soccer ball.

*Scoring Procedure:* The total number of legal kicks during the 30-second period is recorded. The student's score is the better of the two trials.

▶ **FIGURE 6.18** Layout for soccer wall-volley test.

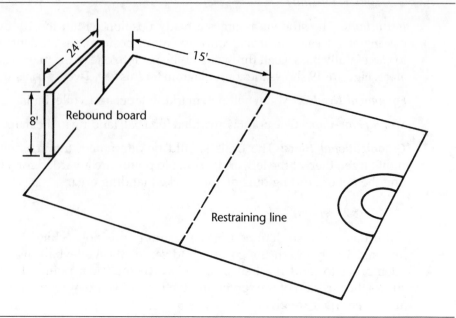

Reprinted by permission of J. L. Yeagley, Indiana University, Bloomington, Indiana.

*Organizational Hints:* Failure to keep the nonkicking foot behind the restraining line results in no credit for that attempt. Extra balls should be readily available in case the student loses control of the ball.

For information on other tests that measure soccer skills, see the *Representative Readings* list at the end of the chapter.

## Measuring Volleyball Skills

### AAHPER Volleyball Skills Test (1965)

*Purpose:* The purpose of this test battery is to measure student performance of selected volleyball skills.

*Description:* The test battery comprises the following four items: passing, serving, setting, and volleying.

*Validity:* Not reported.

*Reliability:* Not reported.

*Age Level:* Ages 10–18.

*Norms:* Normative information for each of the four tests is available in the testing manual.

*Test Area:* Gymnasium with unobstructed wall space.

#### Test 1: Passing

*Instructions:* The student assumes a ready position within the 10- by 6-foot passing area located near midcourt. From this position, the student attempts to successfully pass a ball thrown over the net into one of the marked landing areas. Figure 6.19 shows the court diagram for this test. Twenty trials are given.

*Equipment Needed:* Volleyball net, marking tape, and volleyballs.

*Scoring Procedure:* One point is awarded for a ball landing in the marked area.

*Organizational Hints:* The trials should be alternated, aiming first at the right target, then at the left, and so on. No points are awarded for a ball hitting the net or landing outside the marked landing area.

#### Test 2: Serving

*Instructions:* The student assumes a standing position behind the serving line midway between the corners and serves the volleyball over the net, attempting to land the ball in areas worth the most points. Figure 6.20 shows the position of the server and the respective point values for marked areas. Ten trials are given.

*Equipment Needed:* Volleyball net, marking tape, and volleyballs.

▶ **FIGURE 6.19** Layout for volleyball passing test.

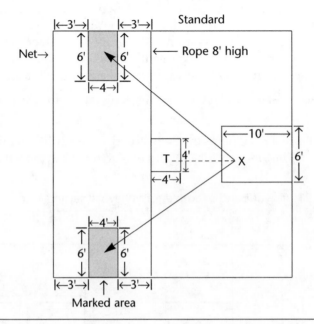

Reprinted by permission of American Alliance for Health, Physical Education, Recreation and Dance, Reston, Virginia.

▶ **FIGURE 6.20** Layout for volleyball service test.

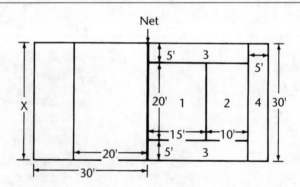

Reprinted by permission of American Alliance for Health, Physical Education, Recreation and Dance, Reston, Virginia.

***Scoring Procedure:*** The total points accumulated in the 10 trials is reported as the student's score.

***Organizational Hints:*** The distance from serving line to net should be shortened from 30 feet to 20 feet for children younger than 12 years of age.

### Test 3: Setting

*Instructions:* The student assumes a ready position inside one of the six-by-five-foot receiving areas located near the net at approximately midcourt and attempts to set a ball thrown from a designated area over the net into the six-by-four-foot target area. Ten consecutive trials are given to the right side and ten to the left. Figure 6.21 indicates the specifications for the testing area.

*Equipment Needed:* Volleyball net, marking tape, tape measure, and volleyballs.

*Scoring Procedure:* One point is awarded for each ball landing in the targeted area. The total score is the sum of hits from both the left and right sides.

▶ **FIGURE 6.21**    Layout and example for volleyball setting test.

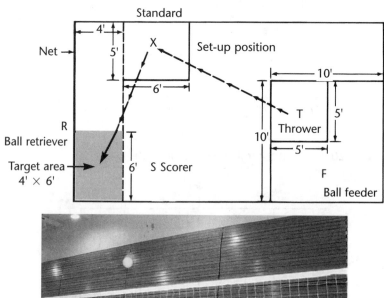

Diagram reprinted by permission of American Alliance for Health, Physical Education, Recreation and Dance, Reston, Virginia.

▶ **FIGURE 6.22**   Layout for volleyball volleying test.

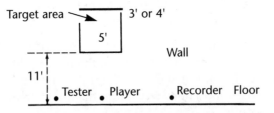

Reprinted by permission of American Alliance for Health, Physical Education, Recreation and Dance, Reston, Virginia.

**Organizational Hints:** Any throw that does not land within the setting area may be repeated.

### Test 4: Volleying

**Instructions:** The student assumes a ready position next to a wall with volleyball in hand. The student begins the test by throwing the ball against the wall and attempting to hit the ball into a target area that is 5 feet wide, 3 to 4 feet long, and 11 feet from the floor. Figure 6.22 shows the specifications for the testing area. One 60-second trial is given.

**Equipment Needed:** Volleyball, stopwatch, marking tape, and tape measure.

**Scoring Procedure:** The number of volleys landing in the target area during the one-minute time limit is recorded as the student's score.

**Organizational Hints:** If the student catches or loses control of the ball, the test must be restarted by throwing the ball against the wall. Only legal hits are allowed.

## High Wall-Volley Test
(Cunningham and Garrison, 1968)

**Purpose:** The purpose of this test is to measure the student's ability to pass the ball into a target area.

**Description:** This test is similar to the volleying test for the AAHPER Volleyball Skills Battery.

**Validity:** Validity coefficients derived from judges' ratings of the test ranged from .62 to .72.

**Reliability:** The test-retest reliability coefficient for college women was .87.

**Age Level:** Although the test was originally devised for college women, it is appropriate to use with youth ages 10–adult.

*Norms:* Not available.

*Test Area:* Gymnasium area with unobstructed wall space and at least a 20-foot ceiling.

*Instructions:* The student stands anywhere in front of a target composed of a 3-foot horizontal line located 10 feet from the floor and two 3-foot vertical lines connected to the end of the horizontal line. Using legal hits, the student attempts to pass and volley a ball into the target area as many times as possible in 30 seconds. Two trials are given.

*Equipment Needed:* Volleyball, tape measure, and marking tape.

*Scoring Procedure:* One point is scored each time the ball hits in the target area or on the lines, including extensions of the 3-foot vertical lines. To be counted, the hit must be legal. The student's score is the better of the two trials.

*Organizational Hints:* If the student loses control of the ball, it may be retrieved and the student may start by tossing the ball off the wall. The student should rest between trials.

For more information on other tests measuring volleyball skills, see the *Representative Readings* list at the end of the chapter.

# Individual and Dual Sports

The following sections describe tests that are designed to assess specific skill performance in individual and dual sports.

## *Measuring Badminton Skills*

### *French Short Serve Test*

(Scott, Carpenter, French, and Kuhl, 1941)

*Purpose:* The purpose of this test is to measure the student's ability to execute a badminton serve accurately, short, and low.

*Validity:* A validity coefficient of .66 was obtained using a criterion of ladder tournament rankings.

*Reliability:* Reported correlational coefficients range from .51 to .96.

*Age Level:* Ages 10–college.

*Norms:* Not reported.

*Test Area:* A regulation badminton court with appropriate target markings.

*Instructions:* The student stands behind the short service line and executes 20 consecutive legal short serves, attempting to hit the shuttlecock between

**FIGURE 6.23** Layout for French short serve test.

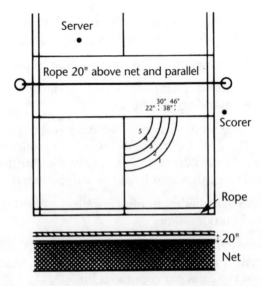

Reprinted by permission of American Alliance for Health, Physical Education, Recreation and Dance, Reston, Virginia.

the rope (strung the length of the net and 20 inches above it) and the net and land it in the target area shown in Figure 6.23. Two practice trials are permitted.

*Equipment Needed:* Tape measure, two dozen shuttlecocks, badminton racquets, rope to stretch above the net, and marking tape.

*Scoring Procedure:* The score is recorded for each successful serve that passes between the rope and net and lands in the target area. No points are awarded for serves that fail to pass between the net and the rope or shuttlecocks landing outside the target area. Twenty trials are administered. The total accumulated points are recorded as the student's score.

*Organizational Hints:* The rope used should be highly visible to assist in determining the flight of the shuttlecock. If the shuttlecock hits the rope, it is re-served and counts as a retrial.

### Badminton Wall-Volley Test

(Lockhart and McPherson, 1949)

*Purpose:* The purpose of this test is to measure the performer's ability to volley a badminton shuttlecock.

*Validity:* Reported validity coefficients range from .60 to .90.

*Reliability:* A test-retest reliability coefficient of .90 was reported using college women.

*Age Level:* This test was originally devised for use with college women, although it could also be used with youth ages 12–18.

*Norms:* Normative information can be found in the original source.

*Test Area:* Gymnasium with unobstructed wall space. Figure 6.24 shows the floor and wall markings for this test.

*Instructions:* The student stands behind a restraining line located 6 feet 6 inches from the wall. On the signal "Go," the student executes a legal serve above the net line on the wall and volleys the shuttlecock continuously for 30 seconds. Three 30-second trials are administered.

*Equipment Needed:* Badminton racquet, new shuttlecocks, stopwatch, tape measure, and marking tape.

*Scoring Procedure:* The number of legal volleys accumulated during each of the three trials is recorded as the student's score. Placing the shuttlecock in play with a serve does not count as a hit.

▶ **FIGURE 6.24**  Layout for badminton wall volley test.

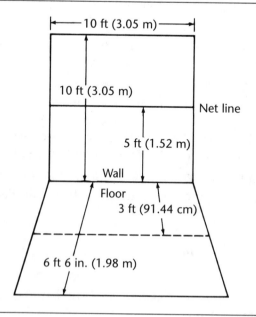

Reprinted by permission of American Alliance for Health, Physical Education, Recreation and Dance, Reston, Virginia.

*Organizational Hints:* Only shots that are hit from behind the restraining line are counted. If the player loses control of the volley, it may be restarted with a legal serve. Rest times are permitted between trials.

## Poole Long-Serve Test

(Poole and Nelson, 1970)

*Purpose:* The purpose of this test is to assess the student's ability to serve high and deep into the opposing backcourt.

*Validity:* A validity coefficient of .51 was derived using the results of tournament play as a criterion measure.

*Reliability:* A correlational coefficient of .81 was obtained using the test-retest method.

*Age Level:* Originally designed for college students, this test may also be used with high school students.

*Norms:* Not available.

*Test Area:* Regulation badminton court.

*Instructions:* The student assumes a position behind the short service line and attempts to serve the shuttlecock over the extended racquet of an assistant standing in a marked area 11 feet from the net (see Figure 6.25) into the five marked target zones. Twelve trials are given.

► **FIGURE 6.25**   Layout for Poole long-serve test.

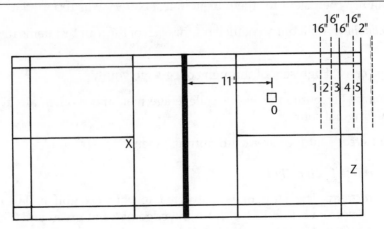

*Equipment Needed:* Badminton racquet, two dozen shuttlecocks, tape measure, and marking tape.

*Scoring Procedure:* The point value of the target area in which each shuttlecock lands is recorded for each attempt. The sum of the 10 best trials is recorded as the student's score.

*Organizational Hints:* Shuttlecocks landing on a line are awarded the higher point value. One point is deducted for any shuttlecock failing to clear the racquet of the opponent (point 0).

For information on other tests that measure badminton skills, see the *Representative Readings* list at the end of the chapter.

## Measuring Golf Skills

### Green Golf Skills Test Battery

Green, East, and Hensley, 1987

*Purpose:* The purpose of this test battery is to measure the fundamental skill components of golf: chipping, pitching, putting, and using the approach shot.

*Description:* The full battery of four test items was designed to measure golfing ability in college males and females, but it appears to be appropriate for high school–age youth. To reduce administrative time, shortened versions of the test may be utilized. The two most accurate predictors of overall golfing ability are the middle distance shot and chip shot.

*Validity:* Using the score from 36 holes of golf as the criterion measure, a validity coefficient for the four-item test battery was reported as .77.

*Reliability:* Reliability coefficients for each of the four test items ranged from .65 to .93.

*Age Level:* High school through college-age youth.

*Norms:* Percentile norms for college-age men and women are available in the original source.

*Test Area:* Outdoor area with putting green.

#### Test 1: Chip Shot

*Instructions:* The student is instructed to chip six golf balls toward the flagstick from a line 10 feet from the edge of a flat green and 35 feet from the flagstick. Six trials are given.

*Equipment Needed:* Golf balls, golf clubs, measuring tape, and flagstick.

*Scoring Procedure:* The sum of the measured distance (to the nearest foot) between the point at which each of the chip shots came to rest and the flagstick is recorded as the student's score.

*Organizational Hints:* Students are allowed to change clubs anytime during the test.

### Test 2: Long Putt

*Instructions:* The student assumes a putting position over one of six balls equally spaced around the cup on a circle with a 25-foot radius. Students are instructed to putt the first ball as close as possible to the hole (or into the hole) and proceed in a clockwise manner to the next ball, and so on, until all six balls have been stroked.

*Equipment Needed:* Golf balls, putters, measuring tape, and hole.

*Scoring Procedure:* The student's score is the sum of the measured distance (to the nearest inch) that each putt came to rest from the cup for all six attempts.

*Organizational Hints:* Students should be encouraged to putt the ball as close as possible or into the hole. Be sure to remove balls from the green after each student's trial.

### Test 3: Middle Distance Shot

*Instructions:* Students are instructed to hit four golf balls down a smooth, open fairway toward a line of flags placed as targets across the fairway. Target flags for females should be placed 110 yards from the teeing area and 140 yards for males. Four shots are given.

*Equipment Needed:* Golf balls, 10 flagsticks or boundary cones, measuring tape, and golf clubs (middle to short irons).

*Scoring Procedure:* The score is the sum of the measured perpendicular distance (to the nearest yard) from the line of flags at which each ball came to rest.

*Organizational Hints:* Students are allowed to change clubs anytime during the test. For safety purposes, the scoring should take place after the student has completed hitting all four shots. The students should be encouraged to use a full swing.

### Test 4: Pitch Shot

*Instructions:* Students are positioned behind a restraining line 40 yards from a simulated green marked with a flagstick and instructed to pitch six golf balls toward a flagstick using either a seven, eight, or nine iron, pitching wedge, or sand wedge.

**Equipment Needed:**  Golf balls, seven, eight, or nine irons, pitching and sand wedges, measuring tape, and flagsticks or boundary cones.

**Scoring Procedure:**  The student's recorded score is the sum of the measured distance (to the nearest foot) from the flagstick at which each of the six pitch shots came to rest.

**Organizational Hints:**  To avoid unnecessary damage due to repeated landings, a simulated green that provides a soft landing area should be used. Balls should be scored and removed from the impact area after each attempt. Students are allowed to change clubs anytime during the test.

### Indoor Golf Skill Test
(Shick and Berg, 1983)

**Purpose:**  The purpose of this test is to measure the golf skills ability of junior high school boys.

**Validity:**  Using a criterion measure of the best of three scores reported for a par-three nine-hole course, a validity coefficient of .84 was reported.

**Reliability:**  A reliability coefficient of .91 was obtained using the test-retest method.

**Age Level:**  Junior high school–age through college.

**Norms:**  None available.

**Test Area:**  This test can be conducted either outside or inside in a small gymnasium or multipurpose area.

**Instructions:**  The student is instructed to hit a plastic golf ball off a driving mat, with a five iron, as far as possible toward a boundary cone located 68 feet from the hitting area directly in front of the student. Figure 6.26 shows the arrangement for the target and scoring zones. Two practice trials are followed by 20 test trials.

**Equipment Needed:**  Several five irons (at least one left-handed), fluorescent boundary cone to mark target and scoring zones, tape measure, marking tape or rope, and driving mat.

**Scoring Procedure:**  The score for each trial is the point value of the area where the ball first hits. Balls landing on a line are given the higher (or highest, if at an intersection of three scoring areas) point value. Balls that travel beyond the scoring areas are awarded either a 4 or 6 depending on the line of flight. Any topped ball passing through the target area is awarded one point. A "whiff," or a ball landing outside the target areas, scores 0. The student's score is the sum of all 20 trials.

▶ **FIGURE 6.26** Layout for indoor golf test.

| | | | |
|---|---|---|---|
| 4 | 6 | 4 | 15' |
| 2 | 4 | 2 | 15' |
| 1 | 2 | 1 | 15' |
| 1 | 1 | 1 | 23' |

○ ←Cone

←15'→ ┊ ←15'→
Student
←————45'————→

Reprinted by permission of American Alliance for Health, Physical Education, Recreation and Dance, Reston, Virginia.

**Organizational Hints:** It is possible to have two or more stations in a gymnasium. The safest and best vantage point for the scorer is a position on either side of the scoring area where the 1 and 2 zones meet.

For information on other tests that measure golf skills, see the *Representative Readings* list at the end of the chapter.

### Measuring Racquetball Skills

### Racquetball Skills Test

(Hensley, East, and Stillwell, 1979)

**Purpose:** The purpose of this test is to measure the speed and power components of racquetball.

**Description:** The test battery consists of the following two test items: a short wall-volley test (speed component) and a long wall-volley test (power component).

**Validity:** Using instructors' ratings of students as the criterion measure, the validity coefficients for men and women combined were .79 for the short wall-volley test and .86 for the long wall-volley test.

**Reliability:** The estimated reliability of the short wall-volley test for the sum of trials over two days was determined to be .76 for men and .86 for women.

Correlational coefficients for the long wall-volley test were .85 for men and .82 for women.

*Age Level:* Originally designed for college students, this test is appropriate for use with high school students.

*Norms:* College T-score norms for men and women are available in the original source.

*Test Area:* Racquetball court.

### Test 1: Short Wall-Volley Test

*Instructions:* The participant stands behind the short service line, drops the ball, and volleys it against the front wall for 30 seconds. A one-minute practice period is followed by two 30-second trials.

*Equipment Needed:* Racquetball racquet, four new regulation racquetballs, marking tape, and a stopwatch.

*Scoring Procedure:* One point is awarded each time the ball legally hits the front wall during the 30-second period. The recorded score is the sum of legal hits of the two trials. No points are awarded when the participant steps over the restraining line to hit the ball or when the ball skips on the floor on the way to the wall.

*Organizational Hints:* There are no restrictions on the number of times the ball bounces before being volleyed. The participant may retrieve the ball in the front court but must return to a position behind the restraining line to put it back in play. Any type of stroke can be used to keep the ball in play. The scorer should be in the court and have two additional balls available in case the original is put out of play. The stopwatch is started when the dropped ball hits the floor for the first time.

### Test 2: Long Wall-Volley Test

*Instructions:* The long wall-volley test is administered in the same manner as the short wall-volley test except for the location of the student on the court. For this test, the participant must volley the ball from behind a restraining line located 12 feet behind and parallel to the short service line.

*Equipment:* Racquetball racquet, four new regulation racquetballs, marking tape, and a stopwatch.

*Scoring Procedure:* One point is awarded for each time the ball legally hits the front wall during the 30-second period. The recorded score is the sum of legal hits of the two trials. No points are awarded when the participant steps over the restraining line to hit the ball or when the ball skips on the floor on the way to the wall.

*Organizational Hints:* Same as in the short volley test, except that the two extra balls may be conveniently placed in the backwall corners.

## Measuring Tennis Skills

### Revision of the Dyer Backboard Test
(Hewitt, 1965)

*Purpose:* The purpose of this test is to measure the rallying and serving ability of students.

*Validity:* Converted *r*'s ranged from .68 to .73 for beginners and .84 to .89 for advanced players.

*Reliability:* Test-retest procedures resulted in correlational coefficients of .82 for beginners and .93 for advanced players.

*Age Level:* Ages 12 through college.

*Norms:* Not reported.

*Test Area:* A smooth gymnasium wall or rebound wall at least 20 feet high and 20 feet wide.

*Instructions:* The student takes two tennis balls and assumes a position behind a restraining line located 20 feet from unobstructed wall space. When ready, the student serves a tennis ball so it hits above the marked net line on the wall and continues to rally using any type of ground or volley stroke. Three 30-second trials are given.

*Equipment Needed:* Basket of tennis balls, tennis racquets, marking tape, tape measure, and a stopwatch.

*Scoring Procedure:* One point is scored each time the ball is hit above the three-foot net line on the wall (balls hitting on the line are considered good). No point is awarded if the student steps over the restraining line while executing the shot. The sum of the three trials is recorded as the student's score.

*Organizational Hints:* If the student loses control of the rally, one of the spare balls should be put in play by serving. This serve does not count as a point and no points are deducted for using the additional tennis balls. Lines on the wall should be one inch wide. A warm-up period on an adjacent wall area is allowed.

### Hewitt's Tennis Achievement Test (1966)

*Purpose:* The purpose of this test battery is to measure the student's skill at executing ground strokes and serving the tennis ball.

*Description:* The battery consists of the following three items: test for forehand and backhand drive, service placement, and speed of service.

*Validity:* Coefficients ranged from .52 to .93.

*Reliability:* Correlational coefficients ranged from .75 to .93.

*Age Level:* The test is appropriate for high school through college students.

*Norms:* Normative information is available in the original source.

*Test Area:* Tennis court.

### Test 1: Forehand and Backhand Drive Test

*Instructions:* The student assumes a position at the baseline at point X (see Figure 6.27), while the test administrator stands on the other side of the net on the center service line at point Y. Using a tennis racquet, the test administrator hits five practice balls to the student's forehand just beyond the service court. The student moves into proper position and attempts to return the ball over the net and under a seven-foot-high rope, strung above net parallel to it, so the ball lands as near to the baseline as possible in one of the target zones. Figure 6.27 shows the placement of the scoring zones for this test. Ten trials are given. The test is repeated to the backhand side.

▶ **FIGURE 6.27**    Layout for Hewitt's tennis forehand and backhand drive test.

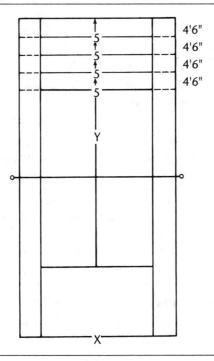

*Equipment Needed:* A basket of tennis balls, tennis racquet, measuring tape 7' × 2" × 2" poles, rope to span above net, and marking tape.

*Scoring Procedure:* The point values earned for each hit (forehand and backhand side) are totaled. The student's score is the sum of these values. Balls hit long, wide, or into the net are scored as 0. Shots that pass over the seven-foot rope and land in a scoring area are counted one-half of the score for that area. All lets are repeated.

*Organizational Hints:* To ensure consistency, the same test administrator should hit balls to all students.

### Test 2: Service Placement Test

*Instructions:* The right service court is marked according to specifications described in Figure 6.28. A rope seven feet from the ground is strung directly over the net. After a 10-minute warm-up, the student serves 10 balls into the marked right service court. The ball must pass through the area marked by the top of the net and the rope.

*Equipment Needed:* A basket of tennis balls, tennis racquet, measuring tape, two-inch-square poles seven feet long, and marking tape.

▶ **FIGURE 6.28**  Layout for Hewitt's service placement test.

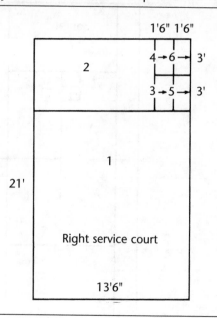

***Scoring Procedure:*** The point value for the target zone in which the ball hits is the score. The sum of the 10 trials is recorded as the student's score.

***Organizational Hints:*** The instructor should demonstrate the proper service technique prior to administering the test.

### Test 3: Speed of Service Test

***Instructions:*** After considerable experimentation, it was determined that the distance a served ball traveled between its first and second bounce was a determinant of the speed of the ball. The court is marked in accordance with specifications detailed in Figure 6.29. This test should be conducted simultaneously with the Service Placement Test and should use the same rules.

▶ **FIGURE 6.29**   Layout for Hewitt's speed of service test.

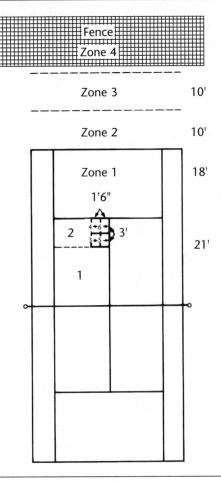

*Equipment Needed:* A basket of tennis balls, tennis racquet, measuring tape, two-inch-square poles seven feet long, rope, and marking tape.

*Scoring Procedure:* The target zone in which the ball hits on its second bounce (after a good serve) is noted. The point values for each serve are recorded. The sum of the 10 trials is recorded as the student's score.

For information on other tests that measure tennis skills, see the *Representative Readings* list at the end of the chapter.

## SUMMARY

This chapter reviews the components of skill-related physical fitness and briefly describes selected field-based tests designed to measure agility, balance, coordination, reaction time, speed, and various individual, dual and team sports skills. Descriptions of tests include purpose, instructions for test administration, validity and reliability, age level, test area, equipment needed, scoring procedures, norms, and organizational hints. The tests cited in this chapter are appropriate for youth of all ages, require little expense, and can be administered in most school settings.

## ► DISCUSSION QUESTIONS

1. Cite characteristics of psychomotor performance. How do these characteristics differ from components of health-related physical fitness?

2. What are the fundamental skills necessary for children to acquire? In what order do you think mastery of these skills occurs?

3. List the components of skill-related physical fitness. Which component is the most important in performing sports-related skills? The least important? Why?

4. Which test or test battery would you select to measure the general motor ability of students in your class? Why?

5. Cite some advantages and disadvantages of incorporating tests to measure sports skills into the physical education curriculum.

## ► REFERENCES

American Alliance for Health, Physical Educa-tion, Recreation and Dance. (1984). *AAHPERD skills test manual: basketball for boys and girls.* Reston, VA.

American Association for Health, Physical Education, and Recreation. (1965). *AAHPER skills test manual—volleyball for boys and girls.* Washington, DC.

_____. (1966). *AAHPER skills test manual for football.* Washington, DC.

_____. (1966). *AAHPER skills test manual—softball for boys.* Washington, DC.

_____. (1966). *AAHPER skills test manual—softball for girls.* Washington, DC.

_____. (1976). *AAHPER youth fitness test manual.* Reston, VA.

American Heart Association in Texas, and Governor's Commission on Physical Fitness. (1986). *Texas physical and motor fitness development program*. Austin, TX.

Barrow, H. M. (1954). Test of motor ability for college men. *Research Quarterly* 25:253–60.

Barrow, H. M., and McGee, R. (1979). *A practical approach to measurement in physical education*. 3d ed. Philadelphia, PA: Lea and Febiger.

Bass, R. I. (1939). An analysis of the components of tests of semi-circular canal function and of static and dynamic balance. *Research Quarterly* 10:33–42.

Baumgartner, T. A., and Jackson, A. S. (1987). *Measurement for education in physical education*. 3d ed. Dubuque, IA: Wm. C. Brown.

Bennett, C. L. (1956). Relative contributions of modern dance, folk dance, basketball, and swimming to motor abilities of college women. *Research Quarterly* 27:256–57.

Collins, D. R., and Hodges, P. B. (1978). *A comprehensive guide to sports skills tests and measurement*. Springfield, IL: Charles C. Thomas.

Corbin, C. B., ed. (1980). *A textbook of motor development*. 2d ed. Dubuque, IA: Wm. C. Brown.

Corbin, C. B., and Lindsey, R. (1988) *Concepts of physical fitness with laboratories*. 6th ed. Dubuque, IA: Wm. C. Brown.

Cratty, B. J. (1979). *Perceptual and motor development in infants and children*. Englewood Cliffs, NJ: Prentice-Hall.

Cratty, B. J., and Martin, M. M. (1969). *Perceptual-motor efficiency in children*. Philadelphia, PA: Lea and Febiger.

Cunningham, P., and Garrison, P. (1968). High wall volley test for women's volleyball. *Research Quarterly* 39:486–90.

Cureton, T. K. (1947). *Physical fitness appraisal and guidance*. St. Louis, MO: C. V. Mosby.

———. (1951). *Physical fitness of champion athletes*. Urbana, IL: University of Illinois Press.

———. (1964). Improving the physical fitness of youth. *Monographs of the Society for Research in Child Development* 4(Serial No. 95, 29).

De Oreo, K. L. (1971). *Dynamic and static balance in preschool children*. Unpublished doctoral dissertation, University of Illinois.

———. (1980). Performance of fundamental motor tasks. In C. B. Corbin, ed., *A textbook of motor development*. Dubuque, IA: Wm. C. Brown.

Di Nucci, J. M. (1976). Gross motor performance: A comprehensive analysis of age and sex differences between boys and girls ages six to nine years. In J. Broekhoff, ed., *Physical education, sports and the sciences*, Eugene, OR: Microform Publications, University of Oregon.

Espenschade, A. (1947). Development of motor coordination in boys and girls. *Research Quarterly* 18:30–43.

Fleishman, E. A. (1964). *The structure and measurement of physical fitness*. Englewood Cliffs, NJ: Prentice-Hall.

Frederick, S. D. (1977). *Performance of selected motor tasks by three, four and five year old children*. Unpublished doctoral dissertation, Indiana University.

Fulton, C. D., and Hubbard, A. W. (1975). Effects of puberty on reaction and movement times. *Research Quarterly* 46:335–44.

Gallahue, D. L. (1982). *Understanding motor development in children*. New York: Wiley.

Gates, D. D., and Sheffield, R. P. (1940). Tests of change of direction as measurement of different kinds of motor ability in boys of the 7th, 8th, and 9th grades. *Research Quarterly* 11:136–74.

Govatos, L. A. (1966). Sex differences in children's motor performance. In *Collected papers of the eleventh interinstitutionalized seminar in child development*. Dearborn, MI: Michigan Education Department.

Green, K. H.; East. W. B.; and Hensley, L. D. (1987). A golf skills test battery for college males and females. *Research Quarterly for Exercise and Sport* 58:72–76.

Hensley, L. D.; East, W. B.; and Stillwell, J. L. (1979). A racquetball skills test. *Research Quarterly* 50:114–18.

Hewitt, J. E. (1965). Revision of the Dyer backboard tennis test. *Research Quarterly* 36:153–57.

———. (1966). Hewitt's tennis achievement test. *Research Quarterly* 37:231–37.

Jackson, A. B., and Baumgartner, T. A. (1969). Measurement schedules of sprint running. *Research Quarterly* 40:708–11.

Jensen, C. R., and Hirst, C. C. (1980). *Measurement in physical education and athletics*. New York: Macmillan.

Johnson, B. L., and Leach, J. (1968). *A modification of the Bass test of dynamic balance*. Unpublished study, East Texas State University, Commerce.

Johnson, B. L., and Nelson, J. K. (1986). *Practical measurements for evaluation in physical education*. 4th ed. New York: Macmillan.

Keogh, J. F. (1965). *Motor performance of elementary school children.* Los Angeles: University of California.

Kilday, K., and Latchaw, M. (1961). *Study of motor ability in ninth grade boys.* Unpublished manuscript, University of California at Los Angeles.

Lockhart, A., and McPherson, F. A. (1949). The development of a test of badminton playing ability. *Research Quarterly* 20:402–05.

Lockhart, A., and Mott, J. A. (1951). An experiment in homogeneous grouping and its effect on achievement in sports fundamentals. *Research Quarterly* 22.

McCloy, C. H., and Young, N. D. (1954). *Measurements in health and physical education.* 3d ed. New York: Appleton-Century-Crofts.

McDonald, L. G. (1951). The construction of a kicking skill test as an index of general soccer ability. Unpublished master's thesis, Springfield College, Massachusetts.

Milne, C.; Seefeldt, V.; and Reuschlein, P. (1976). Relationship between grade, sex, race and motor performance in young children. *Research Quarterly* 47:726–30.

O'Connor, M. F., and Cureton, T. K. (1945). Motor fitness tests for high school girls. *Research Quarterly* 16:302–14.

Pangrazi, R. P., and Dauer, V. P. (1995). *Dynamic physical education for elementary school children.* 11th ed. Boston: Allyn and Bacon.

Peterson, K. L., et al. (1974). *Factor analyses of motor performance for kindergarten, first, and second grade children: A tentative solution.* Paper presented at the Annual Convention of AAHPER, March, Anaheim, CA.

Poole, J., and Nelson, J. K. (1970). *Construction of a badminton skills test battery.* Unpublished manuscript, Louisiana State University, Baton Rouge.

Safrit, M. J. (1990). *Introduction to measurement in physical education and exercise science.* 2d ed. St. Louis, MO: Times Mirror/Mosby.

Schilling, F., and Kiphard, E. J. (1976). The body coordination test. *Journal of Health, Physical Education, and Recreation* 47:37.

Scott, M. G. (1939). The assessment of motor abilities of college women through objective tests. *Research Quarterly* 10:63–83.

Scott, M. G.; Carpenter, A.; French, E.; and Kuhl, L. (1941). Achievement examinations in badminton. *Research Quarterly* 12:242–53.

Seils, L. G. (1951). Agility-performance and physical growth. *Research Quarterly* 22:244.

Shick, J., and Berg, N. G. (1983). Indoor golf skill test for junior high school boys. *Research Quarterly for Exercise and Sport* 54:75–78.

State of North Carolina. (1977). *North Carolina motor fitness battery.* Raleigh, NC: Department of Public Instruction.

Van Slooten, P. H. (1973). *Performance of selected motor-coordination tests by young boys and girls in six socio-economic groups.* Unpublished doctoral dissertation, Indiana University, Bloomington.

Yeagley, J. (1972). *Soccer skills test.* Unpublished manuscript, Indiana University, Bloomington.

Zaichkowsky, L. D.; Zaichkowsky, L. B.; and Martinek, T. J. (1980). *Growth and development: The child and physical activity.* St. Louis, MO: C. V. Mosby.

## ▶ REPRESENTATIVE READINGS

## General

Barrow, H. M., and McGee, R. (1979). *A practical approach to measurement in physical education.* 3d ed. Philadelphia, PA: Lea and Febiger.

Bass, R. I. (1939). An analysis of the components of tests of semi-circular canal function and of static and dynamic balance. *Research Quarterly* 10:33–42.

Chelladurai, P. (1976). Manifestations of agility. *Journal of the Canadian AHPERD.* 42:36–41.

Corbin, C. B., and Lindsey, R. (1988). *Concepts of physical fitness with labora-tories.* 6th ed. Dubuque, IA: Wm. C. Brown.

Cratty, B. J., and Martin, M. (1969). *Perceptual-motor efficiency in children.* Philadelphia, PA: Lea and Febiger.

Gates, D. D., and Sheffield, R. P. (1940). Tests of change of direction as mea-surement of different kinds of motor ability in boys of the 7th, 8th, and 9th grades. Research Quarterly 11:136–74.

Gates, D. P., and Sheffield, R. P. (1940). Tests of change of direction as measurement of different kinds of motor ability in boys of the 7th, 8th, and 9th grades. *Research Quarterly* 11:136–47.

Kirby, R. F. (1971). A simple test of agility. *Coach and Athlete* June, pp. 30–31.

Larson, L. (1941). A factor analysis of motor ability variables and tests. *Research Quarterly* 12:499–517.

McCloy, C. H., and Young, N. D. (1954). *Measurements in health and physical education.* 3d ed. New York: Appleton-Century-Crofts.

Miller, D. K. (1994). *Measurement by the physical educator: why and how.* 2nd ed. Dubuque, IA: Brown and Benchmark.

Pangrazi, R. P., and Darst, P. W. (1991). *Dynamic physical education for secondary school students: Curriculum and instruction.* 2d ed. New York: Macmillan.

Pangrazi, R. P., and Hastad, D. N. (1986). *Fitness in the elementary schools.* Reston, VA: American Alliance for Health, Physical Education, Recreation and Dance.

Scott, M. G. (1939). The assessment of motor abilities of college women through objective tests. *Research Quarterly* 10:63–83.

## Badminton Skills Tests

Beverlein, M. A. (1970). *A skill test for the drop shot in badminton.* Unpub-lished master's thesis, Southern Illinois University, Carbondale.

Hicks, J. V. (1967). *The construction and evaluation of a battery of five badminton skill tests.* Unpublished doctoral dissertation, Texas Woman's University, Denton.

Johnson, R. M. (1967). *Determination of the validity and reliability of the bad-minton placement test.* Unpublished master's thesis, University of Oregon, Eugene.

Kowert, E. A. (1968). *Construction of a badminton ability test battery for men.* Unpublished master's thesis, University of Iowa, Iowa City.

Popp, P. (1970). *The development of a diagnostic test to determine badminton play-ing ability.* Unpublished master's thesis, University of Washington, Seattle.

## Basketball Skills Tests

Barrow, H. M. (1959). Basketball skill test. *Physical Educator* 16:26–27.

Cunningham, P. (1964). *Measuring basketball playing ability of high school girls.* Unpublished doctoral dissertation, University of Iowa, Iowa City.

Gilbert, R. R. (1968). *A study of selected variables in predicting basketball players.* Unpublished master's thesis, Springfield College, Massachusetts.

Mathews, L. E. (1963). *A battery of basketball skills tests for high school boys.* Unpublished master's thesis, University of Oregon, Eugene.

Moffit, D. (1970). *A measure of basketball skill for fifth and sixth grade boys.* Unpublished master's thesis, Central Washington State College, Ellensburg.

Plinke, J. F. (1966). *The development of basketball physical skill potential test batteries by height categories.* Unpublished doctoral dissertation, Indiana University, Bloomington.

Walter, R. J. (1968). *A comparison between two selected evaluative techniques for measuring basketball skill.* Unpublished master's thesis, Western Illinois University, Macomb.

## Football Skills Tests

Cowell, C. C., and Ismail, A. H. (1961). Validity of a football rating scale and its relationship to social integration and academic ability. *Research Quarterly* 32:461–67.

Lee, R. C. (1965). *A battery of tests to predict football potential.* Unpublished master's thesis, University of Utah, Salt Lake City.

May, L. D. (1972). *A study of the measurement of potential football ability in high school players.* Unpublished master's thesis, Texas Tech University, Lubbock.

McDavid, R. F. (1978). *Predicting potential in football players.* *Research Quarterly* 49:98–104.

Sells, T. D. (1977). *Selected movement and anthropometric variables of football defensive tackles.* Unpublished doctoral dissertation, Indiana University, Bloomington.

## Golf Skills Tests

Brown, H. S. (1969). A test battery for evaluating golf skills. *Texas AHPER Journal* 4:28–29.

Cochrane, J. F. (1960). *The construction of an indoor golf skills test as a measure of golfing ability.* Unpublished master's thesis, University of Minnesota, Minneapolis.

Cotten, D. J.; Thomas, J. R.; and Plaster, T. (1972). *A plastic ball test for golf iron skill*. Paper presented at AAHPER National Conference, March, Houston, TX.

McKee, M. E. (1950). A test for the full-swing shot in golf. *Research Quarterly* 21:40–46.

## Pickleball Skills Test

Wasem, J. (1994). Pickleball: A Comprehensive Skills test. *Strategies,* January 1994: 21–25.

Thompson, D. H. (1969). Immediate external feedback in the learning of golf skills. *Research Quarterly* 40:589–94.

Vanderhoof, E. R. (1956). *Beginning golf achievement tests*. Unpublished master's thesis, University of Iowa, Iowa City.

West, C., and Thorpe, J. A. (1968). Construction and validation of an eight-iron approach test. *Research Quarterly* 39:115–120.

## Racquetball Skills Tests

Buschner, C. A. (1976). *The validation of a racquetball skills test for college men*. Unpublished doctoral dissertation, Oklahoma State University, Stillwater.

Karpman, M. B., and Isaacs, L. D. (1979). An improved racquetball test. *Research Quarterly* 50:526–27.

Shannon, J., Brothers, J., and Ishee, J. (1991). Quick and effective skills test for racquetball. *Strategies,* November/December 1991: 24–25.

## Soccer Skills Tests

Crew, V. N. (1968). *A skill test battery for use in service program soccer classes at the university level*. Unpublished master's thesis, University of Oregon, Eugene.

MacKenzie, J. (1968). *The evaluation of a battery of soccer skill tests as an aid to classification of general soccer ability*. Unpublished master's thesis, University of Massachusetts, Amherst.

Mitchell, J. R. (1963). *The modification of the McDonald Soccer Skill Test for upper elementary school boys*. Unpublished master's thesis, Univer-sity of Oregon, Eugene.

Streck, B. (1961). *An analysis of the McDonald Soccer Skill Test as applied to junior high school girls*. Unpublished master's thesis, Fort Hays State College, Kansas.

## Softball/Baseball Skills Tests

Cale, A. A. (1962). *The investigation and analysis of softball skill tests for college women*. Unpublished master's thesis, University of Maryland, College Park.

Elrod, J. M. (1969). *Construction of a softball skill test battery for high school boys*. Unpublished master's thesis, Louisiana State University, Baton Rouge.

Everett, P. W. (1952). The prediction of baseball ability. *Research Quarterly* 23:15–19.

Fox, M. G. (1954). A test of softball batting ability. *Research Quarterly* 25:26–27.

Kelson, R. E. (1953). Baseball classification plan for boys. *Research Quarterly* 24:304–07.

Shick, J. (1970). Battery of defensive softball skills test for college women. *Research Quarterly* 41:82–87.

Sopa, A. (1967). *The construction and standardization of skill tests to measure achievement in specific softball playing abilities*. Unpublished master's thesis, University of North Carolina, Greensboro.

## Tennis Skills Tests

Avery, C. A.; Richardson, P. A.; and Jackson, A. W. (1979). A practical tennis serve test: Measurement of skill under simulated game conditions. *Research Quarterly* 50:554–64.

Cotton, D. J., and Nixon, J. (1968). A comparison of two methods of teaching the tennis serve. *Research Quarterly* 39:929–31.

DiGennaro, J. (1969). Construction of forehand drive, backhand drive, and serve tennis tests. *Research Quarterly* 40:496–501.

Elliot, B. C. (1982). Tennis: The influence of grip tightness on reaction impulse and rebound velocity. *Medicine and Science in Sports and Exercise* 14:348–52.

Hubbell, N. C. (1960). A battery of tennis skill tests for college women. Unpublished master's thesis, Texas Woman's University, Denton.

Kemp, J., and Vincent, M. F., (1968). Kemp-Vincent Rally Test of Tennis Skill. *Research Quarterly* 39:1000–04.

Powers, S. K., and Walker, R. (1982). Physiological and anatomical characteristics of outstanding female junior tennis players. *Research Quarterly for Exercise and Sport* 53:172–75.

Purcell, K. (1981). A tennis forehand–backhand drive skill test which measures ball control and stroke firmness. *Research Quarterly for Exercise and Sport* 52:238–45.

## Volleyball Skills Tests

Brumbach, W. (1967). *Beginning volleyball: A syllabus for teachers.* Rev. ed. Eugene, OR: University of Oregon.

Clifton, M. (1962). Single hit volley test for women's volleyball. *Research Quarterly* 33:208–11.

Comeaux, B. A. (1974). *Development of a volleyball selection test battery for girls.* Unpublished master's thesis, Lamar University, Beaumont, Texas.

Far ow, B. E. (1970). *Development of a volleyball selection test battery. Unpublished master's thesis,* Lamar University, Beaumont, Texas.

Johnson, J. A. (1967). *The development of a volleyball skill test for high school girls.* Unpublished master's thesis, Illinois State University, Bloomington-Normal.

Kronquist, R. A., and Brumbach, W. B. (1968). A modification of the Brady volleyball skill test for high school boys. *Research Quarterly* 39:116–120.

Liba, M. R., and Stauff, M. R. (1963). A test for the volleyball pass. *Research Quarterly* 34:56–63.

Michalski, R. A. (1963). *Construction of an objective skill test for the underhand volleyball serve.* Unpublished master's thesis, University of Iowa, Iowa City.

Morrow, J. R.; Jackson, A. B.; Hosler, W. W.; and Kachurik, J. K. (1979). The importance of strength, speed, and body size for team success in women's intercollegiate volleyball. *Research Quarterly* 50:429–37.

Puhl, J.; Case, S.; Fleck, S.; and VanHandel, P. (1982). Physical and physiological characteristics of elite volleyball players. *Research Quarterly for Exercise and Sport* 53:257–62.

Ryan, M. F. (1969). *A study of tests for the volleyball serve.* Unpublished master's thesis, University of Wisconsin, Madison.

Shaveley, M. (1960). Volleyball skill tests for girls. In Division of Girls' and Women's Sports *Selected Volleyball Articles.* Washington, DC: American Association for Health, Physical Education and Recreation.

Spence, D. W.; Disch, J. G.; Fred, H. L.; and Coleman, A. E. (1980). Descriptive profiles of highly skilled women volleyball players. *Medicine and Science in Sports and Exercise* 12:299–302.

Thorpe, J., and West, C. (1967). A volleyball skills chart with attainment levels for selected skills. In *DGWS Volleyball Guide 1967–69.* Washington, DC: American Association for Health, Physical Education and Recreation.

# MEASURING THE COGNITIVE DOMAIN

7

## ▶ KEY TERMS

answer
cognitive domain
difficulty index
discrimination index
distractor
essay test questions
halo effect
item analysis
item function
objective test questions
qualitative item analysis
quantitative item analysis
semiobjective test questions
stem
table of specifications
taxonomy of educational objectives

## ▶ OBJECTIVES

*After reading this chapter, the student should be able to:*

1. Understand the importance of proper measurement and evaluation procedures regarding the cognitive domain in school and nonschool programs.
2. Demonstrate the ability to write test items that match stated objectives of the particular unit.
3. Explain the roles and relationship of the taxonomy of educational objectives and the table of specifications in test construction.
4. Compare the relative advantages and disadvantages of various types of test items (e.g., true–false, multiple choice, essay).
5. Perform quantitative item analysis using the difficulty index, discrimination index, and item function to improve the validity of a test.
6. Describe qualitative item analysis and discuss how it can be used to improve the validity of a test.

273

As discussed in Chapter 2, the **cognitive domain** includes intellectual abilities and skills ranging from rote memory tasks to the synthesis and evaluation of complex information. Because physical education is generally an activity-oriented discipline that emphasizes physical skills and physical fitness, administrators, teachers, parents, and students seldom link physical education with the cognitive domain. Likewise, the cognitive domain is often overlooked in nonschool settings. In many instances, little thought or planning is given to ensuring that the individual client in an exercise science setting is receiving and comprehending information needed to understand the treatments, training, and fitness program in which he or she is involved. One of the biggest challenges in the health fitness industry is to motivate clients to adhere to their programs for an extended period of time. Many participants drop out within the first six weeks of a program. Ideally, the individuals in these programs should make lifestyle changes and pursue activity and exercise for a lifetime. Individuals who understand the importance of exercising, eating in moderation, breaking the smoking habit, and so forth, are much more likely to carry out their programs. Athletic trainers, physical therapists, exercise clinicians, and other exercise science practitioners should realize the motivational value of increasing the knowledge as well as health fitness levels of their clients. For this to happen, there must be a strong educational component to the program. Without planned measurement and evaluation procedures in place, the exercise science specialist cannot assess the cognitive component of the programs.

It is understandable that people outside the discipline might associate physical education solely with the contributions it can make to the psychomotor and health fitness domains. However, it is not as easily understood why trained physical educators so often neglect the critical cognitive components of physical education. The cognitive domain is an important area that should be addressed in a quality program at any level. Though the cognitive area is almost always included in the stated objectives of the program, the measurement and evaluation procedures concerning these objectives are often inadequate.

Learning the rules and strategies of a game, knowing the history of a sport, recognizing the benefits of various forms of exercise, designing a dance routine, analyzing and making corrections in the performance of a sports skill, understanding established safety procedures, and planning personalized fitness programs are examples of cognitive activities in physical education and exercise science. Understanding these things can help motivate a person to better performance in a selected activity. Establishing this cognitive link is critical in any good program.

In other subject disciplines, the cognitive domain is the major emphasis. Homework assignments, class activities, and written examinations in mathematics, science, social studies, and English are commonplace in the measurement and evaluation schemes of these disciplines. There is no reason why physical educators cannot use the same strategies to assess cognitive objectives in their field. This is not to suggest that physical education should move from the gymnasium to the classroom. Physical education must continue to emphasize skill/fitness goals in motor activity settings, but it should include strategies to ensure that students also gain a fundamental knowledge about the sports and fitness activities in which they participate.

In many secondary physical education settings, conceptual classes on wellness and exercise are being added into the curriculum. These classes are usually one semester long and teach students through a planned sequence of lecture and activities important information concerning proper exercise, body composition, nutrition, stress control, and other wellness topics. The cognitive component is a critical part of these classes. Even in lower elementary levels, physical education includes important information concerning healthy lifestyle habits. It is essential that the teacher have some measurement strategies in place to assess how much of the information is being processed and comprehended by students at any level.

In many nonschool settings, it may not be desirable to use formalized tests to assess cognitive achievement. However, surveys and questionnaires can be designed to determine clients' knowledge levels. Ensuring the validity of these instruments is as important as making sure tests given in school settings are well constructed. The same procedures for constructing tests can be applied to designing instruments to be used in nonschool settings. It would be desirable in most cases to assess a client's knowledge as she enters the program and then use follow-up assessments to monitor the client's progress in the cognitive area. Ideally, upon leaving a program each person should have the knowledge to continue the program without the supervision of the exercise science practitioner.

# MEASURING COGNITIVE ACHIEVEMENT

## School Settings

There are several ways to measure the cognitive achievement of students. Students may complete projects or homework assignments relative to cognitive goals. Though these types of activities are certainly desirable, they should not be the major criteria for evaluation. Projects and homework assignments done away from the teacher's supervision are not always a true reflection of the work of the individual student. The student may enlist the aid of parents or help from other students. This is not necessarily bad, but overdependence on this type of work for measurement purposes may lead to invalid evaluations. The real value of outside assignments is to familiarize students with the material and, in turn, prepare them for tests that are given under the supervision of the teacher.

Examinations may be oral or written. If oral examinations are used, only one student can be tested at a time. Because of the size of most classes, oral examinations are impractical except in unusual cases. It is recommended that the written examination be the major basis of measuring students' knowledge. The use of written examinations with content that matches the stated cognitive objectives provides a way to evaluate how well the objectives are being accomplished. When properly constructed and administered, the examination should provide valid data that accurately reflect the cognitive achievement of the individual student as well as a means of evaluating students' knowledge relative to the stated objectives.

The written test provides important feedback to the teacher as to whether students are meeting the cognitive objectives. If a majority of a class fails to perform to expectations, this may indicate some shortcoming on the part of the instructor. The test might be too difficult for various reasons: not enough time was devoted to cognitive aspects of the unit in class, homework and class activities did not prepare students adequately for the test, and so forth. Without the results of the written test, the teacher may not be aware of any problems and, thus, be unable to make necessary adjustments in future units.

Scheduling and administering of a written test can be an effective way to encourage students to learn about a given subject. If no tests are given, most students will not study extensively enough to gain an understanding of the material. Further, when the students are given immediate results of their performance on a written examination, they are more likely to learn from their mistakes and be reinforced for their correct responses.

Some students are not highly successful at motor skill activities but excel in the cognitive work. Homework assignments, projects, and written tests give this type of student an opportunity for success in physical education, which may stimulate greater efforts in other areas of physical education. Students should be given the opportunity to demonstrate their knowledge in physical education and be positively reinforced by good performance.

It is sometimes a good strategy to give a test and let the students grade their own tests and make necessary corrections. This type of self-test would not be used for grading purposes but is valuable because it allows students to evaluate themselves and, in some cases, motivates them to learn material on which they did poorly. The self-test might be a shortened version of sample questions that the students could expect on upcoming tests. This is good preparation for an examination that will be administered for grading purposes.

## Nonschool Settings

In nonschool settings, which also should include emphasis of the cognitive domain, giving formalized tests is an option, but may not be the best choice. While a physical education teacher may have a large number of students, the typical exercise science setting does not have as many clients assigned to a practitioner. Also, schools are on set schedules, while programs in nonschool settings are ongoing. For these reasons, surveys and questionnaires may be a better method for checking clients' knowledge. In many cases, an oral questionnaire may be the most desirable option. Whatever method is chosen, the exercise science specialist should make every effort to ensure the validity of the technique being used. The same type of planning that this chapter details concerning test construction should be applied in the design of nonschool surveys or questionnaires. Planned measurement and evaluation strategies that articulate the goals of the program should be in place to assess not only the progress of individual clients but also the program's effectiveness.

## PLANNING THE WRITTEN TEST

Planning a written test is an important step in an evaluation scheme because the resulting examination must have content validity. In order for a test to be valid, the test items should match the instructional objectives. To ensure that a test will have content validity, an educator must link the learning outcome and conditions specified in the test question to the learning outcome and conditions described in the performance objective (Kubiszyn and Borich, 1984).

## Matching Test Items to Objectives

Test items must be written with stated objectives in mind, and those objectives should match the learning objectives. Test items should not be easier or more difficult than the learning objectives. The process of matching test items to objectives may seem somewhat difficult, but with careful planning and a little practice, a teacher can write appropriate test items. Listed below are some examples of test items that do not match the objective. Teachers sometimes make the mistake of including test items that are more difficult than the objective. For example,

> *Objective:* Identify activities and sports as being primarily aerobic or anaerobic in nature.
>
> *Test Item:* Explain why jogging is considered an aerobic activity.

In this case, the objective asks only for identification of various activities as aerobic or anaerobic, yet the test question asks for an explanation. If the explanation is considered important, it should be included in the objective.

Often, test items are much easier than the objective. For example,

*Objective:* From memory, draw a tennis court and label the lines.

*Test Item:* Given the following diagram of the playing surface, label the lines of a tennis court.

In this case, the test item would not accurately measure the achievement of the objective. The test question does not require the student to recall and draw the court.

The best way to gain an accurate measurement of achievement is to ask students to demonstrate mastery of the subject matter in a way that is consistent with the objectives.

*Objective:* Describe how to "block out" when rebounding in basketball.

*Test Item:* When rebounding in basketball, explain how to "block out."

If a student can answer this test item satisfactorily, then the teacher can be certain that the objective has been achieved.

Though the examples given refer to test items in a short answer format, the same guidelines of matching test items with objectives apply to all types of test items, including multiple choice, true–false, matching, and essay. By taking care to match the learning outcome and conditions of the objective and test item, regardless of format, teachers can ensure content validity.

## Taxonomy of Educational Objectives

Cognitive objectives can be stated in terms that range from simple to complex. If an objective requires a student to memorize material, it is relatively simple compared to an objective that requires a student to synthesize information to make an evaluation of some type. The more advanced a student is, the more advanced the objective should become. The **taxonomy of educational objectives** devised by Bloom, Englehart, Hill, Furst, and Krathwohl (1956) is the most popular system of classifying the levels of cognitive complexity. It delineates six levels of varying complexity from the knowledge level (simplest) to the evaluation level (most complex). Figure 7.0 illustrates the various levels of the taxonomy.

According to Bloom et al. (1956), the taxonomy levels are hierarchical in that the higher level objectives include the lower level objectives. Thus, if an objective is written at the application level, the successful completion of this objective would require cognitive processes to take place at the comprehension and knowledge levels as well as the application level. Each level of the taxonomy of objectives has different characteristics, which are

 **FIGURE 7.0**   Taxonomy of educational objectives: cognitive domain.

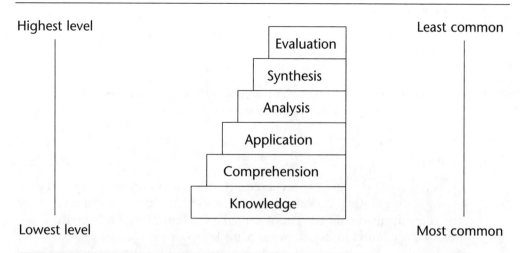

From *Educational Testing and Measurement: Classroom Application and Practice,* 3d ed., by Tom Kubiszyn and Gary Borich. Copyright © 1990 by Scott, Foresman and Company. Reprinted by permission of HarperCollins Publishers.

described below with examples of verbs usually associated with the different levels.

## Knowledge

Objectives at the knowledge level involve recognition and recall. Test items ask students to remember such items as facts, rules, and definitions. Some verbs that are used with the knowledge level are:

| | | |
|---|---|---|
| list | name | label |
| match | select | define |
| recite | state | recall |

Terms such as *who, what, where, when,* and *why* are often included in test items at the knowledge level.

*Sample objective:* The student will be able to define "aerobic" and "anaerobic" in terms of exercise.

## Comprehension

Some level of understanding is required for meeting objectives at the comprehension level, which is considered the lowest level of understanding. To demonstrate comprehension, a student must use knowledge to interpret, restate, or draw conclusions. Some verbs commonly used with this level of objectives are:

| | | |
|---|---|---|
| translate | explain | infer |
| estimate | predict | paraphrase |
| distinguish | summarize | defend |

*Sample objective:* The student will be able to explain the difference between aerobic exercise and anaerobic exercise.

## Application

Objectives at this cognitive level require students to use learning in a variety of settings. Application questions present the problem in a different and often applied context. This means the student cannot rely on the question or the context to decide what prior knowledge must be used to solve the problem. Some verbs used in conjunction with the application level are:

| | | |
|---|---|---|
| develop | organize | modify |
| solve | apply | use |
| employ | produce | prepare |

*Sample objective:* The student will be able to apply the principles of exercise in planning an aerobic workout.

## Analysis

Analysis-level objectives require the student to identify parts or elements, discover interactions or relationships, point out errors of inference or contradictions, or differentiate among facts, opinions, and conclusions. Questions at this level often call for the student to compare and contrast ideas or distinguish relationships. Verbs found in analysis objectives include:

| | | |
|---|---|---|
| analyze | examine | determine |
| identify | relate | point out |
| illustrate | deduce | diagram |

*Sample objective:* Examine the sport of racquetball in terms of the contributions it can make to the various components of physical fitness.

## Synthesis

Objectives written at the synthesis level involve producing something original or unique. Synthesis might involve rearrangement and combining of elements to construct a new whole. Some verbs that describe learning outcomes at the synthesis level are:

| | | |
|---|---|---|
| formulate | create | plan |
| devise | invent | design |

*Sample objective:* Plan a progressive exercise program for a three-month time frame designed to improve cardiovascular fitness and body composition.

## Evaluation

This level of cognition is the most advanced of all levels because all other levels of cognitive activity are prerequisite to making an evaluation. Objectives written at this level require a student to make judgments about methods, materials, ideas, performance, or products with a specific purpose. Test items at this level ask the student to provide a rationale for such judgments. Verbs associated with objectives and test items at the evaluation level include:

| | | |
|---|---|---|
| appraise | interpret | judge |
| defend | justify | criticize |

*Sample objective:* Evaluate the quality of the exercise programs at a local fitness spa.

## Table of Specifications

As we have seen, educational objectives should be written at different levels of the taxonomy and test items should match the objectives. Test items testing student achievement of the objectives should, therefore, represent similar levels of the cognitive domain.

An important step in test planning is making sure that test items and objectives are written at the different levels of the cognitive taxonomy. In order to do this, a **table of specifications** may be created to help the teacher include all details necessary to construct a valid test. This table is analogous to a builder using a blueprint for constructing a building. This blueprint of test construction guides the teacher in selecting items for the test. A good test will include items representative of not just one level of the cognitive taxonomy but items covering several levels of cognitive complexity.

A table of specifications aids the teacher in sampling all the important content areas that a given test covers. Everyone, at some point in his academic career, has taken an exam that did not reflect what was covered and emphasized in class activities. Tests such as these are unfair and do not measure a student's knowledge of the subject. Using a table of specifications can alleviate this problem.

This method of planning a written exam can also be an invaluable aid in planning and organizing instruction because the blueprint should be established before a unit is started. The objectives of the course, the class activities used to meet those objectives, the actual presentation and sequence of the activities, and the testing strategies to measure the degree to which these objectives are met must be thought out in advance so that teaching can be organized and efficient. Minor changes are expected as the unit progresses, but severe alterations from an overall unit plan should seldom be necessary.

An example of a table of specifications is shown in Table 7.0. Steps for constructing such a table are as follows:

1. Determine the educational objectives for the unit.

2. Determine the weighting of the educational objectives in terms of the level of cognitive thinking that is required. For example,

   | | |
   |---|---|
   | Knowledge | 25% |
   | Comprehension | 10% |
   | Application | 35% |
   | Analysis | 20% |
   | Synthesis | 5% |
   | Evaluation | 5% |

3. Determine the approximate time spent in each of the content areas of the specific unit. For instance,

   | | |
   |---|---|
   | History | 5% |
   | Rules | 25% |
   | Equipment | 5% |
   | Etiquette | 10% |
   | Skill and Technique | 35% |
   | Strategies | 20% |

4. After the percentages for cognitive levels and content areas have been determined, set up the table of specifications. The course content areas and their weighting are listed down the left side of the table and the levels of cognition and their weighting are listed across the top.

5. The weight for any cell in the table is determined by multiplying the intersecting values from the left side and top of the cell. For example, the first cell represents knowledge (25 percent) and history (5 percent). Thus, the weighting of the cell would be $.25 \times .05 = .0125$. This figure is multiplied by the number of intended items on the exam to determine how many items should come from this cell. The test illustrated in Table 7.0 has 100 items; therefore, $.0125 \times 100 = 1.25$. Since it is not possible to ask .25 of a question, the weighting of each cell should be used as a guide when writing test items.

6. Adding the values in each cell across each row gives the total number of items for each area of course content. Adding the values in each cell down each column totals the number of items for each cognitive level.

This table of specifications helps the test writer use content areas to implement the different cognitive levels of the educational objectives. A general rule to follow when weighting cognitive levels is to weight introductory-level tests predominantly at the knowledge, comprehension, and application levels. If classes are at the intermediate and/or the advanced levels, the analysis, synthesis, and evaluation levels should be emphasized. It should also be pointed out that items designed to require the higher levels of cognition are more difficult to construct. Good knowledge and comprehension questions are easier to write than synthesis and evaluation items. However, the extra time it takes to construct higherlevel questions pays off as a better designed test to measure cognitive achievement.

Previously in this chapter, we mentioned the importance of content validity in written examinations. By constructing a table of specifications, a teacher ensures that the written test meets the criteria for content validity. As we have seen, constructing a valid test involves a lot of thought and time

► **TABLE 7.0**   Table of specifications for 100-point test in beginning tennis.

**COGNITIVE LEVELS**

| CONTENT AREAS | | Knowledge 25% | Comprehension 10% | Application 35% | Analysis 20% | Synthesis 5% | Evaluation 5% | Total number of points for each content area |
|---|---|---|---|---|---|---|---|---|
| History | 5% | 1.25 | .5 | 1.75 | 1.0 | .25 | .25 | 5 |
| Rules | 25% | 6.25 | 2.5 | 8.75 | 5.0 | 1.25 | 1.25 | 25 |
| Equipment | 5% | 1.25 | .5 | 1.75 | 1.0 | .25 | .25 | 5 |
| Etiquette | 10% | 2.5 | 1.0 | 3.5 | 2.0 | .5 | .5 | 10 |
| Skill & technique | 35% | 8.75 | 3.5 | 12.25 | 7.0 | 1.75 | 1.75 | 35 |
| Strategies | 20% | 5.0 | 2.0 | 7.0 | 4.0 | 1.0 | 1.0 | 20 |
| Total number of points for each cognitive level | | 25 | 10 | 35 | 20 | 5 | 5 | 100 |

to do it right. Unfortunately, many teachers do not take the time to do it right. As a result, tests used often do not reflect objectives and content covered in the unit. However, if teachers are interested in developing quality physical education programs that are useful to the students and to the school, they will realize that the time and effort it takes to construct a valid test is a worthwhile investment.

## SELECTION OF TEST ITEMS

After making decisions about the content areas of the written test, a teacher must decide the format of the test and begin to write test items. Many times the nature of the content area dictates the format of the test items. Certain types of subject matter lend themselves to multiple-choice or true-false format, while an essay-type question is better suited for other types of content information. Generally, higher level cognitive objectives require essay-type questions, while lower level cognitive objectives can be tested with matching, true–false, and multiple-choice questions. Mood (1980) classified the different types of test questions into three general categories: objective, semiobjective, and essay. **Objective test questions** are free from any subjective judgment during grading. True-false, matching, and multiple-choice test items are classified as objective. **Semiobjective test questions** include completion and short answer items. They are so named because very little organization of information is needed on the student's part, and the response is checked to see if it matches the correct answer. Some subjectivity may be included when partial credit is awarded, but grading procedures are usually similar to that of objective questions. When answering **essay test questions**, the student must formulate a response that is graded in a subjective manner since judgmental decisions must be made about the response.

Mood (1980) further points out that subjectivity is present in every test, regardless of the type of questions used. The decisions about the content of the test as well as the format involves subjective decisions on the part of the instructor. Because subjectivity involves biases and experiences of just one person, the amount of subjectivity should be reduced as much as possible in the construction and grading of tests. The use of a table of specifications and the revision of test items after a test is given are two ways to reduce subjectivity.

Knowledge of the advantages and disadvantages of various types of test items is also crucial to the construction of a valid test. Since the teacher has a choice of several types of questions, this knowledge is essential. The following sections discuss the advantages and disadvantages of various test-item formats and suggestions for writing different types of questions.

## True–False

The true–false format is an objective and convenient method of testing. The true–false item consists of a statement that gives a student the choice of two possible answers. It is not time-consuming to write this type of question, and it is easy to score in an objective manner. Further, it allows coverage of a wide range of material, some of which may not be appropriately covered with another type of question. Alternate forms of the true–false format are answering yes–no or right–wrong. The true-false format may also be modified by asking the student to correct the false statements.

The disadvantages of the true–false format is that it encourages guessing. Sometimes students who actually know the material better will interpret the question and "read too much" into the statement causing mistakes that a weaker student will not make. True–false questions tend to test isolated facts (knowledge level) rather than concepts that require higher levels of cognition.

The following guidelines are suggested when writing true–false questions:

1. Clearly explain the desired way of marking true and false answers before the students begin the test. Writing out "true" or "false" can eliminate any confusion in handwriting between a "T" and an "F". Another way to prevent confusion when scoring the exam is to provide a "T" and an "F" on the test sheet and have students circle their response.
2. Make sure that true and false statements are about the same length. There is a tendency for true statements to be lengthier than false statements. Use relatively short statements and eliminate excessive words.
3. Include approximately the same number of true and false items or slightly more false items. Since students have a tendency to mark "true" when they are uncertain, the false statements usually discriminate better.
4. Use statements that are clearly true or clearly false. However, false statements should not be discernible to the uninformed.
5. Avoid the following:
   a. complex or ambiguous statements
   b. double-negative statements
   c. determiners such as never, always, sometimes, or often
   d. items straight from the text that are used out of context
   e. placing items so that answers are in a systematic order

## Matching

The use of matching items is another popular and convenient objective format for testing. They can be used to cover a wide range of material in relatively little space. Like true–false questions, they are quick to write and easy to grade. The matching format consists of two columns of words or phrases, and the student must match each item in one column with the appropriate item in the other. A disadvantage of matching items is that they only test a student's recognition of the material.

When writing matching items, the following guidelines should be followed:

1. It is important that each list include items similar to one another. For example, a list might include dates, names, or terminology but should not mix these things together.

2. A matching section should include about 10–12 items in the description list. The option list should include more items than the description list to reduce using a process of elimination for selection. Every distractor in the option list should be a plausible alternative.

3. There should be only one correct choice for each item in the description list and an alternative from the option list should only be used once.

4. The items in both lists should be arranged in some systematic fashion, usually alphabetically.

5. Each item in the description list should be numbered and each item in the option list should be lettered.

## Multiple Choice

Another common objective format is the multiple-choice question. This format is a little more complex than those previously discussed. Three components make up the multiple-choice question: the stem, the distractors, and the answer. The **stem** is an incomplete sentence or a question; the **distractors** are the incorrect options; and the **answer** is the correctoption.

A unique characteristic of multiple-choice questions is that they can be written to measure levels of cognition higher than the knowledge level. The multiple-choice format has several other advantages: The questions are easy to grade, can cover almost all types of materials, and can be used at virtually all levels of education. Properly written, they discourage guessing more so than other objective formats.

There are disadvantages to this type of question as well. Even though multiple-choice questions can cover higher levels of cognition, they often emphasize isolated facts. They are time-consuming and difficult to prepare when done properly. Writing good distractors can be particularly troublesome. As a rule of thumb, if difficulties arise with devising adequate distractors, it may be that the material being tested lends itself to another format.

The stem of the multiple-choice item should clearly identify the problem in a concise way. Often the use of questions as a stem is more effective than using an incomplete sentence. If the stem is an incomplete sentence, the distractors must be written in a form to conform to the stem. If written in a question form, the alternatives must only conform to each other. A test-wise student will be able to eliminate distractors if there are clues in the content of the question. For example, if the stem ends with the word "an," then the student can deduce that the correct response must start with a word starting with a vowel. In cases such as this, the stem should be ended with "a/an" so as not to give any hints.

Other suggestions for using multiple-choice items are as follows:

1. When possible, the stem should be written in positive terms rather than stated in a negative way.

2. Three or four distractors should be written plus the correct answer for each item. It is not necessary to have the same number of distractors on every question. The distractors should be written in parallel form and be related to the stem in a plausible way.

3. Distractors such as "none of the above," "all of the above," and "both b. and c." should be used sparingly, if at all. There should be one alternative that is clearly the correct answer.

4. The distractors and correct answer should be about the same length. The more similar the content of options, the more difficult the item becomes.

5. The correct answer should be listed with near equal frequency in each of the possible positions of a, b, c, d, e in the list of options. Any sort of pattern that would help the student guess the right answer should be avoided.

6. Ambiguity of distractors can be reduced by having others with knowledge of the test material review it and by modifying or eliminating troublesome test items after administering the test.

7. Giving the correct answer for one question in the stem of another question should be guarded against.

## Completion Items

Completion items are a commonly used semiobjective format on a written test. With this type of question, the student is expected to fill in the blank to answer the test question. This type of item reduces the problem of guessing, and it also requires the student to recall specific information rather than recognize it. In order to complete this type of test, the student must study more intensely.

While this type of item is easy to prepare, it requires the teacher to subjectively decide which areas are to be tested. With some completion items, there may be more than one correct response, which can complicate grading procedures. This causes the grader to make some subjective judgments about the answer, hence the grading procedure is less objective. However, when writing items so that only one answer is correct, the completion items tend to test isolated facts in the material.

For the completion item format, the following guidelines are suggested:

1. When possible, items should require a single-word answer or a brief, definitive statement. Avoid indefinite statements that can be answered correctly by several responses.
2. Limit the number of blanks in the question so that the item does not become indefinite.
3. Prevent awkward sentences by constructing the item so that the blank is located near the end of the statement.
4. Be sure the item clearly defines the problem for the person taking the test. Use precise language to accurately formulate the subject matter of the question.
5. If the correct answer is stated numerically, indicate the unit of measurement and desired accuracy to be expressed.
6. Make sure all blanks are the same length in each question and use "a/an" before blanks to avoid giving any inadvertent hints.

## Short-Answer Questions

Sometimes the short-answer question, another semiobjective test format, can be used in place of completion questions if ambiguity becomes a problem. When the short-answer format is used, it is critical that the respondent understand the limits concerning the length of the answer. The advantages and disadvantages of this format are similar to those of the completion item questions. It is recommended that the short-answer format only be used when there is clearly a correct answer that can be given in one or two words.

## Essay

Unlike objective and semiobjective formats in which the student selects an answer, the essay format requires the student to supply the answer by mentally outlining and composing a response that may be quite extensive. Depending upon the essay question, the student may be required to organize, analyze, synthesize, and evaluate information. In short, any or all levels of cognition may be required to make a suitable response.

Like the objective and semiobjective test items previously discussed, essay items can be well constructed and clearly written or poorly constructed and vague. Well constructed essay questions try to test complex cognitive skills of the students. They ask a student to use information to analyze and evaluate novel situations or provide opportunities for originality and innovation in application and problem solving. A poorly constructed essay question may require the student only to recall information as it was presented in lecture or in assigned reading, or it may be so poorly written that the student does not know what is expected as a satisfactory response.

Properly written essay questions have several advantages over questions in the objective and semiobjective formats. First, because a smaller number of questions is required, an essay test is quicker to construct. Second, when students prepare for an essay test, they must study larger units of information rather than memorize isolated facts. Third, responses to essay questions allow freedom of expression linked with higher order cognitive processes. Students are able to write answers on controversial issues that reflect attitudes and opinions based upon synthesis and evaluation of pertinent information. Fourth, because the student must supply the answer, guessing is eliminated.

However, a number of problems are also associated with essay tests. The major disadvantage of an essay test is the subjectivity of grading. Two different graders may give widely divergent amounts of credit for a certain answer. The same teacher might grade the same question differently on two different occasions. Essay tests are difficult to score because there are often several pages of student handwriting to read and evaluate. Misspellings, grammatical errors, and poor handwriting are elements that can influence grading. In some cases, longer essay answers receive higher marks, which cause students to adopt a rambling, all-inclusive style of writing. Another grading problem is the **halo effect** in which a teacher forms an opinion of a student's ability and is influenced by that opinion when grading the student's paper. Because a large number of items is not feasible on an essay examination, sampling all areas of instructional content can be a problem. From a student and teacher point of view, fatigue can be more of a problem than with objective items, since it takes longer to answer and grade most essay tests.

A number of procedures can alleviate the lack of reliability in grading essay items. The following steps are suggested by Kubiszyn and Borich (1984):

1. Write good essay items. Phrase the questions so that the cognitive processes required to answer the question are clear. Set restrictions on response length.
2. When appropriate, use several restricted-range questions rather than a single extended-range question. This will help scoring reliability and

ensure a wider range of content to be covered. Restricted-range questions are those covering less information and requiring a shorter answer; extended-range questions are broader, requiring a more extensive answer.

3. Specify in advance what is expected in the response and use a predetermined grading scheme. Preparing an ideal answer to the question will help identify the specific criteria for a good answer. Write the ideal response to the question and grade based on this criterion answer.

4. Make sure that the scoring scheme is used consistently. Do not favor one student over the other because of past performance.

5. Use a system so that you do not know what student's paper is being graded. Some sort of simple coding system may be used to ensure anonymity.

6. Score all the answers to one question before going on to the next item. This helps maintain consistency.

7. Establish a method so performance on previous questions is not known. This will help reduce the halo effect.

8. Try to arrange for re-evaluation of the papers before returning them. To truly check reliability, each paper should be graded twice by independent graders and the results compared. If this is not feasible, the same teacher may grade the papers with a time interval of sufficient length so that he or she cannot recall prior scores. If there are serious discrepancies in the ratings, the reliability of the scoring is in question.

With these suggestions for increasing the objectivity and reliability of grading essay items, the following recommendations are made for the construction of essay questions:

1. Use appropriate verbs in the phrasing of the question to specify how the question should be answered.

2. Allow sufficient time to plan and construct the essay item. Keep the objectives and instructional content in mind when writing the essay question.

3. Avoid giving the students a choice of questions to answer. All students should respond to the same questions.

4. Use several short essay questions rather than one question that requires a longer response.

5. Consider the time that students will need to plan and write essay answers. If too many questions are given, students will not have time to adequately formulate answers. Fatigue may become a factor.

6. Set limits on the length of responses. Suggested time allotments for individual questions and time limits for the entire exam are often helpful.

7. Make use of essay questions only when instructional content and objectives make them the best choice. If learning objectives can be effectively tested with objective items, then essay questions should not be used.

## ADMINISTERING THE WRITTEN TEST

When done correctly, planning and constructing a written test is a time-consuming process. It takes a substantial amount of effort to write objectives, put together a table of specifications, select a format for test items, and write the test questions. Nevertheless, it is a necessary process to accurately assess student progress toward cognitive objectives in a valid manner. All of this work may be wasted if the test is not assembled and administered properly.

## Assembling the Test

When the test is assembled, the questions should be grouped by format. For instance, all the multiple-choice items should be put together and all the true-false items should be put together. This will make grading easier and will enable students to work in one format at a time rather than switching back and forth. By following this rule, directions for a given format will only have to be stated once.

All instructions should be printed on the examination, making the directions as clear and concise as possible. Directions should be checked to make certain that they include information about how and where to record answers, the basis for selecting answers, and how many points each item is worth. It is also important to provide a space for the name of the student and to remind students to put their names on the exam. They are more likely to remember to put their name on the exam if there is a space provided.

The teacher should attempt to arrange the test items within each section in ascending order of difficulty. Putting the easier items first allows the student to gain confidence and alleviate tension associated with taking a test. If a test has never been given before, it may be difficult to know which items will prove to be more difficult. In these cases, the items should be randomly arranged within each item format. The test should be assembled so that there is adequate space between items and subsections, and each item is distinct from another. When options for multiple-choice or matching questions are listed, all options should be on the same page. Similarly, students should not have to go from one page to another to finish reading a true–false or completion item. If court diagrams or other illustrations are used, they should be placed directly above the questions to which they refer and, if possible, the illustration and questions kept on the same page.

After the test is assembled, the teacher should prepare the answer key and make sure there is no pattern of answers and that answers are distributed appropriately in multiple-choice and true–false questions. It is important to proofread the test for typographical errors or grammatical mistakes. The exam should be checked for grammatical clues in which elements of one question might answer another. It is a good idea to have another teacher proofread the test to check the clarity of directions and test items as well as to spot any other errors.

## Giving the Test

It is the teacher's responsibility to provide an environment that maximizes the probability that the test results are valid indicators of students' knowledge. With this in mind, an atmosphere should be provided that is quiet, well lit, and comfortable. Students should have adequate space to work and should be arranged so that the possibility of cheating is minimized. Control of cheating is crucial to the validity of test scores and to student attitudes about written tests.

The teacher should plan an efficient way of distributing and collecting the examinations. Any ground rules about time limits, restroom policies, sharpening pencils, and so forth, should be discussed before the test is distributed. Suggestions to students about test-taking strategies, such as "Check your answers before you turn in your test" or "Don't spend too much time on one question," should be made before handing out the examinations. Once the students have the test, they are less likely to listen to what the teacher is saying. Immediately after the exams are distributed, the students should be told to check their copies to make certain that all pages are included and to put their names on the exams.

It is important that the teacher actively monitor the exam. Moving throughout the testing area and carefully watching students discourages copying. The teacher can also help the students pace themselves by periodically advising them about how much time is left in the exam period. Any individual questions should be answered at the student's desk in a quiet manner. The teacher must be careful, however, not to give any advantage to the questioning student over others by the answer that is given.

## Grading the Test

Many teachers make use of a separate answer sheet when using objective or semiobjective tests, enabling them to grade questions very quickly and efficiently. Suggestions for grading essay tests were discussed at length in a previous section of this chapter. Whatever types of items are included on the test, the answer key should be prepared in advance and checked for mistakes. The tests should be graded and returned to students as quickly as possible; however, test scores of individual students should be kept confidential. Students can decide whether to divulge their own test scores.

# ANALYZING THE TEST

Regardless of how much time and effort is spent constructing a written test, there will be items on the test that are ambiguous, inappropriate, or invalid in some way. Some problems will not surface until after the test has been administered. For these reasons, it is important that a test be analyzed to check the effectiveness of the examination. In most cases, certain items on the test will need to be modified or deleted. The end result of this process will be a more valid test. **Item analysis** may be done qualitatively or quantitatively. Both methods are valuable in assessing test quality.

## Quantitative Item Analysis

**Quantitative item analysis** is used very effectively with objective test items. It is a numerical procedure for analyzing test items and is particularly appropriate for multiple-choice formats, since it will give information about the usefulness of both the distractors and the correct answer. Quantitative analysis is also the most appropriate for a norm-referenced test in which the teacher is interested in determining who learned the material and who did not. A valid test will "discriminate" between those students who know the material and those who do not. The results on such a test will be a spread of grades so that the teacher can determine the true knowledge of various students.

A quantitative item analysis provides information about the difficulty index, the discrimination index, and the item function of all possible responses on a test question. With this information, a test can be edited to improve the quality of test questions before it is administered again.

### Difficulty Index

The **difficulty index** refers to the proportion of students who answered the question correctly. This index is calculated by dividing the number of correct responses to a question by the total number of students taking the test. The formula for the difficulty index (p) is:

$$p = \frac{\text{number of correct responses}}{\text{total number of students taking test}}$$

Assume that the test included multiple-choice questions with five alternatives. On a given item, 2 students chose alternative A, 3 chose B, no one chose C, 20 chose the correct answer D, and 10 chose E.

| A | B | C | D* | E |
|---|---|---|----|---|
| 2 | 3 | 0 | 20 | 10 |

Since 20 out of 35 students who took the exam answered the question correctly, the difficulty index would be .57. This is calculated as follows:

$$p = \frac{20}{35} = .57$$

From this information, it immediately becomes apparent that alternative C was not a very good distractor since no one chose it. The item is moderately difficult since 57% of the class answered it correctly.

When the difficulty index is above .75, it is considered to be relatively easy while below .25 is considered relatively difficult. Experts in test construction attempt to have most items fall between .20 and .80, with the average being about .50. The ability of a test to discriminate is the greatest when the overall difficulty index is approximately .50 (Kubiszyn and Borich, 1984).

### Discrimination Index

The **discrimination index** measures the extent to which a test question discriminates between the students who scored well and those who scored poorly on the overall test. A question can discriminate in one of three ways: (1) If it has a positive discrimination index, then the students who did well on the exam answered the question correctly more than students who did not do well; (2) if it has a negative discrimination index, then the students who did poorly on the exam answered the question correctly more than the students who did well on the overall exam; (3) if both the students who did well and those who did poorly on the exam responded correctly with equal frequency on a particular item, then that item has a zero discrimination index. If an item has a negative or zero discrimination index, then it should be modified or discarded.

Though several methods may be used to calculate the discrimination index of an item, the following procedure is recommended. First, if there is a large number of test papers, such as N = 100, the papers are separated into three groups: the upper 27 percent of the scores, the lower 27 percent of the scores, and the middle 46 percent. According to Ebel (1972), the figure "27 percent" is often recommended, though the percentage used can be anywhere between 25 and 33 percent. If a smaller set of test papers is used, such as N = 35, the papers can be split into the upper 50 percent and lower 50 percent. For each question, the number in the upper group and the number in the lower group that chose the correct answer is tallied. The discrimination index (D) is computed with the following formula (Hopkins and Stanley, 1981):

$$D = \frac{\begin{array}{c}\text{Number who correctly} \\ \text{answered the question} \\ \text{in upper group}\end{array} - \begin{array}{c}\text{Number who correctly} \\ \text{answered the question} \\ \text{in lower group}\end{array}}{\text{Number of students in either group}}$$

In the example used to illustrate the difficulty index, 20 out of 35 students correctly answered the question. Using the same example to illustrate the discrimination index, the scores are separated into an upper 50 percent and lower 50 percent. Since 35 students took the test, 18 scores are assigned to the upper group and 17 to the lower group. The following information was tallied for the upper and lower groups:

|        | A | B | C | D* | E |
|--------|---|---|---|----|---|
| Upper  | 1 | 0 | 0 | 13 | 4 |
| Lower  | 1 | 3 | 0 | 7  | 6 |

By inserting the numbers into the formula above, the discrimination index can be calculated. Notice that if the numbers in the upper and lower group are not equal, the larger of the two groups is used in the denominator.

$$D = \frac{13 - 7}{18} = \frac{6}{18} = .33$$

The discrimination index (D) is .33, which is positive. Students who did well on the exam answered this item correctly more often than students who did poorly. Like a correlation coefficient, the value for D can range from −1.00 to +1.00. If $D \geq .40$, the item discriminates well. Between .30 and .39, the item is considered acceptable but subject to possible improvement. If D falls between .20 and .29, it is marginal and definitely needs improvement. Below .19 is a poor discriminator and the item in question should be rejected or undergo major revision for improvement (Ebel, 1972).

Safrit (1990) suggests a simple discrimination method that may be used with a single class. First, the teacher identifies the test score that represents the cutoff between the scores in the high group and the scores in the low group. The teacher then leads the class through each question by asking those in the high group to raise their hands if they answered it correctly. This procedure is repeated with the low group. To avoid possible embarrassment, the teacher may want to refer to the groups as A and B. To keep the entire class involved, the teacher may wish to ask for a show of hands from the middle group even though this information is not used in the calculation. If it is a small class, it may be appropriate to identify the middle score and split the class in half in order to complete this procedure. The number of students from each group (high and low) who answered the question correctly is recorded and used in the formula shown previously to calculate the discrimination index.

Several computer programs have been written for quantitative item analysis. If the proper type of optical scan answer sheet is used, the computer can score the exam as well as provide information about the difficulty index, the discrimination index, and total test reliability. Teachers should take advantage of this type of service not only to improve their examinations but also to save the time it takes to grade exams and do a quantitative item analysis by hand.

## *Item Function*

It has been established that the example test question previously discussed has a difficulty index of .57 and a discrimination index of .33. **Item function** refers to the suitability or effectiveness of a test question. What are other things that should be determined about the item function of this test question? It is known that distractor C should be replaced. Are the other distractors acceptable? If more students in the upper group are choosing a distractor than the lower group, the option should be changed. However, in the example, this is not a problem. The alternatives are probably all right, but as the item is used on future exams, the item can be analyzed more accurately with a larger group of students taking the test.

What other information can a quantitative item analysis provide about the effectiveness of a multiple-choice item? With a little interpretation and a healthy dose of common sense, checks can be made for mistakes in the answer key, guessing, and ambiguity in the alternatives.

In doing an item analysis, suppose that most students in the upper group were missing a certain question. The first possibility is a mistake in the answer key. Every teacher occasionally miskeys the answer sheet. A sample distribution of this situation might appear as follows:

|             | A | B  | C* | D | E |
|-------------|---|----|----|---|---|
| Upper group | 1 | 13 | 2  | 1 | 1 |

The answer key shows C to be the correct option when B is actually the correct choice. A distribution from the upper group such as this is a signal to check the answer key.

Some guessing in a multiple-choice item is inevitable. However, in the group of students who score well on the exam, guessing should be minimized. When excessive guessing occurs in the upper group, the students respond in an approximate random pattern. That is, the answers are somewhat evenly balanced among the options. The following distribution illustrates this situation:

|  | A | B | C* | D | E |
|---|---|---|---|---|---|
| Upper group | 3 | 4 | 4 | 4 | 3 |

A response pattern from the upper group such as this signifies a problem with the test question. It usually means that the information was not covered in class or in assigned readings or that the question was so difficult that even the upper group of students had no idea what the answer was.

Ambiguity between options on a multiple-choice item should be suspected when the upper group chooses one of the distractors about an equal amount as the correct answer. Ambiguity between the correct answer C and alternative A would be suspected in the following example:

|  | A | B | C* | D | E |
|---|---|---|---|---|---|
| Upper group | 7 | 1 | 7 | 1 | 2 |

In this example, a high percentage of students in the upper group who missed this item are attracted to alternative A. With this sort of distribution, the teacher should investigate the possibility of ambiguity between A and C.

Though quantitative item analysis is a valuable way to analyze questions on a test, it does not point out every type of problem. The only way to determine if a test question is poorly written or reflects lack of mastery on the part of the students is through qualitative item analysis.

## Qualitative Item Analysis

**Qualitative item analysis** should be performed on all test items regardless of format. It is the proper technique for assessing usefulness of semiobjective and essay tests and should be used in conjunction with quantitative item analysis on objective questions. The validity and reliability of a test is greatly improved if a combination of these procedures is used. Whereas quantitative item analysis is based on computations and yields numerical indexes, qualitative item analysis evaluates test items on the basis of matching questions to objectives and editing items that are poorly written. If a question seems ambiguous, promotes excessive guessing, is too difficult or easy, or fails to discriminate in a positive manner, the qualitative item analysis helps to point out these problems so the question can either be discarded or changed.

Qualitative item analysis includes a careful appraisal of test questions based on quantitative results. It requires a healthy dose of common sense as test items are being evaluated. While many of these procedures should be carried out prior to administering the exam, they are also performed after the test is given. The results of the test can provide guidance in improving the validity of the exam. Quantitative item analysis can point out problem areas, but some qualitative item analysis must be made in order to modify the test item.

Another method of qualitative analysis is to elicit feedback from students. Although some student reactions are based on emotion of the moment, there may be some justifiable criticisms that students can offer. By asking students to identify problems, the teacher may be able to pinpoint troublesome test questions in a time-efficient way. Students should write down comments about test questions that they found confusing or unfair, and explain why the question is unclear. Having the students put their comments in writing prevents the teacher from having to make on-the-spot decisions. If a decision to delete a question or accept an alternate response is retroactive to the exam already taken, students should be informed if their score is affected. The important thing is that one other resource has been utilized to help analyze and improve the overall quality of the examination.

## SOURCES FOR TEST QUESTIONS

Since most tests given in physical education are teacher-made tests (it would be difficult to find a battery of test questions that matched every teacher's specific objectives), using other sources to provide ideas for test questions may be helpful in constructing an examination. The list below suggests possible sources of test questions for use in physical education. Caution and good judgment must be used in selecting previously constructed test questions to ensure that they are appropriate for a particular situation.

Brown Sports and Fitness Series. Dubuque, IA: Wm. C. Brown Publishers. *This series includes titles of paperback textbooks dealing with 44 separate activities. Each booklet contains various types of test questions at the end. For example, Chet Murphy's third edition of* Advanced Tennis *contains 60 true–false, 30 completion, and 10 matching items, while Virginia L. Nance and Elwood Craig Davis include 125 true–false and 50 completion items in their fifth edition of* Golf.

Corbin, C., and Lindsey, R. *Concepts of Physical Fitness.* 8th ed. Dubuque, IA: Wm. C. Brown, 1994. *This textbook is designed for college-level classes and has an accompanying teacher's manual that includes multiple-choice items for each chapter.*

_____. *Fitness for Life.* Glenview, IL: Scott, Foresman and Company, 1983. *This textbook is designed for use in the secondary school and has an accompanying teacher's edition that includes suggested multiple-choice examination questions covering the material in the textbook.*

McGee, R., and Farrow, A. *Test Questions for Physical Education Activities.* Champaign, IL: Human Kinetics Publishers, 1987. *This book provides*

*250–400 multiple-choice questions for each of 15 different physical education activities. Questions cover beginning through advanced levels and are appropriate for junior high through college physical education classes.*

Mood, D.; Musker, F.; and Rink, J. *Sports and Recreational Activities*. 11th ed. St. Louis, MO: Times Mirror/Mosby, 1995. *Forty activities are included in the textbook. A teacher's manual accompanying this book is available and includes written tests on each unit made up of true–false, multiple-choice, short answer, and essay test items.*

## Other Sources

The AAHPER Cooperative Physical Education Tests. Princeton, NJ: Educational Testing Service, 1970. *This professionally constructed series of tests concentrates on three basic content areas: performance of activity, effects of activity, and factors that modify performance. There are 60 multiple-choice items on each of two alternative and comparable test forms. The tests are available for grades 4–6, grades 7–9, and grades 10–12, with national norms available for each grade.*

Doctoral dissertations, master's theses, and articles in professional journals are also excellent sources for written physical education tests. Both Mood (1980) and Johnson and Nelson (1986) present extensive annotated lists of these sources in their respective textbooks. These lists are organized by topic and are recommended if further information on sources of written tests in physical education is desired.

## SUMMARY

The cognitive area of physical education and nonschool programs is often overlooked. Even when cognitive objectives are listed in programmatic goals, there is little articulation between the actual goal and measurement and evaluation strategies. In many cases, no measurements are done to see if goals in this domain are being met. While people outside the discipline might not recognize the cognitive domain as being critical, professionals in school and nonschool settings should not only incorporate cognitive components into their programs, but also become advocates for the expanding body of knowledge that complements activities associated with physical education and exercise science. While it is important not to stray from the inherent activity-based nature of the discipline, it is equally important to systematically plan, deliver, and evaluate activities designed to meet cognitive goals.

Among the reasons for measuring the cognitive domain in physical education and exercise science programs are evaluating programmatic objectives, monitoring individual progress, accountability, evaluation of components (or units) of a program, and motivation. Additionally, in many school settings, the physical educator is responsible for grading. When a physical educator or exercise specialists administers an instrument (e.g., test, survey, questionnaire) for measuring knowledge, it is important that the instrument used provides a valid indicator of the individual's comprehension of the subject matter. In both school and nonschool settings, much care should be taken in constructing and modifying, as necessary, these instruments. After using the instrument, quantitative and qualitative item analysis should be used to modify and improve the instrument.

In constructing written exams, educators should consider the taxonomy of educational objectives, match test items to objectives, and employ a table of specifications. An understanding and consideration of the relative advantages and disadvantages of various formats is prerequisite to constructing a valid exam. Following proper administrative and grading procedures is also crucial to ensuring valid results. To give written tests that do not possess content validity or to allow improper administrative procedures to bias test results is a waste of valuable class time.

## ► DISCUSSION QUESTIONS

1. What is included in the cognitive domain of physical education and exercise science? Why is proper emphasis on the cognitive domain critical to a quality program?

2. How should assessing the cognitive domain differ between nonschool settings and the school setting? Give reasons for your answer.

3. Discuss reasons that it is important to incorporate sound measurement of the cognitive domain into the school and nonschool programs.

4. Why is it important to match test questions to written objectives? How are the taxonomy of educational objectives and a table of specifications used to construct a written test?

5. List advantages and disadvantages of the following types of test–questions: true-false, matching, multiple choice, completion, short answer, essay.

6. What is the difference between the difficulty index and the discrimination index? Why are both important to consider in analyzing a written test?

7. What role does qualitative item analysis play in test analysis? What facets of test construction does qualitative item analysis consider?

## ► REFERENCES

Bloom, B.; Englehart, M.; Hill, W.; Furst, E.; and Krathwohl, D. (1956). *Taxonomy of educational objectives: The classification of educational goals, handbook I: Cognitive domain.* New York: Longmans, Green.

Ebel, R. L. (1972). *Essentials of educational measurement.* Englewood Cliffs, NJ: Prentice-Hall.

Hopkins, K. D., and Stanley, J. C. (1981). *Educational and psychological measurement and evaluation.* 6th ed. Englewood Cliffs, NJ: Prentice-Hall.

Johnson, B. L., and Nelson, J. K. (1986). *Practical measurements for evaluation in physical education.* 4th ed. New York: Macmillan.

Kubiszyn, T., and Borich, G. (1984). *Educational testing and measurement: Classroom application and practice.* Glenview, IL: Scott, Foresman.

Mood, D. P. (1980). *Numbers in motion: A balanced approach to measurement and evaluation.* Palo Alto, CA: Mayfield Publishing.

Safrit, M. J. (1990). *Introduction to measurement in physical education and exercise science.* 2d ed. St. Louis, MO: Times Mirror/Mosby.

## ► REPRESENTATIVE READINGS

Kirkendall, D. R.; Gruber J. J.; and Johnson, R. E. (1987). *Measurement and evaluation for physical educators.* 2d ed. Champaign, IL: Human Kinetics Publishers, Inc.

Mathews, D. K. (1978). *Measurement in physical education.* 5th ed. Philadelphia, PA: W. B. Saunders.

Verducci, F. M. (1980). *Measurement concepts in physical education.* St. Louis, MO: C. V. Mosby.

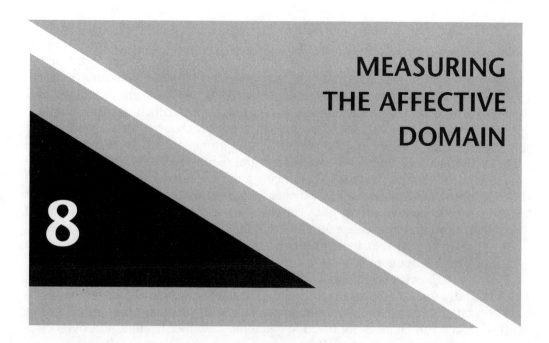

# MEASURING THE AFFECTIVE DOMAIN

## 8

## ► KEY TERMS

affective domain
attitude
Likert scale
self-concept
semantic differential
sociogram
sociometry
two-point scale

## ► OBJECTIVES

*After reading this chapter, the student should be able to:*

1. Identify areas of individual growth in the affective domain in which quality physical education and exercise programs should make positive contributions.

2. Explain the importance of including assessment of the affective domain in the measurement and evaluation scheme in physical education and the exercise science enviroment.

3. Compare and contrast similarities and differences of a Likert scale, a two-point scale, and a semantic differential scale.

4. Discuss methods of measuring attitudes toward physical activity, self-concept, and social competence.

5. Understand measurement problems associated with the various methods of evaluating the affective domain.

Among professionals, there is little disagreement that quality exercise and physical education programs should provide learning opportunities to stimulate growth and development of participants in the physical fitness, psychomotor, cognitive, and affective domains. In movement-based programs, it is apparent that most of the outcomes and program objectives will be directed at the physical fitness and psychomotor domains. Accompanying knowledge and strategies to better understand the how and why of individual activity are associated with the cognitive domain and readily accepted as integral requirements for developing more purposeful movement. Experiencing and understanding movement, developing and maintaining physical fitness, and striving for movement excellence and useful physical skills are any practical goals for physical education and exercise program and inexorably linked. Most professionals also contend that their programs contribute to individual growth in the affective domain.

The **affective domain** includes those characteristics associated with an individual's attitudes, self-concept, and social qualities. Textbooks dedicated to curriculum development usually list several program objectives related to changes in affective behavior. Commonly cited affective objectives for physical education and exercise programs are as follows:

1. Through physical education and exercise programs, the individual should develop a positive attitude toward physical activity.

The assumption is often made that physical education is a viable means to promote the growth and development of positive attitudes toward movement and fitness-related activities. Positive feelings about a physical activity should, of course, promote continuance of regular voluntary participation in physical activity. When youth are asked about their attitude toward physical activity, most will state a positive view. Unfortunately, many of these individuals actually subscribe to a sedentary life-style. In the school and private settings, physical educators must provide instruction and learning experiences that promote good feelings about fundamental movement, fitness-related activities, and sport. Nonschool programs, too, give attention to shaping the attitude participants have toward activity.

2. Through physical education and exercise programs, the individual should develop a desirable self-concept from relevant learning experiences.

**Self-concept** can be defined as how individuals feel about themselves and their ability to cope with life. Sometimes referred to as self-image or self-esteem, self-concept is developed through the responses of people toward the individual. How teachers, exercise specialists, parents, and friends communicate with an individual suggest feelings of being loved or neglected, capable or incapable, intelligent or ignorant, and so on. Teachers and exercise specialists need to understand students and/or clients and assist them in better understanding themselves.

Through physical activity programs, participants have the opportunity to learn more about themselves. Youngsters can experience success and failure, and adults can face challenging physical tasks. Leading experts in pedagogy and curriculum development recommend that physical educators focus on a student's strong points rather than on weaknesses; that children learn how to accept positive feedback from adults and peers; and that students be encouraged to participate in a variety of activities that provide opportunities for successful experiences. (Pangrazi and Dauer, 1992). Achieving self-satisfying levels of skill competency and physical fitness may help make youngsters feel positive and self-assured. Similarly, programs for adults can offer the satisfaction experienced from fulfillment of personal fitness activity goals.

3. Through physical education and exercise programs, individuals should adopt desirable social standards and ethical concepts.

Social development is often considered one of the foremost of all objectives of physical education. By internalizing and understanding the merits of participation, cooperation, and tolerance, youth hopefully will display qualities of good sportsmanship, leadership, followership, social acceptance, and fair play. The teacher can foster these qualities and assist the students in differentiating between acceptable and unacceptable ways of expressing feelings.

Becoming socially competent is an important objective for all phases of a youngster's formal education. Children need to be aware of how they interact with others and how their behavior influences others' responses to them. If students do not receive feedback about negative behavior from teachers and peers, they may never become aware that some behaviors are strongly resented by others (Pangrazi and Dauer, 1992).

It is important for children to become socially competent and learn to cooperate. The nature of many competitive games requires cooperation, fair play, and good sportsmanship. Teachers must emphasize these things during learning experiences to promote socially acceptable behavior. Likewise, adults enrolled in exercise programs have numerous opportunities to strengthen social skills.

As we can see, the development of a positive attitude toward physical activity, positive self-concept, and social competence are worthwhile goals for physical education and exercise programs. All aspects of these programs have a strong impact on promoting behaviors and characteristics associated with affective behavior. How the lesson is organized, the types of activities presented, how the instructor interacts with the client, or how the children are instructed to interact with one another have a great deal to do with attaining program objectives associated with the affective domain.

As with all objectives, it is important to measure and evaluate progress toward attainment of goals in the affective domain. In the physical fitness, psychomotor, and cognitive domains, this task is relatively straightforward and objective. Assessing progress in the affective domain is more problematic because of the subjective nature of the qualities being measured. For example, what is a "good" attitude toward physical activity and how can it be accurately measured? Or, how close is a youngster to displaying a positive self-concept? Or, where is the line between social competence and social incompetence?

To answer such questions, the following sections provide a review of the literature, methods and procedures for gathering and analyzing data, and selected tests to measure qualities and behaviors associated with attitudes toward physical activity, self-concept, and social competence. Because of the potentially sensitive nature of measuring these dimensions, we urge teachers to proceed cautiously. They should obtain permission from their immediate supervisor and administer these types of tests and interpret the results only after they feel confident that they have the necessary skills.

## MEASURING ATTITUDE TOWARD PHYSICAL ACTIVITY

Physical educators and exercise specialists alike recognize the influence attitude has on the performance and exercise behavior of students and clients. Most of the time, the teacher is interested in the student's behavior during active participation in some form of movement experience. For instance, the teacher looks for qualities associated with fair play and genuine interest in physical education class. A coach is interested in the practice and game attitude displayed by athletes. The coach is on the alert to learn about the athlete's sportsmanship and commitment to the strenuous practice regime required to be successful. An exercise specialist is interested in the attitude of the clients toward physical activity and exercise. They look for attitudinal characteristics that demonstrate a participant's pledge to a planned program of physical activity. Regardless of the exercise or activity environment, the practitioner realizes the influence of attitude on performance and recognizes the value of being able to effectively assess and evaluate attitude toward physical activity. The sections below describe methods and techniques to systematically assess and evaluate individuals' attitudes toward physical activity.

## Review of the Literature

Student attitudes toward physical education have been the focus of attention for a considerable period of time. Attitude studies have been reported in the literature as far back as 1933 with the writings of Lapp. Generally, **attitude** refers to feelings about particular social or physical objects such as types of individuals, significant persons, social institutions, and government policy (Nunnally, 1978). Over the past several decades, a number of studies have been published that address the subject of attitudes toward physical activity. Kenyon (1968a) suggests that, although attitude dynamics are not completely understood, and definition and measurement are problematic, progress has been made to warrant their serious investigation in the realm of physical activity. Mostly, these investigations have focused on examination of attitudes toward physical education (Adams, 1963; Richardson, 1960; and Wear, 1950), intensive competition and sportsmanship (McAfee, 1955), and conditioning (Anderson, 1966). Review of these initial studies reveals several shortcomings. First, the studies were limited to a restricted domain and did not examine the much larger domain of physical activity. Second, proper test construction techniques were not always employed. Third, most of the assessment instruments dealt with multidimensional concepts in a unidimensional manner (Simon and Smoll, 1974). However, as a result of these pioneer efforts, researchers have formulated assessment instruments that are appropriately constructed, view attitude from a multidimensional perspective, and are age-specific. Specific tests are described later in this chapter.

## Data Gathering and Analysis

Attitudes are usually measured on scales that require an individual to indicate feelings toward a particular object, person, or policy by providing a response to a written statement. This is most frequently done by using paper-and-pencil instruments. These instruments may be organized into three categories: (1) the Likert scale, (2) the two-point scale, and (3) the semantic differential.

### Likert Scale

Consisting of a series of attitude statements about some person, object, policy, or thing, the **Likert scale** has become one of the most widely used methods of attitude assessment. Respondents indicate the extent to which they agree or disagree with a number of affective statements. Each step of agreement or disagreement is assigned a predetermined numeric value. Totaling the numeric values then suggests whether the individual's attitude is favorable or unfavorable.

The most common Likert scale offers five to seven places along a continuum of descriptors at which the respondent can mark a feeling about a particular statement or object (i.e., agree/disagree). Although it is not particularly important, there is a slight advantage in having an even (4, 6, 8, and so on) rather than an odd number of steps (Nunnally, 1978). Using a scale that has an even number of response locations eliminates the neutral choice necessary with an odd-step scale and forces the respondent to favor one descriptor more than the other.

***Scoring Procedure:*** To complete a Likert scale, respondents simply mark the place on the response sheet that most accurately expresses their feelings toward each affective statement. Figure 8.0 provides a sample Likert scale with choices ranging from Strongly Agree to Strongly Disagree and numeric value assigned to each option. To score the scale, a numeric value is assigned to each space along the continuum depending on whether the item is worded positively or negatively. For example, the numeric value assigned to the options for item 1 in Figure 8.0, which is worded negatively, are SA = 1, A = 2, U = 3, D = 4, and SD = 5. The numeric values for the optional responses associated with item 2, which is positively worded, are: SA = 5, A = 4, U = 3, D = 2, and SD = 1. Summing the numeric values provides the total score for the instrument. Dividing the sum of the scores by the total number of affective statements provides a mean value.

***Advantages and Disadvantages:*** Some advantages and disadvantages of using a Likert scale are listed below.

*Advantages*

1. Furnishes a means for primary and consistent assessment of attitudes with well-devised scales.
2. Adaptable to most attitude measurement situations.
3. Easy to administer, score, and transcribe into quantitative data that can be readily entered and analyzed in a microcomputer.

**FIGURE 8.0**    Sample Likert scale.

| | Strongly Agree | Agree | Uncertain | Disagree | Strongly Disagree |
|---|---|---|---|---|---|
| 1. I have a hard time paying attention in class. (negative) | SA ( 1 | A 2 | U 3 | D 4 | SD 5 ) |
| 2. All students should have to take a course like this one. (positive) | SA ( 5 | A 4 | U 3 | D 2 | SD 1 ) |
| 3. I like learning new sport skills. (positive) | SA ( 5 | A 4 | U 3 | D 2 | SD 1 ) |
| 4. I do not enjoy activities in class. (negative) | SA ( 1 | A 2 | U 3 | D 4 | SD 5 ) |
| 5. I often feel like coming to this class. (positive) | SA ( 5 | A 4 | U 3 | D 2 | SD 1 ) |

4. Compatible with most optical scan sheet formats. This enables the response sheets to be scored by machine.

*Disadvantages*

1. As with most self-report surveys, the respondent is able to convey a false impression of his or her attitude.
2. The distance between points on a scale do not represent equal changes in attitude toward a particular affective statement.
3. Multidimensional concepts may be dealt with in a unidimensional manner.
4. Constructing valid and reliable attitudinal instruments requires time and effort.

## The Two-Point Scale

The **two-point scale** is a variation of the Likert scale. The primary difference between the scales is the number of response options available to the respondent. The two-point scale features yes/no or agree/disagree options, whereas the Likert scale features five or more options. Because it has only two options, the two-point scale is often referred to as the forced-choice scale.

*Scoring Procedure:* Deriving a score from the two-point scale is similar to the process used in scoring the Likert scale. Numeric values are assigned to each of the response options. Usually, a positive response is assigned a +1 and the negative response is assigned either a –1 or 0. While using a +1 and –1 is convenient for defining positive and negative attitude (i.e., any summed score above zero reflects a positive attitude and any summed score below zero reflects a negative attitude), using the 0 enables easier interpretation if the data are subjected to statistical analyses (i.e., correlational procedures).

*Advantages and Disadvantages:* Some advantages and disadvantages of the two-point scale are listed below.

*Advantages*

1. It is easier to understand than the Likert scale.
2. Theoretically, the forced-choice format causes the respondents to provide a more accurate indication of their attitudinal preferences.
3. The likelihood of respondents accidentally marking the wrong step or misunderstanding the choices is small.

*Disadvantages*

1. Having only two diametrically opposed options may be irritating to the respondents. Repeated requests to make a definite response about an affective behavior may create sufficient antagonism toward the instrument to reduce the validity of the results.

## Semantic Differential Scale

The **semantic differential** is a scale that offers two diametrically opposed alternatives at respective ends of a continuum with various steps in between. Sometimes referred to as a bipolar adjective scale, the semantic differential differs from the previous two scales mainly in that it does not use affective statements. Instead, a word or phrase referring to the person, object, policy, or thing in question is presented, along with a list of adjectives that have opposite meanings. Examples of bipolar adjectives would be good/bad, happy/sad, high/low, and so on. Osgood, Suci, and Tannenbaum (1957) provide an extensive list of bipolar adjectives that can be incorporated into a questionnaire. The adjectives are placed at opposite ends of a continuum with steps between offering the respondent various alternatives at which to indicate feelings toward the item in question. An example of the semantic differential scale used to assess a person's attitude toward physical activity can be found in Figure 8.1.

***Scoring Procedure:*** Scoring the semantic differential may be completed in a variety of ways. Two of the more frequently used methods are explained here. The first way is very similar to the procedures described for the Likert and two-point scales. In Figure 8.1, a numeric weight of 1 is assigned to the most negative response and a numeric weight of 7 assigned to the most positive response. Steps between have been assigned appropriate values. The

---

▶ **FIGURE 8.1**   Example of semantic differential scale.

---

**What does the idea in the box mean to you?**

| **Physical Activity** |

**Always think about the idea in the box.**

| 1. | high | ____ : ____ : ____ : ____ : ____ : ____ : ____ | low |
| 2. | awkward | ____ : ____ : ____ : ____ : ____ : ____ : ____ | graceful |
| 3. | meaningless | ____ : ____ : ____ : ____ : ____ : ____ : ____ | meaningful |
| 4. | good | ____ : ____ : ____ : ____ : ____ : ____ : ____ | bad |
| 5. | strong | ____ : ____ : ____ : ____ : ____ : ____ : ____ | weak |
| 6. | beautiful | ____ : ____ : ____ : ____ : ____ : ____ : ____ | ugly |
| 7. | painful | ____ : ____ : ____ : ____ : ____ : ____ : ____ | pleasurable |
| 8. | healthy | ____ : ____ : ____ : ____ : ____ : ____ : ____ | sick |
| 9. | small | ____ : ____ : ____ : ____ : ____ : ____ : ____ | large |
| 10. | slow | ____ : ____ : ____ : ____ : ____ : ____ : ____ | fast |

---

values are summed and a mean score derived. A score of 3.5 or higher reflects a positive attitude; scores less than 3.5 reflect negative attitudes.

The second approach is one endorsed by Kubiszyn and Borich (1984). Numeric values of 7, 6, 5, 4, 3, 2, and 1 are assigned to each step along the continuum regardless of the type of adjective (positive or negative). All the scores for the pairs with the positive adjectives on the left are added together, and all the scores for the pairs with the negative adjective on the left are added. Subtract the score for the left negative adjective pairs from the score for the left positive adjective pairs and divide by the number of adjective pairs. If the calculated mean is greater than zero, a positive attitude is reflected. Similarly, if the average is equal to or less than zero, a negative attitude is reflected.

***Advantages and Disadvantages:*** Some advantages and disadvantages of using the semantic differential are listed below.

*Advantages*
1. The semantic differential can readily be adapted for use in a variety of settings.
2. Its structure allows the evaluation of several different concepts utilizing the same form.
3. The form can be adapted for scoring with an optical scanner.

*Disadvantages*
1. Selecting appropriate bipolar adjectives can be tedious.
2. Without the assistance of an optical scanner, scoring the semantic differential can be both time-consuming and prone to error.

## Uses of Attitudinal Scales

Scales to measure attitude can be utilized in physical education in several ways: (1) to assist the instructor in determining progress toward program or student's goals, (2) to provide a quantitative database to compare the attitudinal scores of individuals or groups (3) to compile information that can be used in planning a physical education or exercise program, and (4) to help evaluate the effectiveness of teaching methods and instructional strategies designed to promote the enjoyment of physical activity (Johnson and Nelson, 1986).

## Problems Associated with Attitudinal Testing

Several problems are associated with attitudinal testing. The validity of attitudinal scales is sometimes questionable, particularly if individuals have limited experience with certain parts of the program and thus cannot make intelligent responses concerning those areas. Many young people, especially below the high school level, lack stability in their attitudes. Young people often will change their attitudes based on recent or new experiences (Johnson and Nelson, 1986). It is important that an instrument measuring attitudes be validated with the population for which it is being used. For example, an attitude survey for preschool children should be validated by (1) experts in the area, (2) test-retest procedures, and (3) concurrent validity tests with an existing instrument. Finally, each statement must be carefully worded to avoid giving any hints of the desired response and to decrease the chance of response distortion by those being measured.

# Tests

The following are examples of testing instruments that can be used to measure attitude toward physical education or physical activity.

### Attitude Toward Physical Activity

(Kenyon, 1968a, 1968b)

**Purpose:** The purpose of the Attitude Toward Physical Activity (ATPA) is to measure various dimensions of an individual's attitude toward physical activity.

**Description:** The ATPA inventory consists of six separate scales designed to measure attitudes toward physical activity as a social experience, aesthetic experience, catharsis, health and fitness experience, ascetic experience, and pursuit of vertigo. Seven-point, Likert-type options ranging from "very strongly agree" to "very strongly disagree" are provided for responses to each of the six subscales. See Figure 8.2 for an example of one subscale.

**Instructions:** The inventory should be administered in a quiet room free of distractions.

**Validity:** Face validity for each dimension was established by a panel of experts. Factor analysis procedures were used to verify the six dimensions of attitude toward physical activity. Except for catharsis, scale scores discriminated between those with strong and those with weak preferences.

**Reliability:** Hoyt reliabilities were calculated for college men and women. Reliabilities ranged from .72 for social experience to .89 for the pursuit of vertigo scale.

**Age Level:** Males and females high school age and older.

**Equipment Needed:** Pencils and ample supply of ATPA inventories.

**Scoring Procedure:** Each scale is scored separately. Therefore, each respondent receives a maximum of six separate scores. Tabulating a quantitative score for each scale is done in the same manner as with any Likert-type scale. The ATPA uses a seven-point scale ranging from "very strongly

▶ **FIGURE 8.2** Attitudes toward physical activity scale.

### HEALTH AND FITNESS SCALE ITEMS

| | | | | | | | |
|---|---|---|---|---|---|---|---|
| VSA | SA | A | U | D | SD | VSD | Of all physical activities, those whose purpose is primarily to develop physical fitness would *not* be my first choice. |
| VSA | SA | A | U | D | SD | VSD | I would usually choose strenuous physical activity over light physical activity, if given the choice. |
| VSA | SA | A | U | D | SD | VSD | A large part of our daily lives must be committed to vigorous exercise. |
| VSA | SA | A | U | D | SD | VSD | Being strong and highly fit is *not* the most important thing in my life. |
| VSA | SA | A | U | D | SD | VSD | The time spent doing daily calisthenics could probably be used more profitably in other ways. |
| VSA | SA | A | U | D | SD | VSD | Strength and physical stamina are the most important prerequisites to a full life. |
| VSA | SA | A | U | D | SD | VSD | I believe calisthenics are among the less desirable forms of physical activity. |
| VSA | SA | A | U | D | SD | VSD | People should spend 20 to 30 minutes a day doing vigorous calisthenics. |
| VSA | SA | A | U | D | SD | VSD | Of all physical activities, my first choice would be those whose purpose is primarily to develop and maintain physical fitness. |
| VSA | SA | A | U | D | SD | VSD | Vigorous daily exercises are absolutely necessary to maintain one's general health. |

### MAXIMUM SCORES FOR ATPA DIMENSIONS

| | Men | Women |
|---|---|---|
| Social | 70 (10 Items) | 56 (8 Items) |
| Health and fitness | 70 (10 Items) | 77 (11 Items) |
| Vertigo | 70 (10 Items) | 63 (9 Items) |
| Aesthetic | 70 (10 Items) | 63 (9 Items) |
| Catharsis | 63 (9 Items) | 63 (9 Items) |
| Ascetic | 70 (10 Items) | 56 (8 Items) |

Reprinted by permission of G. S. Kenyon, University of Lethbridge, Lethbridge, Alberta, Canada.

disagree" to "very strongly agree." It is recommended that the six scores not be summed in an attempt to obtain a composite score. The maximum number of points per scale varies according to the information reported in Figure 8.2. As with other Likert scales, the scoring must be reversed on several items before summing the total score for a particular dimension.

***Norms:*** None available.

*For Additional Information:* G. S. Kenyon, University of Lethbridge, Lethbridge, Alberta, Canada T1K 3M4 or ADI Auxiliary Publications Project, Photoduplication Service, Library of Congress, Washington, DC 20540 (to expedite delivery, request Document No. 9983 and enclose $1.25 for photocopies).

## Children's Attitude Toward Physical Activity

(Simon and Smoll, 1974)

*Purpose:* To measure children's attitudes toward physical activity.

*Description:* The Children's Attitude Toward Physical Activity (CATPA) inventory is based on Kenyon's (1968a, 1968b) conceptual model, which characterizes physical activity as a multidimensional sociopsychological phenomenon, and is modeled after the ATPA. The CATPA, however, employs a semantic differential scale and evaluates each dimension on the basis of eight pairs of bipolar adjectives. This semantic differential is less complex than the Likert-type scale and is more appropriate for elementary and middle school children. The CATPA scale format for health and fitness is shown in Figure 8.3.

*Instructions:* The inventory should be administered in a quiet room free of distractions.

► **FIGURE 8.3**    Scale format for CATPA instrument.

*What does the idea in the box mean to you?*

> **PHYSICAL ACTIVITY FOR HEALTH AND FITNESS**
> **Taking part in physical activities to make your health better and to get your body in better condition.**

*Always think about the idea in the box.*

| | | |
|---|---|---|
| 1. | good ____ : ____ : ____ : ____ : ____ : ____ : ____ | bad |
| 2. | of no use ____ : ____ : ____ : ____ : ____ : ____ : ____ | useful |
| 3. | not pleasant ____ : ____ : ____ : ____ : ____ : ____ : ____ | pleasant |
| 4. | bitter ____ : ____ : ____ : ____ : ____ : ____ : ____ | sweet |
| 5. | nice ____ : ____ : ____ : ____ : ____ : ____ : ____ | awful |
| 6. | happy ____ : ____ : ____ : ____ : ____ : ____ : ____ | sad |
| 7. | dirty ____ : ____ : ____ : ____ : ____ : ____ : ____ | clean |
| 8. | steady ____ : ____ : ____ : ____ : ____ : ____ : ____ | nervous |

*Validity:* It was assumed that the original dimensions of the ATPA were equally representative for children. Language modifications of dimension descriptions were made so that each would be more easily understood by children. The resultant subdomains for the CATPA are described as follows:

1. Physical activity as a social experience. Physical activities that give you a chance to meet new people and be with your friends.
2. Physical activity for health and fitness. Taking part in physical activities to make your health better and to get your body in better condition.
3. Physical activity as a thrill but involving some risk. Physical activities that are dangerous. They also can be exciting because you move very fast and must change directions quickly.
4. Physical activity as the beauty in human movement. Physical activities that have beautiful movements. Examples are ballet–dancing, gymnastics–tumbling, and figure skating on ice.
5. Physical activity for the release of tension. Taking part in physical activities to get away from problems you might have. You can also get away from problems by watching other people in physical activities.
6. Physical activity as long and hard training. Physical activities that have long and hard practices. To spend time in practice you need to give up other things you like to do.

*Reliability:* Reliability coefficients for the six subdomains ranged from .80 to .89. Higher reliabilities were obtained with this semantic differential instrument than with a Likert-type instrument.

*Age Level:* Children in grades 4 through 9.

*Scoring Procedure:* This scaling technique places attitudes on a bipolar continuum. The respondent places a checkmark along the seven-point continuum, which ranges from "extremely favorable" to "extremely unfavorable." The location of the checkmark determines the intensity of the attitude held by the youngster. The scoring procedure assigns the neutral point a score of 0. The extreme ends of the continuum are scored as +3 for "extremely favorable" to –3 for "extremely unfavorable." A +2 score is assigned to checkmarks located in the boxes closest to the "extremely favorable" end of the continuum, while +1 scores were given to checkmarks placed in the boxes closest to the neutral position on the "favorable" side of the continuum. The "unfavorable" side of the continuum follows a similar style of scoring except that minus ranks are assigned to the respective numerals along the scale. The total score for each of the six subdomains is determined by summing all of the scores.

*Norms:* None available.

### CSAPPA: Children's Self-Perceptions of Adequacy in and Predilection for Physical Activity

(Hay, 1992)

*Purpose:* To identify children at risk for hypoactivity and youngsters at risk of becoming obese.

*Description:* The CSAPPA Inventory is designed to measure an individual's adequacy and predisposition toward physical activity. The choices are structured such that activities for which children may be predisposed are described as enjoyable or preferred. Youngsters who view themselves as inadequate in a particular activity will avoid circumstances requiring that behavior and choose not to make efforts to improve. Perceived adequacy, on the other hand, is viewed as the perception of a person's ability to achieve some acceptable standard of success. Ten items begin with active statements, and 10 begin with inactive statements. Eight items address adequacy, the remainder, predisposition toward physical activity. See Figure 8.4.

*Instructions:* The inventory should be administered in a quiet room free of distractions. Children are instructed to read a pair of sentences and then circle the sentence that is most like them. Once finished, they are asked to decide if the statement circled is "sort of true" for them or "really true" for them, and place a checkmark in the proper location. There are no right or wrong answers. Be sure to complete all questions.

*Validity:* The inventory was examined using participation questionnaires, teacher evaluations, and motor proficiency.

*Reliability:* Test-retest reliabilities ranged from .84 (grades 4, 5, 6) to .90 (grades 7, 8, 9).

*Age Level:* Elementary-age children.

*Scoring Procedure:* Items are scored 1-4; 1 is low and 4 is high. Students scoring above 60 are considered to have positive self-perception relating to physical activity.

### Feelings About Physical Activity

(Neilson and Corbin, 1986)

*Purpose:* To provide information about commitment to physical activity.

*Instructions:* The statements may or may not describe an individual's feelings most of the time. Physical activity is defined to include all individual, dual, and team sports and all forms of individual exercise. Persons are

► **FIGURE 8.4** CSAPPA Inventory

INSTRUCTIONS: In this survey you have to read a pair of sentences and then circle the sentence that you think is <u>more like you</u>. For example:

Some kids have one nose on their faces      BUT      Other kids have three noses on their faces!

That shouldn't be too hard for you to decide! Once you have circled the sentence that is more like you, then you have to decide if it is <u>SORT OF TRUE</u> for you or <u>REALLY TRUE</u> for you, and put a checkmark in the right box. Here is another example for you to try. Remember: <u>First</u> circle the sentence that is more like you and then check off if it is REALLY TRUE <u>or</u> only SORT OF TRUE for you.

| REALLY TRUE for me | SORT OF TRUE for me | | | | SORT OF TRUE for me | REALLY TRUE for me |
|---|---|---|---|---|---|---|
| [ ] | [ ] | Some kids like to play with computers. | BUT | Other kids don't like playing with computers. | [ ] | [ ] |

Now you are ready to start filling in this form. THERE ARE NO RIGHT OR WRONG ANSWERS, JUST WHAT IS <u>MOST LIKE YOU</u>. Take your time and do the whole form carefully. If you have any questions just ask! If you think you are ready you can start now. BE SURE TO FILL IN BOTH SIDES OF EACH PAGE!

| REALLY TRUE for me | SORT OF TRUE for me | | | | SORT OF TRUE for me | REALLY TRUE for me |
|---|---|---|---|---|---|---|
| [ ] | [ ] | Some kids can't wait to play active games after school | BUT | Other kids would rather do something else. | [ ] | [ ] |
| [ ] | [ ] | Some kids really enjoy physical education class. | BUT | Other kids don't like physical education class. | [ ] | [ ] |
| [ ] | [ ] | Some kids don't like playing active games. | BUT | Other kids really like playing active games. | [ ] | [ ] |
| [ ] | [ ] | Some kids don't have much fun playing sports. | BUT | Other kids have a good time playing sports. | [ ] | [ ] |
| [ ] | [ ] | Some kids think phys. ed. is the best class. | BUT | Other kids think phys. ed. isn't much fun. | [ ] | [ ] |
| [ ] | [ ] | Some kids are good at active games. | BUT | Other kids find active games hard to play. | [ ] | [ ] |
| [ ] | [ ] | Some kids don't like playing sports. | BUT | Other kids really enjoy playing sports. | [ ] | [ ] |
| [ ] | [ ] | Some kids always hurt themselves when they play sports. | BUT | Other kids never hurt themselves playing sports. | [ ] | [ ] |
| [ ] | [ ] | Some kids like to play active games outside. | BUT | Other kids would rather read or play video games. | [ ] | [ ] |

(continued)

► **FIGURE 8.4**   Continued.

| [ ] | [ ] | Some kids do well in most sports. | BUT | Other kids feel they aren't very good at sports. | [ ] | [ ] |
|---|---|---|---|---|---|---|
| [ ] | [ ] | Some kids learn to play active games easily. | BUT | Other kids find it hard learning to play active games. | [ ] | [ ] |
| [ ] | [ ] | Some kids think they are the best at sports. | BUT | Other kids think they aren't very good at sports. | [ ] | [ ] |
| [ ] | [ ] | Some kids find games in phys. ed. hard to play. | BUT | Other kids are good at games in phys. ed. | [ ] | [ ] |
| [ ] | [ ] | Some kids like to watch games being played outside. | BUT | Other kids would rather play active games outside. | [ ] | [ ] |
| [ ] | [ ] | Some kids are among the last to be chosen for active games. | BUT | Other kids are usually picked to play first. | [ ] | [ ] |
| [ ] | [ ] | Some kids like to take it easy during recess. | BUT | Other kids would rather play active games. | [ ] | [ ] |
| [ ] | [ ] | Some kids have fun in phys. ed. class. | BUT | Other kids would rather miss phys. ed. class. | [ ] | [ ] |
| [ ] | [ ] | Some kids aren't good enough for sports teams. | BUT | Other kids do well on sports teams. | [ ] | [ ] |
| [ ] | [ ] | Some kids like to read or play quiet games. | BUT | Other kids like to play active games. | [ ] | [ ] |
| [ ] | [ ] | Some kids like to play active games outside on weekends. | BUT | Other kids like to relax and watch TV on weekends. | [ ] | [ ] |

PLEASE CHECK TO MAKE SURE THAT YOU HAVE ANSWERED ALL THE QUESTIONS!
THANK YOU!

Reprinted by permission of Dr. John A. Hay.

asked to circle the appropriate letter(s) to indicate how they generally feel about physical activity. See Figure 8.5.

*Validity:* Validity was examined using discrimination indices of item analysis averaged .45.

*Reliability:* Estimates ranged from 0.88 to 0.91.

*Age Level:* This inventory is suitable for a broad age range of individuals.

*Scoring Procedure:* Items 1, 5, 6, 7, 9, and 12 are scored 1 to 5. Items 2, 3, 4, 8, 10, and 11 are scored 5 to 1. Thirty-six is the middle score. The following scale is intended to provide some interpretative information.

54-60   Very favorable feelings about physical activity
42-53   Favorable
30-41   Neutral
18-29   Unfavorable
12-17   Very unfavorable feelings about physical activity

▶ **FIGURE 8.5**   Feelings About Activity Inventory

Directions: The following statements may or may not describe your feelings about physical activity. Physical activity is interpreted to include all individual, dual, and team sports, and all individual exercises. Please circle the appropriate letter or letters to indicate how well the statement describes your feelings most of the time. There are no right or wrong answers. Do not spend too much time on any one item, but give the answer that seems to describe how you generally feel about physical activity.

SD = STRONGLY DISAGREE
D = DISAGREE
U = UNCERTAIN

A = AGREE
SA = STRONGLY AGREE

**THE SCALE**

**Feelings About Physical Activity**

| | |
|---|---|
| 1. I look forward to physical activity. | SD   D   U   A   SA |
| 2. I wish there were a more enjoyable way to stay fit than vigorous physical activity. | SD   D   U   A   SA |
| 3. Physical activity is drudgery. | SD   D   U   A   SA |
| 4. I do not enjoy physical activity. | SD   D   U   A   SA |
| 5. Physical activity is vitally important to me. | SD   D   U   A   SA |
| 6. Life is so much richer as a result of physical activity. | SD   D   U   A   SA |
| 7. Physical activity is pleasant. | SD   D   U   A   SA |
| 8. I dislike the thought of doing regular physical activity. | SD   D   U   A   SA |
| 9. I would arrange or change my schedule to participate in physical activity. | SD   D   U   A   SA |
| 10. I have to force myself to participate in physical activity. | SD   D   U   A   SA |
| 11. To miss a day of physical activity is sheer relief. | SD   D   U   A   SA |
| 12. Physical activity is the high point of my day. | SD   D   U   A   SA |

Scoring: Items 1, 5, 6, 7, 9, and 12 are scored 1 to 5; items 2, 3, 4, 8, 10, and 11 are scored 5 to 1. Thirty-six is the middle score. The following scale gives some interpretative information:

54–60 Very favorable feelings about physical activity

42–53 Favorable feelings

30–41 Neutral feelings

18–29 Unfavorable feelings

12–17 Very unfavorable feelings about physical activity

Reprinted by permission of Dr. Charles Corbin, Arizona State University.

## Physical Estimation and Attraction Scale
### (Sonstroem, 1974)

*Purpose:* The purpose of the Physical Estimation and Attraction Scale (PEAS) is to measure expressed interest in physical activity (attraction) and physical self-esteem relative to physical appearance and performance (estimation).

*Description:* The PEAS consists of 100 randomly ordered statements. Fifty-four of the statements are associated with attraction, 33 with estimation, 2 with socialization, and 11 are neutral. The estimation items require respondents to affirm or deny their physical characteristics, physical fitness, or motor ability. The attraction statements require respondents to affirm or deny their interests in various physical activities. The questionnaire is found in Figure 8.6. The responses to the statements are limited to true (the student agrees with the statement), false (the student disagrees with the statement) or neutral.

*Instructions:* The inventory should be administered in a quiet room free of distractions.

*Validity:* The relationships between the estimation scale to actual fitness and self-esteem as measured by the Tennessee Self-Concept Scale are moderate (Sonstroem, 1978). The attraction scale has been reported to correlate with self-reported participation in physical activity (Neale, Sonstroem, and Metz, 1969; Sonstroem, 1976).

*Reliability:* Coefficients of reliability for internal consistency and stability ranged from .87 to .94 (Sonstroem, 1974; 1976).

*Age Level:* The validity studies have been conducted primarily with adolescent boys. However, the scale has been used with male and female adults.

*Equipment Needed:* PEAS forms, pencils or pens, and scoring key.

*Scoring Procedure:* The answer key, provided with the scale, indicates the response to each statement that demonstrates a positive attitude. Each response consistent with the scoring key receives one point. The total score is the sum of all the individual scores. The higher the score, the more positive the attitude toward physical activity. The estimation and attraction scales can be scored separately.

*Norms:* None available. Mean scores for the scales as derived from Sonstroem's research are available.

► **FIGURE 8.6**   Physical estimation and attraction scale.

| KEYED RESPONSE* | SCALE† | ATTITUDE STATEMENT |
|---|---|---|
| X | N | 1. I would rather see a play than a movie. |
| T | A | 2. I prefer exercising to reading. |
| X | N | 3. I generally prefer talking with friends to playing a family table game such as Monopoly. |
| T | A | 4. I would much rather play softball than go for a ride in a car. |
| F | E | 5. Most of my friends work harder than I do. |
| T | E | 6. My body is strong and muscular compared to other boys my age. |
| X | N | 7. I would be interested in learning to play a musical instrument. |
| F | A | 8. Most sports require too much time and energy to be worthwhile. |
| X | N | 9. I would have made a good accountant. |
| T | E | 10. I am in better physical condition than most boys my age. |
| X | N | 11. The mechanical properties of motors interest me a great deal. |
| X | N | 12. On a Sunday afternoon, I would prefer to go to a movie rather than to go on a picnic. |
| T | E | 13. I am quite limber and agile compared to others my age. |
| X | N | 14. I often stick up for my own point of view even when no one agrees with me. |
| X | N | 15. I enjoy people who talk a great deal. |
| T | A | 16. I prefer team sports to individual sports because of the experience of playing with different people. |
| F | A | 17. I like to be in sports that don't require a great amount of running. |
| T | A | 18. I know that my health improves when I exercise. |
| F | E | 19. I just don't have the coordination necessary to look like a graceful skier. |
| X | N | 20. I prefer woodworking to tinkering with a motor. |
| X | N | 21. One of my favorite interests is listening to music. |
| T | A | 22. I would enjoy participating in activities such as cross-country skiing and channel swimming. |
| F | A | 23. Music, art, or intellectual pursuits are more refreshing to me than physical activity. |
| F | A | 24. I would rather visit an amusement park than watch a tennis match. |
| T | A | 25. I like the social opportunities afforded by physical activity programs. |
| T | E | 26. I am better coordinated than most people I know. |
| T | A | 27. I would enjoy difficult mountain climbing. |
| X | N | 28. I love to go to jazz or rock concerts. |
| F | A | 29. I don't think that I'd enjoy participating in a judo program. |
| T | A | 30. I enjoy the feeling of physical well-being one gets after a day's tramp in the woods. |
| F | A | 31. I would rather watch a good movie than a hockey match. |
| T | A | 32. I would like to belong to some type of exercise group. |
| T | E | 33. I am a good deal stronger than most of my friends. |

(continued)

► **FIGURE 8.6**   Continued.

| KEYED RESPONSE* | SCALE† | ATTITUDE STATEMENT |
|---|---|---|
| F | A | 34. I would rather play poker than softball. |
| F | E | 35. Compared to other people I am somewhat clumsy. |
| T | A | 36. I enjoy hard physical work. |
| F | A | 37. I like to engage in recreational exercise rather than in organized competitive athletics. |
| T | E | 38. I am stronger than a good many of my friends. |
| T | E | 39. Most people I know think I have very good physical skills. |
| F | E | 40. My friends seem to be more physically active than I am. |
| F | A | 41. I would rather walk than run through an open meadow or field. |
| T | A | 42. Sports provide me with a welcome escape from the pressures of present-day life. |
| T | A | 43. I like the rough and tumble of athletic competition. |
| F | A | 44. I prefer to watch an exciting basketball game to playing it myself. |
| T | A | 45. I rather enjoy the physical risk involved when I play football. |
| T | A | 46. I would enjoy participating in a vigorous weight-lifting program. |
| T | A | 47. Long distance running would seem to be an enjoyable activity. |
| F | E | 48. I doubt that I could ever get into good physical condition. |
| T | E | 49. My legs have as much spring as those of champion high jumpers. |
| F | A | 50. I don't enjoy doing things that get me sweaty and dirty. |
| F | A | 51. I prefer not to participate in physical activities that involve risk of injury. |
| T | A | 52. I would enjoy belonging to a whitewater canoe club. |
| F | A | 53. When tensions are high, I prefer to lie down and rest rather than to absorb myself in physical activity. |
| T | E | 54. If I wanted to, I could become an excellent tennis player. |
| T | A | 55. I enjoy performing gymnastic stunts because of the coordinated movements involved. |
| F | A | 56. It makes no difference to me how strong or fit I am. |
| T | A | 57. I would like to meet more people by engaging in various types of physical activities. |
| F | A | 58. After a day at school, I prefer to take it easy instead of participating in vigorous sport activities. |
| F | E | 59. It is difficult for me to catch a thrown ball. |
| T | E | 60. With a fair amount of practice I could maintain a high bowling average. |
| T | A | 61. I enjoy the discipline of long and strenuous physical training. |
| T | E | 62. I can run faster than most of my friends. |
| T | A | 63. Watching an athletic contest provides a welcome relief from the cares of life. |
| T | E | 64. With practice I could become a very good golfer. |
| F | A | 65. I have more important things to do than to spend time on developing and maintaining physical fitness. |

(continued)

**FIGURE 8.6** Continued.

| KEYED RESPONSE* | SCALE† | ATTITUDE STATEMENT |
|---|---|---|
| T | A | 66. I would rather run in a track meet than play badminton. |
| T | E | 67. I could do better at long distance hiking than the average boy of my age. |
| T | E | 68. I exhibit a fair amount of leadership in a sports situation. |
| F | E | 69. I lack confidence in performing physical activities. |
| F | E | 70. Even with practice I doubt that I could learn to do a handstand well. |
| T | A | 71. Playing tennis appeals to me more than does golfing. |
| T | E | 72. I can run for longer distances than most boys of my age. |
| T | E | 73. I am a natural athlete. |
| F | A | 74. The thought of getting sweaty and dirty often keeps me from exercising. |
| T | A | 75. I love to run. |
| F | A | 76. Getting into good physical shape takes too much effort to be really worth it. |
| T | E | 77. I have a strong throwing arm for baseball or softball. |
| T | A | 78. Karate competition must be fun. |
| F | E | 79. It would be very difficult for me to learn to do a back dive. |
| F | A | 80. I would prefer to listen to a concert than to watch a gymnastics match. |
| T | E | 81. I am well-equipped to excel at physical activities. |
| F | A | 82. Being strong and highly fit is not really that important to me. |
| T | A | 83. Absorbing myself in a good sport activity provides an escape from the routine of a school day. |
| F | E | 84. Even with practice I doubt that I could ever learn to do a cartwheel well. |
| T | A | 85. Exercise relieves me of emotional strain. |
| F | A | 86. I would play sports more often if I didn't get so tired. |
| T | E | 87. Probably I could get into good physical condition faster than most fellows my age. |
| F | E | 88. I often doubt my physical abilities. |
| T | A | 89. I would rather play touch football than go to an amusement park. |
| X | S | 90. Participation in physical activity improves me as a social person. |
| F | E | 91. I'm not very good at most physical skills. |
| T | A | 92. I enjoy the exhilarated feeling one gets after doing calisthenics. |
| X | S | 93. I'm not able to meet many worthwhile people through participation in sports. |
| F | E | 94. Poor timing handicaps me in certain physical activities. |
| T | E | 95. I am a natural leader in sport activities. |
| T | A | 96. I would rather play active sports like soccer and basketball than participate in activities like badminton and softball. |
| T | A | 97. I believe it is important that a person belongs to a group that participates in sport activities together. |

(continued)

▶    **FIGURE 8.6**    Continued.

| | | |
|---|---|---|
| T | A | 98. I would rather watch either a baseball or basketball game than visit a museum or art gallery. |
| F | A | 99. Target archery appeals to me more as an activity than does tennis. |
| T | A | 100. I believe one of the greatest values of physical activity is the thrill of competition. |

*T when True is the positive response; F when False is the positive response; X when the statement is unscored (neutral).

†E is the physical estimation scale; A is the physical attraction scale; S is social; N is neutral.

Reprinted by permission of R. J. Sonstroem, University of Rhode Island, Kingston, Rhode Island.

### Richardson Scale for Measuring Attitudes Toward Physical Fitness and Exercise

*(Richardson, 1960)*

**Purpose:** To measure attitudes toward physical fitness and exercise.

**Description:**
This inventory employs two equivalent forms of an equal-appearing intervals attitude scale and was constructed around the topic of "physical fitness and exercise." Respondents are asked to circle the number opposite each item with which they agree. Numeric scale values used in the scoring process have been assigned to each statement. Examples of statements and the respective values are included in Form A shown in Figure 8.7.

**Instructions:** Respondents are to read each statement and circle the number opposite each item with which they agree. They are to make no marks on the numbers opposite the items with which they disagree. There is no time limit, but students are encouraged to work rapidly.

**Validity:** Twenty experts were employed to render an opinion regarding the validity of this instrument. Consensus opinion indicated that the instrument was valid.

**Reliability:** Repetition and parallel forms were used to determine reliability. The test-retest coefficient of correlation between scores was .83 +/−.03, which suggests a high degree of internal consistency.

**Age Level:** High school and college students.

**Equipment Needed:** Appropriate forms, pencils or pens, and scoring key.

**Scoring Procedure:** Scoring is relatively simple. The numeric values assigned to each statement to which the respondent indicated agreement are listed and the median, or middle, score is identified. The median value represents the relative position of that student on the selected attitude scale

▶ **FIGURE 8.7** Richardson scale for measuring attitudes toward physical fitness and exercise.

---

(1.1) Physical fitness activity is the lowest type of activity indulged in by individuals.

(1.3) People have outgrown the need for physical fitness programs.

(1.5) Physical fitness activity programs are necessary only in wartime.

(1.7) Physical fitness activities are the least civilized of people's activities.

(1.9) Physical activity should not be stressed so much in our present culture.

(2.1) Planned physical activity programs have limited value.

(2.3) Physical fitness activity is unnecessary.

(2.5) The values of physical activity are debatable.

(2.7) Physical fitness activity should be left to the individual.

(2.9) Physical fitness programs are too soft.

The scale values in parentheses are listed with decimal points only for presentation purposes. In actual testing, items are given three numbers (without decimals) for convenience in scoring. The first of the three refers to item number on the test; the last two indicate scale values. Thus, the subject sees the numbers 111, 213, 315, and so on to the left of each item. This method of numbering is used to minimize the possibility of a suggested response pattern for the subject. (From C. E. Richardson, "Thurstone Scale for Measuring Attitudes of College Students Toward Physical Fitness and Exercise." *Research Quarterly* 31:638–643, December 1960.)

---

Reprinted by permission of American Alliance for Health, Physical Education, Recreation and Dance, Reston, Virginia.

range and is recorded as the score. For example, if the values corresponding to all statements marked "agree" are 113, 115, 129, 127, and 145, the middle value, or 127, is recorded as the student's score.

*Norms:* None available.

## Wear Attitude Scale

*(Wear, 1955)*

*Purpose:* To measure attitudes toward physical education.

*Description:* This scale, one of the first developed to assess attitude toward physical education, is composed of statements about physical education and is divided into two forms, A and B. Students are asked to check the response that best describes their feelings about each statement. There are five response options ranging from "strongly agree" to "strongly disagree" for each statement. Respondents are encouraged to let their prior experiences influence responses and are informed that their answers will in no way affect their physical education grades. Examples of statements can be found in Figure 8.8.

*Validity:* Face validity has been established for the scales.

▶ **FIGURE 8.8**  Wear attitude scale.

Student's Name _____ School _____

|  | Strongly Agree | Agree | Undecided | Disagree | Strongly Disagree |
|---|---|---|---|---|---|
| 1. If for any reason a few subjects have to be dropped from the school program, physical education should be one of the subjects dropped. | _____ | _____ | _____ | _____ | _____ |
|  | _____ | _____ | _____ | _____ | _____ |
| 2. Physical education activities provide no opportunities for learning to control the emotions. | _____ | _____ | _____ | _____ | _____ |
| 3. Physical education is one of the more important subjects in helping to establish and maintain desirable social standards. | _____ | _____ | _____ | _____ | _____ |
| 4. Vigorous physical activity works off harmful emotional tensions. | _____ | _____ | _____ | _____ | _____ |
| 5. I would take physical education only if it were required. | _____ | _____ | _____ | _____ | _____ |
| 6. Participation in physical education makes no contribution to the development of poise. | _____ | _____ | _____ | _____ | _____ |
| 7. Because physical skills loom large in importance in youth, it is essential that a person be helped to acquire and improve such skills. | _____ | _____ | _____ | _____ | _____ |
| 8. Calisthenics taken regularly are good for one's general health. | _____ | _____ | _____ | _____ | _____ |
| 9. Skill in active games or sports is not necessary for leading the fullest kind of life. | _____ | _____ | _____ | _____ | _____ |
| 10. Physical education does more harm physically than it does good. | _____ | _____ | _____ | _____ | _____ |
| 11. Associating with others in some physical education activity is fun. | _____ | _____ | _____ | _____ | _____ |
| 12. Physical education classes provide situations for the formation of attitudes that will make one a better citizen. | _____ | _____ | _____ | _____ | _____ |
| 13. Physical education situations are among the poorest for making friends. | _____ | _____ | _____ | _____ | _____ |
| 14. There is not enough value coming from physical education to justify the time consumed. | _____ | _____ | _____ | _____ | _____ |
| 15. Physical education skills make worthwhile contributions to the enrichment of living. | _____ | _____ | _____ | _____ | _____ |

(continued)

**FIGURE 8.8**   Continued.

| | Strongly Agree | Agree | Undecided | Disagree | Strongly Disagree |
|---|---|---|---|---|---|
| 16. People get all the physical exercise need in just taking care of their daily work. | ____ | ____ | ____ | ____ | ____ |
| 17. All who are physically able will profit from an hour of physical education each day. | ____ | ____ | ____ | ____ | ____ |
| 18. Physical education makes a valuable contribution toward building up an adequate reserve of strength and endurance for everyday living. | ____ | ____ | ____ | ____ | ____ |
| 19. Physical education tears down sociability by encouraging people to attempt to surpass each other in many of the activities. | ____ | ____ | ____ | ____ | ____ |
| 20. Participation in physical education activities makes for a more whole-some outlook on life. | ____ | ____ | ____ | ____ | ____ |
| 21. Physical education adds nothing to the improvement of social behavior. | ____ | ____ | ____ | ____ | ____ |
| 22. Physical education class activities will help to relieve and relax physical tensions. | ____ | ____ | ____ | ____ | ____ |
| 23. Participation in physical education activities helps a person to maintain a healthful emotional life. | ____ | ____ | ____ | ____ | ____ |
| 24. Physical education is one of the more important subjects in the school program. | ____ | ____ | ____ | ____ | ____ |
| 25. There is little value in physical education as far as physical well-being is concerned. | ____ | ____ | ____ | ____ | ____ |
| 26. Physical education should be included in the program of every school. | ____ | ____ | ____ | ____ | ____ |
| 27. Skills learned in a physical education class do not benefit a person. | ____ | ____ | ____ | ____ | ____ |
| 28. Physical education provides situations for developing desirable character qualities. | ____ | ____ | ____ | ____ | ____ |
| 29. Physical education makes for more enjoyable living. | ____ | ____ | ____ | ____ | ____ |
| 30. Physical education has no place in modern education. | ____ | ____ | ____ | ____ | ____ |

Reprinted by permission of American Alliance for Health, Physical Education, Recreation and Dance, Reston, Virginia.

*Reliability:* The reliability coefficients were .94 and .96 for forms A and B, respectively.

*Age Level:* While the instrument was originally designed for use by college students, it is also appropriate for high school students.

*Test Area:* The inventory should be administered in a quiet room free of distractions.

*Equipment Needed:* Inventory forms, pencil or pen, and scoring key.

*Scoring Procedure:* Positively worded statements are scored from +5 to +1, and negatively worded statements are scored from +1 to +5. The total score is the sum of the points for all the statement responses. The higher the score, the more positive the attitude toward physical education.

*Norms:* None available.

## Cheffers and Mancini Human Movement Attitude Scale
*(Cheffers, Mancini, and Zaichkowsky, 1976)*

*Purpose:* To measure the attitudes of children toward teachers, facilities, and certain processes associated with physical education programs.

*Description:* The CAMHM Attitude Scale consists of pictures that contain situations or occurrences typical of physical education class. Children are asked to respond to the pictures by making a check mark next to one of three facial expressions, either happy, sad, or neutral. Figure 8.9 shows an example of a situation and the response options. Items are situation-specific and may require the use of an artist to draw certain pictures that are descriptive or pertinent to a particular setting.

*Instructions:* Children are instructed to look at the pictures and identify which face they would like to wear when viewing the picture. If they like what they see, they mark the happy face. If they do not like what they see, they place a check mark next to the sad face. If they are indifferent, a mark is placed next to the neutral face.

*Validity:* Validity of this instrument was obtained by oral responses to the pictures of 33 elementary students from grades 1 through 6. If the child had experienced what each picture represented and could tell what was occurring, the statement conveyed by the picture was understood and validity for the CAMHM Attitude Scale was assumed.

*Reliability:* A test-retest format yielded a Pearson *r* of .97. The split-half method resulted in a correlation coefficient of .87. Correlational coefficients for each item ranged from .70 to .99.

*Age Level:* Elementary school children in grades 1–6.

**FIGURE 8.9**   CAMHM attitude scale.

From Victor H. Mancini, "A Comparison of Two Decision-Making Models in an Elementary Human Movement Program Based on Attitudes and Interaction Patterns." Unpublished doctoral dissertation, Boston University, 1974. Copyright by author.

*Test Area:*  Any quiet area free of distractions.

*Equipment Needed:*  CAMHM Attitude Scale and pencils.

*Scoring Procedure:*  A +1 is assigned to a mark by a happy face, a 0 is assigned to a mark by a neutral face, and a −1 is assigned to a mark by a sad face. The total score is the sum of the numeric values. The higher the score, the more positive the attitude toward physical education.

*Norms:*  None available.

## MEASURING SELF-CONCEPT

One of the primary purposes for all domains of physical education is to enhance the self-concept of students (Pangrazi and Dauer, 1995; Pangrazi and Darst, 1991). Similarly, in the exercise setting it is important for the specialist to strengthen participants' self-concepts through exercise and activity. Developing the self-concept is a slow process that requires participants to observe, differentiate, and select until they can understand and accept the image of who they are.

Physical education, exercise programs, and planned physical activity provide environments that can facilitate the development of self. The ability to establish settings that stimulate achievement, enhance health and physical well-being, allow for risks to be taken, and teach responsibility makes physical activity environments effective in promoting active lifestyles and positive self-images. Orchestrating learning experiences that foster a person's self-image and utilizing teaching techniques that promote a feeling of self-worth require a great deal of preparation and skill. Like any other objective, the development of self should be monitored through assessment and evaluation techniques.

## Review of the Literature

In recent years, interest and concern about the affective behavior of individuals has increased. This increased concern is merited because an individual's affective behavior influences their learning and development. The multidimensional characteristics of the self-concept are often cited in the professional literature. Throughout the literature, the self-concept is viewed as a link between observable behavior and the underlying processes of the individual. Some authors contend that self-concept is a directing force for all behavior (Snodgrass, 1977). Others even suggest that it is education's obligation to help youngsters develop better self-concepts (Pangrazi, 1969).

**Self-concept** is a composite view of how one sees oneself, comprising ideas, attitudes, values, and commitments. Rather than originating from within the individual, self-concept is learned. Its development begins soon after birth and continues throughout life, although it is thought to be relatively stable by the age of 11 or 12 (Fitts, 1971). Children and youth develop a view of themselves from the ways in which they are treated by others. Individuals form their self-concept from the types of experiences they have had in life. Youth develop feelings that they are liked, wanted, accepted, and able from the actual experiences of being wanted, accepted, and successful (Combs, 1965). Many experts believe that a sense of belonging, personal competence, and a sense of worth are important parts of total growth and development (Felker, 1974).

Through physical activity, youth are provided with opportunities to participate in learning experiences designed to develop self-concept. Through exploration, experimentation, and structured learning experiences, youth begin to differentiate their capacities and potentials. Establishing a warm, positive learning environment is crucial, and physical educators and exercise scientists must be prepared to measure and evaluate the changes that occur in self-concept as a result of participation in physical activity.

## Data Gathering and Analysis

Data about self-concept are obtained in much the same manner as information about attitude. Pencil-and-paper self-report instruments are designed to elicit information about how individuals feel about themselves.

## Tests

The following section describes tests suitable for assessing and evaluating the progress of self-concept development.

### Cratty Adaptation of Piers-Harris Self-Concept Scale
(Cratty, 1970)

*Purpose:* To measure how children feel about their physical appearance and motor ability.

*Description:* The Piers-Harris (1964) scale consists of statements made by children regarding their likes and dislikes about themselves. Using the Piers-Harris scale as a model, Cratty (1970) developed a scale that focuses on children's view of their physical ability and appearance. The resultant self-report inventory classified statements into five categories: feelings about general well-being, social competence, physical appearance, physical ability, and social achievement. Children are asked to respond to the statements by answering yes or no. The statements can be read to children who are unable to read. An example of this instrument is found in Figure 8.10.

*Validity:* Internal validity was established using item analysis.

*Reliability:* Test-retest procedures resulted in a reliability coefficient of .82.

*Age Level:* Kindergarten through grade 6.

*Test Area:* Any quiet area free of distractions.

*Equipment Needed:* Self-concept scale and pencils.

*Scoring Procedure:* One point is awarded for each positive response. The total score is the sum of expected responses for the statements.

*Norms:* None available.

*For Additional Information:* To obtain information about the Piers-Harris Self-Concept Scale write to: Piers-Harris Children's Self-Concept Scale, The Way I Feel About Myself, Counselor Recordings and Tests, Box 6186 Acklan Station, Nashville, TN, 37212.

▶ **FIGURE 8.10**    Cratty adaptation of Piers-Harris self-concept scale.

Name _____Date _____Grade _____M ___F _____

**Scoring Key†**

| | | | | |
|---|---|---|---|---|
| + | 1. Are you good at making things with your hands? | Yes | No |
| + | 2. Can you draw well? | Yes | No |
| + | 3. Are you strong? | Yes | No |
| + | 4. Do you like the way you look? | Yes | No |
| | 5. Do your friends make fun of you? | Yes | No |
| + | 6. Are you handsome/pretty? | Yes | No |
| | 7. Do you have trouble making friends? | Yes | No |
| + | 8. Do you like school? | Yes | No |
| | 9. Do you wish you were different? | Yes | No |
| | 10. Are you sad most of the time? | Yes | No |
| | 11. Are you the last to be chosen in games? | Yes | No |
| + | 12. Do girls like you? | Yes | No |
| + | 13. Are you a good leader in games and sports? | Yes | No |

†Plus sign (+) indicates questions stated in a positive way. A "yes" response indicates good self-concept. A "no" response on unmarked questions indicates good self-concept.

From B. Cratty, *Movement Activities, Motor Ability, and the Education of Children,* 1970. Courtesy of Charles C. Thomas, Publisher, Springfield, Illinois.

## Nelson-Allen Movement Satisfaction Scale

(Nelson and Allen, 1970)

*Purpose:* To measure an individual's satisfaction with movement.

*Description:* This scale consists of 50 statements pertaining to movement. Respondents are asked to consider each statement and indicate the degree to which the statement describes their feelings. The response scale consists of five options: "strong negative feelings," "moderate negative feelings," "no feeling one way or another," "moderate positive feelings," and "strong positive feelings." Numeric values for the responses range from +5 for the most positive option to +1 for the most negative option.

*Validity:* Face validity is assumed.

*Reliability:* The Kuder-Richardson technique resulted in a reliability coefficient of .95.

*Age Level:* High school students and older.

*Test Area:* Any quiet area free of distractions.

*Equipment Needed:* Self-concept scale and pencils.

*Scoring Procedure:* The sum of all marked options is the total score.

*Norms:* None available.

## Coopersmith Self-Esteem Inventory
(Coopersmith, 1967)

*Purpose:* To measure the self-esteem of children.

*Description:* This inventory is published in either a short or long form. The short form, shown in Figure 8.11, comprises 25 statements about how an individual feels about a particular situation. Students are asked to read each statement and indicate whether the statement describes how they usually feel ("like me") or does not describe how they usually feel ("unlike me"). There are no correct or incorrect answers.

▶ **FIGURE 8.11**   Coopersmith self-esteem inventory (SEI).

**University of California, Davis**

Name _____ School _____

Class _____ Date _____

Please mark each statement in the following way:

 If the statement describes how you usually feel, put a check (✔) in the column, "LIKE ME."

 If the statement does not describe how you usually feel, put a check (✔) in the column, "UNLIKE ME."

There are no right or wrong answers.

| | LIKE ME | UNLIKE ME |
|---|---|---|
| Example: I'm a hard worker. | | |
| 1. I often wish I were someone else. | | |
| 2. I find it very hard to talk in front of the class. | | |
| 3. There are lots of things about myself I'd change if I could. | | |
| 4. I can make up my mind without too much trouble. | | |
| 5. I'm a lot of fun to be with. | | |
| 6. I get upset easily at home. | | |
| 7. It takes me a long time to get used to anything new. | | |
| 8. I'm popular with kids my own age. | | |
| 9. My parents usually consider my feelings. | | |

(Continued)

► **FIGURE 8.11** Continued.

| | | |
|---|---|---|
| 10. I give in very easily. | | |
| 11. My parents expect too much of me. | | |
| 12. It's pretty tough to be me. | | |
| 13. Things are all mixed up in my life. | | |
| 14. Kids usually follow my ideas. | | |
| 15. I have a low opinion of myself. | | |
| 16. There are many times when I'd like to leave home. | | |
| 17. I often feel upset in school. | | |
| 18. I'm not as nice looking as most people. | | |
| 19. If I have something to say, I usually say it. | | |
| 20. My parents understand me. | | |
| 21. Most people are better liked than I am. | | |
| 22. I usually feel as if my parents are pushing me. | | |
| 23. I often get discouraged in school. | | |
| 24. Things usually don't bother me. | | |
| 25. I can't be depended on. | | |

From *The Antecedents of Self-Esteem* by Stanley Coopersmith. Copyright © 1967 by W. H. Freeman and Company. Reprinted with permission.

*Validity:* Face validity is assumed.

*Reliability:* Test-retest reliability obtained for the Coopersmith Self-Esteem Inventory over a five-week interval with a sample of 30 fifth-grade children was .88, and the reliability after a three-year interval with a different sample of 55 children was .70. The total scores on the long and short forms correlate .86.

*Age Level:* Ages 8–10.

*Test Area:* Any quiet area free of distractions.

*Equipment Needed:* Self-concept scale and pencils.

*Scoring Procedure:* The score is the total number of responses marked in the direction that indicated high self-esteem. One point is awarded for each positive response.

*Norms:* None available.

# MEASURING SOCIAL COMPETENCE

The physical education environment should offer an instructional setting that fosters positive social behaviors and should teach children desirable social standards and ethical concepts (Pangrazi and Dauer, 1995). Youth must experience and understand the value of cooperation, participation, and patience through guided physical activities. By utilizing proper teaching methodologies, the instructor can help students differentiate between acceptable and unacceptable social behavior.

Physical education is one way that youth become aware of how they interact with others and how others view them. In this environment, students need to receive feedback from significant others about their behavior; otherwise, they may never realize what actions are considered socially inappropriate. A teacher must continually be alert to reinforce youngsters' proper social behaviors and discourage improper actions.

Many factors influence a student's behavior: peer pressure, stages of emotional development, and type of home life are just a few examples. Though teachers cannot control outside factors, they can strive to establish a positive, healthy environment in physical education. By establishing appropriate behaviors for students in activity settings, the teacher can contribute to their development of social competence. Teaching social competence may be difficult, but it is a worthwhile goal. Whatever the outside circumstances, teachers should insist on proper student behavior in class. Progress toward the attainment of this goal should be monitored.

This chapter has discussed the use of paper-and-pencil inventories to assess and evaluate students' attitudes toward physical activity and self-concept. In the case of social competence, however, overt social behaviors are of greater interest than the manner in which experiences have been internalized. Social factors certainly influence learning outcomes of physical education and can be identified. As a consequence, many instruments to measure the social behavior of youth have been developed.

## Data Gathering and Analysis

Several methods are accepted for obtaining information describing the social behavior of students. Regardless of the method selected, the assessment and evaluation processes cited provide the means to focus on outcomes in terms of measurable increments.

### Anecdotal Records

Anecdotal records are sequential, brief reports that record a teacher's observation of a student's behavior. The information contained in these records may contribute much toward gaining insight about the conduct exhibited by students. These records usually contain the student's name and space for comments about observed behavior. Because physical education programs provide a variety of social situations, the anecdotal record can be a useful tool in charting progress toward attainment of goals. Recording events as they occur, or shortly thereafter, avoids the pitfall of forgetting. Mood (1980) and Mathews (1978) offer the following suggestions for anecdotal recording:

1. Record the anecdote as soon as possible after the occurrence of the incident. Be sure that the student is unsuspecting of the recording.
2. Describe the incident accurately. Add a note of interpretation of the observation.
3. Include enough background information to give the incident meaning.
4. Be sure the evaluative statement is clearly identified and based on observed behavior.
5. Indicate whether the incident is important because it is representative of the individual or very much different from usual behavior.
6. Record anecdotes frequently in order to establish accurate trends. More frequent recordings result in a better understanding of the student.
7. Establish a system of recording anecdotes so that filing and sorting is easily accomplished. Using the microcomputer may assist in this function.
8. Summarize findings from time to time to determine trends in behavior.
9. The anecdotal record sheet should accompany the student's personnel file throughout the school years.

## Checklists

Checklists have long been used as a system of reporting observed behaviors. A regular class list with predetermined behaviors listed across the top of the sheet is a means of monitoring the occurrence of selected behaviors. Frequent tabulation of the tallies can alert the teacher to students who are displaying too much or too little of a selected behavior. Checklists are usually most effective when social behaviors are listed sequentially. In this way, the teacher can direct the teaching process toward diagnosed needs.

## Rating Scales

Rating scales used in the evaluation of social behaviors contain certain descriptive criteria of selected traits. In measuring remembered or perceived behavior, the teacher uses an observation system in the form of a rating scale and assesses an individual on one or more characteristics. Assessments are made on the basis of past observations or on the basis of perceptions of what the student is like and how the student will behave.

Several traits, such as "ability to get along with others," "listens to instructions," "is viewed favorable by peers," and so on, are common to most rating scales. Usually, the rater scores the student by assigning a numeric ranking (e.g., 0 to 5), which describes the frequency of the criterion social behavior being displayed by the student. For example, in rating a child on good sportsmanship, a score of 5 might be recorded if the youngster is consistent in displaying proper conduct during game-type activities; a score of 2 indicates that the student occasionally displays unsportsmanlike actions.

Rating scales are easy to devise and, more importantly, quick and easy to use. Unfortunately, the apparent ease of construction is deceptive and carries a heavy price: lack of validity due to a number of sources of bias that enter into rating measures (Kerlinger, 1973). Still, with knowledge, skill, and care, rating scales can be a valuable evaluative tool.

## *Sociometry*

The technique of sociometry was pioneered by Moreno (1934) and Jennings (1948) and has become a popular method of evaluating and understanding social outcomes. **Sociometry** is a scientific method of studying groups and examining the interrelationships among the individuals making up these groups (Kozman, 1951). Data obtained through sociometric technique can be easily quantified and graphically depicted to show the relationships existing at a given time among members of a particular class. Use of a test-retest format allows teachers to note changes in individual and group status. The ability to objectively assess and evaluate social behavior can assist teachers in structuring lessons, managing classes, and evaluating progress toward development of acceptable social behavior.

Basically, sociometric technique asks respondents to choose, based on predetermined criteria, with whom they would like to live, study, work, play, and so on. Questions are written so that each relates to an activity or lesson that the students have experienced. For example, a teacher might ask children to list three classmates they would like to include on their softball team.

Sociometric choices should be organized in an understandable manner if they are to be properly used and interpreted. The matrix chart, or tabulation sheet, shown in Table 8.0 represents one method to tabulate sociometric results. To design a simple matrix chart, students' names are listed down the left side of the chart and across the top. Each student's level of choice is listed in the appropriate box. From Table 8.0 the following are Rebekah's choices:

1. Sarah L.
2. Michael M.
3. John S.

▲ **TABLE 8.0**   Sociometric tabulation form.

| CHOSEN → \ CHOOSER ↓ | 1. Jacob H. | 2. Sarah L. | 3. Rebekah H. | 4. Markell M. | 5. John S. | 6. Kyle T. | 7. Deanna M. | 8. Ryan T. | 9. Michael M. | 10. Megan K. |
|---|---|---|---|---|---|---|---|---|---|---|
| 1. Jacob H. | | 1 | | 2 | | 3 | | | | |
| 2. Sarah L. | | | 3 | | 2 | | | 1 | | |
| 3. Rebekah H. | | 1 | | | 3 | | | | 2 | |
| 4. Markell M. | | | 2 | | | 3 | | 1 | | |
| 5. John S. | | 3 | | 2 | | | 1 | | | |
| 6. Kyle T. | | 2 | | | 3 | | 1 | | | |
| 7. Deanna M. | | | 1 | | | | | | 2 | 3 |
| 8. Ryan T. | | | | | | | 1 | | 2 | 3 |
| 9. Michael M. | | | | 1 | | 3 | | 2 | | |
| 10. Megan K. | 1 | 2 | 3 | | | | | | | |
| Total 1st Choices | 1 | 2 | 1 | 1 | 0 | 0 | 3 | 2 | 0 | 0 |
| Total 2nd Choices | 0 | 1 | 1 | 2 | 1 | 0 | 0 | 1 | 2 | 0 |
| Total 3rd Choices | 0 | 1 | 2 | 0 | 2 | 3 | 0 | 0 | 0 | 2 |
| TOTAL | 1 | 4 | 4 | 3 | 3 | 3 | 3 | 3 | 2 | 2 |

Rebekah's choices are recorded on the matrix chart next to her name in her horizontal row. The number one is placed in the column under Sarah's name; number two is placed in the column under Michael's name; and so on. After the tabulating is completed, each choice (regardless of number) is given a point value of one. The total number of choices a student receives on a sociometric question indicates the degree to which the student is accepted by classmates.

## Sociogram

Although the matrix chart is useful to organize raw data and determine the level of social acceptance of group participants, it does not provide a total picture of the group's social fabric. The **sociogram** graphically depicts the raw data in a form that is easily understood and interpreted. The sociogram is devised from information contained on the matrix chart. For example, look at the data recorded on the matrix chart in Table 8.0. The sociogram developed from this data is depicted in Figure 8.12. Developing a sociogram from this information requires the following steps:

1. Determine those group members chosen most often and place them near the center of the sociogram. Those chosen least often should be located near the perimeter.
2. Plot the placement of individual cells in pencil and expect to rearrange the location of individuals on the chart.

▶ **FIGURE 8.12**  Sociogram.

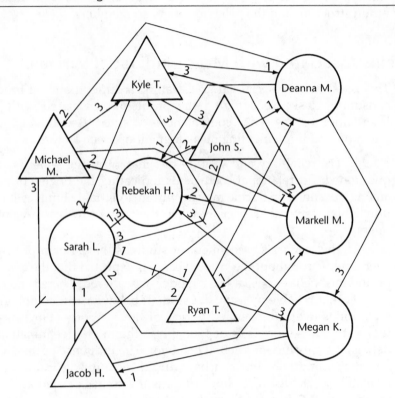

**Legend**
1. ○ Girl  △ Boy
2. → Unreciprocated choice to 2nd level choice
3. The numbers "1," "2," "3" reflect preference.
4. $\frac{2}{+}^3$  Mutual choice
5. ○ or △ Near center—high # of choices, ○ or △ Away from center—low # of choices

3. Identify various classifications of participants by certain figures. For example, all boys would be circles, girls triangles, and mainstreamed youngsters a square. The number assigned to the student on the matrix chart is the identification number for the sociogram.

4. Choices indicated on the matrix chart are represented by lines connecting cells on the sociogram. Arrows ($\rightarrow$) from one cell to another indicate choices that are in one direction only. Perpendicular lines (—|—) indicate mutual choices. Rejections can be identified with a broken line (– – –).

5. To keep the chart from getting unnecessarily cluttered, plot only mutual and unreciprocated choices.

Sociometric testing can be a valuable tool for the physical education teacher. Using sociometric techniques will assist in better understanding group structure and the behavior of group members.

## Problems Associated with Measuring Social Variables

The assessment of social variables can be a difficult and, at times, a time-consuming task. Recognizing the problems associated with collecting information on the social competencies of students will assist teachers in planning and implementing measurement of social factors.

1. The reliability and validity of behavior rating scales is continually questioned. Correlational coefficients indicating the degree of consistency among questions on a scale may be within acceptable limits, yet may prove unreliable over time, especially when the rating involves several different raters.

2. The teacher's assessment of students' behavior probably changes over time. Throughout the school year, it is expected that the teacher's view of students' behavior is, at least, moderately altered. There is no research to suggest that reliable measures of student behavior can be obtained with a few ratings over an extended period of time. Woody (1969) has reported that a student's score is as dependent on the rater's feeling about the student as it is on student's actual behavior. The influence of the "halo effect" on interpreting behavior can be reduced by utilizing trained raters. The availability of video recording equipment also has created an opportunity for teachers to monitor the behavior of students on a regular basis and should provide the means to conduct validation and reliability studies on social behavior scales.

3. Physical educators often are viewed as unskilled in observational techniques, thereby rendering results invalid. Increasingly, studies are being completed by physical educators that utilize systematic observation.

Systemic observation is a way of collecting quantifiable data by observing student and/or teacher behaviors. Advances in research methodologies and technology now afford physical educators the means to systematically analyze students' behavior in their classes. More information about these techniques is in Chapter 10.

4. The appearance of some behaviors during formal observation may be fleeting or nonexistent. Students need time to exhibit certain social characteristics. Their ability to get along with classmates may not have a chance to avail itself during self-testing units. Similarly, on-task persistence may not be evident during a large group activity. Regardless, observations of student behavior should be scheduled to allow the student every chance to display the behaviors sought.

5. Social behavior scales are limiting. It is impossible to categorize the many different types of social behaviors that can be displayed in a physical activity setting. Selecting an instrument that includes the behaviors of interest in the assessment is the key to the successful evaluation.

6. The social behaviors being measured may not be related to physical education. The learning experiences in physical education may not provide instruction or activities that foster specific behaviors. If the physical education curriculum is not structured to promote certain behaviors, attempts should not be made to measure those traits.

## SUMMARY

The affective domain is often overlooked in the measurement and evaluation schemes of physical education and exercise programs. Though program objectives usually include affective goals, the achievement of these goals is rarely assessed. If affective objectives are included, they should be evaluated.

A quality physical education and exercise program can positively influence many areas of the affective domain. This chapter includes selected instruments to measure an individuals' attitudes toward physical activity, self-concept, and social competence. A brief review of the literature, description of instruments, and information concerning advantages and disadvantages of the various methods are included.

Though measurement and evaluation in the affective domain may not be as precise as in other domains of physical education and exercise science, it is still an important area to assess. By selecting proper instruments, following proper protocols of administration, and carefully interpreting results, physical educators can more thoroughly substantiate their claims of contributing to positive attitudes toward activity, improved self-concepts, and socioemotional development of students and participants.

## ► DISCUSSION QUESTIONS

1. In what facets of an individual's growth should physical education and exercise science make contributions? Which of these facets can be classified as belonging to the affective domain? What are the problems associated with measurement and evaluation of these affective areas?

2. In your opinion, what area of the affective domain is most important in terms of the contributions that physical education and/or exercise science should make? Give reasons for your answer.

3. Why are measurement and evaluation of affective goals often overlooked in physical education and exercise science? Is it important that this situation change? Why or why not?

4. What are the similarities and differences between the Likert scale, the two-point scale, and the semantic differential scale? What are advantages and disadvantages of each scale?

5. Suppose you are a junior high physical education teacher with coeducational classes. What two instruments would you select to assess attitudes toward physical activity and what two instruments would be used to measure the self-concept of students? Briefly describe each instrument and explain why you chose the particular instrument.

6. What is meant by the term "sociometry"? How can sociometric techniques be used to help a teacher understand group dynamics of a class and, in turn, aid in the development of social competence of students?

7. Suppose you are a fitness instructor at a health club. You teach several classes of strength training to adults. What two instruments would you select to assess attitudes toward physical activity, and what two instruments would you use to measure the self-concept of the participants? Briefly describe each instrument and explain why you chose the particular instrument.

## ► REFERENCES

Anderson, M. L. (1966). *Measurement of changes in attitudes of high school girls toward physical conditioning following an intensified physical fitness program.* Unpub-lished master's thesis, State University of Iowa.

Cheffers, J. T.; Mancini, V. H.; and Zaichkowsky, L. D. (1976). The development of an elementary physical education attitude scale. *The Physical Educator* 3:30–33.

Combs, A. W. (1965). *The professional education of teachers.* Boston: Allyn and Bacon.

Coopersmith, S. (1967). *The antecedents of self-esteem.* San Francisco, CA: W. H. Freeman.

Cratty, B. (1970). *Movement activities, motor ability, and the education of children.* Springfield, IL: Charles C. Thomas.

Felker, D. W. (1974). *Helping children to like themselves.* Minneapolis, MN: Burgess.

Fitts, W. H. (1971). The self-concept and self-actualization. *Monograph #3.* Nashville, TN: The Dade Wallace Center.

Hay, J. A. (1992). Adequacy in and predilection for physical activity in children. *Clinical Journal of Sport Medicine*, 2, 192–201.

Jennings, H. (1948). *Sociometry in group relations*. Washington, DC: American Council on Education.

Johnson, B. L., and Nelson, J. K. (1986). *Practical measurements for evaluation in physical education*. 4th ed. New York: Macmillan.

Kenyon, G. S. (1968a). A conceptual model for characterizing physical activity. *Research Quarterly* 39:560–565.

_____. (1968b). Six scales for assessing attitudes toward physical activity. *Research Quarterly* 39:566–73.

Kerlinger, F. N. (1973). *Foundations of behavioral research*. New York: Holt, Rinehart and Winston.

Kozman, H. C., ed. (1951). *Group processes in physical education*. New York: Harper & Brothers.

Kubiszyn, T., and Borich, G. (1984). *Educational testing and measurement*. Glen-view, IL: Scott, Foresman and Co.

Lapp, V. W. (1933). Pupil objectives in high school physical education. *Research Quarterly* 4:157–67.

Mathews, D. K. (1978). *Measurement in physical education*. 5th ed. Philadelphia, PA: W. B. Saunders.

McAfee, R. (1955). Sportsmanship attitudes of sixth, seventh, and eighth grade boys. *Research Quarterly* 26:120.

Mood D. P. (1980). *Numbers in motion: A balanced approach to measurement and evaluation in physical education*. Palo Alto, CA: Mayfield.

Moreno, J. L. (1934). *Who shall survive? A new approach to the problem of human relationships*. Washington, DC: Nervous and Mental Disease Publishing Co.

Neale, D. C.; Sonstroem, R. J.; and Metz, K. F. (1969). Physical fitness, self-esteem, and attitudes toward physical activity. *Research Quarterly* 40:743–49.

Neilsen, A. B., and Corbin, C. B. (1986, June). Physical activity commitment. Conference Abstracts, North American Society for the Psychology of Sport and Physical Activity Conference. Scottsdale, AZ, p. 93.

Nelson, B. A., and Allen, D. J. (1970). Scale for the appraisal of movement satisfaction. Perceptual and Motor Skills 31:795–800.

Nunnally, J. C. (1978). *Introduction to psychological measurement*. New York: McGraw Hill.

Osgood, C.; Suci, G.; and Tannenbaum, P. (1957). *The measurement of meaning*. Urbana, IL: University of Illinois Press.

Pangrazi, R. P. (1969). Developing a climate for success. In *Promising practices in elementary school physical education*. Washington, DC: American Association of Health, Physical Education, and Recreation, pp. 24–28.

Pangrazi, R. P., and Darst, P. W. (1991). *Dynamic physical education for secondary school students: Curriculum and instruction*. 2d ed. Boston: Allyn and Bacon.

Pangrazi, R. P., and Dauer, V. P. (1995). *Dynamic physical education for elementary school children*. 11th ed. Boston: Allyn & Bacon.

Piers, E. V., and Harris, D. B. (1964). Age and other correlates of self-concept in children. *Journal of Educational Psychology* 55:91–95.

Richardson, C. E. (1960). Thurstone scale for measuring attitudes of college students toward physical fitness and exercise. *Research Quarterly* 31:638–43.

Simon, J. A., and Smoll, F. L. (1974). An instrument for assessing children's attitudes toward physical activity. *Research Quarterly* 45:407–15.

Snodgrass, J. (1977). Self-concept: A look at its development and some implications for physical education teaching. *Journal of Physical Education and Recreation* 48:22–23.

Sonstroem, R. J. (1974). Attitude testing: Examining certain psychological correlates of physical activity. *Research Quarterly* 45:93–103.

_____. (1976). The validity of self-perceptions regarding physical and athletic ability. *Medicine and Science in Sports* 8:126–32.

_____. (1978). Physical estimation and attraction scales: Rationale and research. *Medicine and Science in Sports* 10:97–102.

Wear, C. L. (1955). Construction of equivalent forms of an attitude scale. *Research Quarterly* 26:113–19.

Woody, R. H. (1969). *Behavioral problem children in the schools*. New York: Appleton-Century-Crofts.

## ◤ REPRESENTATIVE READINGS

Adams, R. S. (1963). Two scales for measuring attitude toward physical education. *Research Quarterly* 34:91–94.

Annarino, A. A.; Cowell, C. C.; and Hazelton, H. W. (1980). *Curriculum theory and design in physical education.* St. Louis, MO: C. V. Mosby.

Blanchard, B. E. (1936). A behavior frequency rating scale for the measurement of character and personality in physical education classroom situations. *Research Quarterly* 7:56–66.

Edgington, C. W. (1968). Development of an attitude scale to measure attitudes of high school freshman boys toward physical education. *Research Quarterly* 39:505–12.

Verducci, F. M. (1980). *Measurement concepts in physical education.* St. Louis, MO: C. V. Mosby.

Willgoose, C. E. (1984). *The curriculum in physical education.* 4th ed. Englewood Cliffs, NJ: Prentice-Hall.

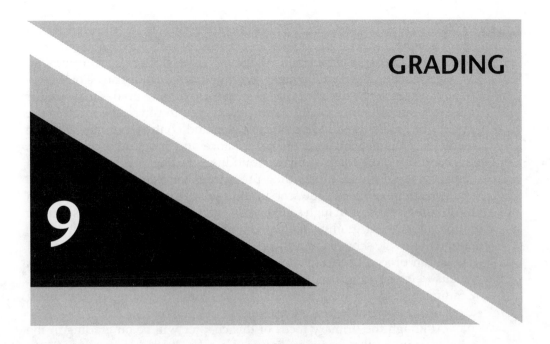

# 9

# GRADING

## KEY TERMS

checklist
contract grading
criterion-referenced
goals
grade
group goal setting
norm-referenced
peer evaluation
percentage method
percentile equivalent method
performance standards
personal interview
portfolio
self-evaluation

## OBJECTIVES

*After reading this chapter, the student should be able to:*

1. Discuss the arguments for and against grading in physical education.
2. Understand the intent and use of predetermined performance-based objectives in the decision-making process.
3. Identify and discuss key issues associated with decision-making.
4. Differentiate between norm-referenced and criterion-referenced grading.
5. Use various methods to calculate grades.
6. Cite and discuss assorted ways student performance can be exhibited.

Physical educators are responsible for assessing performance and assigning grades to students. A **grade** is a symbol to denote progress and serves as a permanent record of a student's achievement. Measurement and evaluation are means by which a grade can be objectively (and subjectively) derived. On the surface, assigning grades may appear relatively simple and straightforward. However, in physical education the process of grading is a source of confusion and controversy, and with the increased emphasis on student performance and program accountability, the confusion and controversy surrounding grading practices have been compounded. Further, the grading procedures for elementary schools differs from those of the middle school, and each of these probably differ from the grading practices in high school. As a practitioner you must be sensitive to the impact that grading has on youngsters. Also, you need to become familiar with the school's procedure. Then you need to identify testing and evaluation procedures to fit the scheme. While most prospective teachers would welcome some foolproof strategies for grading, none are available. Grading requires careful scrutiny and an understanding of the many aspects that contribute to a fair appraisal.

Although the primary focus of this chapter will be on grading in the schools, many of the processes discussed can be applied to exercise science settings. Practitioners in health clubs, hospital settings, and various other exercise and physical activity programs can assess and evaluate participants for the purposes of decision making. In the schools, this decision-making process commonly results in a grade. In the nonschool setting, the process may result in the formulation of a written individual profile that details progress toward goals, performance relative to other participants, and a general summary of "how things are going." We will discuss possible applications of the evaluation process in the nonschool setting in the section "Other Methods to Determine Grades."

## CONTROVERSIES OF GRADING

The calculations associated with determining a numerical rating for grading purposes are not that complex. In fact, the steps involved seldom require more than a calculator and a basic understanding of fundamental arithmetic. Recent innovations in microcomputer software have made the calculations of grades accurate and virtually instantaneous. Why, then, does grading pose such a difficult task for the physical educator? The answer, in large measure, lies in (1) the intricacies associated with the decision-making processes related to how a student is to be evaluated and what criteria are to be used in determining a final grade and (2) the fact that physical education has long been considered separate from the academic mainstream when it comes to grading and, therefore, as a discipline, does not have a position statement on whether to assign grades to students. The following sections discuss the pros and cons of grading in physical education, elaborate more fully on these two multifaceted problems associated with the grading process, and offer suggestions that may alleviate some of the problems associated with grading.

## To Grade or Not to Grade

Physical educators have long debated the issue of whether or not to assign grades to students. While there appears to be no definitive answer to the dilemma, arguments both for and against the practice of grading in physical education can be cited. Identifying these arguments should assist in developing a clearer understanding about the practice of grading in physical education.

### Reasons Not to Grade

1. Physical education is not an academic subject matter discipline. The assignment of grades to a nonacademic area is unnecessary and inappropriate. Grades should be used only to show achievement in subjects such as math, social studies, history, science, and other knowledge-based subjects.

2. The diversity of objectives makes grading in physical education virtually impossible. The goals of physical education are so broad and, at times, vague and difficult to measure, that attempts to assign a grade would be time-consuming and invalid.

3. Existing standardized tests and testing procedures for physical education are extremely time-consuming. This creates a time management problem for teachers who are already saddled with large classes, restricted activity, space, limited class time, and inadequate assistance.

4. Physical education should assume a leadership role in an attempt to make sweeping changes regarding the manner in which youth in school systems are evaluated. Elimination of traditional grading practices would be a step in the right direction for educational reform. By leading the way, physical education would improve its image and gain stature within the total educational experience.

5. Due to the conflicting ways physical education teachers view certain tasks, grades become meaningless and in no way reflect a consistent appraisal of performance. Physical educators are unreliable in their assessment of students. Consequently, in response to inconsistencies among teachers in the assessment and evaluation phases of physical education, grades should not be given.

6. Professional preservice and inservice preparation in the area of measurement and evaluation is lacking. This makes it difficult, if not impossible, for practitioners to do an accurate job of assigning grades.

7. Assigning a grade as a result of performance measure can cause children to become discouraged from active participation in physical activity. If participation in sport and activity is the most important outcome of physical education, then grading would be counterproductive for those less skilled and naturally fit.

8. Grades mean different things to different teachers. The simple fact that individuals view the world differently is evidence enough to support the case that grades are only as good as the teacher who assigns them.

## Reasons to Grade

1. Grading is a means to communicate information about student achievement to parents, teachers, administrators, and students. It is an evaluation process that is readily understood by all.

2. Grades have long been, and will continue to be, the common means to signify a student's performance. Grading is an accepted and expected part of school that cannot be altered.

3. By assigning grades, physical education has been able to maintain the status quo within the school environment. The practice of grading is the common denominator for all classes.

4. The current prevalence of criterion-referenced tests makes it easier to assign a grade to a specific performance. Students demonstrate skills and competencies rather than selecting one of several answers on a written exam. This type of assessment allows discrimination among students and opportunities to assign letter grades accordingly.

5. Historically, physical education has been criticized for the indifferent manner in which tests are utilized. Tests selected are oftentimes not specific and lack the objectivity and standardization necessary for accurate measurement. Grading affects this perception and supports the desired image of conscientious instruction.

6. By not grading, physical education would separate itself even further from the traditional evaluation protocol. Physical education has strived to become an equal partner in the educational mainstream and must continue to follow standards practiced by other subject matter disciplines.

The issues concerning the advantages and disadvantages of grading in physical education are numerous and complex. However, physical educators often become such strong advocates of one point of view about grading that they become overly simplistic and fail to recognize the "bigger picture." As a result, some fundamental realities about the practice of grading in physical education are often ignored. Ironically, it is precisely these realities that must be dealt with in deciding whether or not to grade.

The question of whether or not to grade is usually rendered moot by school policy. Like it or not, physical educators are generally expected to comply with some type of grading practice. After considering the pros and cons, it becomes apparent that currently there are no other viable alternatives to grading. For example, grades serve as a predictor of performance and interest. This information assists teachers and guidance personnel in providing sound advice to students. Parents rely on grades to describe their child's level of achievement. Students have come to view grading as a common practice. As such, it can be of considerable use in formally describing the abilities of a student. State educational agencies and local administrators are imposing mandates on education programs to increase accountability. Grades can serve as a benchmark to verify the strengths and weaknesses of programs.

The practice of grading is not going to disappear. With this in mind, it is inappropriate to ask whether or not we should grade. Rather, it is now time to seek the best ways to evaluate our students' performance in a manner that accurately reflects their performance. Because of the importance placed on grades, a precise system for grading and reporting marks is imperative.

## Issues in Grade Determination

Physical educators are more aware than ever before of the importance of using assessment and evaluation to measure progress toward predetermined program objectives. It is important for practitioners to effectively link grading practices with program goals, unit outcomes, and performance-based objectives (these were generally described in Chapter 2). Doing so not only informs students about what is expected of them, but also demonstrates a logical connection between what is expected and the fundamental goals, unit outcomes, and performance-based objectives. In this day of concern about quality of student performance, it is essential that grading practices reflect an identifiable relationship with expectations and learning experiences. We believe it is a questionable practice to determine a grade based on anything other than measurable performance or observable behavior directly related to predetermined objectives. Clearly defined outcomes, valid and reliable assessment techniques, and sound professional judgment form the basis for acceptable grading procedures.

Educational reform, with its renewed emphasis on accountability, has cemented the link between objectives and evaluation. Debate continues, however, on a variety of issues pertaining to grading. The following sections identify these key issues, offer differing viewpoints associated with the issues, and propose recommendations about grading for consideration.

## Educational Objectives Versus Student Responsibilities

**Goals** for physical education are predetermined targets that are distributed among the four learning domains (see Chapter 2): health-related physical fitness domain, psychomotor domain, cognitive domain, and affective domain. It is assumed that grading in physical education should be based on a student's accomplishments relative to stated goals. This, however, appears to be the exception rather than the rule.

Many physical educators ignore objectives and tend to award grades based on student responsibility details such as showering after class, dressing in the appropriate uniform, being in class on time, and various other tasks. The use of affective factors such as attitude and effort seem to form the foundation of the typical practitioner's assessment and evaluation model (Hensley, 1990). In fact, many physical educators opt to base a student's grade solely on participation, meeting the required dress code, and behavior in class (Imwold et al., 1982). These student responsibilities are by no means trivial but are unrelated to progress toward educational objectives. Using the approach that rewards students for complying with school policy (e.g., arriving at class on time) does not promote learning associated with program goals and becomes simply another way of isolating physical education from other curriculum areas within the school. Grading on effort, participation, and improvement is frequently much too subjective and often becomes a self-fulfilling prophecy. Moreover, a norm established in one year would be of questionable validity (Laughlin and Laughlin, 1992).

A problem arises when students receive a grade in physical education that is earned in a manner significantly different from the rest of the school's subject matter disciplines. For instance, performance in a science class is based on academic achievement, not the student's punctuality, attire, or physical appearance. A teacher who has a problem with a student's behavior may seek to improve the situation by visiting with the student's parents or utilizing school policy to reprimand the student. The teacher will not fail the student because of noncompliance with the school's student behavior code if the student has received passing grades on all the course projects, examinations, papers, and so on. Similarly, a student who fails all the requirements for a course but was always in class, tries hard, and displays a positive attitude should not earn a passing grade.

No longer can physical educators base a grade on student responsibilities such as number of absences, the number of times a student was improperly attired, the number of times a student was tardy, or whether a student took a shower after an activity. In this day and age of accountability, even physical education must rely on objective evidence that reflects progress toward goals in determining a grade.

*Recommendation:* Grades should be awarded on the basis of performance and progress toward stated educational objectives and should not be influenced by behaviors or actions that are enforced through school regulations.

## Process Versus Product

Another issue to contend with in determining grades is whether the process or product of education is a more important criterion. This is a difficult issue to resolve and a point of regular debate among professionals. The process involves activity and participation rather than scores and awards. Often, students who focus on the product (i.e., how fast, how far, how long) rather than the process run the risk of early burnout. Those who support the notion of grading on process assert that it is important for students to leave school with a warm and positive feeling toward physical education. The assumption is that students who enjoy the class will take that feeling with them and continue to participate in physical activity on a voluntary basis throughout their lifetimes. Emphasizing product outcomes for children can cause them to become discouraged during their adult years, when they witness slower improvement or a decline in scores. (Pangrazi and Corbin, 1993). Most of the time, teachers who subscribe to the process approach to evaluation give more weight to factors such as effort, participation, and attitude in determining a final grade. Process-oriented teachers are more likely to award a higher grade to a poor performer who tries hard than to a skilled performer who puts forth a minimal effort.

On the other hand, there are those educators who endorse the importance of performance and claim that product is the best determinant of a grade. They are quick to point out that students who score highest on history tests receive the highest grade. People on this side of the issue view attainment of performance based on outcome statements as the primary criterion for grading. They further attest that process is important but view it as an expected part of the educational experience. In other words, a teacher is responsible for providing a positive learning environment in which the student can grow through encouragement and a multiplicity of activities. Process is not viewed as something that is deserving of a grade.

The arguments for grading on product and on process are both somewhat defensible. This makes it difficult to resolve the issue to everyone's satisfaction. As Pangrazi and Darst (1991) suggest, perhaps the best solution is to develop a grading system that rewards achievement and to deliver the program in a positive manner. It then would be the instructor's responsibility to explain to students that the performance levels within the class are diverse. Just as in a math, reading, or social studies class, better grades in physical education will be awarded to those students who more closely reach the performance-based objectives. Giving all As cheats the outstanding student. Grades should discriminate among good, fair, and poor students. In this setting, instructors indicate that each student will receive quality instruction within a positive learning environment in order to move them toward stated goals.

*Recommendation:* Grades should be awarded based on performance, while instruction should be given in an arena filled with encouragement and effective teaching.

### Psychomotor Domain Versus Health-Related Fitness Domain

Clearly, physical education should provide educational experiences to meet the unique goals of achieving movement excellence and developing health-related physical fitness. Due to such factors as limited space, large class size, and insufficient time allocation for class, physical education programs are forced to establish priorities. Practitioners must make decisions about the relative emphasis to be placed on certain learning experiences. Will more time be directed to health-related fitness activities? Or should more time be spent learning the skills associated with tennis? These are not easy decisions to make. The issue becomes even more problematic when it comes time to determine a grade. Which domain, if either, should receive the greatest weighting?

Practitioners who choose to place more emphasis on skill-related activities in the grading process run the risk of being accused of slighting the fitness dimension. Further, the usually short length of time set aside for each unit is seldom sufficient to significantly improve skill. On the other hand, ignoring skill development and placing a premium on developing fitness is not without problems. Many physical educators believe the heart of any physical education program is skill development. To focus on anything else would be inconsistent with the primary purpose of the profession. In this era of concern about the deteriorating fitness of Americans, however, it seems a major oversight not to focus on fitness development.

Justifying a grade for an individual's performance on fitness tests is also a source of controversy. After all, most health-related fitness qualities are the result of genetic predisposition. To award a grade on someone's "ability to select parents," rather than a legitimate alternative of health-related fitness, is inconsistent with most accepted grading practices.

*Recommendation:* Any viable physical education program must be able to demonstrate attainment of goals in the psychomotor domain and the health-related physical fitness domain. Somehow practitioners must strike a balance of learning experiences and assessment procedures that relate to each of the domains. It is important, therefore, to consider each factor in the determination of the grade.

## Improvement Versus Achievement

Many physical educators believe that grades should be based on relative improvement. Relative improvement is the difference between a student's entry- and exit-level performances on a standardized measure of performance. Grading on improvement stems from the teacher's desire to reward those students who put forth the greatest effort in class. However, following this approach to grading can create a situation in which the most highly skilled students do not have an opportunity to receive the best grade. This relative improvement approach to grading contrasts sharply with grading on absolute performance.

For those who choose to grade solely on improvement, it is recommended that they use a method that recognizes that students scoring poorly on the initial test of performance have a much greater potential for improvement than those who display a high level of performance. The following formula takes into account the potential for improvement relative to the highest score in class.

$$\frac{\text{Student's Posttest Score} - \text{Student's Pretest Score}}{\text{Highest Score for All Students} - \text{Student's Pretest Score}} = \text{Improvement Score}$$

For example, a student's pre- and posttest scores on the sit-and-reach test for flexibility are 20 and 40 centimeters, respectively. If the highest attained score in class is 70 centimeters, the equation would look like this:

$$\frac{40 - 20}{70 - 20} = .40$$

This student's 100 percent improvement on raw score would be converted to a more equitable improvement score of .40. By using this approach, the teacher has some flexibility in determining improvement and creates a situation that is more equitable to those students who score high on the pretest (Illinois State Board of Education, 1982).

Grading only on improvement has some serious drawbacks that should be considered before a decision is made about its role in the evaluation process. Grading on improvement is time-consuming and requires that the same test be given at the beginning and end of the semester, block, or unit. Devoting this much time to testing detracts from valuable instructional time, creates additional clerical duties for the teacher, and becomes a logistical nightmare if pre- and posttest scheduling is dependent on weather or availability of facilities.

A second problem associated with grading on improvement is that students could be placed in a dangerous situation if asked to perform a pretest before any proper conditioning or skill acquisition has occurred. For example, asking children to complete the 12-minute run on the second day of class in order to obtain a pretest score is ill-advised. Similarly, expecting a youngster to perform a test of balance on a beam before gaining some fundamental experience with the apparatus is not prudent teaching and places the child in a potentially hazardous situation.

Third, taking a pretest without the advantage of some knowledge or skill will, in all likelihood, result in inconsistent and inaccurate data. For instance, administering a test of distance and accuracy using a 5-iron to students who have never held a golf club before would not yield the type of results necessary to determine real improvement.

Fourth, once students realize that improvement is the primary criterion for grading, they may be inclined to purposefully decrease their performance on the initial test, thus creating more room for improvement. As we all know, it does not take students long to figure out ways to challenge the system.

Fifth, grading solely on improvement is simply unfair to those individuals who are highly skilled or conditioned performers. Performance is easier to improve at lower levels. Consequently, basing a grade on improvement favors those who have the "longest way to go." A skilled performer may be at a level where improvement is difficult to discern (e.g., how do you measure improvement in a student who made 15 out of 15 on a basketball freethrow pretest?).

Sixth, a youngster's performance on a test of physical fitness skill may improve simply due to physical growth or maturity that occurred between the pretest and posttest. For instance, a child who grows taller and gains weight can certainly be expected to increase performance of measures of strength and endurance. In this case, it becomes difficult to attribute improvement of performance to learning.

Finally, grading on improvement is not in compliance with societal practices or procedures used in other subject matter areas. Society does not reward people for improvement, but rather for achievement. Teachers of English, math, social studies, and the academic disciplines do not base a grade relative to the abilities of the student when they entered the class. The standard in other classes is achievement.

There is an increasing need for schools to demonstrate student achievement. The report card for schools nationwide in most subjects is less than adequate. The achievement of students is being measured against predetermined standards of performance. If we are to have responsible citizens, education must provide learning experiences in all subject disciplines that encourage students to reach higher levels of achievement. In most cases, deriving grades based on established criteria promotes achievement.

*Recommendation:* Since grading solely on improvement is compromised by inequities and inconsistencies, it should not be given serious consideration in the evaluation process.

## Potential Versus Observed Performance

Interestingly, some teachers choose to base a grade on potential rather than observed abilities. This type of evaluation is highly subjective and is unfair to those students who are able to perform. The sophisticated testing equipment necessary to even begin to assess potential performance is not available to the practitioner and remains accessible only to a few elite performers. Furthermore, by using potential as a factor in grade determination, teachers place themselves in an indefensible position if challenged on the manner in which the grade was derived.

*Recommendation:* It is difficult to grade on unobservable characteristics; therefore, observable behavior and performance should be relied on in determining a grade.

## Negative Versus Positive Point Systems

Employing a point system to determine grades is a common practice. Many educators believe that the practice of assigning a numeric value to a particular activity facilitates the grading process. Determining grades based on a point system is easily adaptable to the physical education environment. Utilizing a point system is an attempt to make a grading system justifiable. In most point systems, both performance-based objectives and administrative details are considered in determining the student's total points. However, as Pangrazi and Darst (1991) suggest, a point system can have a negative effect on students when handled inappropriately. If, for instance, a teacher starts each student with a total number of points and subtracts points each time a student does not meet a standard, students will begin to avoid behavior that can result in the loss of points. This may mean that a youngster loses the initiative to perform tasks that are not point-oriented, thereby making the entire learning system dependent on the teacher's grading criteria. This may also lead to the teacher becoming a monitor of behavior and paying more attention to negative behavior, which results in the loss of points, than to positive behavior.

In positive grading systems, students know there will be rewards for performance of tasks and they display behaviors that are in compliance with predetermined objectives or standards. The emphasis is still on performance and behavior but instead of students losing points, a system is established whereby they can earn points. Students are placed in a situation that allows them the opportunity to control their own destiny. They know what behaviors and standards must be met in order to accomplish the goal and understand that the attainment of such is dependent more on them than on the teacher.

*Recommendation:* Grading systems that utilize points should be structured to reward positive behavior, not to punish undesirable or negative behavior.

## Failing Grades Versus Social Promotion

One of the more emotional issues associated with the practice of grading is acknowledging a failing student. No teacher finds satisfaction in assigning a grade of F. Many teachers feel a sense of personal failure for each student who fails to meet expected standards. In many cases, this has led to an unwillingness on the part of teachers to give failing grades, and many adopt an attitude that social promotion or advancement is in the best interest of the students.

A failing grade reflects totally unsatisfactory progress toward objectives. A student who receives a failing grade can be affected in one or more of the following ways: (1) the student may be forced to repeat the course and earn a passing grade, (2) the grade may deprive a student from earning the appropriate number of credits necessary to be promoted, and (3) the grade is absorbed within the cumulative grading system and thus reflects overall performance in a particular grade level.

Regardless of the effect, a failing grade represents failure. During the past several decades, many teachers have argued that failing a youngster can cause undue emotional trauma and does not ensure that the child will learn more during a repeat of the failed course. Many educators have subscribed to this notion and have forsaken the failure system in favor of social promotion. Social promotion has shifted the focus from subject matter learning to the conditions and processes associated with education. As Johnson and Nelson (1986) point out, the premise has been to keep children with their classmates and that "every child is a success."

Social promotion is rooted in noble intentions. Who can question the uniqueness and importance of each child? Who could enjoy informing a youngster of failure? Who does not want every child to be a success? More fundamental questions, however, are now being raised by state governments, educational agencies, school boards, colleges of education, and school administrations. Is it fair to expect students who are unable to read, write, or perform simple arithmetic to function effectively in our society? Should students learn that achievement is synonymous with performance? Or should teachers simply reinforce the concept that says "hang in there, and you will be rewarded"? Throughout the country, these fundamental questions are being answered in the form of educational mandates and legislation directed at applying quality control measures to the students who attend our schools. The public no longer accepts the tenet that there is no failure.

*Recommendation:* If physical education is to maintain its affiliation with the mainstream of other subject matter areas, it is important to initiate a grading system that attends to the realities of failure and does not acquiesce to the notion of social promotion.

## Teaching for Testing Versus Teaching for Learning

The increased emphasis on testing programs designed to demonstrate accountability has caused many educators to plan their lessons according to information covered in competency tests. Teaching only material that is included as part of a state or nationally standardized test for the sake of having students rank high on normative comparisons is a practice based on a false assumption. Certainly, teachers are responsible for directing learning toward attainment of mandated outcomes. However, legislated student performance objectives are usually no more than statements linked to broad program goals. It is important for teachers to realize that learning experiences should be developed according to the needs and interests of students and further refined according to the procedures outlined in Chapter 2. Quality learning experiences and effective instruction directed at predetermined goals will result in successful performance on standardized tests.

*Recommendation:* Physical education programs should use standardized testing programs and legislated performance goals as guidelines for program development and should not "teach for the test."

### Single Observation Versus Multiple Observation for Grading

A physical educator should not rely on one method of evaluation or a single assessment tool to derive grades. Given the diversity of program and student objectives (see Chapter 2), it would be unfair to grade a student based on performance in only one learning domain. For example, using the results of a written test as the sole evaluative tool in determining a grade for a unit on soccer could be viewed as unfair. Since most of the class time would have been devoted to the practice of soccer skills, it only seems reasonable to include some form of skills assessment in the grading process. It would be a difficult and indefensible task to explain to a highly skilled soccer player who received a lower grade than a lesser skilled soccer player that the grade was based on performance on the sole evaluative criterion, a written test. Teachers place themselves in a more defensible position when grades are based on a variety of evaluative criteria.

*Recommendation:* Grade determination should be based on proper evaluation technique, which includes assessment in the areas of all four learning domains.

## METHODS OF GRADING

Grades should be based on measurable factors that reflect a student's achievement or performance in one or more of the four learning domains. It is the teacher's responsibility to utilize appropriate testing techniques in determining the student's progress toward goals in the health-related physical fitness, psychomotor, cognitive, and affective domains. In selecting assessment instruments, the teacher should be mindful that it is helpful to the grading process if techniques used to assess level of performance or behavior provide the teacher with information that can be easily quantified.

Information that cannot be quantified is often difficult to objectively interpret and usually becomes problematic in the grading process. Determining grades is most commonly accomplished in one of two ways: the norm-referenced approach or the criterion-referenced approach. The following sections explain features of these two methods.

# Norm-Referenced Approach

The **norm-referenced** test is sometimes referred to as a test of *relative achievement*. Its purpose is to place students as accurately as possible along a continuum ranging from the lowest to the highest possible scores. This system is based on the normal probability curve that represents a theoretical distribution of data based on a mathematical formula.

As explained in Chapter 3, a normal distribution of interval/ratio data is graphically depicted by the "bell-shaped" curve, in which there is a clustering of scores around the mean and a gradual tapering of scores in the tails of the curve. The entire area under the curve is 100 percent. If you were to divide the area under the curve into sections representing a percentage of the curve, the sum of all sections would still equal 100 percent. The most important consideration in evaluating students based on the norm-referenced approach is careful identification of the areas under the curve that will represent each grade and their corresponding percentages. For the purposes of grading, norm-referenced standards can be used in several ways.

## Standard Deviation Method

As discussed in Chapter 3, the standard deviation is a measure of the relative variability of test scores around their mean and is graphically represented as a linear distance along the X axis of a distribution measured above and below the mean. Mathematically, the standard deviation is defined as the square root of the mean of the squared deviation scores of a distribution. Using this derived measure for purposes of grading requires following several steps. The first step, of course, is to calculate the mean and standard deviation for the group of scores. Secondly, it is necessary to divide the distribution into six sections using the standard deviation values. For example, in Figure 9.0 notice the area under the curve that is 1.5 standard deviations above the mean or higher. Scores falling in this area would receive a grade of A. Assume that the teacher administered a test of softball throw for distance and the mean performance score for the class (N = 30) was 125 feet with a standard deviation of 10. Using Figure 9.0, a score of 132 feet would fall between +0.5 and +1.5 standard deviations above the mean and would fall into the B letter grade range.

It should be clear that grading "on the curve" is often viewed as an unfair practice. The calculated curve may be based on only a small number of students (e.g., a class of 30–40 students). In this case, the distribution of scores might be badly distorted. It is best to pool raw scores and develop

► **FIGURE 9.0** Example of grading on a curve for a test of softball throw.

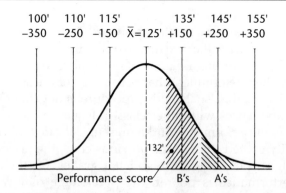

standard deviation grading scales from the test results of several classes. Even if this process takes several semesters, the resulting curve will more accurately reflect a normal distribution and will become a more fair way to determine letter grades.

An advantage of using the standard deviation method to determine letter grades is that scores for different types of tests can be converted to a common scale. Since standard deviation units only reflect relationships to the mean scores and not the units of measure (e.g., distance in feet and inches, centimeters, number of made free throws), teachers can compare, and even average, letter grades derived via this method on different tests (e.g., motor ability and health-related physical fitness).

A drawback to using the standard deviation method to determine grades is that individual student grades become dependent on the performance of classmates rather than on their own achievement or progress toward performance-based objectives. Remember, this type of grading system implies a normal distribution, and grading is determined by the performance of students, not by criteria the teacher establishes. It may be that the particular group of scores that comprise the total distribution has been obtained from students who are not representative of the normal population. For instance, assume that most students in a given class are members of the cross-country team, and the class is a distance run to measure aerobic ability. Conceivably, students who are not members of the team could perform well when compared to predetermined goals yet, due to the influence of the team members' scores, they would receive unusually low letter grades.

When using the standard deviation method, many other factors must be considered. Certainly the general level of proficiency of the group itself needs to be taken into account. A low score in a superior group is not the same as a low score in a less able group. The teacher should be prepared to use good judgment in making grading decisions about students who perform well yet rank at the low end of a highly skilled class.

## Percentage Method

Another method of norm-referenced grading is called the **percentage method**. Somewhat similar to the standard deviation method, the percentage method requires the teacher to rank the performance or collective performances on various assignments and/or requirements of all students. The teacher then determines what percentage of the students are to receive As, Bs, and so forth. Usually, this procedure is dependent on the teacher's previous experiences with other classes. For example, if the teacher feels that the overall performance of the present class in various tests of general motor ability exceeds that of the previous class, the teacher may choose to award a higher percentage of high letter grades. On the other hand, if the overall performance is poorer, the percentage of low grades may be increased. The decision about what percent of students in class earn As, Bs, and so on is in this case arbitrary, usually subjective, and depends on the teacher's professional judgment. In any case, this method of norm-referenced grading places more responsibility in the hands of the teacher than the standard deviation method does.

## Percentile Equivalent Method

The **percentile equivalent method** is rapidly becoming a popular mechanism to determine letter grades. One reason is that most people have some understanding of percentiles. Simply stated, the percentile rank of a score is defined as the percentage of scores lying below the given score. Further, percentiles provide a quick and convenient means to determine individual achievement compared to others of similar background. For example, we can differentiate performance levels of two 10-year-old male students who ranked in the 75th and 30th percentiles on a test of running speed. The student who performed at the 75th percentile scored better than 75 percent of all other 10-year-old boys who composed the normative database, whereas the youngster ranked at the 30th percentile performed more poorly than 70 percent of all other boys of the same age.

Using percentile equivalents also provides a means to compare raw scores from different sets of data. If the mile is run in 12 minutes and 34 seconds, putting the runner in the 15th percentile, and the softball is thrown 175 feet, which places the thrower in the 89th percentile, it is easy to determine the better performance.

Percentile equivalents based on large populations (i.e., national or state norms) are considered valid and provide students with the information necessary to determine their relative performance. Table 9.0 is an example of a percentile table for 10-year-old girls. Test items are from the AAHPERD *Health Related Physical Fitness Test*. This table is representative of an entire set of norms for youth ages 6–18 years developed as part of a special project funded in part by the Illinois Association of Health, Physical

**TABLE 9.0**   Percentile table from Illinois health fitness database.

### GIRLS: AGE = 10

| %Tile | Tricep Skinfold N = (0882) | Sum of Skinfolds (0534) | Sit & Reach (0882) | Sit-ups (0848) | Mile Run (0828) | %Tile | Tricep Skinfold N = (0882) | Sum of Skinfolds (0534) | Sit & Reach (0882) | Sit-ups (0848) | Mile Run (0828) |
|---|---|---|---|---|---|---|---|---|---|---|---|
| 99 | 5.0 | 10.0 | 41 | 58 | 6:38 | 73 | 9.0 | 16.0 | 32 | 40 | 9:15 |
| 98 | 6.0 | 11.0 | 40 | 54 | 7:06 | 72 | 9.0 | 16.0 | 32 | 39 | 9:19 |
| 97 | 6.0 | 11.0 | 39 | 52 | 7:21 | 71 | 9.0 | 16.0 | 32 | 39 | 9:21 |
| 96 | 6.0 | 11.0 | 38 | 50 | 7:39 | 70 | 9.0 | 16.5 | 32 | 39 | 9:23 |
| 95 | 7.0 | 11.5 | 38 | 49 | 7:48 | 69 | 9.5 | 16.5 | 32 | 38 | 9:28 |
| 94 | 7.0 | 12.0 | 37 | 47 | 7:57 | 68 | 9.5 | 16.5 | 31 | 38 | 9:30 |
| 93 | 7.0 | 12.5 | 37 | 47 | 8:02 | 67 | 10.0 | 17.0 | 31 | 38 | 9:34 |
| 92 | 7.0 | 12.5 | 36 | 46 | 8:06 | 66 | 10.0 | 17.0 | 31 | 38 | 9:38 |
| 91 | 7.0 | 13.0 | 36 | 46 | 8:15 | 65 | 10.0 | 17.0 | 31 | 37 | 9:39 |
| 90 | 7.0 | 13.0 | 35 | 45 | 8:22 | 64 | 10.0 | 17.0 | 31 | 37 | 9:42 |
| 89 | 7.5 | 13.0 | 35 | 45 | 8:24 | 63 | 10.0 | 17.0 | 31 | 37 | 9:45 |
| 88 | 8.0 | 13.5 | 35 | 45 | 8:30 | 62 | 10.0 | 17.0 | 30 | 37 | 9:50 |
| 87 | 8.0 | 14.0 | 35 | 44 | 8:32 | 61 | 10.0 | 17.0 | 30 | 36 | 9:52 |
| 86 | 8.0 | 14.0 | 34 | 43 | 8:34 | 60 | 10.0 | 17.5 | 30 | 36 | 9:55 |
| 85 | 8.0 | 14.0 | 34 | 43 | 8:39 | 59 | 10.0 | 18.0 | 30 | 36 | 9:59 |
| 84 | 8.0 | 14.0 | 34 | 42 | 8:41 | 58 | 10.0 | 18.0 | 30 | 36 | 10:02 |
| 83 | 8.0 | 14.0 | 34 | 42 | 8:43 | 57 | 10.5 | 18.0 | 30 | 36 | 10:06 |
| 82 | 8.0 | 14.0 | 34 | 42 | 8:48 | 56 | 10.5 | 18.0 | 29 | 35 | 10:09 |
| 81 | 8.0 | 14.5 | 33 | 42 | 8:50 | 55 | 11.0 | 18.5 | 29 | 35 | 10:10 |
| 80 | 8.5 | 15.0 | 33 | 41 | 8:53 | 54 | 11.0 | 19.0 | 29 | 35 | 10:14 |
| 79 | 8.5 | 15.0 | 33 | 41 | 8:58 | 53 | 11.0 | 19.0 | 29 | 35 | 10:17 |
| 78 | 9.0 | 15.0 | 33 | 41 | 9:02 | 52 | 11.0 | 19.0 | 29 | 34 | 10:18 |
| 77 | 9.0 | 15.0 | 33 | 40 | 9:05 | 51 | 11.0 | 19.0 | 29 | 34 | 10:20 |
| 76 | 9.0 | 15.0 | 33 | 40 | 9:08 | 50 | 11.0 | 19.5 | 29 | 34 | 10:24 |
| 75 | 9.0 | 15.5 | 32 | 40 | 9:11 | 49 | 11.0 | 20.0 | 28 | 34 | 10:26 |
| 74 | 9.0 | 15.5 | 32 | 40 | 9:13 | 48 | 11.5 | 20.0 | 28 | 34 | 10:27 |

*continued*

**TABLE 9.0** Continued.

**GIRLS: AGE = 10**

| % Tile | Tricep Skinfold N = (0882) | Sum of Skinfolds (0534) | Sit & Reach (0882) | Sit-ups (0848) | Mile Run (0828) | % Tile | Tricep Skinfold N = (0882) | Sum of Skinfolds (0534) | Sit & Reach (0882) | Sit-ups (0848) | Mile Run (0828) |
|---|---|---|---|---|---|---|---|---|---|---|---|
| 47 | 11.5 | 20.0 | 28 | 33 | 10:30 | 23 | 15.0 | 27.0 | 24 | 27 | 12:00 |
| 46 | 12.0 | 20.5 | 28 | 33 | 10:33 | 22 | 16.0 | 27.0 | 24 | 27 | 12:06 |
| 45 | 12.0 | 21.0 | 28 | 33 | 10:35 | 21 | 16.0 | 28.0 | 24 | 27 | 12:11 |
| 44 | 12.0 | 21.0 | 28 | 33 | 10:41 | 20 | 16.0 | 28.0 | 23 | 26 | 12:14 |
| 43 | 12.0 | 21.0 | 28 | 32 | 10:45 | 19 | 16.0 | 28.5 | 23 | 25 | 12:19 |
| 42 | 12.0 | 21.5 | 28 | 32 | 10:47 | 18 | 16.5 | 29.0 | 23 | 25 | 12:25 |
| 40 | 12.0 | 22.0 | 27 | 32 | 10:56 | 17 | 17.0 | 30.0 | 23 | 25 | 12:29 |
| 39 | 12.5 | 22.0 | 27 | 31 | 11:00 | 16 | 17.0 | 30.5 | 23 | 24 | 12:32 |
| 38 | 13.0 | 22.0 | 27 | 31 | 11:03 | 15 | 17.0 | 31.0 | 23 | 24 | 12:38 |
| 37 | 13.0 | 22.5 | 26 | 31 | 11:08 | 14 | 18.0 | 32.0 | 22 | 24 | 12:45 |
| 36 | 13.0 | 23.0 | 26 | 31 | 11:13 | 13 | 18.0 | 32.0 | 22 | 23 | 12:56 |
| 35 | 13.0 | 23.0 | 26 | 30 | 11:16 | 12 | 18.5 | 34.0 | 22 | 23 | 13:00 |
| 34 | 13.0 | 23.0 | 26 | 30 | 11:19 | 11 | 19.0 | 35.0 | 21 | 22 | 13:09 |
| 33 | 13.5 | 23.5 | 26 | 30 | 11:22 | 10 | 19.0 | 36.0 | 21 | 22 | 13:22 |
| 32 | 14.0 | 24.0 | 26 | 30 | 11:28 | 9 | 20.0 | 37.5 | 20 | 21 | 13:34 |
| 31 | 14.0 | 24.0 | 26 | 30 | 11:31 | 8 | 21.0 | 38.0 | 20 | 20 | 13:48 |
| 30 | 14.0 | 24.0 | 25 | 29 | 11:33 | 7 | 21.0 | 39.0 | 19 | 20 | 13:59 |
| 29 | 14.0 | 24.5 | 25 | 29 | 11:36 | 6 | 22.0 | 40.0 | 19 | 19 | 14:08 |
| 28 | 14.0 | 25.0 | 25 | 29 | 11:40 | 5 | 23.0 | 42.0 | 18 | 18 | 14:20 |
| 27 | 14.5 | 25.0 | 25 | 28 | 11:43 | 4 | 24.0 | 45.0 | 18 | 17 | 14:42 |
| 26 | 15.0 | 26.0 | 25 | 28 | 11:47 | 3 | 24.0 | 46.0 | 17 | 14 | 15:09 |
| 25 | 15.0 | 26.0 | 25 | 28 | 11:51 | 2 | 25.0 | 52.0 | 16 | 12 | 15:27 |
| 24 | 15.0 | 26.5 | 24 | 28 | 11:55 | 1 | 29.0 | 56.0 | 14 | 6 | 16:32 |

From D. N. Hastad, J. R. Marett, and S. A. Plowman, *Evaluation of the Health-Related Physical Fitness Status of Youth in the State of Illinois*, Northern Illinois University, DeKalb, IL. 1983.

Education, and Recreation and the Department of Physical Education at Northern Illinois University. In the example, it is easy for students to locate their scores and relative percentile performance.

For a teacher responsible for grading large numbers of students, conversion from raw scores to standard percentiles can be time-consuming and can turn into a logistical nightmare. It used to be that the only way to complete this process was to have a booklet or chart with raw scores and norms available for teachers. It then became their task to make the conversions by hand. From a teacher's perspective, this method of assigning grades is not appealing. Today, however, there are many different types of microcomputer software available that instantaneously convert raw scores to percentile equivalents. There is even microcomputer software that creates normative tables from raw scores. This advance in technology has made the use of percentiles as a method of grading much more realistic. A more thorough review of microcomputers and specialized software for physical education is given in Chapter 14.

## Advantages of Norm-Referenced Grading

1. This method provides the criteria by which a teacher can group the class for instruction according to ability.
2. It is most appropriate for the first-year or novice teacher who is not yet familiar with appropriate criterion standards for a particular skill, health fitness level, behavior, or cognitive expectation.
3. If the norms are derived from a class (or classes) where poor performance is the result of inferior instruction, then using norm-referenced grading would not penalize students.
4. Norm-referenced grading yields maximum variability among students and the largest possible range of scores.
5. Raw scores can be transformed into standard scores that reflect performance rankings between and among various types of tests.

## Disadvantages of Norm-Referenced Grading

1. Since students ultimately set the standard, a letter grade of A may be awarded to students who are not remotely close to a performance level deemed worthy of an A grade by the teacher.
2. This type of grading focuses on the rate of learning rather than students' ability to learn, so the quickest learners receive the highest grades.
3. While students vary from semester to semester and year to year, grading on the curve forces teachers to award a certain percentage of each letter grade to a certain number of students. This does not apply to percentile equivalents based on a large sample of students.

4. Grading on the curve is not consistent with evaluation based on performance-based objectives and does not indicate a student's progress toward mastering skills or behaviors.

## Criterion-Referenced Approach

The **criterion-referenced** approach to evaluation utilizes measurement of students' performances as they compare with a predetermined standard, such as a score, number of tasks completed, number of successful attempts versus unsuccessful attempts, or difficulty of tasks completed. The criterion, or standard, is established in advance by the teacher and, in most cases, reflects experiences with previous learners in a similar situation. Generally this criterion is set at something less than perfect performance to allow for a certain measure of unreliability in student performance, and stated as a certain proportion or percentage of the items successfully completed on the test, such as 75 percent. Once the performance criterion is established, students scoring above the standard are given a specific grade (such as Pass), those scoring below the standard are given another grade (such as Fail). Since most school districts use the five-point letter grade system, the teacher will be required to identify four cut-off points to determine five grade categories.

Criterion-referenced grading is sometimes referred to as mastery grading and can be used for evaluating student performance or behavior in any of the four learning domains. The success or failure of this method of grading depends on the teacher's ability to set appropriate standards. Standards must be challenging, yet attainable.

The criterion-referenced system is most frequently used as a means of formative evaluation, measurement that occurs during a unit or a course of instruction rather than at the end. Once a letter grade has been determined for a particular unit, it is recorded in the grade book. At the end of the grading period the teacher can weight all the letter grades, convert them to a numerical scale, and arrive at a final letter grade. If a student received a C+ for skill performance, an A for health fitness, a B- for attitude, and a C on the knowledge component, the grade may be determined according to the example shown in Figure 9.1. Following are two methods using the criterion-referenced system for the purposes of determining grades.

### Trials Successfully Completed

A common standard in criterion-referenced grading is percentage of items correct or trials successfully completed. Using this method, the teacher establishes the criterion required to earn a particular grade. For example, to receive an A on a written test, a student would have to answer correctly 90 percent, or 90 out of 100, of the questions. Or, to receive an A on a test of free throw shooting accuracy, a student would have to make 80 percent, or 12 of

► **FIGURE 9.1**   Calculating final grade from multiple criterion-referenced letter grades.

If a student achieved a C+ on skill, A on fitness, B– on social skills and attitude, C on knowledge, the grade would be averaged as follows:

| | |
|---|---|
| If A + = 12 | 35% C+ = .35 × 6  = 2.10 |
| A   = 11 | 35% A  = .35 × 11 = 3.85 |
| A – = 10 | 15% B– = .15 × 7  = 1.05 |
| B + =  9 | 15% C  = .15 × 5  =  .75 |
| B   =  8 | 7.75 = B– |
| B – =  7 | |
| C + =  6 | |
| C   =  5 | |
| C – =  4 | |
| D + =  3 | |
| D   =  2 | |
| D – =  1 | |

15, attempts. Many school districts, particularly at the senior high school level, are using the percentage correct method as a means of evaluating progress toward performance-based objectives.

## Performance Standards

Another way to use the criterion-referenced method for grading is by setting **performance standards**. Performance standards are preestablished criteria that must be met to receive a particular grade. Since performance-based objectives are an important part of the curriculum-building process, it is only fitting that we use some form of assessment to evaluate progress toward the successful attainment of these goals. To effectively use performance standards as a means to assign grades, the teacher must first be able to establish realistic, yet challenging, standards. To do so requires a knowledge about the capabilities of the students. For example, requiring 12-year-old girls to run a mile in 8 minutes and 36 seconds to receive an A may be an unrealistic standard. While this performance would rank at the 75th percentile (meaning that this performance is better than 75 percent of all girls age 12), it may be that these students have not had sufficient opportunity to develop the cardiovascular fitness and running skill necessary to achieve this goal. Likewise, if the teacher is fortunate to be teaching a class of students who meet the standard with relative ease, then perhaps the goal is not stringent enough. In this instance, proper standard setting is a more difficult task than the accompanying assessment and evaluation techniques.

The prevailing notion underlying mastery learning is that if the objectives are clearly stated and made known to the students prior to the beginning of instruction, all students will eventually meet the criterion. Instruction will be designed so that *all* students attain *all* stated criteria. The differences among students will be reflected in the time it takes to attain objectives, not the performance differences that exist over a set period of time.

## *Advantages of Criterion-Referenced Grading*

1. This method can be used to evaluate performance or behavior in the health-related physical fitness domain, psychomotor domain, affective domain, and cognitive domain.
2. Once the standards have been determined, the grading system is easily implemented.
3. Grades are not influenced by high or low skill levels of other students in class.
4. This type of grading system is consistent with measuring progress toward performance-based objectives and is a reasonable approach for teachers faced with meeting local or state performance-based outcome statements.
5. Criterion-referenced grading supports the use of programs that are paced to meet the needs of students and is predicated on the positive assumption that all students can master the material.
6. The self-paced format of this approach helps to reduce student anxiety and eliminate subjectivity in grading. In fact, repeated testing is possible and encouraged.
7. Since there are no restrictions on the number of students who can receive high grades (As and Bs), it becomes possible for most students to enjoy a certain amount of success.

## *Disadvantages of Criterion-Referenced Grading*

1. Establishing standards can be problematic in that performance-based goals cannot always be accurately specified before the unit is taught.
2. It is difficult to differentiate clearly between what is passing and what is failing, or to establish cut-off points between letter grades on the five-point grading system.
3. Standards within a school or district may vary among teachers, creating a situation in which erroneous interpretation of scores may be detrimental to students.

4. Motivation to surpass previous performance may be decreased. Students may lower their level of achievement to the minimum standard for passing.

# Other Methods to Determine Grades

The norm- and criterion-referenced approaches to evaluation are the two most common methods used to determine a letter grade. But many other means exist to assist the practitioner in assigning grades. While some are merely derivatives of either the norm- or the criterion-referenced approaches, several are unique and merit special attention. The following sections describe five such approaches to grading. The use of any of these approaches is situation-specific and depends on the experience and skill of the teacher. In addition, reference is made to how some of these techniques might be employed in the exercise science setting.

## *Student Self-Evaluation*

It is important for physical educators to provide youth with the requisite levels of fitness, skill, and knowledge to voluntarily participate in physical activity and assume an active lifestyle. An important ingredient in the successful attainment of this goal is the evaluative process. Youth should be given the opportunity to conduct **self-evaluation**. Students who are able to assess and evaluate their personal level of performance are more likely to be active participants in physical activity than those who cannot. With this in mind, it becomes increasingly important to teach students how to assess their abilities in relationship to performance-based objectives. Students should be able to administer self-tests on a variety of fitness- and skill-based goals. Once this procedure is established, it becomes possible to integrate a self-evaluation scheme into the grading system.

When student self-evaluation is used, the instructional approach is closely related to the evaluation technique. Educators need to develop lessons that teach students the proper way to conduct self-assessment techniques. While it can be somewhat time-consuming, teaching students how to conduct self-evaluation has long-term benefits for students as well as the program. If done correctly and accurately, self-testing results can be used as a component in determining the overall letter grade.

## *Group Goal Setting*

A variation of the self-evaluation approach to grading is allowing the class to develop performance- or behavior-based goals. **Group goal setting** allows the class to decide what is to be accomplished and the manner in which the progress toward goals will be evaluated. This can even include the identification of cut-off points for letter grades. The teacher is responsible for delivering instruction to attain goals. Both the students and teacher are active participants in the evaluation process and determination of the final grade.

Group goal setting can be used in a variety of exercise science settings. For example, an adult swim conditioning class can agree to swim a certain combined distance over a certain period of time. Another illustration might be in a nutrition/weight loss program. The participants could establish a goal to lose a total of 150 pounds during a six-week period. In each of these cases, participants actively determine a group goal. This not only promotes positive interaction among participants and the exercise specialist, but it also establishes a benchmark by which progress can be accurately measured.

## Peer Evaluation

Another way to get students actively involved in the grading process is through the use of peer evaluation. **Peer evaluation** gives students an opportunity to evaluate their classmates. Like self-evaluation, peer evaluation makes the students feel more involved in the educational process. Students are more likely to believe that the grading system is fair when it manifests itself through teacher, peer, and self-evaluation (Pangrazi and Darst, 1991) Peer evaluation is useful for the exercise science setting. For example, in a strength training session, participants can be paired and conduct an evaluation of lifting technique. Each would demonstrate selected lifts, while the other observed and provided written and oral commentary about the performance. This type of evaluation can provide yet another bit of evidence to assist the performer in better understanding his/her progress toward predetermined goals.

To be effective, this approach must be well conceived and properly planned. The teacher or exercise specialist must have goals and process documented and agreed-upon prior to the beginning of the instructional unit. Personality conflicts cannot enter into the evaluation process. This requires that the teacher or exercise specialist be constantly aware of the individuals interactions and able to contend with any biased evaluation that may result from friendship or ego. Depending on the skill of the practitioner and participants, this approach to grading and decision making can be successful even in the upper grades of elementary school.

## Authentic Assessment

The educational community is constantly seeking methods to assign grades that accurately portray learning and achievement. Authentic assessment is integrated with the teaching effort and provides meaningful information about student learning and achievement. This style of assessment is accomplished by focusing on student outcomes and refers to assessment tasks in which students demonstrate skills and competencies rather than selecting one of several predetermined answers. In addition, authentic assessments take place in a real setting, rather than a contrived situation like most psychomotor or health-related fitness test batteries. An example of an authentic assessment would be asking high school students to practically apply their understanding of the physiological principle of overload. Students could choose several ways to respond. They could write about overload, orally describe the principle to the teacher, or actually demonstrate the principle in an exercise setting. Having students maintain a journal describing their exercise habits is another example of authentic assessment. Individuals could record their participation in and feelings about the activity. Journal entries would serve as summaries of performance and behavior. Authentic assessment may also be used in the nonschool setting. A participant in an exercise program could be asked to conduct a self-assessment. This would require that she analyze her personal progress toward goals by rating her performance and participation in a particular sport or exercise regime. This is quite effective with adults.

Authentic assessment supports actual instruction and the goals of a nonschool exercise program. If used properly, it is an effective observational and, at times, subjective technique used to determine students' understanding and performance in a real situation. As such, it becomes another method of assessment to consider when grading or decision making is necessary.

## Contract Grading

**Contract grading** allows students to progress at different rates toward predetermined goals. As with other types of criterion-referenced grading practices, working with contracts creates opportunities for all students to achieve. While the highly skilled are likely to fulfill the contractual obligations faster than less-skilled students, the less-skilled student is given extra time to practice, receives extra assistance, and ultimately achieves the same level of skill attainment.

As implied, the contract for grading specifies student-based performance or behavior goals that must be accomplished in order to receive a particular letter grade. To avoid potential confusion, performance objectives should be written in behavioral terms. Objectives should also be written in order of difficulty, with both the quantity and quality of performance or behavior clearly understood by students. If students are familiar with the goals and understand what is necessary to fulfill each, then it becomes possible for students to monitor their progress toward the objectives and pass quantitative judgment about what grade they have earned. Figure 9.2 shows an example of a contract for students in physical education.

The contract approach to grading has several advantages. First of all, since the measurement techniques are spelled out in quantifiable terms, subjectivity has been eliminated. Grading can be a much more positive and

▶ **FIGURE 9.2**   Grade contract for lacrosse.

---

### LACROSSE

---

**Core Objectives** (1 point each)

1. With a crosse, throw an overhand shot 4 of 8 times through a target from a distance of 10 yd.

2. Throw an underhand shot 4 of 8 times through a target from a distance of 10 yd.

3. Throw a sidearm shot 4 of 8 times through a target from a distance of 10 yd.

4. Using any throw technique mentioned above, throw the ball through a target 3 of 5 times from a distance of 10 yd.

5. With a partner, catch the ball with an overhand catch 3 of 5 times from a distance of 10–15 yd.

6. Catch the ball with an underhand catch 3 of 5 times from a distance of 10–15 yd.

7. Catch the ball with the backhand catch and reverse pivot 3 of 5 times from a distance of 10 yd.

8. With a partner rolling the ball from a distance of 10 yd, use the side retrieve technique 5 of 10 times.

9. Using the cover retrieve technique, scoop a "dead" ball up 5 of 10 times.

10. Defend 4 of 8 shots taken by a partner from a distance of 10 yd.

**Optional Objectives** (2 points each)

1. With a partner passing the ball from a distance of 20 yd, use a running side retrieve technique 5 of 10 times.

2. Using the cover retrieve technique, scoop up a "dead" ball 5 of 10 times.

3. With a crosse, throw an overhand shot 4 of 5 times through a target from a distance of 15 yd.

4. Throw an underhand shot 4 of 5 times through a target from a distance of 15 yd.

5. Score 1 of 3 shots past a goalie from a distance of 10–15 yd.

---

Reprinted with permission from *Dynamic Physical Education for Secondary School Students,* 2d ed., by Pangrazi and Darst. Copyright © 1991 by Allyn and Bacon.

meaningful experience if students are able to establish the pace at which they want to move toward a goal. This not only reduces stress, it also creates the opportunity for students to select different means of learning the necessary skills or behaviors stated in the contract.

The disadvantages of contract grading focus on writing the objectives and the student's ability to accurately assess performance. Since a performance-based objective should be challenging, yet attainable, the teacher must be able to write a contract that is neither too easy, nor too difficult. If students realize that the goals are well beyond their level of capability, they will become discouraged. If, on the other hand, the goals are too simple, the students will become bored and the teacher will have been unsuccessful in providing learning experiences that enrich the students' abilities.

As with any form of criterion-referenced grading, the success or fail-ure of the process depends on the ability to accurately equate a grade with performance. For this reason, contract grading is only recommended for use by experienced teachers who are familiar with the personalities and capa-bilities of their students.

## Using a Checklist for Grading

The **checklist** is a subjective way to assess the performance of students and is viewed by many as suspect. This is particularly true when evaluating elements of the affective learning domain, which include sportsmanship, attitude, and self-concept. Much of the evaluation takes place by observing students and making qualitative judgments about their performance or behavior. The reliability of this form of evaluation is often questioned but can be improved by training observers. By using a checklist or scorecard a teacher can quantify the observed performance and behaviors into usable numerical data, which can be ranked, averaged, and so on. Even though using the checklist will increase the reliability of the data, the overall approach is still viewed as subjective. Figure 9.3 is an example of a check-list used to record the attainment of predetermined core and optional objectives.

► **FIGURE 9.3**   Performance checklist monitoring form.

**PERFORMANCE OBJECTIVE MONITORING FORM**

| Name | Core Objectives | | | | | | | | | | Optional Objectives | | | | |
|---|---|---|---|---|---|---|---|---|---|---|---|---|---|---|---|
| | 1 | 2 | 3 | 4 | 5 | 6 | 7 | 8 | 9 | 10 | 1 | 2 | 3 | 4 | 5 |
| | | | | | | | | | | | | | | | |
| | | | | | | | | | | | | | | | |
| | | | | | | | | | | | | | | | |
| | | | | | | | | | | | | | | | |
| | | | | | | | | | | | | | | | |
| | | | | | | | | | | | | | | | |
| | | | | | | | | | | | | | | | |

### Personal Interview

A system closely related to the subjective observation system of grading is the **personal interview**, which occurs when the teacher formally visits with students and asks questions that are related to performance and behavior. From the student's responses, the teacher is able to obtain information that can be used in determining a grade for a particular unit, lesson, or semester. In this setting, students have time to share with the instructor what they have, or have not, learned in class. An obvious advantage of this approach is that it creates an opportunity for the teacher to spend some quality time with each student. A disadvantage is that it is extremely time-consuming.

Another potential pitfall of the personal interview is that the final grade may be the result of the quality of the interview rather than the student's knowledge, performance, or behavior. As with the checklist method, the personal interview is more objective if a checklist of questions and performance evaluations is developed prior to each meeting.

From an instructional and counseling standpoint, the personal interview can be a valuable tool. From an evaluation perspective, it should be used judiciously and only in special cases. A teacher has only so much time available for testing and evaluating. A schedule should, therefore, be established and adhered to. Chapter 2 provides examples of implementation strategies for realistic evaluation schemes.

## REPORTING STUDENT PERFORMANCE DATA

Reporting grades is closely linked to evaluation and can be defined as the process of describing the progress toward goals. Meaningful grade reports to students, parents, and others are extremely important if the program is to maintain credibility. The worth of the program is often judged by the performance of the product. Complete student progress reports may include the following information:

1. The performance-based objective or program goal.
2. The content that was taught to meet the objective or goal.
3. The degree of change exhibited by the student relative to skill performance, behavior, fitness, or knowledge.
4. The student's status relative to continuous progress toward performance-based objectives.
5. The student's status relative to peers. Though many formats for reporting progress in these areas are available, the four most popular methods seem to be the report card, personal letter, conferences, and student profile.

## Report Card

Considerable variation exists in the type and amount of information contained on a traditional school report card. Usually, the report card consists of a listing of the subjects, the letter grades received in those subjects, and relevant personal characteristics of the student. Sometimes, especially with physical education, space will be left to make comments regarding the student's behavior (e.g., sportsmanship, fair play) and general attitude toward the class. The following pieces of information should be included in the report card:

1. The name of the child with all other essential personal information.
2. Absence report.
3. Letter grades, checks, or numerical ratings for selected categories.
4. Space for comments by the teacher(s).
5. A place for the parents to sign, if the card is to be returned.

Most school districts have a standard report card format that is computer generated. This process is certainly advantageous in terms of accuracy, expediency, cost effectiveness, and record-keeping capacity. It does, however, depersonalize the grading process. If we are sensitive to the students' needs and wish to use the evaluative process to enhance learning, then a more personal approach to grading should be considered.

## Student Portfolios

**Portfolios** are becoming a popular method to exhibit student work and performance data. In addition to serving as a means to portray student achievement, the portfolio facilitates teacher and student involvement and still maintains academic integrity by satisfying the need to be accountable. Although relatively new to the education arena, portfolios have been standard fare for displaying the works and achievements of artists, photographers, models, journalists, and other professionals. In recent years portfolios have become a popular means to present students' accomplishments in the areas of reading, writing, art, and other creative and performing subjects. According to Melograno (1994) portfolio implementation in physical education is beginning to emerge in the school setting. Several high schools are employing video tapes of student performance, computer simulations, and fitness progress as artifacts of the student profile.

A portfolio includes many elements and should be designed to meet a variety of important student needs. For example, the portfolio should 1) provide qualitative and quantitative information about student performance that allows them to assess their accomplishments; 2) assist the teacher and student in determining the degree to which learning objectives have been met; and, 3) contain information useful in the placement of students and evaluation of total program.

Student portfolios can also be characterized as "student-centered" and contain work completed, work in progress, goals, teacher feedback, self-evaluation commentary, reflection on activity and performance goals, and other achievements of students in each of the four learning domains. It is important to keep in mind that these portfolios are to be kept over time and should follow students through their school years. Physical educators should spend time planning and organizing the physical appearance of portfolios and consider potential contents prior to implementing the system into their evaluation scheme.

## Personal Letter

One method to personalize the evaluation process is to write a letter to each student. In this letter the teacher can speak directly and uniquely to the individual student and his or her parents. In this type of report, parents and students can get a more accurate and personal appraisal regarding the student's actual performance.

At first, the thought of drafting a personal report to all students may appear to be a clerical nightmare. In most cases, the physical educator teaches more students than any other subject matter teacher in the schools. This is especially true in the elementary school, in which some specialists are responsible for the evaluation of hundreds of students. The rapid advancement of microcomputer software and hardware capabilities, however (see Chapter 14), has done a great deal to make the personal report a feasible approach to reporting grades. A standard-form report can be drafted and key sentences that provide the evaluation of the student can be stored and appropriately inserted in each letter so personalized reports can be generated with little time and effort. Most of the instructor's time can be devoted to developing the document and the evaluation statements. Figure 9.4 depicts a personal fitness report generated by specialized microcomputer software.

The personal report has some disadvantages. For example, while the report serves the reporting function very well, it is less useful and much more cumbersome as a permanent record. Information cannot be easily quantified and the amount of paper required to print reports for all students can be enormous. Therefore, it is recommended that the report be used to complement the standard school form and be directed at students who require special attention.

► **FIGURE 9.4** Computer-generated personal fitness report.

## DYNAMIC PHYSICAL EDUCATION FITNESS EVALUATION
### for Rebekah

The following profile shows how you performed on each of the fitness items. Use this chart to help improve your total body fitness. If you scored in the poor category, an explanation will follow with suggestions for self-improvement.

| PHYSICAL FITNESS ITEM | POOR | SATISFACTORY | GOOD | EXCELLENT |
|---|---|---|---|---|
| Cardiovascular Fitness (mile run) | | | *** | |
| Speed and Leg Power (50-yard dash) | | *** | | |
| Abdominal Strength (sit-ups) | *** | | | |
| Power and Coordination (standing long jump) | *** | | | |
| Upper Body Strength (flexed arm hang) | | | | *** |

### How to Improve

For speed, power, and coordination: to improve in these areas, you need to perform activities at an all-out effort. Activities to try include sprinting, jumping and hopping, running stairs, running with ankle weights, basketball, stunts and tumbling, calisthenics, and isometric exercises.

For abdominal strength: to increase abdominal strength, you need to perform exercises that isolate the stomach area. Examples are trunk curl, half sit-ups, curl-ups, curl-ups with a weight held on the chest, crab kicks, and rowing. Try to work up to 25 repetitions.

Reprinted by permission of Robert Pangrazi and PANDAU Media, Tempe, Arizona.

## Conference

The face-to-face conference is an effective way to report grades to students or parents. It is the most personal way to convey the results of assessment and evaluation. In addition, the conference leaves no room for misinterpretation about the grade and offers the opportunity for students and parents to receive immediate responses to questions they may have about the actual earning of the grade. The teacher has time to clarify any misconceptions that a parent or student may have developed. Also, the conference is likely to lead to better rapport between the teacher and parent. Many schools, especially elementary schools, make parent-teacher conferences a regular part of the school calendar and evaluation process.

One drawback of the personal conference is that, as with the letter, the content is neither easily quantifiable nor readily stored on the student's permanent record. Further, teachers may view the conference more as a public relations effort than an evaluation session. If the interview is the practiced mode of evaluation, the teacher should approach it as such by preparing information relative to the student's progress and relation to peers so that it can be shared with those in attendance at the interview.

## Graphic Profile

The graphic profile is a recommended method of illustrating student progress and reporting performance. As shown in Figure 9.5 the graphic profile satisfies many requirements characteristic of meaningful report formats. The old adage "One picture is worth a thousand words" is proven true when using this method. A person can readily observe standards of a student's performance compared to that of other students, percentile equivalents, or the individual's progress over time. Students, parents, and administrators can readily assess the change in performance without having to interpret numerical charts or conversion tables.

Graphic profiles can be generated on a microcomputer or mainframe computer and printed on most printers. This is advantageous for several reasons. First, the physical task of plotting information is reduced to making a few keystroke entries on the microcomputer and having the software do the work. Many software packages that graphically profile data have a storage capacity. As a result, a student's raw scores may be entered and saved for use at a later date. By using such software, a teacher may follow

**FIGURE 9.5**   Microcomputer-generated graphic profile of performance over time.

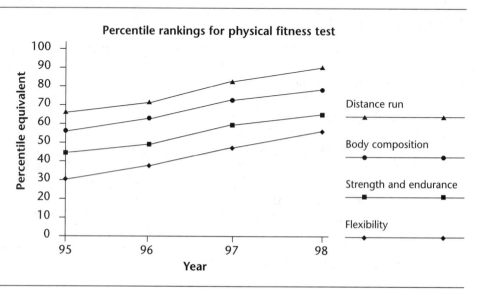

the progress of a student over time. Chapter 14 describes the various software packages that graphically depict raw data scores.

Another advantage of the graphic profile is that the burden of obtaining the printout can be placed on the student. In the elementary and secondary schools, the microcomputer is becoming a tool used by all students. It may be that, once they know their scores from a particular test or battery of tests, students can find some computer time during the school day and generate their own profiles. Since the teacher has records of the raw scores, the student can simply show the printed profile to the teacher to check for accuracy. It can then be sent home for the parents to view. Having the students generate their own profiles adds a personal touch to the evaluation process. Students no longer need to rely solely on the teacher; rather, they can assume an active role in determining their progress toward goals. Also, features of graphic profile software now include prescriptive activities and explanations about the current levels of performance. Because microcomputer software is becoming more sophisticated and less expensive, it is only a matter of time before the graphic profile becomes the most common way to report student progress or grades.

## SUMMARY

Although grading is an integral procedure of teaching, there are differing opinions regarding the relative appropriateness of assigning grades in physical education. Further, a variety of grading practices exist and there is little general agreement among practitioners as to the most appropriate way to grade. The increased attention given to accountability creates a special demand for measurement and evaluation in the physical education curriculum. There needs to be limited, systematic, and objective measurement in the school setting that links goals, outcomes, and objectives with grade determination. This chapter suggests that grading should occur in physical education and cites two basic approaches to determining grades: norm-referenced and criterion-referenced. Norm-referenced tests include the types of assessment that measure relative achievement. Criterion-referenced tests use a single performance and compare it to a predetermined standard. Both types of testing procedures can be used successfully in physical education and the selection of which method to administer is dependent on various factors. In addition to norm- and criterion-referenced tests, other methods may be used to assess and evaluate student performance. The manner of reporting grades is changing with the technological advances in recording, storing, and reporting information, and the computer can now be used to print the traditional report card as well as graphic profiles and personal letters.

## ► DISCUSSION QUESTIONS

1. Explain the basic philosophy underlying your approach to gradingin physical education. What constituencies should be permitted to influence the determination of grades?

2. Cite reasons to link grades with program goals, unit outcomes, and performance-based objectives. From a student's perspective, why would this practice be considered useful?

3. Cite the advantages and disadvantages of grading. Based on the information presented, do you think grading should be used in physical education?

4. Which are the most important issues associated with determining grades? The least important? What factors affect the status of these issues?

5. Cite examples of occasions when the norm-referenced approach to grading would be appropriate to use in physical education. The criterion-referenced approach. Which approach do you think is more compatible with your philosophy of grading?

6. How important is subjective assessment and evaluation in the grading process? Is it a valid means to determine performance? Cite some examples of subjective procedures that you would use in assigning grades.

7. What are the different ways to report grades? In your opinion, which is the best way to communicate performance to the student? Parents? Other teachers?

## ► REFERENCES

Hastad, D. N., Marett, J. R., and Plowman, S. A. (1983). *Evaluation of the health-related physical fitness status of youth in the state of Illinois.* DeKalb: Northern Illinois University.

Hensley, L. D. (1990). Current measurement and evaluation practices in professional physical education. *JOPERD*, 61(2): 32–33.

Illinois State Board of Education. (1982). *Tips and techniques: Ability grouping and performance evaluation in physical education.* Springfield, IL.

Imwold, C. H.; Rider, R. A.; and Johnson, D. J. (1982). The use of evaluation in public school physical education programs. *Journal of Teaching Physical Education*, 2(1), 13–18.

Johnson, B. L., and Nelson, J. K. (1986). *Practical measurements for evaluation in physical education.* 4th ed. Minneapolis, MN: Burgess.

Laughlin, N., and Laughlin, S. (1992). The myth of measurement in physical education. *Journal of Physical Education, Recreation and Dance*, 63: 83–85.

Melograno, V. J. (1994). Portfolio assessment: Documenting authentic student learning. *Journal of Physical Education, Recreation and Dance.* 65: 50-61.

Pangrazi, R. P., and Darst, P. W. (1991). *Dynamic physical education for secondary school students: Curriculum and instruction.* 2d ed. Minneapolis, MN: Burgess.

Pangrazi, R. P., and Corbin, C. B. (1993). Physical fitness: Questions teachers ask. *Journal of Physical Education, Recreation and Dance,*. 64: 14–18.

## ▶ REPRESENTATIVE READINGS

Bosco, J. S., and Gustafson, W. F. (1983). *Measurement and evaluation in physical education, fitness, and sports*. Englewood Cliffs, NJ: Prentice-Hall.

Illinois State Board of Education. (1982). *Tips and techniques: Ability grouping and performance evaluation in physical education*. Springfield, IL: State Board.

Johnson, B. L., and Nelson, J. K. (1986). *Practical measurements for evaluation in physical education*. 4th ed. Minneapolis, MN: Burgess.

Mood, D. P. (1980). *Numbers in motion: A balanced approach to measurement and evaluation in physical education*. Palo Alto, CA: Mayfield.

Pangrazi, R. P. and Darst, P. W. (1991). *Dynamic physical education for secondary school students*. 2nd ed. Boston: Allyn and Bacon.

Pangrazi, R. P. and Dauer, V. P. (1995). *Dynamic physical education for elementary school children*. 11th ed. Boston: Allyn and Bacon.

Wessel, J. A., and Kelly, L. (1986). *Achievement-based curriculum development in physical education*. Philadelphia, PA: Lea and Febiger.

# USING SELF-EVALUATION TO IMPROVE INSTRUCTION

**10**

## ▶ KEY TERMS

Academic Learning Time–Physical
  Education (ALT-PE)
Arizona State University Observation
  Instrument (ASUOI)
checklist
duration recording
event recording
eyeballing
group time sampling
instructional time
instructor movement
interobserver agreement (IOA)
interval recording
management
negative modeling
note taking
placheck recording
positive modeling
practice time
rating scale
response latency
System for Observing Fitness
  Instruction Time (SOFIT)

## ▶ OBJECTIVES

*After reading this chapter, the student should be able to:*

1. Understand problems associated with the
   measurement and evaluation of teacher effectiveness in physical education.

2. Describe traditional methods of evaluating
   teachers and explain why these methods lack
   objectivity and reliability.

3. Identify systematic observation methods used
   for teacher evaluation and explain the advantages these methods have over the traditional
   methods.

4. Demonstrate a basic knowledge of the data
   collection procedures associated with event
   recording, interval recording, duration recording, and group time sampling.

5. Define interobserver agreement (IOA) and explain why it is critical to establish IOA when
   using any type of systematic observation.

6. List and describe teacher and student behaviors that can be observed using systematic
   observation

While instruction is usually considered in relation to school physical education programs, instruction takes place in virtually all activity settings. For example, exercise clinicians teach cardiac rehabilitation patients new health and exercise habits and monitor their workouts, athletic trainers provide feedback to athletes during treatment sessions, personal trainers instruct their clients as they oversee their exercise regimens, and coaches at all levels instruct their athletes in the skills and strategies of their sports. Professionals in all activity settings—both school and nonschool—should strive to provide the best instruction possible. Thus, the emphasis on improving instruction in this chapter is targeted at both physical education and exercise science settings. Further, measurement strategies to gather information on behaviors in this wide variety of activity settings stress the use of self-evaluation methods of evaluating instructional effectiveness. A variety of questions arise when considering appropriate self-evaluation strategies.

1. *Why should efforts at improving instruction focus on self-evaluation strategies?* It is recommended that all physical education and exercise science professionals use some form of self-evaluation to monitor and help improve their effectiveness. While a supervisor or administrator may do an evaluation once or twice a year, this is not adequate to provide substantive information about instruction. These evaluations normally use some type of traditional method to gather data. The problems with these traditional methods are detailed in the following section of this chapter. Multiple observations using more objective techniques are needed for meaningful data to be gathered, but time constraints on outside evaluators usually make repeated observations logistically impossible.

Thus, self-evaluation strategies are much more desirable. Self-evaluation alleviates the time constraints of outside evaluators. The use of a portable cassette recorder or VCR camera to record instructional episodes allows for repeated observations and thorough self-evaluation. In many cases, enlisting the cooperation of a colleague in collecting data for self-evaluation is an excellent strategy. A live observer can sometimes gather information difficult or impossible to get from recorded tapes. By working collaboratively with a coworker, you can observe their instruction in exchange for their observation of yours. Insights into particular situations often surface as instructional episodes are discussed with your peers. What better person to involve with your self-evaluation efforts than a peer who understands the special situations and challenges that you face on a daily basis? While periodic observation made by supervisors and administrators certainly should be considered and may provide valuable information, systematic improvement should be based on self-evaluation.

2. *What type of evaluation instrument should be used in analyzing instruction in activity settings?* It is recommended that systematic observation

methodology be used to gather data on instructional episodes. Later in this chapter, specific information on systematic observation techniques is presented in detail. There are many different ways to design observation instruments for different activity settings. While one instrument may be appropriate for an elementary physical education class, a different or modified instrument likely would be more effective in analyzing instruction in an aerobic dance class at a health club. Whatever instrument is used, information on both instructional behaviors of the practitioner and the nature of activities of the students/clients should be gathered. For instance, what ratio of positive and negative feedback statements does a coach make to his/her athletes? During a workout, what percentage of time is the cardiac rehabilitation patient actually engaged in the prescribed exercise regimen? How many attempts at shooting the basketball does the ninth grade student get during a lesson on shooting? What percentage of instructions or directions from an aerobic dance instructor are targeted at individuals rather than the entire class? Instruments should be designed to answer questions specific to a given setting. Much care must be taken to ensure that the chosen instrument and data collection procedures provide valid and reliable information concerning the instructional episode.

3. *When should the observations be made?* In general, observations should be made at a variety of times with as many observations as possible. Keep in mind that the data collected should be representative of what goes on in the setting. If self-evaluation is based on only one or two observations, it is possible that what occurs is not representative of normal activities. For example, if a teacher wants to evaluate instruction in a six-week weight training unit, she should videotape one class a week during the unit rather than do six observations in the first two weeks. Coaches should do self-evaluation activities during different times of the season. Exercise clinicians should observe their clients' workout behaviors at different stages of their programs. Observations should be planned and conducted to address the issues of interest in the instructional process.

Whenever observations are made, it is crucial that they are carried out in an unobtrusive, objective, and nonthreatening manner. Multiple observations also serve to ensure that behaviors are not altered on the day of evaluation. While each self-evaluation episode provides information about that particular day, a thorough self-evaluation should look at the accumulation of data over multiple observations to observe trends and make possible a summative self-evaluation. Once a baseline is established from initial observations, then specific behaviors can be targeted for improvement, with subsequent observations made to monitor the improvement. This self-evaluation process should be beneficial to all and improve overall program effectiveness.

In a climate of increased demand for accountability, evaluation in activity settings is sometimes linked to student achievement. While achievement should not be discounted, this is not the sole criterion with which to evaluate an instructor. Many variables other than instructor performance may affect achievement, including administrative support, class size or number of clients, availability of facilities and equipment, and socioeconomic background of the participants. An instructor has little or no control over these variables; consequently, self-evaluation should emphasize variables the instructor can control.

Professionals have direct control over the behaviors they exhibit while instructing. This chapter will provide a description of traditional methods of evaluation and an in-depth examination of self-evaluation strategies by focusing on the observable and measurable behaviors exhibited in activity settings. The behaviors exhibited during instructional episodes are critical elements that, in great part, determine instructor effectiveness. Because behavior is an instructional variable that can be analyzed and changed, it makes sense that this should be the focus of self-evaluation.

## TRADITIONAL METHODS OF OBSERVATION

Instruction typically is evaluated by observing the specific setting and using one of several traditional methods of collecting information. The methods detailed below have been used for many years and continue to be employed in many educational and business settings. However, all suffer a major drawback: They are based on the perspective of a single observer making a subjective evaluation.

## Eyeballing

A common method of observation is for the evaluator to merely watch what is being taught and then offer comments and suggestions for improvement. Siedentop (1991) used the term **eyeballing** for describing this method. Feedback to the practitioner is usually in the form of a discussion of the performance at the conclusion of the episode. These verbal intuitions passed on by the supervisor normally lack specificity and are based on the subjective opinions of the evaluator. There is no database and no way to determine changes or improvement in subsequent observations. For these reasons, this particular method falls short of meeting criteria for validity, reliability, and objectivity.

## Note Taking

An observer using the **note taking** technique writes down comments concerning the instructional effectiveness. These notes may be taken as the class is watched or written from memory at the conclusion of the class. Note taking is an improvement over eyeballing since some visible evidence is provided concerning the formulation of the evaluation. These anecdotal records can vary from a few short phrases to long, detailed notes about the observation. The observer still relies on subjective intuition and opinions, but the perceptions are written down. The value of this method depends on the completeness of the notes used for evaluation.

Though this method is superior to eyeballing, the notes taken may or may not be accurate and usually are written in a less than precise style, which inhibits measuring improvements toward specific objectives. Anecdotal records are valuable as a supplementary evaluation tool, but they do not provide enough objective information on which to base a valid evaluation.

## Checklists

A **checklist** is an evaluation tool that offers a series of statements or phrases to which an observer can make yes or no responses. The statements or phrases are characteristics of good instruction, such as "shows enthusiasm" or "good knowledge of subject matter." These characteristics are seldom defined in specific terms, so the observer must interpret each criterion statement. These interpretations inevitably vary from observer to observer, which makes the checklist less than reliable.

The checklist appears to be a more objective evaluation than eyeballing or note taking, but it is still formed by the subjective judgment of a single individual. The evaluation is based on the interpretations and opinions of the observer and offers little in the way of specific information by which to measure future changes (see Figure 10.0). The checklist is valuable for keeping records of steps or jobs completed but should not be used as the major evaluation tool.

## Rating Scales

The traditional method that appears to be the most scientific and objective is the **rating scale**. It is similar to the checklist except that it typically allows the observer a greater range than the yes–no decision of the checklist. An evaluator may assign a score from a range of points, typically one to five, for the characteristics included on the rating scale (see Figure 10.1). Thus, for a characteristic such as "shows enthusiasm," the observer has greater flexibility in making the appraisal.

However, the rating scale is plagued by the same problems as the checklist. The observer must still define the characteristic and then make a subjective decision of how to rate the criterion in question. With a five-point scale for each criterion, it becomes even more difficult to demonstrate reli-

► **FIGURE 10.0**   Example of a checklist.

---

**EVALUATION FORM**

Activity _____Date _____

Student Teacher _____Elementary _____Secondary _____

College Supervisor _____Cooperating Teacher_____

This evaluation of student teaching serves as a tangible basis for discussion among the cooperating teacher, the college supervisor, and the student. The following symbols will be used: Plus (+) indicates a positive feature of the student teacher's work; minus (–) indicates a need for improvement.

**TEACHING COMPETENCIES**

| | | | |
|---|---|---|---|
| ☐ Appearance | | ☐ Planning and organization |
| ☐ Use of language | | ☐ Execution of lesson-teaching technique |
| ☐ Voice | | ☐ Knowledge of subject |
| ☐ Enthusiasm | | ☐ Demonstration of skills |
| ☐ Poise | | ☐ Appropriate progression |
| ☐ Creativeness | | ☐ Provisions for individual differences |
| | | ☐ Class management/control |
| | | ☐ Adaptability, foresight |
| | | ☐ Appropriate choice of activity |

COMMENTS:

---

From *Dynamic Physical Education for Secondary School Students,* 2d ed., by R. Pangrazi and P. Darst. Copyright © 1991 by Allyn and Bacon. Reprinted by permission.

ability with this method. If the rating scale has more than five points, such as a 1–10 scale, reliability becomes more of a problem. The fewer points that are involved, the more reliable the ratings become, but by having fewer points, the instrument becomes less precise.

When the rating scale furnishes general information based on only a few rating points for each characteristic, it can be a convenient way to provide supplementary data on teaching performance. If rating scales are utilized, it is important to understand the weaknesses and limitations of this type of instrumentation.

▶ **FIGURE 10.1**   Example of a rating scale.

| Type (X) in the space that indicates your appraisal of the student teacher: | Superior | Above Average | Average | Below Average | Unsatisfactory | Not Known | | Superior | Above Average | Average | Below Average | Unsatisfactory | Not Known |
|---|---|---|---|---|---|---|---|---|---|---|---|---|---|
| NAME _____ (Last)    (First)    (Middle) <br> SUBJECT OR GRADE LEVEL: _____ | | | | | | | | | | | | | |
| Appearance | | | | | | | Innovativeness | | | | | | |
| Mental alertness | | | | | | | Communication skills | | | | | | |
| Poise and personality | | | | | | | Lesson planning ability | | | | | | |
| Enthusiasm | | | | | | | Rapport with students | | | | | | |
| Health and energy | | | | | | | Classroom control skills | | | | | | |
| Emotional stability | | | | | | | Student motivation skills | | | | | | |
| Tact and judgment | | | | | | | Teaching skills | | | | | | |
| Desire to improve | | | | | | | Provides for individuals | | | | | | |
| Dependability | | | | | | | Understands students | | | | | | |
| Professional attitude | | | | | | | Knowledge of subject | | | | | | |
| Cooperation | | | | | | | Potential as a teacher | | | | | | |

ADDITIONAL COMMENTS:


(Give this completed and signed form to the student teacher)

Name _____(Supervising Teacher) _____Date _____

Name _____(College Supervisor) _____Date _____

To summarize, traditional methods of observing and evaluating teacher performance are based on the intuition and opinion of the observer. These methods are of some value if they supplement an evaluatory tool that exhibits validity and reliability. Eyeballing, note taking, checklists, and rating scales are based on the perspective of a single observer and have proven to be ineffective because they lack precision and offer little or no quantifiable data. Because a database is not created, it becomes quite difficult to evaluate improvement from lesson to lesson (Pangrazi and Darst, 1991).

## SYSTEMATIC OBSERVATION METHODOLOGY

Prior to 1960, most evaluation of instructional effectiveness and research completed on this topic was less than satisfactory because of dependence on inappropriate traditional methodologies. Efforts to observe and evaluate teacher performance were plagued by invalid and unreliable instruments and procedures, some of which were just discussed. As a result, strategies were developed for observing teachers and students in the actual teaching–learning environment in order to obtain more objective and quantifiable information. These tools are called systematic observation instruments.

The advent and growing popularity of systematic observation instrumentation has provided the opportunity to observe, record, measure, and evaluate behaviors in physical education, athletic settings, and clinical exercise environments in a valid and reliable manner. The wide variety of systematic observation instruments allows data to be collected and analyzed on participant and instructor behaviors.

These observational tools range from simple to complex and provide different types of information according to the recording procedures used and the nature of the instrument. The development of these instruments has created new possibilities for improved instructional effectiveness through self-evaluation, improved techniques of supervision, research activities, and innovative models of training and inservice.

Regardless of the complexity or focus of the particular instrument, each observational tool is based on observable behavior categories that are specifically defined to ensure reliability of the observations. Depending on the nature of the instrument, behavioral data can be collected from cassette tapes, from VCR tapes, or by observations made by an on-site data collector. Different recording procedures can be used to collect data—event, interval, duration, group-timed sampling. These procedures will be discussed later in this chapter. Such procedures allow a trained observer to observe and record data that produces quantifiable and objective feedback in a variety of activity settings.

Thus, systematic observation allows for the collection of objective data on instructor and participant behaviors. Subsequent analysis of this information can provide critical insights for teachers, coaches, and exercise science professionals to improve their effectiveness. Data collected with systematic observation procedures is collected by live observers or by using audiotapes or videotapes. Information that can be collected on any part of the instructional process includes the following:

- ▶ type and quality of instructor feedback
- ▶ amount of time devoted to management, instruction, and practice
- ▶ number of skill attempts by a student in a given class period
- ▶ frequency of instructor using first names of students/clients
- ▶ participant off-task and on-task behaviors
- ▶ instructor movement patterns during class

To change and improve instructional practices, the practitioner first must be aware of what is taking place in the activity setting. By becoming more cognizant of the relationship of instructor and participant behaviors to an effective teaching—learning activity environment, the instructor can make changes to improve their effectiveness. Rink (1993) suggests the following steps in using systematic observation:

1. Decide what to look for.
2. Choose an appropriate observational method.
3. Learn to use the observational method in an accurate manner.
4. Collect data.
5. Analyze and interpret the meaning of the data.
6. Make changes to the instructional process.
7. Monitor changes in instruction over time.

## DATA RECORDING PROCEDURES

The use of systematic observation instrumentation provides a way to collect data objectively on instructional effectiveness for purposes of self-evaluation. The methods discussed below have been used not only in studying instructional effectiveness, but also in other areas of research, usually psychological in nature, that examine human behavior. Because of their extensive use, the reliability of these procedures is well documented (Siedentop, 1991).

The following methods are easy to understand and simple to use. The main problem with the use of these methods is deciding what behaviors are to be observed and defining those behaviors in measurable and observable terms. Most problems encountered when using systematic observation systems stem from vague definitions leading to misinterpretations of the behavior categories being observed. The observer must decide on specific definitions of behavior categories, which should be written in a precise manner, preferably with examples, and followed consistently if the data collected are to be accurate and objective. The following represent examples of defined behavior categories that could be used with systematic observation procedures:

*Instruction:* Verbal statements referring to fundamentals, rules, or strategies of the activity, which can come in the form of questioning, corrective feedback, or direct statements.

> Examples: "In soccer, which player is allowed to use his hands?" or "Next time point your toe when you punt the ball," or "Keep your leg straight on that stretch."

*Management:* Verbal statements related to organizational details of the activity not referring to strategies, fundamentals, or content of the activity.

> Examples: "Make five lines on the sideline facing me" or "Please complete your weight-training circuit in 30 minutes."

*Praise:* Verbal compliments or statements of acceptance.

> Examples: "Good job moving your feet on defense" or "That is a perfect pace on the Stairmaster."

*Scolding:* Verbal statements of displeasure.

> Examples: "That was a pitiful effort on defense" or "Stop pushing in the back of that line."

*Use of First Name:* Using the first name or nickname when speaking directly to a participant.

> Examples: "Nice pass, Bill!" "Smitty, you play on the red team today," or "Betty, you are working hard in aerobics class today."

Learning the different systematic observation methods of data collection usually requires nothing more than one or two practice sessions and a thorough understanding of the behavior categories. The methods can be carried out with simple and inexpensive equipment. Paper, pencil, stopwatch, and sometimes a portable tape recorder are all that is necessary. The use of a videotape recording system can also be quite advantageous in the evaluation process. Portable video cameras are commonplace in contemporary settings and the playback feature creates additional possibilities for self-evaluation. In the following section, several methods for observing and recording instructional behaviors will be discussed.

## Event Recording

**Event recording** is a simple procedure providing precise feedback that can be used in the evaluation process. An observer simply records the number of times predefined behaviors occur during a timed observation period. By gathering information on the frequency of a specific behavior, event recording provides a cumulative record of discrete events occurring during the observation period.

Each discrete event, or behavior, exhibited by the instructor or participant is tallied on a recording sheet (see Figure 10.2). It is typically used to count the frequency of instructor behaviors such as use of first name and feedback statements to skill attempts and student behaviors (see Figure 10.12). It is most commonly used to gather and summarize types and frequencies of multiple behaviors. The novice should start by coding a few behaviors at a time because increasing the number of behaviors being recorded makes it more difficult to code the data accurately.

Event recording can also be used to observe participant behaviors. It can be used to count the number of skill attempts (successful and unsuccessful) that students have in a given time period, sometimes called opportunities to respond. Free throws attempted and free throws made is a form of event recording done in basketball statistics. Counting the number of situps a person performed correctly and incorrectly in an aerobics class is a type of event recording. It might be of interest to count how many questions a teacher asked the class or the number of client questions that occurred in a given consultation. Many types of instructor and participant behaviors can be accurately recorded, given a clear definition of the behavior category.

An entire session can be observed using event-recording procedures, or it might be decided to collect data in certain timed segments. For example, if an instructional session is 40 minutes in length, five segments of three minutes each evenly distributed throughout the session would yield representative behavioral data about the lesson without having to record the entire time period. It is often advantageous to combine event-recording procedures with other methods during an observation session.

If segments of a lesson are recorded, the segments should be distributed across the entire session so the data will be representative of the whole class. For example, data collection during the first 15 minutes only of a session typically includes management-type behaviors, such as checking roll, warm-up, and organizing for the day's activity, which would not be indicative of the teaching behaviors exhibited throughout the session. By

▶ **FIGURE 10.2**   Example of event recording.

## EVENT RECORDING TALLY SHEET

Date __11/15__     Coach __Davis_____     Sport __Basketball_____

| Categories | Time __10 min.__ | Time __10 min.__ | Total | RPM | %tage |
|---|---|---|---|---|---|
| First Name | ЖЖ ЖЖ IIII | ЖЖ ЖЖ ЖЖ I | 30 | 1.5 | 15.5 |
| Pre-Instruction | ЖЖ | II | 7 | .35 | 3.6 |
| Concurrent Instruction | III | I | 4 | .2 | 2.1 |
| Post-Instruction | ЖЖ ЖЖ ЖЖ ЖЖ ЖЖ ЖЖ ЖЖ II | ЖЖ ЖЖ ЖЖ ЖЖ ЖЖ ЖЖ ЖЖ ЖЖ IIII | 81 | 4.05 | 41.2 |
| Questioning | IIII | II | 6 | .3 | 3.1 |
| Physical Assistance | II | | 2 | .1 | 1.0 |
| Positive Modeling | III | IIII | 7 | .35 | 3.6 |
| Negative Modeling | II | I | 3 | .15 | 1.5 |
| Hustle | ЖЖ ЖЖ | ЖЖ III | 18 | .9 | 9.3 |
| Praise | ЖЖ | ЖЖ I | 10 | .5 | 5.2 |
| Scold | III | III | 7 | .35 | 3.6 |
| Management | ЖЖ ЖЖ ЖЖ ЖЖ ЖЖ II | ЖЖ ЖЖ ЖЖ IIII | 46 | 2.3 | 23.7 |
| Uncodable | II | IIII | 3 | .15 | 1.5 |

TOTAL            __102__                __92__        __194__ __9.7__

Comments ___Preseason practice — 20 minutes total observation___ spreading the observational segments across the session, data more accurately reflect instructional performance.

## Calculating Rate per Minute for Behaviors

Whether data are collected for the entire session or for distributed timed segments, it is important to note the total time that observations are made and recorded. When using event recording, a stopwatch should be used to time the length of the observation session to the nearest one-half minute. The results of the event-recording data collection can be divided by the number of minutes of observation to calculate the rate per minute (RPM) for each behavior category and a total RPM for all behaviors observed and coded. For instance, if an instructor praises 20 times in 40 minutes of observation, the RPM for the praise category would be calculated as follows:

20 praises divided by 40 minutes = .50 RPM for praise.

This means that the instructor averaged .50 praises per minute during the lesson.

Hopefully, when given this objective information based on systematic observation data, the instructor will realize that future sessions could be made more positive by praising the students more. The instructor could record a future session and count the number of praises used. If 60 praises were recorded in a 40 minutes, the RPM (60 praises divided by 40 minutes) for the praise category would be 1.50. Based on this objective method, it is easy to see that the instructor increased the use of praise in the second observation. Subsequent observations should be made to ensure that the RPM for the target behavior is maintained in the future.

## Calculating Percentages of Behaviors

When an event-recording instrument is designed to record all behaviors of an instructor, the percentage of each independent behavior category should also be calculated. By taking the total number of independent categories and dividing that number into the number of times a specific category was recorded, the percentage for that particular category is ascertained. For instance, if a total of 200 behaviors were recorded of which 40 were tallied as praise, the percentage of praise behaviors would be figured as follows:

40 praises divided by 200 total behaviors = 20%.

This means that 20 percent of all behaviors were praises.

It should be emphasized that this does not mean that 20 percent of the time was spent praising students. Remember that event recording is based on the number of discrete events, not a unit of time. A teacher might praise a student for 10 seconds and later exhibit a praise behavior for one second.

Both are recorded as separate praises. No distinction is made concerning the length of the discrete events. However, a session characterized by discrete behaviors that are lengthy will cause fewer behaviors to be coded, which causes the RPM to be lower.

Consider the practitioner who exhibits only 40 total behaviors in a 40-minute observation. If 20 of these behaviors are in the praise category, then 50 percent of all behaviors (20 praises divided by 40 total behaviors) are praises. Though the figure 50 percent seems high, the RPM for praise is only .50 (20 praises divided by 40 minutes) and the RPM for all observed behaviors is only 1.0 (40 total behaviors divided by 40 minutes). This example illustrates the importance of considering both the RPM and percentage of a given behavior category when analyzing the data for evaluation purposes.

The use-of-first name category is often included on event-recording instruments. The frequent use of first names reflects more individualized attention and specific feedback for the participants. This category is not an independent behavior since it does not occur by itself; rather, it always accompanies another behavior. Because it is used in combination with an independent behavior, the method for calculating percentage of the use of first name category is handled in a slightly different manner.

By dividing the number of times first names are used by the total number of independent behaviors, the percentage for a first name accompanying an independent behavior is calculated. If 40 first names were coded with 200 total independent behaviors, then 20 percent of all independent behaviors were accompanied by a first name. The use-of-first name category is a dependent behavior and is handled separately from the independent behavior categories. If the number of first names is included in the calculation of percentages of independent behaviors, the resulting percentages of each behavior category is decreased, and their true values are distorted. Thus, in calculating percentages, the total of each independent behavior category should be divided by the total number of independent behaviors with the dependent first name category excluded in the total. This treatment of the data yields information that reflects more accurately the behaviors exhibited during the observed teaching performance.

## Interval Recording

Another method for collecting meaningful performance data is **interval recording**. Each behavior category is assigned a number for coding purposes. When the behavior is observed, the corresponding number is written on the coding sheet. Each number recorded is considered a data point. In using this technique, behaviors are observed for short intervals of time and then a short period of time is used to code what behavior best categorizes the observed interval. For example, an observer could observe for five seconds and record for five seconds. Each observe-record is considered a data point. According to Siedentop (1991), it is important to have at least 90 data points for validity to be ensured.

For best results, the length of the interval should be 5–12 seconds. If the interval is too short, it cannot be coded accurately. The interval should be as short as possible and still have reliable data. For beginning data collectors, a longer interval allows the observer to become familiar with the technique. As an observer becomes more comfortable with the method, the interval can be shortened if desired. When using longer intervals, problems are sometimes encountered when several behaviors occur, and the observer has to decide which behavior to record. The observe-record intervals do not have to be of the same length. For instance, the observation can be five seconds, and the record time can be two seconds. The length of the respective intervals depends on the expertise of the observer and the number and complexity of behavior categories utilized. Usually the observe-record intervals should be the same to avoid confusion.

During field-based interval recording, the observer should use an earphone and portable cassette recorder. A tape with cues to observe and record at the selected time intervals helps the observer with data collection. If a teacher can be taped, coding from a videotape can be advantageous. The videotape can be stopped and reversed if any problems in coding arise. Using a videotape also allows teachers to code themselves. Some VCR cameras have a stopwatch function that can be superimposed on the tape, which is convenient to use with interval recording.

An interval coding sheet (see Figure 10.3) is used to collect the behavioral data. Typically, each behavior category is assigned a number, and each cell on the coding sheet represents a data point. To code behavior, the observer starts at the top, left-hand corner and codes in a vertical direction down the column to the bottom before starting on the second column. If five-second intervals are used, then each cell represents the behavior that characterized that five-second observation interval. If a certain behavior is a lengthy one, it may span several data points. Indications of both frequency and duration of behaviors can be derived with interval recording. The number of intervals coded for each independent behavior indicates frequency, while the number of intervals recorded consecutively indicates the duration of a particular behavior.

Because interval recording is based on time, it is recommended that a silence category be added to the behavior categories. An observation interval can pass without the instructor exhibiting any observable behavior other than monitoring the activity. This interval should be coded as silence, which is not used in event recording.

As discussed previously, the use of first name will always accompany an independent behavior. When the first-name category is included, it should be coded in the same cell as the independent behavior it accompa-

▰ **FIGURE 10.3**    Example of interval recording.

## INTERVAL RECORDING CODING SHEET

| 12 | 14 | 14 | 7 | 4 | 13 | 4 | 14 | 10 | $1/12$ | 4 | 3 | 14 | 5 | 14 | 5 | 14 | 14 | | |
|----|----|----|----|----|----|----|----|----|----|----|----|----|----|----|----|----|----|---|---|
| 12 | 14 | 14 | 12 | 4 | 13 | 10 | 14 | $1/10$ | 11 | 4 | 14 | 14 | 14 | 14 | 14 | 14 | 14 | | |
| 12 | 14 | 14 | 12 | 6 | 12 | 14 | 14 | 14 | 9 | 6 | 14 | 14 | 14 | 14 | 4 | 11 | 14 | | |
| 13 | 14 | 14 | 11 | 4 | 12 | 14 | 14 | 14 | 2 | 4 | $1/3$ | 14 | 4 | 13 | 4 | 4 | | | |
| 12 | 14 | $1/3$ | $1/3$ | 7 | 12 | $1/10$ | 14 | 14 | 2 | 5 | 4 | 14 | 4 | 14 | 10 | 4 | | | |
| 12 | 3 | 5 | 4 | 14 | 12 | 9 | 14 | 14 | 14 | 14 | 4 | 12 | 14 | 14 | 4 | 4 | | | |
| $1/5$ | 4 | 14 | 6 | 14 | 2 | 9 | 14 | 14 | 14 | 14 | 5 | 12 | 14 | 14 | 14 | 14 | | | |
| 2 | 4 | 14 | 4 | 14 | 2 | 6 | 14 | Rest | 14 | 5 | 14 | 12 | $1/9$ | 14 | 14 | 14 | | | |
| 2 | 14 | 4 | 4 | 14 | 2 | 7 | 14 | $1/10$ | 14 | 14 | 14 | 12 | 14 | $1/2$ | 14 | 10 | | | |
| 2 | 14 | 4 | 14 | 14 | 14 | 7 | 14 | 14 | 14 | 10 | 9 | 14 | 14 | 2 | 14 | 4 | | | |
| 7 | 14 | 4 | 14 | 14 | 14 | 3 | $1/3$ | 14 | 14 | 14 | 4 | $1/4$ | 14 | 14 | 14 | 4 | | | |
| 2 | $1/10$ | 9 | 14 | 14 | 14 | 4 | 14 | 12 | 14 | 14 | 7 | 4 | $1/10$ | 3 | 14 | 14 | | | |
| 7 | 9 | 7 | 14 | 14 | $1/11$ | 4 | 14 | 12 | $1/4$ | 14 | 14 | 8 | 4 | 14 | $1/10$ | 14 | | | |
| $1/5$ | 10 | 8 | 14 | 14 | 4 | 14 | 14 | 12 | $1/4$ | 14 | 14 | 7 | 4 | 4 | 14 | 14 | | | |

Coach __Clay_____    Date ___4-15_____

School __Indiana State_____    Sport __Tennis (varsity boys)_____

Comments ___10 min. — Rest — 10 min.; mid-season — day after match____

### Behavior Codes

| | | |
|---|---|---|
| 1. Use of First Name | 6. Physical Assistance | 11. Scold |
| 2. Preinstruction | 7. Positive Modeling | 12. Management |
| 3. Concurrent Instruction | 8. Negative Modeling | 13. Uncodable |
| 4. Postinstruction | 9. Hustle | 14. Silence |
| 5. Questioning | 10. Praise | |

nies. If the first name is coded with a 1 and a praise with a 10, then a 1/10 would be recorded in the appropriate cell.

Major patterns of behaviors can be derived from interval recording. The behaviors are entered into a matrix system, and a series of steps are followed to determine dominant patterns of behavior. It is beyond the scope of this textbook to detail this procedure, but the reader is referred to the guidelines of the Flanders Interaction Analysis System (Flanders, 1970) for specific information about this process.

Like event recording, a sampling technique can be used in interval recording. For example, interval recording techniques can be used four different times throughout the session, each five minutes in length. Using a six-second interval, this would yield 100 data points from various parts of the session. The selection of the five-minute segments should be carefully made so as not to create bias in the collected data and should be dispersed throughout the time period. Using segments only at certain parts of the session, e. g., at the start of class, could create bias in the collected data. The collected data should be representative of the instructor's behaviors throughout the entire class episode.

### Calculating the Percentage of Intervals

After data are collected on the interval coding sheet, the number of intervals each behavior has been coded is counted and this information is transferred to the interval worksheet (see Figure 10.4). The percentage of intervals should be calculated for each independent behavior category. The number of intervals coded for each individual behavior is divided by the total number of intervals. This number represents the percentage of intervals that each behavior was observed. Though it is not an exact measure, it gives a general idea of the time spent in each behavior category. Percentage of intervals accompanied by a first name can also be calculated.

## Duration Recording

Whereas interval recording reveals a general idea of time spent in certain behaviors and event recording yields data about the frequency of behaviors, **duration recording** gives exact information about the amount of time that a behavior takes. Time is the measure of the behavior of interest, and the raw data are expressed in terms of minutes and seconds. Exact time spent in activity, in management, or in instruction can be ascertained with duration recording. In certain instances, this type of systematic observation methodology is more appropriate than event or interval recording.

Suppose that a practitioner wants to know how much time is spent in management activities during a class session. The first step is to clearly define what constitutes management. Checking roll, organizing drills, and

▶ **FIGURE 10.4**    Interval recording worksheet.

| CATEGORIES | # OF INTERVALS | % OF INTERVALS |
|---|---|---|
| 1. Use of First Name | 18 | 7.5 |
| 2. Preinstruction | 11 | 4.6 |
| 3. Con. Instruction | 8 | 3.3 |
| 4. Postinstruction | 34 | 14.2 |
| 5. Questioning | 8 | 3.3 |
| 6. Physical Assistance | 4 | 1.7 |
| 7. Positive Modeling | 8 | 3.3 |
| 8. Negative Modeling | 2 | 0.8 |
| 9. Hustle | 8 | 3.3 |
| 10. Praise | 12 | 5.0 |
| 11. Scold | 8 | 3.3 |
| 12. Management | 19 | 7.9 |
| 13. Uncodable | 4 | 1.7 |
| 14. Silence | 114 | 47.5 |

TOTAL  240

transition time between activities are common examples of management time. The observer uses a stopwatch to time each managerial episode throughout the class session. At the end of a 40-minute class, duration recording might indicate that the teacher spent 12 minutes and 30 seconds of time in management behaviors. When first using duration recording, it may be easier to focus on only one behavior. The form shown in Figure 10.5 can be used identify and time a single behavior such as management. The same type of form could also focus on practice time or instructional time. This is valuable information with which to evaluate and make decisions about improving teacher performance.

Duration recording is also advantageous in measuring such things as instructional time and practice time. While event recording is better for

▲ **FIGURE 10.5**   Duration recording sheet for management time.

**MANAGEMENT TIME**

Instructor _____   Observer _____

Class _____ Grade _____   Date and time _____

Lesson focus _____   Comments _____

Starting time _____ End time _____   Length of lesson _____

|  |  |  |  |  |  |  |  |  |  |
|---|---|---|---|---|---|---|---|---|---|
|  |  |  |  |  |  |  |  |  |  |
|  |  |  |  |  |  |  |  |  |  |
|  |  |  |  |  |  |  |  |  |  |

Total management time _____

Percent of class time devoted to management _____

Number of episodes _____   Average length of episodes _____

From *Dynamic Physical Education for Secondary School Students*, 2d ed., by Pangrazi and Darst. Copyright © 1991 by Allyn and Bacon. Reprinted with permission.

behaviors of short duration, duration recording is best for behaviors that typically occur for longer periods of time. With event and interval recording, an observer can collect data on 12–15 behaviors at once. With duration recording, fewer behaviors are observed, but the data are more exact. After practicing duration recording with one behavior, an observer can use a time line (Figure 10.6) to record multiple behaviors. It is recommended that no more than three behaviors be targeted when using a time line. Typically, the behaviors would be management, instruction, and practice. This allows the teacher to examine the percentages of class time devoted to these activities and make changes as needed.

## Calculating Percentage of Total Time

The raw data collected in duration recording is the actual time spent in performing a certain behavior. To say that a teacher spent 12 minutes and 30 seconds in management time means little without knowing the length of observation time. The raw data can be converted into a percentage of time by dividing the time derived from the duration recording by the total observation time. Before this calculation is made, all times are changed into seconds. For example,

$$12 \text{ minutes and } 30 \text{ seconds } = 750 \text{ seconds}$$
$$40 \text{ minutes } = 2{,}400 \text{ seconds}$$

750 seconds of management divided by 2400 seconds of total time
= 31.25% of time spent in management

This conversion to percentage of time permits comparisons between other observations in different settings. Comparisons between classes of different lengths and different instructors can be made. Duration recording offers an excellent way to collect very specific data on behaviors that are essential to effective teaching.

# Group Time Sampling

**Group time sampling** is a method of systematic observation used to collect data on behaviors of all participants over a given time frame. It is similar to interval recording in that observations are made over a given time interval, but is different in that it focuses on the entire group rather than on an individual student. This procedure is sometimes referred to as a **placheck recording** (Planned Activity Check).

At given intervals interspersed throughout the observation session, the coder scans the participants to check how many students are exhibiting a particular behavior of interest. The scan should be done from left to right around the activity setting and can usually be done in about 10 seconds even with large groups. Once the scan observes a particular person, the

► **FIGURE 10.6** Duration recording timeline.

Class _____ Grade _____ Date _____

Lesson Focus _____

Comments _____

Length of Lesson _____

Key word or action used to start class and stopwatch _____

Record the word or action used to signal the beginning of the lesson and start the stopwatch. Keep the watch running continuously. Each time you direct the students in one of the following categories, draw a vertical line through the timeline and place the appropriate letter (I, P, M) above the marked section.

**I**  **Instruction Time:** The initial demonstrations, cues, and explanations that are necessary to get students started on an activity.

**P**  **Practice Time:** When students are working on specific skills during class time (i.e., warm up, fitness, rhythms, games).

**M**  **Management Time:** No instruction or practice takes place during management time. This time includes: giving information, disciplining the class, getting or returning equipment, and the time it takes students t follow those directions.

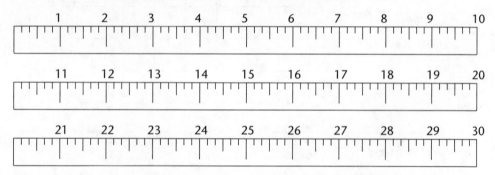

Totals and Percentages: Divide the number of seconds you spent in a category by the number of seconds in class. Multiply by 100 to find the percentage of time spent in each category.

1 = _____ / _____ %  P = _____ / _____ = _____ %  M = _____ / _____ = _____ %

observer should not go back if the behavior in question changes. Group time sampling focuses on behaviors that are characterized by such terms as "on-task/off-task," "appropriate/inappropriate," or "active/inactive" (see

▶ **FIGURE 10.7** Group time sampling recording sheet.

---

## PARTICIPANT PERFORMANCE

Instructor _____   Observer _____

Class _____ Grade _____   Date and time _____

Lesson focus _____   Comments _____

Starting time _____ End time _____   Length of lesson _____

Active/inactive

On task/off task

Effort/no effort

Number of Plachecks _____

Total number of participants in class _____

Average number of participants not on desired behavior _____

Percentage of participants not on desired behavior _____

---

Figure 10.7). The objective of this technique is to quickly observe each individual at a certain time and record the number of people engaged in the defined behavior. The behavior should be predefined in specific and observable terms to ensure accuracy of the recorded data.

The observer should know the total number of participants and should count either the number who are engaged in the productive behavior or the number who are not. It is easier to count the alternative to the defined behavior that the least number are exhibiting. To illustrate, assume that the number of participants who are inactive during an aerobics class is smaller than the number who are active. The number of inactive people can easily be subtracted from the total number in class to derive the number of students who are active.

It should take a maximum of 30 seconds to observe and record the data, and it often take only 10 seconds. The samples should be spaced throughout the lesson at given times. Normally, group time samples are done every three to five minutes. In a 40-minute class, a sample done every four minutes would yield 10 group time observations. If each sample is allotted 30 seconds, only five minutes of observation time would be used with this procedure. If each sample were done in 10 seconds, then only 1 minute and 40 seconds would be used. Even with the five-minute allotment, the time taken for observation is time used wisely to gain valuable information on the behaviors of a group.

Group time samples are normally used in conjunction with another systematic observation procedure. In the time between the samples, for instance, event or interval recording could be used to collect data on teacher behaviors. In this way, an observer would be collecting data on both teacher behavior and the behavior of the class.

## Calculating Percentages with Group Time Sampling

As with other techniques, it is advantageous to convert the raw data into a percentage. A percentage figure can be calculated for each group time sample. The number of persons engaged in the productive behavior is divided by the total number to derive this percentage. If 24 participants out of 30 are observed to be active during an observation, then

24 divided by 30 = 80%

This calculation shows that 80 percent of all participants were active. By converting data to percentages, classes of different sizes can be compared. By adding the percentages for all samples and dividing by the number of samples taken in a given observation, the mean percentage can be figured for all group time samples observed in that particular class. Group time sampling provides valuable input concerning behaviors of the entire class, which can contribute to a more complete evaluation of instructor performance.

# VALIDITY AND RELIABILITY
# OF SYSTEMATIC OBSERVATION

As with any data collection procedure, ensuring validity and reliability of the data is critical. Systematic observation instrumentation and data collection procedures must meet the recognized criteria for validity and reliability if the information derived from these processes is to be of any value in self-evaluation.

## Validity

As discussed in Chapter 4, validity is the ability to measure the attribute that an instrument is designed to measure. In the case of systematic observation instruments, a valid instrument would measure the instructor and/or participant behaviors that the instrument claims to measure. Validity of systematic observation instruments is established by meeting the criteria of content validity.

The behavior categories included in a chosen systematic observation technique should be representative of behaviors exhibited in the teaching–learning environment. Each category is specifically defined in measurable and observable terms. Whether a systematic observation system is simple or complex, it should satisfy the criteria for content validity.

## Reliability

Synonyms for reliability include consistency, repeatability, and precision. A systematic observation system should possess reliability so that confidence can be placed in the collected data. Following established guidelines helps to ensure reliability of data collection procedures. Clear and precise definitions of chosen behavior categories are also crucial. Usually, problems in establishing reliability in systematic observation can be traced to vague or unclear definitions of the behaviors being observed.

When systematic observation procedures are used to determine changes in behaviors, the data must be reliable to ensure that changes are not merely the result of inconsistent data collection by the observer. Confidence in the observations and the resultant evaluation is directly linked to the accuracy and objectivity of the observer.

**Interobserver agreement (IOA)** checks should be done periodically to ensure the reliability and objectivity of the instrument and coding procedures, as well as the accuracy of the trained observers. To complete an IOA check, two independent observers trained in the chosen observation method and thoroughly familiar with the definitions of the included categories observe the same lesson. Typically, a coworker working on self-evaluation with the practitioner can be used to complete IOA procedures. They should be situated far enough apart so that they cannot see how the other observer is coding, thus making them independent of each other. An IOA can be done in a field-based situation, from an audiotape if nonverbal behaviors are not being recorded, or from a VCR tape if both nonverbal and verbal behaviors are being coded.

According to Siedentop (1991), an IOA of 80 percent is necessary to establish reliability for research purposes. With a low number of observations (12 or fewer), 75 percent is sufficient. A slightly lower rate may be acceptable if the data collected are for feedback on which teachers can base improvement.

In general, the percentage of IOA is calculated using the following formula:

$$\frac{\text{Agreements}}{\text{Disagreements} + \text{Agreements}} \times 100 = \% \text{ of IOA}$$

This formula can be applied to calculate the percentage of IOA for event, interval, duration, and group time sampling recording procedures.

For event recording procedures, IOA should be calculated for each behavior category as well as for the total number of events tallied. For instance, suppose the number of praises occurring in a class period are recorded. One observer tallied 30 praises during the class, while the second observer recorded 34 praises. Thus, the two independent observers agreed on 30 praise behaviors and disagreed on 4. By using the formula above, the IOA is calculated as follows:

$$\frac{30}{30 + 4} \times 100 = \frac{30}{34} \times 100 = 88\% \text{ of IOA}$$

If one observer tallied a total of 200 behaviors and the other observed and coded 185, the IOA for all independent behaviors would be as follows:

$$\frac{185}{185 + 15} \times 100 = \frac{185}{200} \times 100 = 93\% \text{ of IOA}$$

If interval recording is the selected systematic observation method, the IOA is calculated in a similar way as in event recording, except that rather than looking at agreements and disagreements on separate events, the calculations are based on agreements and disagreements of how many intervals are coded for the defined behavior categories by the independent observers.

If a tape player is used to give auditory cues during the observation, an extra earphone may be spliced into the line with sufficient cord to allow the observers to be situated at least 10 feet apart. A second alternative is to copy the cassette tape being used and equip each observer with a cassette player and earphone.

If duration recording is used to time a behavior of interest, then the time each observer records for the chosen behavior becomes the variable on which to calculate IOA. Assume that two independent observers were timing managerial episodes for a particular class. One observer timed 7:20 while the other observer recorded 9:55 of management time. First, both times should be converted into seconds.

$$7:20 = 440 \text{ seconds}$$
$$9:55 = 595 \text{ seconds}$$

$$\frac{440}{595} \times 100 = 74\% \text{ of IOA}$$

The IOA of 74 percent is too low for any confidence to be put into the accuracy of recording. In a case like this, there is normally some misunder- standing of what constitutes management. A review of the definition and of coding procedures should improve the IOA on the next check. Because of the straightforward nature of duration recording, a high IOA (>90 percent) should be expected (minimum of 80 percent for other methods).

The accuracy of group time sampling should also be checked for IOA. A group time sample done every 4 minutes in a 40-minute class would yield 10 samples for the observation. Assume that there are 30 students in the class being checked for on-task/off-task behaviors. Table 10.0 shows the raw data recorded by the two independent observers for this class.

The number of students that each observer recorded as being on-task for the 10 samples is summed. Observer A counted a total of 197 students being on-task while Observer B recorded 203 students as on-task. IOA is then calculated as follows:

$$\frac{197}{197 + 6} \times 100 = \frac{197}{203} \times 100 = 97\% \text{ of IOA}$$

Whatever observation method is used, it is crucial that the IOA be calculated to ensure the accuracy of the recorded data. It is a waste of time and effort to collect data without being able to place confidence in the information gathered and the resultant self-evaluation. An advantage of these data collection methods is that they reduce the subjectivity of the observer. Reliability of a systematic observation system is established if the IOA is 80 percent or greater. If this is the case, then both the practitioner and the colleague have evidence as to the objectivity and accuracy of the data.

► **TABLE 10.0** Group time sample data for IOA.

| SAMPLE | OBSERVER A | OBSERVER B |
|--------|-----------|-----------|
| 1 | 17/30 | 19/30 |
| 2 | 21/30 | 19/30 |
| 3 | 24/30 | 24/30 |
| 4 | 15/30 | 14/30 |
| 5 | 19/30 | 21/30 |
| 6 | 21/30 | 21/30 |
| 7 | 16/30 | 18/30 |
| 8 | 23/30 | 24/30 |
| 9 | 23/30 | 24/30 |
| 10 | 18/30 | 19/30 |

# USING SYSTEMATIC OBSERVATION FOR SELF-EVALUATION

The process of systematic observation is not complex. Determining and properly defining the behavior categories is the most difficult task. A data collection procedure or combination of procedures must be chosen, and observers need to be trained to collect the data using the established definitions and procedures. Validity and reliability must be established for credibility of the evaluation plan. Once these things are done, the observers can concentrate on collecting data and adhering strictly to the behavior definitions. The raw data are then analyzed and appropriate calculations can be made for input into the final evaluation. The following discussion provides examples of behaviors that can be observed and the data collection procedures that can best be used. Keep in mind that the following represent some possibilities for the use of the previously discussed data collection procedures. It is not an exhaustive discussion. A systematic observation system should be designed specifically to meet the needs of a particular situation.

As discussed earlier in the chapter, the most useful type of evaluation for a practitioner is self-evaluation. By becoming directly involved with collecting their own personal behaviors, they become much more aware of the instruction process in their activity settings. Becoming more aware opens multiple possibilities for studying and modifying personal instructional behaviors in an attempt to increase the participants' enjoyment and achievement.

Effective instructors give participants time to learn by devoting a high percentage of time to the active practice of the skill being taught. Established routines and organizational structures lead to smooth transitions between activities and low rates of management. Effective practitioners actively teach and communicate clear expectations of performance. High rates of specific skill feedback are present, with student progress being monitored closely so that the task can be modified to fit individual needs. The effective teaching–learning environment will communicate warmth through clear, enthusiastic presentations.

Many behaviors occurring in physical education and exercise science settings are linked to these characteristics of effective teaching–learning environments. The following sections will present a variety of possibilities for practitioners for self-evaluation purposes. All present possibilities of collecting data on the current status of the behavior of interest, analyzing the data to determine how improvements can be made, and implementing new instructional strategies to change the behavior.

## Practice Time

For students to achieve in physical education, they must be on-task a high percentage of the time. For adults or children to improve their fitness, they must be actively engaged in fitness activities for an appropriate amount of time. **Practice time** refers to the time that participants are practicing skills in an environment that allows them to experience a reasonable amount of success. Generally, the higher the amount of practice time, the better chance participants have to achieve to their potential. Since a participant is in the activity setting a limited amount of time, it is important that time be used efficiently. Efficient use of time leads to more meaningful periods of physical activity.

To evaluate practice time, an effective method is duration recording. An observer (student, another teacher, administrator) watches the lesson and times the intervals when students practice skills. At the end of the lesson, a certain amount of time will have been spent in practice time. Frequency and length of time of practice episodes, total time of practice and percentage of practice time can be calculated from duration recording (see Figure 10.6).

Group time sampling can also yield information about practice time. An advantage of group time sampling is that it takes up very little of the total observation period. Event recording can also be utilized to count the number of skill attempts a selected student makes during the observation period. The disadvantage of these two methods is that the data collected are as specific as the information gathered from duration recording.

It should be the instructor's goal to increase the amount of time allowed to practice skills and participate in activity. Decreasing managerial episodes, limiting verbal instructions prior to activity, and creating lessons that encourage maximum participation are ways to increase practice time.

## Instructional Time

It is certainly appropriate that instructors spend some time instructing, whether by lectures, demonstrations, or corrective feedback. In this discussion, **instructional time** refers to explanations, demonstrations, and other information that refers to the content of the particular session. Generally, this type of instruction occurs prior to practice time and helps participants get started on the activity.

While this type of behavior is necessary and desirable, many lessons are plagued by too much instructor talk, which limits the amount of time for active student participation. Instructors must strive to give meaningful instructions in a succinct manner. The right blend of instructional time and practice time differs depending on the type of activity, the maturity and experience of the participants, and whether it is at the start, middle, or end of the unit. These variables must be considered when observing instructional time.

Duration recording can be used to record data on the amount of time spent on instruction. By using a stopwatch and recording the length of instructional episodes, an instructor can receive meaningful feedback about the number of instructional episodes, the average length, and the percent of class time devoted to instruction (see Figure 10.6). A general guideline to follow is to employ short instructional episodes frequently rather than to give lengthy instructions. Also, instructors should try not to exceed 45 seconds when giving instructions in physical education settings (Pangrazi and Darst, 1991).

## Management Time

The **management** behavior category was defined earlier in the chapter. It includes such things as transition time between drills as participants move into various formations, checking roll, any type of recordkeeping, distributing or taking up equipment, choosing teams, or suiting out for activity. Good instructors are highly organized and display efficient management behaviors. A well-planned schedule can help decrease the amount of time spent on management activities, thereby allowing more time for instruction and practice.

Some time must be spent on management, and it can be time well invested when it contributes to the organization of the class. Obviously, a large amount of management time would not contribute to effective teaching and would indicate that class procedures need to be streamlined and/or that participants are not responding quickly enough to managerial directions. By using duration recording procedures (see Figure 10.6), important information about the length of managerial episodes can be determined. A good goal for management time is that it should not exceed 15 percent of a particular class or exercise session.

If event or interval recording procedures are utilized to collect data on other behaviors, a management category may be included to code the observed management behaviors. Though the data will not be as specific as with duration recording, comparisons to other behavior categories are possible with either event or interval recording. Whatever observation method is used, management behaviors are a crucial aspect of effective instruction and should be carefully monitored and evaluated.

## Response Latency

**Response latency** is the time it takes participants to respond to a signal or direction to start or stop an activity (Pangrazi and Darst, 1991). By using duration recording techniques, the amount of time spent to start or stop an activity after a verbal command or signal can be documented. A decision must also be made as to what percentage of students must respond appropriately before stopping the time. Even a small percentage being off-task can lead to a loss of control, so it is recommended that if the criterion is not 100 percent, it should be very near this figure.

As shown in Figure 10.8 the average amount of response latency can be calculated so that the teacher can strive to improve student behavior in future observations. Response latency is wasted time, and class management techniques should be employed to minimize it.

## Instructor Movement

Another facet of teaching that can be examined with systematic observation is **instructor movement**—that is, how the instructor moves around the teaching area when giving individualized feedback to participants. Instructors often fall into the unfortunate habit of teaching from one area of the activity area. Students quickly notice where the instructor is located and position themselves according to their particular attitudes toward the instructor and the activity. If the teacher is relatively immobile, then contact with a great number of students is lost. Usually the students who need the most help and attention move away from the instructor. An excellent example of this phenomenon is typical in aerobic dance classes where the instructor teaches only from the front of the room.

This situation can be avoided if the instructor moves throughout the teaching area in an unpredictable manner. The movement by the teacher can be evaluated by dividing the activity area into quadrants and event-recording the number of moves from area to area. A move should only be tallied if the instructor interacts with a student or students in some way. Merely jogging through a quadrant should not be recorded as a move. Although

▶ **FIGURE 10.8** Duration recording sheet for response latency.

---

**RESPONSE LATENCY**

Instructor _____ Observer _____

Class _____ Grade _____ Date and time _____

Lesson focus _____ Comments _____

Starting time _____ End time _____ Length of lesson_____

---

Starting Response Latency

|  |  |  |  |  |  |  |
|---|---|---|---|---|---|---|
|  |  |  |  |  |  |  |
|  |  |  |  |  |  |  |
|  |  |  |  |  |  |  |

Stopping Response Latency

|  |  |  |  |  |  |  |
|---|---|---|---|---|---|---|
|  |  |  |  |  |  |  |
|  |  |  |  |  |  |  |
|  |  |  |  |  |  |  |

Total amount of starting response latency _____

Percent of class time devoted to starting response latency _____

Number of episodes _____ Average length of episode _____

Total amount of stopping response latency _____

Percent of class time devoted to starting response latency _____

Number of episodes _____ Average length of episode _____

---

From *Instructional Manual for Dynamic Physical Education for Secondary School Students,* 2d ed., by R. Pangrazi and P. Darst. Copyright © 1991 by Allyn and Bacon. Reprinted by permission.

active supervision is important, it is also crucial to consider position. The effective practitioner should teach from the perimeter of the activity area as much as possible. This means that the instructor has his "back against the wall" most of the time. Therefore, participants are not behind the instructor very often and, thus, can be monitored more effectively. Figure 10.9 offers an example of a simple positioning evaluation tool that can be easily used in all types of settings.

Another possibility for analyzing movement is to use duration recording to time the amount of time spent in each quadrant. The amount of time should ideally be relatively equal for each of the four areas. The type of activity occurring when the teacher moves to a different quadrant can also be recorded. Figure 10.9 illustrates a recording instrument that could be used for this technique. When participants are unable to predict where the instructor will be located, they are more likely to be active in appropriate activities. Thus, analyzing instructor movement and location can provide valuable data.

# Specific Instructional Behaviors

Specific instructional behaviors, such as praise, scold, use of first name, and various types of instruction, can be observed and coded by utilizing systematic observation procedures. Typically, event and interval recording procedures are implemented to collect this type of information. Data collection instruments can be designed to record behaviors of interest. With a little practice and precise definitions of behavior categories, an observer can easily record data on a dozen or more behaviors.

## Instructional Feedback

A large percentage of behaviors should be instructional in nature. Instructional feedback can take many forms, including nonverbal behaviors such as **positive** and **negative modeling**. Figure 10.10 shows an event recording form designed to code instructional feedback observed in a lesson. Note that ratios for certain types of feedback can be calculated. Totals for all behavior categories are divided by the total minutes of observations to figure the rate per minute (RPM).

Examples of general feedback are comments like "Nice shot" or "Good block," whereas specific feedback provides more information about the behavior such as "Great job of extending your arm on that shot" or "Billy, you really kept your feet moving on that block." By using first names, the instructor ensures more individualized attention and focuses the comments on the correct students. First name usage can easily be included in the observation data. Since both general and specific feedback can be either positive or negative, positive/negative feedback can also be recorded if desired.

► **FIGURE 10.9** Recording sheet for teacher movement.

---

**POSITION AND SUPERVISION EVALUATION FORM**

When evaluating yourself from tape, keep track of your position when giving instructions (I), management directions (M), and feedback (FB). Each time you are in a quadrant mark:

I—instructions      Ⓘ—instructions, with students behind you

M—management directions      Ⓜ—management directions, with students behind you

FB—feedback      <u>FB</u> —feedback to students in another quadrant

Instructor _____ Observer (if any) _____

Class _____ Grade _____ Date and time _____

Lesson_____

Starting time _____ End time _____ Length of lesson_____

| I | III |
|---|-----|
|   |     |
| II | IV |

Perimeter Instructions _____ Perimeter Directions _____

Circled I or M _____ Scans with Feedback (<u>FB</u>)_____

Quadrant Feedback (FB): I _____ II _____ III _____ IV _____ Total _____

Comments_____

_____

---

► **FIGURE 10.10** Event recording sheet for instructor behavior.

---

## INSTRUCTOR BEHAVIOR EVENT RECORDING

Instructor _____ Observer _____

Class _____ Grade _____ Date and time _____

Lesson focus _____ Comments _____

Starting time _____ End time _____ Length of lesson_____

| | | | | | | | Minutes | | | | | |
|---|---|---|---|---|---|---|---|---|---|---|---|---|
| | | 3 | 6 | 9 | 12 | 15 | 18 | 21 | 24 | 27 | 30 | Event Total |
| General instructional feedback | + | | | | | | | | | | | |
| | − | | | | | | | | | | | |
| Specific instructional feedback | + | | | | | | | | | | | |
| | − | | | | | | | | | | | |
| Corrective instructional feedback | | | | | | | | | | | | |
| First names | | | | | | | | | | | | |
| Nonverbal feedback | + | | | | | | | | | | | |
| | − | | | | | | | | | | | |

Ratio + to −: general instructional feedback _____

Ratio + to −: specific instructional feedback _____

Ratio + to −: nonverbal feedback _____

Ratio + to −: all instructional feedback (verbal and nonverbal) _____

---

From *Instructional Manual for Dynamic Physical Education for Secondary School Students,* 2d ed., by R. Pangrazi and P. Darst. Copyright © 1991 by Allyn and Bacon. Reprinted by permission.

Corrective instructional feedback is also specific by nature. The difference between specific and corrective feedback for the form in Figure 10.10 is that corrective feedback identifies what is incorrect about the skill attempt and also furnishes information about how the skill should be executed. An example would be, "John, you had your head down while you were dribbling. Try to dribble without looking at the ball so you can spot your open teammates." This is a very effective teaching behavior when done in a constructive way. Care should be taken not to comment on every mistake especially when the teacher feels that the student understands the source of the poor skill attempt. Specific feedback merely furnishes information about the skill attempt but includes no correction.

Nonverbal feedback on performance can also be coded. It is sometimes difficult for one person to code both verbal and nonverbal behavior categories. While momentarily recording a verbal behavior, the observer may miss a pat on the back, a frown, or some other nonverbal behavior. The use of videotape can remedy this situation since the tape can be stopped or replayed, or two observers can alleviate the problem in a live situation.

The importance of nonverbal behavior in activity settings should not be underestimated. People learn by mirroring the actions of the instructor much faster than by verbal explanation. Try teaching an aerobic dance routine without using nonverbal behaviors. Negative modeling is an excellent way to show mistakes made by participants when executing a skill. Good instructors depend on positive and negative modeling behaviors to communicate effectively with their students. Systematically observing and recording nonverbal behaviors provide added insight to the teaching–learning process.

## Praise and Scold

Another way to generate systematic information on positive and negative instructional behaviors is to tally the occurrences of praise and scold behaviors. It should be a goal of every professional to establish a positive climate. Every positive statement is coded as a praise, and every negative statement is coded as a scold. Using this information, self-evaluation of current behaviors can be made and goals for maintaining or increasing positive behaviors can be set.

Of course, instructors can go overboard with positive behavior. More is not always better. If a praise is used too much, positive comments will be taken for granted; consequently, the praise statements will lose their value. The same thing happens to the instructor who constantly corrects and nags students about their actions. The students soon tune out and ignore the comments. A general guideline in activity settings is to have a 4:1 ratio of praises to scolds.

◣ **FIGURE 10.11**   Event recording sheet for skill and behavior feedback.

| Feedback Statements | Skill Feedback | | Behavior Feedback | |
|---|---|---|---|---|
| | Positive | Corrective | Positive | Negative |
| Specific | | | | |
| General | | | | |
| Total | | | | |
| Rate per Minute | | | | |

Reprinted by permission of Mayfield Publishing Company from *Developing Teaching Skills in Physical Education*, 3d ed., by D. Siedentop. Copyright © 1991 by Mayfield Publishing Company.

### Behavior Feedback

The previous discussion focused on behaviors that are categorized as feedback to skill attempts. Not all feedback is in reaction to skill attempts. A great deal of feedback is in response to student behavior. Examples of this are such statements as "Super job getting into formation today" or "Nancy, stop hitting Doug." Behavior feedback can be classified in the same ways as skill feedback. Some coding forms allow both feedback to skill attempts and student behavior to be recorded on the same form. Figure 10.11 is an example of this type of form. Self-evaluation of behavior feedback is most appropriate in coaching and physical education settings.

## SELECTED INSTRUMENTS FOR SYSTEMATIC OBSERVATION

Many different systematic observation instruments have been designed and utilized in physical education and athletics. Most of these instruments can be modified to be used with other activity settings as well. An observation instrument should be designed to meet the needs of specific situations. There is no perfect systematic observation instrument. Any instrument will have positive and negative aspects. In considering self-evaluation, decisions about what should be included in the instrument being used must be made. Thought must be given to the behavior categories to be included, how the categories are to be defined, and what recording procedures are to be employed. Using self-evaluation allows the instructor to understand the evaluation procedures more clearly and be less threatened by the process.

Systematic observation instruments vary widely in their complexity. Generally, the more complex the instrument is, the more training is required to use it properly. However, if the instrument is complex, it should yield more sensitive information. An evaluation instrument must be chosen or designed to balance the need for detailed information about instruction with the need for an instrument that can be used in an accurate and reliable manner. Several different systematic observation instruments will be introduced in the following section. Each of the instruments can provide valuable data for evaluating teaching effectiveness, yet they vary in complexity. It is not within the scope of this chapter to give detailed descriptions of the instruments, but references given provide sources for further information. *Analyzing Physical Education and Sport Instruction* (Darst, Zakrajsek, and Mancini, 1989) catalogs over 30 different observational systems, and *Developing Teaching Skills in Physical Education* (Siedentop, 1991, Chapter 16) offers a thorough discussion of instruments for measuring instruction. The highlighting of several instruments in the next section should give the reader a clearer understanding of systematic observation and its many options for self-evaluation.

## All-Purpose Event-Recording Form (Instructor Behaviors)

Figure 10.12 provides a sample of a completed all-purpose event-recording form focusing on instructor reactions to student skill attempts and student behaviors. In nonschool settings, this type of instrument could be used with behavior definitions appropriate for the setting. Note that the observer can change the behavior categories by listing different definitions on the coding sheet. This form limits the observer to four behaviors of interest. Care must be taken to complete demographic data at the top of the sheet, particularly the length of observation. After the frequency of each behavior is totaled, the rate per minute can be calculated by dividing each total frequency by the total length of observation.

## All-Purpose Duration-Recording Form (Student Time Analysis)

When behaviors of interest can last for extended periods of time, the all-purpose duration recording form may be appropriate. Figure 10.13 shows a sample of a completed all-purpose duration recording form. The focus of this observation is analysis of how students are spending their time. Definitions of behaviors of interest are listed on the coding form. A time line is used for the duration recording of the specified behaviors. The time line is divided into 30 minutes, with each minute broken down into 10-second segments. When the behavior changes, the observer checks a stopwatch and

▶ **FIGURE 10.12**    All-purpose event-recording form (instructor behaviors).

Instructor: __Longlin__    Date: __3/9__    School: __Desert H.S__

Activity: __Track__    Time started: __9:05__    Time ended: __9:40__

Length of observation: __35__    Observer: __Cusimano__

Definitions:

1. __Providing exact commendatory information on performance (motor).__

2. __Words supporting students' motor response.__

3. __Providing commendatory statements on behavior, other than motor.__

4. __Teacher comment to terminate behavior.__

| 1  Pos. Skill Fb. (specific) | 2  Pos. Skill Fb. (General) | 3  Behavior Praise | 4  Desists |
|---|---|---|---|
| ЖҤ ЖҤ ЖҤ I | ЖҤ ЖҤ ЖҤ<br>ЖҤ ЖҤ ЖҤ<br>ЖҤ ЖҤ ЖҤ<br>ЖҤ ЖҤ III | ЖҤ II | ЖҤ ЖҤ ЖҤ<br>ЖҤ III |

Totals: __16__    __58__    __7__    __23__

Data Summary:

| Behaviors | Total frequency | Rate per minute |
|---|---|---|
| 1  Pos. skill Fb. (S) | 16 | .45 |
| 2  Pos. skill Fb. (G) | 58 | 1.65 |
| 3  Praise | 7 | .20 |
| 4  Desists | 23 | .65 |

*Comments:*

\* You seem more specific toward male students.

\* Let's work on behavior praise! (crucial this time of year)

\* Be firm when you desist!!

makes a vertical slash through the time line followed by the appropriate abbreviation. The decision of when the behavior changes is often based on what the majority of the class, or 51 percent, is doing. For instance, in the example depicted in Figure 10.13, students were engaged in management

▶ **FIGURE 10.13** All-purpose duration-recording form.

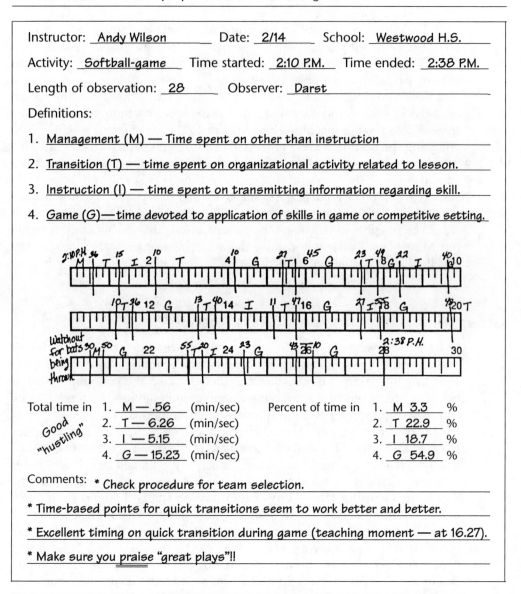

Instructor: __Andy Wilson__    Date: __2/14__    School: __Westwood H.S.__

Activity: __Softball-game__    Time started: __2:10 P.M.__    Time ended: __2:38 P.M.__

Length of observation: __28__    Observer: __Darst__

Definitions:

1. __Management (M) — Time spent on other than instruction__

2. __Transition (T) — time spent on organizational activity related to lesson.__

3. __Instruction (I) — time spent on transmitting information regarding skill.__

4. __Game (G)—time devoted to application of skills in game or competitive setting.__

Total time in   1. __M — .56__ (min/sec)    Percent of time in   1. __M 3.3__ %
*Good*              2. __T — 6.26__ (min/sec)                              2. __T 22.9__ %
*"hustling"*        3. __I — 5.15__ (min/sec)                              3. __I 18.7__ %
                    4. __G — 15.23__ (min/sec)                             4. __G 54.9__ %

Comments: * Check procedure for team selection.

* Time-based points for quick transitions seem to work better and better.

* Excellent timing on quick transition during game (teaching moment — at 16.27).

* Make sure you praise "great plays"!!

at the start of the class period for 36 seconds, were in transition until 1:15, received instruction until the 2:10 mark, and so on. The same procedure can be used with a targeted student rather than the whole class. Note that the observer can record the exact time of behavior change by writing the exact time directly above the slash mark. The total time for each behavior can be calculated from the time line and the percentage of time in each behavior can then be figured as well.

The all-purpose duration recording form can be adapted easily to non-school activity settings and can be used for fewer than four behaviors. If an exercise clinician were monitoring the workout of a cardiac rehabilitation patient performing aerobic activities on a variety of exercise machines, duration recording could be used to measure the amount of time spent engaged in exercise, in moving from one exercise machine to another (i.e., treadmill to rowing machine), and in adjusting each exercise machine (i.e., adjusting the seat on a cycle ergometer, setting speed on a treadmill). This information would provide objective feedback to the patient about the effectiveness of the workout. If too much time was spent in moving from station to station or adjusting machines, further observations would tell the clinician and the patient whether exercise times increased appropriately. It would be possible to videotape the patient, and let her do her own duration recording. This likely would raise the awareness of the patient and be an excellent educational experience.

## Group Time Sampling Form (Class Analysis)

In some situations, it is desirable to gather information about the activities of the entire class. As described earlier, an observer does group time sampling by making a quick scan of the activity area and counting the number of students who are displaying the defined behavior of interest. In the completed group time sampling form shown in Figure 10.14, several types of student behaviors are observed simultaneously. Appropriate behavior refers to students being on-task regardless of the context; the class could be involved in management, instruction, or activity. Engaged behavior denotes that the student is motor-engaged with the subject matter activity. **Academic Learning Time—Physical Education (ALT-PE)** refers to students being motor-engaged with the subject matter activity at a high success rate.

These categories are interconnected in that any given student would have to display "appropriate" behavior to be "engaged." Similarly, "engaged" behavior is a prerequisite of ALT-PE. The observations recorded in Figure 10.14 were made in a class of 30 students. Data were collected every 4 minutes during a 40-minute class, yielding 10 group samples. Across these 10 observations, 78 percent of the class was well-behaved

▶ **FIGURE 10.14** Group time sampling form.

| PARTICIPANT BEHAVIOR ANALYSIS | | | | | | | | | | | |
|---|---|---|---|---|---|---|---|---|---|---|---|
| Class: **5th Period Volleyball** | | Instructor: **Brown** | | | | | No. in Class: **30** | | | | |
| Start Time: **1:30** | End Time: **2:10** | | | Length of Observation: **40 minutes** | | | | | | | |
| Participant Behavior | Appropriate | 20 | 30 | 28 | 26 | 20 | 30 | 30 | 30 | 30 | 20 |
| | Engaged | 4 | 26 | 16 | 18 | 20 | 30 | 28 | 26 | 24 | 16 |
| | ALT-PE | 0 | 0 | 14 | 18 | 0 | 24 | 26 | 22 | 0 | 10 |

Appropriate = **78%**          Engaged = **69%**          ALT-PE = **38%**

Reprinted with permission of Mayfield Publishing Company from *Developing Teaching Skills in Physical Education*, 3d ed., by D. Siedentop. Copyright © 1991 by Mayfield Publishing Company.

(appropriate) and 69 percent was motor-engaged in subject matter activity (engaged), but only 38 percent was motor-engaged at high success rates (ALT-PE). This type of form would also be appropriate to use in adult fitness settings (i.e., aerobic dance class) to ascertain general activity trends of the group.

## General Supervision Instrument

Some systematic observation instruments combine several types of coding to produce a more complete view of the behaviors in a physical education class or nonschool activity setting. Figure 10.15 shows an instrument that has been used to evaluate student teachers. This system uses event recording to code skill feedback statements and reactions to student behaviors. A group time sample is taken every three minutes to measure the number of students behaving appropriately and the number of students engaged in ALT-PE. A time line is included for duration recording of how much class time is spent in management, instruction, and activity. With practice, a single observer can collect data using all three types of observation techniques. Thus, data are collected on both teacher and student behaviors with the same instrument. The data can be quickly quantified and analyzed using the summary statistics on the form, and the information then immediately shared with the teacher to help evaluate the effectiveness of the lesson and to set behavioral goals for future teaching episodes.

▶ **FIGURE 10.15**   A general supervision instrument.

**Record of Time Allotment in Class, Behavioral Interactions, and Skill Feedback Statements**

Observer_____Date_____School_____Grade_____Environment:

Time Started_____ Time Finished_____Total Minutes Observed_____ Experimental_____

Number of Students in Class_____Activity_____Student Teacher_____Generalization _____

(Time Analysis Codes: I = Instruction; A = Activity; M = Management)

| Time Analysis | | Skill Feedback Statement | | | | | |
|---|---|---|---|---|---|---|---|
| Total Management Time ____ | | Positive | | Corrective | | Negative | |
| % Management Time ____ | | General | Specific | General | Specific | General | Specific |
| Total Instructional Time ____ | | | | | | | |
| % Instructional Time ____ | | | | | | | |
| Total Activity Time ____ | | | | | | | |
| % Activity Time ____ | | | | | | | |
| | Total | | | | | | |
| | Rate P/M | | | | | | |

| Group Time Sample Analysis | | Behavioral Interactions | | | |
|---|---|---|---|---|---|
| | | Positive | | Negative | |
| % Appropriate Behavior _____ | | General | Specific | General | Specific |
| % ALT-PE _____ | | | | | |
| | Total | | | | |
| | Rate P/M | | | | |

# System for Observing Fitness Instruction Time (SOFIT)

The **System for Observing Fitness Instruction Time (SOFIT)** is designed to assess variables associated with students' activity levels and opportunities to become physically fit (McKenzie, Sallis, & Nader, 1991). While designed for school settings, the instrument could be easily modified to observe activity levels in virtually any setting (i.e. aerobic dance at a health club, cardiac rehabilitation exercise session, weight training in an off-season athletic workout). SOFIT allows an observer to simultaneously record student activity levels, curriculum context variables, and teacher behaviors. With development and maintenance of physical fitness being a major objective in most physical education programs and many clinical exercise programs, this instrument can be particularly useful for instructors to use to check the activity levels of their students/clients. Many practitioners will be surprised at the low levels of activity that participants exhibit. It is also an interesting instrument to use to code activity levels of students during recess to illustrate the need for structured physical education classes.

This system uses interval recording. A targeted student is observed for 10 seconds and then 10 seconds is allowed for coding. While learning to use the instrument, it is recommended that initially a longer time period be allowed for coding (perhaps 20 seconds), while the time gradually shortened to 10 seconds.

SOFIT is a three-phase decision system as shown in Figure 10.16. Phase 1 is coding the activity level of the preselected student to provide an estimate of the intensity of the child's physical activity. Codes 1-4 (lying down, sitting, standing, walking) describe the body position of the child and code 5 (very active) is used when the child is expending more energy than he or she would during ordinary walking. When the student exhibits two or more of these categories during the 10-second observation, code the higher category. The coder must make one of five choices regarding the activity level of the student and move to Phase 2. If desired, only Phase 1 can be used for coding, with Phases 2 and 3 being eliminated. However, if the instrument is so modified, the time allocated for coding decisions should be reduced. It should also be noted that much valuable information is being lost if only Phase 1 coding is completed.

Phase 2 concerns the context of the lesson. For each 10-second observation, a decision is made whether class time is being used for general content (M) such as managerial activities (checking roll, choosing teams, organizing the class, etc.) or for actual subject matter content. If class time is being used for physical education knowledge content, then it can be coded as general knowledge (K), physical fitness knowledge (P). If the subject being observed is motor active in physical education content, then it should be coded as fitness (F), skill practice (S), game play (G), or other (O). After making a coding decision in Phase 2, the coder moves to Phase 3.

Phase 3 codes teacher behaviors. The first behavior category, promotes fitness (P), is directly related to student involvement in fitness activities and

▶ **FIGURE 10.16**    Coding Phases of the SOFIT Instrument

Phase 1. **Student activity** decision.
What is the physical nature of an individual learner's engagement? What is his/her activity level?

Choices:

1. lying down          3. standing          5. very active
2. sitting             4. walking

Phase 2. **Lesson context level** decision.
What is the general context of the lesson? How is time allocated for the class as a whole (at least 51% of the students)?

Choices:

| General content (M) | Knowlege content | Motor content |
|---|---|---|
| trasition | physical fitness (P) | fitness (F) |
| management | general knowledge (K) | skill practice (S) |
| break | rules, strategy | game play (G) |
| | social behavior | other (O) |
| | technique | |

Phase 3. **Teacher involvement** decision.
What is the teacher doing?

Choices:

(P).   promotes fitness (prompts, encourages, praises, etc.)
(D).   demonstrates fitness (models)
(I).   instructs generally
(M).   manages
(O).   observes
(T).   off-task

**SAMPLE CODING SHEET**

| Interval | Student Activity | Lesson Context | Teacher Behavior |
|---|---|---|---|
| 1 | 1 2 3 4 5 | M K P F S G O | P D I M O T |
| 2 | 1 2 3 4 5 | M K P F S G O | P D I M O T |

From F. L. McKenzie, J. F. Sallis & P. R. Nader, "SOFIT: System for Obsessing Fitness Instruction Time," *Journal of Teaching in Physical Education, vol. 11*, no. 2 (January 1992): 204.

is coded when the teacher prompts or encourages learners for physical fitness engagement. The second category, demonstrates fitness (D), identifies when the teacher models fitness engagement. The four remaining categories instructs generally (I), manages (M), observes (O), and off task (T), are only indirectly related to student fitness opportunities but provide important information on how a teacher spends his or her time.

A sample coding sheet is shown at the bottom of Figure 10.16. This sample shows only two intervals, while a sheet used for actual data collection would include as many intervals as would conveniently fit on the page. When using this instrument, it is recommended that three students be targeted for observation: simply watch student A in the first interval, student B during the second interval, and student C in the third interval, then continue the rotation throughout the observation. The appropriate coding decisions can be circled on the coding sheet. More information on this instrument, which can be used with live observation or videotapes, is available from Dr. Thom McKenzie, Department of Physical Education, San Diego State University.

## Arizona State University Observation Instrument (ASUOI)

The **ASUOI** (Lacy and Darst, 1989) is a systematic observation instrument that can be used to collect behavioral data on coaches, physical educators, or exercise science practitioners. It employs 13 behavior categories that can be used with event-recording procedures. When interval recording is used, the silence category is added. The behavioral categories are shown in Figure 10.17.

▶ **FIGURE 10.17** ASUOI behavior categories.

1. **Use of First Name:** Using the first name or nickname when speaking directly to a student.
2. **Pre-instruction:** Initial information given to the student/s preceding the desired action to be executed that explains how to execute a skill, strategy, etc., associated with the activity.
3. **Concurrent instruction:** Cues or reminders given during the actual execution of the skill, strategy, etc., associated with the activity.
4. **Post-instruction:** Correction, re-explanation, or instructional feedback given after the execution of the skill, strategy, etc., associated with the activity.
5. **Questioning:** Any question to the student/s concerning strategies, techniques, etc., associated with the activity.
6. **Physical Assistance:** Physically moving the student to proper position or through the correct range of motion of a skill.
7. **Positive Modeling:** A demonstration of correct performance of a skill or playing technique.
8. **Negative Modeling:** A demonstration of incorrect performance of a skill or playing technique.
9. **Hustle:** Verbal statements intended to intensify the efforts of the student/s.
10. **Praise:** Verbal or nonverbal compliments, statements, or signs of acceptance.
11. **Scold:** Verbal or nonverbal behaviors of displeasure.
12. **Management:** Verbal statements related to organizational details of practice sessions not referring to strategies or fundamentals of the activity.
13. **Uncodable:** Any behavior that cannot be seen or heard, or does not fit into the above categories.
14. **Silence:** (Used only with interval recording.) Periods of time when the teacher/ coach is not talking or modeling, often while monitoring the activity.

Based on the premise that behaviors of an instructional nature are critical to effective teaching, categories 2–8 are different types of behaviors involved with instruction. This allows an observer to evaluate instructional behaviors in a more sensitive manner. Certainly, the categories could be modified to meet the needs of a particular situation.

Though interval recording may be used with the ASUOI, event recording requires less practice to become a reliable coder. The observer tallies the behaviors on a coding sheet as the lesson is being watched. Figure 10.2 shows an example of an event recording tally sheet. Although the ASUOI is designed to concentrate on the behaviors of the teacher, it may be advantageous to combine it with a placheck recording or some other systematic way of gathering information about student behavior to accompany the information collected on the teacher.

It should be noted that the use-of-first name category is treated as a dependent category because it never occurs by itself, but always accompanies another behavior. All other behaviors are independent categories. For this reason, the totals in Figure 10.2 reflect the total of independent categories. The resulting percentages are calculated by dividing the total of the behavior category by the total of independent behaviors coded. The total number of first names coded are also divided by the total of independent behaviors to calculate the number of independent behaviors that were accompanied by a first name.

The ASUOI is a relatively easy instrument to use. Observers can be easily trained to record teacher behaviors accurately. The instrument can be used in conjunction with videotapes or can be used for field-based coding. More information on the ASUOI is provided in the book *Analyzing Physical Education and Sport Instruction* (Darst, Zakrajsek, and Mancini, 1989).

## Academic Learning Time-Physical Education (ALT-PE)

The **ALT-PE** instrument is based in great part on the results of the Beginning Teacher Evaluation Study (BTES) (Fisher et al., 1980). This extensive study focused on student contact with appropriate curricular materials in the classroom. In this research, Academic Learning Time (ALT) was defined as the portion of engaged time when the student was involved with materials appropriate to his or her abilities. This variable used in the BTES research proved to be a positive predictor of student achievement. With this in mind, the ALT-PE instrument was designed to collect data in physical education settings. The ALT-PE instrument was first introduced by Siedentop, Birdwell, and Metzler (1979) and has been used in a variety of physical education settings (Dodds and Rife, 1983). Student achievement is undoubtedly related to teaching behaviors in physical education. Because ALT provides a measurable criterion strongly associated with student achievement, it offers a way for examining teacher effectiveness in physical education.

The ALT-PE system requires the evaluator to make a two-level decision when observing. First, the evaluator codes the context of the setting under observation. There are 13 context-level categories divided under the "general content" and "subject matter content" headings (see Figure 10.18). This first-level context decision is made by observing the class as a whole. The second decision involves observing the learner involvement of individual students. There are 8 learner involvement categories divided under "not motor engaged" and "motor engaged" headings (see Figure 10.18). The term "motor" refers to motor involvement with the subject matter activities related

▶ **FIGURE 10.18** Academic learning time—physical education category definitions.

## CONTEXT LEVEL

The first level of decision making focuses on the class as a whole (or a subset of the class) and is designed to describe the context within which student behavior is occurring. There are three major subdivisions at the context level. They are:

**General Content** refers to class time when students are not intended to be involved in physical education activities.

**SM Knowledge Content** refers to class time when the primary focus is on knowledge related to physical education content.

**SM Motor Content** refers to class time when the primary focus is on motor involvement in physical education activities.

Each of the three main subdivisions at the context level has categories that describe more specifically the nature of the setting within which individual student behavior is occurring. These categories are defined as follows:

### General Content Categories

**Transition**
Time devoted to managerial and organizational activities related to instruction such as team selection, changing equipment, moving from one space to another, changing stations, teacher explanation of an organizational arrangement, and changing activities within a lesson.

**Management**
Time devoted to class business that is unrelated to instructional activity such as taking attendance, discussing a field trip, lecturing about appropriate behavior in the gymnasium, or collecting money for the yearbook.

**Break**
Time devoted to rest and/or discussion of nonsubject matter-related issues such as getting a drink of water, talking about last night's ball game, telling jokes, celebrating the birthday of a class member, or discussing the results of a student election.

**Warm-Up**
Time devoted to routine execution of physical activities whose purpose is to prepare the individual for engaging in further activity, but not designed to alter the state of the individual on a long-term basis, such as a period of light exercises to begin a class, stretching exercises prior to a lesson, or a cooling down activity to terminate a lesson.

*(continued)*

## Subject Matter Knowledge Categories

### Technique
Time devoted to transmitting information concerning the physical form (topography) of a motor skill such as listening to a lecture, watching a demonstration, or watching a film.

### Strategy
Time devoted to transmitting information concerning plans of action for performing either individually or as a group such as explanation of a zone defense, demonstration of an individual move, or discussion of how best to move the ball down a field.

### Rules
Time devoted to transmitting information about regulations that govern activity related to the subject matter such as explanation of the rules of a game, demonstration of a specific rule violation, or viewing a film depicting the rules of volleyball. (Time devoted to transmitting information about rules governing general student behavior in physical education is coded management.)

### Social Behavior
Time devoted to transmitting information about appropriate and inappropriate ways of behaving within the context of the activity such as explanation of what constitutes sportsmanship in soccer, discussion of the ethics of reporting one's own violations in a game, or explanations of proper ways to respond to officials in a game.

### Background
Time devoted to transmitting information about a subject matter activity such as its history, traditions, rituals, heroes, heroines, records, importance in later life, or relationship to fitness.

## Subject Matter Motor Categories

### Skill Practice
Time devoted to practice of skills or chains of skills outside the applied context with the primary goal of skill development, such as a circle drill in passing a volleyball, one-against-one practice of dribbling a basketball, exploration of movement forms, practicing a dance step, or practicing a particular skill on a balance beam.

### Scrimmage/Routine
Time devoted to refinement and extension of skills in an applied setting (in a setting that is like or simulates the setting in which the skill is actually used) and during which there is frequent instruction and feedback for the participants—such as a half court five-on-five basketball activity, the practice of a complete free exercise routine, or six-against-six volleyball (all with instruction, suggestions, and feedback during the scrimmage).

### Game
Time devoted to the application of skills in a game or competitive setting when the participants perform without intervention from the instructor/coach—such as a volleyball game, a complete balance beam routine, the performance of a folk dance, or running a half-mile race.

### Fitness
Time devoted to activities whose major purpose is to alter the physical state of the individual in terms of strength, cardiovascular endurance, or flexibility such as aerobic dance, distance running, weight lifting, or agility training (the activities should be of sufficient intensity, frequency, and duration so as to alter the state of the individual).

(continued)

▶ **FIGURE 10.18**   Continued.

## LEARNER INVOLVEMENT LEVEL

The second level of decision making focuses on the individual learner(s) and is designed to describe the nature of the learner(s) involvement in a more specific way. There are two major subdivisions at the learner involvement level—not motor engaged and motor engaged.

**Not Motor Engaged** refers to all involvement other than motor involvement with subject matter-oriented motor activities.

**Motor Engaged** refers to motor involvement with subject matter-oriented motor activities.

Each of the two main subdivisions at the learner involvement level has categories that describe more specifically the nature of the learner's involvement. These categories are defined as follows:

### Not Motor Engaged Categories

**Interim**
The student is engaged in a noninstructional aspect of an ongoing activity such as retrieving balls, fixing equipment, retrieving arrows, or changing sides of a court in a tennis match.

**Waiting**
The student has completed a task and is awaiting the next instructions or opportunity to respond such as waiting in line for a turn, having arrived at an assigned space waiting for the next teacher direction, standing on a sideline waiting to get in a game, or having organized into the appropriate formation waiting for an activity to begin.

**Off-Task**
The student is either not engaged in an activity he/she should be engaged in or is engaged in activity other than the one he/she should be engaged in—behavior disruptions, misbehavior, and general off-task behavior, such as talking when a teacher is explaining a skill, misusing equipment, fooling around, fighting, disrupting a drill through inappropriate behavior.

**On-Task**
The student is appropriately engaged carrying out an assigned nonsubject matter task (a management task, a transition task, a warm-up task) such as moving into squads, helping to place equipment, cooling off, doing warm-up exercises, or moving from the gym to a playing field.

**Cognitive**
The student is appropriately involved in a cognitive task such as listening to a teacher describe a game, listening to verbal instructions about how to organize, watching a demonstration, participating in a discussion, or watching a film.

### Motor Engaged Categories

**Motor Appropriate**
The student is engaged in subject matter motor activity in such a way as to produce a high degree of success.

**Motor Inappropriate**
The student is engaged in a subject matter motor activity, but the activity task is either too difficult for the individual's capabilities or the task is so easy that practicing it could not contribute to lesson goals.

**Supporting**
The student is engaged in subject matter motor activity, the purpose of which is to assist others to learn or perform the activity such as spotting in gymnastics, feeding balls to a hitter in a tennis lesson, throwing a volleyball to a partner who is practicing set up passing, or clapping a rhythm for a group of students who are practicing a movement pattern.

Reprinted by permission of D. Siedentop and others, Ohio State University, Columbus, Ohio.

to the goals of the setting. Thus, the observer first codes the context of the class and then codes learner involvement of individual students in the class.

If a general content or subject matter knowledge category is coded at the context level, the learner involvement decision is chosen from the "not motor engaged" group. If a subject matter motor category is chosen at the first level, then the second-level decision can involve any of the learner involvement categories. Any observation in which the "motor appropriate" category is chosen for the learner involvement decision becomes one unit of ALT-PE.

Several systematic observation recording procedures can be used in conjunction with the ALT-PE instrument, including interval recording, group time sampling, and duration recording. Using the ALT-PE system properly requires more extensive training and practice than other instruments presented in this chapter. However, the information derived from the instrument is an important part of evaluating teacher effectiveness, and this instrument has been used extensively in pedagogical research. The historical development of ALT-PE, detailed descriptions of how to use the instrument, and a suggested series of sequential training tasks are included in an ALT-PE coding manual (Siedentop, Tousignant, and Parker, 1982) available from the School of Health, Physical Education, and Recreation at The Ohio State University.

## SUMMARY

In the wide range of activity settings in school and nonschool settings, instruction about exercise and activity is a crucial component of any type of program. There are many different methods and systems to provide evaluation of instruction. While evaluation by a school administrator or work supervisor is a necessary and sometimes valuable form of evaluation of instructional effectiveness, this chapter advocates self-evaluation as the best way to improve instruction in all types of activity settings. The best way to conduct this self-evaluation is dependent on the particular setting and on what aspect of instruction is being examined.

The development of systematic observation instrumentation over the past 25 years provides solutions to many methodological problems associated with evaluation of instruction. These observation tools range from simple to complex and can accurately measure many facets of behaviors in activity environments. The use of event, interval, duration, and group time sampling recording offer many options for instructor evaluation. Regardless of the procedure or combination of procedures used, it is essential that the accuracy and objectivity of the data be established by calculating the percentage of interobserver agreement (IOA).

Properly used, systematic observation methods provide feedback that can be used to improve instructional effectiveness. As with any measurement and evaluation procedure, the data collection must be done properly to ensure valid data. It is hoped that more practitioners in all activity settings will realize the weaknesses of traditional methods and the advantages of systematic observation in the measurement and self-evaluation of instructional effectiveness.

## ► DISCUSSION QUESTIONS

1. List four traditional evaluation methods of instructional effectiveness. In terms of measurement and evaluation theory, what weaknesses do these methods have in common?

2. Describe four systematic observation methods that can be used for self-evaluation of instructional effectiveness. Compare and contrast the advantages and disadvantages of these methods.

3. What is interobserver agreement (IOA)? Explain the importance of establishing an IOA when using systematic observation procedures.

4. What type of instructor behaviors can be measured and evaluated with systematic observation methods? Which are most important? Why?

5. What type of participant behaviors can be measured and evaluated with systematic observation methods? Which are most important? Why?

6. What issues must be resolved when a self-evaluation plan is being formulated in regard to instructional effectiveness? If you were designing a self-evaluation, what procedures would you consider the best?

## ► REFERENCES

Darst, P.; Zakrajsek, D.; and Mancini, V., eds. (1989). *Analyzing physical education and sport instruction.* 2d ed. Champaign, IL: Human Kinetics Publishers.

Dodds, P., and Rife, F., eds. (1983). Time to learn in physical education. *Journal of Teaching in Physical Education,* Monograph 1, Summer.

Fisher, C.; Berliner, D.; Filby, N.; Marliave, R.; Cahen, L.; and Dishaw, M. (1980). Teaching behaviors, academic learning time, and student achievement: An overview. In C. Denham and A. Lieberman, eds. *Time to learn.* (pp. 7–32). Washington, DC: National Institute of Education.

Flanders, N. A. (1970). *Analyzing teacher behavior.* Reading, MA: Addison-Wesley.

Lacy, A., and Darst, P. (1989). The Arizona State University observation instrument. In P. Darst; D. Zakrajsek; and V. Mancini, eds. *Analyzing physical education and sport instruction.* 2d ed. Champaign, IL: Human Kinetics Publishers.

McKenzie, T. L., Sallis, J. F., and Nader, P. R. (1991). SOFIT: System for Observing Fitness Instruction Time. *Journal of Teaching in Physical Education.* 11, 195–205.

Pangrazi, R., and Darst, P. (1991). *Dynamic physical education for secondary school students: Curriculum and instruction.* 2d ed. New York: Macmillan Publishing Com-pany.

Rink, J. E. (1993). *Teaching Physical Education for Learning.* 2nd edition. St. Louis: Mosby Publishers.

Siedentop, D. (1991). *Developing teaching skills in physical education.* 3d ed. Palo Alto, CA: Mayfield Publishing Company.

Siedentop, D.; Birdwell, D.; and Metzler, M. (1979). *A process approach to measuring teaching effectiveness in physical education.* Paper presented at the National Convention and Symposium of the American Alliance of Health, Physical Education, Recreation, and Dance, March, New Orleans, LA.

Siedentop, D.; Tousignant, M.; and Parker, M. (1982). *Academic learning time = physical education: 1982 revision coding manual.* Unpublished manual, The Ohio State University, School of Health, Physical Education, and Recreation, Columbus.

van der Mars, H. (1989). Basic recording tactics. In P. Darst; D. Zakrajsek; and V. Mancini, eds. *Analyzing physical education and sport instruction.* 2d ed. Champaign, IL: Human Kinetics Publishers.

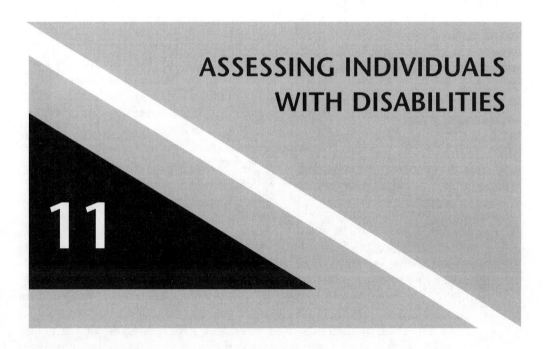

# ASSESSING INDIVIDUALS WITH DISABILITIES

## 11

▶ **KEY TERMS**

adapted or special physical
  education teacher
auditory impairments
inclusion
Individualized Education
  Program (IEP)
long-term or annual goals
mainstreaming
mental retardation
physical disability
present level of performance
short-term instructional
  objective
state education department
  guidelines
transition services
visual impairments

▶ **OBJECTIVES**

*After reading this chapter, the student should be able to:*

1. Describe the roles and responsibilities of physical education teachers for testing and evaluating students with disabilities.
2. Compare the similarities and differences of testing procedures for students with and without disabilities.
3. Analyze administrative concerns and suggested solutions associated with testing students with disabilities.
4. Identify, locate, and administer tests for students with mental, sensory, and/or physical impairments.
5. Discuss characteristics associated with test items used to measure stages of motor development.
6. Identify and contrast the required components of an Individualized Education Program (IEP).
7. Synthesize measurement information into written present level of education performance statements.
8. Write long-term or annual goals and short-term instructional objectives for an IEP.

433

This chapter focuses on students with disabilities, a significant segment of the school population that is often improperly tested or not tested in K-12 physical education programs (Cooper Institute for Aerobics Research, 1994). Such oversight is alarming, since students with disabilities constitute as much as 12 to 15 percent of all school-aged children (Sherrill, 1993). The situation is even more surprising given the fact that physical education, specially designed or adapted if necessary, is required by federal law, which all states and public school districts must comply with, for all eligible students with disabilities. Furthermore, proper assessment or testing procedures are required under this mandated physical education (Dunn & Fait, 1989; Wisconsin Department of Public Instruction, 1988).

Providing quality physical education services for students with disabilities should not be justified solely on the basis of fulfilling a legal mandate, however. Students with disabilities have physical education needs no different from those of their nondisabled peers, and these needs must be met through the same provision of appropriately planned, implemented, and evaluated programs (National Association for Sport & Physical Education, 1995). Obviously, there will be times when the equipment, activities, or methods used to achieve program goals, or the goals themselves, should be modified for specific students. Knowledge of proper techniques and strategies for measurement and evaluation is an important basis for achieving appropriate programming (Fisher, 1988).

Many terms are used by educators, parents, and the general public to describe students with disabilities. Included are words such as *impaired, disabled, handicapped, exceptional, special,* and *unique.* Each of these terms has a meaning that is determined by the knowledge and experiences of the user. However, whatever term is used, the identity of the person should not be hidden in the descriptor. The person should always be described first (i.e., a person with a disability, a student with a unique educational need, or a child with a hearing impairment). This shifts the focus from the disability to the person as a individual with unique physical education interests and needs.

The phrase *students with disabilities* will be used most often in this chapter. This usage is also the most current educational law terminology (U. S. Department of Education, 1992), and is cited as proper usage by professional groups advocating for persons with disabilities. Additional terms such as *impairment* and *condition* will be used in certain instances to provide information that is more specific. Readers must remember that terms used have specific meaning for each student. All students, with or without disabilities, have individual characteristics, abilities, and needs that must be understood and taken into account by teachers when planning physical education experiences.

This chapter is designed for regular physical education teachers responsible for K-12 students with disabilities who are appropriately **mainstreamed** for **inclusion** into their classes (persons interested in physical activity programming for adults with disabilities should consult Lasko-McCarthey and Knopf, 1992; Rimmer, 1994; and Shepard, 1990. This chapter is introductory in nature, and it is recognized that regular physical education teachers may at times need the assistance of an adapted or special physical education teacher. Consulting with an adapted physical education specialist is helpful when the severity and nature of a student's disabilities prevent safe and successful participation in all regular physical education instruction.

Recognition of when and where to seek assessment and programming assistance regarding students with disabilities is important. Regular physical education teachers should remember that persons with expertise in adapted physical education are often available from local special education service centers or programs. Many school districts and/or regional special education programs have adapted specialists on staff for the purposes of providing consultation and/or direct teaching services. Physical educators should never isolate themselves in the gymnasium. Contact and communication with professionals in other disciplines should be a routine activity for all regular teachers, including those in physical education (Lavay, 1988).

The use of testing or assessment for placement decisions is common when working with students who have special or adapted physical education needs. Persons interested in more detailed information about adapted physical education assessment and programming should refer to comprehensive and specialized resources such as texts by Auxter, Pyfer, and Heuttig (1993), Jansma and French (1994), Kelly (1995), Eichstaedt and Kalakian (1993), Sherrill, (1993), Seaman and DePauw (1989), Werder and Kalakian (1985), Wessel and Kelly (1986) and Winnick (1995). It is also recommended that persons responsible for testing many students with disabilities enroll in courses that will provide the skills and knowledge necessary to appropriately work in this specialized area.

The content in this chapter is divided into four sections. The first explains how the curriculum development model presented in Chapter 2 relates to all students, including those with disabilities. The second deals with factors that should be considered when testing students with disabilities. These considerations are included to provide physical educators with guidelines when testing and should be viewed as supplemental to the administrative strategies presented in Chapter 4.

The third section describes features of several tests commonly used with special populations in regular physical education classes and includes valuable practical tips not usually found in the original sources. The final section ties the first three sections together and presents information on how measurement and evaluation data are used to develop long-term or annual goals and short-term instructional objectives for inclusion on a special education student's required Individualized Education Program (IEP).

# LINKING CURRICULUM DEVELOPMENT AND MEASUREMENT OF STUDENTS WITH DISABILITIES

Chapter 2 presented a model containing the phases or steps necessary for quality physical education program development. Phases discussed were (1) establishing a realistic philosophical approach; (2) developing program goals; (3) determining unit outcomes; (4) establishing performance outcomes; and, (5) evaluating and improving the curriculum. Many implications exist for each of these phases related to providing quality physical education instruction for students with disabilities. The following section presents information that links curriculum development to measuring or assessing students with disabilities.

## Phase 1: Establishing a Realistic Philosophical Approach

As mentioned in Chapter 2, accommodating students with special needs in physical education is an important belief and philosophical basis for curriculum development. Given this approach, it becomes important for physical educators to be aware of specific implications regarding all students. All students, including those with disabilities, benefit from and should be included in all aspects of physical education (Block, 1994). Teachers must embrace this philosophy of inclusion when planning and implementing measurement techniques such as devising student interest surveys, considering characteristics and needs of students, and designing program continuity. Additional information should be attained from parents and other teachers of students with disabilities. Parents can assist physical educators to establish realistic and meaningful approaches to instruction and program planning. Physical educators also need to include special education teachers and related service personnel (i.e., physical, occupational, and recreational therapists) when designing a philosophical approach that includes students with disabilities. All of these school professionals work with students on a daily basis and can provide valuable information regarding appropriate physical education. Of course, the students themselves should also be part of this planning stage. These steps insure appropriate inclusion and integration of students with disabilities. This advocacy is a responsibility of every regular physical education teacher.

## Phase 2: Developing Attainable Program Goals

Global physical education program goals guide the development of instructional content. These goals must be devised with local factors in mind, such as available instructional time, equipment, climate, facilities, and other variables. Once a philosophy of inclusion has been established in Phase 1, students with disabilities should be considered and benefit from all of the same program goals as their nondisabled peers. For example, all students should be expected to partake in physical education instruction leading to (1) establishing and maintaining health-related physical fitness; (2) developing competence in movement; (3) understanding the importance of health-related physical fitness and the benefits of an active lifestyle; and, (4) comprehending the rules, strategies, techniques, and safety procedures associated with games and sports.

The attainment of these general program goals may occur at different times, to different degrees, and in different ways for some students with disabilities. For example, a student with a visual impairment may participate in different activities to develop team sports skills or may use different equipment to develop certain fitness components. Analysis of the program goals for students with disabilities may include factors such as where the students are most likely to continue sport and physical activity participation after school years, with whom the students will participate in lifetime sports and fitness, and the availability and willingness of local agencies, programs, and facilities to offer programs for students with disabilities. These factors may lead to physical education instruction that is more community-based (i.e., educating the student at community facilities for the most effective carry over or community transition possibilities). Because most of the same general program goals are appropriate for both disabled and nondisabled students, these modifications are used to individualize the program, not make the program different for students with disabilities. The teacher's creativity and instructional modifications assist all students to achieve these goals.

## Phase 3: Determining Unit Outcomes

Unit outcomes, such as "The student will learn the fundamentals of shooting a free throw," are typically general statements designed for all students participating in a particular instructional sequence. Although appropriate for nondisabled students, special education procedures require that these unit outcomes or learner outcome statements be designed and written for individual special education students. This individualized approach is the key requirement for students receiving special education services and assists the physical educator with measurement, planning, instruction, and evaluation responsibilities. Unit outcomes are known in special education terminology as a student's **long-term or annual goals.** These general or broad statements are important guideposts for designing more specific short-term instructional objectives, with measurable and observable performance criteria. More information regarding long-term goals and short-term instructional objectives is presented at the end of this chapter in the section on the written **Individualized Education Program (IEP).**

## Phase 4: Establishing Performance-Based Objectives

Again, the typical regular physical education performance-based objective is written for an entire group or class of nondisabled (regular education) students. For example, "The student will be able to make 5 out of 10 free throws" is a common objective for a group or class. Students with disabilities must have individualized **short-term instructional objectives** written for each unit outcome or long-term goal. Similar to the linkage between group or class-oriented unit outcomes and performance-based objectives, the short-term instructional objectives for special education students must be directly linked to the individualized long-term goals. These short-term instructional objectives become very important assessment aids for physical educators working with students with disabilities. Guidelines for writing short-term instructional objectives on the IEP are presented later in this chapter.

## Phase 5: Evaluating and Improving the Program

This final, but ongoing, phase of program development includes the effectiveness of instruction being offered to students. Teachers should seek input from others about their instruction and carefully critique their own performance. Regarding instruction for students with disabilities, careful review of individualized long-term goals and short-term instructional objectives is an important part of this global programmatic evaluation. Can you answer the questions, "Have students been successful in and out of class performing and using newly acquired skills and knowledge?" or "Are special education students participating in activities outside of school where they can independently demonstrate and have fun performing skills attained in physical education?" Answers to these questions will provide valuable data for evaluating and improving the physical education curriculum for students with disabilities.

## The Importance of an Individualized Program

Students with disabilities should participate in, and benefit from, physical education in all the same ways as their nondisabled peers. Teachers must commit to a personal and programmatic philosophy of inclusion and integration of all students, and understand that some students will require a more individualized approach to planning, measurement, instruction, and evaluation. Designing a curriculum or program, including goals and performance-based objectives, is most often done for classes or groups of nondisabled students. Physical educators need to implement an individualized approach for students with disabilities. Learner outcomes may be general, but certain students will require different levels of achievement based on varying learning and performance abilities (Pangrazi and Corbin, 1994). For example, a student with a **physical disability** may be working to improve cardiovascular endurance, but may be measured with a different test item than a peer with no disabilities. These two students may also have different cardiovascular endurance goals and objectives. This individualization is appropriate because all students are improving a desired health-related fitness component, but are being measured individually.

## PRELIMINARY CONSIDERATIONS FOR TESTING

Testing in physical education requires considerable teacher planning. Paying careful attention to test administration details, simulating actual testing situations prior to working with students, and practicing can often save much time and avoid unnecessary repetition. These and other practical suggestions can improve testing conditions and will often result in more reliable outcomes when working with the nondisabled and those with disabilities.

Several characteristics unique to students with disabilities can affect the testing process, and consequently, the results. The mental, physical, and/or socioemotional qualities of certain students may require procedures that are not implemented with the nondisabled (Zittel, 1994). The following considerations and suggestions are provided to assist teachers when testing students with disabilities. These suggestions should supplement, not replace, those already discussed in Chapter 4. This information should not suggest that testing students with disabilities is more difficult. Remember, students with disabilities are much more like the nondisabled than they are different from them.

1. *Provide the necessary encouragement and incentive for maximum effort.* Various forms of incentives are often necessary to motivate all students when performing physical/motor tests. Unless otherwise stated in the standardized test directions, verbal encouragement is highly recommended when testing most students with disabilities. The strength of verbal incentive will be different for various circumstances and students. Some students may perform best following a few quiet words of encouragement from the teacher, while others will demonstrate maximum effort when given loud cheers throughout their entire performance by the teacher and/or peers. Incentives for maximum performance may also take the form of tangible rewards such as certificates or participation ribbons. Teachers should be familiar with what works best for each individual student and use incentives to obtain the best possible performance for measurement and

evaluation purposes (Pemberton, 1995). A reward or behavior management program may already be in place with certain students in their classrooms. The physical education teacher should check with classroom teachers regarding carryover to the gymnasium.

2. *Get to know each student.* Teachers who are familiar with their students can generally recognize performance that is less than maximum. This is important when testing, since anything less than maximum would not be a valid indicator of a student's ability. Teachers must be able to recognize when students are not "giving it their best." It also is helpful to obtain as much observational data as possible about students. This should be done in settings besides the gymnasium and gathered from a variety of persons (Jansma and French, 1994). Some students with disabilities may be shy or withdrawn and unwilling to perform to the best of their abilities. A new teacher or one who does not really know the student might not detect subtle behaviors or circumstances that can affect an individual student's motivation and performance levels. Some students may have poor self-concepts and require a more private testing location to avoid what they consider embarrassment in front of their peers. Other students are more likely to perform to their potential in the presence of familiar faces. Although it may require more time, teachers should learn as much as they can about all students in their classes. This may necessitate talking with other teachers and parents. For example, the physical education teacher may discover medical or physical problems that could affect performance and/or attitude by talking with a school nurse or a physical or occupational therapist. The time taken to get to know each student will be a good investment. In addition to significant others, the student is also a valuable source of information for testing and performance.

3. *Provide accurate, motivating, and thorough demonstrations.* Most standardized physical education test items permit a demonstration by the teacher. This demonstration is very important for all students. If given only verbal directions, many students will not understand the test item and what performance is expected of them. A proper demonstration provides additional opportunity to learn what is required through a visual image. A demonstration also allows the teacher to experience the physical demands of the test. The physical demonstration can reinforce a verbal description for items that require specific techniques or requirements. For example, the use of a proper grip when performing the flexed-arm hang is often demonstrated for persons with cognitive deficiencies. A demonstration may also alleviate possible fears students have about certain test items. For example, a proper demonstration with skinfold calipers can relieve unnecessary anxiety about skin pinching or pain. Another illustration of overcoming anxiety is when the sit-and-reach flexibility test is demonstrated. The student can

see that the legs are held down (not forced down) and it does not hurt to do this. A demonstration can also show students what proper pacing means and looks like. This will help prevent some students from fatiguing in the beginning of a distance run or an endurance event such as timed sit-ups or curl-ups. Extra planning may be necessary when demonstrating and/or explaining items with students who have auditory and visual impairments. If necessary, students with **auditory** or hearing impairments should be given written instructions and/or manual communication (e.g., sign language or finger spelling) (Stewart, Dummer, and Haubenstricker, 1990). Students with **visual** impairments can "walk through" the item to become acquainted with the environment and test requirements (Winnick and Short, 1985).

4. *Avoid potentially embarrassing situations.* The nature of much testing in physical education, if not implemented with proper preparation, sensitivity, and common sense, can result in embarrassment for some students. This can have very damaging and long-lasting negative consequences. For example, a student with severe obesity may not be able to perform a flexed-arm hang for even one second or may be unable to run a mile in less than 20 minutes. If administered in the usual group testing situation, these events could be devastating to a student's self-concept. A more individualized approach to testing can avoid these results. The presence of an obvious physical impairment can often lead to similar student discomfort or embarrassment. Many persons with disabilities either lack the ability to perform some tasks due to certain limitations, or may not have the self-confidence to perform in front of others. For example, a student with a motor impairment such as mild cerebral palsy or muscular dystrophy may be reluctant to run a 50-meter dash with an entire class observing. This is not a reason to exclude students from testing in physical education. On the contrary, it is very important to determine present levels of performance in order to set challenging goals, plan appropriate instruction, monitor progress, and encourage students to have fun in physical activity. Testing preparation can avoid potential problems and should include careful analysis of all students for determination of performance capability and personality characteristics. Other precautions can be taken to avoid possible embarrassing situations, including matching persons of equal or near-equal ability to perform partner-type test items such as running sprints or timed curl-ups and assessing skinfolds behind a curtain, an upright tumbling mat, or in an office with appropriate personnel. Unique, but predictable, situations may arise concerning students with prosthetic devices, missing limbs, scars from operations or burns, and conditions such as asthma or epilepsy. Teachers should be aware of all students' unique conditions and arrange appropriate testing situations. Preservation and enhancement of the student's self-concept should be an important consideration in any testing situation.

5. *Test in a nonthreatening environment.* All possible efforts should be made to make the testing environment relaxed and familiar to students—all students, not just those with disabilities. One way to achieve this is to have present authority figures (teachers, aides, or parents) who are in close contact with the students on a regular basis and who can, if trained properly, assist with testing. Having "extra hands" available when testing will likely make everyone's job easier and the process more time-efficient. Persons familiar with students are more likely to know if performance levels represent maximum efforts or if certain individuals are "sandbagging" or inhibited for some reason. Also, most students react better to encouragement or a friendly challenge from a familiar face than from a stranger. It may be difficult for a new person in a situation to determine if a student is in a bad mood, is not feeling well, or is affected by the presence of a newcomer. In addition to having familiar persons present, the testing location should be nonthreatening. Generally, it is best to test students in areas that they recognize. Some students do not react favorably to new locations and this can affect their behavior and test results. If a site different from the usual instructional setting is used for testing, students should have an opportunity to become oriented to the new location before testing takes place. This orientation period may take anywhere from a few minutes to a week with certain students. The time spent, however, will be a good investment in obtaining valid and reliable test results.

6. *Practice or simulate unique items or testing conditions.* Several test items included in this chapter require administrative procedures that are different from those in many regular physical education instruments. The item itself may not be very different, but its performance by students with disabilities may require different movements or execution. It is recommended that teachers simulate or actually perform these items themselves prior to testing students. These simulations allow teachers to experience the movements that students will have to perform and will help avoid many problems during the actual test administration. Based on these simulations, teachers can help students by giving performance tips. Situations that can be simulated include: running blindfolded on a track with a guide wire, running blindfolded while someone holds your arm, performing a distance run or a sprint in a wheelchair, and throwing a softball from a seated position to simulate the performance and physical demands placed on a wheelchair user. Not only will experiencing actual testing situations assist teachers in giving advice and suggestions to students, but it will also show students that the teacher really knows what it is like to perform under their unique circumstances. Students also should be asked for advice about improving test procedures and/or performance skills. For example, a student who uses a wheelchair may be an experienced wheelchair basketball player or track and field athlete. This student could provide assistance and

suggestions to a teacher who is not familiar with performance of physical skills while in a wheelchair. Students enjoy sharing their experiences and will be very helpful, offering many practical suggestions (National Association for Sport & Physical Education, 1995).

7. *Recognize contraindicated activities.* Many students with disabilities possess certain characteristics that require careful attention when performing physical activity. For example, a student with exercise-induced asthma is generally required to take a specific type of medication and do a slow, gradual warm-up prior to participation in cardiorespiratory endurance or sustained aerobic activities. Teachers must be aware of these situations and understand the implications associated with various conditions and participation in physical activity. These conditions are usually discussed in detail in an adapted physical education course but are mentioned here to remind physical education teachers about the importance of constant communication with parents, classroom teachers, and school medical personnel. The regular physical education teacher must implement a communication system with medical and health professionals to stay informed about students with unique conditions. Physical education teachers knowledgeable about common medical conditions are better able to handle the "blanket" medical excuse, which often inappropriately excuses a student from physical education testing and/or class. Students with disabilities should not be excused unnecessarily from physical education programs. If a student is unable to participate in the regular physical education program because of a disability or temporary condition, a specially designed or adapted physical education program must be implemented. The temporary program for individual students should also have goals and objectives that are established after testing. Teachers must be familiar with state education department guidelines concerning medical or health-impairing conditions. Many states publish such resources for teachers and parents (Illinois State Board of Education, 1978, 1987; Johnson and Lavay, 1988; Ohio Department of Education, 1980). Several of these state guides are specifically designed for physical education teachers and address common concerns regarding students with disabilities. Additional guidelines and position statements concerning physical activity participation for students with conditions such as epilepsy and asthma are regularly published by professional groups such as the American Academy of Pediatrics (1983, 1989). Thorough knowledge of the physical activity implications of various medical and health conditions by physical education teachers, coupled with communication among parents, medical personnel, and school staff, can result in physical education testing and instructional programs that benefit all students. Students must participate in physical education to derive its benefits. Physical education teachers are the professional advocates for consistent participation of all students.

# TESTS FOR STUDENTS WITH DISABILITIES

The availability and quality of tests that measure various physical and motor characteristics among students with disabilities have improved dramatically in the past 20 years. This reflects recognition of the need for individual student and program improvements, as well as various state and federal education mandates. Tests range from comprehensive motor development batteries containing over 120 items to practical field-based physical fitness instruments composed of five items.

Tests used in physical education for students with disabilities must be carefully selected. Teachers should ensure that the test chosen is designed to measure the specific components of interest. Since many tests contain items that measure performance in several domains, it may require some very careful picking and choosing among tests to arrive at the best compilation of items for particular students. Of course, only tests with acceptable validity, reliability, and objectivity should be used.

The tests and specific items described below are a very small representation of those that are commonly used with special populations in physical education. Inclusion in this chapter does not indicate that these are the tests of choice for all students. The selection of tests for students with disabilities requires teachers to make informed decisions about measurement based on many factors including the curriculum, Individualized Education Program goals and objectives, and abilities of students.

In many cases, the test descriptions in this chapter have been abbreviated for space purposes. It is important to note that when any test is used for measurement, placement, and/or programming purposes, the original source should be obtained and properly used. The original documents generally contain detailed descriptions of test development, norms, score sheets, interpretation, and other pertinent information. Certain test items that have already been described elsewhere in this text will not be repeated in this chapter unless unique administrative considerations exist for students with disabilities.

Tests presented in this chapter are divided into the areas of physical/ motor fitness and fundamental motor patterns.

## Physical/Motor Fitness Tests

The following section presents selected tests designed to measure physical fitness attributes of students with disabilities. The specific group of students that the tests are designed for is identified in section subheadings. Readers should note that the terms or categories of disabilities identified in the section title will often differ from state to state and even within states or school districts. Refer to the original test instrument (see reference section at the end of this chapter) for descriptions of specific recommended applications.

Some of the following tests include items that measure characteristics other than those generally considered to be in the physical fitness domain.

These additional items will be listed in the *Description* section but will not be explained in the detailed review. The *Reference* section at the end of the chapter includes a list of several other physical fitness tests that can be used to assess students with disabilities.

## Testing Students with Mental Retardation

Many students with mild and moderate **mental retardation** are mainstreamed or integrated into regular physical education. These students will generally be able to perform most test items used with their nondisabled peers. Motivating and clear demonstrations by the teacher are an especially useful technique in assessing students with mental retardation (Eichstaedt and Lavay, 1992).

## Motor Fitness Testing Manual for the Moderately Mentally Retarded

(Johnson and Londree, 1976)

*Purpose:* The purpose of this test is to measure selected physical fitness and motor ability characteristics of students with moderate mental retardation.

*Description:* Physical fitness and motor ability components measured are arm and shoulder strength, abdominal strength, leg power and coordination, arm power and coordination, and running speed. Test items consist of flexed-arm hang, sit-ups, standing long jump, softball throw for distance, 50-yard dash, and 300-yard run-walk.

### Flexed-Arm Hang

*Instructions:* The student is placed at a horizontal bar and uses an overhand (palms away from face) grip to hold the body in position with the chin above, but not touching, the bar. A stopwatch is started once this position is attained and is stopped when the chin touches the bar, falls below the level of the bar, or maintains its height by tilting the head backward. Figure 11.0 depicts proper positioning for the flexed-arm hang.

*Equipment:* Horizontal bar (chinning bar), mat, and stopwatch.

*Scoring Procedure:* The score is the number of seconds the student successfully holds the proper flexed-arm hang position.

*Organizational Hints:* Determine if the student understands that the object of the task is to keep the chin above the bar as long as possible. Check the grip to be sure the palms are facing away from the body. Hands should be approximately shoulder-width apart and no wider. Diameter of bar should not be too large for student's grip. The spotter and timer ideally should be two different persons. Assure the student that there is no danger of a fall. This can be accomplished by lightly touching the student on the waist as the

**◣ FIGURE 11.0**    Flexed-arm hang.

position is held. This touch must not offer any support to aid scoring performance. Use a bar height that does not intimidate students. Adjustable bar units are commercially available or can be constructed. An assistant who is able to move the child to the starting position and serve as a spotter will aid test administration. Give verbal encouragement to "stay up" as long as possible while the student performs.

### Sit-Ups

*Instructions:* A supine, flexed-knee position (knees bent less than 90 degrees) is assumed with soles of the feet flat on mat, heels not more than 12 inches from the buttocks, and hands placed behind the neck with fingers interlocked. The feet are held in contact with the floor by a partner. On the command "Go," the student curls up and touches one elbow to the opposite knee, reclines, and repeats the sit-up motion by bringing the opposite elbow up to the other knee. The student continues this alternate elbow-to-knee curl-up action until time has expired.

*Equipment:* Stopwatch and mat.

*Scoring Procedure:* The score is the total number of sit-ups properly performed in one 30-second trial. One sit-up is counted each time an elbow touches a knee. Situps are not counted if the student does not start from a completely reclined position with elbows on mat, the elbow is not touched to the opposite knee, or the fingers come apart behind the neck.

*Organizational Hints:* Do not permit upward hip thrusts that result in the lower back losing contact with the mat. The student holding down the feet should be strong enough to maintain the person in proper position. Do not allow the student to pull against the neck or back of head with the hands when raising body to sit-up position. Placing arms/hands across chest instead may help avoid possible neck hyperextension. Emphasize the curling motion of the upper body as the sit-up is being performed. Encourage students to pace themselves.

### Standing Long Jump

*Instructions:* Prepare a jumping area by making a restraining line and lines parallel to this line every inch for about 120 inches. Another way to design this jump area is to make a start line and secure a tape measure on the floor perpendicular to the line. The student stands facing forward just behind the jumping line with feet about shoulder-width apart. Body movements in preparation for the jump are permitted as long as the feet do not move. Generally these movements include flexion and extension of the knees, swinging of the arms forward and backward, a strong thrust off the feet as the jump is initiated. The jump is made with both feet leaving the surface and landing at the same time. Allow students sufficient warm-up jumps in order to determine how many jumps are necessary to achieve a maximum performance. With this population, it may be necessary to prepare for testing with weekly charting of 20 to 25 jumps at one time in order to determine how many practices are necessary for optimal jumps.

*Equipment:* Floor or flat outdoor surface and tape measure or premeasured surface.

*Scoring Procedure:* Record the best of three trials to the nearest inch. If several practice jumps are administered as discussed above, be sure student knows which of the three trials are to be measured. For proper performance, both feet must leave the surface and land together. Measurement is made from the restraining line to the heel of the foot closest to the line or other part of the body that touches the surface nearest the takeoff line. Do not count a jump if the student moves feet just prior to jumping.

*Organizational Hints:* Mark the landing point as soon as possible because there is a tendency to move forward with momentum. The takeoff and landing surfaces should be secure and not able to slide in any direction (anchor a mat or other movable surface). Place a marker at the spot of the initial or longest jump to help motivate the student on subsequent trials. Encourage students to swing their arms and to jump "out" instead of "up." Often students will not understand this task and jump more vertically than horizontally.

### Softball Throw for Distance

*Instructions:* The student stands behind a restraining line and throws a softball overhand as far as possible. Three trials are permitted for the test. Students should have a proper warm-up prior to testing, which should include throwing at increasingly longer distances. It is recommended that a procedure similar to that used with the standing long jump be used to determine how many practice throws are necessary for the student to attain a maximum performance. A simple charting procedure during practice sessions will tell at what point, or after how many practice throws, the student performs optimally.

*Equipment:* A large open field or indoor facility, tape measure, a minimum of three softballs (12-inch), and materials to make restraining line.

*Scoring Procedure:* Record to the nearest foot the distance of the farthest throw. Throws must be overhand. Students can make any type of approach to the throwing line but cannot step over it during or after the throw.

*Organizational Hints:* Assign one or two persons to retrieve balls. Use a long tape measure for accurate assessment. Keep side areas clear during testing to avoid possible injury from stray balls. Have extra balls available for practice and efficient testing.

### 50-Yard Dash

*Instructions:* Two students stand behind a starting line and assume a "set" position. The timer stands at the finish line with arms extended sideways. The signal "Go" is given by the timer bringing her arms down briskly. The timer should have a stopwatch in each hand in order to time the two runners.

*Equipment:* Two stopwatches and a straight distance of at least 60 yards that is smooth and solid.

*Scoring Procedure:* One trial is administered. The score is the elapsed time between the "Go" signal and when the student passes the finish line with the body—not the head or arms.

*Organizational Hints:* Positioning someone at the starting line to assist the runners is helpful. Practice the signals "Set" and "Go" prior to administration of the actual test. Encourage students to run as fast as possible until they reach the finish line. Pair runners of equal or near-equal speed so they do not become frustrated. Remind students to run in a straight path. It may help to have lanes or markers for this purpose. Be sure all students understand they should run "as fast as they can."

### 300-Yard Run-Walk

*Instructions:* On the signal, "Ready, go," 5 to 10 students in a single row, and from a standing start, run 300 yards as fast as possible. Some students may be unable to run the entire 300 yards, but walking is preferred to stopping, so students may complete the test at widely varying times.

*Equipment:* A track or solid and smooth surface on which the distance can be marked and a stopwatch.

*Scoring Procedure:* The elapsed time the student takes to complete the distance is recorded to the nearest second.

*Organizational Hints:* This test should be administered after students have had practice in distance running and instruction in pacing. Verbal encouragement should be given.

## Testing Students with Physical or Sensory Disabilities

### Physical Fitness Testing for the Disabled: Project UNIQUE
(Winnick and Short, 1985)

*Purpose:* This test is designed to measure the physical fitness of students with sensory and orthopedic disabilities. (The manual also contains norms for nondisabled students who were part of the original testing program.)

*Description:* The physical fitness components assessed by Project UNIQUE are body composition, muscular strength and endurance, flexibility, and cardiorespiratory endurance. Height and weight measures are also part of the battery. Triceps and subscapular skinfolds are included in the body composition assessment. Items used to measure the physical fitness components vary according to disability. Muscular strength/endurance items include grip strength, 50-yard/meter dash, sit-ups, and the standing broad jump. The sit-and-reach test is used to measure flexibility. Finally, the 9-minute or 1-mile run or the 12-minute or 1.5-mile run is used as the cardiorespiratory endurance measure. Many of these items can be performed on crutches or in a wheelchair.

*Validity:* Factor analysis reveals validity coefficients ranging from .53 to .95.

*Reliability:* Coefficients ranging from .55 to .99 have been reported.

*Age Levels:* Males and females, ages 10-17.

*Norms:* Separate percentile ranking for males and females, by disability, is available for each item, except those with auditory impairments. Normative data for sit-ups are presented for students with auditory impairments, but all other results should be compared to norms for nondisabled students.

*Test Area:* Large indoor gymnasium and outdoor area (ideally with a flat track surface).

### Skinfold Measures

*Instructions:* Triceps and subscapular measures are taken. (See Chapter 5 and Chapter 13.)

*Equipment:* Good quality skinfold caliper. Recommended brands are Lange and Harpenden.

*Scoring Procedure:* Measurements are recorded to the nearest millimeter. Three measures are taken at each site and the average is recorded for each site. The sum of these two averages is also recorded.

*Organizational Hints:* Relieve any fears that students may have about skinfold calipers through discussion and demonstration. Let students with visual impairments feel the caliper before measurements are taken. Do not hesitate to ask students who are physically disabled what the best position would be for item administration. Practice before testing students, use a high-quality caliper that is properly calibrated, and provide privacy for the tests. Privacy is especially important for some persons with physical disabilities, poor self-concepts, or deformities.

### Grip Strength

*Instructions:* Specific instructions are given in Chapter 5.

*Equipment:* Smedley-type hand grip dynamometer and a straight-back, armless chair.

*Scoring Procedure:* Students are given three trials with each hand on an alternating basis. Trials are recorded to the nearest kilogram and the average of each hand is the final score. The two mean scores are added to obtain the sum of grips score.

*Organizational Hints:* Let students with visual impairments feel the equipment and the way this item is performed by having the student hold on to the arm and hand of another person who is performing the test. Take extra care to fit the grip to students who have physical disabilities such as cerebral palsy. Be sure students are properly seated when performing this item; some may require a seat belt or other assistance. Provide adequate performance time.

### 50 Yard/Meter Dash

*Instructions:* The teacher decides which distance to use. Refer to Chapter 6 for administration procedures for nondisabled students. Other methods of ambulation such as propelling a wheelchair may be used for this item. The front wheels of wheelchairs must be behind the starting line at the start of the dash (see Figure 11.1). Timing stops when the front wheels cross the finish line. Students with visual impairments may use a guide wire when running this event (see Figure 11.2). Crutches also may be used.

▶ **FIGURE 11.1**  Wheelchair at start of 50-yard/meter dash.

▶ **FIGURE 11.2**  Guide wire for students with visual impairments in 50-yard dash.

*Equipment:* A flat and smooth straight running area at least 60 yards in length, stopwatch, and start and finish lines.

*Scoring Procedure:* Each student is given one trial and is timed to the nearest tenth of a second. The method of ambulation must also be recorded because different norms are available for various modes of movement (i.e., with or without crutches or wheelchair).

*Organizational Hints:* The use of crutches, wheelchairs, and/or guide wires necessitates great care in the selection of a running surface. Check to see if the surface selected is suitable for use with wheels; some artificial track surfaces may not be appropriate. Do not use string for finish lines. If necessary, provide a spotter for certain students during the dash. Coordinate signs to be used for students with hearing impairments. Equalize ability if running in pairs or small groups. Check physical accessibility to the testing area.

### Sit-Ups

*Instructions:* Refer to page 150 for specific instructions on bent-knee sit-ups. Modifica-tions allowed in Project UNIQUE include clasping the hands behind the head for those who cannot fold their arms across their chest and grasp the opposite shoulders. Another acceptable adaptation is holding down the functional leg of students with lower limb impairments.

*Equipment:* Stopwatch and mat or other comfortable surface.

*Scoring Procedure:* Record the number of correctly performed sit-ups completed in one 60-second trial.

*Organizational Hints:* Allow students with visual disabilities to feel a student while correctly performing sit-ups. Check to ensure that students with abnormal muscle tone (e.g., spastic cerebral palsy) are performing sit-ups correctly. Do not allow upward hip thrusts or rocking motions that permit the lower back to raise off the surface. See additional hints on page 461.

### Softball Throw

*Instructions:* Refer to page 233 for test administration procedures.

*Equipment:* At least three 12-inch softballs and a tape measure.

*Scoring Procedure:* The average of three trials, recorded in feet and inches, is the score.

*Organizational Hints:* Do not conduct this test outdoors in extremely windy conditions. Some students must throw from a wheelchair with brakes locked; others can choose whether to sit or stand for their throws. Refer to the test manual for exact guidelines. Students with deficient balance may use a chair, desk, or other object to stabilize themselves while throwing.

Position students with visual impairments to throw the ball in the correct direction.

### Standing Broad Jump

*Instructions:* Refer to page 222 for administration procedures. This item is administered only to nondisabled students and those with visual or hearing impairments.

*Equipment:* A tape measure.

*Scoring Procedure:* The average of three trials, recorded to the nearest inch, is the student's score for the standing broad jump. A trial in which the student falls backward is not measured and should be repeated.

*Organizational Hints:* Encourage students to fall forward, not backward, when landing. Allow students with visual impairments to feel the jumping area so they can become familiar with the boundaries and surface. They should also be given the opportunity to feel the pattern of someone else jumping in order to understand the necessary body movements. Encourage all students to swing the arms in preparation for take-off and during flight, and emphasize jumping "out," not "up."

### Sit-and-Reach

*Instructions:* Refer to page 136 for detailed instructions.

*Equipment:* Sit-and-reach apparatus (see page 136 for specifications).

*Scoring Procedure:* The average of two trials, recorded to the nearest centimeter, is the student's score. The maximum reach should be held for at least one second.

*Organizational Hints:* Have students practice proper hand and finger placement, preventing either hand from extending further than the other. Place the sit-and-reach box against a wall to avoid movement. Allow students with visual impairments to feel the box to become familiar with the apparatus. Be sure the legs are held down in contact with the floor and that the person holding them is strong enough to hold this position. Certain persons with cerebral palsy (spastic type) should not participate in this item. Refer to the test manual for detailed instructions.

### Long-Distance Run

*Instructions:* Refer to pages 19–20 of the Project UNIQUE manual (Winnick and Short, 1985) for directions for those students who will participate in this test. Some students will compete in wheelchairs. Students between the ages of 10 and 12 years run 1 mile or 9 minutes. Those between 13 and 17 years cover 1.5 miles or run for 12 minutes.

*Equipment:* A stopwatch that scores to the second; fluorescent boundary cones, pins, or flags to mark running course; and beanbags.

*Scoring Procedure:* The time of only one trial is recorded for students between the ages of 10 and 12 who can run a mile in less than 9 minutes and those between 13 and 17 who run 1.5 miles in less than 12 minutes. For students not able to cover the designated distances in the allotted times, the number of laps and partial laps are recorded as their scores. A yards-per-minute score is calculated for runners who do not cover the required distance (divide the distance covered in yards by 9 minutes or 12 minutes). Yards per minute for runners who complete the distance in less than the prescribed time is calculated by converting the time to seconds, dividing this number into the distance covered, and multiplying by 60. Scoring is exactly the same for students who complete this item in wheelchairs. The method of ambulation is important to note, since different norms are used for different methods.

*Organizational Hints:* Have students carry beanbags or other small objects to drop when they finish so they can continue walking to cool down and still have their distances measured accurately. Communication is important for runners with hearing impairments; there must at least be communication signs for starting and stopping. Check to see if the running surface is appropriate for wheelchairs. Many individuals who use wheelchairs will want to use gloves for comfort during the distance push. If necessary, properly secure legs into the wheelchair with velcro straps or other restraints. Ask runners with visual impairments what assistance they desire for the run: a guide wire, running assistant, or some other method.

### Modifications of Prudential FITNESSGRAM
(Cooper Institute for Aerobics Research, 1994)

In Chapter 5, test batteries that measure components of health-related fitness were identified and described. Each of the tests is intended for students who are not disabled. Since health related fitness is important for everyone, practitioners should be able to modify the tests to meet the particular fitness needs of students or clients with disabilities.

The Prudential FITNESSGRAM (1994) illustrates how the health related physical fitness of students with disabilities can be effectively evaluated. Educators should keep in mind that valid and reliable measures of fitness are only obtained when the subject understands each of the tests. Therefore, it is important when working with students with disabilities to allow ample practice time for each test and to be sure that verbal instructions are understood. Suggestions for modifying the Prudential FITNESSGRAM for individuals with disabilities are briefly described in the following sections.

### Aerobic Capacity

Certain physical conditions may prevent a student from running. For example, youngsters may be restricted to the use of a wheelchair, some individuals may require braces, others may have severe visual impairment. Some individuals, although capable of running, may have cystic fibrosis, serious coronary conditions, or acute asthma. In these cases, the practitioner should use some form of submaximal test of aerobic capacity.

*Recommendation:* Use large-muscle exercises such as swimming, stationary bicycling, propelling the wheelchair, or walking/treadmill. Refer to *The Prudential FITNESSGRAM Test Administration Manual* (Cooper Institute for Aerobics Research, 1994) for specific information regarding test modification. Initial scores can be used as baseline data to measure future progress.

### Body Composition

The FITNESSGRAM uses the triceps and calf skinfolds. Normally, these procedures are appropriate for individuals with disabilities. There are however, certain circumstances in which different measures should be used. For example, skinfold measurements should not be taken if scar tissue is present at the site or if the site is otherwise used as a location for medical injections. Limbs that display muscle atrophy also should not be used as skinfold sites. Finally, measures can be made on the left side if problems exist on the right.

### Muscle Strength, Endurance, and Flexibility

There may be occasions when the teacher needs to assess the strength, endurance, and flexibility of students with motor control problems. In these cases, it is important that the teacher remember that any repeated movement may be used to assess these components of fitness. The key is to ask students to reproduce the movement as many times as possible. Students should be encouraged to maintain a rhythmic pace and pause not longer than two seconds between repetitions. Scores obtained can be used as baseline data for subsequent tests to evaluate students' progress.

## Fundamental Motor Patterns

The following section presents selected test items that are designed to measure fundamental skills associated with motor development for preschool and elementary age students, including those in special education classes. The original source offers more detailed descriptions of specific applications (Ulrich, 1985).

### Test of Gross Motor Development

(Ulrich, 1985)

*Purpose:* The purpose of this test is to measure locomotor and object control gross motor skills.

*Description:* Locomotor subtest skills assessed are the run, gallop, hop, leap, horizontal jump, skip, and slide. Object-control subtest skills tested are the two-hand strike, stationary bounce, catch, kick, and overhand throw.

*Populations:* Preschool and elementary school-age students, including those in special education classes.

*Validity:* Content validity was established by expert judgment. Construct validity was determined by factor analysis of the 12 gross motor skills performed by the standardization population. Additional construct validation was established by analysis of cross-age performance and comparisons between subjects with and without mental retardation.

*Reliability:* Test-retest reliability coefficients ranged from .84 to .99.

*Age Level:* Males and females, ages 3-10.

*Norms:* Standard scores and percentiles by age for the locomotor and object control subtests are presented. A separate table allows calculation of a Gross Motor Developmental Quotient (GMDQ).

*Test Area:* A gymnasium, room, or open space at least 60 feet by 30 feet.

#### Subtest 1: Locomotor Skills

##### Run

*Instructions:* The student is instructed to run fast between two marked lines 50 feet apart. The student should run on a line for the full length.

*Equipment:* Some type of marking for lines and a minimum of 50 feet of clear space in a straight line.

*Scoring Procedure:* Students are given credit for: (1) a brief period in which both feet are off the ground, (2) arms moving in opposition to legs, elbows bent, (3) foot placement near or on the line (not flat-footed), and (4) non-support leg bent approximately 90 degrees (close to buttocks).

*Organizational Hints:* Inform students that they do not have to run with their feet on the line. This is a "guideline" only. Observe the performance from both the side and rear. Have at least 10 feet of clear space at the ends of the running path.

##### Gallop

*Instructions:* Mark two lines 30 feet apart. Instruct students to gallop from one line to the other three times, alternating the lead foot each trial.

*Equipment:*  A minimum of 30 feet of open space in a straight line.

*Scoring Procedure:*  Students are given credit for: (1) a step forward with the lead foot followed by a step with the trailing foot to a position adjacent to or behind the lead foot, (2) brief period in which both feet are off the ground, (3) arms bent and lifted to waist level, and (4) able to lead with right and left foot.

*Organizational Hints:*  Observe performance from both the side and rear of student. The tester may have to tap or touch the right and left leg if the student is not yet able to determine left from right.

### Hop

*Instructions:*  Students are told to hop on one foot, then on the other foot, for a distance of 15 feet.

*Equipment:*  A minimum of 15 feet of open space in a straight line.

*Scoring Procedure:*  Students are given credit for: (1) foot of nonsupport leg being bent and carried in back of body, (2) nonsupport leg swinging in pendular fashion to produce force, and (3) ability to hop on the right and left foot (this does not require the performance of the other two criteria).

*Organizational Hints:*  Administer this item in clear, safe space, since balance is required.

### Leap

*Instructions:*  Students are told to leap 30 feet, taking large steps by leaping from one foot to the other.

*Equipment:*  A minimum of 30 feet of open space in a straight line.

*Scoring Procedure:*  Students are given credit for demonstrating the following: (1) taking off on one foot and landing on the opposite foot, (2) a period in which both feet are off the ground (longer than in running), and (3) reaching forward with the arm opposite the lead foot.

*Organizational Hints:*  It may be helpful to place a safe and nonthreatening object such as a tape mark on the floor as a target to leap over. Observe from the students' side.

### Horizontal Jump

*Instructions:*  The student stands behind a line that is marked off with tape or by other means and told to "jump far." Figure 11.3 depicts a student performing this test.

*Equipment:*  A minimum of 10 feet of open space and masking tape.

*Scoring Procedure:*  Students are given credit for: (1) preparatory movement including flexion of both knees with arms extended behind the body, (2)

◣ **FIGURE 11.3**   Horizontal jump.

arms extending forcefully forward and upward, reaching full extension above head, (3) taking off and landing on both feet simultaneously, and (4) arms being brought downward during landing.

*Organizational Hints:* Observe from the side and front on different trials. Be sure that students do not step over the starting line as they initiate the jump.

### Skip

*Instructions:* Two lines are marked off 30 feet apart. Students are told to skip from one line to the other three times.

*Equipment:* A minimum of 30 feet of open space and masking tape.

*Scoring Procedure:* Students are given credit for: (1) a rhythmic repetition of the step-hop on alternate feet, (2) carrying the foot of nonsupport leg near the surface during hop phase, and (3) arms moving alternately in opposition to legs at about waist level.

*Organizational Hints:* Observe from the side and front on different trials.

### Slide

*Instructions:* Two lines are marked off 30 feet apart. Students are told to slide from one line to another three times facing the same direction.

*Equipment:* A minimum of 30 feet of open space and masking tape

*Scoring Procedure:* Students are given credit for: (1) turning the body sideways to the desired direction of travel, (2) a step sideways followed by a slide of the trailing foot to a point next to the lead foot, (3) a short period in which both feet are off the floor, and (4) ability to slide to the right and to the left (this criterion does not require performance of the other three).

*Organizational Hints:* Remind students to keep their heads up while sliding. Areas to side of slide course should be clear of equipment or other objects.

### Subtest 2: Object-Control Skills

#### Two-Hand Strike

*Instructions:* Softly pitch a ball at waist level and instruct the student to hit the ball hard (see Figure 11.4). Do not score tosses that are not at waist level.

*Equipment:* A 4- to 6-inch lightweight ball, a plastic bat, and an open space for hitting.

► **FIGURE 11.4** Striking a pitched ball.

*Scoring Procedure:* Students are given credit for: (1) dominant hand gripping the bat above nondominant hand, (2) nondominant side of body facing the tosser (feet parallel), (3) hip and spine rotation, and (4) transferring weight by stepping with front foot.

*Organizational Hints:* Tell students that they do not have to stand on any certain spot on the floor. Position students so balls are not hit into other testing areas (hit into a wall if available). The tosser should be able to throw accurately. Underhand toss works best with most youngsters.

### Stationary Bounce

*Instructions:* Students are told to bounce a ball three times with one hand.

*Equipment:* A hard, flat surface and an 8- to 10-inch playground ball.

*Scoring Procedure:* Students are given credit for: (1) contacting the ball with one hand at about hip height, (2) pushing the ball with fingers (not a slap), and (3) hitting the floor with the ball in front of (or to the outside of) the foot on the side of the hand being used.

*Organizational Hints:* Inflate the ball properly. Remind students that they can look at the ball while bouncing. Do not restrict students by telling them to stay in one spot.

### Catch

*Instructions:* Student and tosser stand behind lines 15 feet apart. Ball is tossed underhand to student with a slight arc. Instruct student to "catch it with your hands." To be scored, tosses must be between shoulders and waist.

*Equipment:* A 6- to 8-inch sponge ball, 15 feet of clear space, and masking tape.

*Scoring Procedure:* Students are given credit for: (1) preparation, in which elbows are flexed and hands are in front of body, (2) arms extending in preparation for ball contact, (3) catching and controlling the ball by hands only, and (4) bending elbows to absorb force.

*Organizational Hints:* Tosser should stand in open area, free of any visually confusing background against which the student might lose sight of the ball. Do not position student right on the 15-foot line because they often think they have to stand on a specific spot. Have two or three balls available to use time efficiently. Let student feel the ball to alleviate any fear of being hurt by a hard ball.

### Kick

*Instructions:* Mark off two lines, one 20 feet away from a wall and one 30 feet from the wall. Tell the student to stand on the line that is 30 feet from the wall and place the ball on the other line. Instruct the student to kick the ball "hard" toward the wall (see Figure 11.5).

*Equipment:* A slightly deflated playground ball (8- to 10-inch), 30 feet of clear straight space, and masking tape.

*Scoring Procedure:* Students are given credit for: (1) a rapid and continuous approach to the ball, (2) inclining the trunk backward during ball contact, (3) swinging the arm opposite kicking leg forward, and (4) follow-through by hopping on nonkicking foot.

*Organizational Hints:* Observe from side and front during separate trials. Have more than one ball available for kicking. Place the ball on a piece of tape or other material to keep it stationary during kicking.

▶ **FIGURE 11.5** Kicking a ball.

*Overhand Throw*

*Instructions:*  Instruct student to throw the ball "hard" at the wall.

*Equipment:*  A tennis ball, a wall, and about 25 feet of space.

*Scoring Procedure:*  Students are given credit for: (1) a downward arc of the throwing arm to initiate the windup, (2) rotation of hip and shoulder to a point where the nondominant side faces an imaginary target, (3) transferring weight by stepping with the foot opposite the throwing hand, and (4) follow-through beyond ball release diagonally across body toward the side opposite the throwing hand.

*Organizational Hints:*  Tell students they do not have to stand on a line when throwing. Some students may need a reminder to throw the ball overhand. Have extra balls ready for throwing. Encourage students to look at the target when throwing.

# PUTTING IT ALL TOGETHER: THE INDIVIDUALIZED EDUCATION PROGRAM (IEP)

Physical education teachers are important members of school personnel teams responsible for educating all students in several curriculum areas. This responsibility, properly performed, is cooperatively implemented with special education and related service staff members (e.g., physical and occupational therapists). Team members' responsibilities include attending staff meetings, planning interdisciplinary and cooperative educational experiences, providing up-to-date and accurate written reports to document attainment of educational goals and objectives, and working together to assist with, and advocate for, the education of students with disabilities.

A major legal requirement for students age 3–21 who are eligible for special education is the development, implementation, and on-going evaluation of a written **Individualized Education Program (IEP).** The term *individualized* means that each eligible student must have a program specifically written to meet his or her educational needs. Physical education teachers are active and contributing members of IEP teams (Wisconsin Department of Public Instruction, 1985). The IEP is prepared by numerous persons, and the content written by physical education teachers is only part of the total information. An IEP can be as short as 3 pages or as long as 15 or more pages, depending on the student's needs. Not all students with disabilities will have a written IEP; some students with disabilities can perform all educational activities without special education assistance or services.

Physical education teachers should communicate with special education staff at the start of and periodically throughout each school year to determine which students have IEPs, and whether physical education requires written documentation (i.e., present levels of performance, long-term or annual goals, and short-term instructional objectives, etc.). Physical education teachers should acquaint themselves with classroom teachers (regular and special education) to determine who is primarily responsible for each student's IEP. This IEP "team leader" should receive written reports on the physical education program for specific students.

The physical educator should also communicate with the principal and/or the appropriate special education supervisor concerning their roles with special education pupils and procedures for written IEP reports. A schedule is usually distributed to teachers at the start of the school year regarding deadlines for IEP progress reports. Physical education teachers should be on the distribution list for these schedules. They should determine at the start of the year whether they are expected to attend IEP team meetings, or whether written reports will suffice. The best practice is for physical education teachers to attend and participate in IEP team meetings.

A school or school district may have an **adapted** or **special physical education teacher** on staff. In this situation, the regular physical education teacher may assist this specialist with measurement, program planning, and design of goals and objectives for individual special education students. The availability of a specialist will vary from school to school and district to district. Regardless of whether an adapted specialist is on staff, all physical education teachers must understand IEP procedures and be able to perform the roles of measurement, planning, implementing, and evaluating instruction for students with disabilities.

## The Written IEP Document

By law a written IEP must include the following:

1. A statement of the student's present level of educational performance.
2. A statement of annual goals, including short-term instructional objectives.
3. A statement of special education and related services to be provided to the child and the extent to which the child will be able to participate in the regular education program.
4. The projected dates for initiation of services and anticipated duration of the services.
5. Appropriate objective criteria and evaluation procedures and schedules for determining, on at least an annual basis, whether short-term instructional objectives are being achieved.
6. **Transition services** (beginning no later than age 16, or at a younger age if determined appropriate) to include a statement of the needed transition services and, if appropriate, a statement of each public

agency's and each participating agency's responsibilities or linkages, or both, before the student leaves the school setting (Individuals with Disabilities Education Act, Public Law 101-476).

An examination of each of these IEP components will reveal much similarity to measurement and evaluation concepts already presented in this chapter and in Chapter 2. Figure 11.6 presents an example of an actual school district IEP form. This form will be referred to later in this section.

## Statement of Student's Present Level of Educational Performance

This individual student performance information is derived from a variety of formal and informal measurements. The **present level of performance** data is the foundation of a student's IEP because all further goals and objectives are based on individual assessment and the resulting summary statements. In physical education, these statements could include performance scores from health-related physical fitness tests, motor development or ability scales, cognitive knowledge about rules, strategies, and techniques, self-concept regarding movement skills, and many other types of measurements. The types of performance data reported depend on the tests administered.

These data must be collected prior to implementing meaningful instruction for students with disabilities. The student's present capabilities and skills must be known in order to plan and implement activities to further develop skills and knowledge. It is better to report present level of performance data that are objective, observable, measurable, and successful, as opposed to subjective observations and information on what the student is unable to perform (Short, 1995).

Below are sample statements of present level of educational performance that might appear in the physical education section of an IEP:

1. Independently runs 1 mile in 11 minutes and 35 seconds (23rd percentile for age, gender, and disability).
2. Completes 25 curl-ups in 1 minute (58th percentile for age, gender, and disability).
3. Catches a 16-inch playground ball 3 of 10 times when tossed underhand from 10 feet away.
4. Can properly swing a jump rope over head from behind to the front of his body, but can't successfully perform feet-together jump over the rope.
5. Can independently perform all of the following: front dive from knees into deep end of pool, swim to stairs, and exit pool.
6. Can perform an overhand throw with developmentally appropriate arm/leg opposition using a tennis ball.

► **FIGURE 11.6**  Sample school district IEP.

<table>
<tr><td colspan="2">

**SCHOOL DISTRICT OF LA CROSSE**
OFFICE OF STUDENT SERVICES
807 East Avenue South
La Crosse, WI 54601
(608) 789-7688
(608) 789-7603 FAX
(608) 789-7694 TDD

</td><td>

**INDIVIDUALIZED**
**EDUCATION**
**PROGRAM**

Page 1 of __15__

</td></tr>
</table>

| Current IEP Dates |
| --- |
| From _____ to _____ |
|     M/D/Yr          M/D/Yr |

| Name of Student | | D.O.B. | Age | Sex | Race Ethnic | Grade | Building |
| --- | --- | --- | --- | --- | --- | --- | --- |
| Marissa Jones | | 3/23/87 | 9 | F | Caucasian | 4 | State Ridge |

| Parent or Legal Guardian | Address | Telephone |
| --- | --- | --- |
| Martha Jones | 1111 Willow Way South | 608-000-0000 |

| District of Residence | For Transfers: District of Original Placement | IEP Beginning Date | IEP Ending Date |
| --- | --- | --- | --- |
| Lamont | Ona Sparta | (M/D/YR) 10-15-96 | (M/D/YR) 10/1/98 |

| Area of EEN (Handicapping Condition) | __X__ For School Calendar Term | ___ For Summer Term |
| --- | --- | --- |
| Cognitive Delay | | From: |

Document efforts to involve parents in IEP (Dates/Methods/By Whom)        Parents attended 11-14-97
1. 11-3-97 B. Smith, Call  | 2. 11-7-97 B. Smith, Letter | 3. meeting

For students transferring between school districts within the state, IEP Adopted: _____  _____
                                                 (Date)                     (Name & Title of District Representative)

A.  Extent to which student will participate in regular education programs, and nonacademic and extracurricular services and activities; (Describe any modifications the child requires to participate in the regular education programs). (List schedule: Amount of time and Frequency of each class.)

    Attend regular art class (2 days per week – 45 minutes each)
    Attend regular music class (2 days per week – 40 minutes each)
    Attend regular computer lab (2 days per week – 40 minutes each)
    Attend regular physical education class (3 days per week – 45 minutes each)
    Attend regular language arts classes (5 days per week – 45 minutes each)

B.  Please state the specific special education services and the amount of time for each service. (List schedule; Amount of time and Frequency of each class.)

    Marissa will participate in the EEN (cognitive delay) elementary class for ½ of each school day. This will include instruction in math, reading, science, and social studies.

C.  Justification for removal from regular education or regular education environment (include nature and severity of handicap and any potential harmful effects on the child or on the quality of services. (Add additional page(s) as necessary.)

    Testing and observational data reveal that Marissa has a cognitive delay. Her present needs will be best met in the EEN elementary class at State Ridge school. Much of each day will be spent in regular education settings. Marissa has very good social and language skills, and has no behavior problems.

Are any related services **required** to assist the child to benefit from special education?    ☒ Yes ☐ No

| | FREQUENCY/DURATION | | | FREQUENCY/DURATION |
| --- | --- | --- | --- | --- |
| ☐ Occupational Therapy | | ☐ Psychological Services | | |
| ☐ Physical Therapy | | ☐ Recreation | | |
| ☒ Transportation | everyday/45 minutes | ☐ School Health Services | | |
| ☐ Counseling | | ☐ Social Work Services | | |
| ☐ Audiology | | ☐ Parent Counseling/Training | | |
| ☐ Assistive technology | | ☐ Rehabilitation Counseling Services | | |
| | | ☐ Other (specify): | | |

Rev. 8/95      WHITE: EEN Teacher            YELLOW: EEN file            PINK: Parent

▶ **FIGURE 11.6** Continued.

If visually handicapped, does the student need braille instruction?    ☐ Yes  ☐ No    (Justify):

Physical Education    ☒ Regular    ☐ Specially designed

Vocational Education    ☒ Regular    ☐ Specially designed

Are transition services required?  ☐ Yes ☒ No  (If Yes, include transition activities within the goals and objectives, and complete the Summary of Transition Services.)

Will the student participate in standardized testing?

| | | | |
|---|---|---|---|
| Fourth, Eighth or Tenth grade testing under s.118.30, Wis. Stats., | ☒ Yes  ☐ No | ☒ With Modifications _____ |
| Competency based testing | ☐ Yes  ☐ No | ☐ With Modifications _____ |
| Achievement testing (i.e., CTBS) | ☐ Yes  ☐ No | ☐ With Modifications _____ |
| Third grade Reading Test | ☒ Yes  ☐ No | ☒ With Modifications _____ |

| Date of IEP meeting  9–14–97 | Date of IEP Review  10–1–98 |
|---|---|
| IEP meeting participants | IEP meeting participants |
| LEA Representative/Title | LEA Representative/Title |
| Teacher/Title | Teacher/Title |
| Teacher/Title | Teacher/Title |
| Parent/Guardian | Parent/Guardian |
| Private School Representative (when required) | Private School Representative (when required) |
| WSD or WSVH* Representative (when required) | WSD or WSVH* Representative (when required) |
| Community Agency Representative/Title (when required) | Community Agency Representative/Title (when required) |
| Student (if appropriate) | Student (if appropriate) |
| Other/Title | Other/Title |
| Interpreter (when required) | Interpreter (when required) |

This form interpreted by _____ on _____.

*Wisconsin School for the Deaf (WSD), Wisconsin School for the Visually Handicapped (WSVH)

Rev. 8/95

► **FIGURE 11.6**   Continued.

Name of Student

Marissa Jones      (Physical Education objectives)

Present levels of educational performance

Marissa can run 1 mile in 13 minutes and 36 seconds (1-9-97)

Annual goal

Marissa will increase her cardiovascular endurance

| Short-term Objectives | Evaluation Criteria (Expected level of performance) | Evaluation Procedures (Data collection) | Evaluation Schedule (When will this objective be reviewed?) |
|---|---|---|---|
| Following the teacher's directions, Marissa will run 400 meters in less than 2 minutes and 45 seconds. | Run 400 meters in less than 2:45. | Physical Education teacher will observe and time Marissa during physical education class. | 3-10-97 |
| Marissa will ride a stationary bicycle on 3 consecutive days for 15 minutes without stopping. | 3 consecutive days of nonstop stationary cycling for 15 minutes per session. | Physical education teacher will observe and time cycling sessions in gymnasium. | 2-28-97 |
| Marissa will run 1 mile in less than 12 minutes on the outdoor 400 meter track. | Run 1 mile in less than 12 minutes. | Physical education teacher will observe and time Marissa as she runs. | 4-20-97 |

Titles of specific educational staff and related services personnel who will contribute to meeting this goal:

Ryan Cole, regular physical education teacher
Barb Smith, adapted physical education consultant

Parents agreed on importance of this goal - approved                9-14-97

Action taken on this goal at IEP review:                                              Date:

▶ **FIGURE 11.6**  Continued.

---

## SUMMARY OF TRANSITION SERVICES

Date Student Invited and Method of Invitation _____

Transition Services Included in the IEP: (indicate the page and objective number on IEP)

| Yes | No | |
|-----|-----|-----|
| ☐ | ☐ | * Instruction |
| ☐ | ☐ | * Community Experiences |
| ☐ | ☐ | * Employment Objectives |
| ☐ | ☐ | * Post School Adult Living Objectives |
| ☐ | ☐ | ** Acquisition of Daily Living Skills |
| ☐ | ☐ | ** Functional Vocational Evaluation |

* If not included as annual goals and short term objectives in the IEP, write an annual statement of needed services or if not needed, write a statement regarding the basis upon which the service(s) were excluded.

** If not included as goals and objectives in the IEP, these require an annual statement of needed services, if appropriate.

If the child did not attend the IEP meeting, what steps were taken to ensure that the child's interests and preferences were considered in the planning?

Is a statement of each public agency's and each participating agency's responsibilities or linkages, or both, needed?     ☐ Yes  ☐ No

| Participating Transition Service Agencies | Date Agency Representative Invited and Method of Invitation | Statement of Responsibilities/Linkages Related to Each of the Needed Transition Skill Areas |
|---|---|---|
| | | |
| | | |
| | | |

If an invited agency representative did not attend the IEP meeting, what steps were taken to obtain the participation of the agency in the planning of transition services?

---

Courtesy of the School District of LaCrosse.

## Statement of Annual Goals, Including Short-Term Instructional Objectives

Following a determination of the student's present level of educational performance, related goals and objectives must be developed. **Long-term or annual goals** are directly linked to the individual student's present level of performance. Annual goals for a special education student are the same as unit outcomes for a class of students discussed earlier in this chapter and in Chapter 2. These IEP goals are general statements that broadly outline the area(s) of intended achievement and provide focus for planning and teaching with an individual student. See Figure 11.7 for sample long-term or annual goals.

**Short-term instructional objectives(STIOs)** are designed for individual students and are similar to performance-based objectives written for a class or group of students. STIOs are very specific guideposts to determine if measurable and observable progress is made toward the individual student's annual or long-term goals (or unit outcomes). STIOs are derived from examination of present levels of performance (measurement data), and are specific statements written in measurable and observable terms. STIOs should contain the following components:

1. *Who* performs the action (e.g., the student, Marissa, or Ryan).
2. What *performance, action,* or *behavior* is expected or demonstrated (e.g., run, jump, catch, swim, curl-up).
3. *Conditions* under which the performance, action, or behavior is demonstrated (e.g., on an outdoor 400-meter track, with a 16-inch playground ball, following verbal directions from the teacher, after a 2-minute rest, or given a jump rope and teacher demonstration).
4. *Criterion* or *standard* used to evaluate successful or acceptable performance (e.g., 35 curl-ups in 1 minute, or catch 7 of 10 tosses).

Many formats are used for STIOs. The sequence of the four components may vary, but a well-written STIO should clearly communicate what is to be learned and how learning will be demonstrated. Properly worded objectives are important instructional and measurement guides for physical education teachers. In addition, monitoring STIOs provides much of the required written data for IEP reports, team meetings, and other instructional accountability tasks. See Figure 11.7 for sample STIOs.

STIOs can be sequenced to each other or can contain different progress steps related to the annual or long-term goal. Sequencing STIOs may assist with instructional planning and individual student motivation. For example, three STIOs could be sequenced so the student is performing the same action (abdominal curl-ups), but attempts to perform an increased number for each STIO to meet acceptable criteria (from 15 to 25 to 35 after a two-month instructional period).

► **FIGURE 11.7**   Sample STIOs.

Sample annual or long-term goals and STIOs. Note that each annual goal and its STIO directly relate to each other regarding the target physical or motor ability or skill.

1. Annual Goal: Kyle will increase his cardiovascular endurance.

   STIO: Following verbal directions, Kyle will run 1 mile in less than 12 minutes and 30 seconds.

   STIO: On an outdoor track, Kyle will run three, 200-meter sprints in less than 65 seconds each (with 2-minute rest between sprints).

   STIO: Without teacher assistance, Kyle will pedal a stationary bike for 6 minutes without stopping.

2. Annual Goal: Marissa will increase her abdominal muscle strength and endurance.

   STIO: Following verbal directions and a teacher demonstration, Marissa will correctly perform 35 curl-ups in less than 1 minute.

   STIO: Given an exercise mat and a teacher demonstration, Marissa will perform 20 side crunches in less than 1 minute.

3. Annual Goal: Ryan will increase his catching skill.

   STIO: Following a teacher demonstration, Ryan will catch with his hands a 16-inch playground ball tossed at waist height 7 out of 10 times.

   STIO: While in a stationary position, Ryan will toss a tennis ball at least 10 feet in the air over his head (slightly in front of him) and catch 7 out of 10 tosses.

   STIO: While sliding sideways, Ryan will catch a 12-inch playground ball tossed at waist height from 10 feet 7 out of 10 times.

---

Carefully designed long-term or annual goals and properly stated STIOs provide teachers and students with direction for instructional planning and monitoring individual students progress. However, STIOs should not become the lesson plan or activity itself. Lesson plans should present appropriate and motivating content that will assist students to achieve long-term goals and STIOs.

### Statement of Special Services to Be Provided and the Extent of Students' Participation in Regular Education Program

This section of the IEP may includes many educational services. Information regarding physical education should include the type of program (adapted and/or regular class) in which the student is participating. Most often this is a check-off box, followed by an explanation of the type, frequency, and duration of physical education services. This statement would provide the answer to the question, "extent to which the student participates in the regular physical education program." Best practice recommends that the amount of time and frequency of each class also be recorded

in this section (see Figure 11.6). Some students with disabilities will participate in adapted or specially designed physical education, and this placement should be noted on the IEP. Related services, such as occupational or
physical therapy, psychological services, or assistive technology, also must
be listed on the IEP. They are monitored by educational staff other than the
physical educator.

### Projected Dates for Initiation of Services and Anticipated Duration of the Services

Similar to a teacher planning the length of an instructional unit, writing a
student's IEP includes recording dates regarding the length of educational
services. It is recommended that inclusive dates (e.g., from 1/23/96 to
6/12/96) and the amount of time and frequency of classes be included on
the IEP. The physical educator should communicate with other personnel
writing the IEP and provide appropriate dates, amount of time, and frequency of each class or unit.

### Objective Criteria, Evaluation Procedures, and Schedules for Assessing Achievement of STIOs

The IEP must contain information that summarizes how and when educational progress is monitored. Physical educators will participate in this
phase by evaluating each special education student's long-term goals and
STIOs after each instructional unit. This measurement becomes part of each
student's unit evaluation, is recorded on the IEP, and should be communicated to educational personnel responsible for the student's progress.

### Transition Services

The purpose of **transition services** is to prepare eligible special education
students for postschool outcomes such as employment, postsecondary education, adult services, independent living, and community participation
(National Information Center for Children and Youth with Disabilities,
1993). Transition services must be based on individual students' needs and
be a coordinated set of activities. Physical education and resulting life-long
recreation/leisure physical activity participation can play an important part
in transition services for special education students.

Many benefits and goals of the physical education curriculum blend
well with the concept of special education transition services. For example,
one important aspect of physical education programs is for all students to
develop life-long physical activity skills and habits. Participation in lifetime sport and recreational physical activities requires the ability to use
community-based facilities with varying degrees of physical skill, knowl-

edge, and independent behavior. Transition services in physical education for students with disabilities should include instruction in community recreation and physical activity facilities in order to exercise skills learned in the school-based curriculum. For special education students 16 and older (younger if determined), these activities or services should be listed on the IEP and note the responsibilities of all agencies involved.

Appropriate and meaningful transition from school-based physical education instruction to community-based participation for students with disabilities requires planning, communication, and coordination. The physical education teacher should communicate with the special education teacher(s), parents, the student, and participating agencies for coordination all transition goals, services, and activities. Successful transition programming in physical education can assist with goals such as **mainstreaming** and **inclusion** into the community, developing a social network and daily living skills, and developing self-sufficiency and independence.

A trip to the local fitness club or Y could include several aspects of transition programming for students with disabilities. After proper school-based instruction, community-based physical education and recreation/leisure education programming could include many important learning experiences leading to independent and community participation, including

- planning a trip with a friend to a community facility
- arranging and using public transportation
- demonstrating appropriate social skills and behaviors
- application of physical/motor skills learned in school-based physical education,
- self-help and personal skills (dress, hygiene, and locker room functioning), and
- possible employment opportunities related to the experience

The application of physical education skills and knowledge offers a natural and logical learning environment for transition services for special education students. Physical education teachers should provide leadership and work with special education staff to coordinate this part of transition services.

Figure 11.6 presents a sample IEP from a school district (transition services are not included in this sample IEP because of the student's age—below 16—and a determination that these services were not necessary at this time for this individual student). Page 4 of Figure 11.6 represents an example of what a physical education teacher may be responsible to complete for each special education student on an annual basis (with periodic monitoring during the school year). A district may refer to this page as an IEP "goal/objective sheet." Physical education teachers will generally be limited to writing information such as that in Figure 11.6. School districts can design their own IEP forms, but they must contain the required components mentioned above even if they appear different. Many districts use computer programs for IEPs, and physical education teachers should utilize them to organize their IEP records.

## SUMMARY

The process of measurement and evaluation is an integral phase of the physical education curriculum, including instruction for students with disabilities. The availability of standardized tests and curriculum-embedded assessment programs designed specifically for many special populations improves the accuracy of measurement and the quality of instruction for special students in physical education. Teachers must learn to locate, select, administer, and interpret these tests and effectively communicate results to the proper people (parents, students, administrators, classroom and special education teachers, related service personnel, etc.). Of equal importance is the ability to feel confident and comfortable when working with special populations. Physical educators are important members of individual students' IEP teams, and must provide leadership and advocacy for each student's physical education experience. If necessary, regular physical education teachers should seek consultation from those with expertise in adapted or special physical education.

## ► DISCUSSION QUESTIONS

1. What are some disabling conditions likely to be encountered when teaching physical education? What are some of the adjustments, if any, that must be made to accommodate students with disabilities in an assessment and evaluation setting?

2. Cite some administrative considerations that should be addressed before and during testing of students with disabilities.

3. How do test items for batteries designed for students with disabilities differ from those for nondisabled individuals? Are components measured for special populations the same or different from the nondisabled population?

4. How can the test results obtained from assessment of preschool-age children be used? What factors affect a youngster's performance on items measuring fundamental motor patterns?

5. Write one sample long-term goal and three related and sequenced short-term instructional objectives for the present level of performance results in cardiovascular endurance, flexibility, striking, and catching skills.

6. How can the physical education curriculum be used to reinforce and supplement transition services for the special education student?

# ► REFERENCES

American Academy of Pediatrics. (1983). Sports and the child with epilepsy. *Pediatrics* 72:88-85. (Available from AAP, 141 Northwest Point Blvd., PO Box 927, Elk Grove Village, IL 60009.)

———. (1989). Exercise and the asthmatic child. *Pediatrics* 84:392-93. (Available from AAP, 141 Northwest Point Blvd., PO Box 927, Elk Grove Village, IL 60009.)

Auxter, D., Pyfer, J., and Heuttig, C. (1993). *Principles and methods of adapted physical education and recreation.* 7th ed. St. Louis, MO: Mosby.

Block, M. (1994). *A teacher's guide to including students with disabilities in regular physical education.* Baltimore: Brooks.

Cooper Institute for Aerobics Research (1994). Modifications for special populations. In *The Prudential FITNESSGRAM: Test administration manual.* Dallas: Author.

Dunn, J., and Fait, H. (1989). *Special physical education: Adapted, individualized, developmental.* 6th ed. Dubuque, IA: Brown.

Eichstaedt, C., and Kalakian, L. (1993). *Developmental/adapted physical education: Making ability count.* 3d ed. New York: Macmillan.

Eichstaedt, C., and Lavay, B. (1992). *Physical activity for individuals with mental retardation: Infancy through adulthood.* Champaign, IL: Human Kinetics.

Fisher, J. (1988). Measurement in adapted physical education. In P. Bishop, ed. *Adapted physical education: A comprehensive resource manual of definition, assessment, programming, and future directions.* Kearney, NE: Educational System Associates.

Illinois State Board of Education, Department of Special Education. (1978). *Adapted physical education: Related legislation, IEP development and programmatic considerations in Illinois.* Springfield, IL: (Available from Director of Special Education, Illinois State Board of Education, 100 N. First St., Springfield, IL 62777.)

———. (1987). *A parent's guide: The educational rights of handicapped children.* Springfield, IL: (Available from Director of Special Education, Illinois State Board of Education, 100 N. First St., Springfield, IL 62777.)

Individuals with Disabilities Act (IDEA), Public Law 101-476, 20 U.S.C. Chapter 3, 1990. (Available for the Superintendent of Documents, U.S. Government Printing Office, Washington, DC 20402. Telephone: 202-275-3030).

Jansma, P., and French, R. (1994). *Special physical education: Physical activity, sports, and recreation.* 2d ed. Englewood Cliffs, NJ: Prentice Hall.

Johnson, L., and Londree, B. (1976). *Motor fitness testing manual for the moderately mentally retarded.* Reston, VA: American Alliance for Health, Physical Education, Recreation and Dance.

Johnson, R., and Lavay, B. (1988). *Kansas adapted/special physical education text manual: Health-related fitness and psychomotor testing.* Topeka, KS: Kansas State Department of Education.

Kelly, L. (Project Director, NCPERID). (1995). *Adapted physical education national standards.* Champaign, IL: Human Kinetics.

Lasko-McCarthey, P., and Knopf, K. (1992). *Adapted physical education for adults with disabilities.* (3d ed.). Dubuque, IA: Bowers.

Lavay, B. (1988). The special physical educator: Communicating effectively in a tarn approach. In P. Bishop, ed. *Adapted physical education: A comprehensive resource manual of definition, assessment, programming, and future predictions.* Kearney, NE: Educational Systems Associates.

National Association for Sport & Physical Education (AAHPERD). (1995). *Moving into the future—National physical education standards: A guide to content and assessment.* St. Louis: Mosby.

National Information Center for Children and Youth with Disabilities. (1993). *Transition summary: Transition services and the IEP.* 3(1), March 1993. Available from NICHCY, PO Box 1492, Washington, DC 20013.

Ohio Department of Education. (1980). *Improving physical education for the handicapped in Ohio: Guidelines for adapted physical education.* (Available from Ohio Department of Education, Division of Elementary and Secondary Education, 65 S. Front St., Columbus, OH 43215.)

Pangrazi, R., and Corbin, C. (1994). *Teaching strategies for improving youth fitness.* 2nd ed. Reston, VA: American Alliance for

Health, Physical Education, Recreation, and Dance.

Pemberton, C. (1995). Testing: Preparation, administration, recording, and analysis. In M. Safrit (ed.), *Complete guide to youth fitness testing*. Champaign, IL: Human Kinetics.

Rimmer, J. (1994). *Fitness and rehabilitation programs for special populations*. Dubuque, IA: Brown.

Seaman, J., and DePauw, K. (1989). *The new adapted physical education: A developmental approach*. 2nd ed. Palo Alto, CA: Mayfield.

Shepard, R. (1990). *Fitness in special populations*. Champaign, IL: Human Kinetics.

Sherrill, C. (1993). *Adapted physical activity, recreation, and sport: Crossdisciplinary and lifespan*. 4th ed. Dubuque, IA: Brown.

Short, F. (1995). Individualized education programs. In J. Winnick, ed. *Adapted physical education and sport*. 2nd ed. Champaign, IL: Human Kinetics.

Stewart, D., Dummer, G., and Haubensticker, J. (1990). Review of administration procedures used to assess motor skills of deaf children and youth. *Adapted Physical Activity Quarterly*, 7(3), 231-239.

Ulrich, D. (1985). *Test of gross motor development*. Austin TX: PRO-ED.

U.S. Department of Education. (1992). Assessments to states for the education of children with disabilities program and preschool grants for children with disabilities: Final rule. *Federal Register*, 57(189), Tuesday, September 9, 1992, 44794-44852.

Werder, J., and Kalakian, L. (1985). *Assessment in adapted physical education*. Minneapolis, MN: Burgess.

Wessel, J., and Kelly, L. (1986). *Achievement based curriculum development in physical education*. Philadelphia, PA: Lea and Febiger.

Winnick, J. (1995). *Adapted physical education and sport*. 2d ed. Champaign, IL: Human Kinetics.

Winnick, J., and Short, F. (1985). *Physical fitness testing of the disabled: Project UNIQUE*. Champaign, IL: Human Kinetics.

Wisconsin Department of Public Instruction (DPI) (1985). *A guide to curriculum planning in physical education*. Bulletin No. 6230 (Available from Wisconsin DPI, 125 S. Webster St., PO Box 7841, Madison, WI 53707-7841)

—. (1988). *Physical education for exceptional educational needs students*. Information Update Bulletin No. 88.2, December 1988 (Available from Wisconsin DPI, 125 S. Webster St., PO Box 7841, Madison, WI 53707-7841).

Zittel, L. (1994). Gross motor assessment of preschool children with special needs: Instrument selection and consideration. *Adapted Physical Activity Quarterly*, 11, 245-260.

## ▶ REPRESENTATIVE READINGS

Adam, R., and McCubbin, J. (1991). *Games, sports, and exercises for the physically disabled*. 4th ed. Philadelphia: Lea & Febiger.

American Alliance for Health, Physical Education, and Recreation. (1975). *Testing impaired, disabled, and handicapped individuals*. Reston, VA.

Boyd, C., McCubbin, J., and Shasby, G. (1984). *Applied special physical education: A manual for the educator*. Minneapolis, MN: Burgess.

Bundschuh, E. (1983). *Project DART: Physical education for handicapped students*. Northbrook, IL: Hubbard.

DePauw, K., ed. (1982). *Assessment of the exceptional individual: Workshop proceedings*. National Convention of the American Alliance for Health, Physical Education, Recreation, and Dance. Houston, TX, April 22, 1982. (Available from Dr. Karen DePauw, Department of Physical Education, Washington State University, Pullman, WA 99164.)

DePauw, K., and Gavron, S. (1995). *Disability and sport.* Champaign, IL: Human Kinetics.

French, P., Henderson, H., and Horvat, M. (1992). *Creative approaches to managing student behavior in physical education.* Park City, UT: Family Development Resources.

Horvat, M. (1990). *Physical education and sport for exceptional students.* Dubuque, IA: Brown.

Jansma, P. (Ed.). (1993). *Psychomotor domain training and serious disabilities.* 4th ed. New York: University Press of America.

Karnes, M. (1992). *Fit for me: Activities of building motor skills in young children—Teacher's guide.* Circle Pines, MN: American Guidance Service.

Kauffman, J., and Pullen, P. (1987). *What should I know about special education: Answer for parents.* Austin, TX: Pro-Ed.

Kennedy, C., and Bundschuh, E. (1983). *Assessment and evaluation in adapted physical education.* (Available from Project DART, Athens Unit, G. R. C., 850 College Station Rd., Athens, GA 30610, 404-542-8970.)

Kibler, R., Cegala, D., Watson, K., Barker, L., and Miles, D. (1981). *Objectives for instruction and learning.* 2d ed. Boston: Allyn and Bacon.

Mager, R. (1984). *Preparing instructional objectives.* Revised 2d ed. Belmont, CA: Lake Publishers.

Maryland State Department of Education. (1983). *Teacher's helper: Physical fitness for handicapped students.* (Available from Maryland State Department of Education, Division of Special Education, 200 W. Baltimore St., Baltimore, MD 21201.)

Miles, B., Nierengarden, M., and Nearing, R. (1988). A review of the eleven most often cited assessment instruments used in adapted physical education. *Clinical Kinesiology, 42,* 33-41.

Ohio Department of Education. (1983). Integrating the handicapped student. In *physical education: Guidelines for teaching at the secondary school level.* Columbus, OH. (Available from Ohio Department of Education, Division of Elementary and Secondary Education, 65 S. Front St., Columbus, OH 43215.)

Owens, N. (1984). *Teaching golf to special populations.* West Point, NY: Leisure Press.

Paciorek, M., and Jones, J. (1989). *Sports and recreation for the disabled: A resource manual.* Indianapolis: Benchmark.

Roswal, G.; Floyd, R.; Jessup, G.; Pass, A.; Hanson, G.; and Roswal, P. *Alabama Special Olympics sports skills battery test manual.* (Available from Dr. Glen Roswal, Jacksonville State University, Department of Physical Education, Jacksonville, AL 36265).

Salvia, J., and Ysseldyke, J. (1985). *Assessment in special and remedial education.* 3d ed. Boston: Houghton Mifflin.

Seaman. J. (Ed). (1995). *Physical Best and individuals with disabilities: A handbook for inclusion in fitness programs.* Reston, VA: American Alliance for Health, Physical Education, Recreation, and Dance.

Sherrill, C. (1988). *Leadership training in adapted physical education.* Champaign, IL: Human Kinetics.

Vodola, T. (1976). *Project ACTIVE (All Children Totally Involved Exercising).* The following adapted physical education testing and programming manuals are available from Joe Karp, Director, Project ACTIVE, Kelso Public Schools, 601 Crawford, Kelso, WA 98626 (2061577-2463): *Low Motor Ability, Low Physical Vitality, Nutritional Deficiencies, Postural Abnormalities, Motor Disabilities/Limitations, Communication Disorders, Breathing Problems.*

## Test Sources for Measuring Motor Development of Students with Disabilities

Arnheim, D., and Sinclair, W. (1979). *The clumsy child: A program of motor therapy.* 2d ed. St. Louis, MO: C. V. Mosby. (This text contains the Basic Motor Ability Test - Revised.)

Brigance, A. (1978). *Brigance diagnostic inventory of early development.* North Billerica, MA: Curriculum Associates.

Bruininks, R. (1978). *Bruininks-Oseretsky test of motor proficiency: Examiners manual.* Circle Pines, MN: American Guidance Service.

Folio, M., and Fewell, R. (1982). *Peabody developmental motor scales and activity cards.* Hingham, MA: Teaching Resources Corporation.

Loovis, M., and Ersing, W. (1979). *The O.S.U. scale of intragross motor abilities.* Loudonville, OH: Mohican Textbook Publishing.

Werder, J., and Bruininks, R. (1988). *Body skills: A motor development curriculum for children.* Circle Pines, MN: American Guidance Service.

Wessel, J. (1976). *I CAN curriculum.* Northbrook, IL: Hubbard.

Wisconsin Association of Health, Physical Education, Recreation, and Dance (1994). *Gross motor assessment for children ages 3-6: Teacher's manual.* La Crosse, WI: Author. (Available from WAHPERD Executive Directors' Office, University of Wisconsin-La Crosse, 24 Mitchell Hall, La Crosse, WI 54601)

## Test Sources for Measuring Physical Fitness of Students with Mental Impairments

American Alliance for Health, Physical Education, Recreation, and Dance. (1976). *Special fitness test manual for mildly retarded persons.* Reston, VA.

Canadian Minister of State, Fitness and Amateur Sport. (1983). *Canada fitness award adapted for use by trainable mentally handicapped youth: A leaders' manual.* Rev. ed. (Available from Randy Adams, Fitness Canada, 365 Laurier Ave. W., Ottawa, Ontario, Canada K1A 9X6.)

Cooper Institute for Aerobics Research. (1992). *Prudential FITNESSGRAM.* Dallas, TX: Cooper Institute for Aerobics Research.

Dunn, J.; Morehouse, J.; and Fredericks, H. (1986). *Physical education for the severely handicapped: A systematic approach to a data-based gymnasium.* Austin, TX: Pro-Ed.

Jansma, P., Decker, J., Ersing, W., McCubbin, J., and Combs, S. (1988). The project transition assessment system. (Available from: Dr. Paul Jansma, The Ohio State University, Department of Physical Education, 343 Larkin Hall, Columbus, OH 43210)

Polacek, J.; Wang, P.; and Eichstaedt, C. (1985). *A study of physical and health-related fitness levels of mild, moderate, and Down syndrome students in Illinois.* (Available from Dr. Carl Eichstaedt, Dept. of HPERD, Illinois State University, Normal, IL 61761.)

Roswal, G.; Floyd, R.; Roswal, P.; Jessup, G.; Pass, A.; Klecka, L.; Montelione, T.; Vaccaro, P.; and Dunleaw, A. (1985). *Alabama Special Olympics fitness battery test manual.* (Available from Dr. Glen Roswal, Jacksonville State University, Department of Physical Education, Jacksonville, AL 36265.)

Vodola, T. (1975). *Low physical vitality: An individualized program.* (Available from Joe Karp, Director, Project ACTIVE, Kelso Public Schools, 601 Crawford, Kelso, WA 98626, (206) 577-2463. )

_____. (1978). *ACTIVE motor ability and physical fitness norms: For normal, mentally retarded, learning disabled, and emotionally disturbed individuals.* (Available from Joe Karp, Director, Project ACTIVE, Kelso Public Schools, 601 Crawford, Kelso, WA 98626 (206) 577-2463.

## Other Test Sources for Measuring the Physical Fitness of Students with Physical Impairments

Canadian Minister of State, Fitness and Amateur Sport. (1985). *Guidelines for adaptations of the Canadian fitness award: Youth with limited physical abilities.* (Available from Randy Adams, Fitness Canada, 365 Laurier Ave. W., Ottawa, Ontario, Canada K1A 0X6).

Hughes, J., and Riley, A. (1981). Basic gross motor assessment: Tool for use with children having minor motor dysfunction. *The Journal of American Physical Therapy Association* 3:503-11.

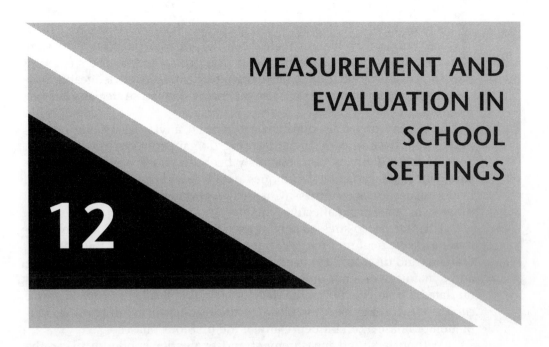

# MEASUREMENT AND EVALUATION IN SCHOOL SETTINGS

## 12

### ► KEY TERMS

content standards

event tasks

National Association of Sport and Physical Education (NASPE)

National Physical Education Standards: A Guide to Content and Assessment

Outcomes of Quality Physical Education

parental reports

portfolios

student journals

### ► OBJECTIVES

*After reading this chapter, the student should be able to:*

1. Identify and discuss factors that affect the design of measurement and evaluation models for implementation in the schools.
2. Describe needs and characteristics of youth in grades K–12.
3. Identify curriculum content for physical education programs at various levels.
4. Critique measurement and evaluation models presented in the chapter and recommend any needed modifications.
5. Design measurement and evaluation models for physical education settings not covered in the examples included in this chapter.

It is hoped that this chapter will help prospective teachers see how measurement and evaluation theory can be put into practice. With state mandates of program accountability, it is critical that teachers entering the physical education profession be prepared to make knowledgeable decisions about incorporating measurement and evaluation strategies into their teaching.

A quality physical education program at any level usually encompasses objectives in each of the learning domains of physical education. Each of these domains has previously been described and various measurement and evaluation techniques detailed with respect to each area: health-related physical fitness (Chapter 5), psychomotor (Chapter 6), cognitive (Chapter 7), and affective (Chapter 8).

Chapter 2 also stressed the importance of measurement and evaluation in the curriculum process. That chapter introduced the four learning domains and discussed the need to view the curricular process as ongoing and dynamic in order to prevent the program from becoming stagnant and outdated. Phase 5 of curriculum development is *evaluating and improving the curriculum*. Turning back to Figure 2.1 the reader will recall that the completion of Phase 5 can influence any of the first four phases.

Without a sound measurement and evaluation model in place, the teacher has no objective data on which to base decisions concerning the curriculum. If there is no way to know how well students are meeting stated program goals, unit outcomes, and/or performance objectives, modifying and improving the curriculum becomes intuitive guesswork at best. By incorporating measurement strategies from each of the four learning domains, the teacher can develop a sound model on which to base evaluation of the program and justification of subsequent curricular and instructional modifications. Therefore, the purpose of this chapter is to present various models of measurement and evaluation as they apply to various school settings.

## NASPE PROJECTS—NEW VISIONS FOR ASSESSMENT

In recent years, the call for accountability in all facets of education has been clear. In response to this demand, the **National Association of Sport and Physical Education (NASPE)** sponsored a project resulting in **Outcomes of Quality Physical Education** (1992) that includes 20 outcome statements (Figure 12.0) culminating in a definition of a physically educated person. The definition includes five major focus areas, specifying that a physically educated person has learned skills necessary to perform a variety of physical activities, is physically fit, participates in regular physical activity, knows the implications of and the benefits from involvement in physical activities, and values physical activity and its contribution to a healthful lifestyle.

▶ **FIGURE 12.0** Outcome Statements from the National Association for Sport and Physical Education (NASPE) Outcome Project.

**The physically educated person:**

▶ **HAS learned skills necessary to perform a variety of physical activities**

1. . . .moves using concepts of body awareness, space awareness, effort and relationships.
2. . . .demonstrates competence in a variety of manipulative, locomotor and nonlocomotor skills.
3. . . .demonstrates competence in combinations of manipulative, locomotor and nonlocomotor skills performed individually and with others.
4. . . .demonstrates competence in many different forms of physical activity.
5. . . .demonstrates proficiency in a few forms of physical activity.
6. . . .has learned how to learn new skills.

▶ **IS physically fit**

7. . . .assesses, achieves and maintains physical fitness.
8. . . .designs safe, personal fitness programs in accordance with principles of training and conditioning.

▶ **DOES participate regularly in physical activity**

9. . . .participates in health enhancing physical activity at least three times a week.
10. . . .selects and regularly participates in lifetime physical activities.

▶ **KNOWS the implications of and the benefits from involvement in physical activities**

11. . . .identifies the benefits, costs and obligations associated with regular participation in physical activity.
12. . . .recognizes the risk and safety factors associated with regular participation in physical activity.
13. . . .applies concepts and principles to the development of motor skills.
14. . . .understands that wellness involves more than being physically fit.
15. . . .knows the rules, strategies and appropriate behaviors for selected physical activities.
16. . . .recognizes that participation in physical activity can lead to multi-cultural and international understanding.
17. . . .understands that physical activity provides the opportunity for enjoyment, self-expression and communication.

▶ **VALUES physical activity and its contributions to a healthful lifestyle**

18. . . .appreciates the relationships with others that result from participation in physical activity.
19. . . .respects the role that regular physical activity plays in the pursuit of life-long health and well-being.
20. . . .cherishes the feelings that result from regular participation in physical activity.

Reprinted from Outcomes of Quality Physical Education Programs (1992) with permission from the National Association for Sport and Physical Education (NASPE), 1900 Association Drive, Reston, VA 20191-1599.

Follow-up work to the Outcomes Project has been the development and adoption of the *Moving into the Future: National Physical Education Standards: A Guide to Content and Assessment* (1995). Content standards from this document are shown in Figure 12.1. Content standards specify what students should know and be able to do and are roughly equivalent to "student learning outcomes" or "student objectives." These content standards, sample benchmarks, and assessment examples have been developed

▶ **FIGURE 12.1**    Content standards in physical education.

**A physically educated student:**

1.   Demonstrates competency in many and proficiency in a few movement forms.
2.   Applies movement concepts and principles to the learning and development of motor skills.
3.   Exhibits a physically active lifestyle.
4.   Achieves and maintains a health-enhancing level of physical fitness.
5.   Demonstrates responsible personal and social behavior in physical activity settings.
6.   Demonstrates understanding and respect for differences among people in physical activity settings.
7.   Understands that physical activity provides opportunities for enjoyment, challenge, self-expression, and social interaction.

From *Moving into the Future: National Physical Education Standards: A Guide to Content and Assessment* (1995) published by the National Association of Sport and Physical Education.

for grades K-12 at two-year intervals. An example of Content Standard #1 for the fourth grade is given in Figure 12.2. Since standards are of little use without precise guidelines to judge whether they have been achieved, NASPE has provided teachers with valid and reliable methods of assessing student progress toward attaining the standards. A major benefit of comprehensive standards and accompanying assessments is that they provide strong rationale that physical education is not "academically soft." The standards show the uninformed that there are meaningful and important areas of achievement in physical education and that these levels of achievement can be measured. These projects provide in-depth illustration of how curricular goals and assessment should be aligned so that the measurement and evaluation activities are relevant and meaningful to students.

While traditional assessment of physical fitness, sport skills, knowledge, and psychosocial characteristics still should be utilized, alternative assessment techniques can be implemented to complement or sometimes replace traditional written, fitness, or skills testing. A short description of a sampling of alternative assessment strategies as detailed in the NASPE (1995) document follows.

**Portfolios** (see Chapter 9 for additional discussion) are collections of a student's work assembled over time. They include various pieces of evidence documenting student achievement of a goal. If the goal was to learn to play soccer, a portfolio might include such things as evidence of playing on a recreational team, a list of drills practiced at home three times a week, a videotape of game play, a critique of offensive and defensive strategies observed in a soccer game, etc.

**Parental reports** provide a record of student participation of some form of out-of-class performance. These reports may refer to play choices,

▶ **FIGURE 12.2**   Fourth grade content standard #1, benchmarks, and assessment examples.

1. **Demonstrates competency in many movement forms and proficiency in a few movements forms.**

Fourth grade students should be able to demonstrate refined fundamental patterns. Attainment of mature motor patterns for the basic locomotor, non-locomotor, and selected isolated manipultive skills (throwing, catching, striking) is an expected exit outcome for fourth grade students. Variations of skills and skill combinations are performed in increasingly dynamic and complex environments (e.g., performing manipulative tasks while dodging, performing a gymnastics sequence with a partner, performing a formal dance to music). In addition, students should be able to acquire some specialized skills basic to a movement form (i.e., basketball chest pass, soccer dribble, fielding a softball with a glove) and to use those skills with a partner.

The emphasis for the fourth grade student is to:

▶ Demonstrate mature form in all locomotor patterns and selected manipulative and non-locomotor skills.
▶ Adapt a skill to the demands of a dynamic, unpredictable environment.
▶ Acquire beginning skills of a few specialized movement forms.
▶ Combine movement skills in applied settings.

**Sample Benchmarks:**

1. Throws, catches, and kicks using mature form.
2. Dribbles and passes a basketball to a moving receiver.
3. Balances with control on a variety of objects (balance board, large apparatus, skates)
4. Develops and refines a gymnastics sequence demonstrating smooth transitions.
5. Develops and refines a creative dance sequence in a repeatable pattern.
6. Jumps and lands for height/distance using mature form.

**Assessment Examples:**

1. Teacher observation—observational record.

Students are asked to receive and send a basketball pass to a partner on the move. The teacher observes the passing and uses a checklist to annotate the performance.

**Criteria for Assessment:**

a. Receives the pass and sends it in one motion.
b. Passes ahead of the moving player (receiver does not have to stop).
c. Receiving student cuts into a space to receive the pass.

2. **Event task—observational record**

Students are asked to combine a balance, a roll, and a traveling action into a gymnastics sequence. The sequence must include all the components and a clear beginning and ending.

*continued*

▶ **FIGURE 12.2**   Continued.

**Criteria for Assessment:**

a. Exhibits a balance, a role, and a traveling action during the performance.

b. Demonstrates a clear beginning and ending to the sequence.

c. Demonstrates smooth transitions between the various skills.

**3. Peer observation**

Have partners observe the preparatory phase of a designated skill in an attempt to ascertain the correct use of critical elements. For example, student A will throw a ball toward a target 5 times using the overhand pattern while student B observes the performance, focusing on a single critical element during the preparatory phase (e.g., opposite foot forward, side to target, arm pulled way back). The observing student gives a "thumb up" if the critical element is correct; if incorrect, the observing student tells what is needed to improve the movement.

**Criteria for Assessment:**

a. Thrower displays the critical element that is the focus of the observation.

b. Observer makes an accurate judgment on the performance.

Reprinted from Outcomes of Quality Physical Education Programs (1992) with permission from the National Association for Sport and Physical Education (NASPE), 1900 Association Drive, Reston, VA 20191-1599.

purposeful practice, formal activities such as sports clubs or lessons in a sport or family activities. They can include anecdotal information and the signature of the person who observed the out of class performance.

**Event tasks** are performance tasks that can be completed within 50 minutes. The task is written broadly enough so there are a variety of correct answers or solutions. An example might be to have a group of students develop a tumbling routine that could serve as a demonstration of skills learned in physical education or plan a five minute routine that could be presented in a school assembly.

**Student journals** provide a student record of participation, results, feelings, and perceptions about events. Entries should be made on a regular basis and serve as indicators of success, failure, enjoyment, or other intangible products of participation. Entries should not be judged as right or wrong, as students describe both positive and negative experiences. Self-analysis and reflections about personal performance are often included. This type of activity can provide valuable insight about student social and psychological perspective concerning their participation and performance in activity.

The four alternative assessment techniques described above are examples of a variety of alternative assessment methods presented in the NASPE (1995) document. All alternative assessment techniques should be characterized by the following:

- ▸ tasks that directly examine the behavior the teacher wishes to measure
- ▸ a focus on product and quality of performance
- ▸ criterion-referenced scoring
- ▸ assessment of higher levels of learning
- ▸ student participation in development of the assessment and ownership of the final product
- ▸ assessment criteria that are given to students in advance (Bartz, Anderson-Robinson, & Hillman, 1994).

## GUIDELINES FOR EFFECTIVE MEASUREMENT AND EVALUATION

Greater demands are being put on assessment in education at local, state, and national levels. At the same time, traditional forms of measurement and evaluation have been used sporadically or not at all. The reform movement in education includes changing measurement and evaluation activities to fully integrate them with the teaching process and objectives for student achievement. The transformation of these assessment programs is toward performance-based outcomes for students. The measurement and evaluation process should be an ongoing process that assesses student progress toward achieving meaningful learning outcomes. The previously discussed NASPE document provides an excellent example of learning outcomes (standards) and assessment strategies.

The following guidelines should be considered regarding what constitutes effective measurement and evaluation.

- ▸ Teacher decisions and grades should be based on a continuous, formative (process) evaluation as opposed to a single score on a fitness, written, or skills test. Evaluation should be integrated into the instructional process, with students being involved with assessment procedures.
- ▸ Assessment should be based on clearly defined educational objectives with distinct criteria for measuring student progress. Students should not be evaluated on subjective measures not central to instructional objectives.
- ▸ Fitness test scores should be used to help students set personal goals and determine individual progress, not for assigning grades. Self-testing can help students learn to assess their own fitness levels and provide more frequent evaluation than time-consuming formal testing procedures. Students can work with partners and work together to develop fitness profiles. The emphasis on self-testing is on the process rather than the product. While self-testing will be less accurate than

formal testing, the value as an educational endeavor outweighs this disadvantage. Self-testing is not meant to replace the formal testing program required at many schools.

▶ Use formative assessment for evaluating skill proficiencies. Formal skills testing can take up too much time, especially with large classes and limited class meetings. A certified physical educator should have the training to apply professional standards to holistically assess student skills. Predetermined performance standards can be used by the teacher, by peers, and by the student for self-evaluation.

▶ Use a wide variety of measurement and evaluation strategies that include all learning domains of physical education. Skills tests, videotape analyses, qualitative teacher or peer appraisals, formal and self-testing of health fitness, group projects, interviews, student journals, student demonstrations, student interest surveys, and written tests are some of the options.

▶ Use the results of measurement and evaluation activities for curriculum planning in daily, weekly, and unit objectives. Instruction should be modified as a result of these activities. In too many cases, assessment activities are used for grading but are not considered in curricular decisions.

▶ Use systematic observation to measure how students spend time in class. If students are to achieve fitness and skill development goals, it is important that they are successfully motor engaged for a high percentage of class time. Using a videotape and stopwatch, teachers should periodically check how much time is spent in activities such as management, transition, listening to the teacher, and appropriate activity. This simple technique can be used to alter teaching strategies in an attempt to increase student engagement. Chapter 10 provided detailed information about how to use systematic observation.

## VARIABLES AFFECTING MEASUREMENT AND EVALUATION MODELS

Every measurement and evaluation model should be specific to the program with which it is linked. Many of the same variables that are considered in designing a curriculum for a given educational setting will affect the amount and types of measurement and evaluation activities that are included. In fact, these measurement and evaluation strategies should be considered part of the curriculum since they take up class time and provide learning experiences for the students. Just as the curriculum will be different at different schools because so many variables affect curricular decision making, the measurement and evaluation scheme should be specifically tailored for that particular setting. Thus, before presenting the measurement and evaluation models, it is important to consider the many variables that can influence these models.

# Characteristics and Interests of Students

The physical, cognitive, and emotional development of students influences the choice of measurement tools. For example, the complexity of measurement instruments changes as students mature physically, cognitively, and emotionally. Thus, the characteristics and interests of students must be considered in designing measurement and evaluation models. While reading the following descriptions of students of different ages, think about the type of instrument that should be used to measure and evaluate the affective, psychomotor, cognitive, and health-related physical fitness domains. Keep in mind that these are general descriptions—there is great variability at every age level in physical and psychological maturity. Pangrazi and Dauer (1992) provide an excellent discussion of characteristics and interests of students in the elementary years. The following discussion concerning the development of students at various grade levels summarizes their thoughts.

## Primary Grades (K–3)

Children in grades K–3 have a relatively short attention span. They are naturally curious about what the body can do, enjoy a challenge, and are highly creative. They are beginning to understand and enjoy the concept of teamwork and are becoming curious about how to move effectively. Still, they usually do better in individual and small-group activities.

Children in this age group enjoy physical contact and rough-and-tumble activities. There are few sex differences in terms of their interests or physical capabilities. They like to perform well, work to please the teacher, are basically truthful and straightforward, and freely express individual views and opinions. They also seek personal attention.

Generally enthusiastic about physical activity, students of this age may tire quickly but recover just as quickly. Basic locomotor skills are being developed while sport-related skill patterns are usually immature. Eye-hand coordination and perceptual abilities are developing, but reaction time is still usually slow. They become increasingly interested in fitness and are naturally rhythmic.

## Intermediate Grades (4–6)

Students in intermediate grades exhibit a number of unique characteristics and interests. At this age, students begin to question the importance of various activities. They want to know the rules and become interested in strategies of games and sports. They also enjoy learning about the importance of both health-related and sport-related physical fitness.

An intense desire to excel in sport skills and physical capacities normally surfaces. Students in this age group accept more responsibility, are more independent, and become more concerned with being a member of a group. These youngsters enjoy group activities and become increasingly competitive. They have more interest in sports and sports-related activities; consequently, maintaining good sportsmanship needs to be stressed.

Steady growth characterizes this age group, with girls often growing more rapidly than boys and boys becoming rougher and stronger than girls. As their coordination and skills improve, the children become interested in learning more detailed techniques. There are often wide differences in physical capacities and skill development.

## Middle School (7–9)

In this age group, students experience a rapid growth spurt which does not follow an even pattern. Usually girls will go through this growth before boys. Tremendous muscular development occurs along with this erratic growth pattern. These physical developments cause periods of poor coordination because motor abilities increase at a slower rate. Posture is often poor. Boys are stronger than girls, run faster, and have slightly more endurance.

Students become very self-conscious and are strongly influenced by their peer group. They become more socially oriented and are increasingly interested in the opposite sex, which results in concern about physical appearance. Emotions can change rapidly at this age, intellectual capacities increase, and adolescents begin to narrow their interests and focus their attention on particular activities.

## High School (10–12)

Students in their high school years continue to mature and develop physically, socially, emotionally, and mentally. Ossification processes are complete and height and weight gains level off. Boys continue to gain musculature and exceed girls in height and weight. Both genders improve their ability to gain motor ability skills.

Students at this age are more secure than their junior high counterparts and have more sense of direction. Specialization and narrowing of interests continue. Their moods are more stable, and a great deal of intellectual development occurs with improved capacity for concentration and reasoning. They are still very concerned with social activities and the opposite sex, and the peer group remains a strong influence. Students are able to handle decision-making responsibilities and become more concerned with achievement and possible pay-offs. There is more interest in high risk/adventure activities, certain fitness activities (i.e., aerobic dance, weightlifting), and lifetime sports.

## Class Size

Class size is an important consideration in measurement and evaluation models. Many physical education teachers are plagued with the problem of oversized classes. While this should not be an excuse for not testing in physical education, it should be considered when selecting and administering measurement strategies. Measurement and evaluation should be a part of any physical education program, but extremely large classes impose limitations.

## Class Time

In planning tests for the various domains of physical education, the amount of time the students spend in class should be considered. Time actually spent in physical education depends on how long the class periods are and how many times per week the class meets. Daily physical education is certainly desirable, but some school districts schedule physical education on an every-other-day basis. Class periods are typically 30 minutes in elementary schools, but may be shorter or longer. Period length at the secondary level is usually 50–55 minutes, but this is not normally all activity time, since students must change clothes at the first and last of each class. The result is somewhere around 30 minutes of activity time at junior high and senior high levels. A certain percentage of that time should be spent in testing activities. If more time is available in class, then more time can be devoted to measurement and evaluation activities.

## Personnel Support

Having people other than the teacher to administer and monitor tests is advantageous to the measurement and evaluation program because more children can be tested in a more efficient manner. Some teachers have teacher aides assigned to physical education. In other instances, more than one physical education teacher may be on staff. Also, it may be possible in some schools to enlist additional personnel support during the administration of measurements. The school nurse can be a valuable resource. Student aides can also be used effectively, as can other teachers. Some teachers have enlisted the help of interested parents. The additional personnel can be used to grade tests, input test scores on optical scan sheets or microcomputers, generate reports to send home with students, or help administer tests. The use of additional personnel not only help the physical education teacher but also can be an excellent source of good public relations.

## Technological Support

Many teachers dislike testing because of the amount of paperwork generated by grading, recording, and reporting the scores. Technological advances can relieve the teacher of much of this tedious work. Word processing makes it possible to create test banks of questions that can be printed quickly for examination. Software is available to average grades, input scores, compute norms, and create individual reports of fitness testing. The personal computer can save many hours of work for the teacher. Optical scan sheets on which students mark their answers allow tests to be machine graded. Some programs also will run an item analysis and provide descriptive statistics concerning test results. The time invested by a physical educator in learning to use these resources will pay dividends of countless hours of work saved in the future. If this type of technological support is available to the teacher, it allows a more thorough measurement and evaluation scheme to be implemented. Chapter 14 provides a broad overview of different types of technological support.

## State and Local Mandates

Many schools have testing requirements mandated by state agencies or local district policies. Obviously, these mandates affect the planning of a measurement and evaluation model, and a physical education teacher may find that certain evaluation decisions already have been made. For example, it may be the policy of a district to do physical fitness testing in September and May of each year, or the district may have a policy dictating the grading method to be used. Some states or districts may decide to use a certain battery of tests for measuring and evaluating health-related physical fitness. In any case, a teacher must be aware of any legal mandates or local policies when planning a measurement and evaluation model.

## Curricular Content

The curricular content of physical education will vary from grade level to grade level. There will be certain similarities between adjoining grade levels, but there should be significant differences when the curricula of diverse grade levels are compared. This is due, in great part, to the differences in student characteristics, needs, and interests. Care should be taken to provide a horizontal progression of learning activities at any given grade level. The proper sequencing of learning activities and units from K–12 grades will provide for vertical progression. A quality curriculum has both horizontal and vertical progression.

## Suggestions for Primary Grades (K–3)

Regardless of grade level, a final result of curriculum planning should be implementation of a program of learning experiences selected based on the needs, characteristics, and interests of children. These experiences must be compatible with program objectives. As discussed earlier, the developmental age of the child dictates, in large part, the type of activities to be presented in the program. Although the process of measuring and evaluating progress toward objectives may vary, the program objectives remain virtually the same.

The learner characteristics of children in grades K–3 make it necessary to create an enjoyable as well as an instructional learning environment. Children should find happiness and reward through properly sequenced movement experiences that nurture a positive approach to physical activity that will last a lifetime.

Learning activities for younger children are individualized and focus on divergent movement. Children begin to learn body management, fundamental skills, and other essential movements that provide a foundation for the transition to more specialized skills. Developmental fitness activities must be designed to accommodate the abilities of the child and should be included as part of each lesson.

During grades K–3, children should have ample opportunities to explore and experiment within their environment and create movement activities without fear. Group activities become more prevalent within the programmatic scheme in grades 2 and 3. In addition to divergent and educational movement, simple rhythmics, appropriate stunts and tumbling activities, and low-organized games are included in the curriculum throughout the early elementary years. Sports skills are introduced in third grade and are intended to establish a foundation that can be built upon during the coming years.

The selection of activities should be directly linked to program objectives. This approach contrasts with selecting an activity because it is fun or because the teacher is good at it or enjoys it. The program should include varied creative movement experiences that can be performed safely by students and contribute to the physical education of the child (Pangrazi and Dauer, 1995).

The process we recommend using to make decisions about what specific learning experiences to include in a program is delineated in Pangrazi and Dauer (1995) and consists of selecting appropriate activities, organizing selected activities into units, allocating units of activity to developmental level, developing a year-long curriculum plan, and delivering a planned daily lesson.

### Suggestions for Intermediate Grades (4–6)

The third grade is a transitional period for children, and physical education activities should provide them the fundamental skills and fitness levels necessary to begin to develop specialized movements. Throughout the fourth, fifth, and sixth grades, the program shifts to an increased emphasis on sports skills and the refinement of previously learned movement competencies. Basketball, football, soccer, softball, track and field, and volleyball become an integral part of the program. This increased emphasis on sports skills prompts a renewed focus on quality of movement and correctness of patterns. Physical fitness development remains a priority, with increasing emphasis on vigorous aerobic activity. During the intermediate grades, the categories of activities remain the same (rhythmics, stunts and tumbling, games, and so on), but the time allocated to each changes.

### Suggestions for Middle School (7–9)

The middle school curriculum often gets overlooked in curriculum planning. Many curricula are designed specifically for elementary and high schools, but in most cases, the middle school curriculum is an adaptation of one or the other. Because of the unique characteristics of the middle school student, the curriculum should be specifically designed for these students.

Most middle school students have a wide variety of interests, so the curriculum should offer the opportunity to participate in many different activities. The curriculum should be balanced with a diversity of team sports, fitness activities, lifetime sports, dance, outdoor adventure activities, and aquatics. The units should be short and may be repeated at different times of the year if student interests dictate. It is recommended that no unit be longer than three weeks with many activities being only one or two weeks in duration. This allows students to explore many activities, allows greater chance of success, and alleviates boredom.

### Suggestions for High School (10–12)

Senior high school programs may vary a great deal from state to state and from large schools to small schools, with differences in facilities and in size of staff. As students mature and narrow their focus in physical activity, they desire more in-depth, specialized instruction. Whereas the middle school curriculum should provide exposure to a variety of activities, the senior high school curriculum should give students as many choices as there are teachers in a given class period.

With increased specialization and student interest, the units should be at least six weeks long. Some schools have nine-week units, while others offer single activities for entire 18-week semesters. More emphasis should be on activities that can be included in an active lifestyle throughout a lifetime.

# EXAMPLES OF MEASUREMENT
# AND EVALUATION MODELS

As previously discussed, there are underlying guidelines that provide the foundation for effective measurement and evaluation strategies. It would be a good idea to review these guidelines before proceeding in this chapter. Many of the variables that affect measurement and evaluation decisions have been delineated as well. When determining what percentage of class time will be devoted to assessment activities, keep in mind that many of these activities should be infused as learning experiences in the curriculum. For instance, peer assessment of the tennis serve can provide feedback as to student progress in serving, but also can be a learning experience in analyzing the important components of this skill. Asking students to keep a daily log of activities outside of physical education class provides an opportunity to assess exercise patterns away from class and makes students more aware of their regular activity patterns. This type of activity could be a starting point for making positive interventions in exercise away from class. Also, keep in mind that there are many different measurement and evaluation activities that can be utilized that are not included in these case studies. Assessment should be continuous. The suggestions in the case studies only highlight the type of activities that can be used; they are not meant to be inclusive.

The case studies that follow are representative of common physical education environments. Careful examination of these case studies will provide insights into the degree and type of testing that are feasible in certain teaching situations. Each case study is illustrated as a yearly plan with suggested measurement and evaluation activities included in each of the four learning domains: health-related physical fitness (HRPF), psychomotor (PM), affective (AFF), and cognitive (COG).

While there are physical education classes (usually elementary) in which the student to teacher ratio may be 60:1 or higher, these are abhorrent situations that are unfair to both the teacher and the students. Measurement and evaluation procedures are severely limited, as is the entire program, by this type of scheduling. Physical educators should have the same number of students as the classroom teacher. The gym is not an oversized classroom, and the scheduling of excessively large classes should not be tolerated.

With excessively large classes, it is tempting to abandon measurement and evaluation. Admittedly, they can be laborious and time-consuming in these settings. However, measurement and evaluation activities are critical to any program, and should not be omitted from the curriculum. Rather, the teacher must choose carefully the types of measurement and evaluation tools and thoroughly organize the administration of the selected tests. Alternative assessments, self-testing, and peer assessment are a few strategies that can be employed in these situations.

The resourceful physical educator should enlist the administrator who schedules the large classes to help with the testing. Other volunteers may come from older children at the school, other teachers, and parents. By giving these volunteers first-hand experience with oversized classes, the physical educator can turn a negative situation into a positive opportunity to inform them of the multitude of problems associated with overcrowded classes. Oftentimes, results of various tests will show that students are scoring below acceptable standards. The oversized classes and resultant shortage of active learning time and individual attention can be pinpointed as major factors in the lack of student achievement. The results of the measurement and evaluation activity can provide important information by which to justify hiring additional physical educators and/or changing the schedule to permit more manageable class sizes.

Measurement and evaluation procedures for children with disabilities are not addressed in the case studies. Detailed information on these special populations and appropriate measurement and evaluation procedures can be found in Chapter 11. Similarly, there is no mention of measurement and evaluation of teacher effectiveness in the case study models. Chapter 10 offers a thorough discussion of this area of assessment.

## Case Study #1

The setting is an elementary school (grades K–6) with a physical education instructor assigned to the school. The coed classes meet daily for 30 minutes with 30+ children per class. Ample indoor facilities are available, as well as outdoor space. Figure 12.3 illustrates a measurement and evaluation model for this situation.

In this model, health-related physical fitness testing is completed twice a year for all grades. The testing done in September serves as a needs assessment and the results, in the form of a graphic profile, are sent home to parents at the end of the first grading period. Sending a graphic profile depicting the student's performance is an excellent way to communicate with the parents. These baseline data provides the information needed to set goals and establish activity schedules for the upcoming year. Students in grades 4–6 should be taught how to self-test themselves on all health-related physical fitness items and encouraged to periodically check their own progress.

During the fall, skill-related physical fitness tests are administered to children in grades K–3. These tests serve as screening devices to identify youngsters who need special assistance. March is devoted to administering skill-related test batteries to the entire school population. The progress of younger students (K–3) is determined, and the older children (grades 4–6) are evaluated against nationally recognized standards. Formative assessment may be appropriate for this assessment.

▶ **FIGURE 12.3**   Suggested measurement and evaluation model for case study #1.

| | HRPF | PM | AFF | COG |
|---|---|---|---|---|
| **Aug.– Sept.** | Health-related fitness testing (K–6) | | Survey—attitude toward activity (4–6) | Written quizzes activity logs, group projects, etc. (4–6) |
| **Oct.** | | Skill-related fitness testing (K–3) | | |
| **Nov.** | | | | |
| **Dec.** | Self-testing (4–6) | | Student interest survey (4–6) | |
| **Jan.** | | | Sociometric test (3–6) | |
| **Feb.** | Self-testing (4–6) | | | |
| **Mar.** | | Skill-related fitness testing (K–6) | Student journal (4–6) | |
| **Apr.** | Health-related fitness testing (K–6) | | | |
| **May– June** | | | Survey—attitude toward activity (4–6) | ↓ |

A pre- and posttest approach to monitoring the attitudes of older children toward physical activity is suggested. The surveys give the instructor insight into children's feelings about what they do in physical education. The midyear interest survey gives the instructor time to make alterations in the yearly program base. The sociometric test gives the physical education instructor and classroom teachers opportunities to identify youngsters who do not seem to fit in with the class.

Daily physical education classes offer ample time for learning experiences associated with concepts of physical fitness. Time is devoted to written examinations or quizzes that give the instructor an opportunity to assess learning. Periodic quizzes during the fall and spring periods are recommended.

## Case Study #2

The setting is an elementary school (K–6) with a physical education instructor assigned to the school. The coed classes meet twice a week for 30 minutes with 30+ children per class. There are ample indoor facilities and outdoor space available. Figure 12.4 illustrates a measurement and evaluation model for this situation.

In this case study, physical education teaching has been reduced 60 percent compared to the first case study. However, measurement and evaluation continue to be an important part of the yearly program. Because of its important influence on the program, health-related physical fitness testing occurs on approximately the same schedule as in case study #1. Since class time is reduced, the instructor solicits the help of classroom teachers and parents to assist with the collection and organization of test information.

Skill-related fitness testing is limited to screening for motor dysfunction in children grades K–3. Since the majority of instructional time will be devoted to teaching motor skills, the instructor is on the alert to identify youngsters who display immature motor skill patterns. Selected motor

► **FIGURE 12.4**  Suggested measurement and evaluation model for case study #2.

| | HRPF | PM | AFF | COG |
|---|---|---|---|---|
| **Aug.–Sept.** | Health-related fitness testing (K–6) | | | Written quizzes, activity logs, group projects, etc. (4–6) |
| **Oct.** | | Selected tests to screen students who appear motor-delayed (K-3) | | |
| **Nov.** | Self-testing (4–6) | | | |
| **Dec.** | | | | |
| **Jan.** | | | Student interest survey (4–6) | |
| **Feb.** | Self-testing (4–6) | | | |
| **Mar.** | | Skill-related fitness testing (K–6) | Student journal (4–6) | |
| **Apr.** | Health-related fitness testing (K–6) | | | |
| **May–June** | | | Survey—attitude toward activity (4–6) | |

skills tests or test batteries are administered to these children and results are used to make decisions about referral to special programs. Because of the limited time available for instruction, skill-related fitness testing in the spring is limited to children in grades 4–6.

Testing in the affective domain consists of completing a student interest survey before the winter break and an attitude toward activity survey at the conclusion of the year. Results are tallied during nonschool time, and evaluation takes place prior to the start of a new period.

Since activity time is curtailed in this particular case study, it is important to maximize opportunities for movement. Accordingly, the instructor either curtails the written quizzes advocated in Case #1 or makes arrangements with classroom teachers to administer and evaluate cognitive tests in their classrooms for the children in grades 4–6.

## Case Study #3

The setting is an elementary school (K–6) with a physical education instructor who coordinates the classroom teachers for delivery of the physical education program. Each class has physical education three times per week, (30-minute periods) with approximately 25 students per class. The school is located in a district with limited funds. As a result, the facilities and equipment are minimal. There are no indoor facilities, but an asphalt play area and fields outside are available. Figure 12.5 illustrates a measurement and evaluation model for this situation.

Coordinating testing and evaluation in this case is complicated by the fact that usually classroom teachers are not trained to administer tests used in physical education. Although the recommended testing schedule is similar to Case #2, the success of this model depends on the ability of the instructor to train and monitor the performance of the classroom teachers. In-service sessions are scheduled that allow the instructor ample time to teach classroom teachers the proper strategies and techniques associated with testing in a movement-based discipline. The instructor also develops instructional materials that can be used to help the students become more skilled in completing self-tests.

## Case Study #4

The setting is a K–5 elementary school with a single physical education teacher assisted by a teacher's aide. The coed classes meet for 45 minutes daily and are oversized, with in excess of 60 students per class. The physical education class time for each grade level is used as a planning period for those classroom teachers. Thus, when the physical education teacher has all the third graders in class, the third grade classroom teachers have a plan-

► **FIGURE 12.5**   Suggested measurement and evaluation model for case study #3.

| | HRPF | PM | AFF | COG |
|---|---|---|---|---|
| **Aug.–Sept.** | Health-related fitness testing (K–6) | Selected tests to screen students who appear motor-delayed | | Written quizzes, activity logs, group projects etc. (4–6) |
| **Oct.** | | | | |
| **Nov.** | as needed | | | |
| **Dec.** | | | | |
| **Jan.** | Self-testing (4–6) | | | |
| **Feb.** | as needed | | | |
| **Mar.** | | Skill-related fitness testing (K–6) | Student journal (4–6) | |
| **Apr.** | Health-related fitness testing (K–6) | | | |
| **May–June** | | | Student interest survey | |

ning period. The facilities consist of a small gymnasium, a blacktop area, and ample field space. Figure 12.6 illustrates a measurement and evaluation model for this situation.

The physical educator makes every effort to enlist the help of classroom teachers for testing. Volunteer parents are also solicited to expedite testing procedures. Health-related physical fitness testing is done twice yearly as in the previous models. The older grades are tested earlier in the semester, and responsible older students then help test younger students later in the semester. A health fitness test battery that offers microcomputer support to generate reports is used to save time in preparing reports to be sent to parents.

Skill-related fitness testing is limited to screening for motor dysfunction in grades K–3 in the fall. With older children, the instructor tries to spot students who display immature motor skill patterns during various units. Sport skill testing for grades 4 and 5 is not performed because of the num-

▶ **FIGURE 12.6**   Suggested measurement and evaluation model for case study #4.

| | HRPF | PM | AFF | COG |
|---|---|---|---|---|
| **Aug.– Sept.** | Health-related fitness testing (4–5) | Screen for motor-delayed students (K–3) | Survey—attitude toward activity (3–5) | Written quizzes, activity logs, group projects, etc. (4–5) |
| **Oct.** | Health-related fitness testing (K–3) | Formative assessments as needed (K-5) | | |
| **Nov.** | | | | |
| **Dec.** | | | | |
| **Jan.** | Self-testing (4–5) | | Student interest survey (3–5) | |
| **Feb.** | | | | |
| **Mar.** | | | Student journal (4–5) | |
| **Apr.** | Health-related fitness testing (K–5) | | | |
| **May– June** | | | Survey—attitude toward activity (3–5) | |

ber of students involved but formative assessments are used. Student interest surveys are administered to grades 3–5 at midyear. An assessment of attitudes toward physical activity is done twice yearly, once in the fall and again in the spring, for grades 3–5.

Because of the large numbers, written quizzes are less frequent than in other models. Additionally, the physical educator asks the classroom teachers to administer these quizzes because of the overcrowded nature of the classes. The teacher aide and parental volunteers are utilized to help grade quizzes, tally student interest surveys, and score the attitudinal scales.

## Case Study #5

The setting is a middle school with grades 7–9. There are four instructors in physical education. Classes meet daily for 55 minutes, with about 40 coed students per instructor. Students dress out each day. Units are no longer than three weeks. There is a small weight room, a gymnasium, and ample field space. Figure 12.7 illustrates a measurement and evaluation model for this situation.

Health-related physical fitness testing is done twice yearly. Testing in September serves as a needs assessment, and results are sent home with students at the end of the first grading period. The second test administration is done in late April or early May and shows final fitness levels and improvement for the year. This report also is sent to parents and forms the basis for evaluating program objectives in this domain. Students may self-test themselves during the year to check their status in the various components of health-related fitness.

With units no longer than three weeks, time for formal sports-skills testing is minimal. Formative assessments are used, and students evaluate their own proficiency during certain drills (e.g., "Shoot 10 free throws and see how many you can make."). Some units, such as weight training or jogging, lend themselves to testing more easily than others.

► **FIGURE 12.7**  Suggested measurement and evaluation model for case study #5.

| | HRPF | PM | AFF | COG |
|---|---|---|---|---|
| **Aug.–Sept.** | Health-related fitness testing | ↑ | Survey—attitude toward activity (3–5) | ↑ |
| **Oct.** | | Formative assessments as needed | Sociometric test | |
| **Nov.** | Self-testing | | | Written tests every 3 weeks, group projects daily logs, demos, etc. |
| **Dec.** | | | Student interest survey | |
| **Jan.** | | | Sociometric test | |
| **Feb.** | Self-testing | | | |
| **Mar.** | | | Student journal | |
| **Apr.** | Health-related fitness testing | | Survey—attitude toward activity | |
| **May–June** | | ↓ | Student interest survey | ↓ |

Sociometric tests are done early in each semester so that instructors are aware of the social dynamics of the class. Some sort of survey concerning attitudes toward activity is administered at the beginning and at the end of the year. Finally, a student interest survey is given at the end of each semester to help instructors evaluate their curricular offerings and plan for future units. Each of the tests in the affective domain can be administered in one class period.

Written tests are administered about every three weeks. Normally tests are given at the end of a unit. If several short units (one or two weeks in length) are taught, those two units are combined into one test. Multiple-choice questions are usually appropriate for these tests. Other options for assessing the cognitive domain are used as well.

## Case Study #6

The setting is a middle school for grades 7–9. There are two physical education instructors. The classes alternate with the health class, so they occur every other day. There is a 55-minute class period with 35 minutes of actual activity, since the students change clothes at the beginning and end of each period. The coed classes have 30–35 students. There is a small weight room, a gymnasium, an activity room, and ample field space. The activity units are a maximum of three weeks long. Figure 12.8 illustrates a measurement and evaluation model for this situation.

This model differs from the previous middle school model because there are fewer class periods as a result of meeting on alternate days. Because of its importance, testing in the health-related area is done at the end of the year. Self-test procedures should be used to initially assess and monitor health fitness status. Goal setting with students can culminate in year-end formal testing. With less class time, formative skill assessment is done. The affective domain is assessed by a sociometric test shortly after the start of each semester and an attitude survey and student interest survey toward the end of the year. Measurement in the cognitive domain is scheduled every six weeks, and each test covers several units. Homework assignments and other projects should play a role in assessing the cognitive domain.

## Case Study #7

The setting is a high school with grades 10–12. There are six instructors per class period, which meets daily for 55 minutes. Students dress out each day. The coed classes have 30–35 students, who are given a choice of activity. Each activity lasts six weeks, and students are not allowed to enroll for any single activity more than twice during the school year. There is a

► **FIGURE 12.8**    Suggested measurement and evaluation model for case study #6.

| | HRPF | PM | AFF | COG |
|---|---|---|---|---|
| **Aug.–Sept.** | Self-testing for fitness | ↑ | Sociometric test | ↑ |
| **Oct.** | | Formative assessments as needed | | Written tests every 6 weeks, group projects daily logs, demos, etc. |
| **Nov.** | | | | |
| **Dec.** | | | Sociometric test | |
| **Jan.** | Self-testing | | | |
| **Feb.** | | | | |
| **Mar.** | | | Student journal | |
| **Apr.** | Health-related fitness testing | | Survey—attitude toward activity | |
| **May–June** | | ↓ | Student interest survey | ↓ |

weight room, swimming pool, activity room, two gymnasiums, and ample field space. Figure 12.9 illustrates a measurement and evaluation model for this situation.

Formal testing in the health-related physical fitness domain is done at the start of the school year and again at the end of the year. Students are given the opportunity to assess their status with self-testing procedures in the middle of the school year.

Sports-skills testing is performed after each six-week unit. With units of this length, adequate time is available to test the proficiency of each student. In some units, such as gymnastics or dance, formative assessment is more appropriate. Qualitative assessment is ongoing in other units as well. Peer and self-assessments are used effectively. When qualitative assessment is used, students are told the criteria on which the evaluation is based.

Because students are given a choice of unit each six weeks, the composition of each instructor's class changes. Thus, sociometric testing is

► **FIGURE 12.9**   Suggested measurement and evaluation model for case study #7.

| | HRPF | PM | AFF | COG |
|---|---|---|---|---|
| **Aug.–Sept.** | Health-related fitness testing | ↑ | Survey—attitude toward activity | ↑ |
| **Oct.** | | Formative contin-uous assessments | | Quizzes weekly, written tests, projects, daily logs, demos, etc. |
| **Nov.** | Self-testing | Sports skills test at end of 6-week unit | | |
| **Dec.** | | | Sociometric test at the start of each 6-week unit | |
| **Jan.** | | | | |
| **Feb.** | Self-testing | | | |
| **Mar.** | | | Student journal | |
| **Apr.** | Health-related fitness testing | | Survey—attitude toward activity | |
| **May–June** | | ↓ | Student interest survey | ↓ |

done at the start of each six-week unit. Attitude surveys are taken at the beginning and end of the school year. A student interest survey is administered at the end of the year to help instructors evaluate their curriculum and plan modifications for the upcoming year.

A major written test is given during each six-week unit. Quizzes are administered on a weekly basis. Outside projects and homework assignments used effectively in units of this length.

## Case Study #8

The setting is a high school for grades 10–12. There are 4 instructors per class period, which meets daily for 55 minutes. Students dress out each day. The coed classes have about 30–35 students, who are given a choice of activity. Each activity chosen lasts for 1 semester, or 18 weeks. Students must sign up for 4 semesters of physical education credit during high school and can-

◤ **FIGURE  12.10**    Suggested measurement and evaluation model for case study #8.

| | HRPF | PM | AFF | COG |
|---|---|---|---|---|
| **Aug.–Sept.** | Health-related fitness testing | ↑ | Sociometric test | |
| **Oct.** | | Formative assessment and | | |
| **Nov.** | Self-testing | sports skills test as needed for 18-week unit | | Mid-semester exam |
| **Dec.** | | ⏐ | Survey—attitude toward activity | Quizzes, other projects as needed |
| **Jan.** | | Formative assessment and | Sociometric test | Final exam |
| **Feb.** | Self-testing | sports skills test as needed for 18-week unit | | |
| **Mar.** | | | Student journal | |
| **Apr.** | Health-related fitness testing | | Survey—attitude toward activity | Mid-semester exam |
| **May–June** | | ↓ | Student interest survey | Final exam |

not take any activity more than twice. There is a weight room, activity room, one gymnasium, and ample field space. Figure 12.10 illustrates a measurement and evaluation model for this situation.

As in the other secondary models, testing in the health-related physical fitness domain is done in September and again in late April or early May and self-testing is used during the year. With 18-week units, instructors have an opportunity to do more extensive qualitative assessment and sports skills testing than in previously discussed situations. Sociometric testing is done early in each semester, and a survey assessing attitudes toward physical activity is completed at the end of each 18-week unit. Also, a student interest survey is administered at the end of the year. A mid-semester written exam and a final examination covering all units are used to evaluate the cognitive domain. Quizzes and additional projects also are used to assess cognitive achievement.

# SUMMARY

Much national attention has been focused on content standards, benchmarks of performance, and assessment options in physical education. The NASPE Outcomes Project and the Standards and Assessment Document have made valuable contributions to ensuring curricular alignment of objectives, performance, and assessment. Guidelines specific to assessment in school settings are presented in this chapter.

Variables that affect curricular design also affect decisions about measurement activities to evaluate students and the overall effectiveness of the program. Among the variables discussed are needs and characteristics of students, class size, class time, personnel support, legislative mandates, and educational technology. Examples of curricula at the elementary, middle school, and high school are included.

The chapter then presents a variety of measurement and evaluation models in a case study format. These models are suggested for various grade levels and different teaching situations (not necessarily ideal) that are typical in schools today. The models are intended only to present possibilities for measurement and evaluation strategies in each setting. It is hoped that by considering the many variables that impact measurement and evaluation and studying the models presented in the chapter, students can begin to apply information previously learned about measuring and evaluating the four learning domains. Students should be able to formulate solid measurement and evaluation models in a variety of potential physical education situations.

# ► DISCUSSION QUESTIONS

1. Which learning domain merits the most measurement and evaluation time in the elementary physical education setting? The middle school setting? The high school setting? Which merits the least? Defend your opinions.

2. What are the variables that affect measurement and evaluation models? Which variable has the greatest impact on these models? The least? Provide a rationale for your answers.

3. Select one of the eight measurement and evaluation models. What concerns would you have regarding the implementation of your selected model? Suggest changes that would eliminate your concerns.

4. The setting is a high school that offers units lasting one full semester. Classes are coed and average 30 students. Develop a measurement and evaluation model for a semester-long weight training unit and a second model for a one-semester tennis class. Think carefully about the type of curricular activities that would be included in each class before developing a complementary measurement and evaluation model.

### ► REFERENCES

American Alliance for Health, Physical Education, Recreation, and Dance (1992). *Outcomes of quality physical education programs*. Reston, VA: APPHERD.

Bartz, D., Anderson-Robinson, S., and Hillman, L. (1994) Perfomance assessment: Make them show what they can know. *Principal*, 73 (3): 11–14.

National Association for Sport and Physical Education (1995). *Moving into the future: national physical education standards—a guide to content and assessment*. St. Louis: C. V. Mosby Publishers.

Pangrazi, R. P., and Darst, P. W. (1991). *Dynamic physical education for secondary school students: Curriculum and instruction.* 2d ed. New York: Macmillan.

Pangrazi, R. P., and Dauer, V. P. (1995). *Dynamic physical education for elementary school children*. 11th ed. Boston: Allyn and Bacon.

### ► REPRESENTATIVE READINGS

Annarino, A. A.; Cowell, C. C.; and Hazelton, H. W. (1980). *Curriculum theory and design in physical education.* St. Louis, MO: C. V. Mosby.

Corbin, C. B., ed. (1980). *A textbook of motor development.* 2d ed. Dubuque, IA: Wm. C. Brown.

Harrison, J. M. (1996). 4th ed. *Instructional strategies for secondary physical education.* Dubuque, IA: Wm. C. Brown.

Siedentop, D.; Herkowitz, H.; and Rink, J. (1984). *Elementary physical education methods.* Englewood Cliffs, NJ: Prentice-Hall.

Wessel, J. A., and Kelly, L. (1986). *Achievement-based curriculum development in physical education.* Philadelphia, PA: Lea and Febiger.

Willgoose, C. E. (1984). *The curriculum in physical education.* 4th ed. Englewood Cliffs, NJ: Prentice-Hall.

Zaichkowsky, L. D.; Zaichkowsky, L. B.; and Martinek, T. J. (1980). *Growth and development: The child and physical activity.* St. Louis, MO: C. V. Mosby.

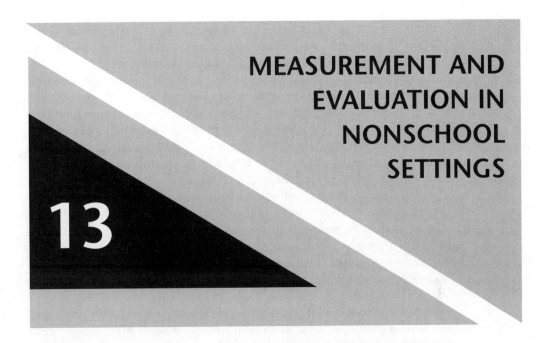

# MEASUREMENT AND EVALUATION IN NONSCHOOL SETTINGS

## 13

### ▶ KEY TERMS

athletic training
blood pressure
body density
cardiac rehabilitation
cardiopulmonary resuscitation
cholesterol analysis
first aid
fitness leadership
fitness management
graded exercise tests
hydrostatic weighing
lung function
maximal oxygen uptake (VO$_2$ max)
nonschool setting
rehabilitation
sphygmomanometer
sports administration
sports injury data
step test
stethoscope
therapeutic recreation
treadmill

### ▶ OBJECTIVES

*After reading this chapter, the student should be able to:*

1. Describe the role of measurement and evaluation in exercise and activity settings outside traditional school physical education programs.
2. Cite similarities and differences among approaches to measurement and evaluation in various nonschool settings.
3. Characterize nonschool fitness, exercise, rehabilitation, and testing programs.
4. Identify and discuss factors that influence the design of measurement and evaluation in the nonschool setting.
5. Design measurement and evaluation models for nonschool settings not included in this chapter.
6. List tests and equipment used in the nonschool setting for the purpose of measuring and evaluating dimensions of movement and health-related physical fitness.

Thus far, this text has focused on the role of measurement and evaluation to strengthen physical education in the traditional school setting. In this era of accountability and reclaiming of public trust in education, it is critical for students preparing to teach physical education to have a working knowledge of, and practical skills in, measurement and evaluation. For students interested in fitness and exercise, some relatively new academic programs are available that prepare students for professions in the **nonschool setting**. These programs have developed in response to increased interest in health and physical fitness among adults seeking to improve their physical fitness through increased physical activity.

Since the early 1980s, professional associations, universities and colleges, private health clubs, and nonprofit organizations have recognized the market impact of strength training for adults. By the mid-1980s this interest had expanded to the medical community. This keen interest in adult exercise programs has blossomed into a burgeoning business. With it comes new opportunities for young people to pursue careers in exercise science.

Many different academic majors can prepare students for careers in **fitness management, cardiac rehabilitation, fitness leadership, athletic training, therapeutic recreation,** and **sports administration.** Each of these options provides the requisite knowledge and training necessary for individuals interested in pursuing a career in health-related professions. Aspiring young professionals can apply their newly acquired skills, knowledge, and expertise to pursue employment in hospital settings, YMCAs or YWCAs, health clubs, university wellness programs, corporate fitness programs, and various other exercise and fitness career options.

Although there are obvious differences between physical education in the schools and exercise/fitness programs for adults in the nonschool setting, at least one common thread is prevalent. Not surprisingly, that is the role of measurement and evaluation. Much like physical education in the schools, the success of fitness programming and exercise prescription in nonschool settings is very dependent on measurement and evaluation techniques. For example, measurement is used to assess initial fitness levels. Laboratory-based testing is the most accurate means to measure components of health-related physical fitness. These tests are conducted on an individual basis in a laboratory setting by trained personnel using sophisticated equipment. For example, maximal oxygen uptake is most accurately determined by measuring expired gases during maximal exercise. Underwater weighing to determine body composition is another lab technique that permits an accurate calculation of body fat percentage. This baseline information is useful in the subsequent testing that assists in charting the progress of individuals. As you already know, multiple measurements are required to provide the information necessary to render an evaluation.

Personalized testing is an expectation of clients participating in specialized exercise programs.

This chapter will describe the role of measurement and evaluation in the nonschool setting, characterize four categories of adult fitness and exercise programs, and discuss special considerations for measurement and evaluation in the nonschool setting. A description of various nonschool exercise and fitness settings also will be provided. Lastly, selected movement and fitness tests will be identified and explained.

## THE ROLE OF MEASUREMENT AND EVALUATION IN THE NONSCHOOL SETTING

Measurement and evaluation play an integral role in any physical activity-based program. Preceding chapters have clearly detailed ways in which testing and evaluating assist the practitioner in a school physical education environment. Looking at the function of measurement and evaluation in the nonschool setting, it comes as no surprise that the fundamental purposes for measuring and evaluating are the same. There are, however, some differences between measurement and evaluation in the school setting and the nonschool settings.

1. The nonschool setting consists primarily of exercise programs for adults. At present, little attention is focused on children and youth.

2. The primary thrust of these programs is toward exercise and fitness activities that contribute to the enhancement of health-related physical fitness. Less attention is paid to enhancing physical skills, cognitive development, or fostering attributes associated with growth in the affective domain.

3. Programs in the nonschool setting are ongoing. There is no academic year to dictate a time frame into which a program must fit.

4. Due to fewer participants and the mature nature of the participants, it is much easier to individualize physical activity programs in the nonschool setting. Likewise, new or complex concepts regarding physical fitness can be understood quickly by a more mature individual.

5. Physical activity programs in the nonschool setting are voluntary. In fact, most participants pay a membership fee for access to and use of facilities and expertise. In contrast, students are required to attend school and participate in physical education. Thus, in the nonschool setting the fitness professional is dealing with adults who have willingly chosen to become actively involved.

6. Most nonschool activity programs are not plagued by space constraints, overcrowding, or the need to meet state or district mandates in

a variety of subjects, as are many school physical education programs. As a result, many school programs are characterized by infrequent and brief class meetings. In the nonschool setting enrollment in exercise and fitness programs can be selective, and the type and duration of activity is of sufficient length to positively alter fitness levels.

7. Programs affiliated with the private, for-profit sector and large business entities (e.g., hospital wellness programs and corporate fitness programs) usually have greater resources than are typically found in the schools.

In spite of these differences, measurement and evaluation in the nonschool setting play the same part in the program's success as in any school-based program. That is to say, the same model for determining curriculum in the schools can be applied in the nonschool setting to ascertain the type of activity needed to improve performance. Just as in schools, the specialist in the nonschool sector must conduct a needs assessment, establish goals, develop performance-based objectives, and provide ongoing evaluation for the purpose of improving the individual's exercise program. The only phase of program development that is required in the school setting but absent from the nonschool environment is the process of defining unit outcomes. Since most nonschool programs are highly individualized and deal with only one form of activity, the absence of unit goals from the larger scheme is generally irrelevant.

Although there are some differences in the settings, the roles of measurement and evaluation in school physical education programs and nonschool exercise and fitness programs are similar. The need to provide quantitative performance benchmarks in order to establish an exercise prescription and to improve various components of the health-related physical fitness domain is critical to the success of any professional physical activity program.

## CHARACTERISTICS OF NONSCHOOL FITNESS AND EXERCISE PROGRAMS

There are a number of different nonschool settings for programs that emphasize fitness and exercise. For the sake of convenience, the many possibilities of nonschool health environments have been classified into four categories. These general areas include (1) athletic training, (2) corporate and community fitness programs, (3) hospital- and university-based health and fitness programs, and (4) therapeutic recreation. The sections that follow will cite distinctive characteristics of each setting and describe the role of measurement and evaluation associated with that particular setting.

## Athletic Training

Athletic training is rapidly becoming a popular choice for students interested in pursuing a health-related profession. This is due in large measure to its affiliation with competitive sports. Potential athletic trainers undergo intensive education designed to provide the requisite knowledge and skills to gain employment in public schools, colleges, or professional sports. Some states require licensure for athletes trainers. Further, it is highly recommended that trainers become board-certified by the National Athletes Trainers Association. To do so requires successful completion of a standard examination. An athletic trainer's primary responsibilities are to prevent, recognize, and treat sports injuries. In addition, trainers must provide assessment, **rehabilitation**, program organization, and education of the athlete. As might be expected, familiarity with and understanding of measurement and evaluation techniques is essential if trainers are to perform their responsibilities effectively. The assessment of sports injuries is a competency that all athletic trainers must possess. Both on and off the field, the athletic trainer is required to render accurate and detailed assessment and evaluation of a variety of circumstances.

Central to the responsibilities of athletic trainers is the ability to prescribe and oversee an appropriate rehabilitation program for an injured athlete (see Figure 13.0). Several criteria must be measured at the beginning, during, and at the end of this process. The following criteria should be considered when determining the status of an injury:

 **FIGURE 13.0** Treatment of Injury.

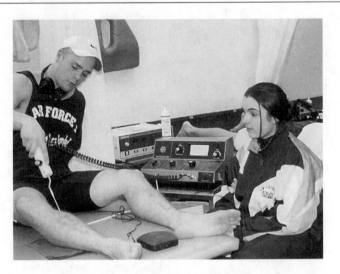

1. strength of each muscle group
2. power of each muscle group
3. endurance of each muscle group
4. balance between antagonistic muscle groups
5. flexibility of the muscles around the rehabilitated joint (Roy and Irvin, 1983).

The assessment and evaluation of sports injuries is the primary function of athletic trainers. Each trainer must develop a systematic approach to measuring and evaluating the extent of an injury. According to the American Academy of Orthopaedic Surgeons (1984), there are three distinct evaluations associated with a sports injury. First is the primary, or on-site, inspection and evaluation. This phase consists of providing necessary **first aid**, the determination of serious injuries, and the proper disposition of the athlete. Second is the off-site evaluation, during which the trainer sequences the procedures that determine the nature, location, and seriousness of the injury. The last phase consists of a treatment regimen, including therapy and, of course, a follow-up exercise program. Once treatment of the injury has been completed, it is the responsibility of the athletic trainer to design a program of exercise to rehabilitate the injured area. An instrument used to aid in the development of an exercise program to rehabilitate an injury is the Biodex (see Figure 13.1). This instrument calculates

▶ **FIGURE 13.1**    The Biodex.

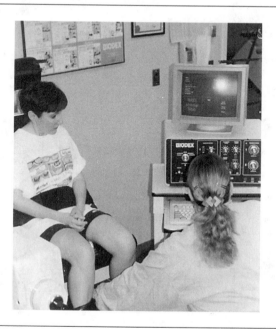

the strength of a muscle or muscle group and can be used to compare the injured area with its uninjured counterparts.

In addition to aiding in the exercise plan, measurement and evaluation techniques are used to assist the athletic trainer in a number of other tasks. Valid, reliable **sports injury data** can materially help decrease sports-related injuries. Properly interpreted, this type of data can be useful in modifying rules and in assisting coaches and teachers to better understand risks associated with participation in certain sports. Quantitative record keeping can also aid in evaluating products designed to protect athletes. In this era of accountability, the public needs to understand the risks inherent in sports.

In sum, the profession of athletic training depends heavily on measurement and evaluation techniques. To be effective in their multiple duties trainers continually assess and evaluate ranging from on-the-scene analysis of an injury to analysis of data accrued over time.

## Corporate and Community Exercise and Fitness Programs

The business world introduced large-scale wellness and health promotion programs to the general public. Many corporations embrace health promotion and have initiated programs of their own that address the many dimensions of healthful living. These programs are founded on the premise that healthy people are more productive, work harder, and spend less time away from the job.

Numerous health and fitness programs and services are sponsored by community agencies. YMCAs and YWCAs, Boys' and Girls' Clubs, health clubs, churches, dance studios, and other local organizations provide educational and exercise opportunities for various community constituencies. Most of these programs offer affordable programs to the local population.

In either the corporate or community agency setting, both the overall operation and individual programming for participants depend on sound measurement and evaluation principles. Fitness specialists are responsible for making decisions about facilities, supplies, overall resources, personnel, curriculum, and fitness testing and reporting. To make such decisions, they rely on measurement techniques that assist in the evaluation of personnel, programs, and facilities and equipment.

## Hospital- and University-Based Health and Fitness Programs

Hospital participation in health promotion dates back to early community education programs. As knowledge of the benefits of early detection of disease and of techniques for trauma treatment grew, hospitals translated this information into offerings of health screening and educational programs. The first of these programs appeared in the 1960s, consisting of **blood**

**pressure** screenings and first aid and **cardiopulmonary resuscitation** (CPR) classes (Burke, 1989). From these humble beginnings has emerged a wide range of educational programs and services designed to promote wellness and change the physical activity and health habits of participants. The American College of Sports Medicine sponsors a variety of certification opportunities for professionals seeking additional training and credentials.

In large part, these programs have been successful due to their affiliations with hospitals. Credibility has been established through programs of high quality, taught by trained professionals with access to sophisticated equipment and resources. Participants in the early programs came from new markets. Outpatients, patients' family members, and community residents who simply thought it made good sense to learn about lifesaving techniques and other health matters began coming to hospitals for education programs. Familiarity with hospital personnel and resources enhanced the hospitals' image in the community and engendered support of such programs (Burke, 1989).

Today many hospitals sponsor exercise and fitness programs. Often sustained through referrals, these programs provide patients with a necessary convenience during the rehabilitation phase of their injury or illness. The programs frequently are housed within the hospital and contain many of the trappings associated with posh health clubs. Like other fitness and exercise programs, hospital-based programs rely on measurement and evaluation techniques to assist in planning and monitoring patients' progress. In addition, multifaceted hospital programs comprise patient recordkeeping, billing procedures, personnel supervision, calibration of equipment and scientific instruments, and curriculum building. Each of these areas requires the application of measurement and evaluation procedures.

With increased interest in hospital health promotion came the need to prepare professionals to work in this area. Universities and colleges began developing programs in fitness leadership and cardiac rehabilitation. In addition, and in order to provide the necessary clinical experiences, some universities and colleges established health and fitness programs of their own. These programs attract adult participants and serve as excellent venues for students to gain valuable practical experience while fulfilling degree requirements.

An example of such a program is the one sponsored by the University of Wisconsin–La Crosse. Established in 1971, this program is for area residents who want to improve their lifestyles. The overall program, which emphasizes cardiorespiratory endurance, muscular strength, flexibility, and proper nutrition, is called the La Crosse Exercise and Health Program. It consists of two distinct, yet interrelated, programs.

The Adult Fitness Program is designed for generally healthy individuals who want to make a commitment to fitness. Upon registration, participants undergo tests to determine their fitness level. The tests are simple and assist the staff in understanding participant limitations and establishing goals. Exercise programs are then tailored to individual needs.

The Cardiac Rehabilitation Program aids individuals who have documented cardiac disease or are at high risk of its development. All workout sessions are closely monitored by trained personnel. For high-risk participants, program sessions are supervised by a qualified specialist. Of course, providing appropriate fitness programming that meets the expectations of paying participants requires knowledge and skill in measurement and evaluation techniques.

In the La Crosse program, skilled staff members use state-of-the-art scientific instrumentation to help participants determine their current level of fitness. Tests include **graded exercise** (stress) tests, body-fat analysis, flexibility and strength assessments, **lung function** measurements, and **cholesterol analysis**. Results of each test are interpreted, discussed with the participant, and used to design an individualized exercise regimen for that member.

## Therapeutic Recreation

Professionals in therapeutic recreation are prepared to develop and implement treatment, education, and recreation programs for individuals with an illness, disability, or special need. Recreational therapists are employed in various treatment centers, such as hospitals, physical rehabilitation facilities, and mental health institutions. Other employment options include residential and community-based health and human service centers, such as long-term care or nursing home facilities. Recreation agencies, including national associations for disabled sports competitors, also offer positions for certified therapeutic recreation specialists. In these positions, recreational therapists must have skills and knowledge to effectively provide activity therapy for a wide variety of persons with disabilities or illnesses. Without appropriate assessment and evaluation techniques these programs could not succeed.

As in other nonschool settings, measurement and evaluation techniques are relevant to multiple dimensions of the job. Assessment techniques are applied in the information-gathering phase to compile records on patients, the number and types of services and programs conducted, attendance, progress, injuries, and the like. According to Wright (1987), specific data collection mechanisms that assist in the measurement phase of therapeutic recreation include the following:

1. *Record review.* This audit uses patient information to assess the practice patterns of recreational therapists.
2. *Utilization review.* This review obtains and analyzes information related to resource utilization.

3. *Direct observation.* This is a systematic approach to observing practitioners' behavior and determining their effectiveness with patients.

4. *Client surveys.* These data collection devices are useful in ascertaining the patients' opinions about practitioner competence.

5. *Research.* As with many other professions, research expands knowledge about the field and practice of therapeutic recreation.

Once the assessment phase is completed, the therapeutic recreation practitioner can evaluate the results and effect any changes warranted by the results.

## CONSIDERATIONS FOR MEASUREMENT AND EVALUATION IN ADULT FITNESS ENVIRONMENTS

Measurement and evaluation are essential for successful exercise, fitness, and rehabilitative programs in the nonschool sector. It is of utmost importance for the professional to be aware of current tests and to understand how each is administered, scored, and analyzed. Some special considerations are found in the private sector that are not always prevalent in the school environment. The following list cites some factors that may influence measurement and evaluation practices in nonschool exercise settings. A brief explanation of why each may deserve special consideration also is provided.

1. *Most subjects in the exercise setting are adults.* With so many already active "baby boomers" reaching middle age, we anticipate increased interest in exercise programs for seniors as well as a dramatic increase in the numbers available to participate in such programs. Exercise practitioners need to be ready and able to accommodate the many special needs this population will demand. This generally means that fitness professionals should expect more questioning about the testing and evaluative process. In addition, adults have higher expectations than children concerning the performance of a practicing professional. Also, with many maximal and submaximal tests, a physician's presence is required during testing. It is strongly suggested that practitioners in this area become familiar with Guidelines for Exercise Testing and Prescription (American College of Sports Medicine, 1991) to learn more about exercise testing of adults.

2. *Adult exercise and fitness programs continue year-round.* Most school programs are bound by a school year. In the nonschool environment, programs are open-ended and scheduled throughout the year. For efficiency and organization, it may be desirable to develop a calendar for testing that is suitable to the various constituency groups.

3. *Most participants expect highly individualized programs.* Unlike school, where a physical educator may teach 25–30 students per class, nonschool classes usually are smaller. In fact, programs often deal with participants on a one-to-one basis. This means that accurate and up-to-date files on all participants need to be established and maintained. Further, testing and evaluation procedures must be tailored to meet individual needs.

4. *Programs depend on revenue generation.* In the public school setting, programs are funded with tax dollars. In the private sector, exercise and activity programs rely on membership dues and fees to support services. This means that testing and evaluation protocols need to appeal to the members. Otherwise, there will not be a sufficient cash flow to support personnel and resource needs. Thus, it is very important that fitness professionals and other program staff consult with the various constituencies about the type of information that would be useful to them. In addition, public relations and marketing programs are critical.

5. *Many participants have experienced some form of serious health problem.* For example, some may have had a heart attack. Some may be undergoing rehabilitation from an injury, while others may be suffering from disease(s) brought on with aging. In any case, a knowledge of how to work with such people is critical to the success of the programs. Testing and evaluating unhealthy individuals or persons recovering from injury requires interpersonal skills unlike those required in the school setting.

6. *The philosophy of business is different from that of the public schools.* Clearly, the purpose of the schools is to educate the future citizenry. Just as clearly, in the private sector the fundamental goal is to make money. This affects the way in which exercise or fitness or rehabilitative specialists approach their jobs. Although many procedures are the same as in schools, this difference in underlying motives may change the decision-making process with regard to measurement and evaluation.

7. *The complexity and sophistication of the clientele require more complex and sophisticated equipment.* This means that all testing equipment and supplies, as well as techniques, must be contemporary and functioning smoothly. Record keeping needs to be emphasized. The ability to show progress of clients is critical to the success of this business. Dues-paying members expect special treatment, and nowhere may this be more evident than in how they are treated in an initial testing session. Exercise specialists can do a number of things to obtain accurate results from testing. For example, they can personally prepare the subject to be tested, personally organize the test session, and be attentive to the smallest details of comfort and convenience.

8. *Many testing procedures will require special certification or training to administer.* CPR training may be required in order to work with older

individuals or those with health problems. Specialized training may be needed to operate a particular instrument. Or, for insurance purposes, the business may require special certification of its employees. In any case, it should be expected that the nonschool setting will impose some certification requirements different from those normally expected of practitioners in schools.

## TESTS USED IN THE NONSCHOOL EXERCISE SETTING

Perhaps the most obvious difference between testing in the school and nonschool settings is that the latter's tests tend to be more individualized and are conducted using more sophisticated measuring devices. The following are examples of tests commonly used in nonschool settings.

## Testing Maximal Oxygen Uptake

Exercise physiologists think the most important variable of physical fitness is cardiorespiratory endurance. Otherwise described as aerobic power, **maximal oxygen uptake**, or $VO_2$ max. Maximal aerobic power ($VO_2$ max) is defined as the maximal amount of oxygen an individual can take in, transport, and use per minute during maximal exercise (Butts, 1992). Maximal oxygen uptake is dependent upon such physiological variables as minute ventilation volume, pulmonary diffusion, blood transportation, cardiac output, distribution of cardiac output, and the physiological state of muscles.

A trained person has a higher $VO_2$ max than the untrained. The degree of improvement that physical training can contribute to cardiorespiratory fitness depends on such factors as initial fitness level, training intensity, duration, and frequency (Butts, 1992). Gender also influences $VO_2$ max. Females are smaller, have less muscle, fewer red blood cells, less hemoglobin, and so on, so their $VO_2$ max is lower than that of the average male.

Maximal oxygen uptake is reported in absolute units ($LO_3 \cdot min^2$) and also in relative units ($mlO_2 \cdot kg^{-1} \cdot min^{-1}$). The relative value is used in order to equate the oxygen consumption of different size people so comparisons can be made between large and small individuals. If only absolute units ($LO_3 \cdot min^2$) were used the largest person would probably have the highest values but would not necessarily have the greatest aerobic fitness. You can convert ($LO_3 \cdot min^2$) to ($mlO_2 \cdot kg^{-1} \cdot min^{-1}$) simply by converting ($LO_2 \cdot min^{-1}$) to ($mlO_2 \cdot min^{-1}$) and dividing by the subject's weight in kgs. The oxygen requirements for any level of activity, including $VO_2$ max can also be expressed in METs. One MET represents an individual's resting oxygen consumption or 3.5 ($mlO_2 \cdot kg^{-1} \cdot min^{-1}$) (Butts, 1992).

Measurement of a person's $VO_2$ max requires expensive equipment, expert personnel, and a willing subject. This makes a "Max Test" relatively impractical for most school settings. In fact, due to cost and time constraints, most nonschool settings are unable to justify using techniques to accurately determine $VO_2$ max. Thus, most measurement techniques to predict cardiorespiratory fitness in the nonschool setting are based on submaximal tests.

### McArdle's 3-Minute Step Test

(McArdle, Katch, and Katch, 1981)

*Purpose:* To predict $VO_2$ max.

*Instructions:* In a **step test**, the subject steps up and down on a 16.25-inch step for 3 minutes. Females step at a rate of 22 steps per minute, males at 24 steps per minute. The beat is established by a metronome at a rate of 88 and 96 for the females and males, respectively. At the conclusion of the 3-minute stepping the subject remains standing while the test administrator counts the pulse rate for a 15-second period beginning 5 seconds after the end of the stepping (5–20 seconds of recovery). Figure 13.2 shows selected phases associated with this particular test.

► **FIGURE 13.2** McArdle step test.

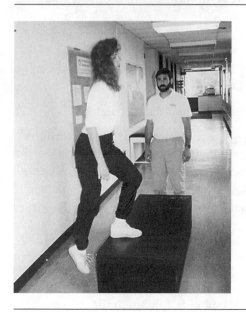 

*Age Level:* Adult.

*Test Area:* Any area spacious enough to accommodate stepper and test administrator.

*Equipment Needed:* Step or bench 16.25-inch high (standard gymnasium bleachers are appropriate substitutes), metronome, digital watch or stop-watch, and calculator.

*Scoring Procedure:* The 15-second value is converted to beats per minute and the following equations are used to determine predicted $VO_2$ max in $mlO_2$ $kg^{-1}$ $min^{-1}$.

> Men: $VO_2$ max ($mlO_2 \cdot kg^{-1} \cdot min^{-1}$) = 111.33 − 0.42 (Heart rate)
> Women: $VO_2$ max ($mlO_2 \cdot kg^{-1} \cdot min^{-1}$) = 65.81 − .1847 (Heart rate)

*Organizational Hints:* A practice session should be used as a warm-up for the subject and an opportunity for the test administrator to obtain a pulse rate. This warm-up should last approximately 15 seconds.

### Kline's One-Mile Walk for Time

(Kline et al., 1987)

*Purpose:* To predict $VO_2$ max.

*Instructions:* Subjects should walk (not run or jog) one mile as fast as possible. During the last quarter mile, subjects should take their pulse rate for 15 seconds while continuing to walk.

*Age Level:* Adult males and females.

*Test Area:* A running track or any flat area suitable for walking that can be marked for distances.

*Equipment Needed:* Digital watch or stopwatch and a calculator.

*Scoring Procedure:* Using weight, age, sex, time for mile walk in minutes and hundredths of a minute, and heart rate in beats per minute during the last quarter mile, the following equation is completed. Results are in L min2 and need to be calculated as $mlO_2$ $kg^{-1}$ $min^{-1}$.

$$VO_2 \text{ max } (L \cdot min^2) = 6.9652 + 0.0091 \text{ X2} - 0.0257 \text{ X3} + 0.5955 \text{ X4} - 0.2240 \text{ X5} - 0.0115 \text{ X6}$$

> Where:   X2 = body weight (lbs)
>          X3 = age (years)
>          X4 = sex (male=1; female=0)
>          X5 = time for 1-mile walk
>          X6 = heart rate (bpm) at end of last quarter mile

### Fox's Bicycle Ergometer Test

(Fox, 1973)

*Purpose:* To predict VO₂ max.

*Instructions:* The height of the bicycle seat should be adjusted for the comfort and proper leg extension of the subject. Metronome is set at 100 beats per minute, and the participant begins pedaling with alternate legs pushing down on each beat to produce 50 pedal revolutions per minute. The workload should be set at 3 (900 kgm) after the subject begins pedaling. Participant rides at this workload for 5 minutes. While subject is pedaling, heart rate is checked for 15 seconds during the fourth and fifth minute.

*Age Level:* Adult males.

*Test Area:* Room large enough to accommodate ergometer and two adults.

*Equipment Needed:* Metronome, bicycle ergometer, digital watch or stopwatch, and calculator.

*Scoring Procedure:* The subject's predicted VO₂ max is calculated according to the following equation:

$$VO_2 \text{ max (mlO}_3) + 6,300 - 19.26 \text{ (Heart rate)}$$

To determine the value in $\text{mlO}_2 \text{ kg}^{-1} \text{ min}^{-1}$ the resultant values are divided by the subject's weight in kg (2.2 lbs/kg).

*Organizational Hints:* To ensure accuracy, the heart rate should be double checked during the fourth and fifth minute. Also, the subject's pedaling rhythm should be monitored during the entire testing session.

## Other Tests

### YMCA Bicycle Test

(Golding et al., 1989)

*Purpose:* To predict maximum physical working capacity.

*Instructions:* The bicycle seat should be set at a comfortable height. Metronome should be set at 100 beats per minute, encouraging the subject to pedal at 50 revolutions per minute. Workload should be set according to the guidelines found in Figure 13.3. The subject should work at each workload for at least 3 minutes. Heart rate should be determined during the second and third minutes. If heart rate differs by more than 4 beats per minute, subject continues working until heart rate stabilizes. Heart rate and workloads are recorded. The second workload is set according to the guidelines in Figure 13.3 and the

### ◣ FIGURE 13.3    YMCA workload guidelines.

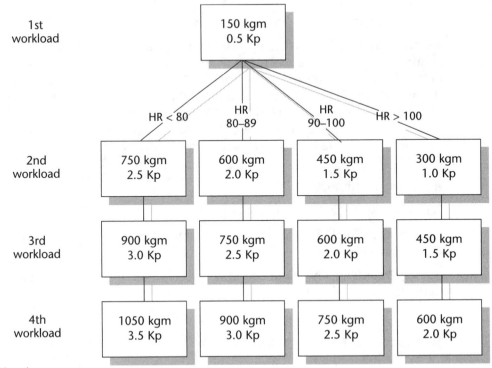

Directions:

1. Set the first workload at 150 kgm/min (0.5 Kp).
2. If the HR in the third min is
   - ▸ less than (<) 80, set the second load at 750 kgm (2.5 Kp);
   - ▸ 80 to 89, set the second load at 600 kgm (2.0 Kp);
   - ▸ 90 to 100, set the second load at 450 kgm (1.5 Kp);
   - ▸ greater than (>) 100, set the second load at 300 kgm (1.0 Kp).
3. Set the third and fourth (if required) loads according to the loads in the columns below the second loads.

directions to determine heart rate are repeated. The third workload is repeated following same instructions. A fourth workload is conducted only if the subject's heart rate response to the third phase did not reach at least 150 beats per minute.

*Age Level:* Adult.

*Test Area:* Any area suitable to accommodate ergometer and two adults.

*Equipment Needed:* Ergometer, metronome, digital watch or stopwatch, and score sheet.

*Scoring Procedure:* The results of the test should be plotted on the scoring graph (see Figure 13.4), according to the directions in the rectangular box.

*Organizational Hints:* If the heart rate during the initial phase was greater than 110 beats per minute, the third workload is not performed.

### Rockport Fitness Walking Test

(Kline et al., 1987)

*Purpose:* To measure cardiovascular fitness.

*Instructions:* Walk one mile as fast as possible.

*Age Level:* Adult.

*Test Area:* Any large open flat area suitable for walking that can be accurately measured. An outdoor running track is preferred.

*Equipment Needed:* Digital watch or stopwatch.

*Scoring Procedure:* The time it takes to walk a mile is recorded to the nearest second. Heart rate per minute is recorded immediately at the end of the mile walk. Using the appropriate Rockport Fitness Walking Test chart for the subject's age and sex (see Figure 13.5), the subject's relative fitness level can be found by going along the horizontal or X axis (time) until reaching the point that represents the subject's time in the mile walk. The vertical or Y axis is followed to the point representing subject's pulse rate. This XY coordinate is within a shaded area that describes the participant's relative level of fitness.

*Organizational Hints:* As part of a pretest warm-up, subjects should practice taking their pulse. An accurate method is to gently place the second and third fingers together on the radial artery just inside the wrist bone. The pulse is counted for 15 seconds (but no more) and multiplied by four to determine pulse rate per minute. For more information about this walking program contact The Rockport Walking Institute, P.O. Box 480, Marlboro, MA 01752.

### YMCA Physical Fitness Test Battery

(Golding et al., 1989)

*Purpose:* To measure the physical fitness components of body composition, cardiorespiratory endurance, flexibility, and muscular strength and endurance.

**FIGURE 13.4**   Maximum physical working capacity prediction.

NAME _____ AGE _____ WEIGHT _____ LB _____ KG

SEAT HEIGHT _____

1ST WORKLOAD HR
DATE _____
USED _____

2ND WORKLOAD HR
USED _____
MAX WORKLOAD _____

PREDICTED MAX HR
MAX O$_2$ (L/min)
MAX O$_2$ (mL/kg)

TEST 1
TEST 2
TEST 3

DIRECTIONS

1. Plot the HR of the 2 workloads versus the work (kgm/min).

2. Determine the subject's max HR line by subtracting subject's age from 220 and draw a line across the graph at this value.

3. Draw a line through both points and extend to the max HR line for age.

4. Drop a line from this point to the baseline and read the predicted max workload and O$_2$ uptake.

| WORKLOAD (kgm/m) | 150 | 300 | 450 | 600 | 750 | 900 | 1050 | 1200 | 1350 | 1500 | 1650 | 1800 | 1950 | 2100 |
|---|---|---|---|---|---|---|---|---|---|---|---|---|---|---|
| MAX O$_2$ UPTAKE (L/m) | 0.6 | 0.9 | 1.2 | 1.5 | 1.8 | 2.1 | 2.4 | 2.8 | 3.2 | 3.5 | 3.8 | 4.2 | 4.6 | 5.0 |
| KCAL USED (kcal/m) | 3.0 | 4.5 | 6.0 | 7.5 | 9.0 | 10.5 | 12.0 | 14.0 | 16.0 | 17.5 | 19.0 | 21.0 | 23.0 | 25.0 |
| APPROX MET LEVEL (for 132 lb) | 3.3 | 4.7 | 6.0 | 7.3 | 8.7 | 10.0 | 11.3 | 12.7 | 14.0 | 15.3 | 16.7 | 18.0 | 19.3 | 20.7 |
| APPROX MET LEVEL (for 176 lb) | 3.0 | 4.0 | 5.0 | 6.0 | 7.0 | 8.0 | 9.0 | 10.0 | 11.0 | 12.0 | 13.0 | 14.0 | 15.0 | 16.0 |

(Graph HR axis values: 200, 190, 180, 170, 160, 150, 140, 130, 120, 110, 100, 90)

***Description:*** This particular test battery is (1) designed to minimize the amount of testing time, (2) relatively easy to administer, score, and interpret; and (3) requires a minimal amount of equipment. Due to the extensive nature of materials associated with this test, it is suggested that the interested reader obtain a copy of the text *Y's Way to Physical Fitness* (Golding et al., 1989). It can be obtained by writing Human Kinetics Publishing, P.O. Box 5076, Champaign, IL 61825-5076.

***Instructions:*** There are nine measurements associated with this test battery. Test items should be administered in the order described.

1.  *Standing height.* With shoes and socks off, the subject stands erect with heels, buttocks, and upper back touching a vertical wall. Measurement is recorded to the nearest quarter inch.
2.  *Weight.* Weight is taken with subject wearing only shorts and is recorded in pounds and kilograms.
3.  *Resting heart rate.* The heart rate is counted for one minute by means of a **stethoscope**. The subject should be well-rested and seated.
4.  *Resting blood pressure.* Systolic pressure and diastolic pressure should be recorded in millimeters of mercury (mm Hg) as indicated on the **sphygmomanometer** scale. (A description of how to take blood pressure can be found on pages 533–534.)
5.  *Body composition.* The Y's method of estimating body fat involves measurement of skinfolds. The sum of four sites, tricep, abdomen, ilium, and calf, is the score recorded. Figures 13.6 to 13.9 show the locations of these sites. Instructions for using the skinfold caliper can be found on pages 174–176 in this text.
6.  *Cardiorespiratory fitness.* The bicycle ergometer test as described on page 521 is used to measure cardiorespiratory fitness.
7.  *Flexibility.* A yardstick is laid on the floor and adhesive tape is placed across it at right angles on the 15-inch mark. The subject sits on the floor with the yardstick between the legs and the feet approximately 12 inches apart with heels resting on the floor at the 15-inch mark. With one hand on top of the other, finger pads on top of fingernails, and arms extended, the subject slowly reaches forward as far as possible along the yardstick, holding the farthest stretch momentarily. Legs should remain straight throughout and the bottom hand should remain in contact with the yardstick at all times. Figure 13.10 illustrates this technique. The score is the most distant point reached on the yardstick. Three trials are allowed. Score is recorded to nearest quarter inch.
8.  *Bench press.* Equipment needed: 35-pound barbell for women and 80-pound barbell for men, metronome, and regular bench for use in completing bench press.

▶ **FIGURE 13.5**    The Rockport Fitness Walking Test.

## FIND YOUR FITNESS LEVEL

The information in the following charts pertains to both the non-treadmill walker as well as the treadmill walker.

Turn to the appropriate Rockport Fitness Walking Test™ chart according to your age and sex. These show the established fitness norms from the American Heart Association.

Using your Relative Fitness Level chart, find your time in minutes and your heart rate per minute. Follow these lines until they meet and mark this point on the chart. This point is designed to tell you how fit you are compared to other individuals of your same age and sex. For example, if your mark places you in the "above average" section of the chart, you are in better shape than the average person in your category.

The charts are based on weights of 170 lbs. for men and 125 lbs. for women. If you weigh substantially less, your relative cardiovascular fitness level will be slightly underestimated. Conversely, if you weigh substantially more, your relative cardiovascular fitness level will be slightly overestimated.

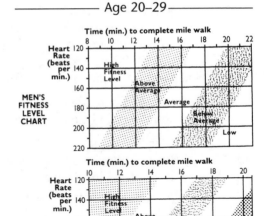

———————— Age 20–29 ————————

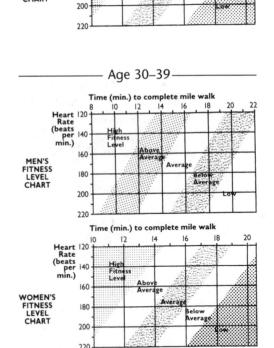

———————— Age 30–39 ————————

*(continued)*

▶ **FIGURE 13.5** Continued.

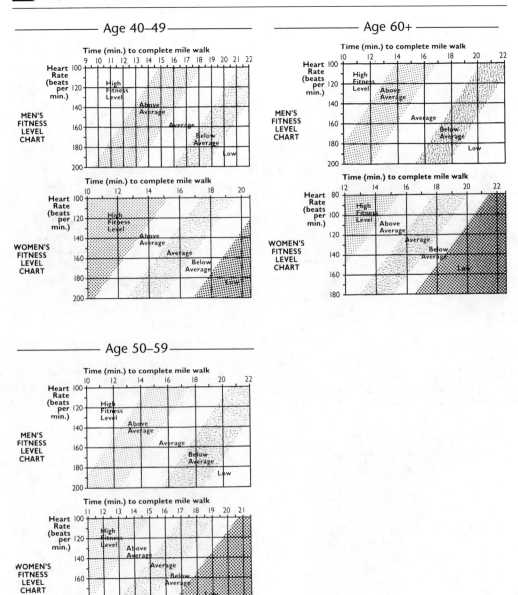

► **FIGURE 13.6**
Triceps skinfold.

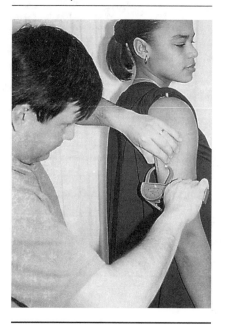

► **FIGURE 13.7**
Abdominal skinfold.

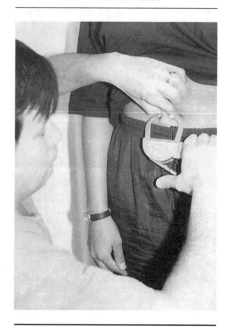

► **FIGURE 13.8**
Ilium skinfold.

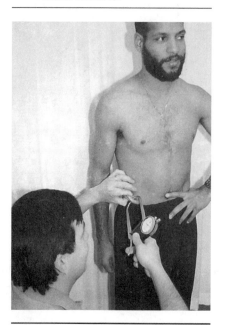

► **FIGURE 13.9**
Calf skinfold.

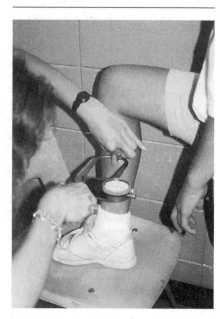

► **FIGURE 13.10** Sit-and-reach using yardstick.

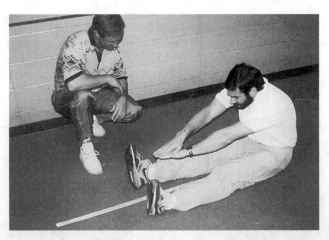

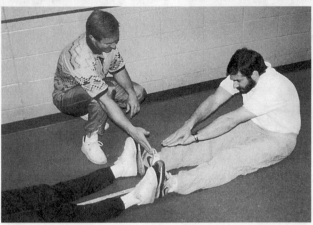

The participant lies on the bench in a face-up position, with legs bent at the knee, and feet flat on the floor. The subject grips the bar with arms and hands shoulder width apart. Figure 13.11 shows proper technique. The subject presses the barbell and weight upward to fully extend the arms. For older individuals it may not be necessary to fully extend the arms. Doing so may place undue stress on joints already suffering from overuse. After each lift the subject returns the barbell and weight to original position. The subject is asked to complete as many repetitions as possible keeping time with a 60-beat-per-minute count on the metronome. The test is terminated when the rhythm is broken or the subject fails to reach full extension. The num-

► **FIGURE 13.11**    Bench press.

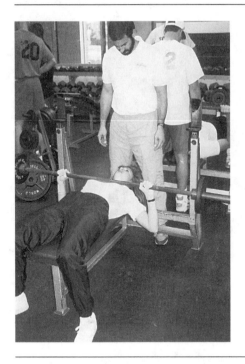

ber of successful repetitions is recorded as the score. For safety purposes a trained spotter should be present at all times.

9. *One-minute timed sit-up.* Subject lies on back with legs flexed at the knees and heels approximately 12–18 inches from buttocks. Arms are bent with fingers next to ears. With a partner holding the ankles, the subject completes as many sit-ups as possible in a 1-minute period. The elbows should alternately touch the opposite knee as subject attains the up position (see Figure 13.12). A mat or piece of carpet should be used to increase the comfort of the subject. The number of successful repetitions completed in the 1-minute timeframe is recorded as the score.

*Age Level:* Adult.

*Test Area:* Areas spacious enough to accommodate each or all of the tests.

*Equipment Needed:* Tape measure, scale, stethoscope, blood pressure cuff with sphygmomanometer, skinfold caliper, bicycle ergometer, yardstick, adhesive tape, barbell and weights, metronome, bench for bench press, and mat or carpet square for sit-ups.

▶ **FIGURE 13.12** Sit-up.

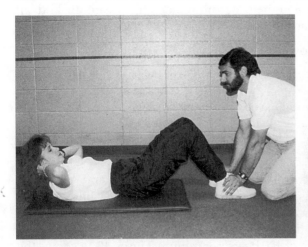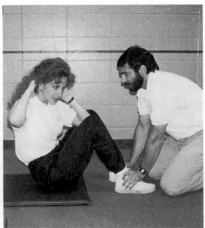

**Norms:** The reader is encouraged to use *The Y's Way to Physical Fitness: The Complete Guide to Fitness Testing and Instruction* (Golding et al., 1989) for norms and relevant standards of performance.

**Organizational Hints:** Subjects are to be informed of the following guidelines prior to the fitness testing:

1. Do not eat, drink, or smoke for 2 hours before testing.
2. Do not drink alcohol one full day (24 hours) before testing.
3. Do not exercise on the day of the testing.

### Treadmill-Predicting VO₂ max from Submaximal Test

(Wilmore et al., 1985)

**Purpose:** To predict maximum oxygen uptake.

**Instructions:** This test permits estimating $VO_2$ max from a submaximal run on the **treadmill**. The subject walks on the treadmill at either 3, 4, or 5 miles per hour for three minutes. The speed should be increased by 1 mph each third minute. The initial treadmill speed is subjectively determined based on the subject's sex and physical activity history. The intent is to obtain a steady state heart rate within a range of 125–175 beats per minute. Treadmill elevation remains level throughout the test.

*Age Level:* Adult.

*Test Area:* A room large enough to accommodate the treadmill and all necessary scientific instrumentation.

*Scoring Procedure:* The following formula is used to predict $VO_2$ max.

$VO_2$ max $(mlO_2 \cdot kg^{-1} \cdot min^{-1}) = 29.7 + 6.665$ TMS4 $- 0.15$ HR $+ 0.31$ RPE

Where:  $TMS_4$ = Treadmill speed during third stage
HR = Heart rate at end of third minute in stage three
RPE = Rating of perceived exertion at end of third minute of third stage.

RPE is a scale shown to correlate highly with heart rate and $VO_2$ max. Created by Borg (1982), this scale (see Figure 13.13) increases linearly with exercise heart rate. The scale ranges from 6 to 20 and was originally calibrated to coincide with heart rate values. For example, RPE rating of 12 corresponded to a heart rate of 120 beats per minute. Figure 13.14 shows the influence of aging on RPE.

► **FIGURE 13.13**    Borg Rate of Perceived Exertion Scale.

| | |
|---|---|
| 6 | |
| 7 | Very, very light |
| 8 | |
| 9 | Very light |
| 10 | |
| 11 | Fairly light |
| 12 | |
| 13 | Somewhat hard |
| 14 | |
| 15 | Hard |
| 16 | |
| 17 | Very hard |
| 18 | |
| 19 | Very, very hard |
| 20 | |

Source: D. G. Borg, Dept. of Psychology, University of Stockholm, Sweden.

▶ **FIGURE 13.14** Influence of aging on RPE.

Change in the heart rate and RPE ratings. Note decrease in maximal heart rate associated with aging. RPE ratings ≥ 18 suggest maximal heart rate has been reached.

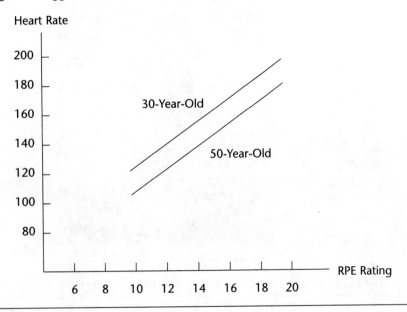

## Blood Pressure
(Butts, 1992)

*Purpose:* To measure the pressure in the arteries exerted by the blood during the systolic and diastolic phases of the cardiac cycle.

*Instructions:* A hollow cuff (blood pressure cuff) is wrapped around the left brachial artery. Inflating the cuff to a pressure higher than the expected pressure in the artery restricts blood flow. Slowly releasing the air from the cuff reduces the pressure in the cuff. The systolic pressure reading is measured at the cuff pressure (mmHg) at which sounds of blood flow are first heard. The diastolic pressure is measured at the point (mmHg) at which the sounds (vibrations) of blood flow cease.

*Equipment Needed:* Blood pressure cuff, sphygmomanometer, chair for subject to sit in, and stethoscope.

*Scoring Procedure:* Both systolic and diastolic blood pressures are measured with the use of a sphygmomanometer. Readings are expressed in units of millimeters of mercury (mmHg). Figure 13.15 illustrates blood pressure being taken. Table 13.0 (Butts, 1992) shows the range of blood pressure values.

▶ **FIGURE 13.15** Blood pressure.

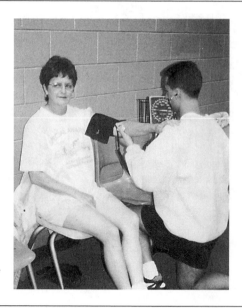

▶ **TABLE 13.0** Range of blood pressure values (mmHg).

|  | SYSTOLIC | DIASTOLIC |
|---|---|---|
| Normal | <140 | <85 |
| High normal |  | 85–90 |
| Mild hypertension | 140–159 | 90–104 |
| Moderate hypertension |  | 105–114 |
| *Severe hypertension | >160 | >115 |

*Confirm (repeat) in a month.

## Hydrostatic Weighing

(As found in Butts, 1992)

*Purpose:* To aid in the prediction of body fat.

*Description:* **Hydrostatic weighing** is a method used to compute body fat percent from **body density**. Although percent fat is only an estimate from the density obtained from underwater weighing, it is still the best available method (Golding et al., 1989). The method is based on the physics principle that mass divided by volume equals density. Archimedes, the Greek mathematician, discovered the physical principle serving as the basis for calculating body density. Simply stated, the weight a body loses underwa-

► **FIGURE 13.16**   Hydrostatic Weighing.

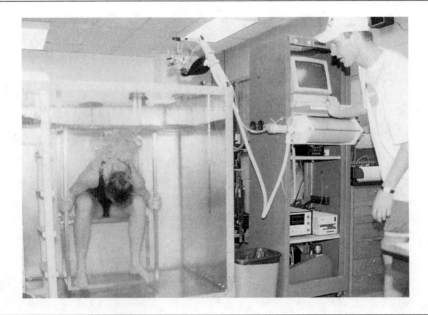

ter equals the weight of the water it displaces. Thus, one can calculate the volume of the water displaced, which equals the volume of the subject. This allows for the determination of body density.

*Instructions:* Lung residual volume is a significant factor in ensuring accuracy and must be measured to correct the underwater weight. Once determined, the subject is asked to be seated in a chair attached to a scale. Then, upon request and while seated in the chair, the subject immerses the body completely underwater. Once submerged, the subject is expected to exhale maximally. At this point, with the subject remaining completely still and submerged, the test administrator reads and records the underwater weight from the scale. Several trials are required in order to determine a consistent underwater weight. Once an accurate underwater weight is known, the test administrator may apply the formula found in the scoring section below in determining body density. This set of instructions is overly simplistic and brief, and is intended to provide only an overview of the procedure to determine body density. Due to the complex nature of this test, the reader is referred to Golding et al., 1989, for more specific instructions regarding densitometry.

*Scoring:* The overall formula for calculating body density is listed below (Butts, 1992).

Formula for calculating % fat from body density.

$$DB = \frac{M_a}{\left[\dfrac{[M_a - M_w]}{D_w}\right]} - RV$$

$M_a$ = Weight in air

$M_w$ = Weight submerged

$D_w$ = Density of the water. 1 at 4 degrees C

$RV$ = Residual volume

$$\% \text{ Fat} = \left[\frac{4.570}{DB} - 4.142\right] \times 100$$

$$\text{Absolute Fat} = \text{Weight} \times \left[\frac{\% \text{ fat}}{100}\right]$$

Absolute LBW = Weight − Fat

Fat and weight expressed in Kgs.

$$DW = \frac{LBW}{\left[\dfrac{[100 - (\text{desired } \% \text{ fat})]}{100}\right]}$$

► **TABLE 13.1**   Conversion of density to percent body fat (Brozek et al., 1963).

| DENSITY | % FAT | DENSITY | % FAT |
|---|---|---|---|
| 1.0200 | 33.8 | 1.0600 | 16.9 |
| 1.0220 | 33.0 | 1.0620 | 16.1 |
| 1.0240 | 32.1 | 1.0640 | 15.3 |
| 1.0260 | 31.2 | 1.0660 | 14.5 |
| 1.0280 | 30.4 | 1.0680 | 13.7 |
| 1.0300 | 29.5 | 1.0700 | 12.9 |
| 1.0320 | 28.6 | 1.0720 | 12.1 |
| 1.0340 | 27.8 | 1.0740 | 11.3 |
| 1.0360 | 26.7 | 1.0760 | 10.5 |
| 1.0380 | 26.1 | 1.0780 | 9.7 |
| 1.0400 | 25.2 | 1.0800 | 8.9 |
| 1.0420 | 24.4 | 1.0820 | 8.2 |
| 1.0440 | 23.5 | 1.0840 | 7.4 |
| 1.0460 | 22.7 | 1.0860 | 6.6 |
| 1.0480 | 21.9 | 1.0880 | 5.8 |
| 1.0500 | 21.0 | 1.0900 | 5.1 |
| 1.0520 | 20.2 | 1.0920 | 4.3 |

Equation: $\% \text{ fat} - \left[\dfrac{4.57}{D}\right] - 4.142\,(100)$

The conversion from body density to percent fat is found in Table 13.1 (Brozek et al., 1963).

*Equipment Needed:* The instrumentation required to conduct underwater weighing varies and is too technical to explain in this text. It is suggested that the reader refer to an exercise physiology text or lab manual for a detailed description of the equipment and supplies necessary for hydrostatic weighing.

## SUMMARY

This chapter focuses on measurement and evaluation in the nonschool environment. Professional careers that require knowledge and expertise in fitness management, cardiac rehabilitation, fitness leadership, athletic training, or therapeutic recreation are briefly described. Career options for individuals trained in these areas are cited and discussed. The relationship between these professions and that of physical education in the traditional school setting is discussed.

Although different in many ways from programs in traditional school physical education, exercise, fitness, and rehabilitation programs in nonschool settings also depend on measurement and evaluation. The role of measurement and evaluation in nonschool settings is clarified and contrasted with testing and evaluation procedures practiced in schools. Characteristics of selected nonschool settings such as athletic training, corporate and community fitness programs, hospital- and university-based health and fitness programs, and therapeutic recreation also are described.

Since there are fundamental differences between activity programs in school and nonschool settings, examples of important items to consider when administering testing and evaluation procedures in the private sector are cited. Lastly, common tests and evaluation procedures that are used in nonschool settings are identified and briefly described.

## ► DISCUSSION QUESTIONS

1. Identify several nonschool settings that have as their mission improving the health and physical well-being of clients. Discuss how measurement and evaluation would enhance the chances of achieving these goals. Which setting is more conducive to your professional aspirations?

2. Cite the main differences between physical education in the schools and exercise and fitness programs in the nonschool setting. What implications do these differences have in the selection of tests and evaluation procedures? What are the similarities between physical

education in the schools and exercise and fitness programs in the non-school setting? What implications do these similarities have in the selection of tests and evaluation procedures?

3. Develop a priority list of the most influential factors in distinguishing between measurement and evaluation in the school and nonschool settings. What circumstances will cause these factors to be altered?

4. Describe a test and/or evaluation procedure that would be exclusively used in the nonschool setting.

► **REFERENCES**

American Academy of Orthopaedic Surgeons. (1984). *Athletic training for sports medicine.* Chicago: American Academy of Orthopaedic Surgeons.

Borg, G. (1982). Psychophysical bases of perceived exertion. *Medicine and Science in Sports and Exercise,* 14:377–81.

Brozek, J.; Grande, F.; Anderson, J. T.; and Keys, A. (1963). Densitometric analysis of body composition: Revision of some qualitative measures to assess weight and loss. *American Journal of Clinical Nutrition,* 31:769–73.

Burke, B. (1989). The historic role of hospitals in health promotion. In N. Sol and P. Wilson, eds. *Hospital health promotion.* Champaign, IL: Human Kinetics.

Butts, N. (1992). *woMAN the incredible machine: Physical education lab manual.* 3d ed. La Crosse, WI: UWL Human Performance Lab.

Fox, E. (1973). A simple, accurate technique for predicting maximal aerobic power. *Journal of Applied Physiology,* 35(6):914–16.

Golding, L.; Myers, C.; and Sinning, W. (1989). *Y's way to physical fitness: The complete guide to fitness testing and instruction.*

3d ed. Champaign, IL: Human Kinetics.

Kline, G.; Porcari, J.; Hintermeister, R.; Freedson, P.; Ward, A.; McCarron, R.; Ross, J.; and Rippe, J. (1987). Estimation of $VO_2$max from a one-mile track walk, gender, age, and body weight. *Medicine and Science in Sports and Exercise,* 19(3):253–59.

McArdle, W.; Katch, F.; and Katch, V. (1981). *Exercise physiology: Energy, nutrition, and human performance.* Philadelphia: Lea and Febiger.

Roy, S., and Irvin, R. (1983). *Sports medicine: Prevention, evaluation, management, and rehabilitation.* Englewood Cliffs, NJ: Prentice-Hall.

Wilmore, J.; Roby, F.; Stanforth, P.; Buono, M.; Constable, S.; Tsao, Y.; and Lowdon, B. (1985). Ratings of perceived exertion, heart rate, and treadmill speed in the prediction of maximal oxygen uptake during submaximal treadmill exercise. *Journal of Cardiopulmonary Rehabilitation,* 5:540–46.

Wright, S. (1987). *Evaluation of therapeutic recreation through quality assurance.* Bob Riley, ed. State College, PA: Venture Publishing, Inc.

► **REPRESENTATIVE READINGS**

American College of Sports Medicine. (1991). *Guidelines for exercise testing and prescription.* 4th ed. Philadelphia: Lea and Febiger.

Arnheim, D. D. (1989). *Modern principles of athletic training.* St. Louis: Times Mirror Mosby.

Gilmore, G. D.; Campbell, M. D.; and Becker, B. L. (1989). *Needs assessment strategies for health education and health promotion.* Indianapolis: Benchmark Press Inc.

Parkhouse, B. L. (1991). *The management of sport: Its foundation and application.* St. Louis: Mosby Year Book.

Railey, J. H., and Railey, P. A. (1988). *Managing physical education, fitness, and sports programs.* Mountain View, CA: Mayfield Publishing Company.

Sol, N., and Wilson, P. K. (1989). *Hospital health promotion.* Champaign, IL: Human Kinetics Books.

# USING COMPUTER TECHNOLOGY

## 14

## ◤ KEY TERMS

Biomedical
　Programs
　(BMDP)
compact disk
computer-assisted
　instruction
database
　management
electronic
　spreadsheet
floppy disk
graphics
hard disk
input
Internet
modem
network
output
peripheral

personal computer
printer
processing
random access
　memory (RAM)
read only memory
　(ROM)
Statistical Analysis
　System (SAS)
software
Statistical Package
　for the Social
　Sciences (SPSS)
storage
video monitor
World Wide Web

## ◤ OBJECTIVES

*After reading this chapter, the student should be able to:*

1. Understand how computer technology relates to the physical education and exercise science practitioner.
2. Describe the essential functions and applications of the personal computer.
3. Identify the hardware components of a personal computer system and understand the relationships of these parts.
4. Provide a general overview of software applications and indicate how each could be used in physical education and exercise science settings.
5. Suggest how to select software specifically designed for use in physical education and exercise science.

Computer technology has transformed the way we operate in the professional world. Whether you aspire to teach physical education in the schools or work in a nonschool exercise environment, you will be expected to have a good working knowledge of how to utilize computer technology. Rapid advances in technology have greatly enhanced the speed, storage, and power of personal computers. Although we visualize a keyboard, monitor, computer, and printer when thinking of computers, the fact is that computers drive the functions of many measurement devices used in physical education and exercise science. High-quality skinfold calipers rely on internal computer chips to calculate body composition; high-speed video cameras are driven by instrumentation that accurately records movement; computer chips are central to the function of over-the-counter heart rate monitors; and many other specialty devices are now commonplace in school and exercise science settings. Microcomputer technology has significantly decreased the amount of time needed to appraise and calculate quantitative procedures associated with measurement and evaluation. For the practitioner, this should be especially gratifying. Tymeson and Fox (1986) cite the importance of the personal computer and suggest that college-level measurement and evaluation courses devote a substantial amount of class time to the theoretical and practical competencies needed to work with the computer.

The computer and other technological devices have become important and permanent tools in physical education and exercise science. Originally designed to handle mathematical computations, the computer has quickly become more than an electronic wizard expediting sophisticated statistical calculations. It is a machine that teachers, students, athlete trainers, coaches, exercise scientists, and clients can use in a multitude of ways to enhance learning and development. It is almost impossible to enter a school building or exercise environment and not find at least one computer being utilized for a variety of tasks. Virtually everyone agrees that the potential of the computer in education is limitless. Even in movement-based disciplines such as physical education and exercise science, the computer is becoming recognized as an essential tool for the practicing professional, and nowhere is the computer more important than in measurement and evaluation.

## USES OF THE PERSONAL COMPUTER IN PHYSICAL EDUCATION AND EXERCISE SCIENCE

In physical education, the **personal computer** can perform many helpful tasks, including

1. managing large quantities of numerical and/or categorical information,
2. generating graphs of students' performance,
3. developing tests and banks of questions,

4. scoring and analyzing the results of health fitness, psychomotor, cognitive and affective tests and/or surveys,
5. providing instructional assistance to students who are having difficulty learning the material in class,
6. scoring tests and assigning grades to students comparing scores with norms,
7. comparing scores with norms,
8. producing personalized profiles and prescriptive activities associated with students' physical fitness or motor ability,
9. monitoring the behaviors of students and teachers in an instructional setting,
10. generating reports to be sent home to parents.

In exercise science environments the microcomputer can be used for

1. communicating with clients and supervisors,
2. enhancing billing, accounting, and mass mailing procedures,
3. analyzing oxygen uptake during a fitness test,
4. publishing a club or agency newsletter,
5. communicating with national networks for the purpose of accessing larger stores of information,
6. recording and analyzing the results of fitness tests,
7. reporting and graphically portraying the results of tests and/or surveys,
8. preparing financial reports for auditors or other agencies,
9. controlling aspects of a graded exercise test to include treadmill speed, grade of elevation, etc.,
10. monitoring exercise and diet,
11. calculating body composition from hydrostatic weighing and impedance techniques.

Computer applications in physical education and exercise science continue to expand at a rapid rate. More and more programs are being developed and marketed to directly assist physical education professionals at all levels and practicing professionals at hospitals, health clubs, and other non-school exercise settings. To function efficiently and effectively in a teaching or exercise environment that relies on computer usage, the professional must have a basic knowledge and understanding of the computer and software.

## BASIC PERSONAL COMPUTING

Being computer literate means different things to different people. A person who works in the corporate setting may need programming skills but little knowledge of commercially produced software. Someone in a clerical position may be fluent in a single word-processing package and have no use for knowledge about other ways to use the personal computer. However, many careers are now embracing a broader view of what is considered computer literate. People selecting careers in education or exercise science are finding out that computer literacy means a great deal more than simply performing rote tasks on the keyboard. High schools and colleges are requiring students to complete a course or sequence of courses providing introductory knowledge about the computer. Further, most preparatory programs for physical educators and exercise specialists now require course work and experience with the personal computer. The knowledge and skills taught in these classes are intended to help individuals develop and broaden the ways in which the computer can be used in educational and exercise settings.

Knowing how to utilize the computer is absolutely essential for the modern physical educator and exercise practitioner. To be prepared for current and future job markets, prospective physical education teachers and exercise scientists should have a functional level of computer literacy. In the largest sense, this means that to be computer literate a person should have a basic understanding of computers and a fundamental knowledge of their application to physical education and related fields. Someone who is computer literate, then, should (1) understand basic functions of the personal computer and accessories, and (2) be able to use software applications in a variety of settings related to the job.

## FUNCTIONS OF THE PERSONAL COMPUTER

In spite of the many recent advances in computing (e.g., improved speed, storage, and appearance), the basic functions of the personal computer remain unchanged. When a computer is instructed to perform a task, it handles the task in a three-part sequence: (1) it accepts the information (**input**) and stores the information (**storage**); (2) it processes the information (**processing**); and (3) it delivers the processed information (**output**).

While this approach is standard operating procedure for the computer, it is also typical of the manner in which teachers and exercise specialists routinely handle information about their students and clients. For example, Mr. Batesky's physical education class completes weekly written assignments about physical fitness. When the students hand in their papers, Mr. Batesky accepts their work (input). Once all the papers have been collected, he puts them into a folder on his desk (storage). At the end of the school day, Mr. Batesky corrects the papers and calculates the grades (processing). The next day, Mr. Batesky returns the assignments to his students (output). The cycle is the same whether a computer is used or not. An example in the exercise science setting is Ms. Butts' measuring a client's body composition using skinfold calipers (input). She records all the values and determines the median for each site (storage). Then, she uses a standard formula to calculate body composition from multiple site skinfold measurements (processing). Finally, Ms. Butts visits with her client and shares the results (output). The logical handling of any information serves as a guideline to the sequencing of software for microcomputers.

The primary differences between doing work by hand and by computer are speed, accuracy, and storage capacity. The microcomputer's components allow it to work with considerable amounts of information in a fast and normally flawless manner. As a result, the tedious tasks associated with teaching and exercise science can be expedited with use of the computer. To better understand the functions of the computer, input, storage, processing, and output will be explained further.

# Input and Storage

Input devices are computer system components that accept processed information. After receiving information, input devices transfer information into the computer's central processing unit. Usually part of the hardware family, several of these devices can also serves as storage devices for data retrieval.

### Keyboard.

A typewriter keyboard is the most common input device and the primary input device for entering new information. It consists of standard typewriter keys, plus a few special function keys that direct the computer to perform specified tasks. As expected, different machines have different keyboards. Some machines have large keyboards with numerous function keys, while others are small, have fewer keys, and rely on multiple keystrokes (using designated combinations of keys) to deliver commands to the computer. The keys are usually sculpted and designed to have a soft feel when depressed.

### Disk drives.

The hard disk drive, floppy disk drive, and compact disk driver are input devices that store information (program or data) so that it is accessible to the central processing unit. A **compact disk** or a **floppy disk** are independent units that are recordlike in appearance and capable of storing large amounts of information in the form of magnetic impulses. When the computer is turned on, the disk drive spins the floppy disk or compact disk at a high speed, much like a compact disk spinning inside a CD player. The metallic pads of the disk drive read the magnetic impulses on the disk and load the information represented by those impulses into the central processing unit. CD-ROM disk technology provides much more storage space for information and affords the user opportunity to play compact disks and access many other media functions otherwise unavailable on floppy disks.

**Hard disks** are larger than floppy disks and stiff—not flexible. A computer with a hard disk storage medium quickly transfers bytes to and from the magnetic surfaces of the hard disk. It is easy to transfer information from the floppy to the hard drive and vice versa. The four most important features of hard disk drive technology, which set it apart from the floppy disk drive, are speed, mass storage capability, long-term reliability, and convenience. Fixed disk technology offers much faster access to stored information than do floppy disks. Personal computers can perform most processing operations many times faster using a hard disk drive than they can using floppy disk drives.

Also, one of the most important features of the hard disk drive is its reliability. Hard drives contain highly advanced micro circuitry, which guarantees long life, and a fixed disk, which is substantially more durable than floppy disks. Information can be stored indefinitely and with less fear of loss, damage, or failure that may accompany working with floppy disks. Finally, the convenience of a hard disk drive cannot be overstated. The rapid advancement of this particular technology has afforded the user many conveniences such as portability, no hassles with floppy disks, and security.

The optical card reader is a popular peripheral input device that reads information from punched or specially marked papers and transfers that data into the computer. The most common type of card is the optical scan form, specially designed cards or sheets of paper composed of variously defined categories and small circles or lines. The categories are determined according to need (e.g., name, address, question number) and the small circles or lines provide space to make a blackened response using a pencil or some other form of marker. Multiple-choice exams are an example of how optical scan forms can be used. Individuals answer questions by filling in the small circles on the answer sheets. These answers are run through an optical scan reader and scored. The reader compares the pattern of marks on the papers to the correct pattern stored in the computer's memory and scores all the exams. The optical scan reader is becoming a popular device to use with the microcomputer and can be a real time saver in large jobs or tasks that are repeated time and time again.

## Processing

The central processing unit (CPU) is linked to the computer's memory and is the piece of electronic wizardry that performs most of the work. The internal workings, referred to as the main circuit board, contain the chips that allow the computer to perform its functions at high rates of speed. The CPU is composed of three primary chips or sets of chips: the microprocessor, random access memory (RAM), and read-only memory (ROM).

### *Microprocessor (central processing).*

The microprocessor is the brain of the computer system. This is the chip that carries out the instructions in the program one by one in the order that they appear. Information stored in memory is processed throughout this central processing unit (CPU) at incredibly fast speed. Machines of different brands may use different processors. The efficiency of the processors dictates the speed at which functions can be carried out. Because the power of a CPU determines the power of a computer system, it is important to consider when purchasing a personal computer.

### *Random access memory (RAM).*

**RAM** is sometimes called main memory, or just memory. RAM chips temporarily store the programs loaded into the computer, as well as data (term papers, individual exercise programs, scientific formulae, budgets, schedules, grades, and so on). The information in RAM is stored as electrical impulses. These impulses are stored in the computer and disappear when the power is turned off. Since the application program used occupies a portion of the RAM, the total amount of RAM available becomes very important. The more RAM, the less a user has to access the slower disk drives to retrieve information. Most microcomputers now offer large amounts of RAM as a standard feature. You can also increase the power and speed of a personal computer by increasing RAM. This is accomplished by adding RAM chips.

### *Read only memory (ROM).*

Whereas RAM chips store application programs and data that change every time a computer is used, **ROM** chips contain information that is permanent and stays intact whenever the machine is turned off. You cannot ordinarily change ROM, add to it, or subtract from it. ROM contains the programs built into the computer by the manufacturer and provides just enough intelligence to do a few simple tasks, such as suggest to a user to load a program. In simpler terms, ROM provides enough intelligence to "understand" a programming language, so that a user can create programs. To the ordinary user, ROM is unimportant.

## Output Devices

An output device displays the information the computer has processed. There are many ways a computer displays processed information but the most common devices are the video monitor and the printer.

### *Video monitor.*

The **video monitor** visually displays information received from the CPU on a screen. Portable computers have screens as small as five inches, and there are monitors 19 inches and larger to accommodate special needs. Most monitors are of high resolution and show characters in color much like those seen on television or video game machines.

### Printer.

A **printer** is an essential component of the microcomputer system. The printer provides a hard copy of the processed information, which gives the user an opportunity to check the accuracy of input data, carefully review generated output, display information, share information with clients, and/or use the printed matter in a variety of other useful ways. For example, on-screen editing of data files and reviewing the results of statistical analyses is a difficult, if not impossible, task. However, by printing a complete copy of the derived information you will be able to carefully check the output. The main features to look for in a printer are speed and quality of character. Speed is a valuable commodity for users who need to print large amounts of information on a daily basis. Let's say, for example, that a fitness instructor needs to print exercise prescriptions for 60 people per day and that each prescription is approximately four pages in length, which is 240 pages per day. If the difference between printing the prescription on a slow printer versus a faster printer was 30 seconds per page, or two minutes per prescription, the total difference per day would be two hours. Multiply that figure by five days per week and the difference is 10 hours. Speed, then, is an important consideration in selecting a printer. However, as is generally the case, the faster the printer the greater the cost. Beyond the appearance of the print and the speed of the printing, several other features must be considered in selecting a printer, including printer width, paper feed capabilities, compatibility with the CPU and software, controls, and print variations.

## Other Peripherals

A peripheral is a device that is located outside the boundaries of the personal computer and is physically connected to the CPU. Peripherals perform specific functions not standard with the computer. While the printer and monitor are technically considered peripherals, these are common items and usually found with most computer systems. Other peripherals serve specific functions central to measurement and evaluation and enhance the capability of the computer system. One peripheral that is of increasing importance in measurement and evaluation for physical education and exercise science is the modem.

### Modem.

A **modem** links the computer by telephone to other computers and information services to send and receive information rapidly. Linking a microcomputer to a mainframe computer via a modem allows a physical educator access to statistical packages usually not available in floppy disk software. Mainframe computers can of perform functions such as calculating group statistics, developing normative data, storing large databases, and other tasks more economically than providing statistical software for all individual microcomputers in an organization. Many exercise science settings and school districts dedicate one phone line to connect computers to a mainframe. This network approach has proven most effective in enhancing communication among users. Networking is a "way of life" for the practicing professional.

## NETWORKING

For the purposes of illustration, a **network** is an interconnected chain, group, or system of computers. Linking individuals electronically facilitates the free flow of information and enhances communication. It is a convenient way to provide multiple access to a huge store of information. Networks may connect a few machines or many. The largest network is the Internet.

The **Internet** is a global network of networks, or inter-network, hence Internet. Its underlying fabric and technologies afford an arena of flexibility, disclosure, and enormous capacity for growth. It is used by tens of millions of people throughout the world. Through the Internet, people access multiple types of information and communicate with friends and associates throughout the world. Physical educators and exercise scientists can capitalize on the easy access and use the Internet for a number of purposes. For example, they can share information with colleagues. Research data, scientific papers, students' fitness scores, and so on instantly can be transferred from one computer to another. Also, the practitioner can search for a variety of subjects and access many different databases. These might include browsing library resources, normative databases, clearinghouses for information, or electronic bulletin boards that post new information daily. Many Internet services are provided by either national services such as America Online and CompuServ or by local area service providers. Most of these services require a fee. In addition, as a user, you can be the source of information and provide the larger community with information about what it is that you are doing. Clearly, the Internet creates an electronic means to navigate a worldwide wealth of information in search of assistance (or answers) to your queries. The **World Wide Web** (WWW) is a particularly useful and popular source of electronic documents. Specifically, by using a browser program (i.e., Netscape) a person can "navigate" between and among a wide assortment of information. Business, colleges and universities, and many individuals are creating WWW pages that contain useful information. The sophisticated computer user will certainly take advantage of all that networks, particularly the Internet, have to offer.

# HOW TO SELECT A MICROCOMPUTER SYSTEM

Purchasing a computer system for use in the physical education or exercise science environments deserves a thoughtful approach. Since many systems of different manufacturers are on the market with all sorts of functions, it is imperative that the primary user acquire a basic understanding of the selection process associated with purchasing a microcomputer system. The selection of a system must be a planned event, not an impulse purchase. The following steps are suggested as guidelines to selecting an appropriate microcomputer system.

*Step 1: Decide how the system will be used.* This is best accomplished by conducting a needs assessment among colleagues and, perhaps, students and/or clients. Components that need to be considered for measurement and evaluation needs are programming capabilities, graphics, storage space, record keeping, grading, and so on. After the primary uses have been determined, move to the second step.

*Step 2: Locate software (programs) that are designed to meet your needs.* Software selection can greatly influence the type of personal computer you choose. Without software, the fanciest hardware setup in the world is useless. When shopping for software, be sure to find out its operating system and version requirements. The operating system controls the overall operation of a computer system and establishes the parameters in which it is able to work. To run a software package requires compatibility between the operating system internal to the machine and the operating system on the disk. A program written for one disk operating system will not run on another. And sometimes, because of incompatibilities among machines, a program written for one machine's operating system will not run on another brand with the same system. There are even situations when an updated version of one operating system will not be compatible with an earlier version of the same program. Advances in technology are eliminating the frequency of this occurrence; however, it is still a common problem among earlier models of microcomputers.

The primary differences among operating systems are in their speed of operation and degree of "user-friendliness." But the most important consideration for the user is the number and quality of application programs available for the operating system. It is not useful to have a machine that runs a limited number of programs.

Remember, operating systems dictate what the machine can and cannot do and control the operation of the disk drives by preparing the disk drive to receive information, maintaining a disk directory that organizes all the information on the disk, copying disks, moving information from disk to disk, and helping to perform many other tasks. An operation can rarely, if ever, be performed in a computer without the assistance of the operating system. Several common disk operating systems are MS DOS, Windows, and Unix, and System 7 for the Macintosh. Many commercially produced programs are written under several operating systems, yet a few specially designed programs can only operate on certain machines. After compiling a list of the software needed, proceed to Step 3.

**Step 3:** *Find a computer with the proper specifications to run the chosen software. Concentrate on the necessities first.* Usually a personal computer with ample speed and sufficient memory and hard disk space, a floppy disk drive, a drive for a compact disk, color monitor, and printer seems to be standard. You can add on as needed later. During the search, let qualified personnel demonstrate how to run the software. Do not take their word that it will run smoothly. Seeing how the software operates is reassuring and educational. Also, speak with colleagues who use the machine(s) you are considering. The insights provided by a trusted user are more valuable than a sales pitch by an overzealous salesperson. Once a system is found that runs the needed software, proceed to step 4.

**Step 4:** *Make sure that the computer system selected is expandable to meet immediate and future needs.* Be certain it is compatible with the machines used by colleagues and that hardware and software support personnel are familiar with the system. Purchasing a system that will grow with the needs of a physical education department or nonschool organization is cost effective in terms of dollars and work hours. Before signing on the dotted line, proceed to step 5.

**Step 5:** *Consider obtaining a service/training agreement.* While most systems are reliable and built to last, breakdowns are inevitable. and protection under some form of service contract may be a good idea. If purchasing a single system, it probably is not prudent to invest in an expensive, long-term service agreement. With the cost of hardware constantly decreasing, it may cost just as much to replace a device as it would to pay the cost of a service agreement. On the other hand, if multiple systems are purchased, the likelihood of something going wrong increases, and a service agreement covering all the systems may be economically sound. Consult the purchasing agent regarding the best or accepted policy and move to step 6.

**Step 6:** *Purchase the computer and necessary peripherals.*

The preceding approach is by no means foolproof. It should, however, provide a logical sequence of events to follow when purchasing a microcomputer system while still leaving room for subjective considerations.

# PERSONAL COMPUTER SOFTWARE

The term software refers to programs that have been written to perform certain functions on the computer. They are sold on floppy disks or compact discs and generally reside (after transfer) on the hard disk drive. Many software packages have been designed with the everyday user in mind.

As might be expected, the market is filled with different types of software. Because the needs of people differ from situation to situation, there will always be marketplace support for new and improved software. Many different types of software can be used to assist physical education and exercise science practitioners in performing day-to-day responsibilities, including communications, computer-assisted instruction, database management, electronic spreadsheet, grading, graphics, interactive video, programming languages, statistics, utilities, word processing, and specially designed functions. The following sections give a brief overview of the various software categories and how each can be applied to measurement and evaluation in physical education and exercise science.

## Communications

Communications software usually contains various utility files and is transferred from a floppy disk to the hard disk drive. Most packages are designed to work with specific machines and operating systems and some work with several operating systems. While appearing more versatile, these programs must first be formatted for a specific system and then can be used only with that system.

Some features of communications software include accessing the Internet, dialing into a central mainframe, answering phone calls, terminating phone connections, creating additional files, sending and receiving files via the phone line, listing files, and sending information to the printer. Use of the Internet is becoming popular among physical educators and exercise scientists. This rapidly growing global network contains millions of users. Due to underlying technologies it has flexibility, openness, and enormous capacity for growth. The availability of World Wide Web browsers and other commercially produced e-mail programs has made electronic communication as easy as using the phone. Using the Internet to solve problems and access huge information bases is commonplace. Communications software can be as simple or as complex as you need. It is an essential tool for you to master.

***Applications in Measurement and Evaluation.***
The primary use of communications software is to facilitate information transfer between and among professionals. This networking can include the exchange of pertinent information. E-mail has afforded practitioners opportunities to link electronically and share information almost instantaneously.

Results of testing, graphic images, surveys, billing procedures and other useful material can be readily transferred. Also, communications software can be used to access larger computers for a variety of purposes. For example, developing norms for fitness or motor ability scores for an entire school or district is much more easily done using a mainframe computer. You can use the memory storage and speed of larger computers without impinging on your personal computing space. Some schools and fitness centers access mainframe computers to generate personalized fitness profiles and individualized exercise prescription programs for students and members. If a task requires massive storage and sophisticated analyses, then using communications software to connect a microcomputer to a mainframe computer is recommended.

### The World Wide Web

The World Wide Web brings a vast array of knowledge right to the desktop. Using a net browser, you are able to access library holdings, professional organizations, colleges, and public schools, and numerous sources of knowledge and useful research information. The once time-consuming task of locating and obtaining information has been replaced by electronic surfing. Time-saving and far-reaching, this technique is clearly the future approach for information gathering.

## Computer-Assisted Instruction

**Computer-assisted instruction** (CAI) software is designed to supplement the teaching process and can be used by individuals to learn more about specific topics. CAI programs can be written in (1) an informational format to provide students or clients with pertinent content about a particular subject , (2) a tutorial format that quizzes persons about a particular topic, or (3) a combination of both instructional and tutorial. One of the primary advantages of CAI is that it can be completed outside of the classroom or exercise setting. This means that teachers can maintain quality instruction in the physical education environment without the potential distraction of youngsters working on microcomputers. Exercise specialists can maximize instruction and still devote time to personal instruction while clients are off working on completing the instructional package.

### Applications in Measurement and Evaluation.
Software is currently available that tutors students about physical fitness, quizzes them on key concepts, asks for raw fitness scores, and provides fitness profiles and exercise prescriptions. Also, a variety of programs have been written about the principles and concepts of successful performance of various sports. Since measurement and evaluation is inherent in deter-

mining level of performance, some knowledge and understanding of how to participate successfully in sports is useful to the participant. Many programs are available that assist in developing exercise prescriptions based on test results, analyze caloric intake and diet, offer information about the value of exercise, and generally provide assistance by giving many useful tips regarding exercise.

## Database Management

**Database management** is analogous to filing. At home one files information such as recipes, holiday card lists, addresses and phone numbers, stamps, coins, and so on. These tasks are relatively easy to perform but become somewhat problematic if, for example, information about coins needs to be cross-indexed according to country, value, decade, and composition. Database management software facilitates this type of task and is relatively easy to use.

Standard features of database management software include displaying information on the screen in a meaningful manner; arranging (sorting) information in any order; selecting and printing or displaying on the monitor only the information that matches certain conditions specified by the user; creating written reports according to an individually designed format; adding, deleting, and editing current records and/or files; and rearranging data to meet current needs. These features and others provide flexibility to manage large (or small) amounts of related information.

### Applications in Measurement and Evaluation.

Database management software can be used to keep records on students or clients. Files may be created to maintain up-to-date student records on written, skill, and fitness tests. The software displays or prints the information in a variety of different ways. If a teacher wishes to show the school board the number of students scoring above the 75th percentile on the distance run, it is a simple process if files are set up properly, to identify those individuals and print out their names. A fitness program manager could use data base management software to create a cohort of certain age/gender individuals or to identify chronic absentees.

## Electronic Spreadsheet

**Electronic spreadsheet** software is similar to database management programs because it is able to manipulate large amounts of information. However, the purpose of a spreadsheet program is to allow the user to work with numbers in rows and columns and perform calculations. Spreadsheets enable users to speculate, forecast, change numbers, and immediately view the effects of the changes.

Spreadsheets have two primary functions. The first function, working with information in spreadsheets, provides the capability to create spreadsheets with numbers and/or formulas in order to maintain up-to-date quantitative analyses of current situations and even to predict the effects of subsequent changes. The second function, displaying the information in an organized fashion, allows the user to create on-screen displays or printed hard copies of the desired information, formatted to specifications. Other features include variable column widths, quick cursor movement around the spreadsheet, on-screen formatting, inserting and deleting columns and rows, and storing information on a data disk. Users can enter in a spreadsheet several fundamental formulas and utilize the copy feature to place the same or similar formulas in other areas of the spreadsheet. Users can alter the form in which numbers in specific areas are displayed, and view the contents from different perspectives, allowing maximum flexibility in number manipulation. The ease in altering information offers efficient and accurate operation.

### Applications in Measurement and Evaluation.

Formula functions give spreadsheet software multiple applications in measurement and evaluation. It can be used to calculate grades, determine standard scores and measures of central tendency, determine mathematical relationships among various other types of quantitative data, and assist in bookkeeping and accounting procedures for a health facility. One of the most useful features is the ability to create a format to suit specific needs instead of having to search for software already designed for a specific purpose.

## Grading

The purpose of grading software is to make compiling students' marks more accurate and efficient. Such programs make grading more flexible by allowing teachers to weight activities according to their importance and provide the teacher with the ability to instantly display to any or all students their grades and progress throughout the year.

It should be emphasized that this type of software is not intended to replace the teacher in the evaluation process. Rather, grading software is designed to expedite the record keeping process. Grading programs can save countless hours of calculations.

Most grading programs allow users to do the following:

1. Maintain separate files for each class
2. Enter and edit student names and identifying codes
3. Duplicate class rosters for students in different classes, but the same homeroom
4. Conveniently enter students' scores as requirements are completed

5. Edit information relative to students and scores
6. Assign weights to individual requirements to reflect their relative importance
7. Display and/or print reports for individuals or entire classes
8. Create a table of grades that show percentage correct
9. Create and print a letter grade scale that corresponds to obtained raw scores

**Applications in Measurement and Evaluation.**
Grading is a major component of measurement and evaluation in the physical education environment. As long as teachers are required to assign grades in physical education, grading software should be used to save time and increase accuracy.

# Graphics

**Graphics** software provides an alternative to the time and effort needed to gather data and prepare graphs and charts. Rather than going to a graphic artist, one only needs to sit down at the computer to convert raw data into attractively crafted graphs that can be used for slides, overhead transparencies, or charts in a report. Features to look for when purchasing graphic software include the following:

1. User-friendliness and simplicity of menus
2. Easy data entry, editing, and storage
3. Capability to accommodate large number of data points per graph
4. Overlay function that allows one graph to be placed on top of another
5. High resolution graphics
6. Lettering kits for labeling
7. On-screen cursor movement when adding information to an existing graph or chart
8. On-screen cursor movement to actually assist in drawing freehand
9. Option to print all or parts of chart in color
10. Print options that can alter the size or position of a chart on the output
11. Interchange of data from spreadsheets to graphics software
12. Built-in slide projector function that allows graphs to be sequentially displayed on computer monitor
13. Ample storage space for raw data

**Applications in Measurement and Evaluation.**
"One picture is worth a thousand words." When explaining the results of quantitative assessment and evaluation procedures, an illustration undoubt-

edly is more helpful than just verbal explanation. Whether a teacher is reporting the breakdown of letter grades, results of fitness or motor ability tests, updated normative ranges, or other forms of numeric distribution, pie graphs, bar graphs, and scatter plot graphs make data much more understandable. Filling the bulletin board with visually appealing computer-generated graphs and pictures can keep the students up to date on progress toward goals and other class-related assignments or projects. Graphic software can be used in the exercise science setting for the purpose of preparing a portrait of the membership in a fitness program, reporting the results of research studies, describing the financial picture of the organization, and interfacing with other types of software (e.g., electronic spreadsheets or database management) to illustrate various characteristics of the operation.

# Statistics

Many software packages offer the user a tremendous amount of statistical calculation power. Certainly statistical packages can be a time-saving addition to a software library.

Most statistics programs allow the user to calculate a wide variety of statistics. Data are usually entered via the keyboard or directly from a data file. The statistics program, then, reads the data and performs statistical calculations. Features to look for when selecting statistical software include:

1. User-friendly and menu driven
2. Clear documentation and explanation of statistical techniques
3. Simple, yet extensive, editing and storage capabilities
4. Printer options and the possibility of graphic generation
5. Fast programs that accommodate large data files

### Applications in Measurement and Evaluation.
Statistical procedures are essential to the measurement and evaluation process. From simple techniques that calculate measures of central tendency to more complex procedures that show mathematical relationships among selected variables, statistics play a key role in measurement and evaluation. The microcomputer will accommodate most everyday needs related to measurement and evaluation in physical education and exercise science. However, the time may come when the size and/or nature of the task is too much for a personal computer. When that is the case, it is time to utilize a mainframe computer.

The mainframe computer performs as a multiuser system that is similar to the microcomputer, but much faster. Composed of large hardware components, mainframe systems are usually housed in specially designed installations at universities, corporations, institutes, or other large organizations. One of the primary functions of mainframe computers is to perform what is affectionately referred to as "number crunching." Number crunching is simply taking many numbers and performing elaborate data handling routines or transformations. The most widely used sophisticated statistical programs for a mainframe computer are the Biomedical Programs (BMDP), Statistical Analysis System (SAS), and Statistical Package for the Social Sciences (SPSS). Most of these statistical software bundles traditionally housed on a mainframe are now available for microcomputers. A brief overview of each program is provided in the following sections.

### Biomedical Programs (BMDP)

Programs supplied by **BMDP** provide a wide variety of analytic capabilities that range from graphics to simple data description to complex multivariate statistical procedures. The BMDP computer programs provide operations ranging from simple data display and description to advanced data analysis.

### Stastical Analysis System (SAS)

**SAS** is a software system for data analysis. SAS provides users with tools for information storage and retrieval, data modification and programming, report writing, statistical analysis, and file handling.

### Statistical Package for the Social Sciences (SPSS)

The **Statistical Package for the Social Sciences (SPSS)** is probably the most commonly used mainframe statistical package and is a comprehensive tool for managing, analyzing, and displaying data. Standard features include inputting from different types of data files, file management (sorting, splitting, and aggregating files), data management (sampling, selecting, and weighing cases), tabulation and statistical analysis, report writing, and graphics.

## Utilities

Utility software is somewhat generic and performs tasks associated with handling existing programs and data files. Utilities frequently used include those for protecting and recovering data, copying files, deleting files, renaming files, listing a directory of files, locking and unlocking files, printing files, formatting a disk, verifying a disk, and other everyday procedures.

### Applications in Measurement and Evaluation.
If computers are used in measurement and evaluation, utility programs are essential.

## Word Processing

Word processing is the most popular function of the microcomputer. It refers to the process of writing, editing, storing, retrieving, formatting, and printing written material using a microcomputer. There are many word processing packages on the market. The following are features that should be considered when selecting word processing software:

1. On-screen editing capabilities
2. Speed in scrolling through document
3. Search and find options
4. Formatting options
5. Pagination options
6. Printing options
7. Storage functions
8. Spell check and thesaurus options
9. Sorting and mail merge functions
10. Grammar checks
11. Bibliography and footnote capabilities
12. Font options

### Applications in Measurement and Evaluation.

Word processing can help in constructing and revising tests, developing multiple forms to be used in the testing process, preparing progress reports to be sent home, publishing newsletters, preparing mass mailings to the membership, personalizing letters to students or members, developing instructions for fitness and motor ability tests, and other written tasks.

## HOW TO SELECT SOFTWARE

As suggested in the guidelines for purchasing a personal computer system, before beginning a software search, some type of needs assessment should be conducted so that the purpose of the software can be ascertained. Be sure to prioritize the features that should be included in the software. Some features will be essential, others nice to have, and some simply extravagant. The final choice will probably be dictated by a combination of price, features, and the components of the microcomputer system.

To aid in the search, several sources of information may be of help, including visiting with friends or colleagues familiar with the type of software being considered, local microcomputer hardware stores, large superstores, browsing the Web, computer magazines and other professional journals, resource books and catalogs, and publishing companies. Since software development is constantly upgrading products, it is imperative that the consumer consult with up-to-date sources in the quest to purchase the right piece of software. An affirmative response to the following questions would suggest that the software being considered is a wise investment.

1. Is the software compatible with my microcomputer system? My colleagues' system?
2. Is it affordable compared to similar products?
3. Is a site license available so others can purchase additional copies at a discount? Can it be upgraded at nominal cost?
4. Are the manuals and tutorials easy to read and understand?
5. Does it have sufficient technical support?
6. Can it reside on the hard disk? Is it modifiable?
7. Does it allow the user the ability to move to and from different sections of the program?
8. Is the content accurate?
9. Does it have audio capability? Graphics?
10. Is it the most current version?

## SOFTWARE FOR MEASUREMENT AND EVALUATION

Many software packages are available to assist physical education and exercise science practitioners in measurement and evaluation. Most software has broad usage in measurement and evaluation, but software available specifically for use in physical education and exercise science environments is on the rise. In fact, there are clearinghouses that disseminate software and information about software to interested professionals. One of the more popular software clearinghouses for physical education is SOFTSHARE, established in 1985 and located at California State University at Fresno. Sponsored by the Physical Education and Human Performance Department at California State University at Fresno, its purposes are to retrieve and disseminate microcomputer software applicable to physical education and related areas. Software available through SOFTSHARE is in the public domain and can be obtained from the clearinghouse for a nominal fee. For a description of physical education and exercise science programs available from SOFTSHARE, contact: Sally Ayer, Physical Education and Human Performance, 5275 North Campus Drive, California State University, Fresno, CA 93740-0028 or e-mail to sally_ayer@csufresno.edu.

Finally, when selecting software we recommend you follow the suggested "tips" previously listed. Technology is advancing so rapidly that to describe software for physical education and exercise science would result in listing some programs that would be out-of-date before this text went to press. Thus, you should obtain advice and information about current programs as you seek to use the microcomputer to assist you with your professional responsibilities.

## SUMMARY

The personal computer is a technological breakthrough that can be utilized in all aspects of physical education and exercise science. Basic computer literacy is becoming a necessity for all practitioners in the schools and the exercise environment. There are many different brands of personal computer systems, but all contain the same essential components: central processing unit (computer), display monitor, disk drive, and printer. Several different operating systems are available to choose from when selecting a computer system. Users also can add additional peripheral devices to perform selected tasks. Various types of software are available for the user and can be classified into the following categories: communications, computer-assisted instruction, database management, electronic spreadsheet, grading, graphics, statistics, utilities, and word processing. Software specially designed for use in physical education and exercise science is available commercially.

## ◤ REPRESENTATIVE READINGS

Beall, B. S. (1983). Computer literacy for health educators. *Health Education* 14: 19–22.

Hastad, D. N., (1984). Microcomputers in physical education and athletics. In *Proceedings of the Fourth Annual Symposium on the Role of the Microcomputer in Education*. Glenview, IL: Micro Ideas, pp. 46–48.

Howley, E.T. and Franks, D.B. (1992). *Health fitness instructor's handbook*. Champaign, IL: Human Kinetics.

Rothstein, A. L. (1985). *Research design and statistics for physical education*. Englewood Cliffs, NJ: Prentice-Hall.

# Index

AAHPERD, 5
  Baseball/Softball Skills
    Test, 230–234
  Basketball Skills Test,
    234–238
  50–Yard Dash, 213, 214
  Football Skills Test,
    238–243
  Volleyball Skills Test,
    248–251
  Youth Fitness Test, 5
AAHPERD Modified Sit-Ups,
  150–153
  bent-knee sit-ups test, 152
  norms-boys, 151
  norms-girls, 152
AAHPERD *Physical Best*, 103,
  107
Abdominal Skinfold, 528
Abscissa, 51
Academic Learning Time-
  Physical Education
  (ALT-PE), 420, 426
Accountability, 7–8
Achievement, 20, 353
Adapted Physical Education,
  463
Adult Exercise and Fitness,
  516
Adult Fitness Environments,
  516
Affective Domain, 31–32, 304
  cooperation, 31
  positive attitudes, 31
  self-concept, 31
Agility, 30, 194, 197
All-Purpose Event-Record-
  ing, 417
Alternate Form Reliability,
  98–99
Anecdotal Records, 335–336
Apparent Limits, 50
Annual Goals, 437, 469
Answer, 286
Anthropometrics, 3
  measurements, 179–180

Arm Curl, 160–161
Arizona State University
  Observation Instrument
  (ASUOI), 425
Assessing Performance, 195
Assessment of Physical
  Activity Assessment of
  Sports Injuries, 512
Assessment Tools, 12–13
Athletic Training, 508, 511
Attitudes, 13, 306, 311
Attitude Toward Physical
  Activity (ATPA), 312–314,
  315
  Kenyon, 1968a, 312
Auditory, 441
Authentic Assessment, 14,
  368–369
  balance, 31

Baseball/Softball Skills, 230
  base running, 231
  catching fly balls, 231
  fielding ground balls, 231
  fungo hitting, 232–233
  overhand throw for ac-
    curacy, 233
  softball throw for distance,
    233
  speed throw, 233-234
  underhand pitching, 234
Back-Saver Sit-and-Reach,
  133-134
Badminton, 252
  French Short Serve Test,
    252–255
  Wall-Volley Test, 253-255
Balance, 194, 203
Balance Beam Walk, 207–208
Bar Graph, 51, 52
Baseline Data, 494
Basketball Skills, 234
  control dribble, 235–236
  defensive movement,
    236–237
  passing, 237

  speed spot shooting,
    237–238, 239
Behavior Feedback, 416
Bench Press, 163-164, 530
Bent-Knee Curl-Up, 136
Bent-Knee Sit-Up,152–153
Biomedical Programs
  (BMDP), 558
Blood, 513
Blood Pressure, 10, 533
Blood Pressure Cuff, 533
Body Awareness, 228
Body Composition, 124, 137,
  172–173
Body Coordination Test,
  209–211
  balance, 209
  hopping, 209–210
  lateral jumping, 210–211
  lateral movement, 211
Body Density, 534
Body Management Compe-
  tence, 192
Body Mass Index, 128
Borg Rate of Perceived Exer-
  tion Scale, 532
Brozek et al., 1963, 536
Butts, N., 533

Calf Skinfold, 528
Cardiac Rehabilitation, 508
Cardiopulmonary Resuscita-
  tion (CPR), 514
Cardiorespiratory fitness,
  124, 137
Catching a Ball, 228
  Distance run, 138
  Field-based tests, 138
Ceiling Effect, 72–73
Central Processing Unit
  (CPU), 546
Central Tendency, measures
  of, 56
  mean, 58–60
  median, 57
  mode, 56

Checklists, 13, 336, 371, 385
Cheffers and Mancini Human
    Movement Attitude
    Scale, 324
Children's Attitude Toward
    Physical Activity
    (CATPA), 314, 315
Children's Self-Perceptions of
    Adequacy in and
    Predilection for Physical
    Activity (CSAPPA), 316
    Hay, 1992 316
Cholesterol Analysis, 515
Class Profiles, 196
Class Size, 489
Class Time, 489
Classification, 20
    of students, 195
Cognitive Achievement, 275
Cognitive Domain, 274, 277
Community Exercise, 513
Competency-Based Testing,
    14
Completion Items, 287
Computers, 15
Computer-Assisted Instruc-
    tion (CAI), 533
Concurrent Validity, 96–97
Conference, 375–376
Construct Validity, 96
Content Validity, 95–96
Continuous Data, 50
Contract Grading, 369–371
Contraindicated Activities,
    443
Converting Scores , 116
Cooperation, 31
Coopersmith Self-Esteem
    Inventory, 333
Coordination, 30, 194,
    208–209
Corporate Exercise, 513
Correlation, 77–79
    Pearson Product Moment
        Correlation, 81–82, 84
    Spearman rho Rank-Order
        Correlation, 79–80
Correlation Coefficient, 77–79
Cratty Adaptation of Piers-
    Harris Self-Concept
    Scale, 331
Criterion Measurement, 100
Criterion-Referenced Tests,
    348, 364

Criterion-Referenced Grad-
    ing, 366–367
Cumulative Frequencies, 53,
    54
Cunningham and Garrison,
    251
Curl-Up, 128–129
Curricular Content, 490
Curriculum, 22
    decision making, 34
    development of, 34–35

Database Management, 554
Data Recording, 389
Decision Making, 34
Demonstrations, 440
Diagnosis, 19–20
Diastolic, 533
Difficulty Index, 293
Direct Observation, 516
Disabled, 434
    disabilities, 436, 444
Discrete Data, 50
Discrimination, 107
Discrimination Index,
    294–296
Distance Run, 138
Distractors, 286
Dribbling, 244–245
Dual Sports, 252–265
Duration Recording, 397, 417
Dynamic Balance, 202
Dynamometer, 158–159

Economy, 104
Educational Objectives, 282
Electronic Spreadsheet, 554
Elementary School, 497
Essay, 288–291
    objectivity, 290
    reliability, 290
    written essay questions,
        289
Evaluating the Program,
    39–41, 438
Evaluating Scores, 117
Evaluation, 2–3, 16, 17–18,
    485
Evaluation of Sports Injuries,
    512
Event Recording, 391–393,
    397
Event Tasks, 484
Examination, 16, 276

Examples of Measurement
    and Evaluation Models,
    493
Exceptional, 434
Exercise Programs, 304, 330
Exercise Science Environ-
    ment, 184, 542
Eyeballing, 384

Face Validity, 95
Field-based tests, 138
First aid, 512
FYT-Fit Youth Today, 135–136
    Bent-Knee Curl-Up, 136
    Body Composition, 137
    Distance Run, 138
    Sit-and-Reach, 136–137
    Steady State Jog, 136
Fitness Centers, 11
Fitness Leadership, 508
Fitness Management, 508
Flexed-Arm Hang, 133,
    154–155
    referenced norms-girls, 156
Flexibility, 124, 164–165
Football Skills, 238
    ball-changing zigzag run,
        240
    catching the forward pass,
        240–241
    football pass for accuracy,
        241
    football punt for distance,
        241–242
    forward pass for distance,
        242
    kickoff, 242
    pull-out, 242–243
    50–yard dash with football,
        243
Fox's Bicycle Ergometer Test,
    521
Frequency Distributions,
    47–48
    grouped, 48–50
    simple, 48–49
Frequency Polygon, 51, 52
Fundamental Motor Patterns,
    455
Fundamental Skills, 192

Goals, 350
Golf Skills Tests, 256–259
    chip shot, 256–257

indoor golf skills, 258–259
long putt, 257
middle distance shot, 257
pitch shot, 257–258
Goniometer, 170–171
Grade, 346, 347
reasons to, 348
Graded Exercise, 515
Grading, 21–22, 346–347,
357–358, 494, 555
Grade Reports, 372
Graphics, 556
Graphs, 50–53
bar graph, 51
frequency polygon, 52
histogram, 51
Grouped Frequency Distribution, 48–50
apparent limits, 50
continuous data, 50
discrete data, 50
real limits, 50
Group Goal Setting, 367–368
Group Time Sampling, 400,
403, 420

Handicapped, 434
Hand Reaction Time Test,
213-215
Heading, 246
Health Clubs, 11
Health-Related Physical Fitness, 8–9, 123-124, 352,
500
body composition, 124
cardiorespiratory fitness,
124
domain, 29–30
flexibility, 124
muscular endurance, 124
muscular strength, 124
Hearing Impairments, 441
Heart Rate, 10
Hewitt's Tennis Achievement
Test, 261
forehand and backhand
drive test, 262–264
service placement test, 263-
264
speed of service test,
264–265
High School (10–12), 488, 492,
501, 503
Higher Skill Attainment, 193

High Wall-Volley Test,
251–252
Histogram, 51
Hitchcock, Dr. Edward, 3
Hospitals, 514
Hospital Based Health and
Fitness Programs, 513
Hydrostatic Weighing, 534

Ilium Skinfold, 528
Illinois Agility Run, 197–199
Impaired, 434
Improving the Program, 438
Improvement, 20, 353
Inclusion, 472
Independence, 107–108
Individual Sports, 252–265
Individualized Education
Program (IEP), 462,
465–469
Individualized Program, 438
Indoor Golf Skills, 258–259
Input, 544
Instructional Episode, 383
Instructional Time, 409
Instructor Movement, 410
Intermediate Grades (4–6),
487, 492
Internet, 549
Interobserver Agreement
(IOA), 404
Interpercentile Range, 61
Interpreting, 110–111
Interpreting Scores, 116
Interquartile Range, 61
Interval, 47
Interval Recording, 394–397
Inventories, 13
Item Analysis, 293
Item Function, 296–297

Johnson Modification of the
Bass Test of Dynamic
Balance, 205–207
Juggling, 246–247
Jumping Ability, 30

Kasch Pulse Recovery Test,
148–150
Kicking a Ball, 227
Kline's One-Mile Walk for
Time, 520
Kraus-Weber Floor Touch,
167–168

La Crosse Exercise and
Health Program, 514
Lat Pull Down, 161–163
Learning Domain, 29
Leighton Flexometer,
171–172
Leptokurtic, 54, 55
Levels of Measurement,
44–45
interval, 47
nominal, 45
ordinal, 45–46
ratio, 47
Likert Scale, 307–309
Long-Term Goals, 437, 469
LSU Step Test, 144–148
Lung Function, 515
Lung Residual Volume, 535

Mainstreaming, 472
Management, 409
Mandates, 490
Matching, 285–286
Maximal Oxygen Uptake,
140, 518
Mean, 58–60, 68
Measurement, 2, 16, 17, 18,
485
Measurement Instruments,
10–11
Measurement and Evaluation
in a Nonschool Setting,
509
Median, 57, 68
McArdle's 3-Minute Step
Test, 519–520
McDonald Soccer Test, The,
243-244
Middle School (7–9), 488, 492,
501
Mode, 56–57, 68
Modem, 548
Modifications of Prudential
FITNESSGRAM, 454
aerobic capacity, 455
body composition, 455
flexibility, 455
muscular endurance, 455
muscle strength, 455
Modified Pull-Up, 131–132,
156–158, 220, 222
norms, 158
Motivation, 21, 195
Motor Fitness Tests, 444

Motor Fitness Testing Manual
   for the Moderately Mentally Retarded, 445
   50–yard dash, 448
   flexed-arm hang, 445
   sit-ups, 446
   softball throw for distance,
      448
   standing long jump, 447
   300–yard run-walk, 449
Multiple Choice, 286
   answer, 286
   distractors, 286
   stem, 286
Muscular Endurance, 124,
   150, 153, 160
Muscular Strength, 124, 150,
   153

National Association of Sport
   and Physical Education
   (NASPE), 103, 408
Needs Assessment, 32–34
   decision making, 32
   Prudential FITNESS-
      GRAM, 33
Negative Modeling, 412
Neilson and Corbin, 1986,
   316
Nelson and Allen 1970, 332
Nelson-Allen Movement Sat-
   isfaction Scale, 332
Network, 549
Networking, 549
9 Minute Run, 143-144
   norms—boys, 145
   norms—girls, 145
Nominal Level, 45
Nonschool Exercise Setting,
   23-24, 508, 510
Normal Curve, 53, 68
Normal Distribution, 75
Norm-Referenced Grading,
   363-364
Norm-Referenced Tests, 358
Norms, 105–107
North Carolina Motor Fitness
   Battery, 216
   Modified Pull-Ups, 222
   Side-Stepping, 222
   Sit-Ups, 216–218
   Squat Thrusts, 223
   Standing Broad Jump, 222
Note Taking, 384–385

Objective Test Items, 289
Objectivity, 100–103
Observed Performance, 355
Odd-Even Reliability, 99
One-Mile Walk/Run, 126
1–Mile Run, 139
   norms—boys, 142
   norms—girls, 142
1.5–Mile Run, 139, 141
Ordinal Level, 45–46
Ordinate, 51
Outcomes of Quality Physical
   Education, 480
Output, 544
Oxygen Consumption, 10

Pangrazi and Corbin, 1993,
   351
Pangrazi and Darst, 1991, 351
Parental Reports, 482
Passing, 248, 249
Pearson Product-Moment
   Correlation, 81–83, 84
Peer Evaluation, 368
Performance-based Objec-
   tives, 38–39, 438
Performance Standards,
   365–366
Percentage Method, 360
Percentiles, 53, 69–73
   ceiling effect, 72
   equivalent method,
      360–363
Personal Computer, 542
Personal Interviews, 372
Personal Letter, 374–375
Personal Values, 13
Personnel Support, 489
Philosophical Aims, 35–36
Physical Activity Patterns,
   9–10, 330
Physical Disabilities, 439
Physical Education, 6–7,10,
   304, 330, 348, 434, 490,
   496, 542
Physical Education Environ-
   ment, 184
Physical Estimation and
   Attraction Scale (PEAS),
   320
Physical Fitness, 5, 30, 122
   agility, 30
   jumping ability, 30
   quickness, 30

speed, 30
   upper body strength, 30
Physical Fitness Testing for
   the Disabled: Project
   UNIQUE, 449
   50–yard/meter dash, 450
   grip strength, 450
   long-distance run, 453
   sit-and-reach, 453
   sit-ups, 452
   skinfold measures, 450
   softball throw, 452
   standing broad jump, 453
Physical Growth Chart,
   180–183
Placheck Recording, 400
Platykurtic, 54, 55
Poole Long-Serve Test,
   255–256
Portfolios, 14–15, 482
Positive attitudes, 31
Positive Modeling, 412
Posture, 228–229
Potential, 355
Power, 30, 194
Practice Time, 408
Praise, 415
Predictive Validity, 97
Present Level of Performance,
   464
Presidents Council on Youth
   Fitness, 5
Primary Grades (k–3), 487,
   491
Printer, 548
Processing, 544
Program Continuity, 36
Program Development, 40
Program Goals, 36–37, 436
   learning domains, 37
Program Standards, 12
Progressive Aerobic Cardio-
   vascular Endurance
   Run-PACER, 127
Prudential FITNESSGRAM,
   126, 103
   Back Saver Sit-and-Reach,
      133–134
   Body Mass Index, 128
   Curl-Up, 128–129
   Flexed Arm Hang, 133
   Modified Pull-Up, 131–132
   One-Mile Walk/Run,
      126–127

Pull-Up, 132
Push-Up, 130–131
Shoulder Stretch, 134
Skinfold, 127
Trunk Lift, 129–130
Psychomotor Domain, 31, 352
  agility, 30
  balance, 30
  coordination, 30
  power, 30
  speed, 30
Public Relations, 23
Pull-Up, 132, 153
  norms—boys, 154
  noms—girls, 154
Pulse, 148
Push-Up, 130–132

Qualitative Item Analysis,
  297–298
Qualitative Measurement, 2,
  94
Quantitative Information, 2,
  94
Quantitative Item Analysis,
  293
Quickness, 30
Quiz, 16

Racquetball Skills Test, 259–261
  long wall-volley test,
    260–261
  short wall-volley test, 260
Random Access Memory
  (RAM), 547
Range, 49, 61
Rating Scales, 13, 336–337,
  385–388
Ratio, 47
Raw Data, 46
Reaction Time, 194, 212
Read Only Memory (ROM),
  547
Real Limits, 50
Record Review, 515
Recording the Scores, 113-114
Regression, 83–85
  simple regression, 83
Rehabilitation, 511
Relevance, 102–103
Reliability, 17, 97–98, 101, 195,
  404
  alternate form, 98–99
  odd-even, 99

Report Card, 373
Reporting, 110–111
Research, 15
Response Latency, 410
Richardson Scale for Measur-
  ing Attitudes, 324
  Richardson, 1960, 324
Rockport Fitness Walking
  Test, 523, 526

Safety, 109–110
Sargent, Dr. Dudley, 3
Scold, 415
Scores, 116–117
  converting, 116
  evaluating, 117
  interpreting, 116
Scoring, 110–111
Selection of Test Items, 284
  essay test questions, 284
  objective test questions,
    289, 294
  semiobjective test ques-
    tions, 289, 294
Self-Concept, 13, 31, 304, 329,
  330
Self-Evaluation, 367, 382, 407
Semantic Differential,
  310–311
Semiobjective Test Items, 289
Serving, 248–249
Setting, 250
Shilling and Kiphard 1976,
  209
Short-Answer Questions,
  288
Short-Term Instructional
  Objectives, 438, 469, 471
Shoulder Stretch, 134
Shuttle Run, 202–203, 225
Side-Stepping, 199, 200, 222
Simple Analysis of Variance
  (ANOVA), 90
Simple Frequency Distribu-
  tion, 49, 49
Simple Regression, 83
Sit-and-Reach, 136, 165–167,
  529
  norms—boys, 166
  norms—girls, 167
Sit-Up, 531
Skewed Negative, 55
Skewed Positive, 55
Skewness, 53-55

Skill-Related Physical Fitness
  Components, 194,
  215–216, 496
  agility, 194
  balance, 194
  coordination, 194
  power, 194
  reaction time, 194
  speed, 194
Skinfold, 127–127, 173-179
  abdomen, 174
  calf, 174
  correlation between skin-
    fold and percent fat,
    177
  scapula, 174
  suprailiac, 175
  thigh, 175
  triceps, 175
Soccer Battery, 244–248
  dribble, 244–245
  heading, 246
  juggling, 246–247
  wall volley, 247–248
Soccer Skills, 243-248
Social Competence, 335
Social Promotion, 356
Social Skills, 5
Sociogram, 338–340
Sociometry, 337–338
Software, 559
Spearman-Brown Prophecy
  Formula, 99–100
Spearman-Brown Prophecy
  Formula, 99
  split-half, 99
  test-retest, 98
Spearman Rho Rank-Order
  Correlation, 79–80, 99
Special, 434
Special Physical Education,
  463
Special Services, 470
Specialized Skills, 192
Speed, 30, 194, 212
Sphygmomanometer, 525
Split-Half Reliability, 99
Sports Administration, 508
Sports Injury Data, 513
Sports Skills Tests, 229–230
Squat Thrust, 199, 201–202,
  221, 223
Standard Deviation, 63–68,
  358–359

Standard Scores, 69
    t-score, 76
    z-score, 73
Standing Broad Jump, 219, 222
Standing with Eyes Open/Closed, 227–227
Standing Long Jump, 226
Static Balance, 203
Statistics, 44, 557
Statistical Analysis System (SAS), 558
Statistical Package for the Social Sciences (SPSS), 558
Steady State Jog, 136
Stem, 286
Stethoscope, 525
Storage, 544
Stork Stand, 204–205
Strength Tests, 159–160
Student Interest Surveys, 35
Student Journals, 484
Student Performance, 19
    achievement, 20
    classification, 20
    diagnosis, 19
    improvement, 20
    motivation, 21
Student Portfolios, 373-374
Students, 487
    high school (10–12), 488
    intermediate grades (4–6), 487
    middle school (7–9), 488
    primary grades (k–3), 487
Subjective Techniques, 13
Supervision Instrument, 421
Symmetry, 53-55
System for Observing Fitness Instruction Time (SOFIT), 423
Systematic Observation, 13, 23, 388–389, 407, 416
Systolic, 533

Table of Specification, 281, 283
Taxonomy of Educational Objectives, 278
    application, 280–281
    Bloom et al. (1956), 278
    comprehension, 279–280
    evaluation, 281
    knowledge, 279

Teacher Effectiveness, 22–23
Teacher Performance, 21
Technological Support, 490
Tennis Skills, measuring, 261
    Dyer Backboard Test, 261
    Hewitt's Tennis Achievement Test, 261–265
Test, 16–17, 18, 94, 104, 331
    recording the scores, 113
    reliability, 17
    validity, 17
Test Batteries, 125
    health-related physical fitness, measures of, 125
Test of Gross Motor Development, 456
    catch, 460
    hop, 457
    horizontal jump, 457
    kick, 460
    leap, 457
    locomotor skills, 456
    overhand throw, 462
    skip, 458
    slid, 458
    stationary bounce, 460
    two-hand strike, 459
Testing Area, 112
Testing Large Groups, 110
Test Questions, Sources of, 298–299
Test-Retest-Reliability, 98
Tests Used in the Nonschool Exercise Setting, 518
Texas Physical Motor Fitness/Developmental Tests, 223
    body awareness, 228
    catching a ball, 228
    kicking a ball, 227
    posture, 228–229
    shuttle run, 225
    standing long jump, 226
    standing with eyes open/closed, 226–227
    throwing a ball, 227–228
    walking a line forward/backward, 226
Therapeutic Recreation, 508, 515
Throwing a Ball, 227–228
Time, 104–105
Transition Services, 471

Treadmill-Predicting VO2 Max, 531
Triceps Skinfold, 528
True-False Format, 285
Trunk Extension, 168–169
Trunk Lift, 129–130
T-Score, 76–77
T-Test
    dependent samples, for, 88–89
    independent samples, for, 86–85
12–Minute Run, 141, 143–144
Two-Point Scale, 309

U.S. Center for Disease Control, 6
U.S. Department of Health and Human Services, 9
Unique, 434
Units of Instruction, 22
Unit of Outcomes, 37–38, 437
University Based Health and Fitness Programs, 513
Upper Body Strength, 30

Validity, 17, 94, 101, 194, 404
    concurrent, 96–97
    construct, 96
    content, 95
    face, 95
    predictive, 97
Variability, 60–61
Variance, 62–63
Volleying, 251

Walking a Line Forward/Backward, 75, 226
Wall Volley, 247–248
Warming Up, 115
Wear Attitude Scale, 325
    Wear, 1955, 325
Wilmore et al. 1985, 531
Word Processing, 559
World Wide Web, 553
Written Test, 276, 277, 291

Yeagley, 244
YMCA Bicycle Test, 521
YMCA Physical Fitness Test Battery, 523

Z-Score, 73